DRINKS

DRINKS

VINCENT GASNIER

PHOTOGRAPHY BY IAN O'LEARY

LONDON · NEW YORK · MUNICH
MELBOURNE · DELHI

Produced for Dorling Kindersley by

cobaltid

The Stables, Wood Farm, Deopham Road,
Attleborough, Norfolk NR17 1AJ
www.cobaltid.co.uk

ART EDITORS	EDITORS
Paul Reid, Lloyd Tilbury, Darren Bland,	Marek Walisiewicz, Kati Dye,
Pia Ingham, Annika Skoog	Maddy King, Jamie Dickson

PHOTOGRAPHY ART DIRECTION	PHOTOGRAPHY
Paul Reid, Lloyd Tilbury	Ian O'Leary

For Dorling Kindersley

SENIOR ART EDITOR Joanne Doran	SENIOR EDITORS Simon Tuite, Gary Werner
MANAGING ART EDITOR Marianne Markham	MANAGING EDITOR Deirdre Headon
DTP DESIGNER Louise Waller	PRODUCTION CONTROLLER Sarah Sherlock

ART DIRECTOR Carole Ash

First published by Dorling Kindersley in 2005
THE PENGUIN GROUP
Registered offices: Penguin Books Ltd, 80 Strand,
London, WC2R ORL

Penguin Group (USA) Inc., 375 Hudson Street, New York,
New York 10014

Penguin Group (Canada), 10 Alcorn Avenue, Toronto,
Ontario, Canada M4V 3B2
(a division of Pearson Penguin Canada Inc.).

Penguin Books Ltd, 80 Strand, London WC2R 0RL, England.

Penguin Ireland, 25 St Stephen's Green, Dublin 2, Ireland
(a division of Penguin Books Ltd).

Penguin Group (Australia), 250 Camberwell Road, Camberwell,
Victoria 3124, Australia (a division of Pearson Australia Group Pty Ltd).

Penguin Books India Pvt Ltd, 11 Community Centre,
Panchsheel Park, New Delhi - 110 017, India.

Penguin Group (NZ), Cnr Airborne and Rosedale Roads, Albany,
Auckland, New Zealand (a division of Pearson New Zealand Ltd).

Penguin Books (South Africa) (Pty) Ltd, 24 Sturdee Avenue,
Rosebank, Johannesburg 2196, South Africa.

2 4 6 8 10 9 7 5 3 1

A CIP catalogue record for this book is available from the British Library.

ISBN 1-4053-0617-1

DD129
Colour reproduction by Colourscan, Singapore
Printed in China by SNP Leefung

Discover more at
www.dk.com

CONTENTS

FOREWORD

Drink has brought pleasure to the world for many thousands of years, and never before have there been more styles of wine, beer, spirits, liqueurs, and cocktails to enjoy and celebrate. Despite (or perhaps because of) this bewildering diversity, many of us stick to our old trusted favourites. We feel it is easy to make an expensive mistake, or to embarrass ourselves through a lack of knowledge. This is a shame, because there is a universe of drink to explore, and it is a wonderful journey! I have written this book to give you the confidence and knowledge to be adventurous – to taste and appreciate a wider range of drinks – because I feel strongly that this pleasure should not be reserved for the select few.

What, you may ask, qualifies one person to write about such an astonishing and wonderful range of drinks – from Polish vodkas to Alaskan smoked beers, from Bordeaux wines to chic Manhattan cocktails? Well, it is about passion. I grew up in the Loire region of France, where from an early age I was enthralled by the whole process of winemaking, and by the fervent commitment of the local growers and producers. Through my training as a sommelier, I worked at some of the best restaurants in the world, with some of the most knowledgeable and hard-working professionals in the business, and picked up some of their knowledge about spirits, cocktails, and other drinks. When I moved to the UK, I carried on learning, and developed a love affair with that most English of drinks – beer. It is an affair that – I'm afraid – I cannot kick!

My great hope is that, in this book, I can pass some of this passion to you. The information on its pages may not make you a drink expert, but might just make you a drink lover. Santé!

Vincent Gasnier

Vincent Gasnier

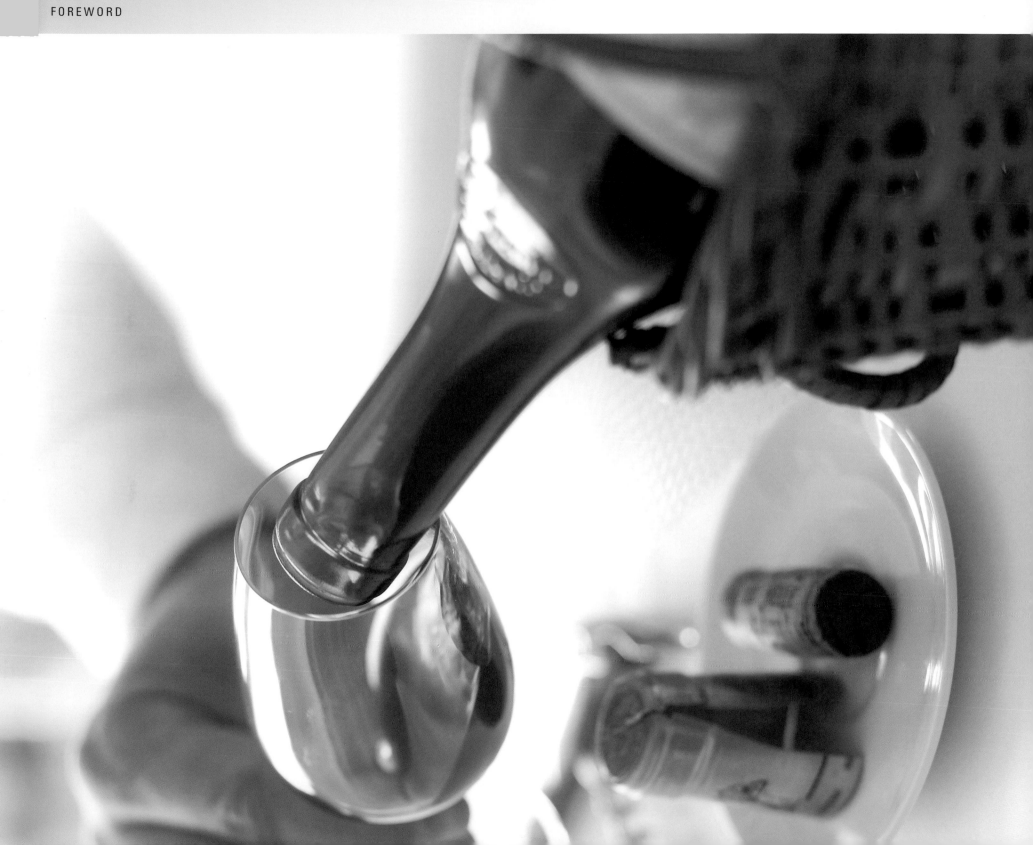

INTRODUCTION

Whether you are choosing wine in a restaurant, or buying beer for a barbecue, I hope that this friendly, accessible, sometimes opinionated guide will help you navigate through the huge universe of drink.

The pages of this book contain descriptions of hundreds of different wines, beers, spirits, cocktails, and liqueurs from all over the world. But even a quick glance at the stacked shelves of a liquor store will tell you that this is in no way a complete account of the thousands of different brands and producers that make up today's drinks market. Even in a book of this size, I have had to be very selective. I hope that I have also been fair by including not only those drinks that I find particularly enjoyable or interesting, but also those that I think will enhance your knowledge and understanding of a particular style of drink – that will wake up parts of your senses that you didn't even know you had! I have not forgotten to include the well-known, global brands, which you are very likely to find at your local store, and which make up such an important part of the drinks industry.

A FASHION FOR LIQUEURS *The drinks world never stands still for long. Liqueurs are no longer "fusty" drinks for after dinner, but are being mixed and enjoyed over ice by a much younger crowd.*

COLOUR, AROMA, AND TASTE
My approach to drink is simple. Whatever I have in my glass – from a mass-produced lager to a vintage port – I always ask myself the same questions: how does it look, smell, and taste? The structure of this book follows the same logic. The description of each drink begins with a summary of its colour, aroma, and taste, after which follow details of its character and background, as well as my own opinions about its quality and its uses – what food the drink complements, whether it works as an apéritif or a digestif, and so on. Wherever appropriate, I give a short list of my favourite, best-value producers; these are my personal views, and I do not mean to suggest that others are not as good or are not worth trying.

Individual accounts of the drinks are grouped together into larger categories – again according to their taste and character. Light, crisp wines, dark and creamy beers, and sour and tangy cocktails are, for me, evocative and useful categories, which reflect how most people choose the right drink for the right moment. These categories of drink are then collected together into chapters – dealing in turn with wine, spirits, liqueurs, cocktails, beer, and cider. At the start of each chapter is a sketch of the drink type – its history, culture, and methods of production, and a quick survey of the most important styles. My tips on how to buy, taste, and serve the drink won't turn you into an expert overnight, but they will help you enjoy and appreciate each drink to the full.

BEER RENAISSANCE *Beer is the new wine! With hundreds of exciting styles, both traditional and new, it is increasingly drunk with food, or sampled at tastings, with friends.*

COCKTAIL CLASS *Over the past two decades, the cocktail has reclaimed its glamorous crown. Stylish new bars and innovative mixologists have elevated cocktail-making to an urban art form.*

"Great drinks don't have to be expensive – you can find real quality, even on a budget."

A USER'S GUIDE TO DRINK

The world of drink – especially of wine and fine spirits – can be quite exclusive, even a little snobbish. The specialist vocabulary of the wine connoisseur and the labyrinthine systems of classifying drinks don't make things easy, and it is not hard to feel lost. I have not avoided such issues in this book; in the following pages I explain, for example, the difference between an XO and a VSOP Cognac; what makes a wheat beer distinct from an ale; and how wine is classified in France. But that is not my main focus. There are already plenty of great books that discuss the technicalities of drink – special vintages, obscure grape varieties, niche producers, and the like. What I really want to know is: can I buy good wine from my supermarket or off-licence? What beer should I try when I get tired of my usual brand? What does a drink really taste like, and is it worth its price tag? If I like Sancerre wine, what else will I like? I hope this book answers these questions and many more. If I have done a good job, it will certainly make you more curious about the diverse world of drink; it will give you the confidence to experiment more, to appreciate better, and to buy more adventurously. Above all, it will help you enjoy drink more than ever before.

PICK OF THE CROP *Packed with orchard-fresh flavours, cider is justly popular in Europe and the US.*

CHANGING TIMES

The world of drink is a dynamic mixture of tradition, innovation, and hard business. New products are launched daily, even faster than old ones are withdrawn; brands change hands, and companies are bought and sold.

To the best of my knowledge, the contents of this book were correct at the time of going to press, but by the time you read this, it is likely that some brands described will no longer exist, or may be known by different names; and new products will have been launched that certainly merit space on these pages. I can only apologise for these inevitable omissions and errors, and remind the reader that it is precisely this pace of change that makes the world of drink so exciting.

SENSIBLE DRINKING

I have one final – and very serious – point to make. This book is overwhelmingly positive about drink. It reflects the enormous pleasure that I have experienced from tasting wines, beers, spirits, liqueurs, and cocktails, both as a professional sommelier, and as a consumer at home and in restaurants. But my pleasure is always tempered by the certain knowledge that alcohol can be highly destructive – physically and psychologically – if its consumption is not controlled. I would advise you to treat alcohol with care and respect; drink is there to be enjoyed and appreciated in moderation, not abused. Drink sensibly – and it will enhance your life as it has mine.

GLOBAL SPIRITS *Some spirits define a nation's character: Russia has its vodka, France its Cognac, and Mexico its tequila. Thanks to improved distribution, premium examples of these classic spirits can now be bought at your local store.*

TRADITION *New technology applied to age-old products improves the drinking experience for all.*

WINE

VINE TO WINE

To take a simple bunch of grapes and turn it into the magic of wine – intoxicating, beautiful to look at and to savour, and infinitely varied – is surely one of humankind's greatest achievements.

CHABLIS *One of my favourite sights – a glass of light, crisp Chablis from Burgundy, France. Vines have been growing in the Burgundy region since Roman times.*

A wonderful thing about wine is that its story is constantly evolving. There are already a myriad types of wine to discover, but new styles are emerging all the time. This is not only due to improvements in technology and production techniques, but a result of new grape varieties and the emergence of new winemaking regions with their own unique soils and climates.

Wine is about far more than production and consumption. At the celebration of a marriage, a birthday, or Christmas, we raise a glass to toast happy times. When we settle down to relax after a hard day at work, or unwind at our favourite restaurant, we often do so with a glass of wine. Of course wine is to drink, but it is also about enjoyment, exploration and, most of all, passion.

THE HISTORY OF WINE

The precise origins of wine are lost in time, but the first certain records of winemaking are Ancient Egyptian tomb paintings, which date as far back as 4000BC. From these we know that the Egyptians harvested grapes with curved knives and carried the fruit in wicker baskets, before pouring them into wooden vats (made of acacia wood) and crushing them by foot.

The Greeks inherited this winemaking culture and transmitted it throughout the Mediterranean, most importantly to Italy. From about 500BC the Romans carried winemaking into much of the rest of western Europe, especially to the Moselle and Rhine Valley regions of France and Germany, and the Danube River valley in Austria. The Romans even introduced winemaking to England, where a small crop of vines provided the Roman legionnaires with their ration of one litre of wine a day.

After the fall of Rome in the 5th century AD, monks took over the care of European vineyards, refining their knowledge of viticulture as they went.

EXQUISITE QUALITY *Some of the finest and most expensive wines in the world are the sweet wines of Bordeaux, such as this Sauternes from Château Rieussec.*

" The wine industry has boomed over the past two decades, and there has been no better time to learn (and taste) more."

THE NAPA VALLEY *Missionaries planted the first vines in California in the 18th century, but planting did not begin in the state's famous Napa Valley until the middle of the 19th.*

ANCIENT HARVEST *This limestone relief, dating from 1400BC, shows Ancient Egyptians harvesting grapes.*

" The practice of drinking wine for pleasure is centuries old – dating at least as far back as Ancient Egypt."

WINE AND RITUAL *In the Christian communion ceremony, red wine symbolizes the blood of Christ. Confirmed members of the congregation take a sip from a chalice such as this.*

As landowners left tracts of land to the monasteries, the French vineyard system began to take shape.

In the 12th century, with the union of Henry II of England and Eleanor of Aquitaine of France, the English began importing wines from Bordeaux, and the commercialization of wine began in earnest.

It was the Spanish who brought the vine to South America, making their first plantings in the 16th century. From there, the European grape travelled to North America to join the continent's own indigenous species of vines.

Then, in Europe in the 19th century, disaster struck. In 1847, the powdery mildew fungus (oidium) attacked many vineyards throughout the continent, causing the grapes to split and become unusable. A second blow followed in the 1860s, when phylloxera – a plant louse, accidentally imported from North America – invaded European vineyards. This pest eats away at the roots of vines and eventually kills them. By the time viticulturists had identified the pest and found a solution (grafting their

vines on to phylloxera-resistant rootstocks from America), enormous damage had been done to the European wine industry: in France, for example, production was slashed by three-quarters in the 1870s, and took decades to recover.

QUALITY CONTROL

As trade in wine grew into a significant economic activity, individual wine producers sought to improve the quality of their products, and to protect them from inferior imitations. In 1855, the Bordeaux Chamber of Commerce classified the region's wines in a hierarchy that matched a wine's price against a set standard of excellence; and in 1905 the French government passed the first anti-fraud law, the cornerstone of the Appellation d'Origine Contrôlée (AOC) system, which classifies French wine to this day. Similar systems of regulation were then introduced in Italy, Germany, Spain, and the US.

Wine is now produced on all the inhabited continents, from Europe through Asia and Australasia to the Americas. Suitable microclimates can be found in the most unlikely places – vines seem to recognize no boundaries – although grapes for use in wine cannot be grown if the average annual temperature is less than 10°C (50°F).

HOW WINE IS MADE

Wine is essentially fermented grape juice. Grapes contain the sugars fructose and glucose, and when the skin is broken and the grape juice left to ferment, these sugars are converted into alcohol. Fermentation is an entirely natural process that is carried out by yeasts – microscopic fungi. Yeasts survive by breaking down sugars to release energy, in the same way that we digest food to sustain life. The key difference is

MODERN WINEMAKING *Like many other New World producers, the Opus One winery in the Napa Valley, California, uses state-of-the-art, industrial winemaking techniques to produce excellent wines of quality and character.*

HARVESTING BY HAND *Hand-picking the grapes, as shown here at St-Émilion in Bordeaux, France, ensures that only perfectly ripe bunches make it to the presses, and minimizes damage to the fruit.*

that the waste product of their digestion is alcohol. Yeasts are present in the air, and some winemakers rely on these natural yeasts as agents of fermentation; however, most use specially cultured yeasts, which behave more predictably and produce wines of greater consistency.

Of course, winemaking is not that simple! For a start, there are more than 4,000 different grape varieties, each with its own characteristics. Of these, just over a dozen rank as the most important for winemaking. The chief white varieties are Riesling, Chardonnay, Sauvignon Blanc, and Sémillon, with Muscat, Gewürztraminer, and Viura following closely behind. Of the red varieties, the most important are Cabernet Sauvignon, Merlot, Grenache, Tempranillo, Syrah (or Shiraz), Sangiovese, and Pinot Noir.

One of the first lessons to learn when buying and enjoying wine is that the character of the fruit from the vine, rather than the country, vintage, or producer, is the most crucial factor in determining the qualities of the drink.

But while each grape variety has its own personality (for example, a Sauvignon Blanc tends to be dry and crisp), the *terroir* (the soil, topography of the region, and climate in which the vines grow) will impart its own influence. For example, one variety of grape may produce peach flavours when grown in a

warm climate, and gooseberry flavours in cooler conditions. Even the position of a vine on a hillside, whether it faces toward or away from the sun, and whether it is in a river valley or on the coast, can have dramatic effects on the taste of the wine. Generally, a warm climate will produce a full style of wine, and a cool climate, a light style.

In the Northern Hemisphere, grapes are usually harvested (by hand or machine) between August and November, and in the Southern Hemisphere between February and May. Hand-harvesting is used whenever it is important not to damage the grapes' skins – in the production of Champagne, for example – or because steep hillsides or other geographical features prevent the use of mechanical harvesters.

At the winery, the grapes are stemmed and crushed to create a pulpy mixture called "must"; this is usually pasteurized or treated with sulphur dioxide

GRAPES IN THE NEW WORLD *Riesling grapes (above), most famous for producing Rhineland wines in Germany, are well suited to the cool climate of South Island, New Zealand, and have had great success there.*

CHARDONNAY *This grape variety has been successfully planted all over the world. It makes Chablis, the famous white Burgundy, as well as lovely wines from California, Chile, Australia, New Zealand, and South Africa.*

FERMENTATION *Oak vats, such as these at the Louis Jadot winery in Burgundy, are traditionally used to ferment wine. However, nowadays many wineries use vats made of stainless steel.*

to suppress the growth of wild yeasts and other micro-organisms in the grapes that might interfere with the production of the wine.

Fermentation can now begin. As a rule, in red-wine production, the skins, seeds, and juice are all fermented together; in white, the juice is separated from the skins and seeds and is fermented alone. Yeast is added to the juice to begin the conversion of sugars to alcohol, which takes from five to 15 days, after which the wine is racked (drawn off) to separate it from the lees – the sediment of dead yeast cells and, in the case of red wine, skins and pips. In red wine, the longer the period of fermentation, the darker and more tannic the wine. If the skins are removed quickly before fermentation begins, white wine can be made from red grapes (for example, most Champagne is made using some Pinot Noir).

Most wine is aged in wooden barrels or casks, often made of oak, giving the wine an extra layer of complexity. Oxygen penetrates the casks and softens some of the wine's harsher characteristics, such as its tannins (in red wine), while water and alcohol escape, concentrating the acidity and flavours of the wine. Before bottling, wine may require blending (where wines from two or more grape varieties are mixed together), filtering (to remove sediment), and stabilizing (adding sulphur dioxide to the wine to prevent the growth of residual yeast or bacteria).

MATURING THE WINE *Many great wines are matured in oak barrels – the smaller the better – which improves the character and complexity of the wine, adding flavours of sweet vanilla and butter.*

CATEGORIES OF WINE

The primary categories of wine are table wines, fortified wines, and sparkling wines. Table wines, also called still or natural wines, are the most common and come in three basic colours: white, red, and rosé (a pale pink). They range in taste from sweet to very dry, and alcohol content varies from seven per cent to 15 per cent. Fortified wines (such as sherry, port, and Madeira) have extra alcohol, usually a grape brandy, added to them, giving them an alcohol content ranging from 14 to 23 per cent. Colours may be white, amber, bright red, or dark red. Sparkling wines are usually white, but may be red or rosé, and have an alcohol content similar to table wines.

DISCOVERING WINE

It is common practice to make distinctions between wines from the "Old World" (Europe) and those from the "New World" (the Americas, Australasia, South Africa, and so on). Both regions produce great, and not-so-great wines, so it is dangerous to make generalizations. However, as a broad rule New World wines tend to be more openly fruit-driven, up-front, and exuberant, and Old World wines more austere, drier, and generally lighter. At the cheap end of the market, New World wines will almost certainly provide the better value for money, but the opposite is not necessarily true at the top end! The key to discovering wines that you love is to be led by your nose and your palate. Remember that for every disappointment, there is always the promise that next time you will discover the perfect wine – the one you have always been waiting for.

CELEBRATIONS *What better way to celebrate than with a glass of Champagne? The most important thing about wine is that it is for enjoying – especially with friends.*

"Wine does not have to be expensive to be good; sometimes taste is simply a matter of being in good company."

GLOBAL PRODUCTION

Wine has always been an important part of European culture, but production has spread all round the world in recent years, bringing wonderful new styles and grape varieties to light. The finest growing regions are situated in two broad bands of latitude, one between 30° and 50° North, the other between 30° and 50° South.

SPAIN

Spain has a surprisingly wide climatic range, which means its wines are equally diverse. The seasonal extremes are tempered by the influence of mountains in many winegrowing areas, like Rioja and Navarra, while Rías Baixas wines are moderated by cool sea breezes. Sherry is made in hot southern Spain.

KEY:
■ WINE PRODUCING REGIONS

UNITED STATES

The heartland of US wine production is California, where the warm, sunny climate is balanced by cool breezes and mists from the ocean. Further north, Oregon and Washington State are fast becoming key wine areas. New York State and Pennsylvania both make good wines on the east coast.

NORTH AMERICA

TROPIC OF CANCER

CARIBBEAN

CENTRAL AMERICA

SOUTH AMERICA

CHILE

Parts of Chile have a Mediterranean climate, and the country has also benefited by being free from phylloxera. As a result, Chilean wine production has soared. The Rapel Valley region produces the best red wines, while the Casablanca Valley makes fine whites.

ARGENTINA

The driving force behind the success of Argentinian wines is the Malbec grape variety, which has been backed by lots of investment in new technology. The region around Mendoza has the perfect climate, with the heat of the continent balanced by cool mountain breezes coming down from the Andes.

FRANCE

France has myriad grape varieties and styles of wine, plus an illustrious winemaking heritage. Producers all over the world make reference to French styles, even if their vineyards are on the other side of the globe, and regions such as Champagne, Bordeaux, and Burgundy will always have a special mystique.

GERMANY

It is time to end the idea that Germany makes mainly sweet wines. Some of the finest dry wines in the world come from the wine-producing regions of Mosel-Saar-Ruwer, Rheinpfalz, and Rheinhessen. Superb grape varieties like Riesling and Spätburgunder thrive in the gentle and productive southwest German climate.

EUROPE

MIDDLE EAST

NORTH AFRICA

EUROPE

MIDDLE EAST

ASIA

AFRICA

EQUATOR

TROPIC OF
CAPRICORN

ITALY

Italy has many long-established vineyards, and makes a fantastic variety of wines. Steeped in history and tradition, these classic styles are influenced by Italy's enormous climatic range, from the cool Alpine Alto Adige and Veneto regions in the north, to the heat of Puglia and Sicilia in the south.

AUSTRALIA

In the past 15 years, Australia has developed into one of the driving forces in New World wines. It also pioneered the listing of grape varieties on wine labels. Victoria, New South Wales, and South Australia are the key wine-growing regions.

AUSTRALIA

SOUTH AFRICA

South Africa's wines rank among the finest from the New World. The best are produced in areas that benefit from the cooling influence of ocean breezes. The regions around Stellenbosch and Constantia are excellent examples of the right kind of supportive and balanced climate.

NEW ZEALAND

New Zealand wines lean towards a European style, thanks to the cool climate. The most important regions are Hawkes Bay and Gisborne on the east coast of North Island, the southern part of North Island near Wellington, and the Northern part of the South Island around Marlborough.

CHOOSING AND STORING WINE

Most people buy their wine from a supermarket as part of their weekly shop, or choose a bottle from a restaurant wine list. Price alone is not always a guide to quality, and a little knowledge about how wines are labelled will pay rich rewards.

The international wine trade has blossomed over the past 20 years and – in theory – it has never been easier to buy good wine. If you have deep pockets, a private wine consultant can help you put together a great cellar; and there are plenty of books, magazines, websites, and wine clubs that can guide you to a good bottle. But, inevitably, we still find ourselves in that familiar position – staring at a wall of wine labels in a store, wondering which to choose. Decoding a wine label is not an easy job, because there is so much variation in the type and amount

DECODING A LABEL *As a very general rule, good wines carry more information on the label than do poor wines, but always take care – the producer will try to hide the wine's weak points. The images here show typical label content for a French white and an Australian red.*

PRODUCER The name of a reputable producer is the single most important indicator of quality on a wine label.

REGION OF ORIGIN This wine is from a named valley in South Australia.

NAME The name of the wine is followed by the grape variety.

TASTING BEFORE BUYING *Some vineyards let you taste different vintages and styles before buying. This is one of the best ways to learn about wine, but be careful – the wine always tastes better in the vineyard than back home, and import and carriage costs can soon mount up.*

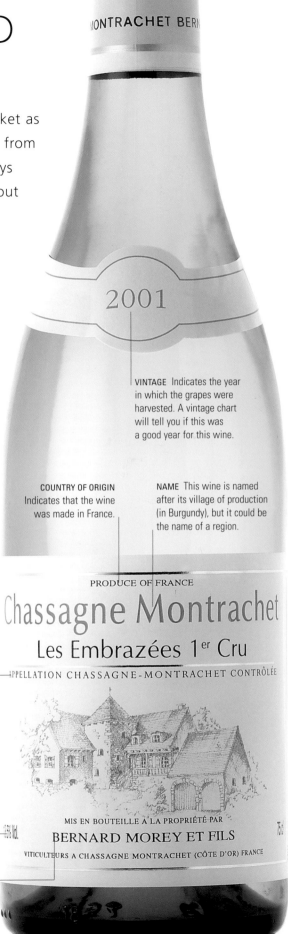

VINTAGE Indicates the year in which the grapes were harvested. A vintage chart will tell you if this was a good year for this wine.

COUNTRY OF ORIGIN Indicates that the wine was made in France.

NAME This wine is named after its village of production (in Burgundy), but it could be the name of a region.

DESIGNATION Appellation Chassagne-Montrachet Contrôlée shows that the wine meets set AOC standards. "Les Embrazées" is a designated area within the AOC region. 1er Cru (*premier cru*) means the wine is classified as a "First Growth" – a high quality standard.

ALCOHOL Indicates the alcohol content by volume.

PRODUCER Above the name of the producer is confirmation that the wine was bottled at the estate – a good sign.

HOW MUCH TO BUY

When buying wine for a dinner or drinks party, I always assume that one bottle is enough for four generous glasses. I allow two glasses of red wine and two of white for each person. Serving Champagne, I allow six glasses per bottle, and plan for two glasses per person.

of information given. Typically, a label will carry the name of the winery or producer, the country and region of origin, the style of the wine, its alcohol content, and details of bottling. It may include the name of the vineyard, the grape variety (or varieties) used to make the wine, and details of the vintage (the year the grapes were grown). It may also carry some form of quality classification, awarded by the government of the country of origin. There is no global classification of quality; each country, or region within a country, may have its own system.

FRENCH WINE

The highest quality classification for French wines is Appellation d'Origine Contrôlée (AOC or AC), which covers about 40 per cent of the country's production. If you see AOC on a label, you will know that the wine has been made in a specific named region (the appellation), and according to set quality standards. Depending on the region, AOC wines may have additional designations: Burgundies, for example, carry the titles *grand cru* and *premier cru* to reflect the top and second highest quality respectively, and Bordeaux wines have their own distinct classifications *(see box, p109)*.

The next level of classification is Vin Délimité de Qualité Supérieure (VDQS), which covers just one per cent of wines, most of which are consumed in France. This classification is commonly seen on wines aspiring to AOC status. Below this is Vin de Pays (VdP; country or local wine), which covers 25 per cent of French production. This classification, which always states the region of the wine's origin, was established in 1968 to reward improvements in quality by producers of more humble wines *(see box, p96)*; Vin de Pays wines are usually at least drinkable, and some are truly excellent. The lowest category,

Vin de Table (VdT; table wine), covers 28 per cent of production, almost all of which is consumed in France. Also known as *vin ordinaire*, this wine is not for keeping, and is often drunk mixed with water.

The French system is a reasonable guide to quality and is most reliable at the top and bottom ends of the scale. In between, there are many VDQS or Vin de Pays wines that you might well enjoy more than an AOC wine, so don't be snobbish. My advice is to first identify the style of wine you like, then go up a notch in terms of quality, and see whether you like, or even notice, the difference.

ITALIAN WINE

Like French wines, Italian wines are differentiated primarily by region (or appellation). Chianti is from Tuscany; Barolo and Barbaresco are from Piemonte; Soave, Amarone, Valpolicella, and Bardolino are from the Veneto in northern Italy; and so on. As in France, the wines are classified by quality, the lowliest being Vino da Tavola (VdT, or table wine), followed by Indicazione Geografica Tipica (IGT, similar in level to the French Vin de Pays). Higher classifications are Denominazione di Origine Controllata (DOC) and the top quality Denominazione di Origine

COLLECTOR'S ITEM
Wine can be a good financial investment. If you are buying wine to lay down, it is vital to know about its provenance. Buy at specialist wine auctions; it is risky to buy privately without taking advice.

PLACE AND PRODUCTION

Throughout the world, wines are associated with specific regions of greater or lesser size. In Europe, these are called appellations (such as Bordeaux and Burgundy); in Australia, they are called Geographical Indications (GIs). The Margaret River GI in Western Australia is a small area producing top-quality wines, notably great Cabernet Sauvignon and Chardonnay *(right)*. In contrast, wines labelled South Eastern Australia (another GI) could come from any of three enormous states, and are unpredictable in quality.

MARGARET RIVER

Controllata e Garantita (DOCG) – wines that adhere to quality standards similar to the French AOC. There may be huge differences in quality within one appellation; my tip is to look for good producers, rather than putting too much faith in designations.

SPANISH AND PORTUGUESE WINE

A Spanish wine designated Denominación de Origen (DO), like a French AOC, comes from a named area and has been quality-checked by an independent standards committee. It is worth looking out for two variants of the DO designation: Denominación de Origen Calificada (DOCa), which identifies the best wines from the regions of Rioja and Priorat; and Denominación de Origen de Pago (DO Pago), which is used for some excellent single-estate wines. Vino de la Tierra identifies some good regional wines (rather like the French Vin de Pays designation) while Vino de Mesa is a basic table wine. Spanish wines can also be classified on the basis of the length of time they are aged in the barrel; the shortest is *joven*, followed by *crianza* and *reserva*, and the longest, *gran reserva*.

CORKS AND CLOSURES

Cork has been used to seal wine bottles for over 3,000 years, and for me, pulling and sniffing a cork is a crucial part of enjoying wine – especially a good bottle. Plastic closures and screw caps are fine for everyday wines, though they are less friendly to the environment than cork.

Portugal follows a French-style classification system. Denominaçao de Origem Controlada (DOC) is the highest category, equivalent to the French AOC; Indicação de Proveniencia Regulamentada (IPR) indicates a wine with DOC potential. Vinho Regional denotes a regional wine from a defined area (as Vin de Pays), while Vinho de Mesa is a table wine.

THE INFLUENCE OF THE GRAPE

The character of a wine – its aroma, taste, and structure – is shaped by the grapes from which it is made. The grape variety (or varieties) used are usually given on the label of the bottle of New World wines, but not always on European wines. The influence of the grapes can be illustrated by contrasting wines made from different varieties.

SAUVIGNON / CHARDONNAY

Sauvignon Blanc grapes *(left)* produce light, dry, aromatic, and citrusy wines with a refreshing feel. Chardonnay grapes *(right)* make richer, more "oily" wines thanks to their thicker structure.

GAMAY / CABERNET SAUVIGNON

Gamay *(left)* are juicy grapes that make light, lively, and fruity wines for early drinking. Cabernet Sauvignon grapes *(right)*, which are thick-skinned and grow in solid bunches, make full, firm, complex wines.

MUSCAT / SÉMILLON

With its big berries and sweet juice, Muscat *(left)* is the classic aromatic grape, making great medium-sweet wines. Sémillon *(right)* can cope with "noble rot" *(see p141)*, and makes some of the finest dessert wines.

GERMAN WINE

The German government has a complicated system of quality classification in which there are four basic categories. Deutsche Tafelwein is ordinary table wine (with no named vineyard). Landwein is a wine that comes from one of 17 approved regions, and must contain at least 5.5% ABV. Qualitätswein bestimmter Anbaugebiet (QbA) denotes a wine from any one of 13 approved regions, which is made only from certain grape varieties, and is at least 7.5% ABV; the name of the vineyard may be given if at least 85 per cent of the grapes were grown at the vineyard. Qualitätswein mit Prädikat (QmP) is the top grade; these wines come from a specified region and grape variety, and are quality tested according to their residual sugar level and sweetness.

NEW WORLD WINES

Labels of New World wines tend to emphasize the grape variety and brand name over the region; the label on the back of the bottle also gives much more information than appears on wines from Europe – the precise location of the vineyard, and a description of how the wine has been aged, for example. However, the lack of independent quality standards means that knowledge of good producers is even more important than for European wines. You may seem terms like "Reserve" and "Estate" on a New World wine, which mean respectively that the wine is the highest quality from that particular vineyard, and that it is bottled on the same estate where it is grown; however, these terms are often used loosely, and are far from a guarantee of quality.

VINTAGE WINES

The word "vintage" on a wine label simply means the year in which the grapes were grown – it does not carry with it any judgment of quality. Good vintages are those years when weather conditions in a particular wine-growing region were just right to produce good wine. In parts of the world with a consistent and predictable climate – Australia, California in the US, and Languedoc in

SHIRAZ GRAPES *Dark and intense, this grape variety originated in the Rhône Valley of France, but is now also responsible for fantastic deep and fruity wines from Australia and California.*

France, for example – vintage makes little difference, but elsewhere, the quality of the wine can be greatly influenced by weather. Specialist wine magazines and websites publish charts that rank the vintages for different regions according to quality; these charts – coupled with expert advice – can be a useful guide when buying wines at the upper end of the price range, especially if you are planning to lay them down *(see below)*. However, vintage charts should be used with caution; a localized hailstorm may devastate vines on one side of a valley, but leave the other side untouched. And a good producer can make a fine wine in a "bad" vintage, but a bad producer will still struggle in a "good" vintage. The key, as ever, is to seek out wines made by reputable producers.

STORING AND CELLARING WINE

Cheap and mid-priced wines should, as a rule, be drunk within one or (at most) two years of purchase. When choosing wines to "lay down" you need to do some serious research or take expert advice and only select the best wines from the best vintages – it is a myth that all expensive wines get better with age.

The ideal place to keep wine is in a cellar *(below)* where the humidity is around 70 per cent and the temperature is 12–18°C (54–64°F). The room should be dark, with no vibration. To store wine at home, especially if you do not have a cellar, keep bottles horizontal in wine racks *(right)*. Terracotta drain pipes can work well as homemade racks. Position the racks as low as possible in a cool, dark location, ideally against a north-facing wall. Wrap the bottles individually in newspaper, and avoid agitating them too often.

TASTING AND APPRECIATING WINE

Anyone can drink and enjoy a glass of wine, but tasting wine is an art. It takes experience and a little knowledge of technique to fully appreciate the complex flavours and textures of this unique drink.

Ultimately, wine is a matter of taste, but just because you dislike a particular wine does not mean it is bad. Such judgments are subjective, and it is crucial to analyse the wine more systematically on the basis of its colour, aroma, and taste, and whether it is a good example of its particular style. Appreciation of wine

grows with experience – the ability to recall, compare, and categorize tastes and aromas – but it starts with a systematic approach to tasting.

I always taste wines from a plain, thin-walled, stemmed wine glass, rinsing it thoroughly in water before moving from one wine to another; restricting the wines sampled to one style or region is helpful because it helps fine-tune the senses. Ideally, the tasting should take place in a brightly lit room, free from strong odours, such as cigarette smoke and cooking; I like to taste in the morning, before my taste buds become jaded, and always taste wines at their correct serving temperatures *(see p29)*.

HOW TO TASTE WINE

1 Check the colour of the wine against a sheet of white paper; examine the colour at the rim, and also when looking down on the wine from above.

2 Swirl the glass to bring the wine into contact with air and release its aromas.

3 Keep your nose at the rim of the glass, take one long sniff and analyse the aromas of the wine.

4 Gently sip a small amount; hold the liquid in your mouth and draw in some air over the wine; most of the "taste" of the wine comes from the detection of aromas at the back of the throat.

5 Spit the wine into a bucket (if you are tasting several wines). Make detailed notes of your observations of colour, aroma, and taste.

1 Check the colour in natural light (not direct sunlight)

2 Gently swirl the liquid in the glass

3 Analyse the aroma

4 Sip and taste the wine

5 Record your observations

DRINK ANALYSIS

COLOUR

Wines in good condition should be bright, vibrant, and clear – never cloudy. Tiny bubbles at the rim are acceptable in some wines, such as Vinho Verde and Muscadet, but should not be evident in others. Colour is usually a good indicator of body – pale whites and reds are usually light in texture. The classic colours for white wines are: straw yellow for dry whites; gold for medium and aromatic whites; dark gold for full, sweet whites. Reds range from garnet to a darker ruby red; the richest dense wines may tend towards purple or even black. Rosé wines are hardly ever a true pink colour, but range from pinky-blue to pinky-orange.

The colour at the rim of the wine is a good indicator of age. Young white wine will have a silver or green rim, which becomes more golden with age. Young red wines have a ruby or purple rim, which becomes tile-red with age.

Still, dry wines should have no residual sugar, and should be low in viscosity. Viscosity will vary with temperature (wines are "thicker" when colder), and even differs with the condition and cleanliness of the glass.

AROMA

The aroma of good wine should be fresh and not sour, and you may be able to detect any of a host of complex aromas: there are thousands of distinct smells and describing them is highly subjective, but they broadly fall into a few "classes". These classes are shown here, alongside an example of wine that typically displays the aroma. In general, dry white wines should have a pleasantly citrus nose, and a grassy or green fruit aroma. Fuller whites might display vanilla or butter in the nose. The lighter reds typically have aromas of red fruits, and the heavier reds, black fruits. Aged reds will have fantastic aromas of leather, earth, smoke, oak, and spice, or even "animal" smells. Young wine will have lively aromas; aged wine will have more ripe and complex aromas.

FRUIT	ANIMAL	SMOKE	SPICE
Gamay	Aged red Burgundy	Bordeaux	Shiraz
HERBS	FLOWERS	WOOD	VEGETABLES
Sauvignon Blanc	Muscat	Chardonnay, Rioja	Saumur, Chinon

TASTE

The spectrum of tastes in wine is so vast, and people's perception of taste varies so greatly, that it is hard even to imagine a vocabulary adequate to describe the flavours in wine. It is, however, useful to analyse the taste of a wine in terms of its balance between fruit, acidity, and alcohol, and (in the case of red wines) tannin – the mouth-drying chemical that comes from the skins of the grapes and from the wood in which the wine is aged. It is just as unsatisfying to have a dry white that is too acidic, as it is to have a rich red that is too "jammy" and tannic.

ACIDITY • ALCOHOL • TANNIN • FRUIT

RED WINE TASTE MAP
A good red balances the key elements of acidity, alcohol, fruit, and tannin. Cheaper wines will lack the complexity of more expensive bottles.

ACIDITY

WHITE WINE TASTE MAP
A good white balances the fruit/sugar, acidity, and alcohol. Serving the wine too cold not only numbs the taste buds, but alters the taste characteristics.

ALCOHOL • FRUIT / SUGAR

OPENING AND SERVING WINE

Choosing the right wine to match your food, preparing and opening the bottle, sniffing, pouring, tasting, and approving are all part of a ritual that transforms the simple act of drinking into an event.

CORKSCREWS
The classic "waiter's friend" is a portable and effective corkscrew; there are countless other designs, including ones with teflon-coated spirals, and even ones that use gas pressure to expel the cork. My advice, as ever, is to keep it simple!

Serving wine at its peak condition takes a little forward planning. Each style of wine has an optimum serving temperature at which it releases its aromas and flavours to best effect *(see box, opposite)*, so you may need to cool or warm the bottles before serving. The easiest way is to place the bottle in the refrigerator where it will cool by about 2°C (4°F) every ten minutes; conversely, the wine will warm up at about the same rate when removed from the refrigerator and left at room temperature. If you need to chill wine quickly, 30 minutes in the freezer, or in an ice bucket, will be ample. You may wish to invest in a rapid chill sleeve, which you can slide over the bottle; this will also keep your wine cool during your meal. Never warm red wine on a hot oven hob or in the microwave; over-warm wine tastes like cough medicine, and if it reaches body temperature, you won't taste it at all! Instead, warm it gently in an ice bucket filled with tepid water. Some light, young reds, such as Pinot Noir, Beaujolais, Valpolicella, or Loire Valley wines, actually benefit from 30 minutes in the refrigerator before serving.

Many people open a bottle of wine a couple of hours before serving to let it "breathe". This is not particularly effective because so little of the wine is in contact with the air; instead, simply serve the wine in a generously sized glass and swirl for a few moments. This will help to release its aromas and

OPENING, DECANTING, AND POURING RED WINE

A day or so before you plan to serve a fine red wine, stand the bottle upright to allow any sediment to settle to the bottom. In my role as a sommelier, I start by presenting the wine to my guests – I name the wine, the producer, and the vintage. When serving fine red wine, hold the bottle at the shoulder or the base – never by the neck – and do not agitate the bottle as this will stir up the sediment.

1 Using a sharp knife, cut the capsule at the top of the bottle and remove it carefully.
2 Pull the cork steadily and gently, keeping the corkscrew straight so that it draws the cork vertically. Don't tug at the cork – let the corkscrew do the work! Clean the neck of the bottle with a white napkin, then pour a little of the wine into a tasting glass.
3 Smell the wine to check that it is not corked *(see p31)*; a corked wine will smell like dirty wet socks, and should be discarded.
4 Pour all the wine from your tasting glass into the glass decanter.
5 Swirl the wine in the base of the decanter; this will clean the decanter of any residual flavours. Pour the wine into your tasting glass.
6 Taste the wine to check its condition.

7 If the wine meets with your approval, you can begin decanting. Slowly pour the wine from the bottle in a steady stream down the side of the decanter. Position the bottle about 10cm (4in) above a lighted candle; this will allow you to see when the sediment arrives in the shoulder of the bottle. At this point, stop pouring; you will inevitably have to sacrifice a little wine to avoid sediment in the decanter.
8 Pour the wine from the decanter into your guests' glasses. It is good etiquette to serve from the right and to fill a red wine glass to only one-third capacity.

1 Remove the capsule

4 Pour the contents of the glass into the decanter

5 Swirl the wine around the decanter

IDEAL SERVING TEMPERATURES

Temperature has a big impact on the taste of a wine. Use a wine thermometer to test the temperature of the liquid, but remember that there are exceptions to the guidelines given below; for example, you can serve cheap wines cooler to hide their imperfections.

TYPE OF WINE	TEMPERATURE
Light, crisp whites	4–6°C (39–43°F)
Juicy, aromatic whites	6–8°C (43–46°F)
Full, opulent whites	10–12°C (50–54°F)
Rosé	4–6°C (39–43°F)
Fruity, lively reds	12–14°C (54–57°F)
Ripe, smooth reds	16–18°C (61–64°F)
Rich, dense reds	18–20°C (64–68°F)
Sparkling	6–8°C (43–46°F)
Sweet and fortified	6–8°C (43–46°F)

FILLING A GLASS *This picture shows the appropriate glasses and filling levels for sparkling wine, red wine, dessert wine, and white wine (from left to right).*

2 Open the bottle using a corkscrew

3 Sample the aroma in a tasting glass

6 Taste the wine

7 Decant the wine

8 Serve and enjoy

flavours, and may soften the harsh tannins present in some young red wines. Pouring the wine into a decanter will also bring the liquid into contact with the air, but the main reason to decant a wine is to separate the liquid from any sediment in the bottle. You only need to decant wines that throw a lot of sediment – notably some older (over 10 years old), full-bodied reds, and port.

EXPANDING CORK *The neck of a Champagne cork expands once it is pulled from the bottle – don't attempt to push it back in!*

EQUIPMENT

You don't need to spend a fortune on fancy equipment and glassware. It is worth investing in a good corkscrew that will not fragment corks – I favour designs that use a smooth metal spiral, rather than a sharp-edged "screw". Many corkscrews incorporate a sharp blade for cutting the capsule over the cork, but

a short, sharp kitchen knife will do just as well. You could buy some good quality white linen napkins, and use these to wipe the bottle and clean up any spills – they add a real air of professionalism. Glassware should be plain and unfussy, to allow the colour of the wine to shine through, and thin-walled – a chunky glass psychologically prepares you for a coarse wine. Wine glasses should always have a stem – if you drink from a tumbler-style glass, the heat from your hands will warm the wine. You can buy a different glass for just about every style of wine, but you only really need four: a large-bowled glass that allows "big" reds to breathe; a smaller tulip-shaped glass for white wines – the smaller volume means that the wines have less time

OPENING AND SERVING CHAMPAGNE

Champagne is bottled to the pressure of a car tyre, and needs to be opened with care. Don't "pop" the cork unless you've just won the Grand Prix – it is dangerous and wastes precious liquid.

1 Carefully cut the foil below the level of the cork, and gently remove it from the bottle.
2 Keeping your thumb pressed on the cork, turn the wire ring six times and open the cage wide.
3 Remove the cork by gripping it tightly and twisting the base of the bottle.
4 Clean the neck of the bottle.
5 Pour steadily, into a flute, inclining the glass to control the building mousse.

1 Cut the seal with a sharp knife and remove

2 Open the cage with thumb covering the cork

3 Twist the bottle, not the cork

4 Wipe the rim of the neck to clean

5 Pour gently and enjoy

MATCHING FOOD AND WINE

There are no strict rules when it comes to pairing wine with food. Old conventions are being eroded by the spread of world cuisine and "fusion" cooking. The table below is merely a set of suggestions, based on my experience as a sommelier, but if you like your Lemon Sole with a full, tannic red, go ahead and enjoy, with my blessing!

○○○ avoid
●○○ acceptable
●●○ good match
●●● perfect match

FOOD STYLE	LIGHT, CRISP WHITES	JUICY, AROMATIC WHITES	FULL, OPULENT WHITES	FRUITY, LIVELY REDS	RIPE, SMOOTH REDS	RICH, DENSE REDS
Smoked	●●●	●●●	○○○	●●●	●●○	○○○
Spicy	●●●	●○○	○○○	●●○	●●○	○○○
Salty	●●●	○○○	○○○	●●○	○○○	○○○
Rich and creamy	●●○	●●●	○○○	●●●	○○○	○○○
Light fish and shellfish	●●●	●●○	○○○	●●●	●○○	○○○
Meaty fish	○○○	●●○	●●●	●●○	○○○	○○○
Poultry	○○○	○○○	●●○	●●●	●●●	○○○
Game	○○○	○○○	○○○	○○○	●●○	●●●
Red meat	○○○	○○○	○○○	●●●	●●●	●●○
Stews and casseroles	○○○	○○○	○○○	○○○	●●●	●●●
Hard cheese	○○○	○○○	●●●	○○○	●●●	●●○
Blue cheese	○○○	●○○	●●○	●○○	○○○	○○○
Soft and creamy cheese	●●●	○○○	○○○	●●○	●●○	●●○
Grilled fish	○○○	●●●	●●○	●●●	●●○	○○○
Grilled meat	○○○	○○○	●●○	●●○	●●○	●●○
Cold meat and charcuterie	○○○	○○○	○○○	●●○	●●●	○○○
Soup	●●○	○○○	○○○	●●○	○○○	○○○
Vegetable dishes	○○○	●●○	○○○	○○○	●●○	○○○
Pasta and pizza	●●○	○○○	●●○	●○○	●●●	○○○
Egg dishes	○○○	●○○	○○○	●○○	○○○	○○○

to warm up; a tall, slender Champagne flute, which reduces the surface area of the drink open to the air, and so preserves the bubbles longer; and a shorter, stemmed glass for dessert wines, port, and sherry.

KEEPING WINE

Once a bottle of wine is opened, it quickly begins to oxidize and will not last more than three days. To slow down the rate of spoilage, push the cork firmly into the bottle, and keep the wine (even a red) in the refrigerator; don't forget to raise it to the right temperature before serving. Specialist devices are available that inject gas (or create a vacuum) in the bottle, but I'm not sure that they do a much better job than simply placing the bottle in the refrigerator.

DIAGNOSING PROBLEMS

Always smell and taste your wine before pouring it for your guests. Occasionally, contamination of the cork will give the wine an unpleasant, musty, damp odour, which only increases with aeration. Such "corked" wine should be discarded (or sent back, if ordered in a restaurant). Another problem is oxidation; excessive contact with the air results in a flat and tired taste, and a loss of fruitiness. Extreme oxidation makes the wine taste like nutty sherry. To slow oxidation, producers routinely add a preservative – sulphur dioxide – to their wines. Heavy-handed use of this chemical can give wine a "rough" feel, which is most obvious at the back of the throat, or may even make the wine taste like bad eggs.

66 Fresh, clean, and zesty; these refreshing white wines are perfect at any time and for any occasion. **99**

LIGHT, CRISP WHITES

INTRODUCING LIGHT, CRISP WHITES

From Italy's Pinot Grigio to South Africa's Chenin Blanc, there is wonderful variety in light, crisp wines. Favourites are often a matter of personal taste – and may even come down to a memory or mood that a particular wine conjures up for you.

CRISP APPLE *Key tastes in light whites include apple and citrus.*

The grapes that make light, crisp wines (among them Aligoté, Trebbiano, and Pinot Grigio) typically have big berries and thin skins. As these wines tend to be produced in cooler climates (such as northern Europe), or in the cooler mountainous regions of hotter countries such as Italy, Portugal, and most parts of the New World, a thin skin is essential to ensure that the grapes ripen early, before they are at risk of being damaged by frost. Light whites tend to be vinified using modern techniques and stainless steel vats, which maintain their freshness.

The characters of light, crisp whites vary according to the particular grower, the region's climate, the soil in the vineyards, and the wine's vintage. The best and most expensive light whites are brilliantly fresh, with a perfect balance between acidity, alcohol, and fruit. They have a complex character that offers citrus, mineral, and apple aromas, and a deliciously long finish. While less expensive light whites can often lack character and personality, some careful choosing will reveal wines that are fresh and clean, with an acidity that is distinct, but not too pronounced. They may have subtle floral or pear flavours and medium length. Some cheaper light white wines can match very well with strongly flavoured, spicy food.

THAI CURRY *Portuguese Vinho Verde, which can be tart and aggressive, is well matched with spicy Thai cuisine.*

DRYNESS AND ACIDITY

The overall style of light, crisp white wines is neutral and dry – but that is not to say that they are bland. Although the dryness is often the first thing to hit the tastebuds when we drink a light white, the dry flavours should be something to grow on the palate and to be enjoyed, and should never be confused with sharpness. The key to a good light white wine lies in its acidity, which should have enough presence to make the wine refreshing, but not so much as to produce tartness in the taste. Overall, dry whites, far from being boring, are fun and youthful. They are wines for drinking (rather than laying down) and so are perfect for enjoying at dinner parties and socially among friends.

GRAPE VARIETIES

The following varieties are the best for making wines that are light, dry, and crisp. Their ripened grapes offer unique characters as well as delicious floral and citrus flavours. Typical examples of light, crisp varieties include, in France, Muscadet from the Loire Valley and Aligoté from

Burgundy. Italy offers Pinot Grigio – known as Pinot Gris in Alsace *(see p45)*, where it makes a fruity, aromatic wine – and the Trebbiano grape (known as Ugni Blanc in France), most notably present in the earthy wines of Soave and in easy-going Frascati.

GRAPE	BEST REGIONAL EXAMPLES	COMMENTS
CHARDONNAY	France: Chablis, Mâcon. Australia: Tasmania. Austria.	A very versatile grape, especially in cold climates, Chardonnay makes refreshing wines with notes of minerals, green apple, and citrus and grapefruit. In France, it is used to make one of the great, classic, light white wines – Chablis.
ALIGOTÉ	France: Burgundy (Bouzeron). Bulgaria. Moldova. Ukraine. Romania. Russia.	Enjoying increasing popularity, the Aligoté grape produces light, lemony wines and is a key ingredient in the famous Burgundy apéritif Kir *(see p37)*.
PINOT GRIGIO	Italy: Northeast (Friuli).	Pinot Grigio is the Italian name for the French Pinot Gris; grown in Italy, it is a dry-wine grape with little aroma, but a refreshing lemony acidity. It makes the perfect easy-quaffing dry white.
MUSCADET	France: Loire Valley.	Muscadet is a dry-wine grape that is not strongly flavoured. It is also known as Melon de Bourgogne in the most western part of the Loire Valley vineyards.
LOUREIRO	Portugal: northern regions. Spain: Galicia.	Loureiro makes a lightly structured wine that is slightly fizzy, zesty, and clean. In Portugal, it is used to make Vinho Verde, while in Spain, it is part of the blend making Rías Baixas.
CHASSELAS	Switzerland. France: Alsace. Germany. Austria. Romania. Hungary. Chile.	Some of the finest white wine in Switzerland is made from this grape, with great apple and citrus aromas.
CHENIN BLANC	South Africa. France: Loire Valley (Anjou-Saumur). USA: California.	A major grape in South Africa, where it is known as Steen. It makes lean and light wines, with notes of apple and citrus.
PINOT BLANC	France: Alsace. Germany. Austria. Italy: Trentino-Alto Adige, Friuli, Lombardia.	The wines made from Pinot Blanc are generally unoaked, and at their best, are fruity and well balanced.
MÜLLER-THURGAU	Germany. Luxembourg. Switzerland. Slovenia. New Zealand.	Known as Rivaner in Luxembourg, the quality of this grape is fast improving. At its best, it is fresh, aromatic, and expressive.
RHODITIS	Greece.	This variety has a pink-skinned berry and is often blended with other grapes. It is used as the base for the Greek wine retsina.
SYLVANER	France: Alsace. Italy. Austria. Switzerland. Germany.	Sylvaner is the Alsace version of Muscadet – dry and steely, with citrus flavours.
VIURA	Spain: Rioja, Navarra.	The most-planted grape in northern Spain, Viura makes wines that are floral with citrus and a balanced acidity.
VERDICCHIO	Italy: Marches.	Verdicchio has a naturally high level of acidity. The best wine made from this grape is Verdicchio dei Castelli di Jesi.
TREBBIANO	Italy. France. South America. Spain.	Trebbiano is known for its acidity even in hot climates. The wine it makes is increasing in importance in the world market.

FRANCE

France produces some of the world's greatest light, crisp wines. I consider Chablis – a dry, unoaked Chardonnay from Burgundy's northern outpost – to be one of the greatest of all. Other examples come from the Loire and Alsace, and all of these wines make excellent partners for food – especially fish and shellfish.

CHABLIS

C COLOUR Very pale straw; clear, bright, and light.

A AROMA Floral and grassy, but delicate and not too highly perfumed.

T TASTE Apple, citrus fruits, and minerals, with notes of flint or steel.

Chablis is a reliable wine, and offers some of the best value to be found in Burgundy. It is a perfect partner to white fish and the classic match for oysters. Take care not to overchill it, though – 11°C (52°F) is the ideal drinking temperature.

Chablis is best known for its steely, dry qualities, so people are often surprised to find out that it is 100 per cent Chardonnay. The wine's distinctive character is a product of climate and *terroir*. Chablis comes from the northernmost part of the Burgundy region near Auxerre, not far from Champagne, where the the flinty soils impart a definite mineral, smoky quality typical of the appellation.

The wines are classified into four quality levels. The Chablis appellation covers the bulk of production, and describes the wine produced in most of the vineyards around the town of Chablis, and

CHABLIS
Domaine Laroche

BOTTLE TIME *Ageing improves a good Chablis. The grands crus age best and longest while Petit Chablis, which is more citrusy, and less complex, needs to be enjoyed young.*

facing north and east. Petit Chablis comes from the same area as ordinary Chablis, but from poorer soils and aspects. The seven *grands crus* – which can be truly outstanding – are all produced on one hill to the northeast of the town, facing south and west. *Premier cru* is also produced on the south- and west-facing slopes; it has at least a half degree of alcohol less than a *grand cru*.

Chablis production has historically been vulnerable to devastating spring frosts, and as recently as ten years ago, when I visited the district, 60 per cent of the year's crop had been wiped out. A tragedy! Technology has come to the rescue, and today, night sprinkler systems are used to protect the buds against the cold with a sort of "ice jacket".

RECOMMENDED PRODUCERS
▸ Domaine Jean-Marc Brocard
▸ Domaine Laroche
▸ Domaine Vincent Dauvissat
▸ Domaine Defaix

MUSCADET

C COLOUR Bright; a pale lemon yellow with green tinges.

A AROMA Youthful; lemon, pear, and apple with notes of lime and minerals.

T TASTE Light and elegant, with a lemony acidity and slightly fizzy feel.

Muscadet comes from the part of western France where the Loire River meets the sea, and the influence of the Atlantic gives mild winters and temperate summers. Muscadet wine is made from the grape of the same name, which is also known as Melon de Bourgogne because of its melon-shaped leaves. The vine was originally brought from Burgundy to the Nantes region because of its resist-ance to cold weather. I owe a lot to this wine; I was brought up harvesting Muscadet grapes to earn a few francs.

MUSCADET
Château du Cléray

The basic Muscadet is light and lively and should be consumed while young. Saying that, I have also tasted some excellent aged Muscadets which had a lovely smokiness with hints of flowers and pineapple. This wine is known around Nantes as "health wine", due to its lack of residual sugar and moderate alcohol content.

In my view, the best Muscadets are produced in the Sèvre-et-Maine district. These wines have a mineral character and are easy to drink. If you want to go another notch up the quality scale, try a Muscadet Sèvre-et-Maine Sur Lie. The name "Sur Lie" is not an appellation, but describes a vinification technique: after fermentation, the lees – a heavy sediment of dead yeast cells, pips, and grape pulp – settle to the bottom of the tank. The lees contain flavours and aromas, and allowing the wine to rest on

FOOD MATCH

OYSTERS AND SEAFOOD Muscadet, well chilled, works with nearly all fish. Try it with oysters, moules marinières, or grilled sardines.

the lees (*sur lie* in French) brings out these characteristics, making it slightly fizzy, and accentuating its freshness, crispness, and fruity flavours. Many Muscadets are sold in distinctive long, thin bottles – look out for them on the shelves of your wine merchant or supermarket.

RECOMMENDED PRODUCERS

▸ Château du Cléray
▸ Château la Perrière
▸ Château de Geuline

BORDEAUX BLANC SEC

C COLOUR Pale gold with silvery tinges; medium intensity.

A AROMA Clean and delicate; pear, quince, peach, and flowers.

T TASTE Subtle and harmonious with a refreshing acidity and good length.

For many years, Bordeaux whites were overshadowed by the region's great reds. They were often semi-sweet, over-sulphured, and lacking in character. Today, new techniques have transformed the wines, and some represent great value for money. Try the crisp, dry Entre deux Mers (literally "between two rivers") made from Sauvignon Blanc, or AOC Bergerac wines: this region is usually associated with sweet wines but dry whites are on the up.

RECOMMENDED PRODUCERS

▸ Château Montdoyen
▸ Château Thieuley

ALIGOTÉ

C COLOUR Pale lemon to very pale straw yellow with silver tinges.

A AROMA Green fruits, such as gooseberry and lemon, with a nutty feel.

T TASTE Dry and clean with citrus flavours. Straightforward and easy to enjoy.

Give this a wine go if you have a soft spot for Muscadet and Chablis. Aligoté grapes are cheap to grow and produce, so the wines are often

excellent value, and are becoming widely available. I think the best ones come from the Burgundy region (especially from around Bouzeron in the Côte Chalonnaise) but the vines are also grown in Bulgaria, Moldova, Romania, and California. Expect the wine to be very dry, lean, crisp, and refreshing; match it with seafood, or use it in a Kir (*see below*).

RECOMMENDED PRODUCERS

▸ Hugues Goisot
▸ Domaine Guy Roulot

CULTURE AND TRADITION

THE PERFECT KIR Aligoté really comes into its own as an apéritif. Mixed with a splash of Crème de Cassis (*see p287*) – a blackcurrant liqueur – it becomes a Burgundian Kir. Of course, you can make a Kir with any dry white but those in the know will be really impressed if you use an Aligoté. The drink is named after Canon Felix Kir, who, when mayor of Dijon, promoted the apéritif. For a special occasion, try a Kir Royal (*see p380*), which uses Champagne in place of the wine.

SYLVANER

C COLOUR Bright, pale yellow with green nuances.

A AROMA Subtle aromas of pear, lemon, apple, hints of herbs, and beeswax.

T TASTE Simple but amazingly refreshing and zingy, with a long citrusy finish.

This wine is a bit like a Muscadet but with more flavour. The Sylvaner grape was introduced into France from Austria around 200 years ago, and is now grown in the cool climate and flat lands of Alsace. Much of the wine is consumed locally, although it has become much more widely available in recent years. Sylvaner has a fresh, fruity taste, with a Riesling-like character, although it is neither as elegant as Riesling, nor as complex. This wine should be drunk young. Serve it as an apéritif, or with any grilled fish.

RECOMMENDED PRODUCERS

▸ Domaine Schaetzel
▸ Domaine Ostertag

PINOT BLANC

C COLOUR Very pale straw; clear and light and very attractive.

A AROMA Not deeply aromatic, but soft hints of peach, pear, and flowers.

T TASTE Fresh and lively, with white fruits and notes of minerals on the finish.

Often called "poor man's Chardonnay", Pinot Blanc from Alsace has its own character. Fresh, clean, and smooth to the finish, it is medium-bodied with good fruit acidity. Enjoy it when young – less than five years old. When buying, look out for the words *clos* (solely owned vineyard) and *réserve* on the label.

PINOT BLANC
Domaine Marcel Deiss

RECOMMENDED PRODUCERS

▸ Domaine Marcel Deiss
▸ Domaine Schaetzel

ITALY

Some of Italy's best wines are light, crisp whites, typically made from a blend of grape varieties. Soave and Verdicchio are very dry, and are great wines to drink with fish and seafood. Orvieto and Frascati – essential Roman wines – are more complex, and are perfect as partners for pasta. Pinot Grigio, the Italian name for Pinot Gris, is a delicate wine and a great alternative to Chardonnay.

PINOT GRIGIO

C COLOUR Pale lemon yellow, with silvery-grey tinges.

A AROMA Youthful and fresh; green fruits, flowers, and hints of minerals.

T TASTE Elegant, slightly fleshy, with a subtle texture; lemony at the finish.

If you enjoy the lightness of Chablis, then you will love Pinot Grigio. The wine has more flavours than Chablis (the grape is grown in warmer climates than the Chardonnay grape that makes the French wine), and where Chardonnay typically displays flavours of apple and lemon, a Grigio will suggest pear or melon. Nevertheless, the wines have the same freshness and minerality.

Italian Pinot Grigio is dry, light, and youthful, charac-teristics also found in Pinot Grigio originating from Oregon in the US. By comparison, the equivalent Pinot Gris wine from Alsace is richer and fruitier –

PINOT GRIGIO
Mezzacorona

as is its counterpart produced in the US state of California.

Prices of Pinot Grigio have risen in recent years, despite its popularity and mass-production. Alas, I am not sure that the quality has followed. The consistency of the wine is key – a good Pinot Grigio should express flavour, crispness, and a delicate body. You should expect to get some excitement out of the bottle, not just the effects of the alcohol!

THE GREY GRAPE *Grigio*, or *gris* in French, means "grey", which refers to the greyish hue of the grape. However, beneath the uninspiring name lies an exciting wine that is experiencing a real boom. In the US it is the best-selling imported table wine, surpassing imports of Merlot and Chardonnay from various origins, and selling twice as much as the next-largest single type, Australian Shiraz.

The wine is at its best when chilled. Drink it within two years of bottling. Pinot Grigio is ideal for a party or drinks reception; or, alternatively, try it over dinner with any type of white fish. I like to enjoy it with baked cod drizzled in *beurre blanc*.

RECOMMENDED PRODUCERS
▸ Mezzacorona
▸ Colli del Sori
▸ Beltrame

SOAVE

C COLOUR Straw yellow, occasionally with a touch of green.

A AROMA Fresh green and citrus fruits with delicate hints of almond.

T TASTE Delicate and light, with a nutty flavour and a slightly bitter finish.

Soave is Italy's most common dry white and is produced around the town of the same name, which lies to the northeast of Verona. Pronounced "swah-vey", the name Soave may derive from *Svevi* or *Suavi* after the Swabians who invaded Italy in the 6th century. The name has nothing to do with "suave" – the wine is too light and fresh for that! The *classico* (a term that denotes a wine from the original winemaking region, and usually of the best quality) comes from a small zone around the hills to the north and east of Soave town.

Most Soave is made from a blend of Garganega and Trebbiano grapes, and has an earthy character. When Chardonnay grapes are added into

the mix, the wine is softer. Look out for *Superiore* on the label – this indicates a stronger, more aged wine.

Soave is great with soups, stir-fry vegetables, or simple pasta dishes. For an Italian theme serve it with seafood linguine. And beware – this wine is so light that you can easily drink too much without noticing!

RECOMMENDED PRODUCERS
▸ Pieropan
▸ Anselmi

FOOD MATCH

APPETIZERS I love to drink Soave with hors d'oeuvres. Try serving the wine as an apéritif to accompany assorted bruschetta.

TREBBIANO

C COLOUR Bright lemon yellow with highlights of silver.

A AROMA Subtle; with green fruits and hints of almond and white flowers.

T TASTE Dry; refreshing with a marked acidity and good balance of alcohol.

The Trebbiano grape is a basic component of Chianti (*see p97*) and also blends perfectly in many Italian whites – it is too neutral in flavour to produce good wine on its own. The finest Trebbiano is from central Italy. Try Trebbiano Toscano, Romagnolo, Soave, and Giallo; also Trebbiano d'Abruzzo – perhaps the most interesting. Chill the wine well and try it with a spicy risotto – delicious.

RECOMMENDED PRODUCERS
▸ Valentini
▸ Thaulero

FRASCATI

C COLOUR Straw yellow, sometimes with greenish tinges.

A AROMA Citrus fruits, flowers, perhaps with a hint of ripe pear.

T TASTE Delicate, with a good balance of citrus and acidity.

FRASCATI *Colli di Catone*

Produced on the beautiful slopes of the volcanic Albian Hills and within sight of Rome, Frascati is a versatile, easy-going wine with a world-wide reputation. It was a favourite among the Romans, and was later promoted by the Church in Italy. Frascati is made from a blend of grapes, including Trebbiano, and is perfect for summer drinking. It is happily matched with any light food dish.

RECOMMENDED PRODUCERS
▸ Colli di Catone
▸ Fontana Candida

VERDICCHIO

C COLOUR Pale gold with sparkling glints of silver; very bright.

A AROMA Fresh and light; green apple and lemon; hints of pear or melon.

T TASTE Clean and characterful with almond and pear; medium length.

The Italian version of Portuguese Vinho Verde, Verdicchio is grown around Ancona on the Adriatic coast of eastern central Italy, in the Marches region. The relatively cool coastal climate allows the berries to ripen slowly, producing a wine with a dry, crisp character.

The best-known of the Verdicchio wines come from the DOC of Verdicchio dei Castelli di Jesi. Here, the wines have a lemon–lime acidity and lingering chalky taste – rather like a Chablis,

VERDICCHIO *Monte Schiavo*

but better value. Verdicchio dei Castelli di Jesi is labelled *classico* when it is produced in the oldest sector of the DOC zone.

The wines from the smaller, less well-known DOC of Verdicchio di Matelica are produced farther inland, in the warmer hills. Here the wines have greater body than those of Castelli di Jesi, with a softer texture and a more melon flavour.

All these wines are well worth trying. Drink them with white meat dishes and white fish. (They even taste good with a light tartare sauce.) Verdicchio makes great company for salads, too – try it in summer with lemon-dressed artichokes.

RECOMMENDED PRODUCERS
▶ Monte Schiavo
▶ Umani Ronchi
▶ Bucchi

ORVIETO

C COLOUR A medium-intense straw yellow, with tinges of green.

A AROMA Delicate; soft flowers with appealing fruits and roasted almond.

T TASTE Fresh, elegant; lemony acidity, medium alcohol, and medium length.

"The sun of Italy in a bottle" – at least according to 19th-century Italian poet Gabriele d'Annunzio. For me it is not that simple. This is a wine you either love or hate; and while personally I enjoy Orvieto, conflicting opinions among my customers make this wine difficult to recommend!

Produced in southeastern Umbria (central Italy), where it has enjoyed great success, Orvieto – made from a blend of grape varieties – is the most important wine in the region. In the Middle Ages, Orvieto became a papal favourite. According to one legend, 19th-century Pope Gregorio XVI requested that his body be

ORVIETO
Castello della Sala

washed in Orvieto before being interred. (However, this Pope was clearly someone who enjoyed God's gifts: he was also a champion of the rival wine Frascati!)

Make sure you pay attention to the label when buying this wine. To breathe new life into the denomination, producers have supplemented the most important *secco* (dry) Orvieto with less favourable *abboccato* (semidry or semisweet), *amabile* (medium sweet), and *dolce* (sweet) versions. It is worth spending a little extra for the best – Orvieto Classico. Enjoy it young with any tomato pasta dish.

RECOMMENDED PRODUCERS
▶ Castello della Sala
▶ Luigi Bigi
▶ Barberani – Vallesanta

SPAIN

Most people praise Spain for its great red wines, such as Rioja and Ribera del Duero, but it also produces some fine, delicate, lemony white wines. Spanish dry whites, such as Viura, can be well made, straightforward, and easy to drink, without too much complexity.

VIURA

C COLOUR An unusual pale greenish yellow, with tinges of silver.

A AROMA Discreet, subtle, and light, with flowers, lime, and hints of nuts.

T TASTE Dry, refreshing acidity, balanced alcohol, and a medium finish.

Most people think of Rioja as a red wine, but this region also produces white wines and they are beginning to win a strong reputation around the world. The success has been due in part to the Viura grape (also known as Macabeo), which has helped to create interesting, fruit-driven, citrusy wines that are improving all the time. As Maccabéo

or Maccabeu, Viura is also an important grape variety in the Languedoc-Roussillon region of southern France.

The best Viura wines are fresh and crisp with a strong floral character and distinctive nutty aroma. The wine is low in acidity, and has a medium alcohol content.

Enjoy Viura chilled with a seafood paëlla. This is a fun wine for drinking while it is still young – try it as an alternative to Bordeaux or Italian whites. If you see it on a supermarket shelf, why not give this interesting wine a try?

RECOMMENDED PRODUCERS
▶ Marques do Monistrol
▶ Marques de Riscal

TOP VARIETY *Viura is now the most widely planted grape in the Rioja region of northern Spain, thanks to its ability to withstand oxidation in the cask.*

PORTUGAL

Portugal is perhaps best known for its red table wines, such as Dão, and its world-famous fortified wines. However, it is also well worth seeking out its very dry, slightly sparkling "green wine" or Vinho Verde, which is a great summer drink, perfect with spicy Asian dishes. Vinho Verde comes from the north of Portugal and represents about 15 per cent of vine planting in the entire country.

VINHO VERDE

C COLOUR Bright; distinctive pale lemon with green tinges.

A AROMA Youthful, fresh, delicate, with green fruits, flowers, and hints of pear.

T TASTE Dry, with a slight sparkle on the tongue; refreshing; medium length.

Portugal has never been famous for its white wines (rather, for its Port). However, the quality of Vinho Verde has greatly improved over recent years, and if I were to give a medal for the best Portuguese white wine, it would go to Vinho Verde!

The Vinho Verde region, in the north of Portugal, produces mainly white wines of characteristic lemony or straw colour. The grapes are picked while they are still young, to create wines that are fruity and fresh, with low alcohol. The name Vinho Verde literally means "green wine" – the "green" refers not to the wine's colour, but to its youthfulness.

The region's mild climate with a good deal of rain during winter and spring means that plenty of water is

VINHO VERDE
Quinta da Aveleda

absorbed into the grapes, making them perfect for producing wines with a low alcohol content.

The most sought-after Vinhos Verdes derive from the Alvarinho grape. Slightly higher in alcohol and more expensive than other wines from the region, they classify as a semi-sparkling wine and have a biting or prickly quality, similar to Muscadet Sur Lie *(see p37)*. When buying this wine in a supermarket, be careful; some supermarket wines are not as young as they should be, and so do not have the characteristic bracing freshness. My tip is to buy and drink this wine as young as possible – while it is slightly fizzy, and very fresh. As a rule of thumb, in summer (the best time to drink Vinho Verde) you should be drinking wine from the previous year's vintage. On the

back of the bottle is a serial number, then a slash, then a date. That date tells you the year in which the wine was bottled. If the number reads, say, 349871/2004, you have a wine from the 2003 vintage, bottled in 2004.

RECOMMENDED PRODUCERS
▸ Quinta da Aveleda
▸ Quinta Altissimo
▸ Quinta de Tamariz

FOOD MATCH

LIGHT, SPICY FOODS The biting freshness, sherbet fizz, and low alcohol of Vinho Verde make it perfect for drinking with dishes such as Thai fish soup or lemon chicken.

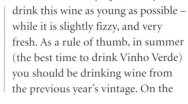

GREECE

The hot dry climate of Greece provides ideal climatic conditions for growing light, crisp grape varieties. Greek wines are uncompromising, and the grape varieties used to make them retain their acidity in the hot climate – the key to a crisp and refreshing wine.

ASSYRTIKO

C COLOUR Usually greeny yellow, with medium intensity.

A AROMA Delicate, with lemon, green apple, honeysuckle, and minerals.

T TASTE Well-balanced with a lemony acidity; fresh at the finish.

Often thought of as Greece's best white wine, Assyrtiko has an excellent structure and a citrusy flavour. Try it as an alternative to dry French or Italian wine: indeed, you might compare it to an Alsatian Riesling or a Pinot Grigio.

The Assyrtiko grape has now established itself as the

ASSYRTIKO
Boutari

foremost quality Greek variety. It is normally associated with the Aegean Islands, particularly the island of Santorini. The Assyrtiko grape is said to have been growing on Santorini since about 1600BC, and the island's rich volcanic soil helps to bring out the grape's special smoky, flinty flavours. However, Assyrtiko is increasingly being planted through-out the Greek wine regions; this expansion is thanks largely to the grape's distinct ability to retain its personality and

high acidity even in the most extreme warm weather conditions. The acidity of the grape is important because, in the case of Assyrtiko, it helps to create a wine with a high alcohol content, but that retains its complexity and balance.

RECOMMENDED PRODUCERS
▸ Boutari
▸ Santorini Co-op
▸ Hatzidakis

FOOD MATCH

FETA SALAD Give yourself a little taste of Greece: match Assyrtiko with chunks of rich feta cheese on a bed of ripe cherry tomatoes and crisp, fresh cucumber – delicious!

RHODITIS

C COLOUR Bright; pale yellow with tinges of gold and straw.

A AROMA Complex, with pineapple, lemon, freshly cut grass, and walnut.

T TASTE Delicate, well-balanced, and subtle; a long, slightly resinous finish.

Not from Rhodes but native to the Peloponnese, Rhoditis keeps a reasonably good acidity even in the hot climate of this southern part of the Greek mainland. The resulting wines have a great harmony between fruit and acidity, and are among the best-quality whites in Greece.

Historically, winemakers have produced Rhoditis for the domestic market, but a new generation is improving the wine, making it easier to recommend. Give it a try with grilled sea bream or mullet, served with a lemon and olive oil sauce.

RECOMMENDED PRODUCERS
▸ Tsantalis
▸ Boutari

SOUTH AFRICA

South Africa's diverse production of light whites reflects its varied climate – from coastal areas cooled by the ocean to hot, dry regions. The South Africans have adopted Chenin Blanc, originally a French grape, as one of their own, and it is now the most-planted and successful grape variety in the country.

CHENIN BLANC

C COLOUR Bright; pale lemon yellow with slight tinges of green.

A AROMA Young and pleasant, with green fruits and notes of melon.

T TASTE Dry, fresh, well-structured; well-balanced, with a floral finish.

In 1655 Chenin Blanc found its way from France to South Africa. Here, it is often known as "Steen", but whether the label says Chenin Blanc or Steen is up to the producer.

South Africa's most prolific grape variety, Chenin Blanc is extremely versatile, which has led to a great deal of variation in style, with many producers introducing oak fermentation and maturation to the winemaking process. When the wine has been matured in oak, it develops a richer feel, a deep yellow colour, and a nutty flavour. However, this is not typical of Chenin Blanc, and in my opinion does not suit the wine. More typically, South African Chenin Blanc is fresh and fruity in style. The great paradox of Chenin Blanc is that it can taste of both steel and honey at the same time.

Overall, South African Chenin Blanc is light and crisp with a fresh structure and represents good value for money. Good Chenin Blancs make for easy drinking. Buy one from a specific region (generic South African Chenin Blanc can be very lean and watery, as well as too acidic) – the best and most famous is Stellenbosch in the Cape.

Chenin Blanc is a social wine: enjoy it with friends at a party.

RECOMMENDED PRODUCERS
▸ Kanu
▸ Ruitersvlei
▸ Fairview

CHENIN BLANC
Kanu

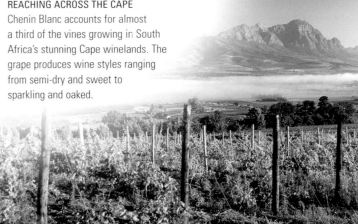

LAND AND PRODUCTION

REACHING ACROSS THE CAPE
Chenin Blanc accounts for almost a third of the vines growing in South Africa's stunning Cape winelands. The grape produces wine styles ranging from semi-dry and sweet to sparkling and oaked.

GERMANY

The most famous of all German wines are the medium-dry whites, especially the great Rieslings. But Germany has pioneered the development of new varieties and crosses, such as Müller-Thurgau, which makes a drier and crisper wine.

MÜLLER-THURGAU

C COLOUR Usually straw yellow, sometimes with a touch of green.

A AROMA Fresh green and citrus fruits; flowers and almond.

T TASTE Delicate and light, sometimes with a nutty flavour; finish slightly bitter.

Müller-Thurgau is a grape variety created in 1882 by Dr Hermann Müller (born in the Swiss canton of Thurgau). His idea was to mix the quality of Riesling with the early ripening of Sylvaner, although evidence now suggests that his cross was actually of two Rieslings.

Müller-Thurgau has a reputation for excellent productivity, and its early ripening makes it hardy even in the coolest wine areas of the world, such as England.

A great deal of Müller-Thurgau production forms the basis of characterless, mass-market German wines such as Liebfraumilch and Niersteiner. This is sad because the grape has the potential to produce wine that is light in body (but not too light), with a delicate, dry taste that is well sustained by crisp acidity. I recommend Müller-Thurgau with a light lunch, perhaps in the German style – with cold meats or a savoury strudel, and a potato salad.

RECOMMENDED PRODUCERS
▸ Meersburger
▸ Rudolf Furst

SWITZERLAND

Most Swiss wine is consumed at home rather than exported, so many people are simply not aware that Switzerland produces some excellent wines. At their best, Swiss whites can rival French Chablis in their style and complexity.

CHASSELAS

C COLOUR Pale yellow, with a faint sparkle and silvery lights.

A AROMA Young, fresh, and delicate; lightly perfumed with lemon.

T TASTE Dry; impressive texture with good balance, charm, and a long finish.

Swiss Chasselas is known by a variety of names depending upon its region of origin. They include Fendant (the best-known Chasselas, from the Valais region, southern Switzerland), Dorin, Gutedel, Marzemina Bianca, Perlan, and Weisser Gutedel. Whatever name it goes by, the grape produces fresh, dry, fruity wines, low in acidity and high in alcohol.

The most elegant and distinctive versions of the wine are likely to come from the vineyards of the Lavaux or Chablais, both of which lie in the Vaud wine region, along the north shore of Lake Geneva.

Definitely one to look out for, this wine is perfect after a long day's skiing, and also makes a great apéritif. In the summer, try it at lunchtime with barbecued prawns.

CHASSELAS *Rouvinez*

RECOMMENDED PRODUCERS
▸ Rouvinez
▸ Hammel

JUICY, AROMATIC WHITES

66 Vibrant, with plenty of exotic fruit to make your mouth water. The secret of these wines is their gentle exuberance, delicate lemony acidity, and wonderful length. 99

INTRODUCING JUICY, AROMATIC WHITES

Bursting with bags of fruit and distinct personalities, juicy, aromatic white wines range from fresh and grassy to deeply perfumed and exotic. Even once you have found a favourite, I urge you to try more – there is so much to discover.

The most important thing to remember about juicy, aromatic whites is that the word "aromatic" does not imply that the wine is sweet. Although the aroma of some of these wines might imply sweetness, this is a reflection of the ripe fruit that has gone into the wine and is not a measure of the sweetness of the wine itself. Juicy, aromatic wines are dry, and differences in their styles are like the different characters you would expect from members of the same family – each one is unique, but ultimately they all share a common bond.

LYCHEE *Exotic fruits fill the nose of an aromatic Muscat.*

The differences, of course, are a result of the grape variety that has gone into the wine, as well as the soil, climate, and viticulture that has gone into the winemaking. For example, Muscat wines are naturally aromatic; while others, such as Gavi di Gavi from Italy, receive their aromas through careful vinification. Like many light, crisp wines, styles that are aromatic and juicy are vinified at low temperatures to bring out their fruitiness, and in stainless steel vats to maintain the wine's freshness. Juicy, aromatic wines are typically produced in cool, temperate climates. Regions such as Alsace in eastern France, New Zealand's South Island, or the mountainous Rueda in Spain present the perfect conditions for creating excellent wines.

CHOOSING YOUR WINE

Moderately priced juicy, aromatic wines will be fairly light, but they should still have lots of character and expression. The flavours and aromas, although probably not profound or even necessarily obvious, will be lemony and floral, and the wines should have a pleasant, medium length. The more you spend, the more exuberant the wines become. Good wines have

SMOKED SALMON *A zesty Sauvignon Blanc is an excellent match for light, smoked fish.*

medium weight and a clean, juicy texture; their flavours are fresh, but full of character and with a perfect balance of alcohol and acidity. The bouquet will be intense, full, and beautiful – and will immediately make an impact on you. You will know when you have a great wine: it will be like walking into a wonderful perfumery!

DRINKING AND SERVING

DRINK PROFILE Juicy, aromatic white wines have a slightly thicker viscosity than light, crisp whites. These are exuberant wines with great, all-round harmony.

C COLOUR Ranging from lemon to pale gold, depending mostly on the vinification technique and grape variety. You will also often see green or silver tinges in young wine.

A AROMA The grapes give their own character to the diverse aromas found in these wines – from the citrusy, grassy aroma of a Sauvignon Blanc to the grapey nose of Muscat.

T TASTE These wines should be reminiscent of ripe peaches – mouthwateringly fresh and juicy. They generally have good acidity to balance the fruit and a long, pleasant finish.

BUYING AND STORING Look for examples from cool regions, where a long ripening season gives the grapes plenty of opportunity to develop their fruit. The ideal wine is fresh and clean, but has a pungent, full flavour. With the main exception of Riesling, these are not usually wines for ageing and are best consumed within two years.

SERVING SUGGESTIONS Enjoyment of this wine lies in its fruitiness. Chilling is essential: the colder the wine, the fresher it will feel.

FOOD COMPANIONS Seafood is perfect with all these wines. Drier versions are great with fish and salads; sweeter, with Asian food. As a rule of thumb, enjoy them with the local food of the wine's origin: goat's cheese with Sancerre, for example, is an unbeatable combination.

GRAPE VARIETIES

There are two great classics in this group of aromatic grape varieties: Sauvignon Blanc and Riesling. Sauvignon Blanc makes great wines in the Loire, the Marlborough region of New Zealand, Australia, and South Africa. Riesling (which, exceptionally, is suitable for ageing) is the distinctive fruity grape from Alsace, Germany, and Austria, and in more recent years Australia and New Zealand. Other superior wines come from grapes such as Albariño (Spain); the up-and-coming Grüner Veltliner (Austria); and most aromatic of all, Muscat.

GRAPE	BEST REGIONAL EXAMPLES	COMMENTS
RIESLING	Australia: Clare Valley. France: Alsace. Germany. Austria.	A classic German variety, Riesling has great floral and lime characters. It makes expressive, elegant wine that is flinty and smoky and among the longest lived, thanks to the perfectly balanced acidity and fruit.
SAUVIGNON BLANC	France. New Zealand. Australia. South Africa: Paarl, Constantia.	Sauvignon Blanc has a high acidity, medium alcohol, a mineral character, and citrus flavours. In France, this important grape makes the superb Sancerre and Pouilly Fumé.
ALBARIÑO	Spain: Galicia (Rías Baixas).	The Albariño grape makes aromatic, peachy Viognier-like wine, with the freshness of Sauvignon. This expressive grape is a great alternative to Sauvignon Blanc from the Loire Valley.
GRÜNER VELTLINER	Austria: Wachau.	Austria's most important grape, Grüner Veltliner makes world-class wine that is elegant and characterful, with floral and spicy notes and medium alcohol.
PINOT GRIS	France: Alsace, Loire. New Zealand. Canada. Germany. Switzerland: Valais.	Pinot Gris makes fantastic wine, with intense colour and distinct aromas, and that is well-balanced, with complex fruit and good texture.
ARNEIS	Italy: Piedmont.	A dry and delicate wine, Arneis has characters of juicy apple, almond, and citrus, and a balanced acidity.
TORRONTÉS	Argentina. Spain: Galicia.	Subtle, aromatic, and not too heavy, Torrontés has Muscat-like aromas underlined by a soft, lemony acidity.
VIOGNIER	France: Languedoc.	Viognier is highly perfumed and floral but retains a clean acidity. It makes a fabulous summer wine.
VERDEJO	Spain: Rueda.	Verdejo has floral and citrus characters, with notes of pear, peach, and mango.
VERMENTINO	France: Languedoc, Corsica. Italy: Sardinia, Liguria. Australia.	Increasingly popular, Vermentino makes charming, floral wine with a good balance between acidity, fruit, and alcohol.
RIVANER	Luxembourg.	and expressive wine with great complexity and balance.
ROBOLA	Greece: Cephalonia.	One of the finest grapes in Greece, Robola makes lemony, minty, and flowery wine that is dry with juicy structure.
LEN DE L'ELH	France: South of France (Gaillac).	This variety is well-perfumed, with notes of apple, pear, and citrus, but it lacks natural acidity and can make flabby wines.
MUSCAT	France: Alsace, Rhône Valley.	Muscat is very aromatic, delicate, and full of flavour, with grape, exotic fruit, peach, apricot, and floral aromas.

FRANCE

France makes a fantastic variety of juicy, aromatic white wines. These are produced mainly in the centre of the country, where the climate allows slow but full ripening of the grapes, bringing out the complexity of the flavours and aromas. The classic regions for these medium-bodied wines are the upper Loire Valley around Sancerre, and the Alsace region in the east of the country.

SANCERRE / POUILLY FUMÉ

C COLOUR Bright lemon yellow to pale straw, with tinges of green.

A AROMA Youthful and aromatic, with green fruit, elderflower, citrus, and grass.

T TASTE Intense with a refreshing, persistent acidity and a clean, long finish.

The Queen of the Loire Valley! If you like aromatic, refreshing, yet restrained wines, then this is for you.

Sancerre, located in the upper Loire Valley, is famous worldwide for its white wine, although it also produces some great rosé and light reds from the Pinot Noir grape.

The style of the wine varies somewhat between adjacent producers, ranging from thinner, acidic wines to more fleshy, mineral varieties. For me, the best white Sancerre AOC wines come from producers in the villages of Bué, Chavignol, Ménétréol, and Verdigny, rather than from the village of Sancerre itself; try to look out for one of those villages on the label.

There are a few satellite appellations in the shadow of Sancerre which fight for – and deserve – recognition. Some offer exceptional quality and value for money. One of the best known is the more mineral and smoky Pouilly Fumé, Sancerre's direct neighbour, just across the Loire River.

Both Sancerre and Pouilly Fumé are made from Sauvignon Blanc – instantly recognizable by its piercing aroma. This has attracted many descriptions, from gooseberry, nettle, and green fruits, to cats' pee (not desirable!). The best Sauvignon Blancs, such as those from Sancerre, are always fresh, zesty, and full of life.

POUILLY FUMÉ
Château de Tracy

YOUNG DRINK Sauvignon Blanc from the Loire sometimes benefits from three to four years of ageing, but is typically drunk young to savour its zesty character.

FOOD MATCH

GOAT'S CHEESE Sancerre and Pouilly Fumé are great companions for a creamy, salty goat's cheese. Look out for Sancerre goat's cheese to keep the flavours local.

Historically, the region around Sancerre used to produce white wine from the Chasselas table grape, but in the 1970s and 80s it found greater success with Sauvignon Blanc – a success that boosted the local economy. The *terroir* is perfect for this classic grape variety, which is often called Blanc Fumé ("smoky white") in the region, a reference to the minerality of the soils, a mixture of clay, limestone, and flint. The cool, temperate climate allows for long ripening and brings out all the characteristic flavours of the Sauvignon Blanc, with local variations reflecting the various soils and microclimates. Sancerre has been called the Sauvignon capital of the world – although this might now be disputed in some parts of New Zealand and South Africa! For me, it is still the best – but then again, I'm biased because I grew up in Touraine and agree 100 per cent with Balzac: "Shame on him who does not admire my joyous, beautiful, brave Touraine whose seven valleys stream with water and wine."

RECOMMENDED PRODUCERS
▸ Château de Tracy
▸ Domaine Alphonse Mellot
▸ Domaine Bernard Baudry
▸ Domaine Henri Bourgeois
▸ Domaine JC Chatelain
▸ Domaine Jean-Max Roger

ALSACE MUSCAT

C COLOUR Pale straw or golden yellow, with green highlights.

A AROMA Expressive rich scents of flowers, musk, and exotic fruits.

T TASTE Dry, light texture; delicate and subtle, underlined by a lemony acidity.

The Muscat grape is linked with the exotic aromas and flavours of sweet wines. Alsace is one of few regions of the world able to produce a complex dry wine from the grape, thanks to its cool climate. Alsace Muscat is at once rich and inviting, and dry and fresh. Low in alcohol and acidity, it is a great apéritif – ideal for sipping in summer with a plate of asparagus.

RECOMMENDED PRODUCERS
▸ Domaine Weinbach
▸ Domaine Rolly-Gassman

ALSACE PINOT GRIS

C COLOUR Bright golden yellow, with a distinct green tinge.

A AROMA Complex, dry, and elegant, with crystallized fruit, apricot, and raisins.

T TASTE Well-balanced, with spicy touches, a hint of oak, and a long finish.

ALSACE PINOT GRIS
Marc Kreydenweiss

This wine, at its rich, honeyed, and aromatic best, can compete with the Pulignys *(see p60).* Pinot Gris is making a comeback in Alsace, driven by a new wave of dynamic winemakers. The wine can be kept for five to eight years, mellowing to a spicy, smoky richness. It is a good match for fish or white meat, but try it with monkfish or warm truffle – heaven!

RECOMMENDED PRODUCERS
▸ Marc Kreydenweiss
▸ Domaine Zind-Humbrecht

ALSACE RIESLING

C COLOUR Bright yellow, with a silver tinge; pale to medium intensity.

A AROMA Very expressive and intense; citrus and exotic fruits, and minerals.

T TASTE Well-balanced and clean, with a great complexity of flavours and texture.

Riesling is the most elegant grape of the Alsace region. The wines vary from the world-class and pricey *grands crus* to the very undistinguished, and from bone-dry and steely examples to more rich and opulent styles. The best bottles improve with age; they are rarely oaked, but are most often aged in the bottle, where they develop gunflint acidity and intense fruit.

ALSACE RIESLING
Domaine Ostertag

RECOMMENDED PRODUCERS
▸ Domaine Ostertag
▸ Trimbach

SAVOIE ROUSSETTE

C COLOUR Pale golden yellow, with a silver tinge.

A AROMA Intense, with dried apricot, peach, ripe pear, and roasted almond.

T TASTE Complex and dry; fleshy with a fresh texture and a mineral touch.

If you ever visit the Alps, try this wine because it is among the finest of the Savoie whites. Production is limited due to the location and climate, and most of the wine is drunk by the locals or thirsty tourists. Who can blame them; this wine continues to improve year by year, and is a perfect social drink to be enjoyed over a fondue or with a cheese soufflée.

RECOMMENDED PRODUCERS
▸ Prieure St. Christophe
▸ Domaine Louis Magnin

JURANÇON SEC / PACHERENC

C COLOUR Pale, becoming darker with age; gold with green tinges.

A AROMA Peach, pineapple, citrus, almond, blossom, and minerals.

T TASTE Dense, underlined with lemon acidity; lingering finish.

Produced in southwestern France, around the town of Pau in the foothills of the Pyrenees, Jurançon sec (be careful – straight Jurançon is a sweet wine) is an exotic dry wine with mineral, smoky flavours, and a fleshy texture. Its close neighbour – in style as well as geography – is the lesser-known but equally interesting Pacherenc du Vic-Bilh, made in the region of Madiran.

I am a great fan of Jurançon. It is an exquisite blend of three grape varieties all grown locally around

PACHERENC DU VIC-BILH
Château d'Aydie

Pau. They are Gros Manseng, Petit Manseng, and Courbu, and they give the wine its characteristic rich texture. Pacherenc is blended using the same grapes, with the addition of Ruffiac, Sémillon, and Sauvignon. The flavours of the two dry wines may be so similar that it can be hard to tell them apart.

Drink either wine within two or three years of harvesting, and serve it lightly chilled (enough to bring out the complexity of its aromas, but not too much to reduce the juicy texture).

This is a must-try for anyone who is out to impress. Drink it in your garden, with bowls of green olives at hand; or with any fish or white meat.

RECOMMENDED PRODUCERS
▸ Château d'Aydie (Laplace)
▸ Domaine Cauhape
▸ Château Castera

GAILLAC

C COLOUR Pale to medium intensity; golden yellow, with a hint of green.

A AROMA Delicate: quince, orange peel, fresh hay, pineapple, blossom, spice.

T TASTE Elegant and slightly oily; complex flavours with a refreshing acidity.

Thought to be one of the first wine-producing regions in France, the appellation of Gaillac has, in the past decade, found renewed dynamism. Wine production has almost doubled, although most of the wine continues to be drunk by locals – and connoisseurs!

Gaillac is produced along the Tarn River, about 30 miles (48km) to the northwest of Toulouse, in southwestern France. The main grape varieties used to make this dry white are the local Len de L'Elh

GAILLAC *Domaine Rotier*

(Gascon dialect for *Loin de l'oeil*, meaning "far from sight") and Mauzac, as well as locally grown Sauvignon Blanc and Sémillon.

Len de L'Elh lacks natural acidity and, when not well cared for or in poor climatic conditions, it can make quite flabby, unbalanced, oily wine. However, the better wines are full of character; delicate and intense. Mauzac produces wines with a flourish of flowers and sweet apple, and a refreshing touch of lemon.

Gaillac represents great value for money, and at its best is exceptionally complex. Enjoy the wines young (less than five years old), with a smoked haddock salad, or monkfish on a bed of saffron risotto.

RECOMMENDED PRODUCERS
▸ Domaine Rotier
▸ Domaine des Tres-Cantous
▸ Domaine des Causse-Marines

VIOGNIER (LANGUEDOC)

C COLOUR Bright and clear; yellow to light gold.

A AROMA Intense, with grapefruit, peach stones, and apricot.

T TASTE Fleshy and full; perfect balance of alcohol and acidity; long, clean finish.

VIOGNIER *Les Perles de Méditerranée*

A grape with a distinctive, blossomy perfume, Viognier is famous as a traditional variety of the northern Rhône, and more recently of the New World, especially California. However, Languedoc-Roussillon, in southern France, also produces Viognier and its style is very different from its Rhône and Californian cousins – the wine is much drier and

more refreshing, with a lighter texture and more citrusy flavours. Nevertheless the grape retains the aromatic intensity and fresh structure that make the Viognier wines so popular with modern winemakers and wine lovers alike.

Until the 1980s Viognier had seen a steady decline in demand – largely owing to low grape productivity from the Rhône vines. However, I think the more reasonable prices of New World stock, and the general excitement about New World wines, has helped influence Viognier to recover its position as a single grape variety of great character and worthwhile drinking.

The delicacy of the fruit is the most important feature of Languedoc Viognier, so this wine should be drunk when it is young. Try it on its own to relax after a busy day. It is also great with delicious gravadlax.

RECOMMENDED PRODUCERS
▸ Les Perles de Méditerranée
▸ Vignerons des Troi Terroirs
▸ Domaine Saint Hilaire

BELLET

C COLOUR Pale; lemon yellow, with fresh green tinges.

A AROMA Expressive, with white flowers, ripe white fruits, and ripe peach.

T TASTE Round and delicate, balanced by lemony acidity and a harmonious finish.

Over the years all the greatest wines of the world will have been tasted in the fabulous restaurants and hotels of Nice, the famous city on the French Riviera. But how many people know that Bellet is Nice's very own local white wine?

Produced on the Alps-facing slopes of the hills around Nice, this wine is fresh, fruity, and aromatic. Its main grape variety is Rolle, which flourishes in the cooler climate of the hills and gives the wine its distinct floral aromas and natural citrusy acidity.

Bellet has to be ranked among some of the great white wines, but its production is strictly limited. This in turn makes the wine highly

sought after, and expensive to buy – rather like everything else in this beautiful part of the world.

Finding a bottle of Bellet is a formidable task – I could not even find one at Nice airport! However, this is a wine well worth searching for. Good luck and happy hunting!

RECOMMENDED PRODUCERS
▸ Clos St Vincent
▸ Château Bellet

FOOD MATCH

SEAFOOD AND TUNA If you are lucky enough to find a bottle of Bellet, save it for a meal with crab or langoustines – or, even better, savour it with a salad Niçoise.

SPAIN

Excellent aromatic whites like Rueda and La Mancha are made at high altitude in the heart of Spain, where cold winters contrast with intensely hot, dry summers. Wonderfully complex wines are also made in the northwest, on the cool Atlantic shores of Galicia.

MOUNTAIN-TOP VINES Like Sauvignon Blanc, Verdejo can ripen fully at high altitudes. Rueda's location, on plateaux at around 900m (3000ft), gives the wine its refreshing acidity and fine aromas. It also means that, although output is low, quality is consistently high.

RUEDA

C COLOUR Bright; light straw yellow, sometimes with a tinge of green.

A AROMA Intense and smooth, with flowers, grass, and lemon.

T TASTE Clean, zesty; ripe texture, crisp acidity; very long finish.

When we think of Spanish wine, we often automatically think of it as red. However, the small town of Rueda (meaning "wheel"), to the northwest of Madrid, has given its name to an excellent white.

Often thought of as the white wine of the Duero River,

RUEDA
Cuevas de Castilla

which flows alongside many of the Rueda vineyards and has its own influence on the character of the wine, Rueda must be drunk while it is still young – its fresh aroma is, after all, its most important feature.

Rueda is produced primarily from the local Verdejo grape. Until the 1970s, the Spanish *bodega*s (wineries) of the Duero valley, particularly of its former capital Valladolid, focused on making sweet, sherry-like wines. (Some of these wines, and some sparkling wines, are still

produced there today.) However, during the process of updating old winemaking equipment with new versions made of stainless steel, the *bodega*s realized that the native Verdejo was capable of creating good-quality, light, dry white wine.

I love the character of this wine and I often recommend it over a Sancerre or Pinot Grigio. In fact, as production of the wine is fairly

limited, I urge you to stock up as soon as you can. Enjoy the wine on its own or with a fish dish, such as grilled sole or pan-fried sea bass, dressed with fennel and green vegetables. Such a treat!

RECOMMENDED PRODUCERS
▸ Con Class de Cuevas de Castilla
▸ Bodegas Matarromera
▸ Jose Pariente

GALICIA

C COLOUR Bright; straw yellow, with silvery highlights.

A AROMA Intense, citrusy, and herbaceous; green apple and flint.

T TASTE Full of character; refreshing acidity with a long, lemony finish.

GALICIA
Casal Caeiro

Tucked away in the far northwestern corner of Spain, and bordering northern Portugal to the south, Galicia is perhaps Spain's most isolated wine-producing region. It is sometimes known as España Verde, or "Green Spain", and includes the peninsula of Finisterre – "the end of the world".

The wines of Galicia are made primarily from the native Albariño grape (a variation of the Portuguese Alvarinho, the major component of

Vinho Verde). At its best, Albariño produces wines that are complex, with balanced acidity and fruit, and that improve in the bottle (unlike Vinho Verde). The Albariño vines flourish in the region's humid climate, which is dominated by the high rainfall coming in off the Atlantic Ocean.

Within Galicia, the denominations of Rías Baixas, Ribeiro, and Ribeira Sacra produce wines that are particularly delicious and aromatic. My personal favourites are the wines from Rías Baixas. (The name comes from the deep inlets – *rias* – that cut into the region's coastline.) Here, Albariño accounts for more than 90 per cent of the vines. Production is limited, but these vines nevertheless produce Galicia's most superior and most sought-after (and therefore most expensive) wines.

Rías Baixas is itself divided into three subzones: Val do Salnes on the

GALICIA
Martín Códax

west coast; O Rosal, bordering the Atlantic to the west, and Portugal to the south; and Condado do Tea, inland and on the Portuguese border. Look out for Val do Salnes – these wines are the purest form of Albariño dry white and they are worth spending a little more on.

Similar to the wines of Rías Baixas, with the same straw yellow colour, are those of Ribeiro. Here, the wines are elegant, fresh, light, and aromatic with good acidity.

In my opinion, the wines of Galicia are the most representative of juicy, aromatic whites as a whole. They never cease to amaze me, and it is time to bring them to the world market – Galician wines are a must!

RECOMMENDED PRODUCERS
▸ Casal Caeiro
▸ Martín Códax
▸ Pazo de Senorans
▸ Pallazio de Fefinanez

LA MANCHA

C COLOUR Pale intensity; bright lemon yellow, with tinges of green.

A AROMA Delicate; pear, lemon, minerals, honey, flowers, and grapes.

T TASTE Clean with good acidity and medium alcohol; apple at the finish.

A sleeping giant, La Mancha is the largest single wine region in Europe.

La Mancha wine is made from the Airén grape, which is particularly suited to the hot, dry climate of central Spain. New producers to the region have begun to harvest the grape as early as possible, to keep both the acidity and the fruit. Vinification in stainless steel at low temperatures helps the wine to keep its aromatic character.

This wine is simple, well-made, inexpensive, and fun to drink at a barbecue or picnic with your friends.

RECOMMENDED PRODUCERS
▸ Finca Antigua
▸ Señora de Rosario

ITALY

Italy's great reds, Barolo and Barbaresco, from the mountainous Piemonte (Piedmont) region, have their white counterparts in Arneis and Gavi di Gavi. Piemonte's complex climate allows depth and richness to come into its wines. On the warmer Ligurian coast, and on Sardegna (Sardinia) and Sicilia (Sicily), the Vermentino grape produces a wine with refreshing acidity.

ARNEIS

C COLOUR Straw yellow, with green or light amber reflections.

A AROMA Herbaceous, with apple, pear, lemon, peach, and almond.

T TASTE Dry with a light, lemony acidity. Elegant with a long, persistent finish.

Recent, growing demand for a white wine to match the quality of reds such as Barolo and Barbaresco has saved the Arneis grape from virtual extinction – it had almost disappeared by the early 1970s. Now, however, the grape is making first-class wines, similar in style to Chablis, but with a fruitier aroma, as well as an elegant, refreshing structure. The wine has a herby, nutty character and flavour, although sometimes it can be low in acidity. (Arneis is often blended with Nebbiolo in order to temper the tannin and acidity of this red wine.)

The best Arneis wines are sold under the denomination Roero Arneis. These come from the Roero hills, north of Alba, in Piemonte (Piedmont; northwestern Italy), but sadly, despite their quality, they are in short supply. Although Arneis has started to perform well in Australia, this grape variety is generally not well-known outside Italy.

Arneis has earned itself the nickname Barolo Bianco (meaning "white Barolo"), but the word *arneis* actually means "stubborn little rascal". This refers to the fact that the grape has a delicate skin and a tendency for its stems and shoots to break.

Arneis is best drunk when young – the wine does not have the minerality and acidity required for ageing and so older vintages tend to have no spine. This is a perfect wine to enjoy in the summer. I think it is excellent with sea bass, accompanied by new potatoes and baby leeks.

ARNEIS
Prunotto

RECOMMENDED PRODUCERS

▸ Prunotto
▸ Azienda Agricola Negro
▸ Bruno Giacosa
▸ Carlo Deltetto

VERMENTINO

C COLOUR Bright; straw yellow, glinting with light green.

A AROMA Subtle, aromatic, and floral, with notes of rosemary and sage.

T TASTE Intense, with a lemony acidity and a refreshing kick.

Primarily an Italian grape, Vermentino is similar to a good Sauvignon Blanc, although it is perhaps more exuberant, and less complex and profound.

Most notably producing wines on the island of Sardegna (Sardinia), the grapes are picked early to ensure good acidity, and the best wines are Vermentino di Gallura (awarded DOCG status in the mid-1990s) and Vermentino di Alghero.

You may also find Vermentino from the French island of Corsica.

RECOMMENDED PRODUCERS

▸ Cantina Gallura
▸ Contini

GAVI DI GAVI

C COLOUR Bright; lemon yellow, with highlights of green.

A AROMA Medium intensity; pear, apple, citrus, and roasted almond.

T TASTE Fleshy; ripe peach; harmonious with a long, clean finish.

I love this unpretentious wine, which has developed a niche as one of the finest whites made from the Cortese grape variety, grown in Piemonte (Piedmont).

The Gavi region is long and narrow and the name "Gavi di Gavi" refers to wine made close to the town of Gavi in the far southeast of Piemonte. This wine is tangy, zesty, and refreshing; and crisp and intense. The alternative, Cortese di Gavi (made elsewhere in the region) tends to be a thinner, more steely wine.

In parts of Italy, quantity has become more important than quality and Piemonte is no exception. With the introduction of modern winemaking techniques, it has become easier for producers to churn out large amounts of white wine that is good value and good to drink as a refreshing wine, but lacks character and body. When choosing Gavi it is important to stick to the recommended producers, who care more for the quality of their wine than the amount they can make.

Try not to drink the wine too young. Gavi is often better – richer, with stronger, more mineral flavours – when it is drunk two years after its vintage. I would choose to drink Gavi with a fresh tomato salad, feta cheese, and basil, or even with a tuna-pasta bake.

GAVI DI GAVI
Broglia La Meirana

RECOMMENDED PRODUCERS

▸ Broglia La Meirana
▸ Fontanafredda
▸ Nicola Bergaglio

LUXEMBOURG

This tiny country lies next to Germany's Mosel Valley and French Alsace, so it is no surprise that it has a fine wine-making tradition. Its classic grape is Rivaner, which is responsible for refreshing and aromatic white wines.

RIVANER

C COLOUR Bright and crisp; pale lemon yellow with silvery tinges.

A AROMA Clean; mainly citrus and green fruits, such as apple; also minerals.

T TASTE Well-structured, elegant, and delicate, with a mellow touch.

If you like the idea of an aromatic Chablis, then you should try Rivaner. The wine is able to combine freshness and minerality with slightly richer and more complex aromas – so it is quite special!

The Rivaner grape is a cross between Riesling and Sylvaner, and is known in Germany as Müller-Thurgau. It is the most widely produced grape in Luxembourg. However, as the wine is consumed mainly locally, Rivaner has seen its production decline in recent years and you may have to make a special effort to find a bottle.

The best Rivaners are so distinctive and delicate that they match happily with any seafood, or even with wild Scottish smoked salmon – for a special treat.

RIVANER *Domaine Mathis Bastian*

RECOMMENDED PRODUCERS

▸ Domaine Mathis Bastian
▸ Wormeldange

GERMANY

Germany will forever be associated with the Riesling grape, which grows beside the Rhine River, and its most important tributary, the Mosel. Its aromatic whites are fresh, fruity, and fantastically complex – a far cry from the reputation created by the glut of Liebfraumilch. In the warmer regions of Germany, Ruländer is a fine up-and-coming grape variety, making fine quality wine.

RIESLING

C **COLOUR** Clear and bright pale straw yellow with tinges of green.

A **AROMA** Intense and complex; peach, pineapple, citrus, flint, and smoke.

T **TASTE** Harmonious, deep; great finesse; tangy when young; mineral finish.

Riesling is undoubtedly Germany's finest grape variety, producing some of the best and most long-lived white wines in the world.

Mosel-Saar-Ruwer is the capital of German Riesling. Its wines are low in alcohol, pale, light, and juicy, with good acidity and fruit, and often slightly fizzy. The region's slate soil imparts a distinctive taste to the wines, from fine-fruity to earthy, or "flinty". They may also be described as smoky, or even, after ageing, as having a hint of petrol.

Riesling from the Rheingau (on the east bank of the Rhine) has a slightly richer texture, and more depth and body than the Mosel wine. Drink it while it is still young.

On the opposite bank of the Rhine lies the Nahe. Here, the highest quality Reislings are pure and crystalline, with flavours ranging from passion fruit, guava, apricot, and vanilla, to red berries and minerals.

Pfalz, bordering France in the southwest of Germany, is second only to Mosel in importance. The Rieslings from here are full-bodied with an essential touch of minerality.

Enjoy German Riesling with cold meats or seafood; I particularly enjoy it with goat's cheese salad.

RIESLING
Fritz Haag

RECOMMENDED PRODUCERS

▸ Fritz Haag
▸ Carl Loewen
▸ Weingut Egon Müller-Scharzhof
▸ Reichsgraf von Kesselstatt

IN A CLASS OF ITS OWN *Riesling from Germany is one of the finest wines in the world – and often exceptionally good value.*

LAND AND PRODUCTION

THE MOSEL VALLEY More than half of the Mosel-Saar-Ruwer Riesling vines adorn the slopes of the Mosel Valley. However, producing wine from the steep valley sides is expensive and this has limited the expansion of the region, despite the high quality of its wine.

RULÄNDER

C **COLOUR** Pale straw yellow, with lemony highlights.

A **AROMA** Dense and rich with flowery hints of acacia and freesia.

T **TASTE** Smooth and finely tuned, with a distinct spiciness on the finish.

Ruländer, cousin to Pinot Gris, makes good wine with more flesh and less exuberance than others in Germany. The wines can be kept for two or three years, and will develop exotic, flinty flavours.

Mostly grown in Pfalz and Baden (in warmer southwestern Germany), Ruländer needs deep, heavy soils in order to produce wine that fulfils its potential for complexity and a full bouquet. Stick to the recommended producers and you will surely discover some classy wines.

RECOMMENDED PRODUCERS
▸ R und C Schneider
▸ Weinhaus Heger

HUNGARY

This country is well on the way to recovering its reputation after years of releasing inferior quality wine (except for the excellent Tokaji dessert wine). The Furmint grape variety, used in the blend to make Tokaji, is now being used to make fine wines on its own.

FURMINT

C **COLOUR** Intense wheat-gold, with tinges of green.

A **AROMA** Pronounced; grapefruit peel, minerals, and warm bread.

T **TASTE** Dense but harmonious, with marked acidity.

Furmint is perhaps most famous for the fact that it is blended into the great sweet wine Tokaji (see p146). However, in its own right the grape produces a fiery dry wine that is intensely aromatic, powerful, and complex, and rich with flavours of apple, citrus fruit, and smoke.

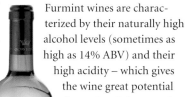

FURMINT
Crown Estates

Furmint wines are characterized by their naturally high alcohol levels (sometimes as high as 14% ABV) and their high acidity – which gives the wine great potential for ageing. It is normal for a Furmint to undergo a minimum of two years maturing in small-sized casks. The result is a wine with a distinctive, spicy aroma, and a slightly harsh-flavoured or tart taste with a strong acidity.

Although Furmint is predominantly a Hungarian grape, some of the best examples of the wine tend to be from the Austrian region of Burgenland, which borders western Hungary. Furmint is widely sold throughout central Europe, and, at its best, is quite unique. Try it with the food suggestions above, or on its own as an apéritif.

RECOMMENDED PRODUCERS
▸ Crown Estates
▸ Bataapati
▸ Chapel Hill

FOOD MATCH

SMOKED FISH Try Furmint with a light lunch of smoked trout, or with other seafood. The wine also goes well with roast chicken or pork, or with a mushroom risotto.

AUSTRIA

Austria makes some great aromatic whites, but relatively few are exported. Look out for Grüner Veltliner, a wonderful crisp and complex white wine, and at the top of every sommelier's wine list!

GRÜNER VELTLINER

C **COLOUR** Pale, straw yellow or pale green, perhaps with silvery tinges.

A **AROMA** Complex and subtle; citrus fruits, white flowers, and flint.

T **TASTE** Dry, delicate, and balanced, with a persistent peppery finish.

Grüner Veltliner (often marketed as simply GV, and in the US as "Groovy"!) is a fine, delicate, and high-quality wine, which can rival even the best white Burgundy.

The wine is a clear, pale straw colour, and has a dry, light feel, with a distinctive, pungent aroma, an array of fruit, herb, and spice flavours, and a range of mineral and acidic characters, with a long finish.

Grüner Veltliner ripens late in the year, and therefore its cultivation is unsuited to the cooler parts of northern Europe. But it flourishes in central Europe, where the summers last for longer and the autumns tend to be slightly milder.

As a result, Grüner Veltliner is the star among Austria's grape varieties and is grown in almost every Austrian wine region. (It accounts for more than one third of Austrian wine production.) The best wines come from Austria's northeastern wine regions. Look out for names like Kamptal; and

GRÜNER VELTLINER *Weingut Dr Unger*

Wachau and Kremstal, which lie along the Danube River. This wine is best while still young, although its high acidity does lend it the character to withstand some ageing in the bottle.

Grüner Veltliner is gaining a great reputation, and it is becoming more readily available outside Austria. Some of the world's top restaurants are adding it to their wine lists, so it is definitely one to look out for. However, you also need to look out for the price: the wine can be expensive, but is well worth it.

Drink Grüner Veltliner on its own, or with light meals of meat or fish; it will set off a dinner party on absolutely the right note.

RECOMMENDED PRODUCERS
▸ Weingut Dr Unger
▸ M & E Triebaumer
▸ Prager
▸ Roman Pfaffl

LAND AND PRODUCTION

DRINKING ROCKS According to some, drinking Grüner Veltliner is like drinking "liquid stone". "Why should we drink fruit when we can drink stone?" say the Austrians when describing the cool, refreshing feel of the wine. The hints of minerals and flints in the wine's flavour come from the combination of soil, climate, and grape variety.

BULGARIA

It comes as a surprise that Bulgaria is one of the world's biggest wine producers. Much of its wine is made from foreign grape varieties, but Dimiat is one of its indigenous grapes, and makes a fine aromatic wine.

DIMIAT

C COLOUR Bright; deep gold with a silvery tinge on the rim.

A AROMA Intense, deliberately scented; pear, flowers, spice, and mango.

T TASTE Subtle, with good balance of alcohol, fruit, and acidity; clean finish.

Dimiat produces both dry and sweet wine. Dry Dimiat is uncomplicated, and when well-made is an aromatic, fresh, and tangy wine with lots of spice and few pretensions.

Most of the wines exported from Bulgaria are made with grape varieties such as Chardonnay, Merlot, and Cabernet Sauvignon.

DIMIAT
Boyar Estates

However, Dimiat could not be more local. A copper-coloured grape native to Bulgaria, it is grown mainly in the eastern and southern parts of the country, along the coast of the Black Sea.

Drink Dimiat within two years of the vintage. Try it as an alternative to a white Italian or Greek wine, with some grilled fish or a salad.

RECOMMENDED PRODUCERS

▸ Boyar Estates Blueridge Winery
▸ Lambol
▸ Suhindol

GREECE

Many Greek wines from the mainland or the Aegean islands are quite dry, and sometimes fairly thin, but there are wines from other parts of Greece with more subtlety and complexity; Robola, which comes from the slightly cooler Ionian islands, is one of the latter.

ROBOLA

C COLOUR A soft but bright gold with green hues.

A AROMA Complex; flowers, honey, lemon peel, peach.

T TASTE Moderately rich; mineral touch at the finish.

Originating in the heart of the Greek Ionian island of Cephalonia, Robola (or Ribolla in Italy) has achieved enormous success in both the quality and quantity of the wine it produces. Increasingly, the grape is recognized as a variety with great potential for making fine aromatic wines.

ROBOLA *Gentilini*

At its best, the Robola grape produces wine with good acidity and a distinct lemony character.

Robola can be drunk when very young, or can be kept for up to four years from its vintage. Serve it chilled, perhaps with some squid or octopus, or a Greek salad, and allow it to take you back to sun-filled days in Greece.

RECOMMENDED PRODUCERS

▸ Gentilini
▸ Ktima Mercouri
▸ Kefalonian Wine Co-operative

ENGLAND

Under the Romans, significant amounts of wine were made in England, but production all but disappeared when continental wines began to be imported in the 16th century. In recent years, production has taken off again, assisted by new grape varieties and crossings.

BACCHUS

C COLOUR Bright; pale lemon yellow with green highlights.

A AROMA Young, intense, and distinct; gooseberry, green apple, and flowers.

T TASTE Lean but delicate; refreshing with marked acidity; moderate alcohol.

What better name for a grape than the Roman god of wine!

I remember the first time I tried wine from this grape without being told what I was drinking. I was convinced that it was a Sauvignon Blanc because of its grassiness and citrus flavours. However, Bacchus is a cross of two German grapes: Sylvaner and Riesling. The fruit ripens extremely early, and so can produce quality wines even in the cool British climate. As a result Bacchus is now the fourth most-planted grape variety in the UK (after Müller-Thurgau, Seyval Blanc, and Sylvaner).

Wines from the Bacchus grape are clean, zesty, aromatic, and youthful. A well-made Bacchus wine can be top class – and exceptionally good value for money.

CHANGING LANDSCAPE
England is now home to several hundred vineyards, mostly growing German grape varieties.

Until the mid-20th century commercial vine-growing in the UK was virtually non-existent. So English wines are fairly new, but they are improving all the time thanks largely to better quality control.

But, watch out – check the label when you buy an English wine. Wines that state "English" on the label are produced from grapes actually grown in England, and are carefully monitored for quality. Wines labelled "British" come from imported, unfermented grape juice, which is more difficult to monitor.

RECOMMENDED PRODUCERS

▸ Chapel Down
▸ New Wave Wines
▸ Sandhurst

NEW ZEALAND

New Zealand now ranks among the great wine-producing countries of the world. It has a cool climate, good levels of sunshine, and a go-ahead attitude, which has really driven results. The Marlborough region produces arguably the best Sauvignon Blanc in the world. There are other fine wine-producing regions on both Islands; look out for South Island Pinot Gris – a rival to Alsace.

SAUVIGNON BLANC

C COLOUR Bright and lively; pale straw yellow with green tinges.

A AROMA Powerful, with bags of fruit: citrus, melon, gooseberry, pineapple.

T TASTE Dry, ripe flavours; marked, balanced acidity; clean, infinite length.

New Zealand's Sauvignon Blanc is a formidable rival to that of France – and rightly so!

Sauvignon Blanc is a grape that takes on the characteristics of its region, and there are distinct differences in the wines from New Zealand's North and South Islands. The northern wine (made in Hawke's Bay and Gisborne) tends to be ripe and rich, with flavours of melon and other similar fruit. Southern styles (Marlborough and Wellington) are light and crisp, with higher acidity, and an exuberant taste of passion fruit, gooseberry, citrus, and herbs.

Most New Zealand Sauvignon Blanc is cold-fermented in stainless-steel tanks to produce freshness and to retain the grape's pungent fruit flavours. The style is similar to that of a Sancerre, but is more "obvious" with a juicy feel. Vintage is less of an issue than it is with a Sancerre.

New Zealand Sauvignon Blanc has established itself as the flagship wine of the New World – with prices to match its reputation. You will not find this wine in the bargain bins, but it is well worth a little extra.

SAUVIGNON BLANC Wither Hills

RECOMMENDED PRODUCERS
▸ Wither Hills
▸ Villa Maria
▸ Cloudy Bay

LAND AND PRODUCTION

COASTAL VINES Marlborough is New Zealand's most acclaimed region for Sauvignon Blanc. The effects of the sea on the climate and the long ripening season work together to produce perfectly balanced, high-quality, aromatic wines.

PINOT GRIS

C COLOUR Attractive, pale gold, reflecting the rich colour of the grape.

A AROMA Honey, apple, lemon, pear, peach, white flowers, and minerals.

T TASTE Fleshy, complex; a ripe texture and a long, aromatic, and clean finish.

New Zealand's Pinot Gris is the modern alternative to unoaked Chardonnay. A mutation of the Pinot Noir grape, Pinot Gris is best known in Alsace, France. However, it is now increasingly grown on New Zealand's South Island, particularly in the wine regions of Marlborough (in the northeast) and Canterbury (in the southeast).

Perhaps the richest in colour of all white grapes, Pinot Gris produces a beautifully golden wine that is also intensely aromatic. New Zealand

PINOT GRIS Matakana Estate

Pinot Gris wines are very fruity, but they also have a firm mineral or stone character, making them particularly distinctive.

Pinot Gris prefers cooler climates, which is why New Zealand, and specifically South Island, has been more successful than other parts of the New World at its cultivation.

South Island's temperate, maritime climate has given the wines a fresher taste than Alsace Pinot Gris, while retaining the grape's characteristic viscous or slightly oily texture.

This is a great summer wine, and is excellent on its own or with light food such as fettucine in a tomato and basil sauce, or sushi.

RECOMMENDED PRODUCERS
▸ Matakana Estate
▸ Morton Estate
▸ Seresin

SOUTH AFRICA

Some of the cooler parts of this country, such as Paarl and Constantia on the Western Cape, are just right for complex Sauvignon Blanc – not as austere as the French versions, and not quite so full as other New World wines.

SAUVIGNON BLANC

C COLOUR Pale lemon yellow, with tinges of luscious green.

A AROMA Elegant, expressive; gooseberry, green pepper, pineapple, passion fruit.

T TASTE Refreshing, balanced; lightly structured; steadied by a citrusy spine.

I particularly like the fact that the fresh and invigorating South African Sauvignon Blancs are richer and more luscious than their French equivalents, but also less exuberant than those from other parts of the New World: their style lies somewhere between the two. This makes them perfect if you want to have the best of both worlds!

SAUVIGNON BLANC Buitenverwachting

Sauvignon Blanc thrives in the regions of Paarl and Constantia, producing wines of great quality and expression – thanks to the cooling influence of the Atlantic Ocean. This allows time for the complexity of flavours to develop as the grapes ripen, and adds concentration and acidity to the wines. Perfect on their own, as an apéritif, these wines also go well with any type of fish.

RECOMMENDED PRODUCERS
▸ Buitenverwachting
▸ Klein Constantia Estate
▸ Vergelegen

AUSTRALIA

One of the great centres of world wine, Australia is justly famous for its big reds, and for its white Chardonnay and Sémillon. South Australia also makes wonderful Riesling, particularly from Clare Valley near Adelaide, and some fine Sauvignon Blanc from the nearby Adelaide Hills.

RIESLING

C COLOUR Pale straw yellow, with silver and green highlights.

A AROMA Intense, delicate, with lime, peach, pineapple, and hints of smoke.

T TASTE Dense and rich, underlined with citrusy and steely acidity; long finish.

If you like exuberant New Zealand Sauvignon Blanc wines, you will be completely bowled over by Australian Riesling.

I have friends who will not buy a Riesling wine on principle, but they do not know what they are missing! Throughout the world Riesling's reputation has suffered from mass-market wines such as Germany's sickly sweet Liebfraumilch, and other "Riesling" wines from eastern Europe.

However, now is the time to look at the full picture and rediscover Riesling. This wonderful grape variety has found a new home and

FOOD MATCH

SHELLFISH Give yourself the ultimate taste of Australia and drink an Australian Riesling with barbecue prawns (great on skewers with courgette). The wine also mixes well with crab and other seafood, as well as light salads of chicken or bacon.

a new style in Australia, and is ready to compete with other world-famous varieties such as Chardonnay and Pinot Grigio.

I particularly like the juicy style from the Clare Valley. An area to the north of Adelaide (in the state of South Australia), the Clare Valley is home to wineries with distinct German and Austrian influences. For example, in 1851 Jesuits, fleeing religious and political persecution in Austria, established the valley's oldest winery, Sevenhill Cellars, in order to make their own altar wine. Today, the Clare Valley wineries produce some of Australia's best Rieslings. With their full lime and citrus flavours they are definitely wines to make your mouth water. In the warm climate around the town of Clare itself (in the north of the region), the wines are full-bodied and round. In the cooler area around Watervale (lying farther south), they are crisp, tangy, and delicate.

The best Clare Rieslings are zesty, extremely floral, and aromatic. They age beautifully and will improve for ten years or more. If you can wait that long, you will find a wine rich with flavours of lime syrup and buttery toast.

So, hold your head up high and seek out an Australian Riesling! You will not be disappointed.

RIESLING
Pewsey Vale Vineyard

RECOMMENDED PRODUCERS
▸ Pewsey Vale Vineyard
▸ Knappstein
▸ Leasingham

SAUVIGNON BLANC

C COLOUR Light straw yellow, with silvery tinges.

A AROMA Fresh and pungent, with grass, gooseberry, tropical fruit, and pear.

T TASTE Full-flavoured and complex with a long, crisp finish.

As a general rule, Australian Sauvignon Blanc tends to be too rich, with the exotic fruits dominating – sometimes to the point of eliminating – the natural freshness of the grape.

An exception to this is the Sauvignon Blanc produced in the winemaking region of Adelaide Hills (lying directly to the east of the town of Adelaide), which has the coolest climate of all vine-growing regions of South Australia. When they are grown in a climate that is too warm, Sauvignon Blanc grapes can over-ripen and the resulting wine is often oily. Most of the vineyards in the Adelaide Hills lie above an altitude of 400m (1300ft). They have the highest rainfall in the state and a strong, cold southerly wind, making the conditions perfect for Sauvignon Blanc.

Most important is that the climate gives the grapes a long, cool ripening period. This enables them to hang on to their zesty freshness, which will in turn create a really exciting wine with distinctive aromas of grasses and citrus fruit, and full, crisp flavours.

Overall, the Sauvignon Blanc from this part of South Australia is exceptional and I love it! I will drink it happily on its own, but partnered with food it is great with light dishes, such as grilled white fish, a ripe avocado salad, or stir-fry vegetables.

SAUVIGNON BLANC
Shaw and Smith

RECOMMENDED PRODUCERS
▸ Shaw and Smith
▸ Nepenthe Wines
▸ Stafford Ridge

ARGENTINA

This country – the sleeping giant of winemaking – is now developing its own grape varieties and styles. Look out for the home-grown Torrontés.

TORRONTÉS

C COLOUR A refined golden yellow hue, with pale intensity.

A AROMA Floral, exotic, and spicy, with fresh grapes, lychee, and flowers.

T TASTE Zesty, full of spice, with a distinctive and refreshing acidity.

The Spanish word *torrontés* means "torrent" in English, and so it is with this wine – the aroma from Torrontés is a tumultuous outpouring that is heavily reminiscent of Muscat: grapey fruit, lychee, and hints of flowers. Its flavours remind me of Sauvignon Blanc.

The Torrontés grape is well-suited to Argentina's arid climate and produces a wine with good acidity and a light body. Nevertheless, the wine has to be carefully vinified to retain its freshness and the subtlety of its fruit, and to avoid oxidation.

TORRONTÉS
Etchart

The grape may have arrived in Argentina from Galicia in north-western Spain, although there is no direct evidence that links the two. In any case, Torrontés has certainly carved its niche, and is gaining the same level of respect for Argentinian white wine as that enjoyed by Malbec for the country's reds.

Refreshing, not over-complex, but nonetheless exciting, Torrontés wines are perfect for summertime drinking. Try them with crisp, green salads or a light lunch of warm, grilled chicken on a bed of leaves.

RECOMMENDED PRODUCERS
▸ Etchart
▸ Santa Julia
▸ La Nature

66 Delicate, smooth, and intense but dry; the best of these wines are perfectly balanced and ideal to enjoy with food. **99**

FULL, OPULENT WHITES

INTRODUCING FULL, OPULENT WHITES

With a firm, full structure, subtle texture, and expressive fruit, these wines appeal to millions of wine drinkers in their "popular" forms – New World Chardonnays and Viogniers – and in their classic incarnations – the great Burgundy whites.

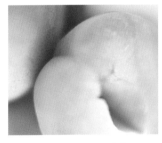

RIPE APRICOT *Many full, opulent whites burst with fruit aromas, such as apricot.*

Full white wines are a real treat, and if you have deep pockets, you can buy yourself a taste of heaven. A great wine will be delicate, and have finesse, balance, and concentration. Its vast, complex, and intense taste will linger, stamping the wine's class into your palate. But do not worry if you are on a tighter budget; unpretentious full whites can be rewarding too. They should feel grapey and well balanced, with a clean finish that is not too oaky. Full whites typically have a firm structure and may feel oily in the mouth, a sensation derived either from the grape variety used – especially Marsanne or Sémillon – or from ageing in oak.

The grapes used to make full whites have relatively small berries with thick skins. They are less productive than other grape varieties, yielding less juice, but the result is a wine that is naturally fuller. The whites often originate in warmer climates – Western Australia, California, and south-central France, for example – or from warmer microclimates in other regions. Full whites are typically vinified in oak barrels. New oak results in a richer wine than old oak, and toasted oak gives the richest finish of all – sometimes too rich. Generally, the more the oak is toasted, the more pronounced the woody flavour in the wine will be.

VARIETY AND STYLE

The full white category includes world-famous wines, such as some of the best Burgundies – Chassagne-Montrachet, Puligny-Montrachet, Meursault, and the like – made from the Chardonnay grape. New World Chardonnays from South Africa or California are now competing with these renowned Burgundies, giving the French a real headache. Other notable full whites include Sémillon from Western Australia or the Hunter Valley, Gewürztraminer from Alsace, Viognier from the USA, the austere Chenin Blanc from the Loire Valley (such as Savennières), and Marsanne from the Rhône Valley.

FISH DISHES *Sea bass comes alive with a Burgundy; but avoid oily fish, which can clash with oaky whites.*

GRAPE VARIETIES

These grape varieties are the best for making full and opulent white wines. Their special character is their body, strength, and weight, balanced with fruit and acidity to keep the wine in harmony. They are often matured in oak, but this should not mask the subtlety of the wine. The classic varieties are Chardonnay and Viognier, in their complex French and openly fruity New World styles, and Sémillon, mainly from Australia. There are also spicy varieties, like Gewürztraminer from Alsace and New Zealand, and Marsanne from the Rhône.

GRAPE	BEST REGIONAL EXAMPLES	COMMENTS
CHARDONNAY	France: Burgundy. Australia. Chile: Casablanca. South Africa: Stellenbosch. USA: California (Napa Valley, Sonoma, Alexander Valley).	The classic full white grape variety, producing wonderful wines from Burgundy, such as Meursault and Montrachet, as well as the finest New World wines from Australia, South Africa, and the USA.
VIOGNIER	France: Rhône Valley, Condrieu. USA: California (Napa Valley).	The main grape to rival Chardonnay, Viognier makes big and muscly wines with notes of exotic fruits, such as mango, peach, and pineapple.
SÉMILLON	France: Bordeaux, Graves, Pessac. Australia: Margaret River, Hunter Valley.	Sémillon makes robust white wine with a more appealing exotic fruit style in Australia, compared to the more reserved but extremely complex Bordeaux style.
MARSANNE	France: Rhône (Châteauneuf-du-Pape, Hermitage, and Crozes-Hermitage). USA: California (Santa Barbara).	Marsanne has an amazing complexity, and ranks among the finest grape varieties in the world. It is enjoying increasing popularity in the world market.
CHENIN BLANC	France: Loire Valley.	This variety, also known as "Pineau de la Loire", favours a more temperate climate, which can make the wine quite austere when young.
GEWÜRZTRAMINER	France: Alsace. New Zealand. Australia. California.	Gewürztraminer makes off-dry white wine, with charming notes of exotic fruit, such as lychee, and a spicy character.
ALBANA	Italy: Emilia-Romagna.	Albana is a key variety of the Emilia-Romagna region, and one of the finest whites from Italy, although difficult to grow well.
GRENACHE BLANC	Spain: Priorat, Rioja. France: Rhône, Provence.	Grenache Blanc, at its best, expresses oiliness, power with finesse, a juicy acidity, and a nutty finish.
SAVAGNIN	France: Jura. Germany. Hungary. Austria.	This grape makes a famous, nutty and lemony wine that can be quite austere, but has great complexity.
ZIERFANDLER	Austria: Vienna. Hungary (known as Cirfandli).	This variety is gaining popularity in the world market. The finest Zierfandler wines are made in a blend with Rotgipfler.
ROTGIPFLER	Austria: Vienna region.	The Rotgipfler grape makes very distinctive wine – full-bodied, spicy, and full of character.
SCHONBURGER	Germany. England.	This pink-berried variety is limited in production, but its tendency to lack acidity makes it successful in a cool climate.
GRECCHETTO	Italy: central Umbria.	Often used in a blend, Grecchetto is becoming more important in Umbrian white wines, such as Orvieto and Torgiano.
GRECO	Italy: Campania, Capri, Gravina. Greece.	This grape makes a dry white wine that is full-bodied and, despite its weight, very elegant.

FRANCE

Great opulent white wines can be found in many regions of France. Some of the all-time classics of the world, such as Puligny-Montrachet and Meursault, are full white wines from the Côte de Beaune, Burgundy. A number of wonderful AOCs stretch down the Rhône Valley – Condrieu, the great Viognier wine, and the complex blends of Hermitage and Châteauneuf-du-Pape. Alsace is famous for its Gewürztraminer, while the Loire Valley and the mountainous Jura also make fabulous white wines.

CÔTE DE BEAUNE

C COLOUR Pale to deep straw yellow, with green to golden tinges.

A AROMA Delicate, with apple, peach, bread, hazelnut, honey, and minerals.

T TASTE Round and elegant; balanced with a persistent, refreshing finish.

If there is one place where Chardonnay produces some of the finest wine in the world, it is the Côte de Beaune, a small area around the town of Beaune in the centre of the Burgundy region. Here, the principal white wine appellations are Meursault, St Romain, St Aubin, Puligny-Montrachet, Chassagne-Montrachet, and Aloxe-Corton. Three of these have made Côte de Beaune world famous.

CÔTE DE BEAUNE
Bernard Morey et Fils

The first, Puligny-Montrachet, produces some of the greatest whites in the world. Pure gold, with hints of green, the wines have a distinct minerality. Their intense and complex aromas combine citrus, apple, honey, and marzipan. Concentrated and structurally perfect, these wines have an "infinite" finish.

The second is Chassagne-Montrachet, producing wines with a powerful body, fruity flavour, and a steely edge. Balanced, complex, and smooth, they are deep gold, with aromas of ripe fruit, honeysuckle, and hazelnut.

Finally, Meursault produces rich, full, and opulent wines, with clean, fresh tastes, lemony acidity, and a long, complex, fruit finish. The best vintages (and those of Chassagne-Montrachet and Puligny-Montrachet), age for up to 15 years.

However, we must not forget one other great Côte de Beaune wine – Corton-Charlemagne, the *grand cru* of Aloxe-Corton. This wine is medium gold and crystal clear, with aromas of baked apple, nuts, butter, citrus fruits, pineapple, and honey. Its taste is rich, buttery, complex, and powerful, with a perfect balance of fruit and acidity. Drink it no younger than five years old; some vintages will age for up to 25 years.

RECOMMENDED PRODUCERS
▸ Bernard Morey et Fils
▸ Coche-Dury
▸ Chartron-Trebuchet
▸ Domaine Maillard
▸ J M Pillot

FOOD MATCH

SHELLFISH The full, opulent flavours of Côte de Beaune Chardonnay are a wonderful match for seafood, such as dressed lobster or scallops, and also go well with French cheese.

WORLD-FAMOUS WHITE
In the wines of Côte de Beaune, Chardonnay comes into its own, setting standards of excellence to which all the world's producers aspire.

CONDRIEU

C COLOUR Pale to deep golden yellow, with touches of silvery green.

A AROMA Unique; apricot, mango, lychee, peach, pineapple, and hazelnut.

T TASTE Complex and classy; ripe fruit with refreshing acidity; lingering finish.

CONDRIEU
Domaine Georges Vernay

The Rhône's finest white? I think so!

Made only from the Viognier grape, Condrieu is intense but balanced, with fresh acidity and moderate alcohol. Its delicate and floral aromas are backed by a full-bodied, rich wine to be enjoyed in its youth.

The wine is expensive, but great value for a "big league" white. Drink it with rich seafood dishes.

RECOMMENDED PRODUCERS

▸ Domaine Georges Vernay
▸ Domaine Cheze

HERMITAGE / CROZES-HERMITAGE

C COLOUR Golden yellow; green to silver highlights; medium to deep intensity.

A AROMA Ripe and exotic; minerals, honeydew, flowers, pine, and hazelnut.

T TASTE Clean and rich; juicy acidity and an elegant finish; notes of spice and pear.

Hermitage is a hill on the east bank of the Rhône River; Crozes is a village in the plateau that surrounds it. Wines from these areas blend the robust Marsanne grape with Rousanne to increase subtlety and aroma. Marsanne makes rich wines, full of body and texture. It also picks up the mineral flavours of its soils.

Some Hermitage wines develop well with age, but drink Crozes-Hermitage and Hermitage with low acidity when they are young. Try them with fish or white meat.

RECOMMENDED PRODUCERS

▸ Domaine Alain Graillot
▸ Domaine Jean-Louis Chave

CHÂTEAUNEUF-DU-PAPE

C COLOUR Bright; pale golden yellow with greenish tinges.

A AROMA Subtle; exotic fruits, acacia, honey, citrus, almond, and beeswax.

T TASTE Round and creamy; great harmony and depth; long finish.

When we talk of the Rhône, we tend to speak only of red wine. However, this is an extensive wine region, producing wines of all styles and qualities – among them some excellent whites. Châteauneuf-du-Pape, the star of the southern Rhône and famous for its distinguished red wine, produces a small amount of Châteauneuf Blanc – I thoroughly recommend that you try it.

The French have enjoyed Châteauneuf Blanc for many years (locals and connoisseurs like to keep the occasional gem to themselves!), but the wines are now gaining recognition in the rest of the world.

CHÂTEAUNEUF DU PAPE *Château de Beaucastel*

Wine of great quality and finesse, Châteauneuf Blanc is big and rich, with a unique character that comes from the "pudding" stones (*galets*) of the *terroir*. Remnants of the last ice age, these stones soak up the heat of the sun during the day and then radiate it back at the vines at night, speeding up the ripening process. They also help the soil to retain moisture.

Drink Châteauneuf-du-Pape young, or age it for three to four years. Good vintages will continue to improve for a further ten years after that. Serve the wine chilled, at around 8°C (46°F), and match it with foie gras, lobster, or Roquefort cheese. At its best, I think this wine is second to none.

RECOMMENDED PRODUCERS

▸ Château de la Gardine
▸ Château de Beaucastel

SAVENNIÈRES

C COLOUR Pale lemon yellow, to deep golden when aged; good intensity.

A AROMA Persistent yet delicate; quince, citrus, smoke, and minerals.

T TASTE Complex, powerful; fresh acidity; unforgettable finish.

Some may say that I am biased (this wine comes from a village close to my home), but I think that Savennières is one of the Loire Valley's finest white wines, belonging to an elite group of wines with "wow" factor. If you like the style of Mosel Riesling, then I think you will agree with me.

Savennières is an extremely dry and complex wine from the Anjou region of the Loire. Here, the Chenin Blanc grape variety is king, and the *terroir* and the distant breezes from the Atlantic Ocean combine to produce wine of the highest quality.

SAVENNIÈRES
Domaine du Closel

Chenin Blanc's high sugar content gives Savennières flavours of well-integrated alcohol. The grape is also naturally high in acidity and, therefore, Savennières is only at its best after ageing (for at least seven years). A good, long-aged Savennières will simultaneously suggest velvety softness and granite hardness, and will combine a bone-dry character with full flavour. The wine is a perfect partner for oily goat's cheese, and for smoked eels or mackerel. If you want to drink a similar but younger wine, try Saumur Blanc or Anjou Blanc, which are from the same region and have the minerality of Savennières, but are fresher. Try them with beautiful Loire Valley white fish.

RECOMMENDED PRODUCERS
▸ Domaine du Closel (Clos du Papillon)
▸ Pierre Bise
▸ Clos Rougeard

JURA SAVAGNIN

C COLOUR Pale yellow, to more golden with bottle-ageing.

A AROMA Fresh, intense, and full of character; citrus, honey, dried nuts.

T TASTE Dense; marked acidity, medium alcohol, and a nutty finish.

The Savagnin grape variety, grown mainly in the mountainous Jura wine region of eastern France, is best known for producing *vin jaune* (literally "yellow wine"), a light, fortified wine rather like sherry. However, Savagnin also produces some fantastic, even outstanding, dry white wine.

Produced only in small quantities, Savagnin has distinctive nutty, lemon, and peach aromas, and a clean finish. The wine is often blended with Chardonnay to make it slightly fleshier and less acidic. However, thanks to its acidic spine, and its well-structured body,

JURA SAVAGNIN
Jacques Puffeney

Savagnin is one of the longest-lived white wines available.

Some wine experts suggest that Savagnin is closely related to the Traminer grape, the forefather of Gewürztraminer *(see p59)*. There are similarities: Savagnin is dry with a balanced acidity, but it is not quite as spicy as Gewürztraminer. However, if you enjoy Gewürztraminer, you almost certainly will like Savagnin, too.

Serve Jura Savagnin as an apéritif, perhaps with olives to complement its flavour. Over dinner, you can enjoy it with roast chicken in creamy mushroom sauce.

RECOMMENDED PRODUCERS
▸ Jacques Puffeney
▸ Henri Maire
▸ Domaine Aviet

ALSACE GEWÜRZTRAMINER

C COLOUR Pale gold to amber, with tinges of green.

A AROMA Lychee, pineapple, ginger, white pepper, roasted almond, flowers.

T TASTE Big and rich with lots of muscle and explosive flavours; long, clean acidity.

Gewürztraminer is one of the great specialities of Alsace, in the east of France. The grape is easy to identify by its pink berries, and has powerful and distinctive aromas of flowers, fruit, and spice.

The wine is round, rich, oily, and fleshy, with low acidity and high alcohol. In good-quality Gewürztraminer, the flavours explode in your mouth, giving the sensation of an exceptionally long, refreshing, and clean finish. All this, despite the wine's heavy, rich texture!

Drink the wine young, although the best examples improve for up to 15 years. And rest assured – once tasted, it is impossible to forget!

RECOMMENDED PRODUCERS
▸ Leon Beyer
▸ Chateau d'Orchwihr
▸ Domaine Zind-Humbrecht

FOOD MATCH

ASIAN SPICES Gewürztraminer makes a perfect partner for spicy food, especially from Asia. Try it while tucking into ginger-spiced pork on herby rice. Gewürztraminer also goes well with Munster – a strong, creamy cheese, which, like the wine, is also from Alsace.

AUSTRIA

Austrian wine tends to be drunk locally but deserves a place on the world stage. There are a number of distinct wine regions in the country, including the area around Vienna itself, which makes fine, rich, white wine.

ZIERFANDLER

C COLOUR Deep lemon yellow, with golden highlights.

A AROMA Unique and ripe; pineapple, spice, walnut, and apple.

T TASTE Powerful and firm; good acidity and well-integrated alcohol; spicy finish.

With the potential for making fine, elegant, and complex wines, Zierfandler is one of the most notable white grape varieties in Austria.

The grape (which in some areas is known as Spätrot) is naturally high in acidity. This means that it makes great wine for ageing.

However, Zierfandler is often blended with another successful

white grape called Rotgipfler. Together they create a wine full of character and strength.

I would usually recommend drinking Zierfandler with meaty fish, such as tuna or marlin, or any white meat. Alternatively, for a really healthy match, try it with a salad of field mushrooms and green vegetables.

ZIERFANDLER
Weingut Stadlmann

RECOMMENDED PRODUCERS
▸ Weingut Stadlmann
▸ Franz Kurz
▸ G Schellmann

SPAIN

The Rioja and Penedès regions of Spain make opulent, buttery whites using the Garnacha Blanca grape. The key to their quality is ageing in a warm climate, maturation in oak barrels, and expert vinification.

RIOJA / PENEDÈS

C COLOUR Mellow, pale golden yellow, with straw tinges.

A AROMA Very clean; pineapple, lemon, grapefruit, walnut; hints of spicy oak.

T TASTE Rich and opulent with integrated acidity and alcohol; long nutty finish.

Although most of the best Spanish wines are reds, there are some very fine white wines, especially those made from the Garnacha Blanca grape (Grenache Blanc in France). This variety is used as a component of white Rioja wines, and to a greater extent in the white wines of the up-and-coming Penedès region of

RIOJA *López de Heredia*

northeastern Spain. When carefully vinified, these wines can be polished, subtle, rich, and waxy, with intense flavours of spice, nuts, sweet pear, and exotic fruits such as pineapple, and a satisfying lemony finish. Try them with tapas.

RECOMMENDED PRODUCERS

▸ López de Heredia
▸ Barbara Fores
▸ Torres

GARNACHA BLANCA *At the winery, white Rioja grapes are handled as little as possible to help prevent oxidization.*

ITALY

Though less well known than the reds, the full whites of Italy can have great depth and character. The best are from the south, where the warm climate adds to the richness of the fruit flavours of the wine.

GRECO DI TUFO

C COLOUR Bright; pale orange-straw, with golden tinges when older.

A AROMA Delicate; citrus, peach, honey, spice, hazelnut, and minerals.

T TASTE Marked acidity, balanced alcohol, and a firm structure; clean, long finish.

Greco di Tufo is a full-bodied, dry white wine made in the Campania region of southern Italy, around the village of Tufo. Greco refers to the grape – a versatile fruit (it is used to make sweet wine, too) originating from Greece, hence its name.

This complex wine gathers its aromas during the winemaking

GRECO DI TUFO
Mastroberardino

process. After picking, the grapes are pressed and fermented at cool temperatures, and the wine remains in tanks for three months before bottling.

An austere wine that is not very well known, Greco di Tufo is well worth trying. It is good with spicy Chinese food or Mediterranean dishes. To be loyal to Campania, try it with seafood pasta.

RECOMMENDED PRODUCERS

▸ Mastroberardino
▸ Terredora
▸ D'Antiche Terra Vega

ALBANA

C COLOUR Straw yellow, with silvery highlights; medium to full intensity.

A AROMA Subtle and elegant; fruit, sage, flowers, almond, and green apple.

T TASTE Full but lean and dry; marked acidity, medium alcohol, spicy finish.

Albana is an intense grape variety, the best examples of which come from around the town of Forlì, in the Emilia-Romagna region of northern Italy.

The Albana grape is vulnerable to diseases such as grey rot, a fungal infection that rots the fruit and causes it to develop off-flavours, and in the past this has restricted the production of good wine. However, Albana grapes have great potential. When the vines have had plenty of water for the developing fruit, the resulting wine should be at its best – smooth yet crisp, with hints of nuts.

Serve the wine well chilled. I particularly like to drink it when I am eating tapas, or with hummus and bread.

Of course, no Italian wine would be complete without a heavy dose of romanticism. In 435AD, in the village of Bertinoro (just south of Forlì) Galla Placidia, daughter of Emperor Theodosius, was offered Albana in a terracotta jug. She tasted the wine and exclaimed, "This wine should be drunk from a jug made of gold, not one made of mere terracotta!" In saying this she gave Bertinoro its name, which means "to drink in gold".

ALBANA
Fattoria Paridiso

RECOMMENDED PRODUCERS

▸ Fattoria Paradiso
▸ Commune Zerbina
▸ Commune di Faenza

USA

If you are looking for consistently reliable full whites, look no further than California. The perfect combination of a large number of sunny days and the cooling, foggy influence of the Pacific Ocean results in wonderful, balanced Chardonnay wines, particularly to the north of San Francisco, and especially in the Napa Valley. The Viognier grape has also established itself in the state.

CHARDONNAY

C COLOUR Golden yellow, often with highlights of green.

A AROMA Complex, intense; mango, red apple; oak-ageing gives toast and vanilla.

T TASTE Rich; great balance of complex flavours and buttery texture; clean finish.

Although Chardonnay has, for many centuries, been the staple grape variety of dry white wines from Chablis and elsewhere in Burgundy, it is now attracting a new generation of wine-drinkers who associate it with the fruity, soft, honeyed wines of the New World, especially those from California, in the western USA.

CHARDONNAY *Newton*

Chardonnay is the most important white grape variety in California. In total there are more than a thousand producers dazzling Californian consumers with their range of Chardonnay wines. As a result there is enormous variation in style. Some Californian Chardonnays are crisp and fresh; others are oily, with butterscotch and vanilla, and all the signs of ageing in new oak; and, of course, there is everything in between.

You might think that as a Frenchman I am predisposed to be negative about these wines. On the contrary, I am overcome by their quality and delighted that wine regions outside France are making memorable Chardonnays.

I particularly love the rich and oily Chardonnays from the North Coast region of California (from appellations such as Alexander Valley, Russian River Valley, and Chalk Hill, all in Sonoma County), which to me are reminiscent of Meursault Chardonnays *(see p60)*.

Of course, there are many others that also draw my attention. Carneros is one of them. This appellation overlaps Sonoma and Napa counties, and its wines have a more defined and lemony acidity than others in California. Their combination of elegance, finesse, and dense flavours is almost unique (comparison can only be made with Burgundy's famous Puligny-Montrachet; *see p60*). Beyond California, there are excellent wines coming out of the Pacific Northwest, from Oregon and Washington State. Here, the climate is colder and more unpredictable, and vine-growing can be tricky; nevertheless the wines are elegantly balanced with rich, natural fruit and lively acidity.

New World Chardonnays will suit almost any occasion. Have a glass on its own – as an apéritif, or socially. They are also delicious with fresh crabs or salmon, and with chicken, lamb, and vegetarian dishes, such as courgette tart.

CHARDONNAY
Stags' Leap

RECOMMENDED PRODUCERS

▸ Newton
▸ Stags' Leap
▸ Duckhorn Vineyards

VIOGNIER / GEWÜRZTRAMINER

C COLOUR Medium straw-yellow, with tinges of silver.

A AROMA Aromatic and youthful; apricot, peach, mango, flowers, and vanilla.

T TASTE Delicacy, harmony, balance; fresh and full of flavour, with a perfect finish.

Viognier arrived in California a mere 20 years ago. Nevertheless (and despite the fact that it is a notoriously hard vine to cultivate), it has made rapid progress. So much so that its depth of character and its complexity are beginning to rival even Californian Chardonnay.

Viognier produces opulent and full-bodied wines, with aromas of spice, flowers, apricot, apple, and peach. The wines have perfectly balanced acidity and fruit.

VIOGNIER *Kendall-Jackson*

Some Viogniers are fermented in stainless steel tanks, which bring out their peach and apricot flavours. Many Californian producers use oak barrels to age the wine, and this adds hints of vanilla and spice.

Viogniers are reminiscent of Gewürztraminer wines, which are also making headway in California. These wines vary from delicate with a sweet edge in the state's warmer counties, to fresh, with citrus tastes in the cooler areas.

Both Viognier and Gewürz-traminer perfectly partner spicy Asian food. Try them with beef or a meaty fish in a spicy black bean sauce. Alternatively, they are great with medium to strong cheeses, such as Munster or Pecorino.

RECOMMENDED PRODUCERS

▸ Kendall-Jackson
▸ Joseph Phelps
▸ Alderbrook

LAND AND PRODUCTION

MISTS OF NAPA COUNTY Despite the fact that, north to south, Napa is only 48km (30 miles) long, there are more wineries here than in any other county in California. There are innumerable soil types across the region and big fluctuations in climate. Indeed, some of the Napa vineyards can be said to have their own microclimate – particular climatic conditions that influence small, distinct areas. However, throughout Napa the mornings and evenings during the vine-growing season are often cold and foggy. The fog helps to steady the climate – which is wonderful for grapes such as Chardonnay because it helps to maintain their characteristic freshness.

CHILE

Chilean wines are almost always great value, and some of their full, opulent whites are equal in quality to any in the world. The most important wine-producing region is the Central Valley, between the Andes Mountains and the Pacific Ocean. Chardonnays from the region below the capital, Santiago, are the best, displaying a fine balance of flavours.

CHARDONNAY

C COLOUR Typically rich, yellow-green with gold tinges.

A AROMA Citrus, apple, exotic fruits (such as pineapple), butter, and vanilla.

T TASTE Fruity, with a perfect balance of fruit, acidity, and alcohol.

You cannot really go wrong by choosing a Chilean Chardonnay. Usually oaked, these wines represent excellent value for money and even at the lowest prices are consistently well-made and rarely disappointing.

This is largely due to the fact that Chile offers the Chardonnay grape its perfect growing conditions, particularly in the Central Valley region. During the daytime there is plenty of sunshine to ripen the fruit. At night, cold air flows down the mountains and cool breezes come in off the ocean, meeting on the valley floor and enabling flavours and acidity to build up in the grapes. The result is wine with a perfect balance between the ripeness of the fruit and a satisfying, refreshing acidity.

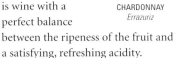
CHARDONNAY
Errazuriz

RECOMMENDED PRODUCERS

▶ Errazuriz
▶ Casa Lapostolle
▶ Santa Rita (Medalla Real)

SOUTH AFRICA

Full whites from this country steer a fine line between the unoaked, more austere European styles and the rich, buttery wines of California and Australia. At their best, they are unbeatable! My favourites come from the cool regions around Stellenbosch and Constantia, where the influence of the ocean makes its mark.

CHARDONNAY

C COLOUR Pale intensity; gold with a hint of green.

A AROMA Rich, complex; honey, lemon, lime, baked apple, vanilla, toasty oak.

T TASTE Delicate and complex, with good acidity and a long finish.

In South Africa, the most successful Chardonnays have some of the weight and intensity of fruit of the New World, and some of the complexity and minerality of the Old. Regions such as Robertson, which is inland and hot and dry, produce bold, Australian-style wines; whereas cooler regions such as Constantia, on the Cape, produce wines that are like those of Burgundy.

Stellenbosch has the perfect climate to get it just right. It is South Africa's "star" wine-producing region, 50km (30 miles) to the east of Cape Town. The mountains and sea that surround Stellenbosch bring cool breezes to the grapes to balance their fruitiness and acidity.

Overall, South African Chardonnay represents great value for all budgets. The wines make an excellent match with delicate fish.

CHARDONNAY
Simonsig

RECOMMENDED PRODUCERS

▶ Simonsig
▶ Jordan Wines
▶ Kanonkop

CASABLANCA CHARDONNAY *Concha y Toro, just northwest of Santiago, Chile, produces Chardonnay reminiscent of the European style. If you find a bottle – or any other from a Casablanca vineyard – buy it! It will not disappoint.*

AUSTRALIA

There are so many regions, and so many excellent full, opulent whites in this country. The best come from the cooler regions like Southern Victoria, Tasmania, or the Margaret River in Western Australia, where the hot climate is tempered by cooling ocean breezes.

SÉMILLON

C **COLOUR** Pale gold to lemon yellow with green tinges; medium to deep intensity.

A **AROMA** Charming and pronounced; pineapple, apple, warm bread, honey.

T **TASTE** Big and rich; amazing complexity, lingering acidity, and "non-stop" length.

The Sémillon grape variety has small berries and a thick skin, and is quite hard to grow successfully. However, when they persevere, growers are rewarded with a complex, intense and rich wine that has a well-defined lemony acidity, and also offers length, finesse, a good balance, and a lingering finish.

Sémillon tends to be blended with Chardonnay or, in Margaret River, Western Australia, with Sauvignon Blanc (and sometimes Chenin Blanc).

Margaret River has the potential to be extremely hot, which is usually unfavourable for producing good grapes. However, the heat is balanced by breezes coming in off the ocean and this ensures that the grapes ripen well while developing fruity, intense flavours. This produces wines that are rich and complex,

SÉMILLON
Rosemount Estate

yet perfectly balanced, and the Sémillon-Sauvignon Blanc blend from Margaret River does not disappoint. Similar to white Bordeaux, it is a crisp, dry white wine, with tangy, herbaceous flavours. This wine represents excellent value – it is definitely one of my must-try wines.

On the opposite side of the country, in southeastern Australia, in the Hunter Valley, New South Wales, growers are producing some exceptional unblended Sémillon wines. Particularly complex, they are some of the best and most distinctive wines of the New World.

Like Margaret River, the Hunter Valley, north of Sydney, is unusually hot for vine-growing. However, the region is also very humid, with low cloud cover during the afternoons. This tempers the evaporation of water from the vines, to create grapes that are bright and fresh, with good flavour. One of the special features of Hunter Valley

WHITE MEAT Sémillon is the perfect food partner for all white meats. Enjoy it with succulent honey-glazed chicken on a bed of crisp, steamed vegetables; or with roast pork drizzled in apple and sage sauce.

Sémillon is that it is unoaked. Amazingly, after a time, and entirely under its own steam, the wine develops all the richness and complexity of a wine that has been fermenting in oak barrels. The better wines will age safely for between ten and 20 years, becoming

rich and luscious, with flavours of melted butter, honey, and nuts.

If you like Chardonnay, why not try a bottle of Hunter Valley Sémillon? The wine makes an excellent and refreshing alternative, and it is often better value – another reason why I like it!

RECOMMENDED PRODUCERS

▸ Peter Lehmann
▸ Lindeman
▸ Tyrell's Vineyards

THE BAROSSA *Another successful growing region for Sémillon is the Barossa Valley, in South Australia. Here, producers make wine with a balance of richness and fresh youthfulness.*

2002
BAROSS
SEMI

CHARDONNAY

C COLOUR Bright; straw yellow with an edge of green.

A AROMA Pronounced and exotic; melon, pineapple, warm bread, and quince.

T TASTE Rich and heavy, but balanced by a lemony acidity and perfect length.

Australian Chardonnay is causing a worldwide sensation and in my opinion there are two regions that make the best: Western Australia, and Victoria in the southeast.

In Western Australia the wines are high in alcohol, but the best manage to balance this with fruit and acidity. Some may be matured in French oak *barriques* (a special kind of barrel famously used in Burgundy) for 12 months. For the best wines, ageing for two to five years helps to develop their complexity, while cheaper wines should be drunk within a year.

Victoria's Chardonnays have a firmer acidity than their Western Australian counterparts. However, they retain their complex flavours, finesse, and elegance – just as a good Chardonnay should.

CHARDONNAY *Leeuwin Estate*

RECOMMENDED PRODUCERS

▸ Leeuwin Estate
▸ Mountadam
▸ Grant Burge (Summers Chardonnay)

MARSANNE

C COLOUR An attractive deep gold with highlights of silver.

A AROMA Exotic, full of character; lemon, smoke, minerals, hazelnut, quince, fig.

T TASTE Muscly, oily texture; medium acidity; complex, elegant, and long.

Not many people know that tucked away in southeast Australia is a special Marsanne wine. The wine is rare, but I could not miss telling you about it!

The Goulburn Valley in Victoria contains some of the oldest and largest plantings of Marsanne in the world.

The top producers are Mitchelton and Château Tahbilk, each with its distinct Marsanne style. Mitchelton is heavily oak-influenced, lemon-accented, oily, and rich, especially after ageing. Tahbilk is unoaked and delicate in its youth. Over time it develops a distinctive honeysuckle bouquet. Both are well worth drinking.

Australian Marsanne is just beautiful, and goes perfectly with white meat.

RECOMMENDED PRODUCERS

▸ Château Tahbilk
▸ Mitchelton
▸ David Traeger

MARGARET RIVER I love the Chardonnays from this region in Western Australia. The area receives a relatively high rainfall, but little of this rain occurs during the October to April growing season, when the grapes need drier weather to develop their flavour. The result is an intense Chardonnay, with (as they say in Australia) high "fruit power". One of the best-known producers in the region is Cape Mentelle, pictured here.

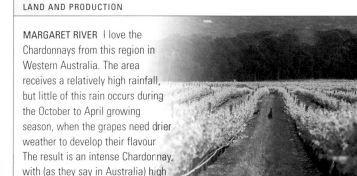

NEW ZEALAND

The cool New Zealand climate favours drier whites, but warmer areas such as Gisborne and Hawkes Bay make great Chardonnays, which are equal to any in the world. New Zealand also makes excellent Gewürztraminer – spicy, fruity, and rich, and a real treat.

CHARDONNAY

C COLOUR Pale; straw yellow, with greenish tinges.

A AROMA Very pronounced; ripe, exotic fruits, vanilla, brioche, and peach.

T TASTE Rich and round; lemony acidity balanced with refreshing length.

New Zealand's climate varies so much between regions that the array of different styles of Chardonnay is dazzling.

Auckland and Northland, New Zealand's warmest regions (in the north of North Island), tend to make rich, ripe, and broad-flavoured Chardonnay. Wines from Gisborne (in the east) are soft and luscious with ripe apricot and melon. South of Gisborne lies Hawkes Bay – my favourite New Zealand Chardonnay. The wine is well balanced, complex, and concentrated, with peach, pineapple, and grapefruit, and a clean length.

On South Island the wines tend to be more citrusy. So, in Marlborough, the country's biggest Chardonnay-producing region, they are zesty with good acidity. In Central Otago, the world's most southerly vineyard, the Chardonnay has a green-fruit and flinty character.

My tip is first to try a few wines from different regions. Once you have found your favourite region, keep trying more from that region until you find your favourite producer.

MARSANNE
Château Tahbilk

RECOMMENDED PRODUCERS

▸ Jackson Estate
▸ West Brook
▸ Morton Estate

GEWÜRZTRAMINER

C COLOUR Deep golden yellow to dark straw or light amber.

A AROMA Exotic; minerals, flowers, lychee, pineapple, ginger, nuts, spice.

T TASTE Big and complex, with a powerful character and excellent acidity.

The German word *gewürtz* means "spiced", and wines made from the Gewürztraminer grape are known for their spicy character.

In the New World the best Gewürztraminer wines come from New Zealand. The country is particularly suited to cultivating this grape as it has a cool climate that encourages slow ripening and enables the complexity of the grapes' flavours to develop fully.

Almost two-thirds of New Zealand's Gewürztraminer plantings are in Gisborne and Hawkes Bay on the eastern shore of North Island, with others in Marlborough in the north of South Island.

The Marlborough wines are less exuberant than those from Gisborne and Hawkes Bay, but here, where the climate is cooler, the wine has a particularly attractive perfume.

Drink the wines young (they will rarely age over five years), and match them with Asian and spicy Pacific Rim foods; or drink them my favourite way – on their own as a summer apéritif.

GEWÜRZTRAMINER
Villa Maria

RECOMMENDED PRODUCERS

▸ Villa Maria
▸ Chifney Wines
▸ Hunters

66 Cheerful and welcoming, these wines add *joie de vivre* to any summer picnic or garden party. **99**

ROSÉ

INTRODUCING ROSÉ

Rosé has not always been taken seriously – mass-market wines of past decades have given the style a bad name. However, attitudes are changing and rosé is again finding its niche. And, with increased demand has come dramatically improved quality.

Rosé is not, as some people assume, simply a mixture of red and white wine. Rather, the wine comes from red-skinned grapes that are vinified using a special technique knowns as *saignée* ("bleeding"). The grapes are macerated with their skins very gently and for only a short time to bleed out the juice, which is then vinified as white wine. The longer the juice remains with the skins, the darker the pink colour of the wine.

STRAWBERRY *Sweet and ripe fruit aromas are prominent in a good rosé wine.*

ROSÉ AROUND THE WORLD

Not all rosé wines are light in body. The lightest rosé tends to come from the Loire Valley – and from California, where it is called blush wine. Fuller rosés come from southern France, particularly Tavel, Corbières, Bandol, and Côtes de Provence; Italy (where rosé is known as *rosato*); Spain (look for *rosado*); as well as from the New World, most notably from Australia.

DRINKING AND SERVING

DRINK PROFILE Rosé wines are not matured in oak, so they should have a refreshing texture. You will also find intense fruit and medium alcohol, and the pleasant finish should be medium to long.

C COLOUR A good rosé wine should be bright, with a light to medium rose-petal colour – almost like a light ruby. Some rosés (particularly those known as "blush") are very pale pink.

A AROMA This should offer well-defined, ripe red fruits, such as strawberry and raspberry. Aromas should be zesty and subtle, with delicate hints of violet, and even some spice.

T TASTE Even though rosé is perceived as a lighter style, this wine should show great complexity. The flavour overall should be fruity and fresh, with balanced lemon acidity.

BUYING AND STORING Rosé wines are meant for drinking young, often the younger the better. You should not store the wine for more than two or three years – age will turn the bright pink wine an unappealing onion brown. Don't be tempted to buy a rosé that is too old – even if it seems a bargain!

SERVING SUGGESTIONS Serve rosé well chilled, and if you are drinking it with a meal, try to keep the wine chilled throughout. These are summery wines, ideal for barbecues; or perhaps they begin as apéritifs, only to become part of a light lunch.

FOOD COMPANIONS With its frivolous image, rosé is too often ignored as a good companion to food. However, great rosé wines, such as Tavel, match perfectly with salads, pasta, and pizza, and even with curry and other spicy foods.

GRAPE VARIETIES

Most fine rosé wines are not made from special rosé grape varieties, but from red varieties, such as Syrah, Grenache, and Pinot Noir. Even some of the most robust varieties, such as Nebbiolo and Cabernet Sauvignon, can be made into fresh and fruity rosé wines.

GRAPE	BEST REGIONAL EXAMPLES	COMMENTS
GRENACHE / GARNACHA	France: Languedoc, Rhône, Provence. Australia. Spain: Rioja, Navarra.	Wines have intense colour, and lovely ripe fruits with spice and good structure.
CINSAULT	France: Languedoc-Roussillon, Rhône. South Africa. USA: California.	Wines are aromatic, fruity, light, and fresh. Often blended with Grenache.
SANGIOVESE	Italy: Tuscany.	Wines are light in colour with marked acidity, balanced alcohol, and plenty of flavour.
SYRAH	USA: California.	Wines have an intense, deep pink colour, and are very fruity and refreshing.
PINOT NOIR	France: Sancerre.	Wines are lightly coloured and refreshing, with fruit intensity. Elegant and popular.

FRANCE

The key areas of French rosé production are the Loire Valley, Provence, Languedoc-Roussillon, and the lower Rhône Valley. The wine is also made in the Jura, Pyrenees, Tarn, Bordeaux, and the Rhône above Tavel, among other regions.

CÔTES DE PROVENCE

C COLOUR From light to salmon pink, and sometimes even light orange.

A AROMA Varied, often herbs (thyme, dill), flowers, and red fruits.

T TASTE Dry and fruity; very bright and refreshing.

The cheerful rosé wines of Provence are instant mood-lifters, and remind me of sunny summer days in one of the most beautiful and prestigious parts of the world.

Côtes de Provence is Provence's largest appellation, covering a wide area in the far south of France, along the shores of the Mediterranean. Made primarily from the Grenache and Cinsault grapes, its rosé wines can vary considerably in style, but are mostly dry. The mountains in the north of the region send cool breezes down to the vineyards, allowing the grapes to retain a lemony acidity, which keeps the wines light and fresh.

Although it is often best enjoyed straight from the vineyard, or at least in the local area, Côtes de Provence rosé is known throughout the world.

I have to say that it has rarely disappointed me – even at bargain prices. They may not be the most exciting, but the modestly priced wines are perfect on a hot day.

For a better-quality rosé at only a little extra cost, try Provence's second-largest appellation, Coteaux d'Aix en Provence, which lies a little inland, further west; or try Coteaux du Varois. Drink the wines well chilled with traditional Provençal dishes, such as tomatoes and peppers roasted in olive oil and garlic, or with baked mushrooms and aïoli.

CÔTES DE PROVENCE
St Roch-les-Vignes

CÔTES DE PROVENCE
Château de Pampelonne

RECOMMENDED PRODUCERS

▸ St Roch-les-Vignes
▸ Château de Pampelonne
▸ Clos St Magdeleine

BANDOL

C COLOUR A delightful colour that varies from deep pink to pale ruby.

A AROMA Subtle; cherry, strawberry, dried herbs, and notes of spice.

T TASTE Dense but elegant with a fresh structure; long and complex finish.

Bandol is the most prestigious wine region in Provence, producing fine-quality rosé, which tends to be fairly full. Its deep colour comes from the local grape Mourvèdre, while adding Cinsault and Grenache into the blend brings fruit flavours and softens the tannins.

Limited production makes this wine highly desirable, and if you have never tasted Bandol you are in for a treat! Try it with seafood, fish soup, and other Provençal dishes.

RECOMMENDED PRODUCERS

▸ Château J P Gaussen
▸ Château Pibarnon
▸ Domaine du Pey Neuf

TAVEL / LIRAC

C COLOUR Light ruby, with subtle nuances of lilac; deepening to copper with age.

A AROMA Fine and complex; flowers, honey, and bursting with fresh red fruits.

T TASTE Well-structured, supple, fresh, and dry with a pleasant round finish.

The appellation of Tavel lies at the lower end of the Rhône Valley, southeastern France, not far from Avignon and close to Châteauneuf-du-Pape. The region makes only rosé wine, and during the 1950s was the most famous rosé-producing region in the world. Even now, Tavel's wine is among the finest in France.

A full body, good length, and deep character, but all the freshness of a good rosé, set Tavel's wine apart from most other "pink" styles of wine. Made mainly from Grenache and Cinsault grapes, the wine is always extremely dry. Its aromas are floral, fruity, spicy, and nutty; and its colour ranges from pink, through to a copper colour for older wines.

The wine's distinctive colour and fruitiness are a result of carbonic maceration, a technique in which the grapes are crushed by their own weight (rather than by a press) in an oxygen-free environment.

This is a classy wine – and one once loved by Louis XIV. It may be expensive, but it is well worth it.

Just north of Tavel lies Lirac. Here, too, the wine is full-bodied for a rosé. Soft pink, with aromas of red fruit and almond, it is also worth a try.

RECOMMENDED PRODUCERS

▸ Château de Aqueria
▸ Domaine de la Mordorée
▸ Domaine Palaquie

LAND AND PRODUCTION

CHALKY SOIL The wine-growing region around Tavel has a dry, chalky soil littered with large, flat stones (*galets*). These absorb heat during the sunny days and slowly release it at night, allowing the grapes to ripen more fully, and this gives Tavel's wine a deep, fruity complexity.

ANJOU

C COLOUR Attractive pale to medium pink with a silver rim.

A AROMA Charming, aromatic; crushed berries, flowers, and gentle spice.

T TASTE Fruity, elegant; refreshing acidity and a long, pleasant finish.

Anjou, in the western part of the Loire Valley, produces two main styles of rosé wine. The first, Rosé d'Anjou, is made from several grapes (including Gamay, Cabernet Franc, and Cabernet Sauvignon) and is light and fresh. The second, Cabernet d'Anjou, is also fresh, but more complex and deep. Made from a blend of Cabernet Franc and Cabernet Sauvignon, this wine is well balanced with a touch of sweetness. It is perfect for a barbecue or with any charcuterie.

RECOMMENDED PRODUCERS

▸ Langlois Château
▸ Domaine Ogereau
▸ Château de Fesles

SANCERRE

C COLOUR Pale pink salmon, with delicate onion-skin highlights.

A AROMA Intense; delicate red berries, spice, and notes of vanilla and leather.

T TASTE Fresh, delicate; harmony of fruit and alcohol; long, complex finish.

A most highly regarded rosé in France, Sancerre rosé is made from Pinot Noir grapes, and is light and refreshing with concentrated fruit. Sancerre can be expensive – check the label to ensure that you have a good producer. (Little else on the bottle will signal the wine's quality.) However, it is truly excellent, especially with grilled fish, such as haddock.

RECOMMENDED PRODUCERS
▸ J M Roger
▸ Lucien Crochet

CORBIÈRES

C COLOUR Bright; deep pink to light purple with a silvery rim.

A AROMA Young, aromatic; hints of strawberry, raspberry, and bilberry.

T TASTE Clean and refreshing; medium weight and well-balanced acidity.

This rosé is fantastic value! Lying in Languedoc-Roussillon (southern France), Corbières has the perfect weather to ripen the fresh grapes (including Cinsault and Syrah) to their full complexity. I love this wine with polenta; or try it with cold meats and black olive tapenade.

CORBIÈRES *Château du Vieux Parc*

RECOMMENDED PRODUCERS
▸ Château du Vieux Parc
▸ Domaine de Fontsainte

COTEAUX DE LANGUEDOC

C COLOUR Dark pink with nuances of red terracotta tiles.

A AROMA Delicate; cherry, red berries, and hints of flowers.

T TASTE Light, fresh, and pleasant; long, clean finish.

France's oldest wine-growing region makes some fine, lighter style rosés, which are good value for money. Try a delicate, floral Costières de Nimes; or even the generic AOC Coteaux de Languedoc will rarely disappoint. They are all perfect with pizza.

COTEAUX DE LANGUEDOC *Château Moujan*

RECOMMENDED PRODUCERS
▸ Château Moujan
▸ Château Creissan

CÔTES DU ROUSSILLON

C COLOUR Bright; charming salmon pink, sometimes with onion-skin tinges.

A AROMA Elegant, fairly intense; ripe strawberry, raspberry, and cherry.

T TASTE Well-structured; refreshing acidity and intense fruit; very long finish.

This up-and-coming region never disappoints: all the rosés of the Côtes du Roussillon are of excellent quality. At their best the wines are intense, deeply coloured, and highly perfumed. Try them with seafood or grilled fish. Their full structure also makes them good with red meat.

Finally, if you are buying rosé, take care not to pick up a Côtes du Roussillon *Villages*. This wine is worth trying, but it will be a red.

RECOMMENDED PRODUCERS
▸ Château du Jau
▸ Château de la Casanove

ITALY

The Italians are experts at making light red wines, and also make fine *rosato* (rosé), especially from the Sangiovese grape variety. Some *rosatos* are made from blends; many have character, depth, and a refreshing acidity.

TUSCAN SANGIOVESE

C COLOUR Bright, ranging from a light ruby red to deep pink.

A AROMA Youthful; heaps of red berries, with sweet spice and notes of violet.

T TASTE Dry and well-structured; harmonious and pleasant; fruity finish.

Thanks to improved vinification techniques and growing consumer demand, the production of Italian rosé (*rosato*) is on the increase.

The Sangiovese grape gives rosé a good spine and a natural lemony acidity. There are two main styles of Tuscan *rosato*, both of which are dry. The first, made with 85 per cent

Sangiovese, is perfectly represented by Cipresseto. This wine is refreshing, upfront, and light. The second, represented by the wines of Bolgheri, on the coast, blends Sangiovese with Cabernet Sauvignon and Merlot, and is more serious and elegant, with good length. Both are great with any light food.

TUSCAN SANGIOVESE *Antinori*

RECOMMENDED PRODUCERS
▸ Antinori
▸ Avignonessi
▸ Guado al Tasso

GREECE

The general improvement in this country's red and white wine output has spilled over into its rosé wines, especially where new technology is making an impact. A country to watch closely in the next decade.

NEMEA

C COLOUR Bright; medium intensity; light to darker salmon pink.

A AROMA Aromatic; strawberry, pomegranate, and wild forest fruits.

T TASTE Pleasant, well-structured, and refreshing; clean acidity; long finish.

Most people would never think to choose a Greek rosé, but new, young winemakers are defying the Greek reputation for poor wine and creating fruit-driven rosés, with the emphasis on quality. These wines deserve a place in the world market.

Produced in the mountains in the north of the Peloponnese, Nemea has great potential for making

elegant, stylish, and complex rosé. The wine is made mainly from the Xynomavro and Agiorgitiko (St George) grapes.

The best Nemea rosés are refreshing and light, and most are made for drinking between six months and a year. They can be great with light Mediterranean cuisine. I especially enjoy Nemea rosé with feta cheese salad.

NEMEA *Ktima Kosta Lazaridi*

RECOMMENDED PRODUCERS
▸ Ktima Kosta Lazaridi
▸ Strofilia
▸ Domaine Porto Carras

SPAIN

Regions like Navarra and Rioja make deep, fruity *rosado* (rosé), full of strength and character. Often, the Garnacha grape is used, making the wine firm and quite strong. Excellent and unusual!

NAVARRA

C COLOUR Deep pink ruby, with onion-skin tinges.

A AROMA Complex, ripe, elegant; forest fruits, blackberry, herbs, and spice.

T TASTE Full and rich, but refreshing; red berries and good acidity; very long finish.

If you like Sangria, then I think you will enjoy Navarra rosé: the wine is well-structured and full of flavour.

Navarra produces rosé mainly from the Garnacha grape. The wine is deep pink in colour and extremely dry and fresh. However, the region lies in the shadow of its neighbour Rioja, and its winemakers have to

fight hard for recognition. The Navarra wines are a much deeper colour than rosé from Rioja, with more intense, slightly sweeter flavours, and a higher alcohol content. Overall, I find that they offer much better value for money; and they create a Spanish ambience that makes them perfect with paella.

NAVARRA
Bodegas Ochoa

RECOMMENDED PRODUCERS

▸ Bodegas Ochoa
▸ De Sarria
▸ Coop San Roque

RIOJA

C COLOUR Deep and distinctive rose-red, with a ruby rim.

A AROMA Youthful and delicate; wild red fruits; strawberry and cherry.

T TASTE Fresh, full flavour, with a slightly creamy texture; long, clean finish.

Rioja has long been Spain's leading wine region, and now finally the rest of the world is waking up to its offerings. Rioja *rosado* (rosé) wines are made primarily from the Garnacha grape variety and they are beginning to really impress me. Although they can sometimes be a bit heavy on the alcohol (a characteristic of Garnacha), they are generally well-balanced. The wines are rich, round, and fruity, with great depth and personality. They have a ripe texture, but manage to retain their underlying acidity to bring freshness to the palate and extend the length of the fruit finish. Once you find a good producer, you can be

RIOJA *López de Heredia*

confident that the winery will normally maintain its style and high quality, so be prepared to spend some time finding your favourite.

All in all, these wines are full of life and very easy to drink – they are superb on the terrace with olives and chillies, or with a delicious feast of cured red meats.

RECOMMENDED PRODUCERS

▸ López de Heredia
▸ Marques de Caceres
▸ Valdemar

PORTUGAL

For some people, rosé wines in the distinctive Mateus or Lancers bottle are as much a symbol of Portugal as its port or Madeira! The success of these wines is a triumph of global marketing – matching demand with just the right product.

MATEUS / LANCERS

C COLOUR Very light pink (Mateus); deep pink with salmon hues (Lancers).

A AROMA Limited; red fruits with a hint of flowers, vines, and peach.

T TASTE Slightly fizzy; fruity, refreshing, and not too sweet; charming finish.

Portugal has two well-known rosé wines – Mateus (found mostly in Europe, but also in the US) and Lancers (which is marketed mainly in the US).

Mateus rosé is produced in the north of Portugal, and is a slightly sparkling, semi-sweet wine.

It is made from a blend of Baga, Bastardo, Touriga Nacional, Tinta Roriz, and Tinta Pinheira grapes, primarily from the Douro and Bairrada DOC regions.

First exported to northern Europe and the US during World War II, the wine reached its selling peak in the 1960s and 1970s. More recently sales have been threatened with decline and producers have had to improve the wine's quality to match their consumers' more sophisticated tastes. Now the wine is well balanced, fresh, and fruity, with just the right level of sweetness.

PORTUGUESE ROSÉ
Mateus

Lancers rosé continues to be one of Portugal's biggest-selling wines. Bottled in a distinctive stone jar, the wine was first introduced into the US after World War II, when American soldiers returned home with a taste for European wine. Produced in the same region as Mateus and using a similar blend of grapes, Lancers rosé is a deep pink colour with a salmon hue.

It has light floral and red-fruit aromas and is light- to medium-bodied on the palate.

Lancers and Mateus are highly versatile wines: serve them at parties, or as apéritifs; or drink them with Oriental or spicy Mexican cuisine.

RECOMMENDED PRODUCERS

▸ Mateus
▸ Lancers

PALACE OF MATEUS *One of Portugal's most recognizable buildings, the Palace of Mateus gave its name to the wine, and is pictured on the label.*

USA

Zinfandel is a red grape that has made its home in California; delicate vinification transforms it into a light rosé or "blush wine". Other varieties, especially Syrah and Grenache, are also used to make these popular wines on the US west coast.

WHITE ZINFANDEL

C COLOUR Bright; extremely pale pink – only a "blush" of colour.

A AROMA Limited; peach, lemon, and red-fruit jam (raspberry, strawberry).

T TASTE Slightly fizzy with a touch of sweetness; long, lemony finish.

WHITE ZINFANDEL *Buehler Vineyards*

In the US, the red grape variety Zinfandel is used to make a rosé known as White Zinfandel or "blush" wine, which became very popular during the 1980s. Sweet and slightly fizzy, this wine is aimed at a youth market, and is sometimes referred to as the "alco-pop" of wine. It is not complex, but when served well chilled, it makes easy sipping if you have a sweet tooth. This wine is charming and friendly in its own way – but not for the connoisseur!

RECOMMENDED PRODUCERS
▸ Buehler Vineyards
▸ Beringer (Stone Cellars)
▸ Cutler Creek

SYRAH / GRENACHE

C COLOUR Elegant deep pink with tinges of darker ruby red.

A AROMA Intense, youthful; cherry, blackberry, and red summer berries.

T TASTE Well-structured and well-balanced; rich flavours; good length.

The Syrah and the Grenache grape varieties have proved extremely successful in the Californian winelands – both are well suited to hot weather, and will produce good yields even in arid growing conditions. The grapes make similarly charming, flavourful rosé wines with all the natural intensity of the grapes' colours and the diversity of their fruit flavours. Both have a full body and a tendency to be quite heavy on the alcohol. Nevertheless, overall these are delicate wines that make excellent, well-balanced alternatives to lightly chilled reds.

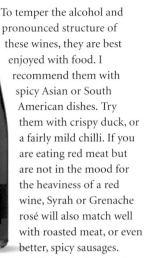

GRENACHE
McDowell

To temper the alcohol and pronounced structure of these wines, they are best enjoyed with food. I recommend them with spicy Asian or South American dishes. Try them with crispy duck, or a fairly mild chilli. If you are eating red meat but are not in the mood for the heaviness of a red wine, Syrah or Grenache rosé will also match well with roasted meat, or even better, spicy sausages.

The rosé wines made from Grenache or Syrah present you with the opportunity to make a discovery – Californian rosé is still in its infancy, but it has great potential for making a big noise in the world of wine.

RECOMMENDED PRODUCERS
▸ McDowell
▸ Cambria
▸ Dehlinger

CHILE

In the world of wine, the Chileans are game for anything. Here, they have successfully used one of the most robust grape varieties, Cabernet Sauvignon, to make a fine and full rosé which is unbeatable value and very satisfying.

CABERNET SAUVIGNON

C COLOUR Rich, deep pink with ruby highlights and a good intensity.

A AROMA Pleasant and youthful; full of red berries and citrus fruits.

T TASTE Ripe and round; fresh, harmonious, and cheerful; good length.

Cabernet Sauvignon is the classic red grape of Bordeaux, and of the big Californian and Australian red wines. However, in the right growing conditions Cabernet Sauvignon is a flexible grape, and the Chileans have succeeded in using it to create delicious, fresh, and fruity rosé wines. They offer a lighter version and a fuller style, both with freshness and complexity, and a host of berry flavours – drinking Chilean rosé is like drinking a glass of pure fruit juice. No wonder that consumers often choose Chilean rosé over, say, a more traditional *rosato* from Italy! This wine is consistently good, and excellent value for money. It is a fun wine for a relaxed lunch, or as a pick-me-up at the end of a hard day.

RECOMMENDED PRODUCERS
▸ Santa Rita
▸ Undurraga
▸ Caliterra

CHILEAN HARVEST *At the Santa Rita vineyards, 40km (25 miles) south of Santiago, the Cabernet Sauvignon grapes are harvested manually to ensure rigorous selection.*

CABERNET
SAUVIGNON
Santa Rita

ARGENTINA

Waves of immigrants from France, Spain, and Italy have shaped Argentina's wine industry in the last two centuries. Since the 1980s, quality – especially of reds – has improved enormously. Rosé is a relatively new, but up-and-coming style, and represents good value.

ARGENTINIAN ROSÉ

C COLOUR Ranges from deep, rich pink to a pale ruby red.

A AROMA Aromatic; cherry, raspberry, and spice.

T TASTE Light to medium-bodied; extremely smooth on the finish.

Argentina's red and white grape varieties (most notably Malbec and Torrontés respectively) have placed the country's wines among the finest in the world – and certainly the best in South America. However, the success of the red and white wines has restricted the potential for great

ARGENTINIAN ROSÉ *Trapiche*

rosé wine, too, and Argentinian winemakers have generally held back on commercial rosé production.

Traditionally, Argentina's pink wines are made using the grape varieties of Criolla and Cereza. These are among the country's oldest vines, and they produce sweet-tasting rosé, sold mostly for local consumption.

However, wineries are now making some interesting Argentine rosés using more commercial grape varieties. Cabernet Sauvignon (a grape that

ARGENTINIAN ROSÉ *Goyenechea*

has been hugely successful all over South America) produces rosé that is bright and fresh. Its crisp acidity balances a host of ripe fruit flavours. However, it is Malbec that is particularly well-suited to the climate and geography of Argentina, especially in the Mendoza region, and it is used to make more than 70 per cent of Argentina's wines. Here, in the foothills of the Andes, the temperate climate gives consistent growing conditions for the grapes, which allows them to develop deep-coloured skins, and full flavours with well-balanced acidity. As a result, Malbec rosé tends to be big rather than delicate, with fruity aromas based on red fruits, such as cherry and raspberry. The wines are rich, lush, and very full.

Argentinian winemakers are also beginning to experiment with rosé

made from Merlot. In vineyards such as the famous Goyenechea, in the Mendoza region, Merlot vines are among the oldest at the winery and, like Malbec, are well-suited to Argentina's dry, warm growing conditions. The wines are fresh and full of flavour with a slightly sweet edge (a result of the liquid being drained off before all the sugar has turned to alcohol). They are created specifically for drinking in their youth – ideally within a year.

The flexibility of Argentinian rosé makes it perfect if you are unsure whether to provide a red or white wine with a meal. They are ideally served in summer, well chilled.

RECOMMENDED PRODUCERS
▸ Trapiche
▸ Goyenechea
▸ Catena (Alamos Ridge)

AUSTRALIA

Australia has the warmth and variety of climate to grow grape varieties that can be hard to grow elsewhere. Nebbiolo, from Italy, for example, has made a new home in Australia, and more durable varieties like Grenache have also been successful.

GRENACHE

C COLOUR Deep rose-petal pink, with tinges of silver.

A AROMA Aromatic, with fresh strawberry, cherry, and herbs.

T TASTE Fresh, fleshy, and intense, with crisp acidity and good length.

With its hot climate providing the grapes with a long ripening season, Australia is particularly well suited to producing elegant, fruity, refreshing, and vibrant rosé wines.

For me, the best are made from the Grenache grape variety, and the wines from the Barossa Valley, in South Australia, are probably the finest of all. These wines express a

lively fruitiness on the nose, but what makes them really special is their perfect balance of acidity and alcohol.

This is a summer wine not to be missed! Enjoy it on its own just to refresh you, or in true Australian style – around the barbecue. It is delicious with grilled shrimp or barbecued steak.

GRENACHE *Geoff Merrill*

RECOMMENDED PRODUCERS
▸ Geoff Merrill
▸ Turkey Flat
▸ Mount Hurtle

NEBBIOLO

C COLOUR Deeper pink than many rosés, with purplish tinges.

A AROMA Young and fresh; bilberry, red berries, spice, and dried herbs.

T TASTE Full, harmonious, and refreshing with a crisp finish.

Nebbiolo is a grape variety traditionally associated with the winemaking regions of northwest Italy, where it produces the big and robust Barolo red wine *(see p114)*. However, in some climatic conditions this berry, which usually is rich in tannins, and has a sharp acidity, can become much lighter and more cheerful, while still offering all its complexity and finesse.

The warm climate of Australia presents perfect growing conditions for this lighter style (although the wine is still rich for a rosé), and Australian Nebbiolo production has become extremely successful. At first producers used Nebbiolo as only part of a rosé blend, but some are

now making the wine with 100 per cent Nebbiolo, with impressive results.

More structured and meaty than many other pink wines, Australian Nebbiolo rosé is especially good with food, where it expresses even more of its great personality. This is thanks to its natural high acidity which perfectly balances the wine. Try it with any tomato-, olive-, or garlic-based dishes, such as penne Siciliana (penne pasta in a sauce of tomatoes and vegetables) or Bourride (a fish stew with a garlic sauce). It is also delicious with peppered steak (from the barbecue for a real taste of Australia), or with seared tuna.

NEBBIOLO *Garry Crittenden*

RECOMMENDED PRODUCERS
▸ Garry Crittenden
▸ Cobaw Ridge
▸ Parish Hill

FRUITY, LIVELY REDS

❝ These are beautifully perfumed wines with loads of firm, crushed berry fruit and a silky smooth finish. **❞**

INTRODUCING FRUITY, LIVELY REDS

Among the greatest and most enjoyable of all wines, fruity, lively reds are easy to drink and flexible – from once-in-a-lifetime aged Burgundy *crus* to lunchtime and barbecue wines such as Valpolicella from Italy or Tarrango from Australia.

DRINKING AND SERVING

DRINK PROFILE There is no significant influence of new oak in fruity, lively red wines, and so the best examples should have a light, airy texture. The wines have a smooth, medium to long finish.

C COLOUR These wines should be bright. They should have an overall colour of light ruby and sparkle with nuances of pink. There may also be pinkness on the rim.

A AROMA The aromas of these wines are quite intense, and are generally dominated by the youthfulness and freshness of the red fruit. There may be banana and spiciness, too.

T TASTE The most significant tastes will be of intense fruit, but the tannins will give a smooth, silky feel on the palate. Expect a balanced acidity and medium alcohol content.

BUYING AND STORING Although these wines are light and not as dramatic as powerful reds, a great deal of care goes into their vinification, which can make them expensive. Drink them within two years, while they are fresh. The exception is a good Pinot Noir, which may be kept for up to 30 years.

SERVING SUGGESTIONS These summer wines are best served slightly chilled (at "cellar temperature") – ideally for 30 minutes in the refrigerator or 10 minutes in iced water. The colder the wine, the more fruity and tannic it will feel.

FOOD COMPANIONS All of these wines are great with light meats, such as charcuterie. Spanish versions go well with tapas; German, with roast pork; New World, with barbecued meat or fish, and vegetarian foods (as well as on their own).

RASPBERRIES *Lively reds burst with red fruit and berry flavours.*

Keeping the tannins under control is the key to creating a fruity, lively red wine. This is why many of the grapes that go into making this style of wine have big berries and thin skins, which give maximum juice but minimum tannin. The wines also tend to be produced in cooler climatic conditions, so ripening is slower, giving the berries plenty of opportunity to develop their distinctive fruitiness. One last essential factor in keeping the tannin levels down comes from the vinification process itself.

Many light red wines are produced using a special technique called carbonic maceration, in which bunches of whole, uncrushed grapes are placed in an anaerobic atmosphere, under a blanket of carbon dioxide. This causes the grapes to produce enzymes that trigger the initial stages of fermentation (removing the need for added yeast). After a few days the berries collapse and the wine is produced in the same way as traditional red wine. The overall result is to keep tannin levels to a minimum, while allowing the best extraction of flavour from the grapes.

Although generally all fruity, lively reds (regardless of their grape variety) will have a bright ruby colour, the best will be a slightly darker shade of ruby, and will have a full bouquet. The wine will feel lively on the palate with tastes of fresh berries and peppers.

PINOT NOIR

The star grape variety of the fruity, lively reds has to be Pinot Noir, although it is notoriously difficult to grow. It also gives low yields, but this is essential if it is to produce wines of good quality. The grape is most typically and exceptionally represented in the light but complex examples of French Burgundy (where Pinot Noir finds its most perfect growing conditions); and also found in wines of California, Australia, South Africa, Chile, and New Zealand. Here, in the New World, the wines are much more "up-front" and voluptuous than their Old World counterparts, and they are quite frankly taking the wine world by storm.

LIGHT PASTA *Fruity Italian reds, such as Valpolicella, Barbera, and Dolcetto, are perfect with pasta.*

GRAPE VARIETIES

The following grape varieties create red wines that are light, fresh, and fruity with distinctive flavours. Other than the classic Pinot Noir, the mainstay of this style of wine, key varieties for fruity, lively reds are Gamay – a vibrant grape, which most famously creates Burgundy's Beaujolais wines; Lambrusco, Barbera, and Dolcetto, which make some of the most famous Italian reds; Cabernet Franc, a variety planted throughout the Bordeaux region, as well as in the New World; and South African Pinotage, which makes light, juicy red wines.

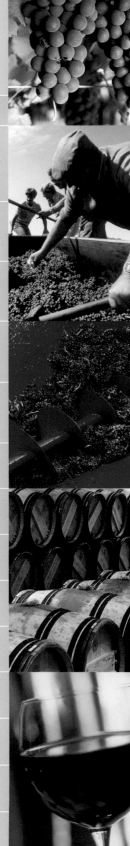

GRAPE	BEST REGIONAL EXAMPLES	COMMENTS
PINOT NOIR	France: Burgundy, Alsace, Sancerre. Australia. New Zealand. USA: California (Carneros), Oregon. Canada.	Pinot Noir grapes produce a silky wine with light colour, which is both highly and delicately perfumed. It ages well and displays a wide range of characters, from black cherry to leather and spice, as well as vanilla and smoke.
GAMAY	France: Beaujolais, Loire Valley. Switzerland: Geneva.	Wines from this grape are very aromatic with soft tannins, high acidity, and low alcohol. Made mainly by carbonic maceration vinification, they are ideal for early drinking.
BARBERA	Italy: Piemonte, Lombardia. Argentina. USA.	This widely planted alternative to Gamay produces wines with lots of fruit flavours and elegance, good acidity (freshness), and low tannins.
LAMBRUSCO	Italy: central regions.	Wines from this grape should be drunk when young. They are simple but well made, full of fruit, and very appealing, with touches of red berries and spice.
DOLCETTO	Italy: Piemonte.	This key grape from the Piemonte ripens early and prefers a temperate climate. It is charming in character, producing soft, easy-drinking, aromatic reds with good balance.
PINOTAGE	South Africa	This cross between Pinot Noir and Cinsault gives wines with soft tannins, smooth cherries, spice, and "meaty" notes.
CABERNET FRANC	France: Chinon, Saumur, St Nicolas de Bourgueil. USA: California. Argentina.	This grape likes a cool climate. In the New World it produces wines with good structure, fruit flavours, and hints of pepper.
ST LAURENT	Austria: Burgenland. Germany: Pfalz. Eastern Europe.	The deeply coloured wines from this grape taste of crushed red berries, have soft tannins, and age very well.
POULSARD/ PLOUSARD	France: Jura.	These large, thin-skinned, and long-ripening grapes produce wines that are relatively perfumed, and typically pale in colour.
MENCIA	Spain: northwestern regions.	This widely grown grape makes light, fruity reds ideal for early drinking. It is famous for Bierzo DO and Galicia wines.
MORISTEL	Spain: Somontano.	The fruity wine from this grape is often blended and should be drunk young. It oxidizes and loses colour fairly quickly.
SPÄTBURGUNDER	Germany.	This is the German version of Pinot Noir; it makes elegant and slightly lighter wines than those of Burgundy.
KLEVNER	Switzerland: Zurich area.	This grape thrives in a cool climate, and makes very complex, world-class wines.
CANAIOLO	Italy: central regions.	This grape produces simple, light, and fruity wines on its own, but is better known as the secondary grape in Chianti.

FRANCE

Burgundy is home to some of the world's most famous lively and fruity red wines, based on the Pinot Noir grape. But France also makes many other superb light reds. The wines of Beaujolais use the Gamay grape, and are fruity and delicious. Chinon, on the Loire, uses the Cabernet Franc variety to make fresh and attractive wines, and fine light reds are also made in the foothills of the Pyrenees.

CÔTE DE NUITS

C **COLOUR** Bright, dense ruby red to purple with mauve tinges.

A **AROMA** Cherry, blackberry, plum, spice, herbs, pepper, earth, leather, figs.

T **TASTE** Powerful yet delicate; soft, silky, rich, fruity, and lively.

Burgundy, with its Pinot Noir grape, has the widest and most varied styles of wine imaginable. Not only are there a vast number of appellations and classifications, but there are many thousands of producers. To me, the key to success when choosing wines from Burgundy is to find a good producer. From the same vineyard, five different domaines will each give you different styles and qualities, and different prices. The key is to find the producer that suits you.

Pinot Noir is a difficult grape to control, even for the very top producers. The best vintages will offer elegance, delicacy, complex fruits, and silky tannins, while in poorer years this grape can produce wine that is acerbic, lacking in fruity berry aromas, and dominated by a herbaceous smell.

The most famous and, in my opinion, the best Pinot Noir wines of Burgundy come from the Côte de Nuits. These wines have the longest life of all red Burgundies and are able to age for at least five years, up to 35 for the best vintages.

The Côte de Nuits contains 23 *grands crus*, grouped into eight communal appellations. Some of the most famous Burgundy reds are from Gevrey-Chambertin; these wines tend to be very deep in colour with an earthy and animal character after ageing. The wines from Morey-St-Denis and Chambolle-Musigny are lighter and particularly elegant and full of finesse. Vougeot reds are floral when young, but develop an earth and truffle character after ageing. Vosne-Romanée is regarded as producing

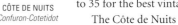

CÔTE DE NUITS
Confuron-Cotetidot

POWERFUL PINOT *Gevrey-Chambertin, in the north of the Côte de Nuits, is renowned for producing intense, deeply coloured wines.*

LAND AND PRODUCTION

ULTIMATE PRIZE Of all the *grand cru* vineyards, La Romanée-Conti in the heart of Vosne-Romanée is the very finest. The wine is fantastically expensive, but it is also totally memorable and unique.

some of the best (and most expensive) wines in the world. Utterly intense, but delicate, the tannins, fruit, and acidity are perfectly balanced. Nuits-St-Georges, and the lesser-known Marsannay and Fixin, have no *grands crus*, but still produce some excellent and world-class wines.

In my opinion, the finest *grands crus* of the Cotes de Nuits – the best vineyards, sometimes owned by a single estate, but more often belonging to a collection of small producers – are the following: Chambertin, Chapelle-Chambertin, Griottes-Chambertin, La Romanée-Conti, Romanée-St-Vivant, La Tâche, Échézeaux, Bonnes-Mares, Clos de Tart, Clos de la Roche, and Le Musigny.

I like to enjoy these wines on their own, but I can also recommend serving a Côte de Nuits with a fillet of venison and a *girolle* mushroom casserole.

CÔTE DE NUITS
Henri Gouges

RECOMMENDED PRODUCERS

▸ Henri Gouges
▸ Confuron-Cotetidot
▸ D Mortet
▸ J L Trapet

JURA POULSARD

C **COLOUR** Varies from a pale red to an orangey-pink.

A **AROMA** Very distinctive; cherry, raspberry, redcurrant, and vanilla.

T **TASTE** Extremely delicate, fruity, and refreshing, with a long finish.

Poulsard is a special and unusual grape from the Jura region. It is very thin-skinned, and so light in pigment that it can also make white wine. You might find this wine marketed as Arbois, where it may be blended with Pinot Noir or Trousseau. In Bugey, another region of eastern France, it is sometimes called Mescle. Poulsard reds and rosés are best served slightly chilled, and this is a lovely wine to drink in summer, with pâtés or even a salad or crudités. And I always say "Poulsard for poultry"!

RECOMMENDED PRODUCERS

▸ Jacques Puffeney
▸ Domaine Rolet

CÔTES DU FRONTONNAIS

C **COLOUR** Bright ruby red, with vibrant pinkish tints.

A **AROMA** Intense raspberry, cherry, lilacs, fresh plum, spice, and liquorice.

T **TASTE** Subtle fruitiness and earthy flavours; medium length.

This up-and-coming appellation of southwest France has caught my attention. It has two styles; the first is traditional: austere, full, and tannic, based on the blend of the Bordeaux grapes Cabernet Sauvignon, Cabernet Franc, and Malbec, with Syrah; the second style is modern, light, and more fruit-driven, mainly using the local Negrette grape. Imagine you are in the mountains with a glass of one of these wines, some grilled or roast meats, and a soft, delicate Pyrenean cheese – heaven!

RECOMMENDED PRODUCERS

▸ Château Plaisance
▸ Château le Roc

SANCERRE ROUGE

C **COLOUR** Distinctive pale ruby red, with an orange rim.

A **AROMA** Delicately perfumed, with fresh red berries, earth, and spice.

T **TASTE** Dry and pleasant; high acidity; balanced tannins; medium to long finish.

I cannot say I have been impressed very often by a red from Sancerre, the Loire region famous for Sauvignon Blanc (*see p46*). However, some producers are

SANCERRE ROUGE *Jean-Max Roger*

taking the red grape as seriously as their white varieties and making wine that matches some of the lighter Burgundies for charm and elegance. The fruity aromas are very similar, but this wine will rarely age.

RECOMMENDED PRODUCERS

▸ Jean-Max Roger
▸ Domaine Henri Bourgeois

SAUMUR-CHAMPIGNY / CHINON

C **COLOUR** Profound deep ruby to crimson, with a purple rim.

A **AROMA** Intense; raspberry, strawberry, dark fruits, and sweet spice.

T **TASTE** Soft, delicate, and aromatic, with a satisfying length.

The regions of Anjou-Saumur and Touraine make a wonderful setting for vineyards, surrounded by the beautiful châteaux of the Loire Valley, and Saumur-Champigny and Chinon are some of their best red wines. On a base of chalk soil, called *tufa*, this is the home of the Cabernet Franc grape, known locally as Breton. A typical Cabernet Franc wine perfectly combines blackcurrant and green pepper with a succulent lemony acidity. Try to find the best vintages, as in a poor year this grape can make wine of a very herbaceous and leafy character if it has not fully ripened.

ALSACE PINOT NOIR

C **COLOUR** Recognizable pale cherry-red, with a ruby rim.

A **AROMA** Intense and youthful; spice, pepper, earth, and smoke.

T **TASTE** Elegant and full-flavoured, with ripe tannins and good length.

I always look out for alternatives to the big names, and this is one of my latest finds. Pure and clean thanks to new technology and improved grape ripening, Alsace Pinot Noirs have real personality, with rich fruit and a refreshing style combining intensity and finesse. They are quite expensive, but definitely worth a try, especially with cured or grilled meats.

RECOMMENDED PRODUCERS

▸ Trimbach
▸ Domaine Marcel Deiss

Chinon, in the Touraine region, is not only famous in the Loire Valley, but also worldwide, and is an alternative to Italy's Valpolicella (*see p86*) and other similar wines. Within France, these reds are a great alternative to Beaujolais, primarily because of the strawberry and raspberry aromas. The structure of the wine is light, with a concentration of fruit flavours, spices, and flowers. Saumur-Champigny wines are similar to those of Chinon, but usually they are a little less structured.

There is nothing better than enjoying a bottle of Saumur-Champigny or Chinon with a picnic or barbecue, or with lighter roast meats and game.

CHINON
Domaine C Joguet

RECOMMENDED PRODUCERS

▸ Domaine C Joguet
▸ Bernard Baudry

BEAUJOLAIS

C **COLOUR** Bright and light ruby red, sometimes crimson; darker for the *crus*.

A **AROMA** Charming, vibrant; youthful red berry fruits, pepper, violet, and banana.

T **TASTE** Fruity and low in tannins, with a long, refreshing, succulent finish.

What can I say about Beaujolais? It is one of the classic red wines of the world, and is typically richly flavoured, light, and exuberant. This is partly due to the character of the Gamay Noir grape, but is also a result of a vinification process called carbonic maceration *(see p78)*, which considerably enhances the fruit flavours.

Beaujolais is in the Burgundy region of France, and has a number of region-wide appellations. Of these, Beaujolais-Villages is my choice for its superior quality and fruitiness. There are also ten classified *crus* in Beaujolais, which vary greatly according to the *terroir*. The challenge is to pick the right one!

Juliénas and Moulin-à-Vent, the oldest *cru* in Beaujolais, produce deep, intense, and complex wines, which conjure up a mixture of violets, peonies, blackcurrant, and strawberry, and can have a mineral edge. Fleurie wines are popular due to their more floral and delicate style, while Chénas produces wine with intense fruit and flower aromas. I have harvested the grapes in Morgon, and I still love the balance of the juicy crushed berries with the dense and compact structure of the wine.

Lighter *crus* include St-Amour, which produces a charming, ruby-red wine, and fresh, youthful Régnié, Chiroubles, Brouilly, and Côte de Brouilly.

You can drink Beaujolais on its own at any time, with lunch or dinner, and with most meats and vegetables. The stronger wines, such as Juliénas or Moulin-à-Vent, are especially good with game and red meat. For a special occasion, I would choose one of the *crus*, but be careful – the quality of the wine very much depends on the producer.

BEAUJOLAIS
Domaine de la Madone

RECOMMENDED PRODUCERS

▸ Domaine de la Madone
▸ Château des Jacques
▸ Duboeuf

CULTURE AND TRADITION

CELEBRATING WINE Beaujolais Nouveau is wine from this region that is made as quickly as possible, and it reaches the shops only a few weeks after the vintage. It has very little complexity – I always think it is just like smelling a bag of sweets! The arrival of the first bottles of this youthful wine is celebrated on the third Thursday of November every year.

COOL RED *Beaujolais wines should not be drunk if they are too warm – slightly chilled is best, especially when accompanied by cold meats.*

SPAIN

Spain is famous for its fuller reds like Rioja and Ribera, but there are also some lighter styles, where climate and grape variety allow. The main fruity, lively reds are Mencía, Somontano, and Valdepeñas. These offer ripe berry fruitiness and soft tannins.

MENCÍA

C COLOUR Deep garnet colour with a purple rim; medium intensity.

A AROMA Hints of oak and red fruits, with prominent dark cherry.

T TASTE Intense, with fragrant red fruits, chocolate, and minerals in the finish.

The Mencía grape variety is mostly grown in Galicia, an up-and-coming region in northwestern Spain, and in neighbouring Bierzo. I find this an underrated grape, capable of making fruity red wines of great quality. Bierzo is fairly new as a DO, and production is very limited owing to the steepness of the vineyard terraces as they rise from the river banks. This wine is rich, aromatic, and very well structured – if you want something brighter and fresher than a Rioja, try this, particularly with tapas or grilled meats. One of my favourite pairings is Bierzo with goat pâté and goats' cheese – a taste of the real Spain. Valdeorras, in eastern Galicia, is very similar in style, but the vineyards benefit from a special microclimate thanks to the Atlantic breezes, which keeps the alcohol content relatively low, while maintaining a good natural acidity.

RECOMMENDED PRODUCERS
▶ Bodegas CA del Bierzo
▶ Pérez Carames

VALDEPEÑAS

C COLOUR Medium crimson with a pinkish rim and good intensity.

A AROMA Fresh ripe berries, with notes of leather and vanilla.

T TASTE Richly flavoured, balanced, and refreshing, with a long finish.

The red Tempranillo grape, known locally as Cencibel, thrives in the roasting hot summers of high-altitude central Spain, giving wines from the Valdepeñas region a great balance between the fragrant ripe fruit and a rich soft texture. Ageing in American oak barrels lends an attractive taste of vanilla, cherry, and butter. A lovely, easy-to-drink wine, ideal for tapas.

VALDEPEÑAS
Bodegas los Llanos

RECOMMENDED PRODUCERS
▶ Bodegas los Llanos
▶ Viña Zara

SOMONTANO

C COLOUR Deep, bright cherry red, sometimes with violet hints.

A AROMA Ripe red and black fruits; notes of vanilla, chocolate, and spice.

T TASTE Beaujolais-like velvety texture, light structure, fruit, and soft tannins.

Make a note now – I promise this will be a new winner for Spain. Somontano, meaning "under the mountains", is located at the foot of the Pyrenees. This area produces wine from Moristel grapes, better known as Mourvèdre, often blended with Tempranillo. The result is soft and light, with velvety, rich, fruity flavours, and a really Spanish feel. Drink this on a warm evening with light meats, tapas, and barbecued foods.

RECOMMENDED PRODUCERS
▶ Enate
▶ COVISA

GERMANY

Germany is most famous for white wine, but also makes a light red called Spätburgunder, which is similar to a Pinot Noir.

SPÄTBURGUNDER *Salwey*

SPÄTBURGUNDER

C COLOUR Normally a ruby red, but can be a very light pink.

A AROMA Bright and fresh, with cherry, vanilla, nuts, and pine.

T TASTE Hints of blackberry, herbs, and minerals, with a gentle, smooth finish.

German red wines are quite rare – it is difficult to find them outside Germany. The best wine-producing regions are Rheinhessen, Pfalz, and Baden. Wines made from the Spätburgunder grape can range from a "blush" rosé style red through to a full red wine, similar to a French Burgundy. Generally, Spätburgunder wines are fragrant, light, lively, elegant, and velvety, with a very smooth finish.

As it is a special event to drink a German red, I try to make the effort to match it with German food like pork roast or bratwurst, although this wine also goes very well with game and poultry. Its dry finish suits blue cheeses, and versions with a slightly sweeter finish can serve perfectly well as dessert wines. If you can find one of these wines, grab it – it makes a special change from the usual light reds.

RECOMMENDED PRODUCERS
▶ B Huber
▶ Bernhardt
▶ Salwey

AUSTRIA

Austrian white wines are often excellent, but are not widely known, as most are consumed by the domestic market. Even less well-known is their excellent light red made from the St-Laurent grape, which is similar to Burgundian Pinot Noir and truly top class.

ST-LAURENT

C COLOUR Bright ruby red with a medium intensity of colour.

A AROMA Pronounced and full aromas of fresh blackberry and strawberry.

T TASTE Fleshy and fruity, with balanced acidity and polished tannins.

For me, St-Laurent is really the Austrian version of French red Burgundy. The St-Laurent grape gets its name from the Saint's Day on August 10th – the date around which this early-ripening grape begins to ripen. It is closely related to Pinot Noir, and quite difficult to grow – it needs high rainfall and very warm summers – but it produces what I consider to be some of the finest Austrian reds. St-Laurent wines, like Pinot Noirs, are light in body and lively in texture, with plenty of soft fruit and berries, balanced tannins, and a clean finish. I find this wine fresher than a Burgundy. It is versatile, and should be considered not only for summer. I enjoy it with roasted meat, lamb, game, pasta dishes, and cheese.

ST LAURENT
Umathum

RECOMMENDED PRODUCERS
▶ Umathum
▶ Gipsberg
▶ Gessellmann

SWITZERLAND

Swiss wines are very light and vibrant, and the mountains and lakes of this country create a cool microclimate that adds to their complexity. Buying Swiss wines can be confusing, however, because grape varieties often go by several names, varying from region to region.

SWISS LIGHT REDS

C COLOUR Light red with an orange-pink rim; similar to rosé.

A AROMA Young, lively nose; raspberry, bilberry; hints of mint, spice, and pine.

T TASTE Very fruity and refreshing; moderate tannins, great harmony.

Most people do not think of Switzerland when they are choosing a wine. I think this is a pity, as this country produces some very attractive styles. Switzerland is still mainly known for its white wine, but its lovely light red wines are becoming more popular in the country itself. However, it is quite unusual to see Swiss wines on supermarket shelves (or even in a restaurant) in other countries. One simple explanation for this is tax – it is so expensive to import wines into Switzerland that most of the Swiss production is drunk locally. In addition, this is a small country locked within the Alps, and most of the wine-growing areas are at too high an altitude for the grapes to ripen easily, resulting in a low level of wine production.

Most of Switzerland's wine is produced in the western region, closer to France and around the great lakes, often on south-facing terraced vineyards that trap the sun. Around the lakes, microclimate has a big influence; the natural light winds slow down the ripening process of the grapes, allowing them to develop more flavour and complexity.

The main wine regions to look out for are Valais, in the upper reaches of the Rhône River, and Vaudois. Pinot Noir (also known as Klevner) thrives in Switzerland and is the most-planted grape variety, followed by the Gamay grape. Both of these can be blended together to become the famous Dôle (in Valais) or Salvagnin (in Vaudois).

Swiss Gamays are similar in many ways to young Beaujolais wines – aromatic and smooth, with just a little spice to keep the interest, although sometimes Gamay wines lack the depth, body, and richness of the Burgundy wines. Syrah, as well as some unusual local grape varieties, such as Humagne and Cornalin, may be used to add extra

SWISS LIGHT REDS
Simon Maye & Fils

interest to the blends. The Italian-speaking parts of Switzerland, around Ticino, produce a light style of Merlot, which benefits from the climatic influence of the Italian lakes.

Switzerland does not make the best wines in the world, but they are light, well rounded, and exceptionally refreshing. These Swiss reds are certainly very cheerful and fun to have around the table with friends, especially on summer days overlooking the mountains.

Swiss reds can be enjoyed on their own, slightly chilled, as an apéritif. Even better, drink them with a fresh perch from Lake Geneva, or any light fish, to bring back happy memories of your mountain holiday.

RECOMMENDED PRODUCERS
▸ Simon Maye & Fils
▸ E & G Roduit
▸ Alain Neyroud

ITALY

The reputation of Italian light reds, such as Valpolicella and Lambrusco, has suffered over the years, but they can be excellent and should be given a second chance. Dolcetto and Barbera are great for everyday drinking.

BARBERA

C COLOUR Medium to deep garnet red with a ruby rim.

A AROMA Full, pronounced and aromatic; blackberry, liquorice, spice, flowers.

T TASTE Fruity flavours, with firm, ripe tannins and good length.

Wines made from Barbera come in a wide variety of styles, from intense reds through to a fizzy version, called Verbesco. Barbera is known as the "people's wine" in the Piemonte (Piedmont) region because it makes up the greatest part of the normal daily drinking wine for the locals, and more than half of Piemonte's red wine production.

There are three areas of production: Asti and Alba (the two most important), and Monferrato.

If Beaujolais *crus* stopped being sold tomorrow, I would turn straight to Barbera d'Asti! It is a great bargain: charming and well made, with ripe fruit to the fore in a pleasant, appealing taste. Barbera d'Alba is well structured, with a ripe and chunky texture. If you like Barolo, this is not quite as full, but you will still love this underrated wine. Be patient with it – I would recommend you to keep it for at least three or four years.

BARBERA
Araldica

I love the fact that these wines have such diversity, based on their particular place of origin. As their reputation and quality have improved, I find great excitement in their straightforward approach, which also offers complexity and elegance. They are fleshy, thanks to their ripe fruit flavours, but their acidity still gives a special freshness.

I like to drink Barbera at lunchtime or sitting outside on a very warm evening. It is extremely versatile, and goes well with most Italian and Mediterranean dishes.

RECOMMENDED PRODUCERS
▸ Araldica
▸ Rochetta
▸ Maccario

CULTURE AND TRADITION

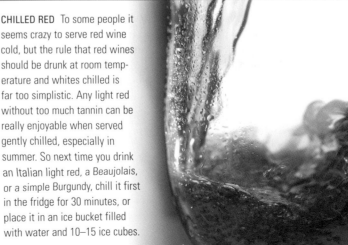

CHILLED RED To some people it seems crazy to serve red wine cold, but the rule that red wines should be drunk at room temperature and whites chilled is far too simplistic. Any light red without too much tannin can be really enjoyable when served gently chilled, especially in summer. So next time you drink an Italian light red, a Beaujolais, or a simple Burgundy, chill it first in the fridge for 30 minutes, or place it in an ice bucket filled with water and 10–15 ice cubes.

DOLCETTO

C COLOUR Deep ruby red through to black cherry; good intensity.

A AROMA Abundant crushed blackberry and raspberry, liquorice, and almond.

T TASTE Delicate and fruity; rich and full-flavoured but light; good length.

Dolcetto is the Piemontese people's most pleasant, everyday wine, and it is said that "half of the blood of people living in Piemonte is Dolcetto". In that case, I wish I came from Piemonte!

Dolcetto is a fantastic grape. It grows where others will not grow and ripens very early. This means that it is rarely acidic or acerbic as it very quickly gets enough sunshine to reveal its full expression of flavour – avoiding one of the major problems

DOLCETTO
Marchesi di Grésy

facing grapes grown in the hilly vineyards of northern Italy.

Dolcetto translates as "little sweet one", perhaps because of the sweetness of the grapes, or because there is a perception of comparative sweetness in Dolcetto wines to the Piemonte palate, even though the wines are in fact dry, without residual sugar. It is softer and fruitier than Barbera, which has a more invigorating acidity.

There are seven DOCs for Dolcetto, all in the Piemonte region. They are Dolcetto d'Alba, Dolcetto d'Aqui, Dolcetto d'Asti, Dolcetto di Diano d'Alba, Dolcetto delle Langhe Monregalesi, Dolcetto di Dogliani, and Dolcetto di Ovada.

The best known, and for me the finest, is Dolcetto d'Alba. Dogliani and Diano d'Alba join it to make a trio of leading regions, while Ovada is mostly

FOOD MATCH

PIZZA Whenever you eat a tomato-based dish, think light Italian reds. Dolcetto was just made to drink with a pizza that is hot from the oven.

very simple and juicy. The term *superiore* can be attached to stronger wines.

Because of the popularity of Dolcetto, and because it is so important to the economy of the region, the style of the wine has been developed to make it easier to drink and even more appealing. The small dark berries have thick skins, which contain a high level of tannins. In

order to control these levels, the maceration process is kept very short. This also has the effect of raising the proportion of acidity in the makeup of the wine, giving a better balance. This process has greatly improved Dolcetto wines in recent years.

Dolcetto makes an excellent all-around red, very versatile and a really reliable standby for drinking with any Italian dish. I particularly like drinking it with risotto, cold meats, pasta, pizza, or pâté.

Do not keep your Dolcettos for long – drink them when young and fresh and fruity, although the very best ones may keep for five years or so. Think of this wine if you want a taste of Italy that is not strong and powerful like Barolo, but is different from Chianti and the Tuscan wines. You will not be disappointed.

RECOMMENDED PRODUCERS

▸ Marchesi di Grésy
▸ Prunotto
▸ Enzo Boglietti

BONARDA

C COLOUR Intense ruby red to purple, becoming lighter at the rim.

A AROMA Very distinctive, with plum and black cherry.

T TASTE Light and fruity, with cherry dominant; smooth texture.

Bonarda grapes are grown in scattered parts of Piemonte and southern Lombardy. In fact, Bonarda is grown more widely in Argentina than in Italy, which is a shame – I would love it if more people were able to enjoy one of my favourite wines, Oltrepò Pavese, made from this grape. These wines are drinkable, smooth, and just right when you want a fruity red. I like to drink them with light foods, such as charcuterie, or one of my favourites, pasta shells with sausage, mozzarella, ricotta, and tomato.

RECOMMENDED PRODUCERS

▸ Alighieri
▸ Loc. Casa Ferrari

LAMBRUSCO

C COLOUR Bright ruby red, with a violet-coloured fizz when poured.

A AROMA Jammy and fruity, with a distinct aroma of violets.

T TASTE Intense flavours of berries; very light, with a vibrant, fresh feel.

Lambrusco has played a very important part in the Italian wine industry. In the 1970s, it became the best-known and most widely consumed Italian wine in the world. Unfortunately, quality began to suffer due to over-production, and it developed a poor reputation. Today,

LAMBRUSCO *Umberto Cavicchioli & Figli*

many people will walk past this wine in the supermarket or avoid ordering it from a restaurant wine list. However, in my opinion, so long as I am careful which I choose, I find that drinking Lambrusco can be a very pleasant experience.

Real Lambrusco is a wonderful red colour – not the white or pale pink of many of the cheaper bottles. It is dry, and suggests sparkle, with lightness, and a low alcohol content, with the kind of brisk freshness and acidity needed to cut through the rich sauces and fatty salamis of its home region of Emilia-Romagna (the area around Modena and Bologna in northeastern Italy).

The first thing I look for in a Lambrusco is the dominant aroma of violets, and then I look at the fizz, which boils up when the wine is poured and leaves a faint ring of white around the edge of the glass when it settles. If this fizz disappears immediately, the wine is authentic.

The best wines are classified DOC, and there are several to choose from; Lambrusco di Sorbara has

the most perfume, while Lambrusco Grasparossa di Castelvetro has a deeper flavour and colour, and more tannin. Richer wines come from Lambrusco Salamino di Santa Croce.

Drinking Lambrusco should be fun, fresh, and stimulating. I really like to pair it with basic Italian dishes like egg pasta, cold meats, or grilled sausages. Do not underestimate this wine; Lambrusco is a robust variety, known for its productivity. Although it has rarely attained anything close to

LAMBRUSCO
Umberto Cavicchioli & Figli

greatness, good quality wines can be found from the best producers. Be careful which Lambrusco you choose, but I think it is worth giving this wine a try.

RECOMMENDED PRODUCERS

▸ Umberto Cavicchioli & Figli
▸ Giacobazzi
▸ Chiarli & Figli

VALPOLICELLA

C COLOUR Bright, charming, ruby red, with good intensity.

A AROMA Black and red berries, with notes of dried herbs and flowers.

T TASTE Fresh and subtle, with cherry and discreet tannins.

Valpolicella is located in the northeastern Veneto region, between Bardolino and Soave, just north of Verona. This is a very famous wine, and in volume terms, it ranks just after Chianti in Italy's total production of quality red wine. The best wine comes from the foothills.

Although it is very popular, people can be very snobby about Valpolicella. It is often thought of as a pouring or quaffing wine, and has suffered from a flood of poor-quality bottles on the world market, which

VALPOLICELLA
Serègo Alighieri

seriously damaged its reputation. One wine critic went so far as to call it "insipid industrial garbage" at one point – not that I agree! Even if over the years the reputation of Valpolicella has suffered, things are looking up. Very few have disappointed me recently, as the quality has really improved.

Regular Valpolicella is light and very fragrant and fruity with a low alcohol content. It has a pleasant touch of acidity, which gives a clean and fresh finish with a charming and easy-drinking feel. This is due mainly to the quality of the Corvina grape. Styles can vary slightly, depending how much of the slightly inferior Rondinella and Molinara grapes are used. Wines labelled *superiore* are stronger and have an ageing period of one year.

The best wines are generally those labelled *classico*, from the heart of

the region. Some big-name stars lead the DOC and keep up the quality image. However, if you see a *classico superiore*, whoever it is made by, then go for it. You should expect a better structured and more complex wine, but still in the light and fruity style. The wine will be aged in big barrels (called *botti*) rather than small casks. This preserves the fruit flavours rather than masking them with vanilla and tannins from the wood of the small barrels.

I love to match this wine with easy foods – pasta, salads, pizza – or else just enjoy it on its own, slightly chilled, on a hot summer's day. I think it is worthwhile giving Valpolicella a fair chance.

RECOMMENDED PRODUCERS
- Serègo Alighieri
- Borghetti
- Tommasi
- Corte Sant'Alda
- Allegrini

CANAIOLO

C COLOUR Delicate pale ruby, with bright highlights.

A AROMA Very exuberant and aromatic; fresh raspberry and strawberry.

T TASTE Soft and light, but with all elements in harmony; very pleasant.

Canaiolo is an important but small part of the blend used to make the famous red Chianti (*see p97*), and is also used in other Tuscan reds. Chianti can be quite green, stalky, and lacking in fruit, but the Canaiolo grape can soften it and bring out the fruit, charm, and subtlety. This grape is also grown outside Tuscany, in Umbria and the Marches, and more recently in Sardegna (Sardinia). Very few major producers use it as a single grape variety – it is difficult to grow and yields are low. However, in some parts of Italy you might come across local wines made with this grape; if you do, drink them with light dishes: strong or spicy food will smother the flavours.

BARDOLINO

C COLOUR Bright ruby red, with medium to pale intensity.

A AROMA Mainly berry fruits, with hints of almonds and spice.

T TASTE Fruity, with balanced acidity and tannins.

This is a cheerful, easy-to-drink Veneto wine, made in large quantities, like Valpolicella. Bardolino's new style is very much fruit-driven, thanks to its successful blend of Corvina, Molinara, and Rondinella. Always drink the latest vintage, ideally within the year, and enjoy the wine at its own level with a straight and simple pizza – nothing over the top.

BARDOLINO
Guerrieri-Rizzardi

RECOMMENDED PRODUCERS
- Guerrieri-Rizzardi
- Lamberti

SAGRANTINO DI MONTEFALCO

C COLOUR Deep ruby red with a hint of purple, tending to garnet.

A AROMA Delicate, with blackberry, black cherry, figs, and spice.

T TASTE Dry, round, and fruity, with balanced tannins; medium length.

Since the mid 1990s, the wines of Umbria have become more popular with wine lovers, including me! Umbria is located at the heart of Italy, bordering Tuscany, Lazio, and the Marches. The most popular Umbrian wine is Sagrantino, and the best example of this is Sagrantino di Montefalco, named after the small hilltop town located southeast of Perugia. This wine is not yet very well known, but it is certainly delicious.

This part of Umbria is more famous for its sweet wine, which is called Sagrantino Passito. The dry wines, however, are on the up;

when vinified with care, they typically show lots of black fruit and softness. There is no doubt that Sagrantino di Montefalco is better produced now than in the past, although there has not yet been a particularly huge investment in modern vinification in this beautiful part of the world. The main change has been the introduction of small barrels for ageing the wine, which gives it a softness, although sometimes with perhaps too much vanilla from the oak.

Montefalco Rosso is a different wine, although from the same region. It is more like a Chianti and is based on the Sangiovese grape, with a small amount of Sagrantino adding character to the blend.

I like to drink the dry version of Sagrantino di Montefalco with light meats and, in the winter, with roasted meats. Excellent!

RECOMMENDED PRODUCERS
- Fratelli Adanti
- Antonelli
- Domenico Benincasa

CANADA

Canadian wines can be excellent, especially from the west coast, where the cool climate produces light reds of great complexity.

CANADIAN PINOT NOIR *Château des Charmes*

PINOT NOIR

C COLOUR Attractive ruby to cherry red; quite pale.

A AROMA Elegant, with fresh red fruits, earth, and spice.

T TASTE Vibrant and fruity, with balanced acidity and subtle tannins.

Most people are surprised when I tell them how good Canadian wines are, but the cooler the climate, the more complex the flavours – up to a point, of course. These wines come from Okanagan Valley in British Columbia, not the Canadian Arctic! The valley has hot, dry, semi-desert conditions in the south, on the US border, but is cooler in the north, with better growing conditions. The region is famous for its sweet ice wines, but Pinot Noir also grows throughout the valley.

Overall, the wines are light and greatly refreshing, with fragrant red fruits and a lively texture. This is definitely a region to watch. It has expanded from only a handful of wineries in the 1980s to more than 50 today. Look out for Okanagan on the label; try these wines with light meats, or meaty fish like sea bass.

RECOMMENDED PRODUCERS
▸ Château des Charmes
▸ Inniskillin
▸ Mission Hill

USA

California makes wonderfully rich and fruity light reds. The combination of warm sun and cooling ocean breezes makes for great quality fruit, which makes great wine! Oregon, to the north, also makes Pinot Noir wines of great depth and complexity.

OREGON PINOT NOIR

C COLOUR Intense, deep ruby colour, with a light ruby rim.

A AROMA Well-defined; cherry, jammy strawberry, fresh herbs, spice, vanilla.

T TASTE Fleshy, balanced acidity, bags of fruit, silky tannins, good length.

The Oregon wine scene has been buzzing since the 1970s, with focused efforts to make its Pinot Noir a truly classy wine. The price is relatively high, but worth every penny. Look for a bottle from the Willamette Valley region, which has the best microclimate due to its relatively low rainfall, resulting in perfect conditions for the grapes. It is one of the best places in the world outside Burgundy for Pinot Noir, and a region I cannot wait to visit.

Oregon Pinot Noir has the bouquet and concentrated fruit of California's Carneros wines, and also the earthy, mineral touch of Burgundy. I cannot recommend these wines enough, and I would love for you to enjoy them as they mature. Try them with a lovely lamb casserole, or with venison.

RECOMMENDED PRODUCERS
▸ Domaine Drouhin
▸ Argyle
▸ Adelsheim

CALIFORNIA PINOT NOIR

C COLOUR Bright deep ruby to cherry red; fairly solid.

A AROMA Intense; ripe berries, cherry, leather, sweet spice, vanilla.

T TASTE Big, rich, and voluptuous, with great balance.

To my mind, Pinot Noir might not be the most successful or representative grape variety in California, but it still has an amazing complexity of flavours and a superb, well-balanced, juicy texture.

In the early years, California winemakers struggled to establish high-quality wines made from Pinot Noir, as the grape is fragile and difficult to grow. But after much determined effort, great success has been achieved, particularly in four districts: Carneros, Russian River Valley, Santa

CALIFORNIA PINOT NOIR
Kendall-Jackson

Ynez Valley, and Santa Maria Valley. All these districts rely on using the cooling influence of fog in the local climate to make wonderfully rich, complex wines with great character. The fog rolls in off the Pacific Ocean each morning, especially in mid-summer, significantly lowering temperatures. This cooling effect allows more time for the grapes to mature and create a wine with a rich complexity of flavours and more character.

Ironically, up until the 1980s growers avoided planting grapes in places like the Russian River Valley, precisely because the fog prevented the kind of full, rich ripening that Californians were used to with their grapes. Instead they concentrated on orchard fruits and dairy farming. It was only at the time when growers began to seek a more European elegance and balance in their wines, that the fog, and the cold winds that

CALIFORNIA PINOT NOIR *Saintsbury*

go with it, started to be seen as the key to overcoming California's warm climate.

The microclimate is even more important than the soil in dictating the style of wine that can be made in a particular vineyard in California. The difference it makes is so great that, unlike many other wine regions, California classifies each area into one of five climatic zones based on the relative heat during a given growing season.

Santa Ynez particularly illustrates these differences. The vineyards quickly change from the cool, fog-influenced Santa Rita Hills near the sea, from where the finest Pinot Noirs come (particularly from the Sanford & Benedict Vineyard), to inland sites, where the climate is much better suited to heat-loving varieties like Cabernet Sauvignon and even the Rhône grape Syrah.

I really like the consistency of quality in California Pinot Noir – these are some of the wines I save for special occasions. One of the most exciting things for me is that Californian producers are so keen to make outstanding Pinot Noir that they make huge efforts to find the best sites to grow it and treat the grapes with the utmost respect. Despite their ability to age well – more than ten years for the best ones – these wines are richer, fruitier, and more upfront than European Pinot Noirs. I just love them with roast meats or even gently spiced dishes.

RECOMMENDED PRODUCERS
▸ Kendall-Jackson
▸ Saintsbury
▸ Sanford
▸ Rex Hill
▸ Sonoma-Cutrer

NEW ZEALAND

This important winemaking country has now focused its expertise on making quality reds. The South Island and the southern end of the North Island make use of their cool climates to make attractive and well-balanced light red wines based on Pinot Noir.

PINOT NOIR

C COLOUR Dark ruby – darker than most European Pinot Noirs.

A AROMA Raspberry, cherry, plum, savoury herbs, and spicy oak.

T TASTE Red berries with hints of oak and vanilla; ripe, round, and sexy!

People (especially the French!) often ask me the difference between Australian and New Zealand wines, and which of them is better. My answer is that they both produce fantastic wines. Australia has a warm climate, so the wine is full of fruit, lively, brash, and "in your face". It is less complicated and great fun to drink on its own or with food. New Zealand is cooler, and this makes the wine less openly fruity and less sweet, but fleshier and more complex. They are both great, but they are very different.

In Marlborough, on New Zealand's South Island, the perfect combination of fine soil, sunshine, and cooling sea breezes makes a particularly fresh Pinot Noir, with a fruitiness that explodes in your mouth. This is definitely my kind of wine! I love these wines, not only because they are new on the market, but because they are a real rival to French Burgundy.

Central Otago, in the southern part of South Island, is, at 45° south, the southernmost vineyard in the world, but also the fastest-growing wine area in the country. The cold climate makes for a long, slow ripening period – a key element for the best Pinot Noir.

Good Pinot Noir is also produced in the Martinborough region of Wairarapa, at the southern end of North Island. There is good soil, low rainfall, and long spells of sunshine, producing fruity and distinctive wines. This is an up-and-coming area, and is one to watch.

New Zealand Pinot Noir should be drunk when it is young, and I like it with light meats or cheese – you will not be disappointed. One way to get the best out of this wine is to drink it

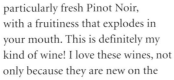

PINOT NOIR *Wither Hills*

MUSHROOM RISOTTO The fresh flavour of a New Zealand Pinot Noir is perfectly complemented by a light dish, such as mushroom risotto.

on its own as an apéritif with any delicate dishes, a few snacks, or even after a meal, to really feel those ripe, rounded flavours.

RECOMMENDED PRODUCERS
▸ Wither Hills
▸ Ata Rangi
▸ Kaimira Estate
▸ Felton Road
▸ Mount Maude

SOUTH AFRICA

South Africa's wide range of climates offers local winemakers the opportunity to experiment with new grape varieties, and this led to the creation of Pinotage, made by crossing Cinsault and Pinot Noir. This fruity, juicy red divides opinion, but can be excellent.

SOUTH AFRICAN LIGHT REDS

C COLOUR Deep red to purple, with a ruby to tile-red rim.

A AROMA Plum, cherry, red berries, chocolate, leather, and spicy oak.

T TASTE Balanced, with high acidity; smooth; long fruity finish.

Red wines have become increasingly important in South Africa's wine industry, but the wines vary in quality and popularity.

The Cinsault (or Cinsaut) grape originates from the Languedoc region of southern France, and produces light, aromatic wines. It is often used in blends to add immediately appealing fruitiness. In South Africa, Cinsault, known locally as Hermitage, became the most-planted red grape up until the 1960s, particularly in the Stellenbosch region, but it has declined in recent years.

Pinot Noir has not been as successful in South Africa as in, perhaps, New Zealand or even Oregon in the US. This grape likes a fairly temperate climate to become as fine and delicate as it is in the most suitable growing regions, and the conditions in South Africa are generally too warm. However, in some exceptional places like Walker Bay, which is further south than the main established wine regions of Paarl and Stellenbosch, there is some very fine Pinot Noir – particularly in the Hemel-en-Aarde valley, close to the whale-watching town of Hermanus.

The Cinsault and Pinot Noir grapes have been overtaken by Pinotage, a successful local cross between the two of them, which was first produced in the 1920s. Pinotage is completely suited to local conditions. I am not surprised that it has become the second-most planted red grape in South Africa. Barring one or two interesting examples in New Zealand and California, plantings of Pinotage are pretty much restricted to this country.

To some people, the jury is still out on this wine. They say you either love it or you hate it, but it is not as simple as that. The styles vary tremendously, as each winery chooses the style that suits its own identity, and this can make understanding these wines pretty difficult. Some are very light wines made to be enjoyed young, while a few are brooding, tannic examples that need to be aged for a while in the bottle before the fruit shows at its best. In general, the fruit is dominant in the wines, and they have a light and juicy feel. The complexity of flavours is important, and the overall feel is of a light and fruity red. I think Pinotage is great to drink with salmon or trout, or even a spicy dish or barbecued meat.

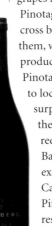

PINOTAGE *Backsberg*

PINOT NOIR *Bouchard Finlayson*

RECOMMENDED PRODUCERS
▸ Bouchard Finlayson
▸ Backsberg
▸ Riebeek
▸ Meerlust
▸ Charles Back

AUSTRALIA

Although bold reds like Shiraz and Cabernet Sauvignon are the flagship wines of Australia, the lighter Pinor Noir thrives in cool microclimates, such as the Yarra Valley in Victoria. Tarrango is another fine, light quaffing wine from the same region.

PINOT NOIR

C COLOUR Intense and attractive; cherry-plum.

A AROMA Black cherry and plum, with hints of French oak.

T TASTE Fresh, youthful, gamey, spicy, and savoury, with a good balance.

Much of Australia is unsuitable for producing good Pinot Noir, which prefers a climate neither too hot nor too cool. However, some pockets of land do have potential, and there is no shortage of winemakers who are avid Pinot Noir fans eager to search out the best sites where their beloved grape can work its bewitching magic. The most established regions for Pinot Noir in Australia are the Yarra Valley, a small area in Victoria northeast of Melbourne, and the island state of Tasmania. Other exciting, up-and-coming regions include Mornington Peninsula, also in Victoria, and Adelaide Hills in South Australia.

The Yarra Valley has a moderately cool climate and good rainfall, and is one of the most suitable regions yet discovered for Pinot Noir – although in a distinctive Australian, rather than Burgundian, style. If you like your wines to burst with fruit, and to be immediate, fresh, and tasty, then go for these. I will often drink Yarra Valley Pinot Noir on its own, or with a lovely plate of cold meats or cheese on a base of lettuce – perfect!

Tasmania was known for many years as the "Apple Isle", a reference to the cold climate that made it more suitable for growing apples than for the heat-loving orchard fruits, such as peaches and oranges, grown elsewhere in Australia. Australia has a great surplus of land that is very hot and dry, and very few of

PINOT'S PROGRESS *The Coldstream Hills vineyard in Australia's Yarra Valley was established by wine critic James Halliday, one of the many champions of Pinot Noir.*

the really cool areas that are ideal to bring out the complexity and special delicacy of flavour in wines. The successful search for a cool climate to make both Pinot Noir and sparkling wines in a Champagne style has made Tasmania more important. This island now has over 60 vineyards and wineries, but many of them are tiny, and the wine they produce tends to be relatively expensive.

The Tasmanian vineyard climate is quite close to that of Champagne and Burgundy. The result is wines of light to medium body, not as rich as those from Victoria, with more subtlety, often with a hint of herbs and spice in the aroma, in addition to the cherry and plum found in Yarra Valley wines. If you are looking for a New World wine that is not too brash and open, try Tasmania.

RECOMMENDED PRODUCERS

▸ Dromana Estate
▸ Mount Macedon
▸ Roaring Forties
▸ Diamond Valley
▸ Spring Vale

PINOT NOIR
Dromana Estate

TARRANGO

C COLOUR Light cherry red, with a medium intensity.

A AROMA Fresh crushed red fruits; simple, but pleasant and youthful.

T TASTE Juicy, charming, and refreshing texture; fruity, with good length.

There are some wines I just can't take seriously, but I still enjoy them for being fun and funky. When I drink Tarrango I feel like I am eating a bag of raspberries! It is light, uncomplicated, and very refreshing, similar to a Beaujolais. This variety was developed in 1965 in Tarrango, Victoria, by crossing Touriga Nacional, a port grape, with the rich white Sultana. This is a great easy drinking red, and best drunk slightly chilled.

TARRANGO
Brown Brothers

RECOMMENDED PRODUCER

▸ Brown Brothers

FOOD MATCH

CHICKEN Light white meat dishes, such as chicken on a bed of salad, give free rein to the fresh, forward fruit of Yarra Valley Pinot Noir.

> **"** The most popular wines in the world – their complex, harmonious personalities mean there's something here for everyone's taste. **"**

RIPE, SMOOTH REDS

INTRODUCING RIPE, SMOOTH REDS

Perhaps the largest and most versatile of all the wine categories, ripe, smooth reds encompasses styles from everyday drinking wines, such as Chilean Merlot, through to prestigious classics, such the *grands crus classé*s of St-Émilion.

This category of wines is a fascinating cross-section through world production. In the past, many of the wines described here would have been considered full-bodied, but in recent years the emergence of intensely rich and heavy New World wines has shifted perceptions, and many are now considered to be "medium" reds. These wines are inevitably characterized by their grape variety, as well as the climate in which the vines grow. Overall, they are riper and more structured than light reds, and tend to be darker in colour with more liquorice and spicy flavours. Many of these wines are aged in oak

DARK FRUIT *Cherries and plums typify the aromas of ripe, smooth reds.*

barrels – but not necessarily new ones – giving them a savoury essence. They are fleshy, but not harsh, and will almost certainly entice you to drink some more!

An inexpensive ripe, smooth red wine should have a rich, fruity bouquet, without too much depth or complexity. Although the emphasis of the wine's taste will be on fruit, the palate should be balanced, as should its texture; the tannins should be discreet. An expensive ripe, smooth red will offer complexity, finesse, and subtlety with a fleshy body and perfectly balanced structure. Flavour rather than weight will dominate the wine, and it will have polished, round tannins.

DRINKING AND SERVING

DRINK PROFILE This category offers an enormous range of wines, all the way from full-bodied to light, but overall they should be smooth and round in texture, with complex aromas, and full flavours.

C COLOUR Expect to find garnet through to dark cherry at the core of these wines. The rim may be lighter – ruby to tile red. As the wines age they may generally become lighter in colour.

A AROMA The complexity of these wines will vary according to country of origin and grape, but generally the aromas are intense, with black fruits, dried herbs, sweet spices, and leather.

T TASTE These wines should exude a harmony of ripe fruit and tannins, with a good balance of alcohol. Expect a long, satisfying finish, lasting between around six to eight seconds.

BUYING AND STORING If you are looking for ripe, smooth reds to lay down, seek advice from your wine seller, as only the best wines and wines from certain vintages are suitable for ageing. Most versions from the New World are intended for drinking while young – within a year or two.

SERVING SUGGESTIONS As a general rule, serve these wines at room temperature, although some, such as Chianti, can be served slightly chilled. There is no need to decant these wines, nor to allow them to "breathe".

FOOD COMPANIONS These versatile wines can be drunk with a huge array of foods, such as pasta and pizza (try a Chianti or Cannonau); light meats (try Montepulciano with sausages or chops) and most vegetarian foods, and fish (try Dornfelder).

PARTNERS *Lamb brings out the flavours of a good Merlot; for heavier meats you can't beat a St-Émilion.*

WINES FOR ALL SEASONS

Ripe, smooth reds are wines for throughout the year, for any occasion – and for any time after midday! While they match beautifully with nearly all kinds of food, don't let that stop you picking up a glass of, say, Washington Lemberger or Chilean Carmenère and drinking it for the pure enjoyment of its delicious fruit and silky texture. Merlot wines and wines such as Rioja will make reliable stand-bys in your wine store, suitable for drinking in summer or winter; although, of course, you might want to keep some Merlots, most notably St-Émilion *grand crus*, for special occasions – and who can blame you? These can be among the most special and expensive wines in the world!

GRAPE VARIETIES

The following grape varieties, which are the best for making ripe, smooth reds, produce more wine than any others in the world. The most important of these is Merlot, which is the grape that goes into the classic wines of St-Émilion and Pomerol, and is also making great medium reds in California, New Zealand, and Chile. Other varieties for special attention are Sangiovese, which is the key grape in the blend that makes Italian Chianti; and Tempranillo, which Spanish *bodegas* use as the main variety in the wines from Rioja and Navarra.

GRAPE	BEST REGIONAL EXAMPLES	COMMENTS
MERLOT	France: St Émilion, Pomerol, Languedoc-Roussillon.	This fine grape is consistently excellent in quality and style. It produces well-coloured wines full of soft fruit, which are velvety on the tongue. Merlots may be very rich, and the grapes are used to produce some of the finest wines of Bordeaux.
TEMPRANILLO	Spain: Ribera del Duero, Rioja.	This is one of the finest Spanish red wine grapes. It makes complex, well-structured wines that can handle long ageing; even the more basic wines are elegant and fruit-driven.
SANGIOVESE	Italy: Tuscany. France: Corsica. California. Argentina.	This classy grape, which is often blended, makes some of the most famous Italian DOCGs, such as Chianti and Brunello. Success of this grape depends a lot on vintage and winemaker.
CARMENÈRE	France: Bordeaux. Chile.	Originally from Bordeaux, this grape has found a new home in Chile. Its wines show great complexity and richness, with dark fruit aromas and flavours, and a clean, dry finish.
BLAUFRÄNKISCH	Austria: Burgenland. USA: Washington.	An up-and-coming variety, which produces well structured wines with intense soft red fruit, sweet spice, and good colour. In the US, this variety is known as Lemberger.
DORNFELDER	Germany.	This grape variety makes fruity wines with a medium texture, and is increasing in commercial importance.
ALEATICO	Italy: Latium, Tuscany, Apulia.	This is a particularly aromatic grape that makes fruity and highly appealing wines.
MONTEPULCIANO	Italy: Abbruzzi, Marches.	Wines from this grape are well perfumed and complex with good structure and distinctive fruitiness. Good ageing.
ZWEIGELT	Austria.	This variety, which produces excellent quality wines, is widely planted in Austria, but little-known internationally.
CASTELAO FRANCES	Portugal.	Also known as Periquita, this grape produces fruity, well structured, and smooth wines.
ROSSESE	Italy.	This grape, which is widely grown in Liguria, makes distinctively flavoured wines.
MONDEUSE	France: Savoie.	Wine from the Mondeuse grape carries blackcurrant and pepper notes. It is similar to a Syrah style, with lighter weight.
CANNONAU	Italy: Sardinia.	Known as Garnacha in Spain and Grenache in France, this grape makes a fine, medium-bodied, fruity wine.
TEROLDEGO	Italy: Trentino.	Famous for the Teroldego Rotaliano wine; deep colours, very fragrant fruits, soft tannins. Charming and elegant.

FRANCE

The Merlot grape is widely used in France to make medium red wines, most notably in the St-Émilion and Pomerol regions of Bordeaux. Wines from these areas are smooth and fruity, but have a balanced, satisfying structure. Less well-known grape varieties, such as Mondeuse from eastern France, offer more spice and freshness and present a spirited alternative to the Bordeaux classics.

ST-ÉMILION / POMEROL

C COLOUR Deep ruby red, becoming black cherry with age; great intensity.

A AROMA Intense fruits and spice; over time cedar, smoke, spice, leather.

T TASTE Perfectly structured: rich, round, velvety, and smooth, yet dense and full.

St-Émilion and Pomerol are active and dynamic Bordeaux regions, with huge complexity and variety. Each has its own philosophy, but the key to their success is the famous Merlot grape, with Cabernet Franc its junior partner. Merlot produces a deeply coloured wine with aromas of ripe black fruit, which is also infinitely complex. These wines are especially smooth and rounded, yet full of power, with a great elegance and finesse. Although they can be drunk young, they reach perfection after five to ten years' ageing in the bottle.

St-Émilion is divided into three classifications: St-Émilion *grand cru*, *grand cru classé*, and *premier grand cru classé*. St-Émilion *grand cru* wines are smooth and pleasant with vibrant fruit. St-Émilion *grand cru*

SEARCH FOR PERFECTION
The classification of chateaux in St-Émilion is revised every ten years.

classé wines are richer and more complex, and usually the best value for money. The highest category, *premier grand cru classé*, is divided into levels A and B. "A" contains only the world-famous châteaux of Cheval Blanc and Ausone.

There are also a number of satellite appellations that can use St-Émilion in their name: Montagne St-Émilion, Puisseguin St-Émilion, Lussac St-Émilion, and St-Georges St-Émilion. These have the classic Merlot style, with a medium body and a spicy finish.

Pomerol has no classification – the wine speaks for itself. It is rich and lush with a tremendous fruit concentration.

RECOMMENDED PRODUCERS

▸ Château Haut Gravet
▸ Château l'Eglise-Clinet
▸ Château Pétrus
▸ Vieux-Château-Certan

LAND AND PRODUCTION

MERLOT COUNTRY This part of Bordeaux is much wetter than the Haut-Médoc, and suits Merlot far better than Cabernet Sauvignon. The chalky soil has a big influence on the wine, as it sponges up water in the winter and releases it during the hot summer. The soil in Pomerol is unique, with gravelly topsoil underlain by layers of clay and sand. Iron oxide in the subsoil gives the wine a special character.

CÔTES DE CASTILLON

C COLOUR Dark black cherry, with a ruby rim.

A AROMA Overripe dark fruits with dried forest herbs, leather, bitter chocolate.

T TASTE Dense and ripe, with well-integrated tannins; smooth, long finish.

Great value-for-money Bordeaux wines from a region that only gained AOC status in 1989! Charming and elegant when still young, these wines offer depth and complexity, and rarely disappoint. Côtes de Castillon is situated on the eastern side of St-Émilion. The soil is quite varied, and the main grape is Merlot. This wine is very flexible; serve it with leg of lamb and roast potatoes, or try it with any white meat – you will see what I mean.

RECOMMENDED PRODUCERS
▸ Château Brisson
▸ Château la Grande Maye

CÔTES DE BOURG

C COLOUR Medium-deep ruby red with a pink rim.

A AROMA Fruit-driven, subtle; red berries, flowers, minerals.

T TASTE Round, velvety, and gentle, with ripe tannins.

This is the most productive region in the Bordeaux Côtes (hillside) appellations, and it has recently improved in quality. Côtes de Bourg wines are made mainly from Merlot and are particularly fruity. You can get the most from this fruity texture with a dish of roast chicken and fresh tagliatelli – very satisfying.

CÔTES DE BOURG
Château Falfas

RECOMMENDED PRODUCERS
▸ Château Falfas
▸ Château Roc de Cambes

CÔTES DE BLAYE

C COLOUR Lively and bright ruby red, with medium intensity.

A AROMA Cherry and other red fruits, with hints of tobacco, spice, and vanilla.

T TASTE Elegant; round and fresh, with supple tannins and a medium length.

If there is one medium red Bordeaux that I would choose, it is definitely Premières Côtes de Blaye – a beautifully structured and elegant wine. Côtes de Blaye wines are mainly produced by co-operatives, but some producers are making challenging, high-quality wines that are great value. Blaye really specializes in white wine, despite the fact that these are excellent reds. Finding the whites may be easy, but it is also worth searching out these reds.

RECOMMENDED PRODUCERS
▸ Château les Bruelles
▸ Château Charron

FRONSAC / CANON-FRONSAC

C COLOUR Garnet red, with a ruby rim and good intensity.

A AROMA Delicate; fresh red fruits with notes of herbs, toast, and vanilla.

T TASTE Finesse and elegance, with suavity and concentration of flavours.

Fantastic wine! This is probably the best Bordeaux region on the right bank of the Gironde, after St-Émilion and Pomerol. If you like the delicacy of St-Émilion and the velvety character of Pomerol, then this wine is for you. It has complexity, intensity, and subtlety of flavour, but without too much weight. Canon-Fronsac is the finest part of the region, and now is the time to get some before the market catches on, and prices rocket.

RECOMMENDED PRODUCERS
▸ Château de la Dauphine
▸ Château Fontenil

MONDEUSE

C COLOUR A deep-coloured red with an opaque texture.

A AROMA Intense and complex; violets, pepper, spice, red fruits, liquorice.

T TASTE Well-structured and juicy; refreshing acidity; long, clean finish.

Mondeuse is a grape variety from Savoie in eastern France, usually sold as Vin de Savoie. For me, this wine is a real winner after a long day's skiing. I would place it somewhere between a Fleurie from Beaujolais, because of its freshness and weight, and a Crozes-Hermitage from the Rhône, because of its fruity and spicy aromas. I love this wine best with calves' liver and mash.

RECOMMENDED PRODUCERS
▸ Domaine Tardy
▸ Domaine Quénard

CORBIÈRES

C COLOUR Dark ruby to garnet, with a pinkish rim.

A AROMA Mediterranean sunshine feel; blackberry, cherry, spice, dried herbs.

T TASTE Complex flavours; rich and dense, but with a long, smooth finish.

You can now find some fantastic wines from Corbières, the leading appellation of Languedoc-Roussillon, and they are becoming more and more complex thanks to the use of Syrah. The best are big, smooth, full of character, and great value for money. These wines are for early drinking, and great with grilled chicken and green peas, or any meat or vegetarian dish that is not too strong.

CORBIERES *Château Auris*

RECOMMENDED PRODUCERS
▸ Château Auris
▸ Château la Voulte-Gasparets

FITOU

C COLOUR Intense ruby red with tile-red nuances.

A AROMA Red berries, pepper, plum, toast, chocolate, and vanilla.

T TASTE Rich and fleshy; balanced tannins and a full-flavoured finish.

Fitou is at the southern end of Languedoc, where it borders with Roussillon. It was the first appellation in Languedoc to be officially recognized, back in 1948, but for red wines only.

Despite the fact that Fitou has been well known in France for some time, it has only really begun to make an impact on the wider market in recent years. At one point, producers made the mistake of concentrating on volume at the expense of quality, but Fitou wines are now making a comeback and the region is rebuilding its reputation.

FITOU
Domaine Bertrand Bergé

Within the appellation, there are two very different areas. The dark, herbal wines from the mountains contrast with those from the coast, where the grapes benefit from the cooling sea breezes.

Production is controlled by four big co-operatives, and the quality of the wines has greatly improved over the past 15 years. Growers are now investing in oak barrels to make their product even more in tune with consumers' demands.

Carignan used to be the dominant grape, but new blends incorporating Grenache, Mourvèdre, and Syrah are making the wines better balanced, with more elegance and fruit character. I still think it has a long way to go, but Fitou is definitely worth trying, especially with a pasta dish, or charcuterie.

RECOMMENDED PRODUCERS
▸ Domaine Bertrand Bergé
▸ Domaine Lerys

ST-CHINIAN

C COLOUR Distinctive deep crimson, with ruby or orange nuances.

A AROMA Rich and powerful; black fruits, pepper, and notes of tar and leather.

T TASTE Dense, round, ripe tannins; good structure, long and complex.

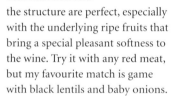

ST-CHINIAN *Château Viranel*

I have never really thought of St-Chinian as part of the Languedoc; it reminds me more of the style of the Rhône Valley. The concentration and the structure are perfect, especially with the underlying ripe fruits that bring a special pleasant softness to the wine. Try it with any red meat, but my favourite match is game with black lentils and baby onions.

RECOMMENDED PRODUCERS
▸ Château Viranel
▸ Domaine Canet-Valette

MINERVOIS

C COLOUR Intense garnet red, with ruby to orange nuances.

A AROMA Rich and complex; blackberry, quince, almond, and cinnamon.

T TASTE Dense and ample but with finesse; long fruity finish.

Minervois produces some great, well-structured wines, with excellent consistency and quality. This appellation lies to the north of Corbières and is named after the village of Minerve. It stretches from the slopes of the Cevennes to the valleys of the rivers Aude and Hérault. Viticulture goes back at least to Roman times, but the area only received AOC status in 1985.

Minervois is a wine full of character, very much like a light St-Chinian, but still very round and dense. Since gaining its AOC, the co-operatives and the small growers have rolled their sleeves up to improve the quality by investing in their wineries, reducing yields, and introducing better techniques of vinification. For example, it is now normal to deal separately with the different varieties of grape, rather than lump them all together. Carignan is now often fermented by carbonic maceration (like Beaujolais) in order to enhance its fruit aromas, and it is blended with more structured grapes such as Syrah and Mourvèdre. The wine might even have a short spell in oak barrels. The resulting wine is incredibly improved and great value. It is ready to drink very early, up to about five years.

FAUGÈRES *Domaine du Météore*

RECOMMENDED PRODUCERS
▸ La Livinière
▸ Château Fabas

FAUGÈRES

C COLOUR Really dark black cherry, with a deep ruby rim.

A AROMA Overripe dark fruits with dried forest herbs, leather, bitter chocolate.

T TASTE Dense; well-structured, with ripe flavours and well-integrated tannins.

Imagine a dry, hot, mountainous region, where the land is beautiful, wild, and hilly, and the wine is a blend of Carignan and Cinsault, backed up by weighty Mourvèdre and Syrah. Faugères is a very classy wine, with a well-defined personality, and the *terroir* lends a meaty character, with serious quantities of dark fruit. This is an underrated region, full of potential.

RECOMMENDED PRODUCERS
▸ Domaine du Météore
▸ Domaine Deshenrys

LAND AND PRODUCTION

VIN DE TABLE AND VIN DE PAYS
French wines labelled Vin de Table are basic, cheap table wines – the ones you will see in plastic bottles on the shelves of a French supermarket. They can be made from any variety of grape from anywhere in France or elsewhere; no information about region, vintage, or grape is given on the label, and quality is patchy! The appellation Vin de Pays (literally "country wine") was established in 1968 to recognise improvements in the quality of regional French wines, allowing producers to give more information on their bottles, such as the place of origin and the grape varieties used. The Vin de Pays appellations are in the third rank behind the top Appellation d'Origine Contrôlée (AOC) and the second Vin Délimité de Qualité Supérieure (VDQS). The Vin de Pays classification is growing

VIN DE PAYS D'OC *Les Perles de Méditerranée*

SHIRAZ CABERNET
La Baume

in importance, and now accounts for about 20 per cent of French wine production. The area covered by each appellation is variable – sometimes it is a large region (for example, Vin de Pays d'Oc covers four French *départements*) and sometimes it is a small zone. Many Vins de Pays are good for everyday drinking; look out for those made by enthusiastic producers from Australia and elsewhere the New World, who are using new technology to breathe fresh life into old established French vineyards, especially in the Languedoc-Roussillon region, southern France *(right)*. These can be real bargains!

ITALY

A warm climate is necessary to produce wines with balanced alcohol, smooth tannins, and refreshing acidity. Italy has one of the best natural environments for winemaking, and the country is home to some classic styles. However, of all the many grape varieties in the country, only a few are either light or emphatically full-bodied, so the rest fall into the ripe, smooth, "medium" category.

FOR THE CELLAR *Chianti Classico is made mainly from the Tuscan grape variety Sangiovese, and has great potential for ageing.*

CHIANTI

C COLOUR Lively, brilliant ruby red, tending to garnet with ageing.

A AROMA Violet, cherry, dark berries, plum, and spice, especially cloves.

T TASTE Medium-bodied; tannic when young, but soft and velvety after ageing.

In the traditional, romantic image of Chianti, it was the basket-bottle wine, standing on a red checked tablecloth next to a candle. Standard Chianti is still very popular but has lost its profile as a wine of quality. Some very special producers still make superbly concentrated and well-balanced Chianti, but the finest are produced in the *classico* zone, the area between Siena and Florence, and only Chianti Classico is generally worth looking at seriously.

Sangiovese is the key grape in the blend, giving brilliant, vivacious fruit that can be aggressive. In *classico* wines the fruit flavours combine with oak ageing to give excellent complexity and personality. Of the seven other, and smaller, Chianti zones, I would recommend Rufina as an alternative to Classico, and probably better value.

A step up from Chianti Classico is the fantastic Chianti Classico Riserva, which has slightly more alcohol than regular Chianti Classico and longer ageing before it is released. Single-vineyard Chiantis are usually of a higher quality and are often aged as *riservas*.

Many people, including me, have spent many a happy hour drinking Chianti with spaghetti, pizza, and the usual international Italian dishes. But you can match it with more: it is also ideal with fish, vegetables, pepperoni, aubergine, and most well-seasoned foods, and Chianti's acidity also matches up well with acidic foods like tomatoes.

RECOMMENDED PRODUCERS

▸ Castello di Fonterutoli
▸ Antinori
▸ Ricasoli (Castello di Brolio)
▸ Marchesi di Frescobaldi

CHIANTI
Antinori

VINO NOBILE DI MONTEPULCIANO

C COLOUR Distinctive deep ruby-red with hints of purple.

A AROMA Intense cherry, minerals, spice, wood, earth, and game.

T TASTE Rich and full, but smooth; firm tannins and good acidity.

This is a wine that has always lived in the shade of its two famous neighbours, Chianti and Brunello di Montalcino. All three are made from the same key grape variety – Sangiovese – but they have very different styles. Vino Nobile sits half way between Chianti and Brunello; it is fuller than Chianti, with a fruitier, sweeter feel, because of the region's sandy soil and warmer climate.

Montepulciano is a small town in the hills of Tuscany, near Siena, and the true Vino Nobile must originate

VINO NOBILE DI MONTEPULCIANO
Poliziano

there. The wines fall into three broad categories – Rosso, Vino Nobile, and Vino Nobile Riserva. The Rosso, a lighter wine, is classified as a DOC, and the other two as DOCG. The medium-bodied, well-structured Vino Nobile ages quite well thanks to its acidity and tannins. The Riserva is a little higher in alcohol, and is aged for longer before it is sold.

Despite being less popular than its two rivals, Vino Nobile was one of the first wines to be granted the coveted DOCG. It is still very popular in Italy, and you will see why if you try it with a pasta dish, lasagne, or a pepperoni pizza. Not too many Italians know this, but this wine also goes perfectly with an Irish stew.

RECOMMENDED PRODUCERS
▸ Poliziano
▸ Avignonesi
▸ Contucci

ALEATICO

C COLOUR Rich, deep, and intense vermilion, with a ruby rim.

A AROMA Very pronounced and refined; sweet spice, black fruits, and violets.

T TASTE Rich, strong, velvety; medium acidity, balanced tannins, good length.

I love the flowery aromas of this rare grape, and I am really sad that it is so little known. Seek out and try Aleatico wines from Tuscany – they are the finest – but it is also produced in Liguria and Latium, northwest of Rome. I really enjoy this wine as a refreshing change, particularly over a light lunch of cured meats or even at a barbecue.

CANNONAU
Argiolas

RECOMMENDED PRODUCERS
▸ Francesco Candido
▸ Felice Botta

CANNONAU

C COLOUR Quite a dense ruby red, with a bright pink rim.

A AROMA Crushed fresh cranberries; elegant, smoky, peppery.

T TASTE Round, fleshy, fruity; medium acidity, integrated tannins, long finish.

I am a great believer in the ability of Sardegna (Sardinia) to produce quality wine. Cannonau is its best-known red grape, generally accepted to be the same variety as the Grenache of France. The sea breezes and the warm temperature create ideal growing conditions, and older bush vines allow the berries to ripen to the full. Try it with a rabbit casserole or chicken.

RECOMMENDED PRODUCERS
▸ Argiolas
▸ Sella & Mosca

TORGIANO

C COLOUR Bright ruby red to garnet, with good intensity.

A AROMA Complex; black cherry, almond, spice, "animal", and oak.

T TASTE Rich and round; refreshing acidity, excellent balance, long finish.

This is a fantastic wine, like a well-structured Dolcetto (*see p85*). Only a short time ago a wine supplier asked me to test a bottle of Torgiano. I loved it, but I had to ask "how much?" I was amazed, not only at the quality, but at the unbelievably good value. I am now convinced that the Umbria region can produce top-quality wines – I just hope the prices will stay low!

Torgiano, named after the castle in its centre – Torre di Giano – is a small town in the central Italian region of Umbria, near Perugia, and was the

TORGIANO *Lungarotti*

first Umbrian wine to receive its DOC, in 1968. The Riserva has been a DOCG since 1990. Along with its growing reputation, Torgiano wine has benefited from the influence of the dominant producer, Dr Lungarotti, who has maintained and developed the quality of the wines, and experimented with new blends.

This is my favourite Umbrian red so far, and a real rival to Chianti. The same grape – Sangiovese – has come into its own to produce a wine that offers density and delicacy, with a rich and smooth finish. Torgiano's potential for ageing makes it even more worth buying and keeping for around four or five years. Great with lamb meatballs and penne, or similar spicy and savoury pasta dishes.

RECOMMENDED PRODUCERS
▸ G Lungarotti
▸ Consorzio Vitivinicola Perugia

NERO D'AVOLA

C COLOUR Deep black-cherry, with a purple rim.

A AROMA Complex; ripe black fruits, plum, chocolate, and spice.

T TASTE Rich and round, with lemony acidity and good tannins.

This highly respected grape (also called Calabrese) is from Sicilia (Sicily), where it grows superbly and shows the island's quality potential. It is also a great asset in blending thanks to its ability to age and its firm structure. Together with Merlot it makes a very fine, elegant, and complex wine. It is fabulous with roast beef or juicy loin of lamb with dried herbs.

NERO D'AVOLA
Santa Anastasia

RECOMMENDED PRODUCERS
▸ Santa Anastasia
▸ Gulfi Vineyards

ROSSESE

C COLOUR Ruby, with purple or dark orange reflections; garnet with age.

A AROMA Fragrant, fruity, and slightly spicy; intense rose when aged.

T TASTE Dry and tasty, with a round, smooth structure; bitter almond finish.

If you like fragrant and delicately flavoured wines, then this is one to try – but be sure to search out a good producer. Rossese di Dolceacqua, from a small DOC zone in Liguria, is very appealing thanks to its elegant aromas of red berries, and is full of character. The wine is at its best in the first three years, although a particularly good vintage can improve when aged. It is superb with rich, full-tasting dishes such as rabbit with herbs, stuffed pigeon, or guinea fowl.

RECOMMENDED PRODUCERS
▸ Cane
▸ Lupi

TEROLDEGO ROTALIANO

C COLOUR Elegant, deep ruby-red, with a pinkish rim.

A AROMA Charming; juicy berries, violets, dried fruits, tar.

T TASTE Flattering; soft ripe fruits, low tannins, balanced.

The perfect summer wine! Teroldego grapes have found their ideal site on the Rotaliano plain in the north of Trentino, where they produce fruity, elegant, and easy-drinking wines similar to Fleurie from Beaujolais. Teroldego is not one to cellar: drink it, slightly chilled, with a home-made lasagne.

TEROLDEGO ROTALIANO
Mezzacorona

RECOMMENDED PRODUCERS
▸ Mezzacorona
▸ Conti Martini

SANTA MADDALENA

C COLOUR Deep ruby, with tile red developing over time.

A AROMA Fresh cherry and blackcurrant; smoke, almond, and walnut.

T TASTE Fleshy, round, and well-balanced, with a medium, slightly bitter finish.

This is the most famous wine from the Alto Adige, in the foothills of the Alps. It is made from a local variety, Schiava, blended with other grapes. The freezing winters and boiling hot summers have the effect of heightening the flavours and aromas of the wine, which is greatly appreciated in Italy, Austria, and Germany – but everyone should share in the pleasure! Keep it for less than three years, and enjoy it with cured meats and charcuterie.

RECOMMENDED PRODUCERS
▸ Kettmeir
▸ Roner

ROSSO CONERO / ROSSO PICENO

C COLOUR Deep, dark ruby red, with reddish-orange tints.

A AROMA Dried herbs, plum, liquorice, black cherry, spice.

T TASTE Harmonious, ripe, and velvet-smooth.

From the Marches region in eastern Italy, these wines have real potential. The main difference between them is the grapes used; Piceno is mostly Sangiovese, like Chianti, and is the fuller wine; Conero is mainly Montepulciano. Their refreshing style cuts through a creamy sauce such as carbonara.

ROSSO CONERO
Monte Schiavo

RECOMMENDED PRODUCERS
▸ Monte Schiavo
▸ Cocci Grifoni

LAGO DI CALDARO

C COLOUR Typically an elegant ruby red to garnet.

A AROMA Fresh and fruity, with hints of almond.

T TASTE Well-balanced fruit and acidity; medium texture and good depth.

This is another star from the Alto Adige region. The wine is made mainly from Schiava (also called Vernatsch) grapes, and quality is greatly increased by the favourable microclimate around the lake after which it is named. Lago di Caldaro is an excellent red wine, despite a very low profile around the world, and it really is a must for you to try. If you are able to find a bottle – ideally two or three years old – then serve it with loin of pork or chicken chasseur.

RECOMMENDED PRODUCERS
▸ Gaierhof
▸ Hofstatter

AUSTRIA

Hardly any Austrian red wines are exported but they are often excellent, with the character of a robust Beaujolais or Burgundy.

AUSTRIAN MEDIUM REDS

C COLOUR Garnet for Blaufränkisch; a deeper, ruby red for Zweigelt.

A AROMA Intense wild berries, spice, violets in both wines.

T TASTE Both have excellent balance, though Zweigelt is less acidic.

Look out for two interesting reds from Austria – Blaufränkisch and Zweigelt. Blaufränkisch is Austria's most planted variety and makes wines like a denser *cru* Beaujolais, characterized by high acidity and intense fruit flavours. It is often gently oaked, and makes a perfect match for white meats or roast lamb.

ZWEIGELT *Lenz Moser*

This is one of those grapes that could make a revolution – soon!

I am also a big fan of Zweigelt, even if its greatest potential has yet to be realized. It is actually a cross between Blaufränkisch, which adds flesh and flavour, and St-Laurent, which provides structure. Zweigelt has a subtle and elegant Pinot Noir style, but with more body and weight. Try it with a summer barbecue, or a plate of charcuterie, or even chicken and chips.

RECOMMENDED PRODUCERS
▸ Lenz Moser
▸ Umathum
▸ Gipsberg

GERMANY

Like the Austrians, German consumers drink most of their own country's red wine output, which means that exports are limited. Germany mostly produces light reds, but there are also some very interesting medium varieties, full of fruit and character.

DORNFELDER

C COLOUR Very intense dark garnet, with a ruby rim.

A AROMA Attractive red fruits and sweet forest fruits.

T TASTE Very fruity; soft, velvety finish with a slight hint of tannins.

Red wines make up a small minority of German wines, and a dark, rather full-flavoured red is even more unusual. Dornfelder produces a very deeply coloured wine with great intensity of aromas and a harmonious, well-structured palate. Not only will the best bottles bring more pleasure than most Spätburgunders, but Dornfelder is being planted more and more. It even has the ability to cope with oak ageing, which adds further complexity to its flavours. Give it a few more years, and it will bear comparison to Merlot and the sweeter Cabernets.

Dornfelder is also a partner for a wide range of foods. It is the ideal companion to borscht and also goes well with medium-rare roast beef, barbecued ribs, lasagne, and meatballs. Roquefort is one of the best cheese matches. I would recommend that it is served slightly chilled, particularly in the summer.

RECOMMENDED PRODUCERS
▸ Meckenhem
▸ Castel Vollmer
▸ Bürklin-Wolf

SPAIN

Spain's most important grape is Tempranillo, which forms the basis of the great Riojas. It is also used in the Navarra region, where it is blended with other varieties to make a smooth wine that draws inspiration from French styles. The use of oak-ageing tends to make Spanish wine soft, spicy, and rich, but in *crianzas*, which are aged for only a short time, fruit flavours come to the fore.

RIOJA

C COLOUR Garnet with a ruby to terra-cotta rim after ageing; deep intensity.

A AROMA Dried plum, raisins, figs, dark cherry, tobacco, spice, vanilla, leather.

T TASTE Rich, round, fresh, fruit-driven, classy; soft tannins; very good length.

When people think of red wine and Spain, they think of Rioja, a name known throughout the world. The name is derived from the Rio Oja, a tributary of the larger Ebro, which flows from northern Spain to the Mediterranean. Rioja is made mainly from Tempranillo (which means "early ripening"), which is native to Spain, and produces deeply coloured, richly flavoured wines with a great potential for ageing. These wines have complex, delicate aromas, and over time they develop leathery, spicy characters.

Crianza, *reserva*, and *gran reserva* wines are aged first in oak barrels, then in bottles before being sold. There are many different producers, but most use American oak barrels to mature the wine, which introduces vanilla and butter aromas. Wines labelled *joven* (young) have little or no oak ageing.

The *crianzas*, having spent a year in the barrel and another in the bottle, offer great complexity but are still dominated by the fruit character, while the *reservas* offer more vanilla, spice, and leathery notes due to an extra year in American oak. The *gran reservas* are the finest and greatest wines, but they are still good value. They are produced only in the best years and

RIOJA
Conde de Valdemar

spend at least two years in the barrel and three more in the bottle. As a result, they have an intense bouquet and the complexity of a good red Burgundy combined with the depth of one of the great wines from Piemonte made with Nebbiolo grapes *(see p114)*.

You might see on the labels some different sub-regions of Rioja. There are three, divided by terrain and climate – Rioja Alta, Rioja Alavesa, and Rioja Baja.

Rioja Alta, sometimes called the Bordeaux of Spain, makes big, assertive wines that need time to soften. When mature, these are the finest and most delicate wines of Rioja. Rioja Alavesa accounts for a small part of the total Rioja vineyard area and makes high-quality, soft, rich, fruity wines. Both the Alta and the Alavesa regions have climates in which the hot, Mediterranean weather is moderated by cooler breezes from the Atlantic Ocean, and therefore make better quality wines. The Rioja Baja region does not have a cooling breeze, and the flat valley floor is too fertile for good-quality grapes. The result is a full-bodied, but more ordinary wine.

Rioja wines are very versatile. I often drink them, not only with Spanish food, but with light meats, such as lamb or veal. The wines of Rioja Baja are less delicate, and are more suited to roasts and red meats.

RECOMMENDED PRODUCERS
▸ Conde de Valdemar
▸ Marques de Griñon
▸ Marques de Murrieta
▸ Artadi

FINE BLEND
Tempranillo may be blended with Garnacha and Graciano grapes to make Rioja.

NAVARRA

C **COLOUR** Black cherry with a ruby to brick-red rim.

A **AROMA** Jammy blackberry, sweet spice, coffee, undergrowth, vanilla, almond.

T **TASTE** Smooth, fleshy, pleasant, good acidity; rounded by American oak.

Navarra (or Navarre in English) is a large region located in the north of Spain, neighbouring Rioja. Most of the wine is red, with some rosé and white. The region has suffered from being in the shadow of the world-famous Rioja wines but is now forging its own identity with modern styles that are neither Rioja clones nor New World copies.

Navarra has worked hard to overcome its past mistakes. When the phylloxera louse devastated the vineyards of Bordeaux in the late 1800s, Navarra thought it would

NAVARRA
Señorío de Sarría

benefit, as Spain was much less affected, but the resulting massive over-production of cheap and inferior wine exported to Bordeaux really damaged the reputation of Navarra wines – a case of a double-edged sword! The region has been trying to recover ever since, and has made some progress in recent years, as quality has improved.

There are five different growing districts with varied terrain and climatic differences within the region – Tierra de Estella, Valdizarbe, Baja Montaña, and the finest two regions, Ribera Baja and Ribera Alta.

Traditionally, Navarra wines have been made from Garnacha grapes blended with Tempranillo and other varieties to produce an inferior version of Rioja, but new techniques, and the blending of Garnacha and Tempranillo with Cabernet Sauvignon and Merlot, have

LAND AND PRODUCTION

SHIFTING INFLUENCES The climate in Navarra ranges from cool and mountainous in the north, where the Pyrenees dominate the horizon, to areas in the west where the Atlantic

Ocean has a moderating influence. The warm Ribera Baja region, in the south, is particularly suitable for Garnacha, and produces wines to rival those from the Rhône Valley.

moved the style of Navarra wines towards that of Bordeaux, rather than the New World. In white wine, Navarra nods to Burgundy, with fine barrel-fermented Chardonnays.

Navarra red wines are worth a try if you want an alternative to both Rioja and Bordeaux. They are smooth and not too overpowering, making them an excellent match for

light cooked meats such as lamb, or for cold meats and vegetables. If you find a good one, you have an experience that is part French, part Spanish, and quite unusual!

RECOMMENDED PRODUCERS
▸ Señorío de Sarría
▸ Bodegas Ochoa
▸ Palacios de la Vega

PORTUGAL

Portuguese producers have really come on in the past five years, and grapes like Touriga Nacional often make excellent wines. If you take a little time to select the best, your care will be amply rewarded.

DOURO

C **COLOUR** Dark and inky, with a purple to ruby rim; good intensity.

A **AROMA** Complex, rich; tar, liquorice, dark chocolate, and black fruits.

T **TASTE** Big, ripe, and smooth; refreshing acidity and a very long, clean finish.

This can still be called an up-and-coming wine region for unfortified table wines, although it has long been famous as the source of port. The style is quite variable, but if you can find the best producers, there are some amazing wines.

As port has become rather less fashionable and has declined in importance in the past few years,

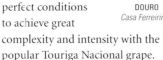

DOURO
Casa Ferreirinha

these excellent wines have begun to fill the gap for producers and wine-lovers alike. The coolest parts of the region have the perfect conditions to achieve great complexity and intensity with the popular Touriga Nacional grape.

Look out for these wines. They age well, for up to about five years, and are fairly well priced, and with a meal like roast rack of lamb they really are hard to beat.

RECOMMENDED PRODUCERS
▸ Casa Ferreirinha
▸ Ramos Pinto
▸ Quinta de la Rosa

GREECE

Greece's wine output is dominated by white varieties, but reds are gradually becoming more important. New technology and better quality control have helped this beautiful part of the world make wines to match. The Rapsani region produces some of the best.

RAPSANI

C **COLOUR** Bright deep ruby with pink or orange tints.

A **AROMA** Elegant and subtle, with sweet spice and dried fruits.

T **TASTE** Round and velvety; juicy, with refreshing acidity and good tannins.

Rapsani is a famous wine in Greece, and is mainly drunk locally. Its heart is on the east coast of Greece, on the foothills of Mount Olympus, where the microclimate is particularly well suited to red wine. According to myth, this is the original source of nectar, the divine drink of the ancient gods of Olympus. The key grape variety is

Xynomavro (see also p118), which here makes a round wine with ripe black fruits and good, mellow tannins. It is aged in oak casks then continues for at least six more months in the bottle; this helps to build the wine's character, and gives it that important little hint of stimulating spice. I love to drink this wine with a moussaka or even a herby, spicy, Greek mutton dish.

RAPSANI
Evangelos Tsantalis

RECOMMENDED PRODUCERS
▸ Evangelos Tsantalis
▸ Biblia Chora
▸ Ktima Mercouri

CHILE

Chile has become more and more important as a wine producer, and certain grapes grow particularly well there. The Chileans have made the "lost" Carmenère variety their own, while its cousin, Merlot, has also been used to excellent effect.

CARMENÈRE

C COLOUR Rich and distinctive dark cherry or garnet, with a ruby rim.

A AROMA Intense figs, plum, cherry, black fruits, sweet spice, and chocolate.

T TASTE Round, harmonious, beautifully structured, with bags of flavour.

At the moment, I just cannot get enough of this wine. This is a new discovery, which the Chileans have adopted as their flagship, and they see it developing to fill the same position as Zinfandel in California, Tempranillo in Spain, Pinotage in South Africa, Shiraz in Australia, and Sangiovese in Italy, giving Chile the opportunity to present to the world its own grape variety, and one of true individual character. Currently, the wines are also excellent value for money.

I just love the story of this grape. Carmenère is not new, but was widely cultivated in Bordeaux in the 18th century. It was transplanted from France to Chile in the late 19th century by French winemakers who were hired by wealthy landowners, and it flourished in South America when it was only a fading memory in Europe.

However, the name and special character of the grape disappeared even in Chile, by being confused with Merlot. It was only in the 1990s that it was discovered that Chile's rich "Merlot" wines were actually being made from Carmenère. Hence it is now widely known as "the lost grape of Bordeaux".

Overall, Carmenère has more fruit than Cabernet, and is as approachable and smooth as Merlot, and just as consistent. This is the kind of wine I often select if I am undecided about what to drink – you must try this wine if you have not already done so. It is pleasant and delicate with appealing fruitiness, but not too jammy or syrupy. Drink it if you are eating duck breast or venison; it is also really great with smoked mackerel.

CARMENÈRE
Santa Rita

RECOMMENDED PRODUCERS
▸ Santa Rita
▸ Undurraga
▸ Canata

MERLOT

C COLOUR Profound with good intensity; rich black cherry.

A AROMA Delicate and powerful; ripe black fruits, cherry, spice, and prune.

T TASTE Rich, round, and smooth; great balance, harmonious tannins, clean finish.

Chilean Merlot has lost some of its impact on the world of wine due to the rise of Carmenère, although its quality is still consistent and can be exceptional. It is at its best in Maipo Valley and Maule Valley. Here Merlot has a richer, denser character, and is less openly fruity than Australian wine – closer to the style of St-Émilion (see p94). I particularly enjoy these good-value wines over lunch with a grilled steak and salad, or even on their own, as they are not overpowering on the palate.

RECOMMENDED PRODUCERS
▸ Viña Alamosa
▸ Casa Lapostolle

AUSTRALIA

Medium red wines, while not as popular as the fuller Shiraz, are gaining ground in Australia. Merlot is the most important, but Italian varieties like Sangiovese have also been grown successfully in recent years.

MERLOT

C COLOUR Deep garnet, with a ruby rim and good intensity.

A AROMA Mulberry, plum, blackberry; hints of spicy oak and cigar box.

T TASTE Smooth, velvety, concentrated; refreshing, with charm and delicacy.

In Australia, Merlot is mainly used in blends with Cabernet Sauvignon or Shiraz, but in recent years single-variety Merlot has taken off. Compared to Californian Merlot (see opposite), the Australian version tends to be bigger, with soft chunky fruit to the fore, especially in hotter areas such as the Barossa Valley. Beyond the typical berry and plum aromas, the best wines have a more complex range of scents, including mint, floral notes of violet and lavender, pepper, and other spices. Australian Merlots are very well structured, very approachable and easy to drink. They are also perfectly balanced, with great length. I recommend you try them with grilled meats or with any type of meat stew or casserole.

MERLOT
Yalumba

RECOMMENDED PRODUCERS
▸ Yalumba
▸ Fermoy Estate
▸ Evans & Tate

NEW ZEALAND

New Zealand has a cool climate, but outstanding medium reds are produced in the country's warmer regions, mainly from Merlot grapes. These high-quality wines are made with the latest technology, but their sophistication can come with a high price tag.

MERLOT

C COLOUR Elegant and intense dark garnet with a ruby rim.

A AROMA Big and juicy; forest fruits, ripe plum, toffee, leather, earth, and spice.

T TASTE Smooth, complex; exceptional balance; full flavours; lingering finish.

For me, North Island's Hawke's Bay is the capital of New Zealand Merlot. Merlot is a recent phenomenon in New Zealand, and the region has made great strides in only the past ten years. Hawke's Bay has a unique warm and sunny climate, making it the driest region in the country. This allows the grape to grow and ripen very slowly, which produces many more flavours in the wine without detracting from the lively and juicy feel that is typical of Merlot.

Most of the best New Zealand Merlots are blended with other grapes, particularly Cabernet Sauvignon, where the Merlot is used to soften the intense Cabernet, and provides a particularly smooth feel to the wine. These wines have not yet made their way fully on to the world market, but they are showing great potential. They go well with light or medium meats and cheese – or you can drink them on their own.

RECOMMENDED PRODUCERS
▸ Te Awa Farm Winery
▸ Esk Valley
▸ Morton Estate

USA

California produces some of the finest New World Merlots and the grape is currently enjoying great popularity there. Further north, in Washington State, wine made from the Lemberger grape—a revival of an old Austrian variety called Blaufränkisch—is creating a stir.

CALIFORNIA MERLOT

C COLOUR Distinctive and intense dark garnet with a ruby rim.

A AROMA Juicy black forest fruits, ripe plum, toffee, leather, earth, and spice.

T TASTE Smooth, with great balance, full flavours, and a lingering finish.

To my mind, this is one of the finest Merlots from the New World. Sadly, it is still in the shadow of the huge status given to Cabernet Sauvignon in California. Merlot was brought to California in the 1860s, but it was only in the 1970s that winegrowers in Sonoma Valley started planting it, trying to make wine that was "soft and fluffy", instead of harsh and tannic. For too long, Merlot has been seen as simply great fun to drink, often by the glass, any day, any time, and just too easy to enjoy for it to matter very much. But now Merlot is making a determined comeback, offering complexity, richness, and intense fruitiness, while keeping its smooth personality.

Look out for these Merlots, especially if you are after an affordable St-Émilion style. The best come from Sonoma, but it is also produced in Napa Valley and Santa Ynez Valley. I really enjoy this wine with côte de boeuf, or lamb shank with garlic and mashed potatoes – real class!

CALIFORNIA MERLOT
Newton

RECOMMENDED PRODUCERS

▸ Newton
▸ Bogle Winery
▸ Stags' Leap

WASHINGTON LEMBERGER

C COLOUR Ranges from light to dark red; lighter wines are normally sweeter.

A AROMA Black cherry and just a hint of spiciness and chocolate.

T TASTE Light to medium in body, and very lively and versatile.

Lemberger is a grape variety that I fell in love with after the very first sip. I am not the only one; Lemberger has caught the interest of many people, especially winemakers, as it is a very successful grape in cool climates. This is because it has a natural low acidity, and therefore ripens well in difficult conditions. Grapes of this kind make wine with finely balanced tannins and wonderfully complex fruit flavours.

So far, Washington State is one of the few places in the world where the Lemberger grape is established. It made its appearance only about 30 years ago, but it is actually the same variety as an older, long-established Austrian grape, Blaufränkisch (*see p99*), also known as Kékfrankos in Hungary. However, I expect it to crop up in many other places soon.

This is a top-quality wine, and one of my personal favourites, with its lovely, subtle spicing on top of a core of cherry fruit. Unfortunately, it is not produced in great quantities so it can be a little hard to find, but it is worth looking out for and trying when you get the chance.

If you find some of this wine, do not keep it for too long because its low acidity will prevent it from ageing. Rather, enjoy its youthful charm and complex flavours over a plate of cheese or charcuterie, and you will also fall in love with it.

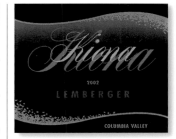

WASHINGTON LEMBERGER *Kiona Vineyards*

RECOMMENDED PRODUCERS

▸ Kiona Vineyards
▸ Thurston Wolfe
▸ Latah Creek

FERTILE DESERT *Plentiful irrigation means vines can flourish where only the sagebrush would normally grow in the arid landscape of Washington State.*

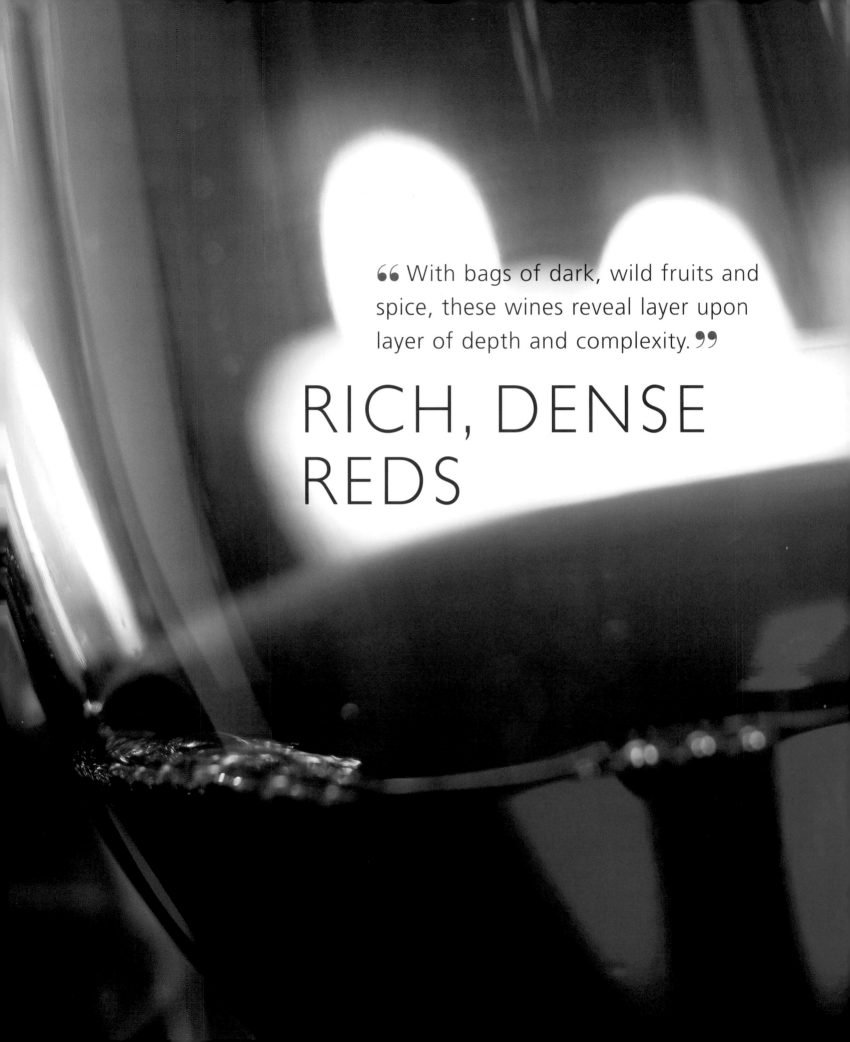

" With bags of dark, wild fruits and spice, these wines reveal layer upon layer of depth and complexity. "

RICH, DENSE REDS

INTRODUCING RICH, DENSE REDS

Big wines with big names, the rich, dense reds are filled with the aromas of forest fruits and feel like liquid velvet on the palate. They are powerful, complex, sophisticated wines, and perfect to enjoy with warming food on cold, winter evenings.

DRINKING AND SERVING

DRINK PROFILE When you swirl a rich, dense red, the wine should leave a gloss on the inside of the glass. Its "legs" (or viscosity) should be thicker than any other style of red. These are big, full wines.

C COLOUR These wines should be a deep, inky, black cherry colour, with nuances of purple for younger versions and red tiles for older – the warmer tones brought out by bottle-ageing.

A AROMA The aroma of these wines should be intense and "jammy", with liquorice, figs, prunes, coffee, chocolate, tobacco (and cigar box), spice, leather, and notes of vanilla.

T TASTE The harmony of alcohol and acidity is key in the taste of these wines. Tannins should balance the structure of complex flavours, and the finish should be fresh and very long.

BUYING AND STORING The best of these wines will be expensive as they will have spent around 18 to 24 months ageing in oak barrels – adding to the cost of caring for the wine before bottling. Some can also be bottle-aged for many years, to bring out their tannins and deep colour.

SERVING SUGGESTIONS Serve these wines at room temperature – they will feel alcoholic if too warm, and overly tannic if too cold. Decant the wine – the air will release the complex aromas, and any sediment will stay in the bottle.

FOOD COMPANIONS These wines suit roast meat, or heavy vegetarian main courses with fleshy vegetables, such as aubergine. Gattinara or Barbaresco match well with veal and game; Shiraz or Zinfandel with spicy foods.

BLACKCURRANTS *Forest fruits fill the nose of rich reds.*

Rich, dense reds are typically made from grapes with small berries and thick skins – the classic example being the grapes of Cabernet Sauvignon. Although these grapes give lower yields of juice, they are rich in colour and also in tannin (which gives the wine structure and also acts as a preservative, enabling the wine to age well). The grape varieties of rich, dense reds need warm climates to develop to their full potential, but not so hot that the grapes are scorched by the sun. This is why they are most successful in the more southerly parts of Europe and in the New World. They must ripen fully before they are harvested, otherwise the wine will be acerbic and harsh. Wherever the grapes are grown, good soil drainage is key to producing superior fruit for full-bodied reds. When the soil is well drained, the vine's roots have to grow downward in order to find water deep underground. As they do so they pick up minerals and trace elements, which then emerge as rich tastes in the grapes themselves. If the soil is soggy, the vines are said to have "damp feet", and the roots grow outward, picking up fewer flavours.

NEW- AND OLD-WORLD AGEING

Warmer climates (such as those in the New World) will give more fruit and "jammy" qualities in the wine, and generally this style benefits less from bottle-ageing. Many New World wines are aged in new oak barrels before bottling. This gives the wines softer, buttery flavours, such as vanilla, which allows producers to release them onto the market quickly, and consumers to drink the wine quite young without missing out on the complexity of its flavours. In the Old World, particularly in the Bordeaux and Rhône wines of France and those of Piemonte (Piedmont) in Italy, the deep, complex, dry flavours often take years to reach their peak. As the wine ages the tannins soften, becoming more integrated into the body of the wine. Ultimately, the wine achieves a perfect balance of ripe tannin, fresh acidity, and rich fruit.

ROAST BEEF *Roast meat is just perfect with Châteauneuf-du-Pape or a New World Shiraz.*

GRAPE VARIETIES

The king of the rich, dense reds is Cabernet Sauvignon, the variety of the great Bordeaux Médoc wines and also of some of the best red wines from California and Australia. Another powerful variety is Syrah (or Shiraz), from the Rhône Valley, which creates elegant, complex wines, not only in the Rhône, but notably in Australia and California, too. Nebbiolo, key to the great Italian reds of Barolo and Barbaresco, is another classic; and there are many other varieties making superb wines – Mourvèdre, which makes Bandol and Châteauneuf-du-Pape, being just one.

GRAPE	BEST REGIONAL EXAMPLES	COMMENTS
CABERNET SAUVIGNON	Very widespread. France. USA. Chile. South Africa. Australia.	The tiny black berries of this variety produce wines with high colour, tannin, acidity, alcohol, and fruit. The finest examples have power and elegance and benefit from oak ageing. This is a key variety for the great wines of Bordeaux.
SHIRAZ	Australia: Barossa and Hunter Valley. South Africa: Stellenbosch.	The Australian and South African name for Syrah *(below)*. This grape makes world class wines with a rich and opulent character that are typically warming and "jammy".
SYRAH	France: Languedoc-Roussillon, Rhône, Provence. Switzerland. Italy. USA: California.	This is one of the finest red grapes in the world, and its tiny berries give wines with firm tannins and acidity, balanced alcohol, and good ageing characteristics.
GRENACHE	France: Rhône, Provence, Languedoc-Roussillon. Spain. Australia.	One of the most widely planted of all varieties, Grenache makes some real blockbuster wines, with lots of flavour and good ageing potential. It is known as Garnacha in Spain.
NEBBIOLO	Italy: Piemonte. Argentina. California.	Grown only in small quantities, this grape produces wine with high acidity, balanced alcohol, high tannins, and lots of fruit. It needs time in the bottle to develop its superb bouquet.
BRUNELLO	Italy: Tuscany.	These grapes make a powerful wine – well structured, with good colour, acidity, and balanced alcohol.
MOURVÈDRE	France: Rhone, Provence, Languedoc-Roussillon. Spain. USA: California.	This variety makes big, powerful, tannic wines, with bags of black fruits and sweet spices. It is often used as a blend.
MALBEC	France: Cahors. Argentina.	This grape makes full-bodied, intense, dark-coloured, and long-lived wines. It has been a great success in Argentina.
ZINFANDEL	USA: California.	A full-flavoured grape making plummy and peppery wine with high alcohol and long ageing potential. A top class grape.
TANNAT	France: Madiran. Uruguay. Argentina.	A "monster" grape, but very elegant. Produces big, intense, rich wines with high level of tannins, that age well in wood.
TOURIGA NACIONAL	Portugal.	Tiny black berries make a deep coloured wine, full of flavours and high tannins, with a balancing acidity. Ages very well.
AGIORGITIKO	Greece.	Also known as Nemea. The wine has dark fruit aromas, but sometimes lacks acidity; ages well.
CARIGNAN	Spain. Italy. France.	This grape produces wines that are high in tannin, acid, and alcohol, but needs time to develop its character.
AGLIANICO	Italy: Campania, Basilicata. Greece.	Makes the great full-bodied and intense wines Taurasi and Aglianico del Vulture from the south of Italy.

FRANCE

Rich, dense reds from France rank among the great wines of the world, with character, history, and prestige that are second to none. They typically have great depth and the ability to be aged for many years – so a dusty bottle often hides a sublime wine.

PAUILLAC

C COLOUR The classic Bordeaux colouring of deep garnet with a ruby rim.

A AROMA Complex; delicate black fruits, chocolate, leather, tar, tobacco.

T TASTE Dense, concentrated, round, and balanced, with unforgettable length.

I call Pauillac the "velvet heart" of the Médoc – and of all Bordeaux. This village has had a unique part to play in the development of the Haut-Médoc region. It is a small port on the Gironde River, and was once very important in the process of loading the wine barrels onto the boats ready for export, so it played a key role in establishing the name of Bordeaux wines around the world.

This wine has always been my favourite style of all the Médoc wines! These are rich, intense, complex wines, full of character and concentration, and a superb finesse and elegance. Pauillac includes three of the four Médoc First Growths (*premiers crus*; *see opposite*): Château Latour, Château Lafite-Rothschild, and Château Mouton-Rothschild.

Overall, there are 18 classified châteaux in the Pauillac appellation, including the celebrated Château Pichon-Longueville-Comtesse de Lalande and Château Lynch-Bages.

These wines are classic Cabernet Sauvignon – dark, opaque, garnet-red, with a profound depth of colour. The aromas are incredibly intense, and become even more complex and varied with ageing. These wines are full, robust, and powerful, with a perfect balance of elegance, smoothness, and structure. They soften very gradually over the years; this can take an average of 15 years – and much longer for the very greatest wines.

Like other Bordeaux wines, Pauillacs are perfect partners for classic French dishes such as roast meats and game. Along with those of St-Estèphe, these are the most robust Bordeaux wines, but Pauillacs are more fleshy, rounder, and richer. Truly the heart of Bordeaux!

PAUILLAC
Château Lynch-Bages

RECOMMENDED PRODUCERS
▸ Château Lynch-Bages
▸ Château d'Armailhac
▸ Château Batailley
▸ Château Clerc-Milon

BENCHMARK WINE
For many people, powerful yet velvety Pauillac is the definitive red wine style of Bordeaux.

LAND AND PRODUCTION

BORDEAUX WINES

The region around the city of Bordeaux, in the southwest of France, produces some of the great wines of the world. A combination of climate, soil, skill, and tradition has maintained the reputation of the region for several hundred years, ever since the original link with the British market (where red Bordeaux wine was called "claret") and later with the markets of the world.

The key to the success of the region is the Cabernet Sauvignon grape, which lies behind the great wines of the Médoc, the area along the banks of the Gironde River. This variety makes the great reds of the famous chateaux, such as, chateaux Latour, Margaux (pictured right), Lafite, and Mouton-Rothschild.

On the east bank of the river, the St-Émilion and Pomerol areas make excellent wines, mainly from the

ST-ESTÈPHE
Cos d'Estournel

Merlot grape, including classics such as Chateau Cheval Blanc.

To the south of the city, the Graves area, named for its gravelly soil, and the Pessac-Léognan area, also make fine reds.

There is no single system that classifies Bordeaux's 57 appellations and thousands of wines – indeed there are several, which, confusingly, use different terms for wines of similar quality. The first of these was devised in 1855 for the Universal Exhibition in Paris, and classified the wines (specifically those of the Médoc) into five quality classes or *crus* (Growths), with *premier cru* (First Growth) being the finest. Other systems use terms like *cru classé*, and *grand cru classé* to denote the best wines of the region.

MARGAUX

C COLOUR Classic and elegant; bright, deep garnet, with a ruby rim.

A AROMA Ripe red and black fruits, cinnamon, earth, and coffee.

T TASTE Complex, smooth, rich; full-flavoured with a savoury finish.

If Pauillac is velvet, then Margaux is the silk of the Médoc; it is a lighter-bodied wine with a heavenly perfume that includes red fruits as well as black. These Bordeaux wines are primarily made from Cabernet Sauvignon, blended with Merlot, Cabernet Franc, and Petit Verdot. They are a deep garnet red, and are world famous for combining complexity, structure, and fullness with elegance and finesse. They are rich, smooth, and rounded, with great depth. They are velvety too, but are above all polished and silky.

MARGAUX *Château Margaux*

Most people have heard of Château Margaux, and quite rightly. This is one of the most famous wines in the world, and also one of the most exquisite. Château Margaux is an ancient and famous name in wine, and was already well established when Médoc wines were classified in 1855.

But look out! The commune of Margaux, the most southerly of the Médoc communal appellations, shares its name with this famous First Growth (*premier cru*) wine. So when you see Margaux on the label, you can easily think that this is the real thing. Take care, look carefully at the label, and make sure you know what you are buying. Although Château Margaux is the only First Growth in

MARGAUX *Château Palmer*

Margaux, this appellation is not short of other fine wines. It is possible to find Third, Fourth, and Fifth Growths that taste truly amazing, and are really great value for money as well. The Second Growths include some classic wines, such as Château Rauzan-Ségla, Château Rauzan-Gassies, and Château Brane-Cantenac.

There are 12 Third Growths in Margaux, and among them the châteaux with the highest reputation are Palmer, Kirwan, Giscours, and Cantenac-Brown. There are also three Fourth Growths and two Fifth Growths. The second wine of Château Margaux is Pavillon Rouge de Château Margaux, which also has a high reputation.

Despite their ability to cope with very long ageing, these wines are lovely after only five years, and sit beautifully alongside meat dishes, such as pan-fried calves' liver, or rare sirloin or rump steak. The best wines are the last word in complexity, smoothness, richness, and elegance. Good Margaux wines are expensive, but you *must* experience them!

RECOMMENDED PRODUCERS

▶ Château Margaux
▶ Château Palmer
▶ Château Monbrison
▶ Château Kirwan

FOOD MATCH

ROAST DUCK When fully mature, at perhaps 15 years old, Médoc wines are a fine match for duck. Drink younger wines with red meat.

ST-JULIEN

C COLOUR Dark, deep garnet with a purple to ruby rim.

A AROMA Complex; myrtle, violet, black fruits, chocolate, vanilla, earth.

T TASTE Savoury and elegant, with depth and concentration.

I believe that St-Julien is a shy and underrated Bordeaux appellation, and it has the fewest classified châteaux. St-Julien has always been in the shadow of St-Estèphe and Pauillac, its neighbours on either side. However, the quality of St-Julien wines is probably the most consistent of all the Médoc appellations.

Many of the St-Julien châteaux have maintained a very high standard over the years, and some are considered to have a quality above their formal classification. St-Julien has no First Growths (*premiers crus*;

ST-JULIEN
Château Léoville-Barton

see p109), but still includes some of the most famous properties in the world. Second Growths include Gruaud-Larose and Léoville-Barton, two names that rank among the greats of Bordeaux. There are also some excellent unclassified properties with a good reputation, such as Château Gloria.

These wines are so complex, and have so much depth and subtlety that the wine needs time to "talk" (develop) before revealing its full character. These are some of the most feminine wines of the Médoc. They are less intense than some, but are rich and particularly elegant. Ageing potential is very good for the best wines, often up to 15 years.

RECOMMENDED PRODUCERS

▸ Château Léoville-Barton
▸ Château Gruaud-Larose
▸ Château Léoville Las Cases

ST-ESTÈPHE

C COLOUR Intense colouring of deep garnet to crimson red.

A AROMA Black cherry mingling with violets, wood, and spice.

T TASTE Robust, with marked acidity and tannins; balanced and well-structured.

I always say that St-Estèphe produces the most austere wines of the Médoc region of Bordeaux. Because of a clay undersoil, grapes are slower to ripen here, and the climate, in the northern Médoc, is particularly cool. The resulting wine has a high acidity, firm tannins, and less fruitiness than those of its neighbours – but it is still great wine. In a good year, these wines can be the best of the whole region, as the slow ripening greatly increases the depth and complexity of the wine.

There are no First Growths in St-Estèphe, but there are some excellent *cru bourgeois* wines (a lower level of classification in the Médoc) worth looking out for, including Château Haut-Marbuzet. The wines of St-Estèphe are classic and extremely long-lived. You may have to wait a long time to really enjoy them – sometimes up to 20 years.

RECOMMENDED PRODUCERS

▸ Château Montrose
▸ Château Cos d'Estournel
▸ Château Phélan-Ségur

FOOD MATCH

SEARED STEAK The best red meat, simply cooked, melds wonderfully with the tannins and richly complex flavours of St-Estèphe.

LISTRAC

C COLOUR Very dark black cherry, with purplish tinges.

A AROMA Dark fruits, spice, and leather; hints of vanilla from oak ageing.

T TASTE Very well-structured; firm and refreshing, exceptional length.

This is the "quiet man" of the Médoc reds. Listrac is the most recently created communal appellation in the region, often marketed as Listrac-Médoc. Listrac has no classified châteaux, although wines such as Château Clarke and Château Forcas-Hosten have an individual reputation, partly due to their popularity among wine connoisseurs as good-value options in this high-priced part of Bordeaux.

Listrac's inland location and heavy soils make for a solid rather than a fragrant style of Médoc wine – closer to that of St-Estèphe than Margaux. These wines are made mainly from Cabernet Sauvignon, blended with Merlot and Petit

Verdot, and as a result are very austere and robust. They age very well, for up to about 20 years.

Very sadly, this AOC has not achieved its full potential yet, and as a result has not won worldwide recognition. Recently, Listrac producers have begun to introduce a greater amount of Merlot into the blend. This makes sense to me – Merlot is a more appropriate grape for such a heavy soil that has more clay than gravel. The higher proportion of Merlot should make the wines more charming and appealing while still young – we will see.

LISTRAC
Château Fourcas-Hosten

RECOMMENDED PRODUCERS

▸ Château Fourcas-Hosten
▸ Château Clarke
▸ Château Fonréaud

MOULIS

C COLOUR Deep black cherry, with a few hints of garnet red.

A AROMA Dark forest fruits, undergrowth, liquorice, tar, pepper, toast, smoke.

T TASTE Perfect harmony; balanced and well-structured; long and pleasant finish.

Moulis wines are the "secret" *crus* of the Médoc region of Bordeaux – Moulis is the smallest of all the communal appellations of the Médoc, and unbelievably has no *cru classé* wines. However, it is well known for producing some excellent *cru bourgeois* wines.

Moulis wines are made from blends of all the usual Médoc grapes – Cabernet Sauvignon, Cabernet Franc, Merlot, and Petit Verdot, and even Malbec. I usually describe these wines as the "baby wines of St-Estèphe", because of their austerity and firm structure. However, they shed their tough tannins much faster than St-Estèphe wines and find the ideal balance

of acidity and tannin at just five or six years. They are often able to age for much longer than this, maybe even for as much as 20 years in the very best vintages.

Moulis and Listrac (*see left*) are often seen as slightly inferior to the most famous Médoc appellations, but Moulis in particular has vineyards with the location and special gravel soils to match those belonging to some of the classified properties in the more esteemed communes. Its reputation is bad luck for Moulis as the price of the wine remains low, but this is great news for wine drinkers!

These wines are real winners – offering great value, consistent quality, great ageing potential, and popularity. What more could you ask for, when you are paying a quarter of the price of most other appellations in the Médoc region?

RECOMMENDED PRODUCERS

▸ Château Chasse-Spleen
▸ Château Baudan
▸ Château Poujeaux

GRAVES / PESSAC-LÉOGNAN

C COLOUR Deep garnet red, with a characteristic purple rim.

A AROMA Classic and very delicate; black fruits, violets, baked bread, leather.

T TASTE Rich, round, powerful; coffee, minerals; great tannins, long finish.

I call this area the Châteauneuf-du-Pape *(see p113)* of Bordeaux. These are truly great wines – voluptuous and deep, with great colour and concentration, and rich, ripe fruit. I am often surprised to find that many people think that Graves mainly makes white wines – although it does make many excellent whites – when some of the world's best reds come from this area of Bordeaux. The dominant red grape is Cabernet Sauvignon, and Graves wines are structured, powerful, and able to endure exceptionally long ageing. The Merlot and Cabernet Franc grape varieties are used in the blend.

Within the Graves appellation is a special sub-region called Pessac-Léognan; this is the finest part of Graves and became an AOC in its own right in 1987. This is the area immediately around (and now partly in) the city of Bordeaux, and includes what were the best châteaux of Graves, including the world-famous First Growth Château Haut-Brion, the only property in the area to feature in the celebrated 1855 classification of properties in the Médoc. Also in Pessac-Léognan are the almost-as-famous Château la Mission-Haut-Brion and all the other *cru classé* wines recognized in the official 1959 classification of properties in the Graves region. The Graves

GRAVES
Vieux Château Gaubert

appellation has a good reputation and has maintained a high standard over the years, consistently performing very well. Under the rules, every château is reviewed every ten years, and either upgraded or declassified, which is great incentive to maintain performance!

The red Pessac-Léognan wines have elegance and class. They are normally matured in new oak barrels, giving them a smooth smokiness.

LAND AND PRODUCTION

PRECIOUS STONES The vineyards of Graves stretch along a narrow band of land on the left bank of the Garonne River between Langon and Bordeaux. Graves translates as "gravel", in reference to the stony soils found here. The temperate climate, due to the proximity of the river and the ocean, also benefits ripening, but it is the excellent drainage and ability of the gravel to retain heat which play a major role in the quality of the wine.

There are some fantastic wines in the Graves and Pessac-Léognan appellations, often little-known to the wider public. They can make a great investment, and are well worth having in the cellar.

RECOMMENDED PRODUCERS

▸ Vieux Chateau Gaubert
▸ Chateau Haut-Brion
▸ Château Bellevue
▸ Château Rahoul

CAHORS

C COLOUR Particularly dark and deep cherry red with a ruby rim.

A AROMA Black fruits, spice, dried herbs, chocolate, truffles, leather.

T TASTE Rich and powerful, with firm tannins, concentration, and finesse.

A blockbuster from southwest France. This is an especially individual wine, with its own distinctive personality, mainly due to its principal grape variety, Malbec, known locally as Auxerrois or Cot. Cahors produces only red wines, and in the past was known for its dense, dark "black wines".

The wine is made in the Bordeaux style, but the fruit is more concentrated, as the Cahors region is further inland and has a warmer, Mediterranean-influenced climate. A true Cahors is austere and muscular, and very big. This is a wine perfectly suited for long ageing, and a special

bottle for a birthday, or to lay down, can be much better value than a Bordeaux. With age the wine becomes more refined, velvety, and concentrated, with marked finesse and a very long, almost infinite finish – a true classic French wine.

Cahors is a dynamic region, with a great wine to promote on the world market. With new wineries and investment, this region is set to break out from the shadows and make a name for itself. Cahors is one of my great favourites. I do not drink it too young, and combine it with some strongly flavoured meats – perhaps roast beef or pork, or a runny cheese like Époisses; or best of all, with a cassoulet de Castelnaudary, a traditional white bean stew.

CAHORS
Château la Coustarelle

RECOMMENDED PRODUCERS

▸ Château la Coustarelle
▸ Clos la Coutale
▸ Château du Cedre

MADIRAN

C COLOUR Opaque and dark inky hue, with a purple rim.

A AROMA Intense; jammy black and red fruits, sweet spice, tobacco, liquorice.

T TASTE Savoury, velvety, dense, well-structured, and complex; long finish.

Madiran is a region of southwest France in the western part of the Pyrenees. Madiran produces only red wine, using a local grape variety – the highly tannic Tannat.

Thirty years ago, you would have to keep this wine for ten years before you could consider opening the bottle – and you would still have to dilute it with water! However, in recent years I have noticed that the style has changed for many of these wines, even though the structure is still very solid. New production techniques brought in by a younger generation have revolutionized the wines of the region, and I now think that the best of them can seriously challenge overpriced Bordeaux.

These days, the wines generally reach their peak after five to ten years, but the best can easily keep for longer.

This is a top-class wine, and one that I believe will grow in popularity thanks to improved production techniques. It is still not very well known, but the region is dynamic, and I think we will be seeing this wine more and more in restaurants and shops over the coming years.

So my advice is to try it when you see it. You will not be disappointed – particularly if you order it with confit de canard, cassoulet, Pyrenean cheese, blue cheese, or game.

MADIRAN
Château Bouscassé

RECOMMENDED PRODUCERS

▸ Château Bouscassé
▸ Domaine Capmartin
▸ Château d'Aydie

HERMITAGE / CROZES-HERMITAGE

C COLOUR Deep and rich; inky black, with a garnet rim.

A AROMA Classic; spice, violets, blackcurrant, smoke, and truffle.

T TASTE Robust, with savoury flavours; firm but ripe tannins; good length.

Hermitage is a classic French wine – the most famous of the northern Rhône Valley – and it is known throughout the world. The appellation is acknowledged as the home of the Syrah grape variety.

Syrah, also known as Shiraz, is a very distinctive variety with small berries, making wine that is deep in colour, and very expressive and full-bodied. It is now very popular worldwide, and is used in many New World wines. But there is a great difference between the New and Old World styles. Rhône Syrah wines are austere, robust, and fairly tannic when young; Shiraz from

Australia, by contrast, is richer and more obvious, full of jammy fruits with a smooth touch.

Hermitage is located at the southern end of the northern Rhône region, not far from Valence. The vines are planted on the hills and terraces along the river, in such a way as to gain the maximum exposure to the sun. A small amount of the white grapes Roussanne and Marsanne may be added to the Syrah to make up the blend for Hermitage wine, which is highly concentrated, with the quality and potential for long ageing.

After ageing, the flavours of the wine are even more complex, with smoke, earth, woody undergrowth, prunes, and pepper, as well as mellow tannins. Like a great Bordeaux, this wine achieves an exceptional balance between power and robustness on the one hand, and elegance and smoothness on the other.

CROZES-HERMITAGE
Gilles Robin

Hermitage wines can easily last for more than 20 years, after which they can match a great wine from the Médoc. A true Hermitage is a complex and delicious wine, and an unforgettable experience.

Crozes-Hermitage is Hermitage's little brother. The same blend of grapes is used, but while Hermitage is made from grapes grown on the valley sides, directly exposed to the sun, those of Crozes-Hermitage are on the plateau around and above. This results in a slightly lighter style, which is more approachable when young – although, as with Hermitage, the deep colour and the tannins will still stain your teeth!

While it is not as famous as Hermitage, Crozes-Hermitage is by far the larger appellation – in fact the largest appellation in the northern Rhône – with ten times the area of vineyards. There is

CROZES-HERMITAGE *Alain Graillot*

inevitably some variability in style and quality, so take care when choosing a Crozes-Hermitage. The best wines are made from grapes grown on outcrops of granite scattered around the region. These are excellent wines and are generally very good value for money.

Both Hermitage and Crozes-Hermitage wines are classic partners for the great French dishes, such as boeuf bourguignon, casseroles, roast meats, and game.

RECOMMENDED PRODUCERS
▸ Gilles Robin
▸ Alain Graillot
▸ Paul Jaboulet Aîné
▸ J-L Chave

CÔTE-RÔTIE

C COLOUR Very deep garnet red, almost black; more orange-tinted with age.

A AROMA Dark fruits, undergrowth, leather, chocolate, spice, flowers, oak.

T TASTE Very rich; deep and full-bodied, with firm tannins.

This is another Syrah-based wine, but this time with up to 20 per cent of the white grape Viognier allowed in the blend, adding to the wine's

complexity with a flowery aroma. I call this the ultimate expression of Syrah. It is deep, dark, rich, and elegant, a dense and full wine, and a match for red meats, strong cheeses, and full-flavoured grilled vegetables.

Probably the finest reds from the northern part of the Rhône, Côte-Rôtie wines age well, but production is limited, so they can be expensive.

RECOMMENDED PRODUCERS
▸ Guigal
▸ Domaine Bonnefond

LAND AND PRODUCTION

ROASTED SLOPES The vineyards of Côte-Rôtie cling to the steep hillsides of twin slopes, the Côte Brune and the Côte Blonde, on the western bank of the Rhône, south of Lyon. The name Côte-Rôtie literally means "roasted hillside", as the southeastern exposure captures the maximum amount of sun. Production is dominated by Guigal, a producer that has improved and promoted the wines of this area.

CORNAS

C COLOUR Very dark, deep cherry red, with a heavy intensity.

A AROMA Intense; pepper, blackcurrant, blackberry, plum, spice, undergrowth.

T TASTE Strong, dense, and tannic when young; very well-balanced.

Cornas is a tiny appellation, making a deep, dark complex Syrah that is a real rival to Hermitage. It is located on the west side of the Rhône, to the north of Valence. Grab a bottle whenever you can, as the production from the awkward terraces along the river is very low. Cornas is great with classic French meat dishes, but it needs quite a few years to soften and reveal its amazing complexity.

ST-JOSEPH *Domaine Chèze*

RECOMMENDED PRODUCERS
▸ Auguste Clape
▸ Jean-Luc Colombo

ST-JOSEPH

C COLOUR Garnet, with a ruby rim; intense and fairly rich and opaque.

A AROMA Complex; pepper, blackcurrant, violet, woody undergrowth.

T TASTE Smooth and delicate, with a firm structure balanced by ripe fruit.

Made in a lighter style than in the other northern Rhône appellations, St-Joseph's Syrah wines are elegant and rich examples, with the tannins not too dominant, and a smooth, harmonious, and velvety texture.

They can age for up to six years and can be very good value for money – but stick to recognized producers. These wines are great fun with a nice meaty lunch or cheese.

RECOMMENDED PRODUCERS
▸ Domaine Chèze
▸ Pierre Gaillard

CHÂTEAUNEUF-DU-PAPE

C COLOUR Classic and intense; deep garnet with a ruby rim.

A AROMA Wild black fruits, sweet cherry, tobacco, leather, smoke, coffee, spice.

T TASTE Voluptuous, round; firm tannins when young; harmonious; long finish.

The papal wine! The vineyards of Châteauneuf-du-Pape are located between Avignon and Orange, and are the most famous wines of the southern Rhône Valley. They are named after the summer residence of the popes during their exile to Avignon in the 14th century, still commemorated by the sign of the papal crossed keys embossed on the special Châteauneuf bottles.

The structure and personality of this wine is unique, thanks to both

CHÂTEAUNEUF-DU-PAPE
Château la Nerthe

the very unusual blend of grape varieties and to the special type of soil found here. Thirteen different grape varieties are allowed in the blend, several of them white, which is very rare for a single appellation. In reality, the great majority of Châteauneuf wines are based on Grenache, with Syrah and Mourvèdre for support, but other varieties such as Cinsault and Terret Noir may be used as a kind of "seasoning", to add complexity, and the Counoise variety is increasing in importance. But the *terroir* also plays a special part. The soil is made up of large pebbles (*galets*) that soak up heat during the day and gently release it at night, ensuring full ripeness of the grapes.

There are two main wine styles favoured by producers of Châteauneuf-du-Pape. The traditional wine is very dark

and spicy and ages well, while modern wines have much juicier fruit flavours. Both are wonderful, heady wines and can be drunk quite young, but I would advise you to put some of them, particularly the traditional style, away in the cellar. I find the most excitement in these wines once they have spent a few years in the bottle, when they reveal all their complexity and the intensity of their bouquet. The tannins melt into the overall texture and everything is held in a subtle balance – superb! At any age, Châteauneuf is a perfect food match for barbecued meats, steaks, or grilled vegetables.

CHÂTEAUNEUF-DU-PAPE
Château de Beaucastel

RECOMMENDED PRODUCERS
▸ Château la Nerthe
▸ Château de Beaucastel

GIGONDAS

C COLOUR Intense, deep black cherry with a ruby rim.

A AROMA Concentrated forest fruits, with pepper, smoke, tar, and liquorice.

T TASTE Rich and round; elegant, ripe tannins; refreshing acidity.

Gigondas is a close relative of Châteauneuf-du-Pape in style and strength. It does not have the same potential for ageing, but is more charming and pleasant when young. It is also cheaper and offers much better value. Trust me, at a time when we are all looking for alternatives to the big names, this underrated appellation is definitely one to go for. Share this wine with friends over some roast meat or game – just unforgettable!

RECOMMENDED PRODUCERS
▸ Domaine de Font-Sane
▸ Domaine Amadieu

VACQUEYRAS

C COLOUR Garnet with a ruby rim; it looks powerful and rich, but also delicate.

A AROMA Red and black fruits; the older wine has spice, smoke, figs, and game.

T TASTE Dark and deeply rich dry flavours, full of black fruits.

Watch out for this new arrival! Vacqueyras was only awarded its AOC in 1990, and is buzzing with dynamism, quality, and passion. The wines produced here get better and better each year. They are rich and solid, but also remain fresh and elegant, with a wonderful balance between fruit and tannins, which allows them to age well for around five years. Vacqueyras is made from similar grapes to its neighbours Châteauneuf-du-Pape and Gigondas, and goes beautifully with grilled meats and stews.

RECOMMENDED PRODUCERS
▸ Archimbaud-Vache
▸ Domaine des Amouriers

LIRAC

C COLOUR Classic deep ruby red to dark garnet.

A AROMA Red berries, black pepper; with ageing, leather, earth, liquorice.

T TASTE Medium-bodied but with full, very fruity flavours.

Lirac is less structured and lacks depth compared with some other wines, but it is still full, elegant, and rich in red fruits. It can be kept for three to five years, during which time it will soften and develop some "animal" flavour characters. Lirac is perfect at lunchtime on a cold winter's day – with a coq au vin or a steak with pepper sauce and baked potatoes.

LIRAC
Chateau de Ségriès

RECOMMENDED PRODUCERS
▸ Château de Ségriès
▸ Château d'Aquéria

BANDOL

C COLOUR Garnet with a purple rim; very deep and intense.

A AROMA Jammy black fruits; earthy, "meaty", spicy, with dried herbs.

T TASTE Velvety, polished, structured; ripe tannins; long, aromatic finish.

This is the king of Provence wines. Bandol is not only popular and acknowledged as the most famous Provence wine, but its quality is fantastic. I like the way this wine from the warm south of France combines power with elegance, depth, richness, and complexity of flavours, without being aggressive. This is due to a clever blend of grapes, and also to long ageing in oak barrels.

The powerful Mourvèdre is the key grape variety, with a smaller proportion of Grenache and Cinsault providing softer fruit flavours. Sometimes there is also a little Syrah. Mourvèdre thrives in this part of the world, and Bandol is

probably the most suitable area of all for it – at least in France – with vineyards laid out in terraces in a natural amphitheatre facing the Mediterranean sea and protected by mountains. Only these conditions can capture all the sun this late-ripening variety really needs. The grape yield varies from one year to the next, which can affect the price, but I think it is still an affordable wine that offers great value.

Bandol can be drunk young, after a short time in a decanter to let it breathe, but it also has the potential to be kept for more than ten years. It makes an excellent partner for beef and other red meat dishes, and spicy sausage.

BANDOL
Domaine Tempier

RECOMMENDED PRODUCERS
▸ Domaine Tempier
▸ Château de Pibarnon
▸ Mas de la Louvière

ITALY

This country makes some of the longest-lived wines, with great character and many layers of flavour. The best come from the country's cooler regions near the Alps. In Barolo, Barbaresco, and Gattinara, Italy makes some of the greatest wines in the world.

BAROLO / BARBARESCO

C **COLOUR** Deep garnet with a purple rim; tile-red after ageing.

A **AROMA** Tight; ripe wild black fruits, plum, liquorice, tar, truffles, spicy oak.

T **TASTE** Unique; firm, high acidity; solid, marked tannins; elegant, infinite length.

These are some of the world's finest and longest-lived wines, boasting power, intensity, depth, and character. They are high in alcohol, with marked levels of tannin and acidity, and a distinctive fruit content. Nebbiolo, the grape variety of both Barolo and Barbaresco, is perhaps named after the mists – the *nebbia* – that settle over the vineyards during the cool mornings of Piemonte's harvest season, and help to control the pace of ripening and improve the quality of the grapes.

Barolo is the best known Nebbiolo wine, and one of the greatest ageing

BAROLO
Prunotto

wines in the world. Standard Barolo must be aged two years in oak or chestnut barrels and one in the bottle. The *riserva* must be aged for five years in the barrel and the bottle. Many producers are now making the wine in a more approachable style, though still concentrated, but with rounder tannins when still young, a result of the required long maturation prior to bottling. The quality of the wine carries on rising throughout the appellation. More and more Barolos are now named after individual vineyards to make them distinct and more easily recognizable.

An equally stunning wine, Barbaresco is not as "big" as its neighbour, and can have more elegance and finesse while young. It is the "queen" to Barolo's "king". Barbaresco is more obviously charming and fruitier, with better balanced and more integrated tannins.

I would really call these enthusiasts' wines, as you will need to cellar them for more than a decade. With the long ageing required, it is most likely that you will be opening them for a special occasion, and you would really want to match them with a full dinner menu. They are perfect with roast meats, especially roast pork, and with chicken *cacciatore* and other heavy or strong meats.

RECOMMENDED PRODUCERS
▸ Prunotto
▸ Bruno Giacosa
▸ Azienda Agricola Negro
▸ Giacomo Conterno

FOOD MATCH

TRUFFLES Barolo and Barbaresco often carry a scent of black truffles, so these luxurious fungi are an ideal match for these special wines.

ROYAL STANDARD
Barolo is the best-known Nebbiolo wine, and has been famously described as "the king of wines and the wine of kings".

GATTINARA

C COLOUR Dark cherry, with ruby to orange tinges.

A AROMA Ripe and intense; red and black fruits, smoke and coffee.

T TASTE Well-balanced, charming, and refreshing, with round tannins

The baby Barolo! Gattinara is made in the region north of Turin, where the Nebbiolo grape is locally called Spanna, and is usually blended with about 10 per cent Bonarda. Like Barolo, it is matured for some time in barrels before being bottled, under strictly regulated conditions, and it has the same ability as Barolo to greatly improve with ageing – often up to 15 years. However, even if this wine is able to challenge Barolo in style and structure, there is not too much

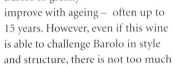

GATTINARA *Mario Antoniolo*

for Piemonte's star performer to worry about. Although Gattinara wines offer a similar personality, with more pronounced fruit characters and softer tannins, they lack the depth and class of the best wines of Barolo.

An important factor for wine drinkers, however, is that Gattinara is cheaper than Barolo and much better value, so, if you want to discover Nebbiolo, this will be the wine for you. Gattinara is fine with all roasted meats, game, or poultry, and also with risottos. However, my special favourite is to drink it with pan-fried calves' liver, mashed potato, and crispy bacon. Now there is a perfect food and wine match!

RECOMMENDED PRODUCERS
▸ Mario Antoniolo
▸ Travaglini
▸ Le Colline

AMARONE DELLA VALPOLICELLA

C COLOUR Deep garnet, with rich nuances of dark, port-like purple.

A AROMA Black cherry, plum, figs, tobacco, leather, earth, bitter almond.

T TASTE Complex, powerful, strong; smooth, full flavours; very long.

Amarone della Valpolicella, or Amarone, is the most famous dry red wine made from dried grapes, and this DOC has made a comeback in its popularity over the past few years.

The system of producing Amarone is very complex and long, and is left to the individual winemaker. Amarone is made from the *orechiette* or "ears" of the grape cluster – the tiny group at the top of the main bunch, which are the most exposed to the sun and experience the most

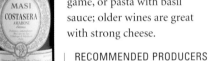

AMARONE DELLA
VALPOLICELLA
Masi

caramelization in the ripening process. The grapes are spread out on straw mats in trays to dry for at least three months before they are ready for vinification. This concentrates their sugars and produces a rich, intense, jammy flavour in the wine, and it also converts the residual sugars into alcohol, creating a very strong and intense dry red – up to 17% ABV.

Overall, this wine tastes very much like a port, but it is dry, with a distinctive bitter finish, which gives it a freshness. Amarone can be drunk young, but it improves with age, and can last for 30 years or more. Try a young Amarone with steak, braised meat, game, or pasta with basil sauce; older wines are great with strong cheese.

RECOMMENDED PRODUCERS
▸ Masi
▸ Serègo Alighieri
▸ Allegrini

AGLIANICO

C COLOUR Deep garnet red with ruby to orange reflections.

A AROMA Dark berries, violet, woody undergrowth, herbs, prunes, chocolate.

T TASTE Great harmony, with marked acidity and concentrated fruit flavours.

I am a great believer in these wines and I still remember the first time I tried them. What I particularly like is their determination, well-defined character, strength, and body, supported by so much ripe fruit flavour that they make your mouth water.

Aglianico is a red grape variety that was brought to Italy by the Greeks more than 2,000 years ago and was used by the Romans in one of their own favourite wines, the Falerno. The name Aglianico is a corruption of the

AGLIANICO DEL VULTURE
Fratelli d'Angelo

Italian word *ellenico*, meaning Greek (Hellenic). The variety has its Italian home in the mountainous region to the east of Naples, and prefers volcanic soil, giving its best results at higher altitudes. It particularly thrives in two parts of the region: Basilicata, and Taurasi in Campania.

Aglianico del Vulture is the star of Basilicata region. When still young, this has the strength and austerity of Italian wines, due to the grape variety and the volcanic soil, but with a gentle, feminine touch because of its concentration of ripe fruit flavours.

This is a special wine – especially after long ageing in oak barrels.

Taurasi is the hero of southern Italy. This Aglianico wine is produced in Campania, around Avellino, to the east of Naples, and is named after one of the villages in the region. Taurasi gained DOCG status, Italy's highest wine classification, in

LAND AND PRODUCTION

MOUNTAIN WINE The volcanic activity of southern Italy, where Vesuvius famously buried Pompeii, has created the perfect soil for growing Aglianico grapes. The cooler nights in vineyards at altitude in the mountains help the grapes to combine freshness and fruit flavours with the power and structure typical of southern Italy, making Aglianico the region's finest wine.

1993, and is the only DOCG zone south of Rome on mainland Italy. It is sometimes called "the Barolo of the South", because of its power and intensity. I am not surprised at this accolade, because this is an under-rated wine of the highest quality. It is well worth buying if you are not after a famous name on the label, but a top-notch wine at a fair price.

I always think of Aglianico wines as winter wines. These are not wines for a lunch in the Italian sun, but for a delicious meal in front of a log fire, after a hard, cold day. They are perfect, especially after long ageing in the bottle. Pair them with robust meals like beef casserole, roast pheasant, or aged sharp cheeses such as Gouda, Jack, Asiago, or Provolone.

RECOMMENDED PRODUCERS
▸ Fratelli d'Angelo
▸ Paternoster
▸ Armando Martino
▸ Botte

BRUNELLO

C COLOUR Opaque black cherry with a purple rim; tile-red with ageing.

A AROMA Intense; dark fruits, plum, leather, forest fruits, spice, and earth.

T TASTE Wonderful complexity; rich, firm structure; round tannins after ageing.

Brunello di Montalcino is one of the driving forces behind the success of Tuscan wines, which have made a real impact all over the world. It is a classic wine, on a par with the leading appellations of Bordeaux or the great northern Italian Nebbiolo wines like Barolo.

In the 1980s, Brunello was one of the original Italian wines to be granted the superior Denominazione di Origine Controlata e Garantita (DOCG) status, alongside four other great wines of Italy: Barolo, Barbaresco, Chianti, and Vino Nobile di Montepulciano. Brunello is a top-quality DOCG and the wine has many special characteristics, the foremost of which is its great potential for ageing.

Brunello is the local name for the Sangiovese Grosso grape, a strain of Tuscany's Sangiovese that thrives around the town of Montalcino. The Italian word *bruno* means dark, and Brunello is so called because of its dark skin. The Brunello grape is similar to the Sangiovese of Chianti. The key difference between Brunello and Chianti is the climate in which the grapes are grown– it is hotter and drier here than in other parts of Tuscany, which gives Brunello its special character, ripeness, and perfect balance.

Young Brunello is impossible to drink as it is so tannic, austere, and firm, but it is still balanced, with bags of fruit. Because of this, it must be aged in the barrel for at least 24 months, and cannot be released until its fifth year. In practice, it is normally kept in wood for three to five years to soften the tannins and allow the sought-after mature aromas such as leather, truffles, spice, and woody undergrowth to develop.

You might also come across the sister of this wine, Rosso de Montalcino, which is made from the same grapes but is not aged for so long. This is also a great wine, but expect it to have more young fruit flavours and less tannin, allowing for earlier drinking.

At its finest, I think Brunello di Montalcino is one of the world's best wines. I am not alone in thinking this, as in 1999 a panel of experts chose the Biondi-Santi 1955 Brunello to be among the top dozen wines of the century, the only Italian wine to be included. If you are lucky enough to have a very old Brunello, you might want to keep it for a special occasion. I always think of this as a winter wine, so a

BRUNELLO
Silvio Nardi

FOOD MATCH

GAME BIRDS Pheasant and other game birds suit aged red wines that are appreciated for their mature aromas, such as Brunello.

Christmas or New Year dinner is an obvious choice. It is perfect with meat, fowl, game, and mixed grills. Serve it in place of a Bordeaux to surprise your guests, and enjoy it!

RECOMMENDED PRODUCERS
▸ Silvio Nardi
▸ Biondi-Santi
▸ Costanti

CARMIGNANO

C COLOUR Intense ruby red to purple; lightens with age.

A AROMA Blackberry, plum, and liquorice, with hints of white pepper.

T TASTE Full-bodied and fruity, with undertones of chalk and lime.

If you like Chianti, you will love its Tuscan neighbour Carmignano. Lower acidity and firmer tannins make this wine more elegant and refined, a perfect match for antipasti, red meats, and strong cheeses, such as Gorgonzola and Pecorino. Best drunk when five or six years old, this wine has a distinctive character – like Chianti, but with a stronger alcoholic kick from the addition of about 10 per cent Cabernet Sauvignon grapes to the traditional Chianti mix of Sangiovese and Canaiolo.

Carmignano holds the coveted DOCG status; with just seven fiercely proud producers it matches great value with high quality. The vineyards are set on low hillsides, which enjoy warm daytime temperatures. This means the grapes can be harvested early, well before the autumn rains, and the wine is reliable and consistent from one year to the next.

It is also worth seeking out the early-maturing bottling of Carmignano, sold as Barco Reale. Lighter, more acidic, and a little smokier than Carmignano proper, it has a charred, bitter streak that lightens its fat, rounded, fruity texture.

RECOMMENDED PRODUCERS
▸ Villa di Capezzana
▸ Fattoria di Ambra
▸ Fattoria di Bacchereto

WARM SLOPES *Carmignano is at a lower altitude and is warmer than Chianti, which gives the wine its special character.*

CARMIGNANO *Villa di Capezzana*

SPAIN

New techniques have recently increased the importance of full reds like Ribera, and they now pose a real challenge to Rioja's dominance. These wines have good intensity, fruit, structure, and acidity, and are currently among the most sought-after in the world.

RIBERA DEL DUERO

C COLOUR Deep garnet with a purple rim; great intensity of colour.

A AROMA Blackcurrant and spice; full, but freshly perfumed.

T TASTE Complex, elegant fruit; thick but rounded.

This is another of my favourites among the full reds. Sadly, this brilliant Spanish wine is often underestimated because of the dominance of Rioja – but it is a beauty, so do not miss it!

RIBERA DEL DUERO
Vega Sicilia

The name Ribera del Duero comes from the Duero River, halfway between Madrid and the Bay of Biscay, which becomes the Douro in Portugal. The climatic conditions in the valley are quite extreme, with hot days and cold nights in summer, and cold winters. Tempranillo is grown under its local name Tinto Fino, and comes into its own in these conditions, which create a higher acidity in the grapes than in Rioja, producing wine with better structure, great intensity and longevity, and a luscious feel. It is a sure sign of success

that more of this variety is being planted along the Duero each year.

This region is producing some star wines, increasingly appreciated around the world, such as Pesquera and Vega Sicilia, which have the greatest longevity of all Spanish wines. Vega Sicilia is made from a blend of Cabernet Sauvignon, Merlot, Malbec, and Tinta del País (another name for Tempranillo). The best wine of the best years – called Vega Sicilia Unico – is aged in oak for five or six years before release.

Try Ribera de Duero with sausage and mash or with braised rack of lamb, or, for a special treat, a tournedos Rossini. Fantastic!

RECOMMENDED PRODUCERS
▸ Vega Sicilia
▸ Pesquera

TORO

C COLOUR Distinctive deep, inky red-black with a purple rim.

A AROMA Ripe dark fruits; blackberry, cherry, smoke, coffee, minerals.

T TASTE Strong, solid, concentrated, powerful; jammy fruits; good length.

TORO
Bodegas Frutos Villar

It is no surprise that in the heart of Spain, the boiling, dry summers and non-existent rainfall produce solid, powerful, "black" wines. Tempranillo has established itself here, but it produces wines that are darker and more tannic than in Rioja, and which have a greater ageing potential. Toro is still on a learning curve, but this is a region to watch, and one that could compete with Australia, and even with Cahors *(see p111)*.

RECOMMENDED PRODUCERS
▸ Bodegas Frutos Villar
▸ Piedra

CONCA DE BARBERÁ

C COLOUR Dark, deep, black cherry, with a ruby rim.

A AROMA Intense, complex; blackberry, chocolate, smoke, liquorice, spice.

T TASTE Firm with elegance and depth; polished tannins; good length.

In Catalan, a *conca* is a basin-shaped valley gouged out of the mountains, which, along with its gravelly soil, creates a perfect microclimate for ripening grapes, and for creating balanced acidity in the wine. Red Conca de Barberá is a blend of Tempranillo, Garnacha and Cabernet Sauvignon, and is an intense and complex wine with plenty of warmth and ripe fruit. I hardly ever find this rare wine, but when I do, I love it with home-made mashed potatoes and black pudding, or a lovely confit of duck breast with black lentils.

RECOMMENDED PRODUCERS
▸ Josep Foraster
▸ Torres

PRIORAT

C COLOUR Very opaque; inky, with a purple rim.

A AROMA Figs, tobacco, herbs, dried fruit, spice, black fruits.

T TASTE Dense, structured, solid, but with a round, ripe texture.

This is a world-class – and expensive – wine that I treat very seriously. Priorat is situated in Tarragona, southwest of Barcelona. The region's poor, stony soil and its very old Garnacha and Carignan vines give low yields and an extreme concentration of fruit. The wines are typically big and powerful, with smooth tannins and good acidity, perfect for long ageing.

PRIORAT
Álvaro Palacios

RECOMMENDED PRODUCERS
▸ Álvaro Palacios
▸ Clos Mogador

TERRA ALTA

C COLOUR Garnet red with a ruby rim; medium to deep intensity.

A AROMA Red berries with spice, smoke, herbs, and woody undergrowth.

T TASTE Refreshing acidity, with ripe flavours, balanced tannins, good length.

This is the least known wine in Catalunya (Catalonia), but this small DO near Priorat is slowly improving in quality. So far, just a few producers have made the most of the potential of the very high altitude. Their wines are concentrated and rich in fruit, but the acidity is fairly pronounced thanks to the mountains and the cooling sea breezes. This is a perfect wine for barbecues or charcuterie, or even with steak and chips. Nice and simple, but very tasty.

RECOMMENDED PRODUCERS
▸ Barbara Fores
▸ Pedro Rovira

TARRAGONA

C COLOUR Quite an opaque wine; silky red with a ruby rim.

A AROMA Intense; a cocktail of black fruits and black pepper.

T TASTE Great balance; harmonious, elegant, well-structured; long finish.

I am convinced that this DO from northern Spain will really make its mark very soon. So far, most of the production is white wine, and it is also well known for its sweet wines. Tarragona reds have a good structure, but often not enough elegance and balance to rival their neighbours Priorat and Conca de Barberá. This is a wine for early drinking, but is still harmonious and very enjoyable. Drink it with nice crusty bread and saucisson or some tapas, and imagine you are there on the mountains overlooking the sea.

RECOMMENDED PRODUCERS
▸ Cellers Scala Dei
▸ Torres

PORTUGAL

If Portugal can continue to introduce new technology and better quality control, then wines like Bairrada and Dão will start to make a real impression on the world market with their powerful flavours. Lively and intense, these wines are a good match for spicy food.

BAIRRADA

C COLOUR Intense black cherry, slightly fading at the edges.

A AROMA Tar, herbs, black cherry, blackcurrant, tobacco, pepper.

T TASTE Big, voluptuous; firm, balanced acidity; rich fruit.

BAIRRADA
Casa de Saima

When people think of Portugal, they naturally think of port, or of relatively recent products such as Mateus Rosé. They forget, or perhaps do not realise, that Portugal has been making wine for many centuries, at least since Roman times. In the north of Portugal, port has always been the main money-maker, and Bairrada has lost out because of this. I do not think it will ever rank alongside the best wines in the world, but Bairrada is now establishing the reputation and quality to be a real rival to its neighbour Dão.

One of the special characteristics of Bairrada is that it has the perfect climate for its main grape variety, Baga (which means "berry"). Baga is Portugal's most widely cultivated red wine grape variety and it thrives in Bairrada, except in poor years, when it produces a rather unripe, astringent wine. Baga is a very tannic grape variety and Bairrada wines have traditionally needed long ageing for the tannins to soften. Nowadays, newer production methods are beginning to help in the search for quality and a more respectable place on the world market.

At their best, Bairrada reds have an intense fruitiness and plenty of vigour, and will age for many years. As they are not too overpowering, I like to drink them with barbecued meat or vegetables, and their slight spiciness makes them a great match for Merguez or other types of spicy sausage.

RECOMMENDED PRODUCERS
▸ Casa de Saima
▸ José Maria da Fonseca

DÃO

C COLOUR Deep and intense ruby, and quite opaque.

A AROMA Pronounced and fairly dry, with blackcurrant, spice, and herbs.

T TASTE Dry, firm tannins, with sufficient fruit flavours; good length.

DÃO
Duque de Viseu

For many years, Dão was controlled by co-operatives, often producing hard, tannic wines lacking in fruit. Fortunately, a number of younger growers have realized the potential of this region, and have begun making wines in a fruitier style with better balance. Portugal's best red grape, Touriga Nacional, grows particularly well here, and plays a key part in the Dão blend. Serve Dão with heavy and meaty dishes, or why not with a bouillabaisse?

RECOMMENDED PRODUCERS
▸ Duque de Viseu
▸ José Maria da Fonseca

GREECE

Greek wines are often thought of as firm, strong in alcohol, and quite hard to drink. However, there has been steady improvement in recent years, and a new generation of excellent, fruit-driven wines with far more finesse has appeared. Greece is on the up!

AGIORGITIKO

C COLOUR Deep garnet red, with ruby at the edges.

A AROMA Very fruity, with blackberry and hints of black cherry.

T TASTE Full, with medium fruit, low acidity and a long finish.

Greece has been producing wines for thousands of years, but very few have reached a level where they are judged to be of world standard. However, since the country joined the EU, more effort has been made to improve the quality.

The Agiorgitiko (St George) grape is a variety of Nemea that grows in the Peloponnese. The wine is locally known as "Blood of Hercules". It is rich, intense, and smooth – similar to Merlot, but with firmer tannins – but it can lack freshness and length due to low acidity.

To my mind, drinking Greek wine is really about the "Greek experience", rather than trying to capture the elegance of, say, a Bordeaux. Enter into the spirit and create a little flavour of Greece by trying this wine with grilled lamb, feta, and salad.

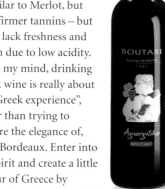

AGIORGITIKO
Boutari

RECOMMENDED PRODUCERS
▸ Boutari
▸ Tsantali

XYNOMAVRO

C COLOUR Deep garnet red, fading to ruby at the rim.

A AROMA Intense and fresh; pleasant ripe fruits; citrus and mineral hints.

T TASTE Full and firm, with pronounced acidity and complex fruit flavours.

Xynomavro is the dominant grape of northern Greece, used in the wines of Naoussa, Goumenissa, and Amyndeo. It has a deep colour and prominent acidity (the name means "acid black"). The tannins can be harsh but the best wines age extremely well, developing a complexity akin to fine Barolo, and in warm years they can be soft and delicious even when young. I recommend that you drink this wine only with food, especially slightly spicy meats.

RECOMMENDED PRODUCERS
▸ Aidarinis
▸ Castanioti

LIMNIO

C COLOUR Attractive, dark black cherry, with a pinkish rim.

A AROMA Dried herbs, cherry, plum, jammy blackcurrant, and white pepper.

T TASTE Full; velvety texture; fruit-driven, with warmth and good length.

The Limnio grape is native to the island of Lemnos but is mainly grown in northern Greece, particularly in the Rapsani district. Limnio produces well-structured wines of considerable body and high alcohol content. They have a very dark red colour and velvet texture, and some wines require at least one year's ageing in barrels. Some of the best wines are made from a blend with Cabernet Sauvignon or Cabernet Franc. I have fond holiday memories of drinking Limnio with grilled lamb under the stars on a warm evening.

RECOMMENDED PRODUCERS
▸ Samos Co-op
▸ Papaïoannou

HUNGARY

Hungarian red wines are now considered better than their well-established whites. One of the most popular is Kadarka.

KADARKA *Takler*

KADARKA

C COLOUR Medium to deep ruby red, with orange tinges.

A AROMA Very fruity, with strong hints of spice and wild flowers.

T TASTE Full-bodied, strong, powerful, and well-structured, with a long finish.

Kadarka is Hungary's most widely cultivated grape and is the most important variety in Egri Bikavér (Bull's Blood), a wine at one time exported in great quantities. Kadarka is essential for a quality Bikavér, but during the Communist era, the mass-production techniques led to the creation of cheap, sour wine that

ruined the image of this famous drink. Now, a new generation of winemakers is producing Bikavér to suit global tastes, and better versions are coming on to the market.

On its own, Kadarka produces full-bodied, tannic red wine that can be very aromatic and spicy and is usually high in alcohol. It is best to drink it young, but if you can find a bottle that has been aged in wood for three or four years, it is excellent with a sirloin. But my favourite is Bull's Blood and lamb chops, after which I can take on the world!

RECOMMENDED PRODUCERS
▸ Takler
▸ Blue Danube

BULGARIA

This country is a large-volume producer – one of the biggest in the world – but for many years its wines were trapped within the economies of eastern Europe. My view is that in five or ten years Bulgaria will be a major presence in the world market.

MELNIK / MAVRUD

C COLOUR Dark garnet with ruby to brick or tile-red nuances.

A AROMA Not too obvious; forest fruits, vanilla, and spicy oak.

T TASTE Firm tannins, solid, heavy; moderate acidity and fruit; good length.

Melnik and Mavrud are the most interesting of Bulgaria's indigenous grape varieties. Melnik is the main town of the southwestern region of Bulgaria along the Greek border, and has given its name to the local grape variety as well as the wine. Melnik is a thick-skinned, blueish variety, that makes weighty, tannic wines in the

Greek style. The Southern region is home to Mavrud, which produces hearty, plummy wines that can benefit from vinification in oak.

Of all Bulgarian wines, Melnik probably ages the best, and ageing brings out the roundness and complexity, with older wines having a similar feel to those from the Rhône Valley. Drink this wine with a local dish, such as savoury stuffed peppers or mutton. With Mavrud, I would recommend you keep to the latest vintages, and drink it with quite strong or even spicy dishes.

RECOMMENDED PRODUCERS
▸ Santa Sarah Privat
▸ Vinazod Assenovgrad

SERBIA AND MONTENEGRO

Serbia and Montenegro has a favourable climate for the production of full red wines. Some of them, such as Vranac, are very popular, but are mostly drunk locally. In recent years, the wines produced by this part of the world have shown signs of great improvement.

VRANAC

C COLOUR Deep ruby red; intense but fading at the rim.

A AROMA Full of character; cherry, prune, green pepper, hints of green walnut.

T TASTE Robust and full, with firm tannins, slight bitterness, and rich fruit.

The quality of wine from Serbia and Montenegro (and of the former Yugoslavia) has been quite variable over the years, but there are some wines that are really interesting and well worth tasting, including Vranacs. Indeed, the best Vranacs have been compared to the wines of Bordeaux, which I know might surprise some people!

Vranac is a red grape native to the mountainous region of Montenegro. It makes a dry red wine, with a rich structure and a full character, and typically it will have quite a pronounced bitterness. This can be counterbalanced by serving it with food that is rich or strong in flavour, or maybe with a creamy cheese.

I would recommend that you do not store this wine for very long, and certainly that you do not lay it down. Despite the fact that this is quite a full wine, it will not improve with age. In the summer, it is lovely to serve Vranac slightly chilled.

RECOMMENDED PRODUCERS
▸ Snova
▸ A D Plantaze

CROATIA

I am very optimistic about this country. Many of their wines are drunk exclusively by the domestic market, but some, like Plavac Mali, are easily good enough to make an impact around the world.

PLAVAC MALI *Dalmacijavino*

PLAVAC MALI

C COLOUR Good, well-balanced colouring of dark garnet with a ruby rim.

A AROMA Fairly simple black fruits; intense, peppery, plummy.

T TASTE Strong; medium acidity, generous alcohol, and rich texture; medium finish.

During the Communist period, most wines sent for export from the former Yugoslavia were white. Today, people around the world are still more familiar with Croatian white wines than reds, and much of the country produces only white wine. However, the Dalmatian coastal region has become a successful red-wine producing area.

Plavac Mali is a grape native to Croatia, and is used to make wines such as Dingac and Postup. It produces deeply coloured, intense, and tannic wine, naturally strong in alcohol, which responds well to ageing. There seems little doubt that this grape is related to Zinfandel, via another local variety, Dobricic, so if you like Zinfandel, you should try this European wine. I always drink Plavac Mali with food, maybe with chops or something from the barbecue.

RECOMMENDED PRODUCERS
▸ Dalmacijavino (Plavac Marjan)
▸ Grgich

USA

California is the heartland of winemaking in the USA, and produces a wide range of full reds, due to its variety of micro-climates. Californian reds can be pricey, but from supermarket favourites to opulent rarities, you can always find a bargain.

NAME GAME *The name Zinfandel is thought to be a corruption of Zierfandler, an unrelated Austrian variety.*

ZINFANDEL

C COLOUR Garnet red with ruby to orange tinges; variable intensity.

A AROMA Distinctive and complex, with plum and green pepper.

T TASTE Rich, round, and heavy, but with refreshing acidity; very long.

At its best, this is a unique and unbeatable wine. Zinfandel has often been planted in unsuitable locations and over-produced, but modern, high-quality examples are complex, dense, rich, and full of flavour, and also have elegance and subtlety. This wine responds well to maturing in oak barrels, which give it a better balance – it can age for up to five years, and the best easily for ten. Zinfandel can be drunk on its own as a fruity apéritif or after-dinner drink, but I like it best of all with barbecued steaks and sausages.

RECOMMENDED PRODUCERS

▸ Nalle
▸ Ridge

CABERNET SAUVIGNON

C COLOUR Deep, dark garnet red with a purple to ruby rim.

A AROMA Cherry, blackberry, leather, smoke, warm bread, coffee beans.

T TASTE Robust, but delicate and classy; perfect balance.

Cabernet was introduced in California before the 1880s and has since become the best-known grape variety produced in the US, making up 15 per cent of California's wine production. The best wines have finesse, complexity, and delicious ripe black fruit with a well-balanced texture. They are clear rivals to the top wines of Bordeaux. There are excellent blends of Cabernet with Merlot, Malbec, Cabernet Franc, and Petit Verdot, in the Bordeaux style, referred to as Meritage, a term that you might see on the label. Most wines are gently oaked, and, as in Europe, the quality of the vintage has an influence on the wine.

The very best Californian Cabernets are from the famous Napa Valley, particularly around Rutherford, Oakville, and St Helena. In the Sonoma Valley, Cabernet has taken a firm hold, thanks to a suitable microclimate, but these tend to be bigger wines with a little less finesse.

I like to drink these wines with any full dinner menu, whether meat or vegetarian. They are perfect with the main course, especially steak, roast meats, or cheese dishes. However, as Californian Cabernets are so rich in fruit, you can also drink them on their own, either before or after a meal.

CABERNET SAUVIGNON
Arrowood

RECOMMENDED PRODUCERS

▸ Arrowood
▸ Stags' Leap
▸ Beringer

CALIFORNIA CLASSIC
The power, structure, and great class of Cabernet Sauvignon shine through in Californian wines.

SYRAH

C **COLOUR** Dark and inky, with a purple to ruby-red rim.

A **AROMA** Elegant, stylish, pronounced; blackberry, spice, cedar, herbs, and mint.

T **TASTE** Voluptuous, smooth, big; complex texture; long and impressive finish.

California makes some very fine, complex, and intense Syrah wines. Production began as recently as 1970, but this wine is very classy, with a wonderful character and an impressive style of its own. California Syrah is more voluptuous and richer than Syrah from the Rhône Valley, but has elements of the European character enhanced with the best New World techniques, making it more subtle than Australian Shiraz.

SYRAH *Araujo*

The best wines have an excellent structure with just enough tannins to give a satisfying and complex finish, which is really important if you want the wine to match well with heavy meats, such as game. My own special favourites for Californian Syrah are duck and black olives, or a tender filet mignon. These exciting, refreshing wines can also be drunk on their own.

RECOMMENDED PRODUCERS
▸ Bonny Doon
▸ Araujo
▸ Bell Wine Cellars

FOOD MATCH

ROAST VENISON The complex and voluptuous texture of California Syrah makes it a worthy match for rich venison dishes.

NEWCOMER *California has been making Syrah for only a few decades, but produces some of the world's best.*

ARGENTINA

The climate of the Andes is central to the quality of Argentine wines. Their flagship red grape is Malbec, and this variety produces some of the best New World wine, in terms of quality and value for money.

MALBEC
Bodega Norton

MALBEC

C COLOUR Intense and very dark, inky red with a ruby rim.

A AROMA Distinctive; blackberry, plum, coffee, game, spice, and oak.

T TASTE Rich, fleshy, refreshing acidity; balanced tannins; good length.

Argentina has adopted the Malbec of Cahors in southwest France (see p111) as its own. However, the Argentinian wines made with this grape are more fruity, intense, and much richer than their French equivalents. In Mendoza, the Andean climate helps to produce a wine that combines the New World fruity style – ripe and upfront – with the more austere European style of higher acidity and firmer tannins, making it perfect for food matching. These wines are usually matured in oak and improve very well with ageing, or they can equally be drunk immediately if preferred. Malbec can reveal its quality with any types of meat, but my special favourite is roast rack of lamb cooked with herbs – fantastic!

RECOMMENDED PRODUCERS
▸ Bodega Norton
▸ Dona Paula

CHILE

Chilean Cabernet Sauvignon is one of the world's best inexpensive wines, and is made by highly skilled producers, such as Santa Rita. Famous Bordeaux houses like Rothschild have made big investments in the country and this bodes very well for Chile's winemaking future.

CABERNET SAUVIGNON

C COLOUR Garnet red with a ruby rim and deep intensity.

A AROMA Blackcurrant, chocolate, sweet spice, hints of mint; ripe but elegant.

T TASTE Charming, delicate, well-flavoured, with perfect balance.

I am a big fan of Chile, especially when I want an easy wine – one that is not too intense, but very well made. Chilean wines are generally very good value, rarely disappoint, and are best for early drinking. Cabernet Sauvignon is the most widely grown grape variety in the country, and is extremely fruity, clean, and concentrated.

The best region is the Central Valley, but my own favourite is the Rapel Valley, with its two sub-regions, Cachapoal and Colchagua. The cool climatic influence of the Antarctic Humboldt Current means that this wine is less fruity than that from the warmer regions – it is somewhere between a Napa Valley wine from California and a Bordeaux.

These are very versatile wines, and can be enjoyed on their own, or with chops, steaks, or sausages.

RECOMMENDED PRODUCERS
▸ Santa Rita
▸ Los Vascos

SOUTH AFRICA

South Africa's wines have characteristics of both the Old and New Worlds, and the best strike a great balance between tannins, acidity, alcohol, and fruit. This country makes some of my favourite New World wines, as they have great quality, character, and consistency.

CABERNET SAUVIGNON
Rustenberg

CABERNET SAUVIGNON

C COLOUR Dark inky red to black, with purple nuances.

A AROMA Blackcurrant, plum, chocolate, hints of spice.

T TASTE Rich and velvety, with perfect balance and great character.

South African Cabernets are half way between the jammy Australian style and the drier, tighter wine of Bordeaux. The wine has a traditional, firm, assertive style, combined with a tendency to be very fruit-driven, with ripe rather than jammy black fruit dominating. The intense fruity aroma is upfront, but also full of elegance and finesse. It shows an excellent balance between the ripeness of the fruit, tannins, and alcohol, and has real depth. This wine is usually aged in French oak, and the result is rather more classy than exuberant, again showing the polished, European side of the wine.

Cabernet Sauvignon is used in blends, often with Merlot and other Bordeaux varieties in emulation of the classic Bordeaux blend, as with Californian Meritage wines (see p120). Some blends are more adventurous, taking in a proportion of Shiraz or South Africa's signature grape variety, Pinotage.

The best wine regions for the production of Cabernet Sauvignon in South Africa are Stellenbosch and the warmer parts of Constantia. Some good wines also come out of Franschhoek, part of Paarl.

South African Cabernet is fantastic with a tasty steak, but it has such great harmony and complexity that you can happily drink it on its own, before or after a meal. This is my favourite New World Cabernet Sauvignon. I love the perfect balance in these wines, and I also find that they offer great value for money.

RECOMMENDED PRODUCERS
▸ Rustenberg
▸ Rust en Vrede

SHIRAZ

C COLOUR Deep plum, typical of the Shiraz style.

A AROMA Rich black fruits; smoke, chocolate, and black pepper.

T TASTE Exuberant and rich, with great depth and complexity.

SHIRAZ Backsberg

South African Shiraz has more of a cool-climate feel than the full, fruit-driven wines from Australia, and is nearer to the French style (some producers prefer to call it Syrah). However, it still has the black-fruit-and-spice exuberance typical of Shiraz, and represents a combination of very good value and excellent quality. You may well see it in a blend with Cabernet Sauvignon – this has been a great success for the South Africans. I like to drink it on its own, or with spicy food.

RECOMMENDED PRODUCERS
▸ Backsberg
▸ Meerlust

AUSTRALIA

Australia is now a world leader in full red wines, especially Shiraz and Cabernet Sauvignon. Many regions, like the Barossa Valley, have a perfect climate for these varieties, and produce wines that have tannins and acidity when young, balanced with bold fruit flavours.

SHIRAZ

C **COLOUR** A rich dark purple to inky red, with a ruby rim.

A **AROMA** Black fruits, spice, dried plum, tar, smoke, eucalyptus.

T **TASTE** Rich, profound, velvety; refreshing tannins; very long.

Shiraz is being planted more and more around the world, but it made its mark in Australia long ago, and established itself as a star performer; it is the most-planted red grape variety in Australia.

Australian Shiraz is a very bold, spicy wine, with ripe,

SHIRAZ
Rosemount Estate

black, upfront fruit. Although these are powerful wines, they are still very approachable and easy to drink, even when young. I find that they are typically much sweeter and riper than the French Syrah wines from the northern Rhône Valley, and can be much more suggestive of spice, eucalyptus, and chocolate, with the tannins less firm than in Australian Cabernet Sauvignon.

Australia has made great investments in its wine industry, and

although these wines have a uniform style and identity linked to sweet blackcurrant, the quality is rarely disappointing thanks to excellent Australian winemaking skills, high technology, and a suitable climate.

The best Shiraz comes from Barossa and the Hunter Valleys, two of Australia's longest-established regions. Barossa is northwest of Adelaide, and just far enough inland to be away from the moderating effect of the sea. The valley is one of Australia's most important wine regions, and, in my view, the ultimate region for Australian Shiraz. Wines such as Penfolds Grange and Henschke Hill of Grace are among the most expensive in the world. I find it hard to believe that the Australian government was encouraging growers here to uproot their old Shiraz vines in the 1980s – but they

SHIRAZ
Grant Burge

fought back by making better and better wines.

The Hunter Valley is north of Sydney, and has a very hot but humid climate, with the vineyards spread out along the valley floor. Shiraz wines from the Hunter Valley tend to be more tannic than those from the Barossa Valley, and consequently age better. However, vintages are more variable, due to higher rainfall.

Many Australian Shiraz wines are outstanding and well balanced. You do not have to spend too much more than a supermarket price to have one of these wines, and it will be worth every penny.

RECOMMENDED PRODUCERS

▸ Rosemount Estate
▸ Grant Burge
▸ Glaetzer
▸ Henschke
▸ Sandford

CABERNET SAUVIGNON

C **COLOUR** Deep, inky dark cherry to garnet with a ruby rim.

A **AROMA** Obvious; dark cherry, cedar, tobacco, blackcurrant, and chocolate.

T **TASTE** Round and rich, but elegant and complex; firm tannins; good length.

This is another winner for Australia, a wine that has a great identity and has really established itself. Australia produces many different Cabernet styles, some unlike any others found throughout the world. In essence, these wines are upfront, jammy, ripe, exuberant, fruit-driven, and very attractive, and are consistently winning friends and devotees. The quality and character of Cabernet shows through, whether it is part of a blend, particularly with Shiraz, or on its own.

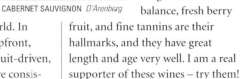

CABERNET SAUVIGNON *D'Arenberg*

Of all the Australian regions, my two personal favourites for Cabernet are Coonawarra in South Australia and Margaret River in Western Australia. Coonawarra wines have really intense aromas, but with complexity and finesse. Nearby Padthaway is slightly warmer, so its wines are slightly fruitier and more open.

I believe that Margaret River is even better than Coonawarra, as the cool maritime climate of Western Australia controls the ripening of the fruit. These wines have subtlety, class, and finesse, rather than weight. Beautiful balance, fresh berry fruit, and fine tannins are their hallmarks, and they have great length and age very well. I am a real supporter of these wines – try them!

RECOMMENDED PRODUCERS

▸ D'Arenberg
▸ Katnook
▸ Wynn's

MATARO

C **COLOUR** Intense garnet red with a purple rim.

A **AROMA** Jammy black fruits; earthy, "meaty", spicy, with dried herbs.

T **TASTE** Velvety, full of character, and well-structured, with ripe tannins.

This is one of those wines that has not yet reached the shelves of the supermarkets, but could be on the verge of making a great impact.

Throughout the world, Mourvèdre, known in Australia as Mataro, is used as part of a blend, where it brings structure and complexity to the finished wine. On its own, however, it is amazing and very individual – firm and solid, with marked tannins and lots of dark wild fruit. You definitely need a strong-flavoured meat or a creamy dish to suit this wine.

RECOMMENDED PRODUCERS

▸ Turkey Flat
▸ Best's

LAND AND PRODUCTION

HEAT SEEKER The Mataro grape likes a hot and dry climate, and is grown throughout Australia. In fact, the warmer the climate, the better it is for reducing Mataro's tannic structure and enhancing the fruit character, which is why the warmer parts of the Barossa Valley are ideal. If Australia can find the perfect microclimate, as France has done in Bandol *(see p113)*, Mataro could really be a new star.

66 Joy, celebration, elegance, and charm –
these are the quintessential party drinks.
A feast for the eyes, too, as tiny creamy
bubbles run up the glass. 99

SPARKLING

INTRODUCING SPARKLING WINES

Sparkling wine is an instant mood-lifter, and, whatever the quality, the first glass always tastes great. You will know a really good sparkling wine by the tiny, refreshing bubbles that caress your palate, inviting you to take another sip.

DRINKING AND SERVING

DRINK PROFILE Sparkling wines should be fresh and light. Aromas should be clean, and not specifically reminiscent of any particular grape variety – most sparkling wines are blends.

C COLOUR The colour of sparkling wines varies from pale yellow through to golden yellow, with silver rims. "Pink" Champagne and sparkling rosé vary from very pale pink to almost red.

A AROMA The aroma of Champagne is subtle and discreet, with pear, apple, citrus, and floral tones. Cheaper sparkling wines may seem slightly metallic on the nose.

T TASTE Light and dry, sparkling wines should leave your mouth feeling refreshed. If there is a hint of mushroom, the wine is "tired": drink it straight away, as it will not improve.

BUYING AND STORING You don't have to buy big brands to get great sparkling wine: as all sparkling wines are blended, store brands can be just as good. Sparkling wines are not intended for ageing; most Champagne is best drunk within ten years.

SERVING SUGGESTIONS Chill the wine for about 30 minutes in the freezer or two hours in the refrigerator. To preserve the bubbles, don't "pop" the cork: hold it and twist the bottle, which should release the cork with a quiet sigh. Serve the wine in tulip-shaped glasses or flutes, which enhance the flow of bubbles; avoid the coupé (saucer) glass.

FOOD COMPANIONS Seafood (particularly oysters) and other very light dishes match well with dry sparkling wines. Sweeter versions, such as Asti or Sekt, should be matched with cakes and desserts.

The term "Champagne" is reserved for sparkling wines made in one particular area of northern France, around the city of Reims and the town of Epernay. Champagne contains the most northerly and so the coolest vineyards in France. When the grapes are harvested they are often only just ripe. This gives them a high acidity, which in turn gives a good balance of fruit and alcohol in the resulting wine. However, Champagne now accounts for a mere one in 12 bottles of sparkling wine. Other parts of the world, and other regions of France, offer some excellent alternatives, notably *crémant* wines from France, Cava from Spain, and Asti from Italy. Australia, New Zealand, and California are making some good fizzes, too.

CITRUS *Zesty flavours are prominent in Champagne.*

ALL ABOUT THE SPARKLE

The best sparkle, with the most delicate bubbles, is achieved through a process known as secondary fermentation. A sugar-and-yeast mixture is added to still, fermented wine, which then begins to ferment again, creating tiny bubbles of carbon dioxide. In traditional methods (those used in Champagne or in wines labelled *méthode traditionelle* or *méthode champenoise*; *see also p129*), secondary fermentation is set off in the bottle itself, and a special stopper (later replaced by a cork) prevents the gas from escaping. More modern techniques are the tank method and carbonation. In the tank method, secondary fermentation occurs *en masse* in a sealed tank. These wines can be good, but tend not to be as subtle as those made by the *méthode traditionelle*. In carbonation, no secondary fermentation occurs at all. Gas is injected into the wine from a cylinder, resulting in large, short-lived bubbles. These wines tend to be of unreliable quality. A good sparkling wine will display the *cheminée* – a chimney of bubbles, rising from the bottom of the flute to the centre of the liquid's surface; the bubbles then move out to form a circle around the inside of the glass.

CAVIAR CANAPÉS *Champagne paired with caviar is the ultimate luxurious indulgence.*

GRAPE VARIETIES

The single most important grape variety in sparkling wine is Chardonnay, but these wines are typically made from blends. The classic Champagne blend is Pinot Meunier and Pinot Noir (both red grapes) and Chardonnay, each of which adds something different to the character of the wine. Spanish Cava uses local grapes such as Macabeo along with an ever-increasing amount of Chardonnay. Local grape varieties tend to be used in Italy and Germany, while in the New World, Chardonnay and Pinot Noir tend to dominate.

GRAPE	BEST REGIONAL EXAMPLES	COMMENTS
CHARDONNAY	France: Champagne, Burgundy. Italy: Franciacorta. USA. California. Canada. Australia. New Zealand. South Africa.	The essential sparkling wine grape is at its best in the coolest regions of its range, where resulting wines express lemony and green apple characters. It combines well with the yeasty character of the style, producing complex but elegant notes of almond, warm bread, and biscuit. Expensive to grow, this grape is usually blended to achieve the perfect balance.
PINOT NOIR	France: Champagne, Burgundy. Italy: Franciacorta. USA: California. Canada. Australia. New Zealand. South Africa.	This grape provides the "backbone" for many sparkling wines, holding together their structure, and bringing body as well as intensity and freshness. It is part of the blend for most of the great names in Champagne, including the finest Dom Perignon and Cristal.
PINOT MEUNIER	France: Champagne. Italy: Franciacorta. Canada.	This grape is part of the classic Champagne blend, adding fruit intensity to the wine. It is usually blended, but when on its own it produces some charming peachy and apple-rich styles that have less finesse and elegance than Champagne, but are great as apéritifs!
MUSCAT	Italy. France: Limoux.	In common with its cousin Clairette *(see below)*, this variety produces light and pleasant wines. It is most popular in Italy, especially the Asti area of Piemonte (Piedmont), where it is known as Moscato. Here, it makes subtle wines with a touch of sweetness and a faintly aromatic character.
CHENIN BLANC	France: Loire Valley. South Africa.	Though very popular for still white wine in South Africa, this grape, which is high in acidity, finds its ultimate expression in France, and particularly in sparkling wines. These tend to be less aromatic than those made from other grapes.
MACABEO	Spain.	This highly productive variety is fairly neutral in character, with high acidity and low flavours. It is often blended with other varieties, including Chardonnay, to make Cava. It adds a fresh, light touch that is essential to good sparkling wine.
PROSECCO	Italy.	This variety produces a light, refreshing style of wine, lower in flavour than many fizzes, but elegant and subtle with notes of almond, pear, and flowers. It is grown in northeastern regions of Italy, such as Veneto and Friuli-Venezia Giulia.
CLAIRETTE	France.	Sparkling wines from this grape are subtle, elegant, fruity, but never too fizzy. Clairette de Die, made in the Rhône Valley from 25-per cent Clairette grapes, is a less expensive but enjoyable alternative to Champagne.
RIESLING	Germany.	Some excellent examples of Sekt, German sparkling wines with a slightly sweet character, are made from this variety, which is often blended. Wines labelled "Deutscher Sekt" are made exclusively from German grapes.

FRANCE

Everyone knows that France is the home of Champagne, the greatest of the world's sparkling wines, made in the region around the great city of Reims. But France also makes other fine sparkling wines in different regions; these cannot be called "Champagne" but are instead known as *crémant* wines. The main centres of production are Alsace, Burgundy, and the Rhône and Loire valleys.

CHAMPAGNE

C **COLOUR** Pale to medium gold, with silver tinges; fine, steady bubbles.

A **AROMA** Elegant; fresh fruit (apple, citrus); biscuit; flowers; mineral hints.

T **TASTE** Complex, refreshing; creamy texture; delicate bubbles; long finish.

Champagne – the "King of the Bubbles"! This most famous of sparkling wines owes much to the cold climate of northern France. The short growing season means that the grapes do not ripen sufficiently to make good still wine – rather, it is low in alcohol and high in acidity. In the 17th-century Dom Pérignon, monk and cellar-master of the Abbey of Hautvillers, inadvertently started a "secondary fermentation" in a bottle of the abbey wine. The result was a more palatable wine with refreshing bubbles – Champagne!

Dom Pérignon's original techniques for making sparkling wine are, of course, now much refined, and the process of making Champagne is long and difficult, but the results are exquisite.

There are three grape varieties that can be blended to produce Champagne, each of which grows best in one of Champagne's three primary regions. Pinot Meunier (a red grape) is grown in the Vallée de la Marne, which stretches westward through Champagne along the banks of the Marne River. This is a robust grape, providing

A PLACE IN HISTORY *In 1918 Winston Churchill said, "Remember... it's not just France we are fighting for, it's Champagne!"*

CHAMPAGNE
Pol Roger

CHAMPAGNE
Laurent-Perrier

fruitiness. It makes up the base for all but the finest Champagnes. Pinot Noir (also a red grape) grows best in the Montagne de Reims region, lying to the south of the city of Reims. This grape provides structure, depth of fruit, and longevity. Chardonnay (a white grape) is grown in the Côte des Blancs, south of the town of Epernay. This grape brings lightness and elegance to the wine, as well as giving it that special "warm bread" taste. The blend of these grapes is known as the Champagne's *cuvée* – the key to a great Champagne.

Most Champagne houses buy in their grapes from the region's growers and then blend them into their own house style. This blending (or *assemblage*) is an artform, remarkably producing house styles that are consistent from year to year.

If you see *grand cru* or *premier cru* on the label, the house has blended the wine using grapes from one or more of Champagne's specially classified villages, where the local variations in the *terroir* have given the grapes a better reputation than grapes from elsewhere in the region.

Apart from the blending, a Champagne's style is affected by a process called *dosage*, in which a mixture of still wine and sugar (known as *liqueur d'expedition*) is added to the completed Champagne to replace any liquid lost during *dégorgement* (see box, below). The amount of sugar added during *dosage* dictates the resulting sweetness of the Champagne. Champagnes with no added sugar are labelled *Ultra Brut*, *Extra Brut*, *Brut Zero*, or *Brut Sauvage* and are

CHAMPAGNE
Charles Heidsieck

extremely dry. *Brut* indicates a very dry wine; *Extra-Sec*, dry; *Sec*, medium-dry; *Demi-Sec*, sweet; and *Doux*, very sweet.

Most Champagne is non-vintage (NV), but occasionally an exceptional summer will result in vintage Champagne – a wine made using grapes from that year alone. Only in vintage years will houses deviate from the normal blend of their house style.

Champagne is the only appellation in France that does not have to place Appéllation d'Origine Contrôllée (AOC) on its labels, but the region is nevertheless governed by strict laws. The label must state "Champagne" and "*Méthode Champenoise*", and give the name of the house along with one of four sets of initials. In descending order of quality these are: "NM" (*Négociant Manipulant*), which indicates that the producer has bought in the

grapes from one or more of the region's growers, or has bought the growers' still wine and has taken over production from *assemblage* onward. Most of the Champagne houses (around 70 per cent of all Champagne production) are *négociants manipulants*. "RM" (*Recoltant Manipulant*) indicates that the grower himself has made the wine from his own grapes. "CM" (*Co-operative Manipulant*) indicates

that the wine has been produced by a co-operative of grower-producers. Be wary of MA (*Marque Auxiliare*), which, while cheaper, is usually Champagne of lower quality.

RECOMMENDED PRODUCERS
▸ Pol Roger
▸ Laurent-Perrier
▸ Charles Heidsieck
▸ Bollinger
▸ Louis Roederer

CULTURE AND TRADITION

THE CITY OF KINGS
If Champagne is the drink of kings, then it is fitting that the wine comes from a city where 25 kings of France have been crowned. The Gothic cathedral of Reims, which took around 80 years to build, beginning in 1211, played host to the coronation of French kings from Louis VIII in 1223 to Charles X in 1825.

LAND AND PRODUCTION

THE TRADITIONAL METHOD
A wine labelled "Champagne" must come from Champagne itself. However, there are many sparkling wines from elsewhere in the world produced using Champagne's techniques. These wines are labelled *méthode traditionelle*. After pressing, the grape juice undergoes a first fermentation, usually in stainless steel tanks. Next comes *assemblage*: a highly skilled blender "assembles" the components of the wine to create a house's own particular

HIGH OUTPUT *Some producers use automated giropalettes to perform the remuage – these can hold up to 45 times as many bottles as a traditional pupitre.*

style, often by taste and smell alone. As the blend is bottled, a small mixture of wine, sugar, and yeast (*liqueur de tirage*) is added. This sets off the second fermentation in the bottle, which, crucially, creates bubbles of carbon dioxide and increases the wine's alcohol. As the wine matures, the dead yeast cells (lees) impart their flavour – the longer the wine spends on its lees (anything between 15 months and seven years), the better its quality. The yeast sediment is then removed from the bottle using *remuage* (or riddling). The bottle is turned (by hand or mechanically) very slowly until it is upside down, causing the lees to slip into a plastic cup in the neck, held in place by a crown cap. The sediment is then removed using *dégorgement*: freezing the wine in the bottle neck to take out the sediment, and the bottle is sealed with a cork.

CHAMPAGNE
Bollinger

Remueurs ("riddlers") hand-turn the wine bottles on a pupitre, a hinged rack that can hold up to 60 bottles at a time.

LIMOUX

C COLOUR Bright medium to pale straw yellow, with silver tinges.

A AROMA Youthful, aromatic; pear, peach, apricot; bread, biscuit.

T TASTE Round and creamy, with a lemony acidity; good length.

LIMOUX *Château Rives-Blanques*

The town of Limoux, lying in the foothills of the French Pyrenees, produces two sparkling wines. The first is Blanquette de Limoux, the region's traditional wine, which its winemakers claim predates Champagne. The second, "new" wine is the classy and elegant Crémant de Limoux, which was given appellation status in 1990.

Blanquette de Limoux must contain at least 90 per cent Mauzac grapes (known as Blanquette, meaning "white", in the region's dialect). The grapes are picked early in the season so that the wine benefits fully from their high acidity. The result is a sparkling wine with a light, bubbly structure and a sweet feel. It is competitively priced and ideal for drinking on a summer's day.

However, Crémant de Limoux is now the flagship wine of the region. This wine is made with a blend of 70 per cent Mauzac (which keeps it fresh and fruity) and 30 per cent Chardonnay and Chenin Blanc, which bring elegance and delicacy to the wine – and top-ranking fine bubbles! As there is no residual sugar in the blend, a sweet touch comes from the grapes themselves. I love this *crémant* as an apéritif, or as a refreshing pick-me-up in the afternoon.

RECOMMENDED PRODUCERS

▸ Château Rives-Blanques
▸ Caves de Sieur d'Arques
▸ Domaine de Flassian

LOIRE

C COLOUR Pale lemon to straw yellow, with silver tinges.

A AROMA Fresh, elegant; green apple, citrus fruits, pear; mineral hints.

T TASTE Charming and delicate; fine bubbles; balanced, clean finish.

With its great still whites, such as Sancerre and Muscadet, and excellent light reds, the Loire does not spring to mind as a region for top-class sparkling wines – but it is!

The Loire Valley's climate and *terroir* are very similar to those in Champagne and so perfect for producing grapes suited to making sparkling wine. The most notable variety is Chenin Blanc, although Pinot Noir, Chardonnay, and Grolleau (among others) are often also used in the blends. Winemakers use the traditional method of making sparkling wine *(see p129)*; and some of the Champagne houses themselves have set up off-shoot wineries in the Loire (Bollinger being perhaps the most famous).

The best of the Loire's sparkling wines come from the town of Saumur, which lies in the wine-producing area of Anjou-Saumur, in the western Loire. Here the *crémant* is outstandingly complex and fresh – and while it is enjoyed mostly by the

LOIRE *Baumard*

locals and is fairly undiscovered by the rest of the world, it is also extremely good value for money. I think this is a great alternative to Champagne, and makes an ideal apéritif; or try it with seafood.

RECOMMENDED PRODUCERS

▸ Baumard
▸ Les Vignerons de la Noelle
▸ Bouvais Ladubay

DIE

C COLOUR Pale golden yellow with tinges of green.

A AROMA Fresh, elegant; apple, pear, white peach, and minerals.

T TASTE Delicate, with light, fine bubbles; clean, beautifully balanced finish.

The Rhône Valley's Crémant de Die has been recognized as a top-class alternative to Champagne only since the early 1990s, because most people knew only of the Rhône's other significant sparkling wine, Clairette de Die. Some say that the Clairette, made from golden Muscat and Clairette grapes, existed before Champagne. It is produced using the *méthode diose*, in which secondary fermentation is set off not by the addition of a sugar-and-yeast mixture (as it is with Champagne),

DIE *Jean-Claude Raspail*

but naturally, because some of the must (the crushed grapes – stems, skins, and pips included) is bottled with the wine. The result is a gently sparkling, sweet wine. It was awarded appellation status in 1942.

Crémant de Die (before 1999 this wine was known as Clairette de Die Brut) is made exclusively from Clairette grapes and secondary fermentation is set off in the traditional way by the addition of sugar and yeast, just as it is with Champagne.

The balance between the flavours and persistent lemony acidity makes this wine an ideal apéritif. However, it is important to drink it within three years of bottling to ensure that you gain the most out of its subtle texture, fine aromas, and complexity.

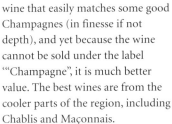

BURGUNDY *Caves de Bailly*

RECOMMENDED PRODUCERS

▸ Jean-Claude Raspail
▸ Cave Monge-Granon
▸ Domaine Achard-Vincent

BURGUNDY

C COLOUR Bright straw yellow, with green tinges.

A AROMA Complex; baked apple, citrus fruit, pineapple, pear; nuts, toast.

T TASTE Smooth and round, with fine, fresh bubbles; long, flavoursome finish.

Crémant de Bourgogne is an exceptional sparkling wine made using Chardonnay grapes in the traditional method. This is a wine that easily matches some good Champagnes (in finesse if not depth), and yet because the wine cannot be sold under the label '"Champagne", it is much better value. The best wines are from the cooler parts of the region, including Chablis and Mâconnais.

RECOMMENDED PRODUCERS

▸ Caves de Bailly
▸ Bernollin

ALSACE

C COLOUR Pale to medium straw yellow, with silver tinges.

A AROMA Young, elegant; apple, citrus, flowers.

T TASTE Clean, pure, light; well-integrated bubbles.

Crémant from the cool Alsace region of eastern France is complex and fresh with lots of personality. The wine is blended using Pinot Blanc, Pinot Noir, Chardonnay, Pinot Gris, and Riesling grapes. Serve Crémant d'Alsace well chilled (to enhance its citrus flavours) as a summer apéritif.

ALSACE *Dopff au Moulin*

RECOMMENDED PRODUCERS

▸ Dopff au Moulin
▸ Gustave Lorenz

SPAIN

Though overshadowed by France, Spain makes some truly excellent sparkling wines, which can be outstanding value. They are marketed under the name Cava and made by the traditional method used also for Champagne *(see p129)*. There are some big producers, including Freixenet and Codorníu, whose products are sold worldwide.

CAVA

 COLOUR Medium lemon yellow with green tinges.

 AROMA Intense and youthful; pear, citrus fruits, and notes of exotic fruits.

 TASTE Refreshing and clean; good, harmonious balance; lemony finish.

Spain is the world's second-largest producer of traditional-method sparkling wine, after France; and, although the country does produce other sparkling wines, Cava is its most famous.

Cava production is limited by law to five of Spain's provinces. These include the famous La Rioja and Navarra regions, but in reality almost all Cava is produced in just one of these five – Catalonia, in the northeast of the country, and specifically around the town of San Sadurni de Noya. For me, these San Sadurni Cavas are the best.

Most Cava is made using a mix of Macabeo, Parallada, and Xarel-lo grapes, with Chardonnay gaining popularity. Producers use Pinot Noir, Garnacha, or Monastrell for Cava *rosado* (rosé).

The techniques for making sparkling wine were imported into Catalonia from France at the end of the 19th century. In 1986 Spain established the Cava denomination, but (as with Champagne) there is no need for Denominación de Origen (DO) to appear on the label – the word Cava is enough. The classification system for Cava is not as rigid as that in France, but generally if you are looking for a very dry wine, buy *Extra Brut*; for dry, buy *Brut*; for semi-sweet, *Extra-Seco*; for sweet, *Seco*; and for very sweet, Sweet! If you are looking for a biscuity, Blanc de Blanc Champagne-style, try Cava Gran Reserva, which is left in the cellars for around three years and is therefore much more complex and aromatic than many other Cavas.

To some extent the marketing and snob-value of true Champagne has undermined the greatness of Cava: people assume that it is second-best. But many Cavas, especially those controlled by the houses of Codorníu and Freixenet, are great value. Try them as apéritifs, or, if you like food with your fizz, with light meals or seafood.

CAVA
Freixenet

CAVA
Codorníu

SPANISH SUCCESS
Subtle and balanced, Cava easily rivals French and New World sparklers.

RECOMMENDED PRODUCERS
▸ Freixenet
▸ Codorníu
▸ Albet I Noya
▸ Marques de Monistrol
▸ Kripta

LAND AND PRODUCTION

TURNING TIMES At the winery of Juve y Camps in San Sadurni de Noya, the Cava undergoes *remuage* (riddling) in traditional *pupitre* racks. Many larger wineries now use mechanical riddlers (*girasols*), developed by the Cava industry in the 1970s.

ITALY

Italy is best known for its light, semi-sweet, sparkling (*spumante*) wines, especially Asti, which is a great, fun drink perfect for parties. Most Italian sparkling wines are made in the far north of the country, especially Piemonte and Lombardia in the northwest, and Veneto in the northeast. These wines should be drunk young and fresh; if the bottles are dusty, buy elsewhere!

ASTI

C COLOUR Bright, pale lemony yellow, with greenish tinges.

A AROMA Aromatic; peach, apricot; flowers; a touch of the exotic!

T TASTE Light, with a lemony acidity and sweetness on the finish.

ASTI
Gancia

Lying in the region of Piemonte (Piedmont), northwestern Italy, the town of Asti produces two sparkling wines – Asti and Moscato d'Asti. If you have tried these wines, then, like many other people, you may have had a bad experience and be reluctant to try more. Mass-production of Asti in the past gave us inferior sparkling wines that undermined a great potential for making something really good.

Thankfully, many small estates in Italy are now taking Asti seriously and the quality of its wines has improved consistently over the last ten years. So, it is time to forgive and forget and to give Asti another chance! Of the two wines, Moscato d'Asti is the more sophisticated, with gentler bubbles. Both are made using a variation of the tank method (*see p126*) – where the secondary fermentation takes place in closed tanks, not in the bottle. For the wines of Asti the first fermentation is halted (in the tank method first fermentation is complete) and a sugar-and-yeast mixture is added to the partly fermented must. This is placed in a tank to finish fermenting, then filtered and bottled. By halting the first fermentation the resulting wine is quite sweet, and low in alcohol (which makes it very easy to drink). I love these wines, and they are perfect with apple tart or peach mousse.

ASTI
Rotari

RECOMMENDED PRODUCERS

▸ Gancia

▸ Rotari (Mezzacorona)

PROSECCO

C COLOUR Bright; pale yellow with greenish tinges.

A AROMA Clean, with citrus, green apple, flowers, and bitter almond.

T TASTE Subtle and well-balanced, with a nutty and ripe, exotic-fruit finish.

The cool climate of the Veneto, in northeast Italy, is perfect for cultivating the Prosecco grape. Some of the crop is made into still wine, but Prosecco's flagship wines are its refreshing *spumantes*, made using the tank method (*see p126*).

Prosecco is slightly sweeter than many other sparkling wines, and can be identified easily by its bitter almond taste at the finish. Overall it is delicious. Drink it as the Italians do – as an apéritif; or as the perfect partner to a light summer dessert.

RECOMMENDED PRODUCERS

▸ Malvolty

▸ Adriano

FRANCIACORTA

C COLOUR Bright; pale straw yellow, with silver tinges.

A AROMA Finesse, intensity; pineapple and hints of other exotic fruit; almond.

T TASTE Elegant, delicate; complex texture with balanced acidity; very long.

After a great deal of effort to establish itself as one of the wine world's serious players, Franciacorta's dry, sparkling wine is the new star of Italy.

The Franciacorta region lies in eastern Lombardia (Lombardy) in northern Spain, near the town of Brescia. Here the mountainous climate offers cool summer nights and warm days, which enable the grapes to ripen with a high level of acidity. (This is important as it gives freshness to the resulting wine.) A cool breeze from Lake Garda further enhances these growing conditions.

Most sparkling Franciacorta (the region makes still wines, too) is made using primarily Pinot Bianco grapes, which produce fresh and fruity wines. In 1995, Franciacorta was awarded Italy's highest wine qualification (DOCG status), so this elegant and delicately bubbly wine is definitely worth trying!

If you prefer creamier sparkling wines, such as the richer Champagnes, try Franciacorta's sparkling Riserva. This wine has to be kept on its lees (the dead yeast cells) for a minimum of three years before it is disgorged, and I think it is fantastic.

These wines provide the perfect accompaniment to roast chicken or any type of fish.

FRANCIACORTA
Fratelli Berlucchi

RECOMMENDED PRODUCERS

▸ Fratelli Berlucchi

▸ Antinori

▸ Bellavista

GERMANY

The Germans are enthusiastic consumers of sparkling wines. Their locally produced fizz for everyday drinking is Sekt, made from Pinot Blanc or Riesling grapes. This is produced on an industrial scale, and is excellent value.

SEKT

C COLOUR Clear; delicate pale yellow with silver tinges.

A AROMA Youthful and freshly aromatic; citrus, green fruit, and pear.

T TASTE Refreshing textures, with integrated fizziness and a medium finish.

Sekt is a fruity wine, usually lower in alcohol than Champagne and slightly sweeter than good sparkling wines from France, Spain, and the US. The best Sekts are bottle-fermented, but most is made using the tank method (*see p126*). Low-priced Sekt is sold as *trocken* (dry) and *halbtrocken* (semi-sweet), and both are great alternatives to Asti.

SEKT
Kupferberg

The base wines that go into a Sekt blend are often imported from France or Italy, and the blend is merely made to sparkle in Germany. However, Deutscher Sekt denotes a wine made in Germany using German grapes alone (usually Riesling or Müller-Thurgau). Single-variety Sekt is often labelled with the name of the variety: if you come across a Rieslingsekt, it could be worth a try!

RECOMMENDED PRODUCERS

▸ Kupferberg

▸ Schloss Wachenheim

▸ Heymann-Lowenstein

USA

The wonderful still wines made in California have been joined by a range of confident and keenly priced sparkling wines. The influence on style is strongly French; in 1973 Moët & Chandon became the first French Champagne house to begin production in California, taking full advantage of the cooler climates in the state's Sonoma and Mendocino counties.

CALIFORNIAN SPARKLING *Mumm Napa*

CALIFORNIAN SPARKLING WINES

C COLOUR Bright; pale straw yellow, with green tinges.

A AROMA Intense, complex; green apple; citrus, pineapple, pear; brioche.

T TASTE Elegant; refreshing, but full of flavour, with good length.

The fact that some of the French Champagne houses have started to set up in California says it all! The state is producing some of my favourite sparkling wines – classy, elegant, and very well balanced with a complexity that is second-to-none. They are less acidic and austere than sparkling wines from elsewhere in the world, and have some of the fruitiness associated with California's still wines.

The Californian wine industry has settled down over the past decade and its cooler microclimates (usually near the ocean) are particularly suitable for the grapes that make sparkling wine (especially Pinot Noir, Chardonnay, and Pinot Meunier). The weather enables the grapes to ripen slowly with a low sugar content and high acidity. In addition, growers and winemakers are using new techniques that permit them to clone the very best Chardonnays and Pinot Noirs (each major grape variety has hundreds of different clones) to go into their wines.

Armed with their ever-increasing knowledge of viticulture, growers and winemakers are looking closely at the soils and sites within the most suitable denominations, and finding the exact places that yield wines of the very highest quality. As the vines age, year by year, they give the grapes, and so the wines, more character. The overall result is that

LAND AND PRODUCTION

CROSSING THE OCEAN Californian growing conditions are perfectly suited to the grapes used in sparkling wine. So much so that even the French Champagne houses, including Mumm (whose Californian vineyards are shown here), Louis Roederer, and Moët, have set up here. What an accolade!

CALIFORNIAN SPARKLING *Domaine Carneros*

Californian sparkling wine is continually getting better and better.

Most of the superior sparkling wines come from four appellations in the North Coast region, which lies north of San Francisco, along the coast and inland to Central Valley. These are Anderson Valley in the wine area of Mendocino County; Green Valley and Russian River Valley in Sonoma County; and Carneros, which straddles the south end of Sonoma and Napa counties. In addition, a few areas lying near the Pacific Ocean in the North Central Coast region (to the south of San Francisco) also produce good quality sparkling wine.

Without question Californian sparkling wines are extremely good value – often up to a third less than equivalent Champagnes – and you will not go far wrong by choosing something from Sonoma or Mendocino counties. If you are looking for a very dry wine, buy Brut. This is California's most popular, and so most prolific, sparkling wine. Second most popular is Blanc de Noir – a white sparkling wine made entirely from Pinot Noir grapes.

I would recommend a Californian sparkling wine as an apéritif to accompany canapés, or with any fine and delicate fish, such as monkfish. Truly excellent!

RECOMMENDED PRODUCERS

▸ Mumm Napa
▸ Domaine Carneros
▸ Domaine Chandon
▸ Scharffenberger Cellars
▸ Roederer Estate

CANADA

Much of Canada is just too cold for winemaking. The temperate regions on the west coast and near the Great Lakes, however, produce some fine sparkling wines – and quality is improving.

CANADIAN SPARKLING WINES

C COLOUR Ranging from light gold to bright pale straw yellow.

A AROMA Fruity (nectarine, apricot), and a hint of nuts, honey, and exotic lychee.

T TASTE Delicate but bright and lively, balanced by a natural lemony acidity.

Only through the slow ripening of its grapes will a sparkling wine develop depth and complexity. A climate with warm days and cool nights is key, which makes Canada a potential hotspot for good sparkling wine.

Canada's thriving wine industry is concentrated in the four provinces of Ontario, British Columbia, Quebec, and Nova Scotia. In all these regions, the grapes tend to be grown near large bodies of water, which balance the effects of severe winters.

The region with the best quality sparkling wine is British Columbia, on the Pacific coast. Here sparkling wine is made in a variety of ways, including the traditional method (see p129). Producers such as Sumac Ridge and Ontario-based Château des Charmes, while not able to call their wine "champagne", use traditional methods and strive to match the best of their French rivals – but at much more affordable prices.

CANADIAN SPARKLING *Blue Mountain Vineyard*

RECOMMENDED PRODUCERS

▸ Blue Mountain
▸ Château de Charmes
▸ Sumac Ridge Estate
▸ Mission Hills
▸ Summerhill Estate

AUSTRALIA

This country is now adding sparkling wines to its vast repertoire. In typical Aussie style, winemakers are experimenting with new ideas, such as sparkling red Shiraz. Some of the great Champagne Houses have also now established themselves in Australia, so we should expect great things in the future.

AUSTRALIAN SPARKLING WINES

C COLOUR Pale straw yellow with silver tinges; good, steady bubbles.

A AROMA Youthful, complex; apple, pear, white peach; a hint of bread.

T TASTE Harmonious and delicate; good, refreshing acidity, and good length.

Everyone now knows that Australia offers a phenomenal range of quality red and white still wines, so it is no surprise that their sparkling wine is brilliant too. Most of Australia's sparkling wines are made in the traditional method (*see p129*), and nearly all wine-makers use the classic Champagne grape varieties of Pinot Noir and Chardonnay. To top it all, the winemakers are bursting with expertise and new technology.

Overall the quality of Australian sparkling wines is second-to-none. However, region of origin and particularly local climate play key parts in the resulting wine, so you should bear these factors in mind when choosing your wine, as well as your taste for the personal style of the particular winery.

The wine from the coolest regions is the finest. Victoria, which lies in the far southeast of the country, has traditionally been the most successful. Here some of the vineyards benefit from the cooling influence of the ocean, while others (most notably those in the Great Western district, whose major sparkling-wine producer is Seppelt) benefit from cool mountain air.

One of the leading producers of Australian sparkling wine is Green Point, established by Moët et Chandon in Victoria's Yarra Valley in the mid-1980s. The vineyards are planted with the three traditional Champagne grape varieties (Chardonnay, Pinot Noir, and Pinot Meunier), but they are supplemented with grapes from other parts of Victoria and Australia.

AUSTRALIAN SPARKLING
Seaview

AUSTRALIAN SPARKLING
Seppelt

If you are looking to make a discovery, the one to watch is the up-and-coming region of Tasmania. As Tasmania is an island (off the southeastern coast of Australia), the ocean breezes are even more influential – cooling the climate to create perfect conditions for keeping the grapes' crisp acidity and low sugar-levels. Although output is small, Tasmania's potential is well-recognized in the wine world – with French Champagne house Louis Roederer having set up a joint venture there. Other excellent Australian producers are Heemskerk, producing Jansz Brut, and Seaview. Hardy's, Seppelt, and others also produce a sparkling red Shiraz.

RECOMMENDED PRODUCERS
▸ Seaview
▸ Seppelt
▸ Green Point (Moët et Chandon)
▸ Heemskerk

NEW ZEALAND

New Zealand has been making sparkling wines from the Pinot Noir and Pinot Meunier grapes since the beginning of the 20th century. Using and adapting traditional methods in the country's cool climate, unique styles have emerged, characterized by subtle fruit flavours. Brands like Cloudy Bay have established themselves at the very top of the market, rivalling even French sparkling wines.

NEW ZEALAND SPARKLING WINES

C COLOUR Bright, pale straw yellow, with silver tinges; fine bubbles.

A AROMA Delicate; green apple; peach; flowers; hints of warm bread.

T TASTE Fresh and elegant; creamy and subtle bubbles; long, lemony finish.

If there is a New World country that has ranked itself among the makers of the very best fizzies, New Zealand is the one. Since the late 1970s several New Zealand wineries have formed alliances with French Champagne houses, such as Deutz, to assist in the development of their premium sparkling wines. These wines have now earned international acclaim, resulting in increased demand in export markets. New Zealand sparkling wines are beautifully balanced with complexity, freshness, and class – true rivals to the French!

The country's great advantage over other New World wine producers is that it is primarily a cool country, and yet it is still warm enough to allow the grapes to ripen. Slow ripening enables the grapes to develop complexity that shows itself in the wine's sophisticated, creamy tastes. Overall, New Zealand sparkling wines offer finesse similar to the best basic Champagne *cuvées* – but at a fraction of the price.

Marlborough, in the north of New Zealand's South Island, is often cited as the best area for sparkling wines, and produces such fine examples as Cloudy Bay Pelorus. Most of these wines are made from Chardonnay and Pinot Noir grapes sourced from several growers and estate vineyards located within the Wairau Valley in Marlborough. On the North Island, Morton Estate produces the fine Morton Brut Methode Traditionnelle. All these wines match well with a wide range of light dishes, especially seafood, such as crayfish, crab, scallops, caviar, and white fish.

I really believe in these wines and I often choose them as alternatives to

NEW ZEALAND SPARKLING
Morton Estate

FOOD MATCH

ALMONDS New Zealand sparkling wine, sipped lightly as an apéritif, is perfectly complemented by a bowl of almonds. Delicious!

Champagne. Some of my clients can tell the difference, but many cannot. Either way, we all agree that New Zealand sparkling wines are among the finest in the New World.

RECOMMENDED PRODUCERS
▸ Morton Estate
▸ Cloudy Bay Pelorus
▸ Deutz
▸ Montana

SOUTH AFRICA

The principal style of South African sparkling wine – Méthode Cap Classique – uses grapes and methods similar to those employed in Champagne itself. The name comes from a 40-year-old accord with France, in which it was agreed that, provided South African wines bore no French names, the French would continue buying South African crayfish.

CAP CLASSIQUE

C **COLOUR** Bright; pale straw yellow, with green tinges.

A **AROMA** Medium intensity; fresh fruit including pear and apricot

T **TASTE** Elegant, delicate; well-integrated bubbles; refreshing finish.

"Méthode Cap Classique" is the South African term denoting that the wine has been made in exactly the same way as Champagne. The Cap Classiques also use the traditional Champagne grape varieties of Pinot Noir and Chardonnay; although Pinotage (a cross between Pinot Noir and Cinsault), Chenin Blanc, Sauvignon Blanc, Riesling, and Muscat may be used, but usually only in lower-quality carbonated wines.

WESTERN CAPE WINERY
The Graham Beck Winery has won several international awards for its sparkling wines.

CAP CLASSIQUE
Graham Beck

Although South African still wines have impressed many wine-lovers with their spectacularly rapid improvement, and are now ranked with the finest New World wines, South African sparkling wine has generally not yet reached the standards of New Zealand or California fizzies. However, South African winemakers are determined to make their wine industry rank with the top New-World producers across the whole range of wines, and Cap Classique is definitely one to watch out for.

As with all sparkling wines, climate is key and the climatic differences in South Africa can be quite extreme. Look out for wines from the cooler areas: the wines from Constantia are among my favourites. Constantia lies in the Coastal Region and

CAP CLASSIQUE
Villiera

is cooled by breezes from the Atlantic Ocean and False Bay, and by the mountains that lie on one side.

Another great region is Paarl – and particularly the ward of Franschhoek, which is cooled by the rivers and hills that lie within its boundaries. Some of the best Franschhoek sparkling wines are produced by the Graham Beck winery (so good that they were chosen to toast Nelson Mandela at his presidential inauguration), which also has another site at Robertson in the Breede River Valley. The Graham Beck Brut NV, a Pinot Noir–Chardonnay blend, has a rich, creamy complexity that is balanced by freshness and finesse. The award-winning Blanc de Blancs is distinctive and full-bodied, for a sparkling. Although it is made entirely from Chardonnay, half of the still wine that goes into the blend undergoes its first fermentation in oak barrels. This is then mixed with Chardonnay that has been fermented in stainless steel vats, before being bottled for its second fermentation. The wine spends at least 48 months on its "lees" (in contact with the yeast) before the sediment is extracted to reveal a wine with lovely yeasty aromas.

The producer J.C. Le Roux, whose winery lies in Devon Valley, Stellenbosch (in the Coastal Region),

FOOD MATCH

SEAFOOD King prawns, oysters, and caviar are delicious with the richer South African Cap Classique wines, which go well with carpaccio, too.

exclusively makes sparkling wines. If you like especially crisp sparkling wine, try the Cap Classique Pinot Noir, which has a zesty taste and refreshing finish. Some of Le Roux's better wines can be stored for up to 10 years in the right conditions.

Although I believe that there is room for improvement in South African sparkling wines (often the bubbles are a little too big and detract from the finesse), there is no doubt that they are on their way up in the wine world. I thoroughly recommend that you give them a try.

RECOMMENDED PRODUCERS

▶ Graham Beck
▶ Villiera
▶ J C Le Roux
▶ Boschendal
▶ Cabriere

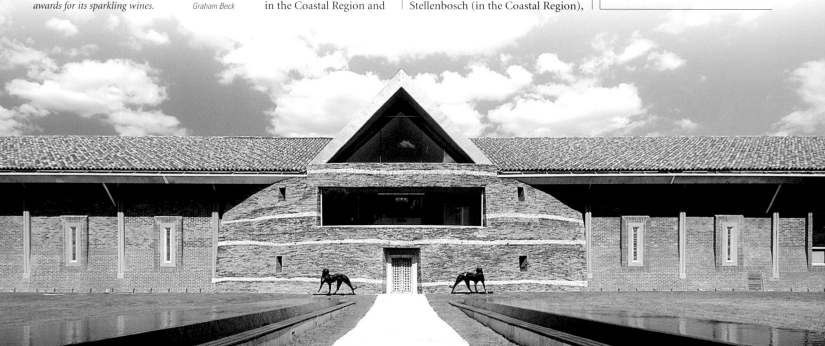

❝ Voluptuous, with a deep intensity, rich bouquet, and a silky, sophisticated structure, the best of these wines have tremendous ageing potential. **❞**

SWEET AND FORTIFIED

INTRODUCING SWEET AND FORTIFIED WINES

In the days when dinner ended with a rich pudding, sweet wines were a normal part of a meal. Even though these wines have lost favour in recent years, they continue to provide some of the best (and most costly) tasting experiences in the world.

DRINKING AND SERVING

DRINK PROFILE These wines should have a high viscosity in the glass, with extremely long "legs". The aromas will change if the wine is botrytized – becoming concentrated, even mushroomy.

C COLOUR Sweet and fortified wines should be bright, and the colour of pale gold or straw, with silver-green nuances in the first five years, turning to hints of gold. Intense opacity in port.

A AROMA These are complex wines, with intense, delicate aromas. Look for hints of figs, marmalade, honey, pineapple, grapefruit, dried apricot, spice, chocolate, and liquorice.

T TASTE Sweet wines are full and rich, luscious and subtle, with a balance of lemony acidity underlying the sweetness. There should be a clean, fresh, and persistent finish.

BUYING AND STORING These wines give excellent potential for ageing, sometimes for up to 50 years. They can be extremely expensive.

SERVING SUGGESTIONS Serve most sweet and fortified wines "colder than cold". This will bring out the wines' acidity, which is the key to their freshness, balancing their sugars and preventing them from tasting sickly. If they are served too warm, the wines will feel heavy and sticky. They are most suitable for serving at the end of a meal.

FOOD COMPANIONS As a general rule of thumb, the wine should be sweeter than the food, or the wine will taste bland. However, don't limit sweet wines to the dessert course. They can make great partners for some blue cheeses, or try the classic combination of Sauternes with foie gras.

ORANGE MARMALADE *Fortified wines have dense, sweet flavours.*

At the lower end of the market, sweet wines are sometimes made by adding unfermented grape juice to dry wine. But in most cases, sweet and fortified wines are created when grapes stop fermenting before all their sugar has turned to alcohol. In the case of sweet wines, such as Sauternes and Tokaji, fermentation either ceases naturally or is made to stop by the addition of sulphur dioxide. In fortified wine, such as sherry and port, the producers add alcohol to kill off the yeast and prevent further fermentation. The best sweet and fortified wines are made from berries that have a super-concentration of sugar. Concentration is achieved in three main ways: first, the grapes may be dried in the sun. Second, they may be left in the frost, freezing the water out of the berries and so leaving a greater concentration of sugar (creating so-called "ice wines"). Finally, many of the greatest sweet wines are a result of the grapes being subjected to a benign disease, known as "noble rot", caused by the fungus *Botrytis cinerea*.

THE NOBLE ROT

Producers of dry wines fear *Botrytis cinerea* because it can discolour grapes and give the wine undesirable flavours. But for the makers of such sweet wines as Sauternes, Barsac, and Monbazillac from France, *Trockenbeerenauslese* wines from Germany, and Tokaji from Hungary, the noble rot is an ally. When the weather is cool and misty in the mornings and hot and sunny in the afternoons, *Botrytis cinerea* mould grows over the ripened grapes as they hang on the vines,

PEAR TART *Desserts that are sweet, but not overly so, will not overpower the rich flavours of sweet wines.*

shrinking and dehydrating the berries without breaking their skins. This concentrates not only the grapes' sugars, but their acid and flavours too. As noble rot will not grow uniformly over the grapes, winemakers need to conduct several pickings (by hand). This and other factors make production of these wines expensive – but the cost is worth it, turning out wines that are sweet but not cloying, and perfectly balanced.

GRAPE VARIETIES

For sweet wines, it is not so much the grape variety that is important, but the process used in production. Most – even the great classics like Barsac and Sauternes – are blends of grapes. Sémillon is the most important, but Riesling, Chenin Blanc, and Muscat are also used.

Fortified wines are also usually blends, with spirit added to increase strength. The key grape varieties in sherry are Palomino, for delicacy; Pedro Ximénez, for a fuller type of sherry; and Moscatel, for sweetness. In port, around 85 different grape varieties are used.

GRAPE	BEST REGIONAL EXAMPLES	COMMENTS
SÉMILLON	France: Sauternes, Barsac, and satellites. Australia. California. Chile.	One of the key grapes in this category, Sémillon is often blended with Sauvignon to balance its oily and rich texture. It supports noble rot extremely well, thanks to the skin of the berries. The resulting wines are very fine, with delicate and intensely complex aromas. They age very well, revealing their true personality after many years. In the New World, wines from this grape tend to be stickier, and ready to be enjoyed sooner.
RIESLING	Germany. Austria. France: Alsace. Australia. Canada. Chile.	This versatile grape is used to make some of the finest and rarest dessert wines in the world. It ages well, improving over decades, thanks to its high acidity.
MUSCAT	France: Beaume de Venise, Frontignan, Rivesaltes. Italy. South Africa: Jerep go. Australia. Portugal: Setúbal, Madeira. Spain.	This successful grape features in a range of vibrant, exotic wines with pronounced grape characters. These range from wines light in weight to much darker and stickier wines, but all have intense flavours. Their lack of strong acidity means that they do not age well beyond a few decades, but fortified styles, such as Madeira and Setúbal will age for centuries. This grape variety is also known as Moscatel.
CHENIN BLANC	France: Loire Valley.	This famous grape makes some great botrytized wines thanks to its high acidity. The wines have intense aromas and include Vouvray, Quarts du Chaume, Coteaux du Layon, and Bonnezeaux.
GRENACHE NOIR	France: Banyuls, Maury, Rasteau. Spain.	This is one of the most popular red grapes for making fortified wines around the Mediterranean. The wines are unusually fresh in taste and possess a delicate bouquet.
GEWÜRZTRAMINER	France: Alsace. Germany. New Zealand.	Gewürztraminer is a grape producing traditionally off-dry wines full of exotic and spicy flavours. As a sweet wine, it offers intensity, and bags of fruit.
VIDAL	Canada.	The thick-skinned and heavy-yielding Vidal grape is a cross between the Ugni Blanc and Seyval Blanc varieties. It is used to make a rich, well-balanced ice wine that has helped to revolutionize the Canadian wine industry.
PEDRO XIMÉNEZ	Spain: Malaga, Montilla. Australia.	This Spanish grape variety is becoming better known thanks to improved vinification. It is used to make fortified wines, notably the sweeter styles of sherry. These wines tend to be very sticky, intense, and flavoursome, but beautifully balanced.
MALVASIA	Italy.	This variety, which is grown throughout Italy, is used to make the famous Vin Santo. It is often blended with the Trebbiano grape, which adds an extra dimension of complexity, comparable with the classic Sauternes blend of Sémillon and Sauvignon. It is also known as Pinot Gris.

FRANCE

France makes some of the greatest sweet wines in the world, especially from blends of the Sémillon grape in the favourable microclimate of the Bordeaux region. Sweet wines are also produced in the Loire Valley and in Alsace, using local grapes, such as Chenin Blanc, Riesling, and Gewürztraminer.

SAUTERNES / BARSAC

C **COLOUR** Deep gold to straw yellow, with silver tinges; bright.

A **AROMA** Intense, complex; honey; dried apricot, pineapple; marmalade; acacia.

T **TASTE** Oily, but balanced by a marked acidity; rich with a long, clean finish.

The king of dessert wines! The region of Sauternes, in southern Bordeaux, produces the most famous of all dessert wines – a luscious blend of Sémillon (the key variety) with a little Sauvignon Blanc to balance acidity and maintain

SAUTERNES
Château de Rayne Vigneau

freshness, and perhaps a small amount of Muscadelle for extra flavour. Sauternes' position between the Ciron and Garonne rivers provides a unique microclimate, perfectly suited to the development of *Botrytis cinerea*, the fungus that produces noble rot. A confluence of the two rivers gives misty mornings; these encourage the fungus to produce spores, which grow in the warm afternoons. As noble rot develops, the grapes shrivel, concentrating their sugars. Adjacent to Sauternes, northward

along the Garonne River, lies Barsac. Here the wines are slightly less sweet than Sauternes, and are lighter and fresher (a result of the limestone soil on which its vines are planted).

Matching sweet wine with desserts is not easy – the sugar combination can sometimes clash. These wines are best with a dessert that is not too sweet, such as apple tart. However, to get the best out of a Sauternes, try it with blue cheese, or make the famous match with foie gras.

LAND AND PRODUCTION

SAUTERNES AT IT BEST
Winemakers at Château d'Yquem have been making the world's best (and most expensive) sweet wines for centuries. The wines are aged for three years before a blind tasting determines the barrels good enough for bottling.

RECOMMENDED PRODUCERS
▸ Château Rieussec
▸ Château de Rayne Vigneau
▸ Château D'Yquem
▸ Suduiraut

LAYON / BONNEZEAUX

C COLOUR Beautiful golden yellow; intense and bright.

A AROMA Complex, expressive; marzipan, peach, apricot, quince, cinnamon.

T TASTE Suave, oily, rich; balanced with marked acidity; full; very long finish.

Coteaux du Layon comes from the heart of the Loire, in the Anjou district, on the banks of the Layon tributary. The Chenin Blanc grapes that go into this wine grow perfectly on the steep valley sides, expressing their very best qualities – including a characteristic high acidity. During the autumn months, the Layon River brings morning mists and humidity, which encourage the development of noble rot, essential for sweet wine production here.

Coteaux du Layon wines are more upfront and easier to enjoy young than Sauternes; they tend to have a lighter texture and are less sticky, with emphasis on fresh baked

CHATEAU DE FESLES
BONNEZEAUX
appellation Bonnezeaux controlée
1998
13 % vol   50 cl

BONNEZEAUX *Château de Fesles*

fruit, such as apple and quince, rather than on jammy exotic fruits.

Within Layon lie two unofficial "*crus*" – Bonnezeaux and Quarts de Chaume – whose wines are by far the best sweet wines in the Loire. In these two regions, the grapes yield less juice than they do in the coteaux (the hillsides in the region), so it is often highly concentrated and flavourful. This means that a well-made, good-vintage Bonnezeaux or Quarts de Chaume might age for between 30 and 50 years. Try these wines with caramelized tarte tatin and vanilla ice-cream – the best!

RECOMMENDED PRODUCERS
▸ Château de Fesles
▸ Château Pierre Bise

ALSACE

C COLOUR Pale straw to golden yellow with green tinges; bright and pleasant.

A AROMA Intense, elegant; ripe, exotic fruit; citrus; flowers.

T TASTE Delicate, fruit-driven; long, harmonious finish.

Alsatian sweet wines fall into two classifications based on their residual sugar content. The lighter wine is *vendange tardives*, while *sélection de grains nobles* is long-aged and syrupy.

The wines are made from four different botrytized varieties: upfront Muscat; complex Pinot Gris; muscly Gewürztraminer; and sticky, lemony Riesling.

ALSACE
Rolly Gassmann

RECOMMENDED PRODUCERS
▸ Rolly Gassmann
▸ Zind Humbrecht

VIN DE PAILLE

C COLOUR Deep, rich golden yellow with orange nuances.

A AROMA Complex; dried fruit (apricot, pineapple, orange); honey; hazelnut.

T TASTE Rich and harmonious; round with "infinite" length.

Literally translated, *vin de paille* means "straw wine" (in German, *strohwein*). The grapes are hand-picked and left to dry in the sun on straw mats. The sun evaporates the water from the berries to concentrate the sugars. Once raisined, the grapes are pressed and vinified. Alsace, Jura, and the northern Rhône all produce a small amount of these wines. They offer fantastic complexity of flavours, with sherry-like notes, and are heavenly with apricot tart and almond ice-cream.

RECOMMENDED PRODUCERS
▸ Domaine Rolet
▸ Jacques Foret

LAND AND PRODUCTION

SWEET WINE PRODUCTION Making sweet wines relies on the extraction of water from the grapes before pressing, which concentrates the berries' sugars. The two most common ways of doing this are through "noble rot" and by freezing the water out of the grapes. In regions with misty, humid mornings and warm, sunny afternoons, a parasitic fungus called *Botrytis cinerea* can attack the grapes, extracting their moisture. In colder climates, the grapes can be left on the

vines into winter. Once the temperature drops below -8°C (17°F), the grapes freeze, which naturally brings the water out of the flesh. The frozen grapes are then picked and pressed as quickly as possible – often during the night.

RACE AGAINST TIME
The grapes used to make ice wine must reach the press still frozen.

NOBLE ROT Botrytis cinerea *desiccates the grapes and turns their skins a purple-brown colour. The fungus looks unattractive, but it is harmless.*

MUSCAT DE BEAUMES-DE-VENISE

C COLOUR Bright straw to lemon yellow with silver tinges.

A AROMA Vibrant; very aromatic; exotic fruits; flowers, honey, and spice.

T TASTE Rich and strong, with a delicate texture and long, fruity finish.

MUSCAT DE BEAUMES-DE-VENISE
Domaine de Durban

This famous sweet wine comes from the Vaucluse, a beautiful part of the southern Rhône Valley. It is made from purely Muscat à Petits Grains grapes, which are well-suited to a hot Mediterranean climate.

Muscat de Beaumes-de-Venise is a Vin Doux Naturel (VDN, literally meaning "natural sweet wine"). VDNs are made in the same way as port: winemakers stop fermentation toward its completion by adding alcohol. This leaves some residual sugar, but also results in a high alcohol level (about 15% ABV).

The finished product is a subtle and delicate sweet wine with an appealing fruit structure. Its orange blossom, floral, and spicy character makes it good enough to eat!

Although the wine can lack bite (there is insufficient acidity) and the locals drink it as an apéritif, it goes well with light desserts, or a fruit salad. Drink it while it is young, and do not worry if you do not finish the bottle in one sitting: its high alcohol means that it will keep in the refrigerator for up to about five days.

RECOMMENDED PRODUCERS

▸ Domaine de Durban
▸ Chapoutier
▸ Domaine de la Pigeade

RIVESALTES

C COLOUR Bright; deep gold to amber with a silver rim.

A AROMA Intense but elegant; quince, fig, apricot, almond, exotic fruits.

T TASTE Rich, oily, and structured, but well-balanced with a long, clean finish.

Rivesaltes lies in southern France, in the foothills of the Pyrenees. The region is home to two appellations making Vins Doux Naturels (VDNs) – Rivesaltes and Muscat de Rivesaltes. Together they represent over half the total production of Muscat wine in the whole of France.

The wines of the Rivesaltes appellation can themselves be split into two categories, white and amber, depending upon the wine's blend of grape varieties (including Grenache, Macabeo, and others). I find the white Rivesaltes to be like a Pineau de Charentes (from the west of France), because of its strong, rich texture. Amber Rivesaltes is more like a fruity Tawny port – it has a delicious character of prunes, cherry brandy, and chocolate.

Muscat de Rivesaltes is made from a blend of two varieties of Muscat grapes: Muscat of Alexandria and Muscat Blanc à Petits Grains. Best drunk when it is young, the wine is delicate and aromatic, with a rich texture and baked-fruit flavours.

I am a big fan of all the wines of Rivesaltes – they are good value, and delicious with chocolate tart.

MUSCAT DE RIVESALTES
Domaine Cazes

RECOMMENDED PRODUCERS

▸ Domaine Cazes
▸ Domaine la Casenove
▸ Domaine Lerys

BANYULS

C COLOUR Opaque; dark garnet with a ruby to red-tile rim.

A AROMA Intense, delicate; fig, quince, prune, chocolate, liquorice, and spice.

T TASTE Full, rich; round, smooth texture, balanced by tannins and a fresh acidity.

Banyuls is produced on the gravelly soil terraces around the town of Collioure, near the Spanish border. High standards among a few dedicated producers result in wines with huge complexity and finesse. For less fruit, but more chocolate and spice, try the *grand cru*; it is more like Châteauneuf-du-Pape than fortified wine!

I love these wines and would even choose them over port to end a meal.

BANYULS *Domaine du Mas Blanc*

RECOMMENDED PRODUCERS

▸ Domaine du Mas Blanc
▸ Castell des Hospices

FRONTIGNAN

C COLOUR Pale gold to straw yellow with green tinges.

A AROMA Youthful, intense, complex; pineapple, passion fruit; flowers.

T TASTE Intense, delicate, and subtle with a great concentration of flavours.

Frontignan is a small appellation between Sète and Montpellier in the Languedoc region of France. Muscat de Frontignan is one of the finest Muscat wines, made from the delicate Muscat à Petits Grains grapes. Its combination of depth and elegance is down to the *terroir* in the region, but also to the sea breezes, which maintain its refreshing acidity and balance. Try it with any summer fruit tart.

RECOMMENDED PRODUCERS

▸ Château de Stony
▸ Château de Six Terres

MAURY

C COLOUR Bright dark cherry, with a ruby rim. Good depth.

A AROMA Powerful and rich; spice, fig, cocoa, blackberry, prune.

T TASTE Ample, rich, vinous, and suave; fresh, balanced by mellow tannins.

A sweet wine of a small appellation in Roussillon, Maury is made mainly with Grenache Noir, and is light, but more complex than its neighbour Banyuls. Vines are grown on a hilly, stony schist, far from the sea, which brings out the grapes' fruit. Serve the wine slightly chilled with chocolate tart, or caramelized duck breast, with *girolle* mushrooms and dried figs.

MAURY
Mas Amiel

RECOMMENDED PRODUCERS

▸ Mas Amiel
▸ Domaine Maurydore

RASTEAU

C COLOUR Deep garnet, with a purple and orange rim.

A AROMA Complex; dried fig, walnut, prune, spice, blackcurrant, dried herbs.

T TASTE Dense, well-structured, and powerful, but harmonious; good length.

Rasteau is a well-structured, virtually undiscovered Vin Doux Naturel (VDN) from the southern Rhône. It must be made from 90 per cent Grenache grapes. Lighter styles make excellent apéritifs, while the heavier Rasteau Rancio (which is exposed to heat and oxygen during vinification) is a dessert wine. Drink it with a rich Black Forest Gâteau.

RECOMMENDED PRODUCERS

▸ Domaine la Soumade
▸ Domaine de Beaurenard

SPAIN

The great Spanish fortified wine is sherry, named after the city of Jerez in Andalucía. Sherry has its own special process of manufacture, and can be dry or sweet. Other great, but lesser-known wines, with their own style and character, include Montilla from Cordoba and Málaga, both cities not far from Jerez.

SHERRY

C COLOUR Pale lemon to deep gold and dark, russet brown.

A AROMA Intense, classy; nuts, citrus fruit, flowers, a hint of caramel.

T TASTE Round and complex; low acidity, balanced alcohol, long finish.

SHERRY
Delgado Zuleta

One of the great fortified wines, sherry is made around the town of Jerez in southern Spain. Three main grape varieties are used to make sherry (individually or in combination). First is Palomino (accounting for all but ten per cent of sherry production), which makes a delicate, dry sherry. Second is Pedro Ximénez (PX). These grapes are dried in the sun to concentrate their sugars, and make a fuller, richer, darker sherry. The last is Moscatel; sherry from this grape tends to be drunk only locally, although some is used to sweeten other fortified wine.

SHERRY
Hidalgo

Every bottle of sherry you find in your local store will fall into one of two categories: *fino* or *oloroso*. A *fino* is made when a type of yeast (flor) begins to develop on the surface of the wine as it ferments. This reduces the wine's acidity, and by providing a "blanket" over the wine, prevents it oxidizing. This gives a more a delicate (*fino*) taste. If flor does not develop, the sherry will become an *oloroso*.

Once fermentation has finished, and the producers can see whether flor has begun to develop, the wine is fortified according to whether it is to be *fino* or *oloroso*. Pure grape spirit is added to to raise the alcohol level to around 18% ABV for *oloroso* sherries (this prevents flor from forming during maturation), and 15.5% ABV for *finos* (a level at which flor will flourish during maturation). The wines are then matured using the *solera* system (*see below*).

There are several kinds of *fino* sherry. Standard Fino is light and dry, while Manzanilla is delicate and pungent, with almond flavours. The darker, nutty Manzanilla Pasada is a Manzanilla that has been bottled after the flor has disappeared – at about seven years. Fino Amontillado is a *fino* that has lost its flor (at around six years), turned amber, and gained a slightly nutty, *rancio* (over-ripe fruit) flavour. A simple "Amontillado" is a *fino*-style wine, which is darker and softer than Fino Amontillado. "Pale cream" sherry is sweetened *fino*.

As *fino* is a delicate and tangy wine, drink the contents of an opened bottle within a week or so, otherwise it will lose its freshness.

Oloroso sherries are oxidized, giving a deep brown colour and rich, nutty flavour. Most Spanish *oloroso* sherries are dry. "Cream" sherry and Amoroso tend to be sweetened, lower-grade *oloroso*. Once opened, *oloroso* sherry will keep well.

To further confuse matters there is the rare, aged (often 20 years or more) Palo Cortado. This begins as a *fino*, with a tangy flor character, then evolves as an *oloroso*, developing a rich nuttiness and a darker colour.

Serve dry sherry chilled as an apéritif, or with tapas. Sweet sherry, by contrast, is best at room temperature, with the cheese course at the end of a meal.

SHERRY
Emilio Lustau

RECOMMENDED PRODUCERS
▸ Delgado Zuleta
▸ Hidalgo
▸ Emilio Lustau
▸ Colosia
▸ González Byass

MONTILLA

C COLOUR Bright; ranging from pale lemon yellow to gold.

A AROMA Fresh; citrus, spice, walnut, pear, flowers.

T TASTE Clean, rich, round; balanced acidity and alcohol.

Montilla wines, from Cordoba in Andalucía, are naturally high in alcohol and tend to be unfortified. Made mainly from Pedro Ximénez grapes, they are similar in style to sherry. Supermarkets will classify them as dry, medium, and cream (or sweet). The dry is similar to *fino* – having aged with flor (a yeast).

MONTILLA
Pérez Barquero

RECOMMENDED PRODUCERS
▸ Pérez Barquero
▸ Alvear

MALÁGA

C COLOUR Dark chocolate brown with orange nuances.

A AROMA Powerful; tobacco, spice, coffee, liquorice, prune, and walnut.

T TASTE Rich and heady; strong but well-balanced; full of flavours and character.

This Spanish fortified wine from the town of the same name is made from either Pedro Ximénez or Moscatel grapes, both of which make it very sweet. First, the grapes are allowed to dry and concentrate in the sun. Once the grapes are pressed, and the juice is extracted, producers usually stop fermentation at the required level by adding grape spirit or *arrope*, which is unfermented, concentrated grape juice.

This is a winter wine to drink with rich puddings; it is also great with mature cheddar.

RECOMMENDED PRODUCERS
▸ Hermanos
▸ Larios

LAND AND PRODUCTION

MATURING SHERRY The "*solera* system" ensures that a sherry's qualities remain consistent from year to year. The youngest wine in the top *criadera* (the name for all but the bottom row of barrels) is mixed with the older wine in the row below, which mixes with the still older wine in the next row, and so on, blending the characters from the different ages. Sherry for bottling is then taken from the bottom row – the *solera* itself.

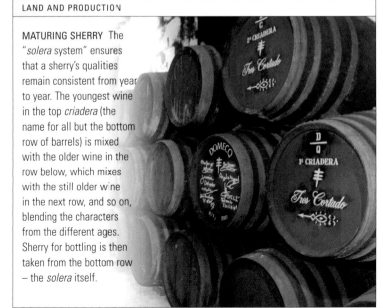

PORTUGAL

Portugal is synonymous with port, the classic fortified wine, made in many different styles around the city of Oporto in the north of the country. Less well known is Setúbal, named after a city near Lisbon, and a fine, rich alternative to port. The Portuguese island of Madeira also makes wonderful fortified wines, using a special process that gives them a burnt character and the ability to endure great ageing.

PORT

C **COLOUR** Deep opaque purple, with a brown rim.

A **AROMA** Intense; dried fruit; spice, liquorice, coffee, almond.

T **TASTE** Suave; vinous with a smooth texture; very well-balanced.

PORT
Quinta do Portal

Port is made in the Douro River valley in northern Portugal. Traditionally, the grapes are crushed by foot, although now most producers use mechanical crushers. The must ferments in closed concrete or steel tanks. When about half the sugar has turned to alcohol, the wine is run off into barrels containing (traditionally) one part brandy to four parts wine – to prevent further fermentation. Ageing and blending occurs centrally at Vila Nova de Gaia, at the mouth of the Douro.

The most basic style of port is called ruby. This is a fruity, non-vintage, appealing wine, for everyday drinking. Tawny ports are smooth, with dry, nutty flavours and are excellent served chilled as apéritifs, perhaps with a bowl of almonds.

The finest and most expensive port of all is vintage port, which comes from a single, exceptional harvest. After two years of cask-ageing, the wine matures in the bottle for between 15 and 50 years! Vintage port requires decanting; before opening, stand the bottle upright for at least 24 hours (longer for older vintages) to allow time for the sediment to settle on the bottom. This is an after-dinner drink, traditionally taken with cheese. I love to savour it on its own, especially when old, with a bar of dark chocolate and a small cigar.

RECOMMENDED PRODUCERS

▸ Quinta do Portal
▸ Taylor's
▸ Vargellas

LAND AND PRODUCTION

MOVING PORT Traditionally, special boats named *barcos rabelos* were used to bring the port wine from the *bodegas* in the Douro valley to Vila Nova de Gaia, for blending and ageing. However, damming of the river means that today the wine must be transported by road.

THE PERFECT GLASS
Serve your port at about 18°C (64°F) in a tulip-shaped glass, filled no more than half way.

SETÚBAL

- **C** COLOUR Distinctive tawny brown with highlights of orange.
- **A** AROMA Pronounced and spicy; raisins, dried fig, and baked fruits.
- **T** TASTE Rich and heavy, but harmonious; syrupy, with intense, complex flavours.

Setúbal, from one of the oldest demarcated wine regions of Portugal, is a fortified wine made using the Moscatel (Muscat) grape. It is produced in a similar way to port: grape spirit is added to fermenting must (crushed whole grapes), which stops fermentation. Rather than the wine being run off at this stage, it is left with the skins for several months, and then aged in casks for between 20 and 50 years (for the best wines), before bottling. For a change from port, why not try a Setúbal?

RECOMMENDED PRODUCERS
▸ Fonseca
▸ Caves Velhas

MADEIRA

- **C** COLOUR Dark brown with gold to red-tile nuances.
- **A** AROMA Intense and delicate; plum, toffee, raisins, quince, hazelnut.
- **T** TASTE Rounded; perfectly balanced; great depth and elegance.

Madeira wines take their names from four local white grape varieties, each of which imparts its characteristics to the wine. They are Sercial (producing the finest dry wines); Verdelho (giving medium-dry, nutty wines); Bual (rich, medium-sweet wines); and Malmsey (the sweetest wines). Most Madeira is a blend of these grapes; to carry the name of a particular variety, the wine must be at least 85 per cent that grape. Otherwise, the wine is marketed under such names as "Island Dry" or "Rainwater".

MADEIRA *Cossart Gordon*

LAND AND PRODUCTION

CLIFFTOP WINES Madeira is an Atlantic island, around 1000km (620 miles) west of Lisbon. It has rich, fertile volcanic soil, and, as there is little level land, vineyards tend to be planted on stepped terraces (*poios*). Vines trail over pergolas, which helps to protect them from fungal disease.

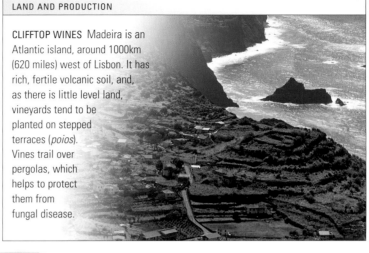

In sweeter Madeira, fermentation is halted by adding spirit, as with port; for drier Madeira, the wine is fortified after fermentation (like sherry). The wine then spends a minimum of three months exposed to heat – either under the sun's rays, or in heated rooms. This process (called *estufagem*, caramelizes the sugars and oxidizes the wine, making it high in alcohol and tannins and able to age almost indefinitely. Drink old Madeiras with rich, mature cheese.

RECOMMENDED PRODUCERS
▸ Cossart Gordon
▸ Blandys
▸ Perreira

ITALY

Italy makes some wonderful sweet wines from the Muscat grape, and Sicily is well known for its rich, fortified Marsala – a drink similar to *oloroso* sherry. But the most famous of all is Vin Santo, which is made from grapes dried on racks to concentrate their sweetness.

VIN SANTO

- **C** COLOUR Amber to deep gold, with a silver rim.
- **A** AROMA Elegant; jammy apricot; pineapple, honey, and almond.
- **T** TASTE Round, delicate; good acidity; good length.

Vin Santo (meaning "holy wine") is an unforgettably complex dessert wine made all over Tuscany, central Italy. The unique method of making Vin Santo begins when the grapes (Trebbiano and Malvasia) are put out to dry. Producers crush the dried, concentrated grapes

VIN SANTO
Antinori

over the winter months. Exactly when pressing occurs depends upon the amount of residual sugar the producer wants for his final wine. (The later the crushing, the sweeter the wine.) The juice is left to ferment, and then mature for three to six years in oak casks, which gives the wine its complexity and amber colour.

Vin Santo is superb! Try it with Italian biscotti or a nougat *glassé*, which will reinforce the slightly oxidized almond and vanilla notes of the wine.

RECOMMENDED PRODUCERS
▸ Antinori
▸ Filigare

MARSALA

- **C** COLOUR Deep amber to ruby, with orange nuances.
- **A** AROMA Full of character; dried fruit through to herbs and spice.
- **T** TASTE A powerful, opulent, and dry texture; intense with a long finish.

Marsala is made in Sicilia (Sicily) in the sherry style – from fermented wine, which is then fortified and sweetened. The wines are labelled according to the amount of ageing they have had, from *fine* (aged for one year), through *superiore*, *superiore riserva*, and *vergine*, to *vergine stravecchio* (aged for more than 10 years). Try good Marsala with blue cheese.

MARSALA
Pellegrino

RECOMMENDED PRODUCERS
▸ Pellegrino
▸ De Bartoli

MUSCATO

- **C** COLOUR Limpid; pale straw to lemon yellow; bright with green tinges.
- **A** AROMA Subtle and charming; mango, lychee, papaya, citrus, and melon.
- **T** TASTE Light, refreshing; pleasant hints of fizz and a clean, fruity finish.

I am a great fan of these vibrant, light-hearted, and sexy wines from the Asti region of Piemonte (Piedmont), northwest Italy. They have a sweetness that makes my mouth water! I think of Muscato d'Asti as a baby Muscat de Beaumes-de-Venise, because it has a lighter structure and a fizziness that enhances its fruity freshness. Perfect on a summer afternoon!

RECOMMENDED PRODUCERS
▸ Dinderralla
▸ Banfi

HUNGARY

The favourite of kings through the ages, Hungary's classic Tokaji (or Tokay) is one of the great sweet wines of the world, made from a particular blend of grapes. After years under a communist regime, when investment in technology and the quality of the wine suffered, this special drink is making a powerful comeback.

TOKAJI

C **COLOUR** Deep golden yellow, with straw to orange tinges.

A **AROMA** Intense; dried apricot, honey, walnut, raisins, prune, sweet spice.

T **TASTE** Rich and voluminous, with good intensity and complexity.

Tokaji (often Anglicized to Tokay) is an exceptional Hungarian dessert wine. The wine is blended from three main grape varieties: Harslevelu (usually the dominant grape, giving the wine its perfumed, spicy character), Furmint, and

TOKAJI
Crown Estates

Muscat. The grapes are grown around the village of Tokaj, which lies in the northeastern corner of Hungary on the Tisza River.

Historically, this area produced dry white wine. However, in the 17th century, a threatened attack by the Turks postponed the harvest leaving the grapes to shrivel on the vines. When eventually these overripe grapes were pressed, they produced the sweet wine we know today. In fact, the region is well suited to producing

sweet wines – warm weather and mists from the Tisza River and its tributaries provide perfect conditions for the growth of *Botrytis cinerea*, the benevolent fungus that causes "noble rot" *(see p141)*.

There are three categories of Tokaji: *szamorodni*, *aszú*, and *aszú eszencia*. *Szamorodni* is made by throwing into the vat all the leftover grapes at the end of the harvest; ripe, overripe, botrytized (affected by noble rot), and even rotten! The resulting strong table wine is dark yellow, sometimes sweet, sometimes dry, and is much more basic than the other Tokajis.

In my view, Tokaji *aszú* wines are the best. These are made using late-harvested grapes that have been botrytized. After the juice is squeezed, the grapes are crushed into a pulp, which is added to dry wine to the right level of sweetness, measured in *puttonyos*.

TOKAJI *Royal Tokaji Wine Company*

Each bottle of Tokaji will give a *puttonyos* rating, ranging from three (least sweet) to six (most sweet). (Incidentally, the figure is only a measure of sweetness and in no way refers to quality.)

Eszencia is an *aszú* made using the best botrytized grapes from the best vineyards. These grapes exude little juice, but it is especially sweet and good. The resulting wine is thick, and yet refreshing rather than cloying. *Eszencia* takes decades to mature and is incredibly rare and expensive.

The best Tokaji wines can age for centuries in the bottle. At the end of World War II, Russian soldiers found hoards of Tokaji that had been bottled in various years between 1668 and 1811 – all still drinkable!

RECOMMENDED PRODUCERS
- ▸ Crown Estates
- ▸ Royal Tokaji Wine Company

AUSTRIA

The Austrian climate can be very warm indeed, and the humid microclimate among the country's lakes and mountains provides near-perfect conditions for "noble rot" *(see p141)*, essential for these fine, sweet wines.

AUSTRIAN SWEET WINES

C **COLOUR** Beautiful deep straw yellow, with golden highlights.

A **AROMA** Concentrated and delicate; apricot, pineapple, flowers, peach.

T **TASTE** Perfectly balanced and structured; ripe flavours; great length.

The finest sweet wines of Austria (and perhaps the world) are produced around the Neusiedl lake near the border with Hungary. Here long hours of sunshine during the growing season and humidity caused by the lake are ideal for the development of noble rot, which concentrates the grapes' sugars.

AUSTRIAN
SWEET WINES
Nikolaihof

There are three grades of sweetness used in Austria, one of which will be on your wine's label. *Auslese* is the least sweet, then *Beerenauslese*, and finally *Trockenbeeren-auslese* (most sweet).

Look out for Ausbruch, a complex dessert wine produced in the town of Rust, with yeast and herbs overlaying rich, ripe fruit. This wine is rare, but if you find a bottle, you will discover the closest thing to perfection!

RECOMMENDED PRODUCERS
- ▸ Nikolaihof
- ▸ Knoll

EISWEIN

C **COLOUR** Distinctive bright gold, with nuances of green.

A **AROMA** Complex, wide-ranging; from crystallized exotic fruit to citrus; flowers.

T **TASTE** Subtle and syrupy; persistent, concentrated, clean finish.

For me, Austria makes the best ice wine *(see p141)*: it has a constant, lemony acidity, and complex flavours. Look out for the eisweins of grower Willi Opitz, who has perfected the technique of getting the frozen grapes to the presses. Austrian eisweins can make a great investment, but I prefer just to get on and drink them – they are delicious with blue cheese.

EISWEIN *Willi Opitz*

RECOMMENDED PRODUCERS
- ▸ Willi Opitz
- ▸ Salomon Undhof

STROHWEIN

C **COLOUR** Bright; deep gold with straw to silver highlights.

A **AROMA** Amazingly intense! Maple syrup, honey, ripe fruits, toffee apple.

T **TASTE** Rich and ample; syrupy, but well-structured and perfectly balanced.

The word *strohwein* means "straw wine" – the grapes are left out to dry on straw mats, usually in the wineries' lofts, to concentrate their sugars.

Strohwein has complex aromas, thanks to its slight oxidation, and delicious flavours – a rare treat! I tasted a Willi Opitz strohwein with a slither of stilton years ago. I remember it like yesterday – remarkable!

RECOMMENDED PRODUCERS
- ▸ Willi Opitz
- ▸ Helmut

GERMANY

German wines may be very sweet indeed, but they also possess high natural acidity, giving them excellent balance. Some of the very best German sweet wines are made from grapes left out in the frost to concentrate their sweetness – a long-established technique.

GERMAN SWEET WINES
Selbach-Oster

GERMAN SWEET WINES

C COLOUR Deep straw to golden yellow, with silver tinges.

A AROMA Intense, elegant; fresh; dried apricot; citrus and exotic fruit; smoke.

T TASTE Rich and opulent, underlined by a pronounced, balancing acidity; complex.

German sweet wines are some of the finest and longest-lived in the world. They can be rich, sticky, and syrupy when young, but have excellent acidity to balance the sweetness; the finish is clean and fresh.

A wine labelled *Auslese* (meaning that the grapes have been selectively harvested) will be sweet, but relatively light. *Beerenauslese* and *Trockenbeerenauslese* wines have been made using grapes that have been left on the vines for longer and are partially raisined. The latter have also been affected by noble rot, making them even more sweet, complex, and delicious. German eiswein (*see p141*) is fantastic – very sweet, but not cloying, and with excellent balance.

RECOMMENDED PRODUCERS
▶ Selbach-Oster
▶ Merkelbach

CANADA

Canada is an up-and-coming country for many varieties of wine, and some of the best are produced by making use of the cold winter climate to freeze the water out of the grapes. The result is wonderfully sweet and rich ice wine, perfect for matching with desserts.

CANADIAN SWEET WINES
Inniskillin

CANADIAN ICE WINES

C COLOUR Lively, bright straw yellow, with green tinges.

A AROMA Elegant; pineapple, peach, apricot, caramelized apple, and citrus.

T TASTE Rich, opulent, and complex; exceptional lemony acidity; long finish.

The best Canadian dessert wine is ice wine, usually made using Vidal grapes (a hybrid of Riesling) or Riesling itself. The winemaker leaves the grapes out late in the season, so that the cold weather freezes out the grapes' water, concentrating the sugars. Canada's Niagara Peninsula has a perfect climate for producing this kind of wine, but also look out for ice wines from British Columbia (which produced the original Canadian ice wine in the 1970s). These wines are particularly sweet, rich, and complex, and great with crème brûlée or caramelized pears.

RECOMMENDED PRODUCERS
▶ Inniskillin
▶ Peller

AUSTRALIA

This great country has an almost infinite range of climates, and the Australians are also willing to experiment with new grape varieties and methods of production. Some of the country's best sweet wines use the Muscat grape to make a rich, sweet, fortified style, called Liqueur Muscat, which is comparable to sherry.

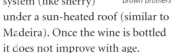

LIQUEUR MUSCAT

C COLOUR Opaque; dark brown with a toffee rim.

A AROMA Intense, pronounced; chocolate, toffee, almond, liquorice, vanilla.

T TASTE Rich, heavy; balanced by a fine freshness and long, complex finish.

If you like sherry made from Pedro Ximénez grapes, or Madeira, you will love Australia's Liqueur Muscat! The Australian Muscat grape has a dark skin and the Australians call it "Brown Muscat" or "Tokay".

The wine is produced by combining several sweet-winemaking techniques. Overripe grapes are partly fermented then fortified with grape spirit (like port). The wine is then matured using the *solera* system (like sherry) under a sun-heated roof (similar to Madeira). Once the wine is bottled it does not improve with age.

LIQUEUR MUSCAT
Brown Brothers

This is an unusual, rich wine. Serve it chilled at the end of a meal – perhaps with a chocolate dessert.

RECOMMENDED PRODUCERS
▶ Brown Brothers
▶ Mick Morris

SOUTH AFRICA

Jerepigo, from the Cape region of South Africa, is a special and unusual wine. It is made by adding spirit to pressed grape juice *before* fermentation. In fermentation, yeast turns fruit sugar into alcohol until the rising alcohol level kills the yeast. If alcohol is already present, as in Jerepigo, the yeast dies sooner, leaving fruit sugars unfermented, and making the finished wine sweeter.

JEREPIGO

C COLOUR Deep gold to straw yellow, with greenish tinges.

A AROMA Elegant, powerful. Dried fig, pineapple, mirabelle plum, flowers.

T TASTE Strong, opulent, oily, and rich; great intensity; flavoursome finish.

Jerepigo is one of South Africa's specialities: a quality dessert wine made principally from Muscat à Petit Grains grapes. To set it apart from similar Old World wines, Jerepigo is fortified before rather than during fermentation. In this way the alcohol content remains high, but it is balanced perfectly by the wine's high level of residual sugar.

Jerepigo's aromas are fresh and youthful, with distinctive dried fig and exotic fruits – the signature of a Muscat. The wine is consumed mostly in South Africa, so it can be hard to locate, but when you do, try it with a fig tart.

JEREPIGO
Du Toitskloof Cellar

RECOMMENDED PRODUCERS
▶ Du Toitskloof Cellar
▶ KWV

66 Versatile wines that offer a pyramid of complex flavours, these great apéritifs will really wake up your taste buds. 99

WINE-BASED BITTERS

INTRODUCING WINE-BASED BITTERS

Wine-based bitters are wonderfully versatile. Primarily apéritifs for serving chilled with a slice of lemon, orange, or other fruit, they are also great at a party, served with lots of ice and some soda water.

DRINKING AND SERVING

C COLOUR Various. If the base wine is red, expect dark red, with nuances of brown; if the base is white, expect yellow, or a greenish colour, with nuances of deep gold or straw.

A AROMA Highly aromatic, with complex layers of fruit, herbs, and spices.

T TASTE The complete range from extremely dry to very sweet. Most wine-based bitters will have a long finish.

Wine-based bitters, which combine wine with spirits, herbs, and spices, developed in three main ways. Some, such as the delicate Noilly Prat from France, came about because these additives were found to preserve wine during storage, especially on long sea voyages. The amère Byrrh began life as a medicine – adding herbs to wine, especially quinine (from the bark of South American cinchona trees), created a medicinal elixir. Finally some of the most famous names – including Chambéry and Dubonnet from France, and Cinzano and Martini from Italy – were created for pure enjoyment, because certain plants, herbs, and spices gave extra dryness or sweetness, and complexity to the wine. Although based on wine, these bitters are stronger than table wines, at around 14–18% ABV.

WALNUT *Many vermouths have a wonderful nutty aroma.*

VERMOUTH

There are two main types of vermouth: the French style, which is usually dry or very dry, with a light, golden hue; and the Italian style, which is relatively sweet and is usually deep red or amber in colour.

CHAMBÉRY

C COLOUR Pale lemon yellow, with delicate tinges of green.

A AROMA Fresh and subtle; citrus fruits, herbs, forest plants, and walnut.

T TASTE Dry and clean, with a splendid structure and well-integrated alcohol.

If you are a fan of *fino* sherry, or of the nutty Savagnin wine from the Jura in eastern France, then you will probably love this sophisticated and delicate apéritif. Chambéry is a premium-quality vermouth from

the Savoie region in the southeast of France. Set in the French Alps, the Savoie is a great place to visit – the local cheeses alone are worth the trip, but the lovely Chambéry is the icing on the cake!

Production of Chambéry began as long ago as the early 1900s. The vermouth has had its own appellation since 1932, but its base wines come from the *département* of Gers in the Midi-Pyrénées, in southwestern France. However, as long as the vermouth itself is

CHAMBÉRY

actually blended and produced in Chambéry, it can carry the name on its label.

Chambéry is produced by taking blended base wines and treating them with a secret mix of herbs and other plants. This is then combined with plant-derived alcohol to create the final blend.

Overall, Chambéry is an extra-dry vermouth, with real delicacy and sophistication, and a crisp texture – like breaking ice. Clean and pure, this apéritif is quite simply beautiful.

The famous Chambéry producer is Dolin, which also makes Chambéryzette, a traditional French strawberry-flavoured vermouth.

NOILLY PRAT

C COLOUR Bright and limpid; pale straw yellow with hints of gold.

A AROMA Delicate, subtle; notes of citrus fruits, walnut, and apple.

T TASTE Oily, mellow; fresh; coriander at the finish.

This world-class vermouth is made from light, fruity white wines, mixed with plants and herbs. First it matures indoors, then is transferred to oak barrels and left outside to develop its flavours, exposed to the sun and winds of the Mediterranean. The result is relaxing, refreshing, and unique. Enjoy it chilled; I love it with green olives.

NOILLY PRAT

CINZANO

C COLOUR Attractive pale gold, through to pale green, orange, and red.

A AROMA Sweet and alluring; notes of herbs and almond.

T TASTE Complex and well-balanced; slightly bitter finish.

Cinzano is a traditional Italian vermouth produced as either Rosso (red), Bianco (white), or Secco (dry), as well as in speciality versions, such as Rosé, Limetto (lemon), and Orancio (orange). The drink is named after the Italian distiller who first created the Rosso in Turin (northern Italy) in 1786. His creation soon became the drink of choice for wealthy Turin socialites, but the big boom came after World War II, when the various versions of Cinzano became popular ingredients in cocktails. Cinzano has been part of the massive Campari group since 1999 and is now the second-biggest-selling vermouth in the world – after Martini – and these days is almost as often enjoyed on its own as it is in mixed drinks.

If there is one rule about Cinzano it is that it should always be served chilled. Whichever version you are drinking, try it on its own with a slice of lemon – or a twist of lemon peel – or even topped up with lemonade (or soda, if you want something less sweet). The Rosso is great on the rocks with a half slice of lemon or orange and makes an excellent mixer in cocktails, as it breaks through other flavours with its spicy character. The two white versions – the full-bodied Bianco and delicate Secco – make especially excellent apéritifs. These are all international products, and deservedly so.

CINZANO

MARTINI & ROSSI

C COLOUR Dark ruby red, through to golden yellow and pale green.

A AROMA Elegant, fresh, and full of ripe aromas, combined with nuts and herbs.

T TASTE Delicate and sweet, with depth and a slightly bitter finish.

In 1863, near Turin (northern Italy), master blender Alessandro Martini and wine expert Luigi Rossi first produced the original Martini vermouth – Martini Rosso. The company gave us the Extra Dry in 1900 and the Bianco in 1910. Now owned by Bacardi, Martini vermouths are the best-selling in the world.

I love the Rosso just as it is as an early-evening apéritif. The Extra Dry – lemon in colour and aroma, with hints of raspberry – is a key cocktail ingredient; while the aromatic Bianco is lovely on its own, or on ice with lemonade or soda.

PUNT E MES

C COLOUR Garnet to deep ruby, with orange hues.

A AROMA Intense; wormwood, bitter herbs, wild blackberry, and spices.

T TASTE Dry, complex, and refreshing, with a nutty finish.

One of the world's most popular red vermouths, the distinctive Punt e Mes originates from Milan. I find it less fruity than Martini or Cinzano, and it has a lovely bitterness at the finish, bringing a freshness to stimulate the appetite.

I love it in a long drink with fresh juice or soda, but it is most popular in cocktails. Look out for the Poca-Hola – Punt e Mes, Campari, Noilly Prat, lemon juice, and cola. Generally, it makes a great alternative to Martini.

PUNT E MES

AMÈRE

Amères are wine-based bitters flavoured with the herb quinine, which is effective in the prevention of malaria. Developed as medicinal drinks for French soldiers, missionaries, and adventurers in the tropics, amères make excellent apéritifs, and are also fine as digestifs.

AMBASSADEUR

C COLOUR Deep, dark red, with tinges of dark orange.

A AROMA Elegant, with orange and hints of spice.

T TASTE A fine balance of orange citrus and herbs, with gentian to the fore.

This classic French apéritif distinguishes itself from other amères by its lightly flavoured texture, dominated by Curaçao oranges and combined with gentian, with its slightly bitter taste.

Ambassadeur is perfect in the summer, perhaps at a lunch with friends, and is best served on the rocks with half a slice of orange.

BYRRH

C COLOUR Dark red, glistening with slight tinges of orange.

A AROMA Distinctive, with citrus fruit, herbs, and red wine.

T TASTE Bittersweet fruit, especially orange, with a herby feel.

Byrrh is produced in Roussillon, in the far south of France. It is red wine treated with quinine, Curaçao, and herbs. The mixture is matured for three years before bottling.

You will either love or hate this distinctive apéritif – its combination of sweet flavours and bitter finish is unique. Serve it either at room temperature or slightly chilled.

DUBONNET

C COLOUR Deep, dark red for the Rouge version; pale yellow for the Blanc.

A AROMA Elegant, with red wine (in the Rouge), sweet herbs, and spices.

T TASTE Rich, with the sweet wine and fruit well balanced against the herbs.

In 1846 Joseph Dubonnet, a Parisian drinks' supplier, mixed dry white wine with Vin Doux Naturel ("natural sweet wine") and flavoured the mixture with quinine, bitter-orange peel, herbs, plants, and caramel. He then matured it for three years. The result: Dubonnet.

There are actually two Dubonnet blends. The richer, sweeter Rouge is red-wine based; the Blanc (or Blond) is drier, and made using fortified white wine. Both blends are very special apéritifs indeed – neither too sweet nor too dry, and with enough body to be refreshing. Perfect!

ST RAPHAËL

C COLOUR A transparent and attractive medium to light orange.

A AROMA Citrus fruit, especially orange, with spicy herbs, and wine.

T TASTE Dry with balanced citrus fruit and herbs, and a fresh finish.

Like Dubonnet, this amère was once labelled *quinquina*, meaning "quinine tonic" – a medicine used to protect against malaria. Originally created in Lyon, France, it now makes an extremely complex amère, and contains, among other things, oranges, cocoa, quasia (a root extract from South America), and colombo (a medicinal root), all macerated in alcohol with red grapes. This is a great alternative to the red amères. Try it over ice with lemon and orange slices.

ST RAPHAËL

SPIRITS

DISTILLED PLEASURE

What could be better than a fresh, sparkling gin and tonic at the end of a working day, or a fine XO Cognac after dinner? Spirits are versatile drinks that can suit every mood, taste, or occasion.

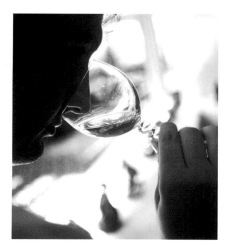

SPIRITS TO SAVOUR *The dense aromas of vanilla, spice, wood, and flowers shine through in a glass of fine Cognac.*

Crystal clear, smooth, smoky, fiery, warming, subtle, refreshing, stimulating, delicate – these are just some of the words used to describe the incredibly diverse flavour palette that spirits present. There is fantastic choice in the world of spirits – too much for one lifetime – and most of us will only sample a few, preferring to stay with our trusted favourites.

My advice, however, is simply to be adventurous. Tasting spirits is one of life's great joys and comforts, and every sip reveals something about the techniques and traditions that shaped the drink's character.

All spirits are made in essentially the same way: first, a base ingredient containing sugar – such as grapes or other fruit, malted grain, rice, or molasses – is fermented, then the liquid is distilled to concentrate the alcohol. Typically, the character of the base shines through in the final product; brandy, for example, has strong notes of grapes, while sugar cane permeates the taste of a good rum. But that is not the end of the story – think about Scotch whisky and London Dry gin, which are both based on the same type of grain but have very different tastes. After distillation, the qualities of the spirit may be modified in a number of ways. For whisky, brandy, and rum, ageing, usually in

oak barrels, shapes the character of the drink, while with gin it is the addition of "botanicals" – herbs and spices – that makes the difference. Finally, the skill and quality standards of the producer exert their own influences on the strength, character, and complexity of the drink, producing the range of styles and brands available on today's market.

A HISTORY OF SPIRITS

The technique of distillation is not new. Thousands of years ago, the ancient Babylonians, then the Egyptians and Chinese, concentrated alcohol for use in perfume manufacture and metal processing. However, the first detailed description of distillation is credited to the brilliant 8th-century Arab alchemist Jabir Ibn Hayyan (known in the West as Geber). Considered by many to be the grandfather of modern chemistry, Geber not only distilled spirit from heated wine, but also invented the alambic still. This apparatus consisted of a pot in which the wine was heated, linked to a condenser, where the alcohol-rich vapour cooled, condensed, and was collected. Similar still designs (sometimes called pot stills) are used to this day, and the Arabic heritage of distillation is evident in the very words "alcohol" and "alambic",

CLASSIC MIXES *Vodka and tonic with a wedge or two of lime is one of the great classic spirit mixes: refreshing, zesty, and sophisticated all at once.*

" Today's distillers are still alchemists, taking a humble base material like grain and shaping it into a magnificent, glowing glass of whisky."

PURE ALCOHOL *The clear product of distillation – alcohol spirit – runs off from an alambic still. It is what happens next that makes all the difference.*

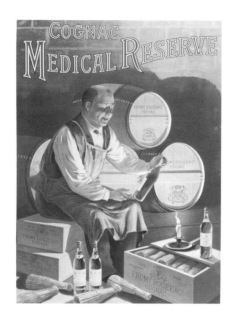

MEDICINAL DRINK *Even in the 20th century, Cognac was promoted for its supposed medicinal value. Few would argue that a good Cognac can make you feel better!*

which are derived from the Arabic *al-koh'l* (meaning "essence") and *al-ambiq* (meaning "still"). The work of the early distillers was developed through the Middle Ages; pioneers like the Frenchman Arnauld de Villeneuve, who lived in the 13th century, gave a detailed description of the production of eau-de-vie ("water of life"), the classic distilled grape spirit.

In the 14th century, European monks began to make spirits infused with herbs, while the Germans and Dutch expanded production of their *Ausgebranden Wasser* or *brandwijn* (literally "burnt wine") – the predecessor of modern brandy. Initially at least, many spirits were promoted for their medicinal benefits and were sold under the name "cordial" (from the Latin word for "heart", because they were administered to stimulate the heart). Soon, however, the medicinal became intertwined with the pleasurable, and spirits came to be enjoyed by a wider public.

The first brandies reached England in 1585, brought back by troops returning from the Low Countries, and by 1638 the economic importance of spirits in England had grown to the extent that

a guild – the Worshipful Company of Distillers – was set up to regulate and supervise their production. By the 18th century, spirits had made an indelible mark on world history: rum had become an important currency in the slave trade, while the consumption of cheap gin in London had terrible social consequences for the city's poor.

Great strides in production techniques, quality control, and regulation took place during the 19th century, and many drink styles and producers familiar to us today had emerged by the beginning of the 20th. Companies like Gordon's, Booth's, Tanqueray, and Gilbey's were supplying London Dry gin to every corner of the British Empire, while advances in blending techniques boosted the fortunes of Scotch whisky manufacturers, such as Ballantine's, Teacher's, Chivas, and Cutty Sark. Jamaica, Martinique, and Cuba became the heart of rum production in the Caribbean, with companies like Bacardi and Appleton established alongside British "Navy rum" producers, such as Lamb's, Captain Morgan, OVD, and other great brands. Though popular in their home countries, vodka and tequila only rose to prominence during the 1920s as the fashion for cocktails spread through the Western world. Today, we are presented with a staggering array of styles and brands, suited to every taste and every budget.

> " Distillation is an almost magical process that turns simple ingredients, like grain or grapes, into aromatic, evocative drinks that delight the senses. "

SMUGGLING RUM *During the period of Prohibition in the US after the First World War, millions of bottles of spirits were smuggled into the country to meet undiminished demand. In this photograph from 1923, rum smugglers from Mexico are caught at the US border.*

RAW MATERIALS *Barley and rye grains, ready to embark on a long journey that ends in a bottle of American whiskey. Whiskey, gin, and vodka all use grains as their base material.*

HOW SPIRITS ARE MADE

The basic raw material for all spirits is a sugar-yielding base. The most common bases are grapes and grape pomace for brandy and grappa; barley, wheat, and maize for whisky, gin, and vodka; sugar cane or molasses for rum; and fruits like apples, pears, and cherries for other spirits. Sometimes the base is a plant, like the blue agave for tequila, or a more unusual substance, such as maple syrup.

The first stage of the process is normally to break down the raw base material into a "mash", which is then fermented by selected yeasts – much in the same way as wine and beer are produced. After fermentation, the liquid is distilled – a process that separates alcohol from the liquid. The principle of distillation is simple; alcohol starts to boil at 78.3°C (172.9°F), whereas water boils at a higher temperature of 100°C (212°F). So when the fermented liquid is heated, an alcohol-rich fraction boils first, and is then condensed and collected. Premium spirits, such as single malt whiskies, Cognac, Armagnac, and some fine rums are distilled in traditional copper alambics (or pot stills). Though slow and labour-intensive, this traditional process allows for fine control over the strength of the spirit (typically 60–70% ABV), and the amounts of organic chemicals carried through from the base, which, in large part, give the drink its character. Many other spirits, such as vodka and gin, are made in a different design of still; known as a continuous, or column,

SHAPED LANDSCAPES *Spirits are made across the world, from the Ardbeg whisky distillery on Islay, off the coast of Scotland (left), to the blue agave fields near Tequila, Mexico (below).*

GIN STILLS *State-of-the-art manufacturing techniques and equipment are used to make some of the best new gins on the market, such as the fashionable Bombay Sapphire, whose Carterhead stills are pictured here.*

still (or Coffey still, after its Irish-born inventor Aeneas Coffey), this consists of several interconnected stainless steel towers into which steam, and the alcohol-rich liquid, are fed. The alcohol has a lower boiling point than the rest of the liquid, and is turned into vapour by the heat of the steam, producing a spirit of around 90% ABV. The Coffey still, which was patented in Dublin in 1831, is less expensive and quicker to operate than an alambic still, and produces a much purer spirit, with fewer oily components from the base. This makes it more suitable for high-volume, industrial scale production of spirits than the alambic.

Both alambic and continuous stills have their place in global spirits production, but it is encouraging to note that ever more small distilleries (even some vodka producers) are using alambic stills to make spirits with care and attention, for sale to niche markets prepared to pay a premium for quality.

The strength of the spirit emerging from the still is much higher than the strength at which it will be bottled (typically around 40% ABV). The strength is often reduced simply by adding water, but in the case of whisky, rum, and brandy, storage in wooden barrels for a period of years allows some of the

alcohol to evaporate, lowering the strength. These barrels, usually made of oak, are sometimes charred on the inside to enhance the interaction between wood and spirit, and so alter its taste and colour. When spirit emerges from the still – whether an alambic or Coffey – it is always colourless.

American whiskey is matured in new oak barrels and, once used, the barrels may be sold on to rum and Scotch manufacturers, who use them for adding character to their own products. Similarly, former sherry casks are also often used to age spirits.

The purity of a spirit (especially in the case of vodka) may be enhanced by filtering the liquid over columns of charcoal, or its character may be changed by redistilling the drink in the presence of flavouring agents (such as juniper berries and other "botanicals" in the case of gin).

THE BLENDER'S ART

Another essential stage in the manufacture of spirits is blending. Working by nose alone – sniffing rather than tasting individual components – a skilled master blender mixes together spirits from different distilleries, from different casks, or of different ages, to maintain the taste and quality standards of a particular brand. Blending whisky is a highly developed art: up to 50 different ingredients may go into a blend, which the blender coordinates with the delicate and creative precision of an orchestra conductor. Some rums, tequilas, and brandies are also subjected to blending, too.

BARRELS OF WHISKY *At the Glen Moray Distillery, Scotland, oak barrels containing Speyside malt whisky are rolled to the storehouse to begin the ageing process. Traditional methods help to maintain the character of the product.*

" Unlike fine wines, spirits do not improve once bottled; the skill of the producer is the key to quality. "

CELEBRATING SPIRITS

The enduring appeal of spirits is their sheer versatility. A gin cocktail is hard to beat as an apéritif, and there is no better after-dinner drink than a brandy – unless of course you prefer a malt whisky, fine rum, or even a glass of calvados. Tequila, vodka, and rum are all great party drinks, either as mixers or shorts. Spirits are not commonly drunk with food, but some cultures enjoy vodka with fish, or whisky with spicy meat dishes like haggis. In Asia, brandy is often drunk with food, usually as part of a long drink. Whatever your own preference, the world of spirits will meet it, with all its generous variety!

FINE MALT *The character and colour of a malt whisky depend on the local conditions, the production process, and the wooden barrels in which the spirit is aged.*

MOOD MATCHERS *From a warming Cognac to an icy clear vodka, there is a spirit to match every mood and every occasion.*

GLOBAL ORIGINS AND PRODUCTION

Distillation is practised all round the world and a fantastic variety of spirits exist, from instant pick-me-ups, to gentle and sophisticated after-dinner digestifs. Some are associated with just one country, while others, like vodka, are truly international drinks.

BRANDY

MAIN PRODUCERS France, Greece, Spain, South America (as pisco), and nearly all wine-producing countries.

BASE Grapes.

SERVING Fine brandies at room temperature in a balloon or tasting glass; others mixed with soda water, tonic, or ginger ale.

NORTH AMERICA

BOURBON

MAIN PRODUCERS USA, notably the state of Kentucky.

BASE Maize, rye, and barley grain.

SERVING Straight, usually with ice, in a rocks glass; can also be mixed with soda water, ginger ale or lemonade, and used as a base for cocktails.

CENTRAL AMERICA

CARIBBEAN

TEQUILA / MEZCAL

MAIN PRODUCERS Mexico: Tequila in Jalisco State, and Oaxaca State for Mezcal.

BASE The blue agave – a succulent, similar to a cactus.

SERVING Straight without ice in a shot glass; mixed with ice and fruit juice in a tall glass; or in cocktails like Tequila Sunrise.

SOUTH AMERICA

RUM

MAIN PRODUCERS Jamaica, Cuba, Barbados, Trinidad, Bahamas, Brazil, Australia.

BASE Molasses or sugar cane.

SERVING On its own, with ice, or mixed with cola or fruit juice. Great in cocktails. Fine rums can be drunk from a brandy balloon, others in a tumbler or tall glass.

WHISKY

MAIN PRODUCERS Scotland, Ireland, USA, Canada, Japan.

BASE Barley, maize, wheat, and rye grain.

SERVING Malt whisky at room temperature in a rocks glass with a splash of water; others can be served over ice, with water, soda water, or other mixers.

AQUAVIT

MAIN PRODUCERS Denmark, Sweden, Norway, Iceland.

BASE Potatoes or grain – mainly wheat or barley.

SERVING Aquavit can be served straight with ice, which allows the spirit's subtle flavours to stand out. It also works well in a tall glass with fruit juice.

VODKA

MAIN PRODUCERS Russia, Poland, Sweden, Norway, Finland, Holland, France, USA.

BASE Grain – mainly barley, rye, or wheat; potatoes.

SERVING Straight with ice, or mixed with fruit juice or tonic water; also in cocktails. Can be served in a chilled shot glass.

EUROPE

ASIA

MIDDLE EAST

TROPIC OF CANCER

AFRICA

EQUATOR

TROPIC OF CAPRICORN

OCEANIA

AUSTRALIA

SAKÉ

MAIN PRODUCERS Japan, where it has a unique ritual status.

BASE Rice.

SERVING Can be served at a wide range of temperatures, from very slightly chilled to warm. It is usually served on its own, traditionally in a *masu*, a type of drinking vessel.

GRAPPA

MAIN PRODUCERS Italy.

BASE Grape pomace (crushed skins, stalks, pips, etc).

SERVING Sometimes mixed with fruit juice; the best can be served on its own with or without ice. Italians sometimes like to add a shot of grappa to an espresso, making what they call a *corretto*.

MARC

MAIN PRODUCERS France.

BASE Grape pomace (crushed skins, stalks, pips, etc).

SERVING Usually mixed with fruit juice in a tall glass, to dilute its sometimes fiery character. Though traditionally a "poor man's brandy", marc has a unique character of its own.

COGNAC / ARMAGNAC

MAIN PRODUCERS Made exclusively in southwest France.

BASE Grapes.

SERVING The classic serving for Cognac is on its own at room temperature in a balloon glass. It can also be mixed with fruit juice or cola, and is used as the base in a variety of cocktails.

GIN

MAIN PRODUCERS UK, Holland, Belgium, USA, Spain, Philippines.

BASE Grain – usually wheat or barley.

SERVING Straight with ice, or mixed with fruit juice or tonic in a tumbler glass with a lime or lemon wedge; also very important in cocktails.

CHOOSING AND STORING SPIRITS

A bottle of spirit can be quite an investment. Understandably, when faced with shelves stacked with bottles, most of us stick to tried and tested favourites or buy big brands, reassured by their reputation. But it doesn't have to be this way!

Throughout the world, sales of spirits are growing. Revived interest in cocktails, plus the opening up of new markets in India and Asia, has meant a boom-time for distillers, who have launched ever more innovative and diverse brands. In the US, where alcohol consumption has actually fallen over the past few years, Americans are drinking "upscale", choosing rarer premium drinks, such as single-malt Scotches, single-barrel Bourbons, and XO Cognacs, over the value brands that used to dominate the market.

DECODING A LABEL *A label is there to help impose a brand, but it contains many clues about the quality of the bottle's contents. The type of information given varies greatly from one drink style to another, but in general, a lack of details may suggest an inferior product.*

DRINK STYLE
The label will state if the whisky is a blend or a single malt, and the place of distillation and bottling.

BRAND NAME
An established name like Glen Grant is a safe bet, but poor spirits often hide behind "pastiche" names.

AGEING
The amount of time a whisky spends in the cask is crucial in determining quality. Ordinary whisky will be three to five years old. If there is no age information, then look out!

PLACE OF ORIGIN
The country of origin may be supplemented with information that locates the whisky in a particular region, such as Speyside or Islay.

SPECIALIST RETAILER *For a huge range of spirits brands, expert advice, and a programme of tastings, visit a specialist retailer. Milroy's store in central London is a magnet for whisky-lovers around the world, with a stock of more than 700 malts, including rare, collectable bottles.*

BRAND NAME
Each spirit brand has its own "house style". This label also states that the company was established in 1749 – a long history is a good sign.

APPELLATION
Appellation Contrôlée, a term more often seen on wine labels, is a guarantee of the place of origin of this Martinique rum.

DRINK STYLE
This label denotes a *rhum agricole* (made from pure sugar cane) and aged in wood (bois).

BOTTLING INFORMATION
Good producers of fine spirit will proudly boast precisely where their spirit is made and bottled.

CONTENT AND STRENGTH
This information is legally required in most countries.

PLACE OF ORIGIN
Martinique rum is famed for its quality: the label trumpets its origins.

Unlike wines, spirits do not improve with age after bottling; however, they will last for many years if unopened. While wine bottles are stored on their side in order to moisten the cork, spirits should be stored upright because the distilled alcohol will destroy a cork. Once the seal is broken, ensure that the bottle is stored in a cool, dark place with the cap or cork firmly in place. Evaporation will not only make the spirit vanish, but will change the balance of its flavours.

Flavour is in fashion and people are looking for more than a drink that simply gives them a kick. But how do you choose a spirit with that extra special something? Really, there is no substitute for experience; by tasting spirits, and reading and talking about them, you will develop the vocabulary and skill to compare their different characteristics and soon identify your preferences. Finding out about their methods of production is also helpful. Knowing the difference between a single malt and a blended whisky, or *reposado* and *añejo* tequila, will help you make a more informed buying decision.

For wines, the region of production is a great indicator of quality, and this goes for some spirits too. Cognac from the Grande Champagne region, for example, will probably be more refined than a bottle labelled "Bois". And as with wines, some spirits are accredited by government bodies – an assurance of certain standards in their production. For example, the words *rhum agricole* on a bottle of Martinique rum are a guarantee from the French government that the drink is distilled only from fresh cane juice, rather than inferior molasses.

WHERE TO BUY

Supermarkets and general drinks stores are stocked with a multitude of brands, many of which are in fact owned by a handful of giant drinks companies. While these familiar bottles are consistently reliable and offer good value, they tend to be promoted at the expense of smaller, and often more interesting

producers. It is worth seeking out independent retailers, who may specialize in one or two styles of spirit, or scouring the internet for smaller boutique brands. Look out for tastings, which may be organized by the distilleries themselves, by their retailers, or by enthusiasts' societies. Just as wine connoisseurs compare different vineyards and vintages, you will be able to sample and contrast the products of different distilleries and of various styles and ageing regimes.

In the following pages of this book, I explore the main spirit styles, their many variants, and how they are made – all of which will help you understand the words printed on the label of a bottle. After that, a selection of spirits of each style is described in greater detail. This selection reflects not only my own preferences, but also the brands you are likely to come across, wherever you live. But don't take my views as gospel. Be adventurous, try new styles, and form your own opinions. That's where the fun starts!

COST AND VALUE *In the world of spirits, price is a fairly reliable – but not infallible – guide to quality. Distillation, ageing, and blending are all fine arts; care, time, and attention all cost money.*

TASTING SPIRITS *There are many clubs and companies that organize spirits tastings. Often these are held* in situ *– whisky tastings at hotels in the Scottish Highlands, for example. At home, miniatures are a great way to discover and compare new brands without spending too much.*

TASTING AND APPRECIATING SPIRITS

Sampling a glass of fine spirit is one of life's great experiences. Locked up in the colour, aroma, taste, and texture of the liquid are the atmosphere, landscape, and tradition behind its production.

Connoisseurs of wine often talk about the importance of *terroir* – the intimate influence of place on the qualities of the drink. It is a term that can be applied just as well to spirits: consider a single-malt whisky that evokes the peat, heather, and salty, craggy coastline of the Scottish Highlands; or a 40-year-old Calvados that smells like fresh apples, which grew in an orchard in northern France before

humans first landed on the Moon. The ability of spirits to conjure up mood is part of their appeal, but to compare drinks and develop your palate, you need to apply a little analysis to the colour, aroma, and taste of a spirit *(see box, right)*.

Tasting a spirit is a little different to tasting a wine; its high alcohol content means that it should be sniffed delicately, and that it cannot be rolled around the mouth like a wine. Some tasters judge spirits by aroma alone; others add water to the liquid before tasting, which arguably allows more subtle notes to come to the fore. I prefer to taste the spirit undiluted, and always use a narrow, tulip-shaped tasting glass rather than a wine glass: this helps to concentrate the aromas of the drink.

TASTING TECHNIQUE

Pour a small amount of spirit into a tasting glass and swirl it around gently. Don't put your nose right into the glass – your senses will be overwhelmed by the drink's high alcohol content. Instead, hold the glass with your nose in line with the rim, and gently take in the aromas mixed with the air. Then take a small sip of the spirit; keeping the spirit at the front of the mouth, draw some air over the liquid and then briefly let the spirit fill your mouth before swallowing. If you are tasting a range of spirits, spit the liquid out, and cleanse your mouth with a dry cracker before sampling the next.

Sampling the aroma

Tasting the spirit

DRINK ANALYSIS

COLOUR

Assess the colour of a spirit in bright daylight (but not direct sunlight) against a sheet of plain white paper. Tip the drink slightly in the glass; you will see that the body of the liquid has a deeper, and sometimes quite different colour to the rim (which may appear silvery). Perception of colour is highly subjective, so try to develop your own vocabulary for describing the hues of drinks.

Clear spirits, such as vodka and gin, should be bright and fresh-looking, without the slightest hint of haze. The colour range of brandies and whiskies goes from yellow through to dark amber or copper, with a light gold as the norm. These colours come from ageing in oak; usually, the longer the period of ageing, the darker the colour. The body should be shining and translucent, not opaque. This also applies to tequila and the lighter rums, although white rum and unaged tequila should be clear.

AROMA

When judging aroma, pour a small amount of spirit into a tasting glass from a freshly opened bottle. I prefer to sample spirits at cellar temperature (even those, like vodka, which are usually served cold). Do not warm a glass of brandy or whisky in your hands or, worse still, over a candle flame. Heat forces aromatic compounds in the drink to break up and vaporize too rapidly. Most people say that whisky smells of whisky, and, rum smells of rum. But with practice, you will learn to pick out specific notes in the aroma of a drink; indeed, their presence is often the very reason why we like one drink, and dislike another. Some of the main aromas present in spirits are identified below; in a good spirit, these aromas should be subtle – never aggressive or with any hint of burning.

COFFEE
Rum

TOFFEE/HONEY
Brandy

FLOWERS
Gin, whisky, rum, brandy

SPICE
Tequila, whisky, gin

FRUIT
Rum, whisky, brandy, gin

PEAT
Whisky

HERBS
Gin

SMOKE
Whisky, tequila, rum

TASTE

The tastes hidden in a fine spirit are so diverse and complex that they cannot easily be put into words, and in some malt whiskies and brandies the taste evolves, unfolding from one sip to the next. A good starting point is to identify opposing taste categories, such as those shown on this taste wheel *(right)*, and picture where your spirit is located on the wheel. The notion of taste also encompasses the spirit's body (full or light, smooth or firm) as well as its length (how the taste persists and develops after the drink is swallowed).

SHORT FINISH · SMOOTH · FULL · BALANCED · DELICATE · LEAN · PERFUMED · TIGHT · POWERFUL · LIGHT · LONG FINISH · FIRM

SERVING SPIRITS

Spirits are surrounded by ritual. Whether pouring a Cognac as a nightcap or toasting friends' health with a round of tequila slammers, the way the drink is presented has a bearing on enjoyment.

Traditionally, gin, vodka, and other clear spirits have been drunk as apéritifs; brandy and aged rum or tequila are considered to be after-dinner drinks, while whisky is enjoyed both as apéritif and digestif. But these traditions are constantly being reshaped by cultural influences from different parts of the world, and by the endeavours of spirits producers, who are continually trying to tailor their drinks to appeal to new markets. Take Cognac as an example: old school Cognac-lovers are horrified to see their

favourite drink served in a highball glass with soda water, tonic water, or ginger ale, but these new habits are taking root, even in France, the home of Cognac. The practice of drinking spirits with food is also spreading; in Asia, brandy is often served by the bottle, its balance of fruitiness, acidity, and mellowness making it a perfect match for rich dishes, such as duck. In northern Europe, vodka is drunk with oily fish, and whisky with red meats, game, and lobster, while in the Americas tequila is drunk with spicy Mexican food, and Bourbon with barbecues.

MEASURE FOR MEASURE

Each drink has its own serving conventions, perhaps the most elaborate of which surrounds tequila. In Mexico, this drink is typically served chilled in a shot glass; before downing the spirit, you take a lick of

MIXED BLESSINGS *Premium gin can be served neat – ideally well chilled, and in a stemmed glass like a truncated Champagne flute. Indeed, this is the best way to sample Dutch Genever. More often, though, gin is mixed with tonic and served with a slice of lemon or lime and plenty of ice.*

SERVING COGNAC

Today, many Cognac makers advise against serving Cognac in the traditional balloon glass, favouring a narrower tulip-shaped glass, which better displays the drink's subtle aromas. It is hard to argue with this, but for me, the big balloon snifter still has its place because it adds a real sense of occasion.

OPENING AND POURING A COGNAC
1 Carefully cut the capsule below the level of the cork. The aim is to avoid "nicking" the cork. Remove the capsule and cork.
2 Using a napkin, remove any dust and debris from the bottle.
3 Lay the snifter on its side. Pour in the Cognac until almost level with the lip of the glass – this technique delivers just the right amount of liquid for the size of the glass.

1 Carefully remove the capsule

2 Wipe the neck of the bottle

3 Place the glass on its side and pour to the rim

salt, and afterwards bite into a wedge of fresh lime. The idea is that the salt and lime mollify the fiery flavours of the drink. This technique may be fun with ordinary tequila, but don't try it with a fine, aged variety, which should be sipped from a brandy balloon. In a similar vein, standard vodka and aquavit should by default be served ice cold in frozen shot glasses, but try this with an aged Polish vodka or a pot-distilled premium brand and you will miss out on a wealth of subtle flavours. Rum, the perfect party drink, is usually mixed with cola or fruit juices in a punch, but aged dark rums should be served straight and unchilled as digestifs.

The general rule is to treat the drink with the respect it deserves. Cheaper brands will usually benefit from a mixer, or being served over ice, while classier variants should be served at cellar temperature in a glass that gives them room to breathe. In these cases I generally pour about 30ml (1oz) into the glass.

SERVING WHISKY

A single malt whisky should always be served at cellar temperature; it is not intended to be a thirst-quenching drink, so avoid ice, which will only numb the tongue to the drink's subtle flavours. A splash of water can help to tame the fire of the spirit, but choose a spring water (rather than tap water) that will not contaminate the flavours. Blended Canadian whisky has a more rounded, fruity taste, and benefits from being served "on the rocks". Bourbon is a highly versatile drink, pairing well with a variety of mixers. Blended whisky is not always just for mixing – some blends are good enough to rival single malts.

CLASS IN A GLASS *Imagine a malt whiskey served in a Martini glass – unthinkable! The shape and quality of the glass is part of the ritual of drinking spirits, and also helps to frame the colour and aroma of the drink. Here are the classic spirits glasses, from left to right: shot glass for chilled vodka; flute or tasting glass for any brown spirit; tumbler or rocks glass for whisky; highball glass for long, mixed drinks; balloon, or snifter, for brandy.*

66 The queen of spirits – rich, subtle, elegant, and distinguished; at its best, the choice of connoisseurs the world over, and the perfect digestif. **99**

BRANDY

INTRODUCING BRANDY

Brandy has been with us for at least 900 years – written records of Armagnac eau-de-vie date back to the 12th century. This style of drink reaches its zenith in southwestern France, but great versions are available from producers around the world.

The word "brandy" is derived from the Dutch word *brandewijn* – literally "burned wine". The name refers to the process of heating wine to concentrate its alcohol and create a spirit – in other words, distillation. The best wine brandies (for other kinds of brandy, see "Other Spirits", *p256*) are noble, smooth, and often very expensive drinks, and it is surprising that they come from a highly undistinguished raw material – the Ugni Blanc grape. This grape is high in acidity and low in sugar, and the wine made from its berries is so acid and so low in alcohol as to render it almost undrinkable. The first Cognac-makers realized that by distilling the unpalatable wine they could increase the alcohol content and balance out the acidity, creating something infinitely more delicious.

FIGS *Ageing in oak imparts fruity fig aromas to a brandy.*

BRANDY AROUND THE WORLD

The most costly brandies, and arguably the best in the world, come from the Cognac and Armagnac regions of southwestern France. Cognac itself is divided into six sub-areas, the two best being Grande Champagne and Petite Champagne. (The names refer to the high level of chalk in the soil and are nothing to do with the famous sparkling wine.) The others are Borderies (the next-best), Fins Bois (the largest), Bons Bois, and Bois.

WARMING BRANDY *Hold the "bowl" of a snifter in the palm of your hand to release the aromas of the drink.*

Armagnac, in the Gascony region, has three sub-areas: Bas Armagnac (producing delicate, fruity, and full-bodied brandies), Ténarèze (where the brandies are lighter and more floral), and Haut Armagnac, although this now produces more wine than brandy.

Both Cognac and Armagnac have Appellation Contrôlée status; the main difference between the two is the way in which the spirit is made. Cognac is made in a pot still. The wine is heated to boiling point in a huge copper "kettle"; the resulting vapour travels along a pipe (called the "swan's neck") and into a condenser, which liquefies the vapour to give concentrated alcohol spirit. In Cognac, this process is carried out twice (double-distillation) to create the right concentration of alcohol. In Armagnac, brandy is made by continuous distillation in a patent still. The patent still comprises two columns. In the first the wine is vaporized and in the second it is rectified (purified) to the right alcoholic strength. This process happens just once.

Brandy produced in France but outside the appellations of Cognac and Armagnac is labelled "*fine*" *(see p179)*. Spirit that is referred to simply as "brandy" often comes from elsewhere in the world – most notably from Spain (Brandy de Jerez), California, Italy, Germany (*Weinbrand*), South America (especially Chile), Mexico, South Africa, and Cyprus. Whether pot or patent stills are used in these regions depends upon the producer, but with the exception of Armagnac, pot-still brandy is generally considered to be the best, producing spirit with lots of character, flavour, and aroma.

UGNI BLANC *This grape has a low sugar-content and high acidity, which makes it an ideal variety for distilling into brandy.*

CLASSIFYING BRANDY

A basic Cognac is classified as VS ("Very Special", a 19th-century term), and must not contain any brandy less than three years old. VSOP ("Very Special Old Pale"), sometimes called VO or Reserve, must not contain brandy less than five years old. XO, Napoleon, Extra Vieux, Vieille Reserve, and other classifications all describe Cognacs more than ten years old, but these distinctions are not strict. Generally XO ("Extra Old") is the best. From Armagnac, brandies labelled simply Armagnac should be two to six years old; those labelled Vieille Armagnac, more than six years old; and those labelled *Millésimes* must be from the vintage displayed on the label. In Spain the basic Spanish brandy (aged perhaps for only six months) is Solera Brandy de Jerez; the higher grade (one year old) is Solera Reserva; and the highest grade (at least three years old) is Solera Gran Reserva. In the New World some producers use the VS system, as for Cognac, but others have devised their own classification systems based on the age of the brandy in the blend.

CASK-AGEING *Immediately after distillation, all brandy is clear. The distinctive golden, browny colours are achieved as a result of ageing the spirit in oak casks, such as these at Courvoisier, in France.*

FRANCE

France is the home of the greatest brandies in the world – Cognac, from western France and exported worldwide; and Armagnac, produced in Gascony, to the south of Bordeaux, and less easy to find outside the country. Other regions of France also produce brandies, marketed as "Fine", and some are also of extremely high quality.

HINE

C COLOUR Ranging from medium old gold to light amber brown.

A AROMA Beautifully balanced, with flowers, nuts, honey, and vanilla.

T TASTE Highly sophisticated and smooth; light and delicate in style.

Hine Cognac is the legacy of Englishman Thomas Hine, who left his Dorset home in 1791 to take up residence in France. Cognac became his passion, and he intended that his own House should focus on quality rather than quantity. Hine is now

part of the LVMH Group – along with Hennessy Cognac (*see p175*).

For export to Britain, some Hine Cognacs are made in the Franco-English tradition of "early landing". Barrels of spirit are delivered to Britain while they are still young. In the cooler, damper climate, maturation is slower producing a smoother drink.

Hine produce Cognacs only of VSOP quality and better. The basic (although it is anything but basic)

HINE ANTIQUE

Hine is the Rare and Delicate VSOP. This is a blend of more than 25 aged Cognacs and is particularly fine and light to drink. The company's flagship Cognac is Hine Antique, which is also light and delicate, but is made from more than 40 aged Grande Champagne and Petite Champagne Cognacs. It has an amber colour,

with aromas of spice, ripe fruits, honey, nuts, and vanilla. Most special of all are Hine's vintage Cognacs. The company declares vintages only in exceptional years (1983 being the most recent), and releases only a few hundred bottles of the resulting Cognac. These are expensive and special. If you are lucky enough to have one – enjoy!

HINE VSOP

BISQUIT

C COLOUR Medium golden amber, with moderate intensity.

A AROMA Fruity with raisin, sweet vanilla, and notes of oak.

T TASTE Quite rounded and full-bodied; fresh and fruity with chocolate notes.

The Bisquit House was founded by Alexander Bisquit in 1863, and is now part of the Pernod Ricard group. Bisquit produce a Classique VS, but their main focus is a VSOP – a lively, fruity Cognac, matured for eight to ten years. It makes perfect sipping at a summer party. The company does produce aged Cognacs (such as a bittersweet XO and the Cohiba Extra), but its strength lies in its younger offerings, so stick with these.

BISQUIT

RENAULT

C COLOUR Distinctive, dark, rich amber, with a good shine.

A AROMA Powerful; vegetable notes, with raisin, chocolate, and ripe fruits.

T TASTE Well-structured and full-bodied; wood, vanilla, and honey flavours.

Founded by Jean-Antonin Renault in 1835, Renault is now the luxury Cognac of drinks giant Pernod Ricard.

Renault Carte Noir Extra is a superior VSOP aged up to 15 years in oak barrels. It has a perfect balance of fruit, flowers, and spice. However, the Carte d'Argent XO (Extra Old) is one of my all-time favourite Cognacs. Aged up to 30 years, it is a dark, rich amber with aromas of sweet fruits, hazelnut, fig, and orange. It has wonderful length, and a perfect, soft finish.

RENAULT

DAVIDOFF

C COLOUR Dark amber with bright, shining golden nuances.

A AROMA Notes of vanilla, oak, woody undergrowth; hints of roses.

T TASTE Round and well-balanced, with flavours of honey and vanilla.

Exceptional (and expensive!), Davidoff is the joint venture of cigar entrepreneur Zino Davidoff and Kilian Hennessy – owner of Hennessy Cognac.

Davidoff Classic, which contains around 40 different eaux-de-vie from the best areas of the Cognac region, is woody and aromatic. Extra is a blend of older, rich, full-flavoured Cognacs (some more than 40 years old). The blend is left to mature for 18 months and, unusually, sold at a strong 43% ABV. It is rich and golden, with notes of leather and orange.

CAMUS

C COLOUR Intense gold with shades of light straw.

A AROMA Fruity; flowers, almond, and hazelnut; tobacco in the older blends.

T TASTE Full-bodied; full-flavoured, including hints of vanilla and oak.

Camus is a large, family-owned Cognac House – and is fiercely independent! The company was founded in 1863, and has been especially noticeable since it hit the duty-free market.

Camus make a full range of products, from the full-bodied VS De Luxe, through peppery Grand VSOP and complex Napoleon XO, to their top-quality product, the smooth and mellow Extra. The company issued New Extra, a richer version of Extra, to celebrate the millennium. This Cognac comes in a beautiful crystal decanter. (Camus often make an art out of their packaging.) These are all fine Cognacs – pure luxury in a bottle.

MARTELL

C **COLOUR** Dark and rich amber with a beautiful golden rim.

A **AROMA** Fruity and elegant; violets, nuts, orange, honey, and vanilla.

T **TASTE** Well-structured; a balanced blend of exceptional Cognacs.

Martell was founded in 1715 by Jean Martell, a smuggler from the Channel Islands. Martell is now one of the "Big Four" (along with Hennessy, Courvoisier, and Rémy Martin), and is the flagship brand of Pernod Ricard.

Jean Martell built up his business through the combination of a shrewd marriage and solid business sense. His strategy was based on making reliable but not outstanding brandies. In 1986 the Martell family sold the company to Seagrams, who greatly expanded the brand's range. (Pernod Ricard acquired Martell in 2002.)

Martell VS, the basic Martell brandy, is available in airports and supermarkets in more than 140 countries. A reliable spirit for everyday drinking or mixing, VS is a blend of five- to seven-year-old Cognacs from different parts of the region, and is fresh and fruity, with aromas of peach and banana. Darker and more complex is Martell VSOP. This Cognac is ten to 12 years old, with floral, grape, and vanilla aromas.

However, to step up your enjoyment of Cognac, try the Cordon Bleu or the XO Supreme. Cordon Bleu is made from 20- to 30-year-old spirit, and is dark amber with aromas of orange, spice, and nuts. XO Supreme is dark, full, and powerful, with dense aromas of almond and vanilla, and a long finish.

Special order Martells include Extra, Classique de Martell, and L'Or de J&F Martell.

If you like fuller, richer Cognacs, this great House will have something for you – and the top end offers just that bit of extra body.

MARTELL VSOP

WORLDWIDE FAME
Martell VS remains one of the best-known Cognacs around the world.

MIXING IT UP

MARTELL AND TONIC
A great drink for the end of the day: fill a tall glass with ice cubes and pour in tonic almost to the top. Finish with a shot of Martell. Sip gently, without stirring. The brandy will relax you, while the tonic refreshes.

DELAMAIN

C COLOUR Bright deep straw yellow with golden tinges, to deep amber.

A AROMA Delicate; vanilla, fruit, dried flowers, and forest plants.

T TASTE Dry and mellow; great finesse; complex; good length.

Delamain was founded in 1762 by James Delamain, a Protestant Irishman who had a long family connection with the Cognac region. After more than 200 years, Delamain is still owned by the family, which has ensured that its reputation as a company focussed on quality has been maintained.

Delamain makes probably the best basic Cognac – the Pale and Dry, which is light, bright, and fruity. Slightly older, and as a result richer, smoother, and darker in colour (closer to amber than gold), is Vesper. This Cognac has aromas of

DELAMAIN

liquorice and woody undergrowth. The Trés Vénerable is a blend of extremely old Cognacs, and is especially rich and delicate. It is amber, and has a wonderful range of aromas: the woody undergrowth and liquorice tones of the Vesper, but with raisins, vanilla, and honey on top.

The best Delamain of all is Réserve de la Famille – a true great, with a price tag to match! This is not a blend, but a selection from a single cask, and from a single local vineyard. Of course, the colour of each selection will vary, but generally, although the Delamain Réserve de la Famille is deep amber, it tends to be lighter and brighter than *special-cru* Cognacs from other Houses. Similarly, its aromas will vary, but they are always powerful and rich. Delamain is also among only a handful of Houses able to sell Cognac that identifies its vintage.

LÉOPOLD GOURMEL

C COLOUR Pale golden yellow to dark, vintage gold.

A AROMA Ripe fruits, such as peach and orange; notes of vanilla, wood, and spice.

T TASTE Fresh and fruity, with a bright and young feel.

This is a newcomer among Cognac Houses. Established in 1979, the House is the brainchild of car engineer and Cognac enthusiast Pierre Voisin, who named the House after his grandfather. Léopold Gourmel is now owned by Olivier Blanc, Voisin's original partner, and his vision is to bring the Cognacs to a new generation of drinkers.

Unusually all Léopold Gourmel Cognacs are vintage – from a single year – and are unblended. The basic Le P'tit Gourmel is aged for five years and is

basically equivalent to a VS. It is bright and fruity and makes an excellent mixer.

The company has three flagship Cognacs: the Age du Fruit – pale gold and aged for around nine years, giving fresh fruit, flowers, and spice; the Age des Fleurs – aged for around 12 years, gaining its name from its complex floral aromas; and the Age des Epices – aged for around 20 years, with a deliberately enhanced spicy nose, and woody hints. This is well worth trying if you enjoy your Cognac spicy.

The House's top brand is Quintessence, which is red-gold in colour and around 30 years old. This is highly complex, well balanced – and very expensive! Nevertheless it is a full, yet fine and delicate drink.

Most styles come not only in regular bottles, but also in distinctive conical or round decanters – worth looking out for.

LÉOPOLD GOURMEL

RÉMY MARTIN

C COLOUR Medium gold through to light amber brown.

A AROMA Vanilla, spice, cigar box, rose, jasmine, almond, and apricot.

T TASTE A classic lighter Cognac; delicate and elegant.

If you prefer lighter-style Cognacs, then Rémy Martin is the one for you.

Established in 1715, Rémy Martin was almost bankrupt when it was bought by Renaud in 1924, who began a great revival based on Rémy's classic VSOP. The company is today part of the group that includes Cointreau, Bols, and Heidsieck (Champagne).

The most basic brand is VS Grand Cru, made only from Petite Champagne. It has been cleverly marketed

RÉMY MARTIN
VSOP

specifically as a Cognac that mixes easily in long drinks and cocktails. Light gold in colour, it is smooth and delicate, with aromas of vanilla, oak, violet, rose, and apricot, and hints of leather and liquorice.

The flagship is, of course, the classic VSOP, known by its frosted green bottle, and the standard to which all other VSOPs aspire. (One in every three VSOPs sold in the world is a Rémy Martin.) The spirits in the blend are from four to 15 years old. It gives a perfect mix of aromas: fruit, cigar box, and spice.

The Club brand is aimed at the cigar smoker. The newish 1738 Accord Royal is a rich, darker Cognac with a copper-amber colour.

Rémy produces two XO brands (XO Special and XO Excellence), and an award-winning Special. All are gold to amber, with an incredible

RÉMY MARTIN
GRAND CRU

range of aromas, and a perfect balance. The Excellence is blended from spirit aged up to almost 40 years, and has a finish of 15 to 20 minutes!

The very best in the range are the Extra (marketed in a decanter), and the unbelievable Louis XIII. The Extra is dark amber and made from spirit up to 50 years old. Its aromas include wood, spice, port, and cigar box. Louis XIII is one of the world's greatest Cognacs. Its constituent spirits are up to 100 years old and kept in a special cellar. Dark amber with hints of red, it has an incredible range of fruity, woody, and spicy aromas and a finish that may last up to an hour! It is marketed in a crystal decanter, and sold in only limited quantities.

Rémy is known for consistent quality throughout the range, and for sheer professionalism. It is one of the favourite Houses of brandy drinkers throughout the world.

A. DE FUSSIGNY

C COLOUR Golden yellow through to caramel; good intensity.

A AROMA Cinnamon, orange, walnut, and vanilla; delicate with a slight sweetness.

T TASTE Rich and smooth; buttery and creamy; long, balanced finish.

Alain Royer established this House in 1987, with a mission to market his product to reach new customers. I particularly love the fact that you can buy single measures of his Cognac in cigar-shaped tubes to carry anywhere – marketing genius!

Despite the gimmicks, the House has established a good reputation, with all its Cognacs originating from the Grande or Petite Champagne districts. The VSOP is smooth and fruity; the Extra, nutty and fruity and made entirely from Grande Champagne spirits. The XO "For Men" comes in an after-shave shaped bottle. This is an excellent Grande Champagne Cognac – rich and smooth, with a growing fan base.

HENNESSY

C COLOUR Golden yellow through to amber and dark mahogany.

A AROMA Wonderfully complex; oak, nuts, vanilla, leather, spice, and grapes.

T TASTE Great balance; rich, dry and smooth; buttery and creamy.

Hennessy was established by Irishman Richard Hennessy in 1765. In 1971 it merged with Moët to create Moët-Hennessy, which is now part of LVMH. The result is that Hennessy is now the world's leading Cognac brand.

Hennessy makes a full range of brandies. At the most basic level, PureWhite, aimed at younger drinkers, is light, floral, and fruity. It is designed to be served in a cocktail or long drink. The VS is bright gold, smooth, and well-balanced, with nuts and oak. This, too, is recommended for cocktails.

CONQUERING THE WORLD
The position of the Hennessy Cognac building on the Charente River in Cognac made exporting a tempting prospect. From its earliest beginnings Hennessy shipped its Cognac to other parts of the world – starting with Britain and Ireland, and from there to Australia, America, and Asia.

HENNESSEY VS

Next up is the VSOP Privilège. Blended from about 60 eaux-de-vie from throughout Cognac, it begins to show the wood, vanilla, and liquorice of ageing. Hennessy tries to promote a young image for this Cognac by recommending it as a "highball mixer", but in my view it is really for drinking on its own.

Hennessy Fine de Cognac is a new blend, again aimed at young consumers, particularly women. It is elegant and floral, with a light, delicate touch. It has hints of orange, lemon, spice, and honey.

However, Hennessy's flagship is its XO – Cognac's original XO, and the benchmark for all other XOs. This is powerful and masculine, with a deep amber colour, a rich and full taste, and woody, spicy aromas.

Hennessy make two exclusive blends – Private Reserve and Paradis Extra. The first is a limited edition of a blend first produced in 1873 and made up of 14 Grande Champagne eaux-de-vie. For a top Cognac it is relatively light, fruity, and floral. The Paradis Extra is a blend of more than a hundred old spirits from the Hennessy warehouse. It is spicy and peppery, and perfectly balanced with fruit and flowers.

However, the Richard Hennessy ("The Richard"), is the jewel in Hennessy's crown. Some of its eaux-de-vie have aged for more than 200 years, giving a complex blend with a perfect balance of wood, fruit, spice, and vanilla, and an infinite finish. This is a drink never to forget!

HENNESSY PUREWHITE

RAGNAUD SABOURIN

C COLOUR Yellow through amber to dark mahogany for the older brandy.

A AROMA Fruit, flowers, vanilla, sweet spice, lime, quince, and liquorice.

T TASTE Rich, smooth, and very full; perfectly balanced.

Ragnaud Sabourin is synonymous with quality, and one of my favourite after-dinner brandies. Its limited production provides brandies with just the right amount of caramel, and lots of fruit, elegance, and complexity. Start with the Alliance No. 20 Reserve Special, which is 20 years old, rich, and buttery; or try the 35-year-old Fontvielle – dark mahogany, full, fruity, and rich, with aromas of liquorice and lime. Florilège is an excellent mahogany blend of aged spirits, with outstanding *rancio* (over-ripe fruit).

RAGNAUD SABOURIN

CHÂTEAU BEAULON

C COLOUR Amber through orange to golden copper.

A AROMA Grapes, flowers, pear, hazelnut, spice, and tobacco.

T TASTE Characterful, balanced, and well-rounded; complex; spice, vanilla, raisins.

This award-winning House is based in Bordeaux, along the Gironde River. Château Beaulon's strength lies in its "specials", which truly live up to their name. The Grande Fine Extra is more than 50 years old, deep copper-red, and woody, with hints of coffee, cocoa, and beeswax. The 1976 (distilled using grapes exclusively from the 1976 harvest) is particularly fruity, spicy, and delicate. The very best is the Rare, which is blended from a selection of the estate's rarest eaux-de-vie, and is mellow, rich, and complex.

OTARD

C COLOUR Golden yellow through to dark amber with reddish tinges.

A AROMA Typically flowery and spicy, with pear, lime, and tobacco.

T TASTE Very fruity, flowery, and spicy; good balance, especially the XO Gold.

Founded in 1795, Otard once ranked with the likes of Hennessy. Now it is a much smaller operation, although it still produces good Cognac. The VSOP Fine Champagne has powerful aromas of flowers, fruit, and spice, while the Napoleon is more delicate and woody, with hints of dried fruit and coconut. The Otard XO Gold is delicate and floral, and is a much darker amber, with a hint of red. The top brand is the 1795 Extra. This special Cognac has great length, and rich aromas of honey, flowers, fruit, and cigar box.

OTARD

AE DOR

C COLOUR Ranges from a dark, deep yellow to light amber.

A AROMA Elegant, with vanilla, aromatic violet, vinewood, and some spice.

T TASTE Rich and elegant; blended with expertise from the finest spirit.

One of my all-time favourites! Established in the 19th century, AE Dor offers an Aladdin's cave of exquisite Cognacs. The most basic Sélection is a light, bright, and fruity blend, and is an elegant all-round brandy. For something richer and darker try the VSOP or the Vieux Napoleon, with its nose of vanilla and violet. Cigar smokers have their own special blend, the Reserve. Most delicate is the delicious and classy Gold. This is so beautifully balanced that you could almost believe that it has no alcohol in it at all.

COURVOISIER

C COLOUR Light amber through to dark, vintage gold.

A AROMA Ripe fruits and flowers; vanilla, wood, and spice.

T TASTE Rich, full, flavoursome, and complex; also subtle and satisfying.

Courvoisier claim to be the brandy of Napoleon, but as the House was established in 1843, the direct connection is with Bonaparte's nephew Louis, rather than the great man himself. The silhouette of the Emperor and the "Josephine"-shaped bottles were introduced in the early 20th century for brand identity. The House has had several changes of ownership over the years, but Courvoisier is now the flagship brand of Allied Domecq.

The Courvoisiers that you are most likely to see on your supermarket shelves are the basic VS (reliable and fruity with an aroma of fragrant herbs); the VSOP Fine Champagne (subtle, with hints of vanilla and flowers), and the higher level VSOP Exclusif. Aimed at the younger market, this last brandy is light, smooth, and exotic, and very approachable (in contrast to the heavy cigar-linked brands). It is one of my favourites as a brandy for any occasion. You will recognize it by its special long, slim bottle.

The Napoleon Fine Champagne is one of the flagship Courvoisier brandies. It is a blend of Grande and Petite Champagne, with a minimum of 50 per cent Grande Champagne, and is aged up to 20 years. This is a classic blend – dark and very

SWIRLING BRANDY *The practice of swirling brandy in the glass releases its aromas; for Courvoisier, this means a full appreciation of rich, ripe fruits, sweet vanilla, and delicious spice.*

INSPECTING THE WOOD Courvoisier believes that attention to detail is essential in the creation of its Cognac. The company uses only aged Limousin oak barrels to mature its brandy, and each piece of wood (taken from trees that are centuries old) is inspected for perfection before it becomes a cask.

rich, with aromas of port, orange, spice, and prune.

Courvoisier's XO (extra-old) brandy is its award-winning Imperial. This Cognac is rich and subtle, with vanilla, chocolate, and spice aromas. This is really something special, and it may be hard to find – if you do, save it for an important occasion!

Another award winner is the Initiale Extra. Like the Imperial it comes in a teardrop-shaped bottle. Initiale Extra is made with spirits up to 50 years old, which give perfectly harmonized aromas of mushroom and cigar box with vanilla and spice. Available for the serious Cognac-lover, and even collector, are Courvoisier's special Cognacs, such as the Erté Collection (eight decanters with images from the French Art Deco painter of the same name); and L'Esprit de Courvoisier, which comes in a Lalique crystal decanter, and is blended from Cognacs dating from the 19th century to 1930. If you ever have the chance just to taste the L'Esprit, you are very lucky indeed!

COURVOISIER VS

CLÉS DE DUCS

C **COLOUR** Attractive, dark, vintage gold through to light amber.

A **AROMA** Aromatic, fragrant, and full; fruit, vanilla, and spices.

T **TASTE** Well-balanced; quite young and fresh; medium smoothness and length.

One of the main differences between Cognac and Armagnac is that for centuries the great Cognac Houses have promoted their product around the world, turning it into a global brandy. Armagnac, on the other hand, has been localized, partly by virtue of the fact that the Armagnac region is further inland than Cognac, and so historically it has been more difficult to export the product. However, the Armagnac House of Clés des Ducs is a subsidiary of the global spirits group Rémy-Cointreau, and is marketed globally.

CLÉS DE DUCS

As a result Clés des Ducs may be the only Armagnac you see on the shelves of your local store.

Clés des Ducs makes a "Napoléon" blend, but probably the best-known blend is the VSOP (sold in a distinctive "shouldered" bottle). This is made from a blend of Armagnacs with an average age of seven years. It has a lovely light amber colour – unusual for an Armagnac, which is often a richer amber than Cognac because of the darker oak traditionally used for its casks.

It is soft, fruity, and spicy. For me it is perhaps released onto the market a little too early. (It does not have the depth you might expect of a classic Armagnac.) But if you like your brandy young and fresh, or you are simply looking for something gentle and easy to drink at the end the day, this Armagnac is one to try.

BARON DE SIGOGNAC

C **COLOUR** Gold through amber, with mahogany highlights.

A **AROMA** Vanilla, cinnamon, ginger, and orange, with woody and nutty notes.

T **TASTE** Full and round; spicy and well-balanced with hints of caramel.

This award-winning House belongs to ADEX, a firm with large stocks of Armagnac eaux-de-vie for blending. The basic brands are the three-star VS Baron de Sigognac (at least two years old), and the floral, fruity VSOP (at least four years old). The ten-year-old is a fine product – round, woody, and spicy – aimed at cigar smokers; and the 20-year-old is light-coloured and elegant. The House is especially successful with its single vintages. These tend to be rich and dark, with truffle, caramel, and vanilla flavours.

BARON DE SIGOGNAC

CHÂTEAU DE LAUBADE

C **COLOUR** Medium amber brown through to dark mahogany.

A **AROMA** Elegant, with vanilla, spice, wood, and notes of nuts.

T **TASTE** Full and round; very smooth and rich with a satisfying finish.

This is the biggest estate in Armagnac, but it is not the market leader. The House concentrates on collecting and selling single vintages – some of which date back to the 19th century (and cost more than $2,000!). The lowest grade is the VSOP. Naturally, the style of the vintages varies, but mostly they are rich, dark, complex, and smooth Armagnacs, with woody, spicy aromas. They are just beautiful! If you are looking for a special gift, Château Laubade will almost certainly have something for you.

CHÂTEAU DE TARIQUET

- **C** **COLOUR** Elegant gold, through amber to bright copper for the aged versions.

- **A** **AROMA** Flowers and vanilla; baked bread, honey, and dark fruits.

- **T** **TASTE** Delicate, floral, and light; elegant and complex.

This 300-year-old estate in Bas Armagnac makes several Côtes de Gascon wines, but also a large range of Armagnacs. Most styles are made using Folle Blanche grapes, producing brandies that are light and floral. They range from basic styles, such as the three-star Classique, through exclusive blends, such as the 18-year-old Hors d'Age, to vintages, such as those from 1982, 1985, and 1988, which are rich and dark.

CHÂTEAU DE TARIQUET

DOMAINE DE BOINGNÈRES

- **C** **COLOUR** Elegant medium gold through to dark amber for older styles.

- **A** **AROMA** Delicate, with flowers and vanilla, honey, and dark fruits.

- **T** **TASTE** Delicate and floral, but also elegant and complex with a light finish.

The Domaine de Boingnères estate, in the Bas Armagnac region, dates back to 1807 and remains under the control of the founding family – the current owner, Madame Lafitte, is a direct descendent of the original Monsieur Boingnères.

The small estate – there are just 22 ha (54.5 acres) of vines – has established one of the highest reputations of all Armagnac producers because of its emphasis on quality rather than quantity. Most Domaine de Boingnères Armagnac is distilled from the base wine of

DOMAINE DE BOINGNÈRES

the Folle Blanche grape. The fruit is turned into brandy using authentic, high-quality production methods, and the spirit is largely aged in new oak, ensuring good colour, with plenty of spice and vanilla. The results are earthy, award-winning Armagnacs that feature on the drinks lists of the world's finest restaurants. Boingnères spirits display deep and focused fruit, while retaining plenty of finesse.

Most Domaine de Boingnères Armagnacs are marketed by vintage and, as a general rule, the older the spirit, the more expensive it will be. Whatever you pay for a bottle, you can be certain you have made an excellent choice.

SAMALENS

- **C** **COLOUR** Medium amber-brown through to shining gold.

- **A** **AROMA** Balanced and elegant; fruit and vanilla; honey and a hint of oak.

- **T** **TASTE** Round and smooth; quite rich, with a lovely vanilla and fruit balance.

These Bas Armagnac brandies come from an estate established in 1882 and still owned by the founding family. The spirits are aged in small casks made from dark, Gascony oak, which give a greater concentration of flavours and make the finished products feel especially rich and smooth. The brandies are packaged in distinctive shell-shaped and shouldered bottles.

The estate produces an excellent VSOP (six years old), Napoleon (12 years old), and Reserve Imperial XO (15 years old), but I think their best product is the 20-year-old Vieille Relique, which is warm, smooth, and full bodied with an excellent finish.

JANNEAU

- **C** **COLOUR** Gold through to amber, with bright notes and nuances.

- **A** **AROMA** Flowers, and fresh, ripe fruit; prunes and nuts.

- **T** **TASTE** Light and bright; spicy, fresh, and well-balanced.

Pierre Etienne Janneau founded his Armagnac distillery in 1851, making it the oldest of the *Grandes Maisons d'Armagnac* (Armagnac "Houses"). However, over the years the firm has been sold to a variety of large owners who have not cared for the brand in the way that it deserves – until now. Janneau is now owned by the Italian Giovinetti family, from Milan, which has already made a name for itself through its promotion of malt whisky in Italy. The family employs Willy Phillips – most successfully

JANNEAU VS

linked to The Macallan malt whisky – to manage Janneau. The result is that this Armagnac has made a great recovery in the marketplace.

Janneau now offers an excellent range of mass-market Armagnacs – all of which are extremely reliable and increasingly well respected throughout Europe and the world.

The distillery uses wines from both the Ténarèze and Bas-Armagnac regions to make its brandy. The wines from Ténarèze offer flowers, such as jasmine and rose, to the blend; while those from Bas Armagnac give richer and more spicy effects, such as aromas of leather and cinnamon. The proportions of each wine will determine the overall mood of the brandy.

Most of the company's products are blended from brandies made in both the traditional way (known sometimes as the *méthode armagnacaise*, using a single, continuous

still), and those made by the Cognac process, using double distillation in copper pot stills (*see pp170–1*). The latter method is more expensive and tends to produce brandies that are of finer quality – they are more full bodied and rounder, with more layers of aroma and flavour.

Janneau's most basic brandy is the VS. A blend of four-year-old spirits, it is gold, light, floral, fresh, and fruity on both the nose and the palate. Next up is the VSOP – also known as the Seven-Year-Old – a blend of Armagnacs aged for at least seven years in barrels made from local oak. The result gives a hint of vanilla to the layers of fruit.

If you are looking for a brandy to drink over ice or to use as a mixer in a long drink, I recommend the Janneau five-year-old blend. This brandy is part of the company's "Double Distillation" range and it is specifically aimed at the cocktail

JANNEAU VSOP

market. It is aged for a minimum of five years in new oak casks.

For something more spicy and nutty, with the richer flavours of dark fruits such as black plums, try the outstanding Janneau XO. The Très Vieille Grande Fine Armagnac is extremely smooth, with the special complexity that comes with long-ageing. The pride of the House, this reserve is blended using eaux de vie that are up to 30 years old. The result is deeply rich and earthy, and one of the finest blends on the market. Janneau also produces vintage Armagnacs from several years dating well back into the 20th century.

If you are not familiar with Armagnac, Janneau's products are a good place to start. The basic brands are completely reliable and widely available, and I would advise you to gradually work your way up through the list to the exclusive blends at the very top.

THE MARK OF FRENCH BRANDY

The term "*fine*" is used to describe high-quality French grape brandies that are not from the exclusive regions of Cognac or Armagnac. Usually *fine* brandies will be named according to their area of production. So, for example, you might find a Fine de Bourgogne (from the Burgundy region), a Fine de Champagne (from Champagne), or a Fine de Bordeaux (from Bordeaux).

Fine de Bordeaux is made from grapes that must come from the Bordeaux area – usually Ugni Blanc and Colombard – which are double distilled, and then aged in oak casks.

You may also come across brandy labelled Fine de la Marne. This comes from Champagne, and is a by-product of the production of the great

VIELLE FINE DE LA MARNE

sparkling wine. To get its bubbles, Champagne is bottle-fermented *(see p129)*: during the process, a small amount of lees-rich wine must be removed (disgorged) before the Champagne is fit for sale. Some Champagne houses recycle this disgorged wine to make a *fine* brandy. The results have toasted-bread flavours (from the yeast), and a beautiful amber colour (from ageing in oak).

Some *fine* brandies are labelled *Eau de Vie de Vin* (literally meaning "wine brandy") and are made from some of the most famous wines in France. For example, Château La Nerthe, a producer in the Châteauneuf-du-Pape appellelation, in the southern Rhône, makes a Fine de Châteauneuf du Pape, which it calls Eau de Vie de Vin des Côtes du

EAU DE VIE DE VIN DES CÔTES DU RHÔNE

Rhône. At Château La Nerthe, the brandy is aged in old oak barrels for eight years. The result is a deep golden spirit, with aromas of sweet, dried fruits and a palate rich with butter and spice. As with all brandies, the quality of the drink depends as much on the skill of the distiller as on the raw materials, so it is vital to buy from established, reputable producers.

MARQUIS DE MONTESQUIOU

C COLOUR Light gold with sparkling highlights, through to deep amber.

A AROMA Fruity and appealing, with apricot, peach, vanilla, and oak.

T TASTE Well-balanced; smooth, rich texture, and a firm finish.

The Montesquiou family has owned this estate since the 11th century (the family's most famous member was d'Artagnan – one of the Three Musketeers), but the brand is now owned by Pernod Ricard, and is making its brandy for the mass market.

Look for the reliable and award-winning Napoleon (five years old) and XO (ten years old), as well as the superior, single-vintage Armagnacs, including those presently available from 1965, 1971, and 1976.

MARQUIS DE MONTESQUIOU

LABERDOLIVE

C COLOUR Medium amber-brown through to dark copper.

A AROMA Intense and complex, with balanced fruit, vanilla, and oak.

T TASTE Perfectly balanced; smooth and rich with infinite length.

This is Armagnac at its best! Established in 1866, Laberdolive is one of the most prestigious Armagnac houses in the world and has, since its beginnings, set the standard for single-estate and single-vintage Armagnacs.

Each vintage is carefully produced using a blend of Ugni Blanc, Folle Blanche, and Colombard grapes. The key vintages are 1942, 1946, 1954, 1962, 1964, 1970, 1976, and 1979. The most powerful of these is the 1970, and the most fruity come from 1976 and 1979.

CHÂTEAU LABALLE

C COLOUR Light, shining, bright gold, through to dark amber.

A AROMA Fruit, such as apricot; earthy wood and sweet vanilla.

T TASTE Well-made with good balance; smooth but not too rich.

Established in 1820, Château Laballe makes a fine range of excellent Armagnacs, aged in new oak barrels, and primarily marketed according to vintage. The estate is managed by a family who also produce Bordeaux wine.

Some of the vintages that are currently available include one from as long ago as 1973, as well as the more recent years of 1985, 1986, 1987, and 1989. One of the distinctive features of this château is that it sells some of its brandies in larger-sized bottles, including a 150cl-bottle (a magnum) of the XO.

CHÂTEAU LABALLE

LA CROIX DE SALLES

C COLOUR Golden yellow through to dark amber-brown.

A AROMA Fruity and complex; peach, apricot, wood, and vanilla.

T TASTE Good balance; smooth and moderately rich, with a soft finish.

Owned by the Dartigalongue family and established in 1838, La Croix de Salles is situated in Bas Armagnac. In 1870 the family acquired the current estate, where they set up a modern vineyard and installed a distillery. Over the years five generations of the same family have prided themselves on high-quality production, using both modern technology as well as traditional techniques (especially for the older vintages). The VSOP blend is excellent and makes a perfect introduction to Armagnac, and the vintages are simply first-class.

SPAIN

Spanish brandy has a history longer than that of Cognac, and tends to be richer and more fruity than its French counterpart. The industry has grown in conjunction with that of sherry, and many Spanish brandies are made by sherry producers.

OSBORNE

C **COLOUR** Dark golden through to dark amber brown.

A **AROMA** Extremely rich; plum jam, orange, prune, nuts, wood, and vanilla.

T **TASTE** Full-bodied and luscious; really smooth, with fruit and vanilla.

A family-owned firm, Osborne began producing brandy in 1772 and is today the world's largest supplier of Brandy de Jerez.

Although Osborne Brandy de Jerez has links to sherry (the word sherry is a corruption of Jerez – the town around which sherry is made), it does not come from the same region. The links lie in the grape varieties and the *solera* system of maturation and blending *(see p143)*. The brandies also undergo a secret process involving the addition of prunes, nuts, and other, undisclosed items.

The result is that Osborne brandies tend to be darker, richer, and more fruity than those from Cognac or Armagnac, although they are perhaps not quite as sophisticated. The closest match is the Gran Reserva, marketed as Conde Osborne, and the firm's flagship product. This is aged for 15 to 20 years, and has all the signature fruity, aromatic qualities of Osborne, but is much smoother and more delicate. If you are looking for a mixer, try the excellent Veterano, while the longer-aged Magno, a best-seller in Spain, is good on its own.

OSBORNE VETERANO

THE BLACK BULL *The famous black bull on the Osborne label was first introduced in 1956 during an advertising campaign for Veterano.*

EMILIO LUSTAU

C COLOUR Medium amber brown through to a darker copper.

A AROMA Rich and fruity; chocolate, prune, dark sugar, oak, and vanilla.

T TASTE Full and smooth; extremely creamy, but delicate and satisfying.

Founded in 1896, the firm of Emilio Lustau began life as a producer and distributor of sherry – a job that it continues to this day. As a result, the company's Brandy de Jerez was somewhat overshadowed – consumers identified Lustau with sherry, not brandy. However, in 1990 the company came under the ownership of the brandy firm Luis Caballero, and this has been a happy combination. Luis Caballero has improved the company's financial base, marketing,

and distribution, giving Lustau brandies a new lease of life.

Lustau offers four brandies – all of very good quality. The basic Lustau is the Decano. This is a good, regular brandy, best for mixing in cocktails or for long drinks. The Reserva, if not outstanding, is also good. This brandy can be drunk on its own, but is more frequently used as a base for cocktails.

The company's flagship product is the Millenario Gran Reserva. This brandy is very deep, rich, and smooth. For something really opulent and creamy, try the Señor Lustau, which is noted for being quite delicate and complex, unlike many other Spanish brandies, and is often justifiably compared with Cognac or Armagnac. Señor Lustau is perfect for sipping on its own, and is an excellent match for a good cigar.

EMILIO LUSTAU

GONZÁLEZ BYASS

C COLOUR Light golden amber, through to a light brown.

A AROMA Fruity and complex; nuts, baked apple, sultanas, wood, and vanilla.

T TASTE Delicate and complex; extremely smooth, but with a distinct freshness.

Formed in the middle of the 19th century, González Byass is the result of a merger between sherry-producer Manuel González Angel and his English agent Robert Byass. The company, the largest in Jerez, in Spain's sherry-producing region, is now known throughout the world through brands such as Tío Pepe sherry.

González Byass's most successful brandies are the blockbuster Soberano range – known to every young Spaniard as their favourite brandy mixers.

The Soberano Solera – Spain's best-selling brandy and usually the basis of a long drink – is light, fresh, and fruity, and has a prominent flavour of sultanas.

However, the company's flagship brandy is the Lepanto Gran Reserva, marketed in a slightly garish decanter-type bottle. This is at least 15 years old, quite dry, and pale in colour (a light golden amber). It can be compared to a young Cognac, and is usually drunk on its own.

The Lepanto PX and Lepanto OV are also at least 15 years old, and each matures in its own type of ex-sherry cask. These brandies are darker, richer, and more raisin-influenced.

González Byass has everything! I love the bright and lively Soberano for a party; but to savour when I settle down after a meal, a Lepanto is easily as good as a Cognac.

GONZÁLEZ BYASS

DOMECQ

C COLOUR Dark amber through to a bright mahogany.

A AROMA Fruity and rich; plum, sultanas, herbs, toffee, caramel, and oak.

T TASTE Rich and smooth, with a fine fruit balance; elegant but fresh.

The name Domecq is synonymous with spirits – as part of the massive conglomerate Allied-Domecq, the company now owns world-famous brands such as Courvoisier, Malibu, Teacher's, and Canadian Club. However, Domecq is actually a very old firm, and its origins lie in sherry-making. It started making Spanish brandy very early in its history.

In France in the late 19th century, the phylloxera blight wiped out huge numbers of vineyards, including many in Cognac, bringing the Cognac industry to a standstill. In 1874 Pedro Domecq, seizing the open market, launched his Fundador brandy. This spirit, aged for three years, and bright mahogany in

colour, is one to buy if you want a popular, no-frills Spanish brandy.

For something similarly popular, but light, try Centenario. This brandy is aged for three years using the *solera* system, which is also used to age sherry *(see p143)*. Centenario has an intense amber colour, with a slight herbal aroma and delicate sherry notes.

If you are looking for a Gran Reserva, one of the better premium brands is Don Pedro. This is medium amber in colour with complex aromas of nuts, caramel, raisins, toffee, and oak. However, Domecq's best Gran Reserva is Carlos I. This is much darker than the Don Pedro, having been aged in *oloroso* sherry casks for at least 12 years. It has a long finish, and hints of dried fruits and vanilla. The taste is complex and satisfying, and if you like a touch of dryness, then this is one for you.

TORRES

C COLOUR Vintage gold through to dark amber for the mature versions.

A AROMA Fruity with prune and plum; caramel, nuts, and oak.

T TASTE Smooth, rich, full, and satisfying, with a lovely balance of fruit and wood.

Torres is the largest producer of wine in Catalonia (around Barcelona), but also makes a number of Catalan-style brandies, which tend to be less rich than brandy from Jerez. The dry 10 Gran Reserva is similar to Cognac, but somewhat less sophisticated. The 20 Imperial is richer and darker, with flavours of deep fruits, vanilla, and oak, and a touch of sweetness. The flagship is Jaime I. At least 30 years old, this brandy is strong, dark, and sweet – and perfect as something rich and luscious after dinner.

TORRES

MASCARÓ

C COLOUR A pale golden colour, through to light amber.

A AROMA Fruits, such as pear, as well as vanilla, nuts, and oak; hints of toffee.

T TASTE Delicate and fine; well-balanced with good length.

Mascaró is a family business based in Catalonia, the region surrounding Barcelona, with a distinct personal style. The basic brandies are the three-year-old VO and the five-year-old Narciso – both are golden, uncomplicated, and quite woody. The flagship is the EGO, the Mascaró version of XO (extra-old) and intended as a direct competitor to Cognac. Aged for at least eight years in oak barrels, this is a delicate and complex brandy and I love it!

For the millennium, Mascaró produced a special cuvée (blend) of selected spirit of at least 20 years old. The company issued only 2,000 numbered bottles – if you find one of these, please let me know!

PORTUGAL

The best Portuguese brandy is made with the white grape varieties used for making Vinho Verde, and is very rich and fruity.

PALACIO DE BREJOEIRA

C COLOUR Dark amber brown through to deep copper.

A AROMA Complex; dried fruits, fig, coffee, orange, and chocolate.

T TASTE Well-concentrated; warm, rich, and ripe; medium length.

Palacio de Brejoeira produces an excellent *bagaceira* (pomace brandy) from the pressings of the Alvarinho grapes used in Vinho Verde, but its best *aguardente* (grape brandy) is Velha Alvarinho – a fine example of Portuguese brandy, with complex aromas and a warm, rich taste.

AVELEDA

C COLOUR Ranges from dark, vintage gold to light to medium amber.

A AROMA Complex; vanilla, earth, lemon peel, baked bread, herbs, flowers.

T TASTE Warm, ripe; complex flavours; good length.

Quinta de Aveleda, based in northern Portugal, produces the country's most highly regarded brandies. The best is Aguardente Adega Velha. Aged for more than ten years in French oak, this award-winning brandy has a complex range of aromas, including earth, herbs, and flowers, with darker hints of coffee and chocolate. For me, Adega Velha is an altogether superior brandy, and is well worth trying.

AVELEDA

ITALY

Although better known for its grappa, Italy has a fine brandy tradition using grapes such as Trebbiano, also used in Cognac.

BUTON

C COLOUR Light to medium amber; extremely intense.

A AROMA Fruit, such as prune and plum; vanilla and oak.

T TASTE Warm and delicate, with a slightly dry feel and a satisfying finish.

Buton's brandies are close to Cognac in style, but slightly stronger. The most famous is the Vecchia Romagna – the only Italian brandy made in pot stills and matured in old oak barrels. Look out for the aged brandies, such as the Vecchia Romagna Riserva Rare, which contains spirits up to 15 years old.

STOCK

C COLOUR Light orangey yellow, through to amber; intense, deep.

A AROMA Well-balanced; a perfect combination of grapes, vanilla, and oak.

T TASTE Fresh and fruity; quite warm and lively; smooth in the older versions.

Established in 1884 and now owned by the German company Eckes, Stock produce the world's best-selling Italian brandy, Stock 84. (The name refers to the company's foundation year.) This is their VSOP, produced from Trebbiano grapes and matured in seasoned oak casks. Stock Original is the company's basic offering. This brandy is light gold in colour and best drunk as a mixer.

STOCK

GERMANY

German brandies are quite light and fragrant with a fine balance, and comparable to medium Cognacs in style and quality. Most of the grapes and base wines used for production are imported into Germany from France and Italy for ageing and blending.

ASBACH

C COLOUR Dark, vintage gold, through to light amber brown.

A AROMA Sweet, with vanilla, apple, coffee, cake, jammy fruit, and minerals.

T TASTE Light and fresh, with medium length and a satisfying finish.

Hugo Asbach founded his company in the late 19th century, and in 1907 came up with the word *Weinbrand*, which has now become the accepted German term for brandy.

Asbach's flagship is Uralt – and whenever I think of German *Weinbrand*, it is always the Uralt bottle that pops into my head! The wine used for Uralt comes from

Charente in southwestern France, and the brandy is aged in Limousin oak for three years or so – much longer than the minimum stated by German law.

Asbach also makes a Privatbrand – its VSOP – which is aged for eight years, and the 15-year-old Spezial-brand, equivalent to an XO. The Selection, aged for 21 years, is a gift product, and comes in a decanter. To celebrate the year 2000, the company produced the limited-edition 1972 Vintage. This is a collector's item – look out for it!

ASBACH

ECKES

C COLOUR Dark browny red through to vintage gold.

A AROMA Not overpowering and quite neutral; fruit, vanilla, and oak.

T TASTE Light and fruity; fresh character with medium length.

This is definitely a company to look out for if you like German "Cognac". An international production and distribution company for the drinks industry, Eckes was founded in Germany in the 1850s, and after World War II expanded rapidly into Austria, Italy, and eastern Europe. Its wine-and-spirits arm is known as Eckes and Stock, and controls more than one hundred brands of brandy.

One of its flagship products is Chantré – named after the chairman's wife – a range of Cognac-style brandies, and the biggest-selling brandy in Germany. Chantré Cognac (the term Cognac can be used because the raw spirit that produces this version of

Chantré originates from there, although it is blended in Germany) is VSOP-quality, and matured in oak barrels for at least four years. The result is a silky-smooth brandy, with well-integrated fruit and vanilla flavours. The basic brandy is Chantré Weinbrand, while Chantré Cuvée Rouge is an under-strength brandy – at 30% ABV – distilled entirely from red wine. This is a delightful, subtle spirit with a glorious red colour. Others of Eckes' under-strength brandies include the mild and gentle Goldbrand and the subtle Attaché.

The oldest Eckes brand is Mariacron, which the company acquired in 1961, but which has been produced since 1894. This is another big seller – one of the top five brandies in Germany. It is a light, warm, first-class mixing brandy.

ECKES

SPIRIT AND SMOKE Like brandy, cigars should set your senses alight, especially in aroma and taste, but also in colour too – a good cigar should be of uniform colour, without "patches". Match fine brandy with a medium to full Havana (handmade Cuban) cigar, as their spicy, fruity, woody, and mellow characters will complement each other perfectly.

DECKER

C **COLOUR** A light amber colour, with golden highlights.

A **AROMA** Jammy fruits, toffee, spices, wood, and sweet vanilla.

T **TASTE** Fresh, spicy, and a little warm at the finish.

This small family company has tried to take seriously the idea that although the Cognac region has a monopoly over the magic word "Cognac", it cannot monopolize quality. Decker brandies are oak-aged and made using methods as near as possible to those of traditional Cognac. The results are normally extremely smooth, and of superior quality. They are like Cognac, but all have a spicy touch.

The basic Decker is the Kaiserberg, which is lively and fresh, and best as a mixer. Next is the sweetish Dupont. At the top is the Steinhalter, which is aged for seven years and is fruity and complex.

RACKE

C **COLOUR** Bright and appealing light to medium amber.

A **AROMA** Very attractive and elegant; caramel, vanilla, dried fruits, honey, oak.

T **TASTE** Medium intensity; quite smooth and slightly sweet on the finish.

Although Racke's priority is wine, about a quarter of its sales are in spirits. Racke introduced the first ever German whisky in 1959, and also makes Pott rum – a big seller.

Racke's best-known brandy is Dujardin Imperial, made in Germany from French-sourced wine and matured in French-oak barrels. This is a brandy of medium intensity, either for mixing, or to enjoy on its own as an everyday digestif.

The company's other brand is Scharlachberg – created in 1920, Scharlachberg Meisterbrand is the third-biggest-selling brandy in Germany. This is a mild, medium brandy, and is best used as a mixer.

CYPRUS

Brandy is very popular among Cypriots – some even enjoy it with food. Cypriot brandies are deeply flavoured with a sweetish tinge.

SODAP

C **COLOUR** Light gold through to medium amber for the older versions.

A **AROMA** Appealing; wood, dried fruit, vanilla, and herbs.

T **TASTE** Not too rich; quite delicate and smooth; fresh finish.

Established in 1947 in Cyprus, SODAP is a large wine co-operative. Its basic brandy is VO 47, which is young and fiery. The VSOP, matured in oak casks for at least 15 years, is delicate and fairly complex. Best of all is the Adonis – richer and smoother, it can be drunk on its own.

KEO

C **COLOUR** Medium gold with amber tinges and amber on the rim.

A **AROMA** Grapes, vanilla, and wood, with some notes of honey.

T **TASTE** Softly sweet, and extremely silky smooth.

With branches in Greece, Cyprus, and Italy, Keo produces brandy distilled mainly from the white Xinisteri grapes. The Keo VSOP, which should never be confused with the Cognac VSOP grade, is a basic brandy, and really suitable only for mixing. Much better is Keo's flagship product, the Five Kings. The spirit is double-distilled in pot stills, and then aged for 15 years. The result is a smooth, aromatic brandy rather like a young Cognac, and altogether very drinkable.

KEO

GREECE

Greece's brandy market is dominated by one product – Metaxa. First made in 1888, the company now sells over a million cases each year worldwide. Metaxa is typical of the Greek style – not over-complex, but with a rich and deeply fruity texture.

METAXA

C **COLOUR** Soft, dark, honey gold through to amber.

A **AROMA** Muscat grapes, raisins, herbs, rose, and wood.

T **TASTE** Extremely well-balanced, quite mellow and woody, with a long finish.

Some say that because Metaxa is made from a mixture of spirit, wine, and herbs, it is not a brandy but a liqueur. However, I treat it as a brandy: all brandies have something added to them – sometimes it might be caramel, sometimes just the flavour from an oak barrel – and if you go to Greece and ask for a brandy, you will be served Metaxa.

Metaxa is produced using a blend of red grapes, and is aged in oak casks for between three and 15 years. After ageing, it is blended with Muscat wine and herbs, stored for not less six months in larger oak barrels, and then bottled.

Metaxa comes in three main versions: Three Star, Five Star, and Seven Star – each star represents a year's ageing. Beyond the basic models is the Private Reserve. This is at least 20 years old, and is smooth, rich, and complex – a very satisfying brandy.

METAXA

ISRAEL

Israel is the largest kosher brandy producer in the world, although France, Italy, and the US make it as well. The industry was established by French Jewish families like the Rothschilds, and has now become very popular in Israel.

CARMEL MIZRACHI

C **COLOUR** A deep, dark gold, with nuances of amber.

A **AROMA** Dried fruit, especially raisins; earthy wood, and honey.

T **TASTE** Mellow, fruity, and quite sweet, with medium intensity.

Founded by the Rothschild family (owners of Bordeaux's Château Lafite wine) in 1882, Carmel Mizrachi is the biggest exporter of Israeli brandy. Using its good connections with brandy producers in Italy, Carmel has gradually built up a reputation for quality, largely as a result of growing its own grapes,

which produce a firm base for the spirit.

One of the best of the company's products is the fruity and lively Carmel 777 (a VSOP), aged for three years.

CARMEL MIZRACHI

The prize-winning 777 Gold is six years old, and although a little sweet is extremely well balanced. However, best of all are the award-winning Brandy 100, which is nine years old and has a full, mellow fruit flavour and good balance; and the 110 XO, which is 15 years old and particularly smooth and graceful.

GEORGIA

The Republic of Georgia, in eastern Europe, has long been a producer of wine, and, since the 19th century, of excellent brandy. Producers use methods that are essentially the same as those of Cognac – brandy is double-distilled, and then aged in oak barrels.

ENISELI

C **COLOUR** A shimmering dark gold to the darker side of medium-amber.

A **AROMA** Open and attractive; vanilla, caramel, grape, dried fruit, and oak.

T **TASTE** Reasonably dry; sophisticated; velvety and well-balanced.

The award-winning Eniseli brandies are produced by a drinks company founded in 1884 by chemist David Saradjishvili. Not only is the brand said to have found its place at the table of Tsar Nicholas II of Russia, it was also a favourite of the Russian dictator Joseph Stalin, and was savoured by British Prime Minister

Winston Churchill at the conference in Yalta, Crimea, in 1945.

The basic Eniseli brandy is three years old, uncomplicated, and perhaps a little sweet; while the five-year-old Dr Saradjishvili (named after the company's founder) is a little more complex and well balanced. For something drier and richer with a fruity, smooth palate and a hint of caramel, try the VO (blended from brandies between ten and 21 years old), and the Tbilisi (blended from brandies aged between 15 and 20 years).

Other Georgian brandies that I think are worth trying include Sakartvelo, OC, and Kazbegi – all of which are very good.

CHILE

The origin of Chilean brandy, known as pisco, dates back to the Spanish invasion of the country in the 16th century. The conquerors planted grapes to produce wine for church services and later distilled the juice.

CAPEL

C **COLOUR** Clear through to light gold for the aged versions.

A **AROMA** Not too rich; dried fruit, wood, and a hint of vanilla.

T **TASTE** Delicate and quite dry; smooth with a medium finish.

Established in the 1930s, Capel is the largest co-operative of Chilean distillers producing pisco – Chile's national spirit, which since the early 19th century has been regarded as a brandy to rival some of the basic Spanish blends.

The low-end Capel piscos – Tradicional and Especial – are really suitable only for mixing; try them in

a Piscola (a brandy and cola), or in a Pisco Sour *(see p350)*, an apéritif cocktail made with egg white, sugar, and lemon juice.

Both the Capel Reservado (40%

PISCO CAPEL

ABV), and the strong Capel Gran Pisco (43% ABV), have a much better flavour, with the grape balanced by spicy notes.

For other good brands of pisco, not made by Capel, check out Los Artesanos de Cochiguaz, as well as Alto de Carmen, which is made entirely from Muscat grapes, and is really quite smooth and delicate.

ARMENIA

Although Armenia is a tiny country in the Caucasus Mountains, it has a well-deserved reputation for fine brandies. Armenian varieties tend to be refined, light, and smooth and are very popular in Russia. Only a small quantity of Armenia's output is exported to the West.

ARARAT

C **COLOUR** Light amber through to darker copper-bronze.

A **AROMA** Nuts, vanilla, chocolate, pine, cedar, cigar box, liquorice, and spice.

T **TASTE** Fresh and bright, through to complex, smooth, and full.

The Ararat Distillery in Yerevan, Armenia, has been producing quality brandy for over 100 years, and has been part of the massive Pernod-Ricard group since 1998.

The company's basic brandy is Hayk, which is light and fresh, and ideal as a mixer, as is the similar Ararat Three Star, which is aged for three years. The Ararat Five Star is

aged for five years, and is the smoothest of the three. It is also fruitier, nuttier, and more complex, and excellent on its own over ice.

Ani is aged for six years, and Otborny for seven, but the best Ararat brandies are the ten-year-old blends Akhtamar and Dvin. These are powerful, full, award-winning brandies, excellent for drinking on their own. The company's top grades are Prazdnichny, Vaspurakan, and Nairi, which are blended from brandies up to 20 years old.

Overall, Ararat offers a broad range of brandies, but nevertheless consistently produces spirits of great quality. Try the best examples next time you want something new – I love them!

MEXICO

Mexicans love their brandy, drinking over 150 million bottles a year! Contrary to popular myth, they prefer it to tequila – Presidente and Don Pedro are the largest-selling brandies in the world. Mexicans like to drink the spirit on the rocks, with cola.

DOMECQ

C COLOUR An attractive dark gold to deep amber colour.

A AROMA Fruity and woody, with caramel and vanilla notes.

T TASTE Quite clean and light, with a touch of sweetness; smooth.

The production of Domecq brandy in Mexico began just after World War II, when Don Pedro, head of the Spanish brandy producer Domecq (see p181), visited Mexico with the intention of creating a purely Mexican brandy. In the late 1950s, Presidente was launched, and it grew to become one of the top 20 spirits worldwide, and the biggest-selling imported brandy in the US. This brandy is aged, using the *solera* system (see p143), for only six months, making it young and fiery, especially on its own! Domecq followed up its success with Don Pedro, a richer, smoother, and also very popular brandy, aged for a year, and a great way to end a meal.

In the 1970s, Domecq introduced the Azteca d'Oro. A high quality brandy aged for 12 years, it is blended to become darker, richer, and more satisfying, and is woody and spirited. Azteca d'Oro is very popular in the US, and has already established a reputation as the best Mexican brandy.

ANGOVES

C COLOUR Dark gold through to a dark chestnut-brown.

A AROMA Complex; butter, spice, oak, coconut, and vanilla.

T TASTE Rich and satisfying; well-balanced, clean, and quite dry.

Founded in 1886 by a British doctor named William Angoves (and still run by his family), Angoves began producing brandy commercially in 1925 and since then has established a strong reputation as one of Australia's best brandy houses.

Based near Adelaide, South Australia, the company is best known for its St Agnes range of brandies, which are made using the traditional Cognac methods of double distillation in pot stills and ageing in oak casks. The basic St Agnes Three Star is young, fresh, and lively and great at a party in a long drink with soda water or cola. There are two Five-Star brandies: the more recent VSOP and the Old Liqueur. The latter is a flagship product for the company and is richer, more rounded, and more mature (at least ten years old) than Angoves' other brandies.

The award-winning favourite of the St Agnes range is the Seven-Star XO, which contains brandies that are at least 20 years old. This is dark and rich, and full of complex aromas and flavours. It makes a truly wonderful digestif.

In March 2000 Angoves released the Anniversary Show Brandy to commemorate 75 years as brandy producers. The company issued only two thousand numbered bottles of the anniversary brandy, each of which contains a special blend of spirits that are at least 30 years old. These are wonderful collectors' items – if you are lucky enough to see a bottle, grab it!

ANGOVES

AUSTRALIA

Australia's brandies can be quite pleasant, though few are classics. Brandy has been distilled and aged there for many years. Much of it is sold within the country, although recently some producers have exported, hoping to emulate the success of Australian wines.

BRL HARDY

C COLOUR Pale amber through to apricot and deep amber.

A AROMA Complex; well-balanced; oak, grass, chocolate, and honey.

T TASTE Slightly oily in texture; full, rounded; intense.

Since its establishment in 1853, BRL Hardy – now known as the Hardy Wine Company – has played a key role in the development of Australian wine. Along the way it has branched out into brandy production, to take advantage of the vast numbers of fruit-producing vines on its estates and using the Cognac methods of double distillation in pot stills and oak barrel-ageing.

BRL HARDY

The company's basic brandy is Black Bottle, made from Doradillo and Grenache grapes. It is matured in oak for a minimum of two years and has a sweet palate and well-balanced finish.

One of my favourite non-French brandies is the BRL Hardy XO. This blend has an average age of 20 years, and complex aromas of vanilla and oak, with hints of chocolate.

McWILLIAMS

C COLOUR Translucent, shimmering light gold, through to amber.

A AROMA Complex, delicate; grape, oak, butter, and vanilla, with nutty overtones.

T TASTE Firm and well-balanced; very smooth and satisfying; great length.

Founded in 1877, this is a well-established, award-winning Australian family firm, based in New South Wales, southeastern Australia. The company has a good reputation and a large portfolio of brandies. It is well respected for its high standards of quality and for introducing new techniques to its brandy production.

Whereas most brandy is made from grape varieties such as Ugni Blanc and Folle Blanche, McWilliams uses the Sémillon grape in its blends. This grape variety – which was once the world's most widely planted – creates a base wine that is quite neutral in flavour, but beautifully susceptible to the rich flavours of oak-ageing, creating distinctive brandies of consistently high quality.

McWilliams offers a basic Max Three Star blend, which is light, but quite rich, with good vanilla and buttery hints; this is perfect for a long drink, such as brandy and soda water, or in a cocktail. The Four-Star Chairman's Reserve is, like the Max Three Star, extremely well made, with a similarly light, fresh, and fruity feel. The difference lies in the fact that the Four Star is smoother, as a result of longer ageing.

McWilliams' star product is the Five-Star Show Reserve Deluxe Liqueur. This is not only one of the very best Australian brandies on offer, but one of the best in the world! A blend of the 1963 and 1973 vintages, the Show Reserve is distilled three times and is, quite frankly, pure joy in a bottle.

McWILLIAMS

USA

Brandy has been distilled and aged in the USA since the mid-1800s, but the success of California wine has put new life into the industry. Attempts are being made to match the sophistication of French brandies through traditional ageing and blending techniques.

E & J GALLO

C COLOUR Delicate light gold through to a firmer amber for the older versions.

A AROMA Fruity, especially cherry and prunes; wood, sherry, nuts, butterscotch.

T TASTE Well-balanced; quite light, crisp, and clean; medium length.

Ernest and Julio (E & J) Gallo is one of the world's biggest winemakers and distributors, with a large slice of the US wine market, as well as a good presence worldwide. Since 1968 the company has also been a major brandy producer.

E & J Gallo's most basic product is the VS Brandy, the biggest-selling brandy in the US. Well made and reliable, it is light, golden, quite fruity, and buttery. If you are looking for a good mixer or a good-value, steady, after-dinner drink, the VS would certainly be worth a try.

The VSOP is smoother and richer, with more signs of ageing, and thus greater complexity, than the VS. The aromas of vanilla and sherry are much more distinct, and they are mixed with the richness of wood and fruit. Overall, this is a really good, well-balanced brandy.

The E & J Cognac is spicy and woody, but not too heavy. It is a complex, good-quality brandy with a light style (and light colour), and is perfect for everyday drinking.

JEPSON

C COLOUR Dark, golden, and intense; clear and appealing.

A AROMA Complex and floral; almond, baked apple, caramel; smoky overtones.

T TASTE Delicate; quite dry; smooth with a long finish; excellent balance.

Like most California brandy-makers, Jepson is known primarily for its wine. However, far from viewing the brandy as a secondary product, Jepson takes its spirit extremely seriously – and as a result Jepson brandies are thoroughly enjoyable.

Jepson makes some of the best brandies in the US. The company uses Colombard grapes, which have a flowery aroma and high acidity, perfect for making good brandy. The grape comes originally from France, where it was used by Cognac-makers only in the shadow of the Ugni Blanc and Folle Blanche varieties. In the 1970s, California winemakers transported the grape home, and now it is hugely successful in Mendocino County (in the California North Coast wine region, above San Francisco), where it is mainly used to make crisp white wine.

Of Jepson's products the Rare Brandy Alambic is the most widely available. Aged for at least five years in French oak casks, this is a regular prize-winner. The Jepson Old Stock is darker, smoother, spicier, more expensive, and very satisfying indeed. However, the top product is a special reserve called Signature Reserve. This is a superior and genuinely rare product, with all the complexity of the other blends, combined with a hint of smoke. At around $100 a bottle, it is one to have as a special treat!

JEPSON

CHRISTIAN BROTHERS

C COLOUR Dark, translucent gold through to a medium amber.

A AROMA Orange and almond; vanilla; dominated by fruit.

T TASTE Light and delicate, with a touch of sweetness; extremely pleasant.

Established in 1882, Christian Brothers is one of the oldest California brandy producers. It is now part of the US drinks group Heaven Hill Distilleries.

The company's popular, good-value brands include a basic, fruity VS, a smoother VSOP, an XO Premium, and Christian Brothers' White (presented in a frosted glass bottle). These brandies are all noted for their light and fruity style, and are not too ambitious or complex, making them excellent mixers.

CHRISTIAN BROTHERS

RMS

C COLOUR Deep gold to almond with hints of orange.

A AROMA Complex and delicate; pecan nuts, caramel, spice, orange, and oak.

T TASTE Delicate and fine; smooth and round; medium- to full-bodied.

Set up in the 1980s by the French Cognac house Rémy-Martin, RMS is an attempt to recreate the sophistication of Cognac in California – and it has been a great success. RMS uses several grape varieties in its blends – including Colombard, Pinot Noir, Chenin Blanc, Muscat, Palomino, and even the classic Armagnac grape, Folle Blanche – to create a range of excellent brandies, some of which, such as the fabulous Pinot Noir XO, are deliberately identified with one grape variety.

One of the US's biggest-selling brandies is the RMS Special Reserve. This award-winning, "basic" brandy – although it is anything but basic – uses spirits that are up to eight years old. The result is fruity and nutty, and light and delicate.

For something richer, and more like a traditional Cognac, try the prize-winning Quality Extraor-dinaire. Packaged in a tasteful decanter, this is a 14-year-old brandy, and is dark and complex, with aromas and flavours of spice, pepper, and butterscotch. I am confident that, left to age for a few more years, this brandy would be almost indistinguishable from a superior Cognac.

The Folle Blanche brandy is one of the company's "single-variety" spirits and the only brandy in the US made exclusively from Folle Blanche grapes. This is another excellent brandy: it is dark in colour – like unpeeled almonds – light and floral, with a perfect blend of vanilla, tobacco, and dark fruits.

LAND AND PRODUCTION

RMS PINOT NOIR XO Brandy made from red grapes is extremely rare, particularly Pinot Noir grapes from California, where the hot weather makes them difficult to grow. This is why RMS's Pinot Noir XO is really special. Aged for ten years, the brandy is light apricot in colour, with aromas of blueberry, orange, spice, nuts, and tobacco, and floral aromas of lilac, jasmine, and orange blossom.

PINOT NOIR

SOUTH AFRICA

South African brandy is produced mostly for the mass-market but many distillers have extended their range and now make top-quality spirits. This has led to a new generation of appealing South African brands, some of which have reached world-beating standards.

KWV

C COLOUR Dark gold through to apricot and dark amber.

A AROMA Distinctive and intense; nuts, vanilla, pepper, baked apple, apricot.

T TASTE Slightly sweet; quite warm and full; well-balanced.

5 STAR VO BRANDY

KWV is easily the biggest brandy producer in South Africa – and bigger than all the others put together! It also has significant market presence in the rest of the world.

Over the years KWV has produced some quite ordinary brandies, but since the mid-1990s (with the advent of the end of Apartheid and the relaxing of trade sanctions against South Africa), the company has seriously improved the quality of its products.

KWV is a large company with a broad range of brandies. The basic Three Star is quite light and nutty, and makes a reasonable mixer. The Five Star VO is a fun, fruity, golden brandy and great for everyday drinking and for serving up in cocktails at parties.

However, things improve dramatically with the complex ten-year-old. KWV brandies almost always have a good balance between fruit, nuts, vanilla, and general sweetness, and the ten-year-old manages to combine all these elements really well, to create a brandy that feels like nougat with attitude! It is also a little richer than the more basic blends, with a hint of port.

At the upper end of the range are an XO and a 20-year-old. These are dark and rich brandies, which have a good body, and complex aromas of black fruits, apricot, and brown sugar.

The company's top product is the award-winning Diamond Jubilee. This great brandy is made from a blend of 10-, 12-, 15-, and 23-year-old superior, pot-still brandies (added together the brandies have a combined maturation of 60 years – hence "diamond jubilee"). The result is rich, dark gold, and extremely

IMOYA VSOP ALAMBIC BRANDY

complex in both its aromas and flavours. It has a great balance between fruit, wood, vanilla, and overall sweetness, with apricots in abundance. Presented in a smart cut-glass decanter, this brandy easily ranks with the best offerings from France, Spain, and California.

KWV's biggest new product is Imoya VSOP Alambic (*imoya* means "the ancient wind of Africa"). Aimed at the younger end of the market, it is a blend of double-distilled, pot-still brandies aged for up to 20 years in small French-Limousin oak casks. The result is a deep, golden amber brandy, dry and fresh, and yet also very strong and complex. It has rich flavours of dried fruits, a smooth palate, and a long finish. Early signs are that Imoya has been extremely well received, and KWV itself hopes that it will introduce brandy to a whole new generation of drinkers.

BACKSBERG

C COLOUR Attractive and shimmering; medium to vintage gold.

A AROMA Elegant; flowers, peach, apricot, nuts, liquorice, and spice.

T TASTE Smooth, nutty, and warming with a medium finish.

This is a small distillery run by the Back family who emigrated to South Africa from Lithuania in 1916. The company is situated in the Western Cape and has established an excellent reputation as a winemaker.

Brandy was first distilled on the estate in the 1800s, and the original Back settlers continued to use the old still until well into the 1920s. At the end of the 1980s, the family bought a French still and began making brandy again. The results are two really good spirits, produced just like Cognac *(see pp170–1).*

BACKSBERG

The grape variety used by Backsberg is Chenin Blanc, which produces refreshing, dry, and crisp white wine that is perfect for drinking in hot climates. The wine is also fairly high in acidity, and these two character-istics make it a natural choice for distilling into good-quality brandy.

For something rich and floral, with a complex aroma, try the four-year-old Sydney Back Estate Brandy. In 1995, the year of its first release, this brandy won the Domecq Trophy at the International Wine and Spirits Competition in London, as "The Best Brandy in the World" – so it is definitely worth finding!

The older, Sydney Back Ten-Year Estate Brandy is again rich and complex, with a perfect mingling of fruit, spices, and nuts. This is a very warm and satisfying spirit, and is lovely for drinking on its own at the end of a meal, although I particularly like it with a drop of water.

MIXING IT UP

BRANDY COCKTAILS Traditionally thought of as a spirit to sip neat after dinner, brandy also makes some excellent cocktails. Among them are the Side Car *(see p349)*, with triple sec and lemon juice; the Brandy Alexander *(see p363)*, with chocolate liqueur and cream; and the Champagne Cocktail *(see p379)*, with a sugar cube and lots of fizz!

The water of life, with fantastic depth and subtlety; there is an amazing range of flavours and styles.

WHISKY

INTRODUCING WHISKY

In the cooler parts of the world, where fruit can be difficult to grow, people learnt to distil grain. The earliest recorded whiskies seem to come from Ireland in the 15th century. In the 21st century, whisky is the most important grain spirit of all.

The name "whisky" comes from the Gaelic *uisge beatha* – "water of life", which is thought to refer to the fact that the drink was once valued for its supposed medicinal properties.

Whiskies are generally marketed in two styles: single malt and blended. Single malt whisky is a premium product; it is made only from malted barley – no other grains – and at a single distillery. Most of the world's malt distilleries – around one hundred – are in Scotland, and their products typically contain all the personality of their geographic origins. Blended whiskies, by contrast, are created by mixing together a range of malt and grain whiskies to give a spirit with a desired colour, flavour, and character. You may also see other terms used to describe whisky: "vatted malt whisky" is simply a blend of malt whiskies from different distilleries; and "Scotch" is used to describe a whisky from Scotland.

VANILLA *Oak-ageing gives whisky distinct vanilla aromas.*

SINGLE MALT WHISKY

To create malt whisky, the grain is steeped in spring water, which can impart distinct characteristics to the spirit; for example, water from Islay (southwestern Scotland) gives peaty flavours, and water from the Highlands (central-eastern Scotland) gives notes of heather. The moistened grains are allowed to germinate, traditionally on a "malting floor", although many whisky-makers now use mechanized systems. During germination, starch in the grain is converted to sugar – the raw material for fermentation. Once the grains have sprouted, they are dried in a kiln – a process that also adds flavour to the final product. The dried grain, or malt, is then ground, and infused in hot water. The infused liquid is run off and the whisky-maker adds yeast to begin the fermentation process. It is this fermented

HAGGIS *Whisky is not often partnered with food, but the spicy, oaty flavours of traditional Scottish haggis match perfectly with certain single malts, such as well-aged Glenlivet.*

liquid, called the "wash", which is distilled to make malt whisky. Scottish single malt is distilled in a pot still – a huge, copper, kettle-like vessel, which heats the wash and turns it into whisky distillate. This is then distilled at least once more, before being left to mature in oak for at least three years. The oak barrels are usually former sherry casks, which impart a sherry sweetness to the whisky. Ireland produces single malt whiskies, too; these tend to be more mellow than Scottish malts, largely because they use a proportion of unmalted barley and are distilled three times rather than twice.

OTHER WHISKIES

Many people think of blended whiskies as inferior to single malts. However, this is not always true! Some of the most important and significant of the world's whisky brands are blends. As with fine Champagne, blending is an art of the highest form, because the blender must keep the product consistent from batch to batch and year to year.

The most readily available blended whiskies, other than those from Scotland, come from Ireland, the US, Canada, and Japan. Irish blended whiskey (note the spelling – whiskey from Ireland and the US is spelt with an "e") is usually made from barley (both unmalted and malted), oats, or wheat. Each individual spirit is usually triple-distilled in a pot still, before the blender selects and refines his blend.

Bourbon is whiskey from the US, and originally from Bourbon County, Kentucky, but now made all over the country. This style must contain at least 51 per cent maize and is aged in new oak barrels – often charred on the inside to give a smoky flavour to the spirit – for a minimum of two years. The US also gives us rye whiskey, which must contain at least 51 per cent rye mash and tends to be quite full-bodied, and Tennessee whiskey, which is blended from maize and rye, and charcoal-filtered, making it particularly clean and smooth. Canadian spirit has no designated grain quantities, but is usually a blend of whiskies mainly made from rye. Finally, in Japan, the blends are made from rye and barley. Japan also makes single-grain whiskies and is home to the largest malt distillery in the world.

CHARCOAL FILTERING *At the Jack Daniel's distillery in Tennessee, in the US, maple wood is burned for charcoal. The unique feature of Tennessee whiskey is that it is charcoal-filtered to give pure, clean flavours.*

TASTES OF THE SEA *The Lagavulin distillery, at Lagavulin Bay on the south coast of the Isle of Islay, Scotland, ages its whisky in warehouses lying next to the sea. The salty sea air adds its own flavours to the distillery's distinctive single malts.*

SCOTLAND

The home of "Scotch", Scotland is today the heart of a great world whisky industry. The main producing regions include: Campbeltown, once "the whisky capital", on the Mull of Kintyre in the southwest; the Highland region to the north and east; and the island of Islay, which lies just off the west coast. Fine whiskies are also made on Speyside on the northeast coast, and in the Orkneys.

SPRINGBANK

C COLOUR Light gold through to deep russet for the special whiskies.

A AROMA Aromatic; peat, spices, and honey; excellent balance.

T TASTE Smooth and mellow; complex, full-flavoured; slightly smoky and spicy.

Established in 1828, the Springbank distillery, in Campbeltown (western Scotland), offers a fine range of single malt whiskies blended from the distillery's own spirits. The Springbank ten-year-old is light gold; the 15-year-old, darker and more complex. Also available are the lighter, sweeter Campbeltown Loch and the darker, heavier Mitchell's 12-Year-Old.

Several special whiskies, sold as "Wood Expressions", offer the opportunity to compare single malts that have been matured in different wooden casks once used for other wines and spirits (sherry, port, Bourbon, and rum). Finally, the limited edition Springbank 1966 is really top class – you must try it!

SPRINGBANK

GLENGOYNE

C COLOUR Light to medium gold, through to bronze for the older whiskies.

A AROMA Clean, bright, sunny; flowers, apple, sherry, orange, malt, smoke.

T TASTE Subtle and well-balanced; delicate and fruity with a great subtlety.

Based in a beautiful glen near Glasgow, Glengoyne produces spirit that is used in mass-market blends such as Cutty Sark and Famous Grouse, but also smooth ten-, 17-, and 21-year-old single malts. They also make limited-edition older whiskies, cask vintages (you can have the labels personalized on these bottles – a perfect present), and special-edition whiskies, such as the Millennium 2000. The company launched a new single malt in 2004, the 12-Year-Old Cask Strength. All Glengoyne whiskies are known for their finesse, subtlety, and balance.

GLENMORANGIE

C COLOUR Pale gold, deepening to vintage gold for the longer-aged whiskies.

A AROMA Complex, elegant; butterscotch, vanilla, and citrus, with hints of yeast.

T TASTE Medium-bodied, creamy; smoke, spices, nuts, flowers; clean finish.

Established in the 1840s, Glenmorangie produces Scotland's best-selling malts (third in the world). The basic products are the Glenmorangie ten- and 18-year-old single malts. The ten-year-old is light, refreshing, and elegant, with hints of spice and citrus fruits, and a clean finish. The 18-year-old, matured in sherry casks, is darker, richer, and smoother, with a very long finish.

GLENMORANGIE

Glenmorangie's other offerings include the 15-year-old, of which I am a fan. This is matured in oak casks formerly used for Bourbon, and is warm, with hints of cinnamon and liquorice. The 15-year-old Sherry Wood Finish (matured in Bourbon casks, but finished in sherry butts) is quite sweet and luscious, with honey and caramel. The Port Wood Finish is very full, with hints of chocolate and blackcurrant. The Madeira Wood Finish is also rich and complex, and has an extra "burnt" taste. A newer product is the Burgundy Wood Finish, with notes of rich red fruits. Glenmorangie has also made many "specials", such as the Distillery Manager's Choice, usually from particular vintages. It produced a Millennium Malt in a limited edition of 2000 bottles. This 24-year-old is a rare treat: the aroma is rich and complex, with oak, sherry, and coffee. It is smooth and full-bodied, with a slightly sweet finish. If you see a bottle, grab it!

DALWHINNIE

C COLOUR Light golden; very bright with lively yellowish tinges.

A AROMA Quite dry and nutty; orange, flowers, and smoke.

T TASTE Medium-bodied; fresh and fruity with a slightly sweet finish.

Dalwhinnie is the highest distillery in Scotland. It lies in a cold, wild place, chosen for the clear spring water in which to steep the barley. The distillery is now owned by drinks multinational Diageo. The main Dalwhinnie is a light, flowery 15-year-old single malt, with a sweet finish. It would make gentle supping on a summer picnic. Look out for the special editions, such as those matured in *oloroso* sherry casks – these are very special.

DALWHINNIE

OBAN

C COLOUR Dark golden yellow, with a traditional whisky feel.

A AROMA Quite peaty and fruity, with hints of salt and smoke.

T TASTE Rich, but medium-bodied; hints of honey and spices; smoky, salty finish.

The Oban distillery, in Scotland's Western Highlands, dates back to the end of the 18th century, but is now owned by Diageo. The whisky comes with a unique history – remains of prehistoric man have been found in caves just behind the Georgian distillery buildings!

Oban's main brand is a 14-year-old malt, but better are the special editions, such as a 14-year-old sherry cask edition from 1985. This whisky is well balanced, with a great combination of spice, smoke, and sweetness.

THE DALMORE

C COLOUR Dark gold through to amber for the older whiskies.

A AROMA Quite rich and fruity, with notes of sherry, orange, nuts, and marzipan.

T TASTE Full-bodied, with honey, spices, nuts, and a dry finish.

The Dalmore distillery lies in the east of Scotland, near the Cromarty Firth. It is owned by drinks company Whyte & Mackay. Dalmore produces three fantastic single malts, all of which are smooth and delicate with loads of flowers. They are the 12-year-old, matured in sherry butts and so dark and rich; the more complex 21-year-old; and the 50-year-old – a real treat! I like to drink these as digestifs – as an alternative to Cognac. There is also a Cigar Malt, which is rich and luscious, as its name suggests.

DALMORE

ENDURING QUALITY
Despite being a bestseller, Glenmorangie retains its distinction. This is at least in part down to the knowledge of the families of Muir and MacDonald, who took over the brand in the 1920s and are still involved in its production.

STRATHISLA

C COLOUR Deep yellow, through dark, vintage gold, to coppery bronze.

A AROMA Very aromatic; summer flowers, fruit, peat, and spice.

T TASTE Medium-bodied, sweet; caramel, peat, malt, nuts; long, fruity finish.

Founded in 1786, the Strathisla distillery claims to be the oldest in the Highlands. It is now owned by the Pernod Ricard group.

Much Strathisla whisky goes into the blend that makes Pernod Ricard's best-selling Chivas Regal (see p200). Strathisla bottles only one single malt under its own name – a spicy 12-year-old, with hints of nuts and sherry. It is matured in American oak barrels formerly used for Bourbon and sherry – both of which give the flavours a strong fruity element. Other Strathisla whiskies are available bottled by Gordon and MacPhail.

GLENFIDDICH

C COLOUR Very pale gold deepening to old gold for the longest-aged whiskies.

A AROMA Aromatic; quite light; pear and citrus, with hints of heather and pine.

T TASTE Light style; flowery and fruity with hints of peat.

A Highland distillery, Glenfiddich has been independently owned by the Grant family since its foundation in the 1880s.

The family like to call their whisky "Château-bottled" as Glenfiddich is one of only a few distilleries to bottle its whisky on site. The distillery might be said to be the foremost single-malt producer in the world, not only because its whiskies are available in more than 200 countries, but also because in the

GLENFIDDICH
SPECIAL RESERVE

mid-1960s Glenfiddich took the unprecedented step of promoting its single malt internationally, despite heavy competition from big-name blended brands. Its success opened the way for other single-malt producers to do the same.

The best-selling 12-year-old Special Reserve is light, delicate, fruity, and refreshing, with a distinct pine aroma. I love to drink it as an apéritif. The 15-year-old Solera Reserve is matured in *oloroso* sherry casks using a version of the *solera* blending system. Casks of differently aged spirit are stacked in rows on top of one another, with the oldest along the bottom. Spirit from the top row is mixed with spirit from the row below it, which is mixed with the row below that, and so on, until the final blend is drawn off from the casks on the bottom. The result is

a complex, creamy, fruity malt; great for after dinner.

A recent addition to the Glenfiddich range is the Havana Reserve, a 21-year-old matured in casks originally used to make Cuban rum. The result is a sweet, rich, and fruity blend with spicy notes. Glenfiddich also produces the 18-year-old Ancient Reserve, the 21-year-old Gran Reserva, as well as 30-, 40-, and 50-year-olds. All of these are excellent and, if you have deep pockets, they

GLENFIDDICH
HAVANA RESERVE

are worth seeking out. The 50-year-old is one of the most expensive whiskies ever sold at auction: in the 1990s a bottle fetched about $70,000 at an auction in Milan. There is also a range of specials, including a 1937 vintage whisky. This is a very special single malt: there are only 61 bottles in the world and each will set you back around $16,000.

THE GLENLIVET

C COLOUR Light gold, through to dark amber for the older whiskies.

A AROMA Soft, light, and delicate, with honey, flowers, spice, and malt.

T TASTE Medium-bodied; honey, fruit, and flowers, with sweet overtones.

The Glenlivet distillery lies in an isolated part of Speyside, in the valley of the Livet River. It has a long history of making excellent whiskies – the original distillery was founded

by crofter George Smith in 1824. Smith was the first whisky-maker in Scotland to have a legal distillery.

Since these earliest beginnings, The Glenlivet has established a top-quality name for itself throughout the world. Part of the Pernod Ricard group, it is now the biggest-selling single malt in the US, and one of the biggest in the world.

The basic brand is the 12-year-old – a light, golden, flowery, and fruity whisky that is quite subtle and

WELL-WATERED *The mineral-rich water used to make The Glenlivet comes from Josie's Well, a natural spring high in the Speyside mountains.*

well balanced. There are also two other 12-year-olds. One is marketed as The Glenlivet French Oak Finish – the whisky finishes maturing in French oak, increasing its woody and spicy notes and giving a darker, richer whisky. The other is the American Oak Finish (available only in airport duty-free shops), which is heavily oaked, rich, and exclusive.

The 18-year-old, winner of several awards, is complex, with wood, nuts, spice, and toffee. Its style is magnified in the 21-year-old.

The brand's top range is the "Cellar", with some rare special treats, such as the 1959 Limited Release, which sells for between $1500 and $6000 a bottle; and the 1967 vintage, released for 2000–2001 and now very hard to find. If you come across any of The Glenlivet special editions, they are simply wonderful.

MIXING IT UP

ON THE ROCKS Drink any of the offerings from The Glenlivet and you are in for a treat, whatever way you take it. I like to drink mine on the rocks – poured over a few ice cubes in the bottom of a whisky glass. Drink the whisky slowly so that, as the ice cubes melt, their water mingles with the spirit to release its flavours.

THE GLENLIVET.
George Smith's Original 1824
Pure Single Malt
Scotch Whisky

AGED **12** YEARS
Aged only in Oak Casks

GEORGE & J. G. SMITH
Distilled in Scotland at
The Glenlivet Distillery, Banffshire
PRODUCT OF SCOTLAND
70cl 700ml 40%vol 40°GL 40% alc./vol

THE MACALLAN

C COLOUR Dark old gold, to sherry-coloured and mahogany.

A AROMA Quite light and fragrant; dried fruits, toffee, cloves, and peach.

T TASTE Full-bodied, rounded, fruity; vanilla, sherry, smoke; good length.

This old Speyside distillery is famous for using Spanish-oak sherry casks. The distillery buys the oak in Spain, has the casks made there, and then loans them to certain Spanish sherry *bodegas* before bringing the empty casks to Scotland to use for maturing The Macallan whisky. The casks are used throughout the Macallan range, and the result is to create a rich, full, and fruity style of spirit.

The Macallan whisky was once used mainly for blending. However, in the 1970s the producers decided to market their product as a single malt, and it is now one of the top five single malts in the world. Its biggest claim to fame is that it is the single malt of choice for the House of Commons, the seat of British politics.

Unlike most other single-malt producers, The Macallan makes a young seven-year-old specifically for the Italian market, where lively and fresh whiskies are in great demand. The basic UK flagship brand is the ten-year-old, which has the distillery's signature sherry richness and fruitiness. The floral, fruity 12-year-old is well-respected internationally, as is the 1990-vintage Elegencia, which is a lighter colour and style than most of the other The Macallans.

The Macallan Cask Strength is a successor to the 15-year-old, and is the main product for the US market. It is a strong, well-rounded, and spicy whisky in the typical Macallan style. However, more interesting perhaps is one of the company's other flagship whiskies, the 18-year-old. This great product is dark and rich, and very well balanced. The 25-year-old is similar, and still richer. The top product is the 18-year-old Gran Reserva, which is one of the greatest The Macallans ever produced – so much so that demand continually exceeds supply. If you spot a bottle, buy it quickly! It is very rich and dark, with powerful flavours of syrupy orange marmalade and a deep oaky woodiness.

Macallan also produces a wide range of special whiskies, from the mellow, complex, and dark 30-year-old in its blue packaging, through the extremely old vintages of 50 years and beyond, to the 1841 Replica and 1861 Replica – great malts that replicate bottlings from those years.

THE MACALLAN

AUCHENTOSHAN

C COLOUR Lemon to light gold and copper; bright and clear.

A AROMA Fragrant and lively, with fresh fruit, flowers, citrus, and spice.

T TASTE Light, quite sweet, and smooth, with orange, nuts, malt, and raisins.

Auchentoshan is a distinctive, award-winning brand that uses triple-distillation to create a smooth, light, and fresh whisky. Maturing in both sherry casks and Bourbon barrels adds complexity and sophistication. The basic product is a ten-year-old Lowland Single Malt, which is light, citrusy, and fresh. Older products are 21-, 22-, and 25-year-olds, which are darker and richer.

AUCHENTOSHAN

THE BALVENIE

C COLOUR Pale straw yellow through to dark coppery amber.

A AROMA Sweet, spicy, and pungent, with hints of sherry and honey.

T TASTE Very rich, mellow; spice, flowers, and malt; caramel notes at the finish.

The Balvenie is owned by the same family as Glenfiddich (the Grant family), and is made next door, but this is where the similarities end. Whereas Glenfiddich generally offers a light, dry, citrusy whisky, The Balvenie tends to be rich, sweet, honeyed, and floral. The flagship product is the ten-year-old Founder's Reserve, which is golden, spicy, and fruity, with an excellent, long finish. This is a

THE BALVENIE

frequent award-winner, with a great reputation. The 12-year-old Doublewood (also an award-winner) is matured in both Bourbon and sherry casks, and as a result is rich, nutty, and fruity (especially orange).

The Port Wood 1989 reflects the deeper influence of port wine. The Single Barrel 15-Year-Old is made in batches of only about 350 bottles, and (as its name suggests) comes from one barrel. Both are complex whiskies, with aromas of vanilla, oak, and honey and a perfect balance of malt and spice.

A couple to look out for are the award-winning Thirty (smooth and mellow with hints of dark chocolate, plum, marzipan, and caramel), and particular vintages, which The Balvenie offer as limited editions. The Balvenie Cask 191 is one of these – it is a 50-year-old whisky and is deeply fruity and rich. Delicious!

LAND AND PRODUCTION

CARING FOR THE STILLS
The distillation room at The Balvenie produced the first of the company's whiskies in 1993. The copper stills are replaced every 15 years or so, but the replacements are always identical to the originals – after all, the shape of the still works its own magic on the character of the whisky. At Balvenie, the stills are cared for by a dedicated "still man".

MORTLACH

C COLOUR Dark amber; darker than most comparable whiskies.

A AROMA Fruity and deep with hints of peat and smoke.

T TASTE Full-bodied; honey, fruit, caramel, sherry, spice, and a long, dry finish.

This Speyside distillery dates back to the early 1820s, but is now part of drinks conglomerate Diageo. The whisky has a peaty, smoky style, and is used mainly for blending (in the Johnnie Walker blends, for example).

However, there are also single-malt Mortlachs (or "Morties" as they are known locally). The main brand, marketed by Diageo, is the 16-year-old, which is a lovely, fruity, and smoky-rich whisky with a distinct sherry character. Other Mortlachs are marketed by independent bottlers. Some of these are better than others, and one of the best is Gordon and Macphail's 1980 Cask Strength, which is rich and peaty, and great at the end of a meal.

GLENTURRET

C COLOUR Very light, with a delicate, bright golden hue.

A AROMA Light and fresh with hints of smoke, flowers, and pepper.

T TASTE Quite smoky and spicy with a sweet and nutty feel.

Glenturret is a small but highly respected distillery making excellent single malts. It is situated not far from Crieff in Perthshire, and claims to be Scotland's oldest and also its most visited distillery. Glenturret whisky is made in small quantities using pot stills, and is used in the Famous Grouse blend.

The most available Glenturret single malt is the 10-year-old, which is fresh and clean with hints of honey and ginger, and is well worth a try. Glenturret also produces a number of other versions, including single vintages, such as the 1972, which has a great vanilla character. The single vintages can be difficult to find.

GLENROTHES

C COLOUR Medium gold; bright and clear with light amber highlights.

A AROMA Very appealing, with hints of caramel, sherry, vanilla, peat, and toffee.

T TASTE Full-bodied and quite sweet, with spice, caramel, and honey; long finish.

This Highland distillery is said to lie on the site of the 14th-century murder of the daughter of the Earl of Rothes. However, despite its dark history, the distillery produces a lovely, full-bodied 12-year-old whisky, with a beautiful balance of peat, spice, and honey.

Glenrothes will also occasionally release single vintages, as well as single-cask bottlings, many of which come from the 1960s – these are very special whiskies indeed.

ROYAL LOCHNAGAR

C COLOUR Dark gold to light amber; a traditional whisky look.

A AROMA Rich and fruity, with smoke and spice in fine balance.

T TASTE Complex, with fruit, spice, and malt, and hints of sherry and honey.

The Lochnagar distillery lies not far from the royal family's Scottish

seat at Balmoral. It received its "royal" prefix in 1848 following a visit from Queen Victoria and her consort Prince Albert. It is now owned by the Diageo group.

Overall, Lochnagar whiskies are full, fruity, and satisfying. The 12-year-old is also quite sweet, while the brilliant 23-year-old is big and powerful, with complex spice and liquorice flavours.

ROYAL LOCHNAGAR

EDRADOUR

C COLOUR Deep gold to medium amber and bronze.

A AROMA Delicate and sweet, with peat, fruit, and nuts.

T TASTE Dry with a sweet and nutty finish; fruity and well-rounded.

This is Scotland's smallest distillery, located in the southern Scottish Highlands near Pitlochry. No bigger than a small farm, the Edradour distillery is run by only three men, and makes whisky using traditional methods and equipment. Its output is just 12 casks a week. Nevertheless, it is a modern operation, formerly owned by Pernod Ricard, but now part of the Signatory Vintage Scotch Whisky Company. The only available Edradour is a ten-year-old single malt, which is very aromatic, with a distinctive character of sweetness, peat, and nuts. This is a beautiful whisky – but extremely hard to find outside the distillery itself.

CLYNELISH

C COLOUR Deep, vintage gold with good intensity.

A AROMA Complex and rich; smoke, fruit, tobacco, and spice.

T TASTE Very full-bodied; complex and dry, with nuts, spice, peat, and earth.

One of Scotland's most northerly distilleries, and established in 1819 by the Duke of Sutherland, Clynelish produces whiskies that are included in the Diageo group's "Flora and Fauna Malts". Most of the Clynelish whiskies are uncompromising: peaty, smoky, and spicy, not too sweet, and full-flavoured. The 14-year-old has a good, full body; and the 24-year-old is especially complex and oaky. Clynelish is also marketed by private bottlers, such as Blackadder.

BLADNOCH

C COLOUR Light, bright, and golden with amber highlights.

A AROMA Very aromatic and exciting, with citrus, lemon, and flowers.

T TASTE Light to medium-bodied, with flowers, malt, spice, and honey.

Bladnoch dates back to 1817. After several changes of ownership and a period of closure, it was re-opened in 2000 by Raymond Armstrong, who agreed to keep it as a specialist Lowland distillery. While we wait for

BLADNOCH

Armstrong to release his first whiskies, controlled stocks are available from Diageo. The range includes a gentle, aromatic ten-year-old; and the excellent 15- and 23-year-olds. Bladnoch is also available in Gordon and Mac-Phail's Connoisseur's Choice series.

ABERFELDY

C COLOUR Ranging from dark golden amber through to light gold.

A AROMA Appealing and warm, with sherry, citrus, and spice.

T TASTE Quite fresh; dry and peaty; hint of smoke; medium-bodied.

The Aberfeldy distillery is owned by Bacardi and the whisky is used in the blend for Dewar's White Label. Of the Aberfeldy single malts, the 12-year-old is smooth, oily, peaty, full, and satisfying. The 15-year-old is a lighter colour, with some pine and peat in the taste, and not too fruity. The 1980

ABERFELDY

vintage is pale gold, with aromas of pine and heather, and a smooth, oily texture, with a dry finish. All make great after-dinner, sipping whiskies.

GLENFARCLAS

C COLOUR Medium to dark gold, through to amber for the older whiskies.

A AROMA Light and flowery, with fruit, sherry, and peat.

T TASTE Delicate and creamy, with nuts, fruit, and spice at the finish.

Glenfarclas is one of the few remaining independent distillers in Scotland. Its award-winning whiskies are aged mainly in sherry casks and are typically fruity and delicate. The ten-year-old is bright gold, medium-bodied, and fruity; and the 12- and 15-year-olds are similar, but deeper, darker, richer, and stronger. The special 105 Cask Strength is 60% ABV, dark amber in colour, and smooth and powerful. The 40-Year-Old Millennium Edition is legendary because of its exquisite quality – if you see one, grab it – or tell me!

GLEN GRANT

C COLOUR Ranging from very pale lemon gold to full amber red.

A AROMA Dry and floral with a hint of sherry and fruit.

T TASTE Clean and dry; quite crisp; malt, nuts, and a hint of fruit at the finish.

Glen Grant has been producing quality whisky since 1840, and recently passed into the ownership of the giant Pernod Ricard group. The brand was one of the first single malts to hit the international market, and is now well-established in several countries, particularly in Italy, where it is the market leader.

Glen Grant produces excellent, dry, crisp, and delicate whiskies that are light and subtle on the palate.

GLEN GRANT

Even the youngest examples are well-respected and popular, with fruity aromas and a nutty palate. These include a Glen Grant that carries no age statement, but is actually five years old, and another marketed as Glen Grant Five-Year-Old. The main, aged brand is the ten-year-old, which is matured in Bourbon and sherry casks, but is not at all rich, and has a clean, fresh feel.

Most other Glen Grants are marketed by independent bottlers such as Gordon and Macphail and Adelphi. These vary in quality, but some very old and rare vintages (some more than 50 years old) are great if you can find them. Overall, if you like light, delicate whisky, you will almost certainly love Glen Grant. I really enjoy it as an apéritif, or on its own with the tiniest drop of water, just to bring out its character.

ABERLOUR

C COLOUR Medium vintage gold through to dark amber.

A AROMA Very aromatic; malt, caramel, sherry, and spice.

T TASTE Smooth, rich; peat, honey, toffee; smoky finish.

The perfect after-dinner whisky, Speyside's Aberlour is a serious alternative to Cognac. (It is no accident that this brand is one of France's favourites.) Founded in 1879 by philanthropist James Fleming, Aberlour is now owned by the Pernod Ricard group, giving the whisky a well-deserved high profile throughout the world.

The water used in making the whisky is soft, helping to give the drink its gentle, medium body. Aberlour is matured in Bourbon and *oloroso* sherry casks, which impart fruit and depth of flavour.

ABERLOUR

Try the delightful, award-winning ten-year-old, which is golden, spicy, and fruity, with a complex taste that combines nuts, malt, flowers, and spice. The 15-year-old Sherry Finish is amber in colour and has the darker aromas and flavours of black fruits, as well as orange and spice. The A'bunadh is a cask-strength (59.6% ABV) single malt, made in the 19th-century style – unfiltered and undiluted! This robust and powerful whisky is dark amber, and is full of the tastes and aromas of the old sherry casks used for its maturation.

The 12-year-old Double Cask Matured (soft, aniseedy, and fresh) and 15-year-old Cuvée Marie d'Écosse (sweeter and smoother) are made for the French market and are definitely well worth trying.

BENROMACH

C COLOUR Clear straw yellow through to dark gold.

A AROMA Distinctly fruity and fresh; citrus (orange), with hints of peat.

T TASTE Rounded; spice, smoke, and malt with a peppery finish.

Following a long period of closure, Benromach was re-opened in 1998 (the distillery's centenary year) by its newest owners, Gordon and MacPhail.

Benromach produces excellent Speyside malt whiskies, which are smooth and round with a hint of spice and peat. I love their complexity – you never know what is coming next!

In 2004 Benromach launched a new single malt as its leading brand. (This was the first brand distilled under the Gordon and MacPhail

BENROMACH

ownership.) Known as Benromach Traditional, it is a well-balanced, fresh, and quite citrusy whisky, with a dry, spicy finish.

If you prefer your whisky darker, richer, and fruitier, try the 18-year-old; or for lightness with spicy pepper, try the 25-year-old. The 1980 Cask Strength is a powerful whisky that is light gold in colour, and perfumed, dry, and oily. Otherwise, try the Vintage 1973 for a fragrant whisky full of exotic fruits and spice. As part of the centenary celebrations (and re-opening), three rare sherry casks (used since 1886, 1895, and 1901 for sherry-making) were filled with Benromach 15-year-old and left for two years. The distillery released only 3,500 bottles of the resulting Centenary whisky – they may be almost impossible to find, but it would be worth a try!

BOWMORE

C COLOUR Ranging from gold through to amber, bronze, and red.

A AROMA Distinctive; smoky with a hint of salty sea air and sherry.

T TASTE Rounded and very satisfying; peat, heather, and sea salt with fruit.

This great old Islay distillery is the flagship of its owners Morrison Bowmore of Glasgow (itself part of the global Japanese group Suntory). Founded in 1779, Bowmore has been a well-established favourite in Canada, the UK, and Ireland since the turn of the 20th century. The distillery stands by the sea, and the sea air seems to find its way into the barrels, giving the whisky just a hint of its coastal origins.

Unlike most Islay whiskies, Bowmore whiskies tend not to be too peaty. The spirit is matured in sherry and Bourbon casks, which give the malt fruity, rich tones with a hint of sherry. If you have never tasted Bowmore before, begin with

the Bowmore Legend (no age given) or the 12-year-old, then work your way up through the various ages (including 15-, 17-, 21-, 25-, and 30-year-olds). These whiskies are all very different, but they share a smoothness and richness, and the warmth of sherry. The Cask Strength (56% ABV) is deeply dark, oaky, and sweet. You will either love or hate the Darkest Islay (one of Bowmore's specials) – it is finished in sherry casks and is so rich and dark that it is ruby red in colour. The range also includes Dusk, Dawn, and Surf – these each have individuality, but are all quite deep, complex, and rich.

Overall, Bowmore offers a fantastic range of great whisky – it will almost certainly have something for you to love. I like to drink the younger versions as apéritifs; the older, as digestifs. Perfect!

BOWMORE

LAPHROAIG

C COLOUR Light yellow through to darker old gold with red highlights.

A AROMA Distinctive; peaty, smoky; a hint of medicine, sweetness, and salt.

T TASTE Complex, robust; peat, smoke, salt, nuts, caramel; long, warm finish.

The Islay distillery of Laphroaig is in a realm of its own. Laphroaig is not just a distillery or a whisky, but a whole culture, with a fan club, and a note on its bottles inviting drinkers to buy a square of land next to the distillery itself. (In return buyers are invited to the distillery each year to enjoy a tot of the whisky.) A number of happy owners have proposed marriage on their square of Laphroaig land; others have taken pieces of grass back to their homes, travelling over oceans and continents to get there. This is some whisky!

Established in 1815, the distillery has been closed, re-opened, owned by the British Army, and managed by Bessie Williams, one of the first female managers to venture into the whisky business. It is now the top-selling malt brand of Allied Domecq.

This is an uncompromising whisky (giving rise to Laphroaig's own slogan "You'll either love it or you'll hate it"), which gives a pure feel of the Scottish islands – there is very little fruit, only a hint

AMERICAN COUSINS Laphroaig is very particular about the casks used for the maturation of its whisky. Believing sherry casks to give whisky an unnatural, alien flavour, the company uses only American-oak Bourbon barrels. Once the barrels are filled, they are date-stamped and labelled. As the whisky matures inside the casks, the oak "breathes in" the sea air, giving this special whisky its unique salty taste.

of sweetness, and lots of peat, smoke, and salt.

The classic and most famous Laphroaig is the ten-year-old, which is raw, full, peaty, and totally satisfying. For me this is a "must-try". The 15-year-old is darker and more complex, and has not generated the same level of enthusiasm among its drinkers as that shown by drinkers of the ten-year-old. Nevertheless, this is an award-winning whisky and is certainly worth a try.

At the top end of the range lies the 30-year-old, which can be hard to find in retail outlets, but is available directly from the distillery. This is rich and smooth, with a little more fruit and sherry than other

Laphroaigs. However, one of the world's greatest whiskies has to be Laphroaig's 40-year-old – it is also rich and smooth, with a perfect balance of spice, malt, and sea salt, and a finish that goes on forever.

MIXING IT UP

TASTING PURE ISLAY There is only one way to really savour the purity of Laphroaig – straight up, no ice, with a tiny dash of cool water to release the spirit's complexity.

ISLAND PEAT *Laphroaig is made by drying the malt over an Islay-peat fire, giving all its whiskies a taste of the island.*

BRUICHLADDICH

C COLOUR Light to medium gold, deepening to full gold with age.

A AROMA Fragrant and fruity, with flowers and a hint of sea salt.

T TASTE Fresh and light; quite dry with nuts, malt, and honey.

Bruichladdich – also known as "The Laddie" – is one of Scotland's most westerly distilleries, on the island of Islay, tucked away and almost forgotten until a group of investors revived its fortunes in 2000. Try the fresh and complex ten-year-old in a long drink as an apéritif; or relax with the award-winning 15-year-old and its fruity, sweet aromas. The star is the 20-year-old – The Flirtation – a great digestif, neat or with a tiny dash of water.

BRUICHLADDICH

CAOL ILA

C COLOUR Light to medium gold, often with tinges of green.

A AROMA Moderately peaty and smoky; hints of nuts and spice.

T TASTE Quite dry and rounded with salt and a hint of sweetness on the finish.

This Islay distillery is owned by Diageo and, as well as being used in the Johnnie Walker and Bell's blends, Caol Ila single malts are marketed in Diageo's "Hidden Malts", "Flora and Fauna", and "Rare Malts" series. These include a bright, peppery, slightly oily, but well-balanced 12-year-old, which is not as peaty as other Islay whiskies. Some excellent old vintages are available through independent bottlers, such as Gordon and MacPhail and Cadenhead.

ARDBEG

C COLOUR Distinctive and clear; light to medium gold.

A AROMA Rich aromas; peat, salt, orange, medicine, and smoke.

T TASTE Rounded, dry, and full; smoke, peat, spice; long, satisfying finish.

This classic Islay malt offers no flowers or honey and very little fruit. Instead you get peat, smoke, "medicine", and body. Owned by Glenmorangie, Ardbeg's reputation is second-to-none. Try my favourite – the peat-influenced ten-year-old, a fantastic oily, spicy whisky; or the cask strength (58% ABV) Very Young. The most readily available top brand is the Lord of the Isles: at 25 years old it is a developed version of the basic style, and expensive!

THE ARRAN MALT

C COLOUR Light golden yellow, through to amber for the blends.

A AROMA Complex; citrus fruits, vanilla, honey, flowers, and apple.

T TASTE Oily and fruity with hints of toffee, lemon, sherry, and honey.

This is a young distillery, opened in only 1995, but is definitely one to watch. The isle of Arran's soft water makes a distinctive whisky, which is quite sweet and fruity, with a smooth, oily texture. The Single Island Malt is five years old and fresh and citrusy, while the Robert Burns – the Arran distillery's flagship single malt – is full but also fresh. Both make excellent apéritifs. There is also a blended version of the Robert Burns, which makes a dark and rich digestif.

THE ARRAN MALT

LAGAVULIN

C COLOUR Ranging from pale lemony gold to dark amber brown for the 16-year-old.

A AROMA Powerful and peaty, with a hint of seaweed and salt.

T TASTE Very full-bodied; peat, sherry, smoke; long and slightly sweet finish.

The Lagavulin distillery dates back to the 18th century, but is now owned by Diageo.

If you are looking for a full, rich, smoky, and peaty whisky to settle back with after a meal, then this Islay malt is for you. Look for the multi-award-winning 16-year-old, a member of Diageo's "Classic Malts" series. Or, try the special 1986 Distillers' Edition, which has less peat and a hint of sherry.

LAGAVULIN

HIGHLAND PARK

C COLOUR Dark old gold to rich, deep amber for the aged whiskies.

A AROMA Complex and rich, with heather, smoke, and peat.

T TASTE Medium-bodied; sweet and peaty with honey notes.

Founded in the 18th century, this Orkney distillery is the most northerly in Scotland. Its whisky is made using hard water and the malt is dried over peat fires; the spirit matures in both sherry and Bourbon casks. The overall result is a multi-layered whisky of real distinction. The 12-year-old has really well-balanced fruit, peat, and heather; the similar 18-year-old is a bit more oily and chewy. Both are great. Try the 25-year-old as an alternative to Armagnac – it is very rich, with spice, wood, and fruit.

HIGHLAND PARK

TALISKER

C COLOUR Rich old gold to amber; very intense.

A AROMA Full, sweet, pungent, and peaty, with pepper, sea salt, and sherry tones.

T TASTE Full-flavoured and well-rounded; peat, honey; a very long, peppery finish.

Talisker is the only distillery on the Isle of Skye, off the northwestern coast of Scotland. Founded in 1830, the distillery's whisky was made famous later in the 19th century by the writer Robert Louis Stevenson, who described it as the "King o' drinks". It was a staple of the British Army in India during the 19th century. The distillery is now owned by drinks giant Diageo and its single malt is offered as a member of the "Classic Malts" range.

The most important Talisker is the multi-award-winning ten-year-old (to date it has won six gold medals in various competitions), which manages to create a perfect harmony of fruit, peat, pepper, and smoke. However, more powerful, but equally well-balanced is the 20-year-old, which is matured in sherry casks (unusually for Talisker) and has achieved an outstanding reputation as a whisky of real quality.

Other, older Taliskers are hard to find, but if you can find a Talisker 25-year-old single cask, or other limited edition from this distillery, you have found pure liquid gold – and should hang onto it, if you have the necessary cash.

Talisker does not make whisky to sip idly. Think big when you drink it, savour it with purpose and roll the spirit around in your mouth to release its full flavours. It is perfect with a cigar at the end of a meal.

TALISKER

TEACHER'S

C COLOUR Bright medium gold; richer than many other international blends.

A AROMA Distinctive and full; caramel, heather, grain, and malt.

T TASTE Very full-bodied; spice, caramel, vanilla, smoke, honey; long, malt finish.

William Teacher was the first whisky-maker to dispense with a cork stopper and use a screw-cap. Now Teacher's Highland Cream (owned by Allied Domecq) is one of the world's greatest brands of blended whisky – recognition it truly deserves. The two core single-malt components of Teacher's are Glendronach and Ardmore. Powerful, but not aggressive; fruity but not too sweet; and malty and peaty, but not at the expense of all the other flavours, this reliable whisky is one of my top choices.

TEACHER'S

BALLANTINE'S

C COLOUR Light, bright gold through to deeper, medium amber.

A AROMA Elegant, delicate, and creamy, with wood, honey, nuts, and smoke.

T TASTE Well-rounded and warming; smoke, vanilla; long finish.

Nineteenth-century master blender George Ballantine believed that blended whiskies were as important as single malts and should aspire to reach the same standards.

Ballantine's is now owned by Allied Domecq. The Finest is clean, soft, and beautifully balanced, as is the delicate Gold Seal 12-Year-Old. I think the best is the fantastic 17-year-old, with its endless flavours of nuts, honey, coffee, herbs, vanilla, flowers, and smoke. If you want to taste a great blend, try this one!

JOHNNIE WALKER BLACK, BLUE, RED, AND GOLD LABELS

C COLOUR Ranging from medium gold through to dark amber.

A AROMA Fresh and lively; smoke, malt, vanilla, toffee, and fruit.

T TASTE Full; malt, honey, toffee, peat, and smoke; warm finish.

This is the biggest international blend of them all. As far back as 1924 Johnnie Walker was selling in 120 countries – some call it the first truly worldwide brand – made distinctive by its striding figure, square bottle, and slanting label.

The company is now owned by Diageo, and Johnnie Walker whisky is simply everywhere! All the different labels (red, blue, black, and gold) have their individual styles, but all are big-sellers. Biggest of all is the Red Label, which the company introduced in 1909. It is a perfect day-to-day blend – well-balanced and satisfying.

The Black Label, aged for 12 years, is oily, and deeper, darker, and richer than the Red, with a perfect balance of sherry, malt, and fruit. By comparison the Gold Label is light and creamy, with a honeyed sweetness, and peat and smoke. Diageo suggests serving it frozen!

The Blue Label has a little more peat than the other blends. It is also more expensive – a pity, because I think this, and even the company's excellent special single malts, do not quite live up to the Johnnie Walker "Label" classics.

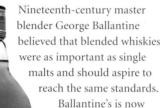

JOHNNIE WALKER BLACK LABEL

CHIVAS REGAL

C COLOUR Light amber through to deeper, luxurious bronze.

A AROMA Floral and delicate; malt, vanilla, herbs, sherry, and spice.

T TASTE Very smooth; fruity, sweet, and rich, with flowers, butterscotch, and nuts.

Launched in 1909 by two brothers, Chivas Regal holds tight to the principle that only single malts of 12 years old or older should be used in a blend. Rich and luxurious, it is now a flagship brand for Pernod Ricard, and a worldwide product.

The Chivas Regal 12-year-old is the height of smoothness, and is sweet and fruity. However, the decadent 18-year-old is the award-winner: dark, complex, and smoky.

CHIVAS REGAL

CUTTY SARK

C COLOUR Extremely pale gold – almost natural yellow.

A AROMA Oak and malt, with hints of sweetness and flowers.

T TASTE Very smooth and delicate; vanilla, peat; a fresh, crisp finish.

Cutty Sark was launched in 1923, specifically for the US market. The blend is made from around 20 single malt whiskies, including Glenrothes, The Macallan, Glengoynes, and the Islay malt Bunna-habhain. The overall result is a great, light, fresh, crisp whisky, which avoids the addition of caramel to give it colour, and has just the right amount of fruit. It makes a perfect apéritif or lunchtime whisky. Others to try are the richer, fruitier 12-, 18-, and 25-year-old versions.

THE FAMOUS GROUSE

C COLOUR Ranging from dark gold through to light amber.

A AROMA Warm, elegant, and aromatic; peat and smoke, with fruit.

T TASTE Fresh, smooth; slightly smoky and peaty; long, caramel finish.

The Famous Grouse, introduced in 1895, is the most popular blend in Scotland, and I love it for day-to-day drinking. Elegant and well-balanced, it is warm and fruity, and slightly peaty, but without too much malt.

Try the 12-year-old Gold Reserve, which is luscious and full-bodied with strong hints of oak and caramel; or the excellent Vintage Malt, which has sherry and orange. I love the Islay Cask Finish, which has an extra layer of smoke and peat; and the Cask Strength, which is robust, complex, and satisfying.

THE FAMOUS GROUSE

GRANT'S

C COLOUR Medium to old gold; darker amber for aged blends.

A AROMA Complex and elegant; malt, raisins, peat, and oak.

T TASTE Light, dry, fresh; malt, caramel, peat, and hints of chocolate; great finish.

The Grants are one of whisky's most famous families. William Grant, having fought in the battle of Waterloo in 1815, returned to Scotland to create whiskies such as Glenfiddich and The Balvenie.

The most successful Grant blend, said by some to be the greatest blend of all, is William Grant's Family Reserve, which is light, fresh, peaty, fruity, and malty, reflecting the great single malts that have gone into it.

Other blends, all worth a try, include Clan MacGregor, Robbie Dhu 12-Year-Old, and all the Grant specials.

BELL'S

C COLOUR Attractive dark old gold to light amber.

A AROMA Fragrant; warm and nutty; malt and spice.

T TASTE Medium-bodied; full-flavoured with spice and honey.

Established in the early 19th century by Arthur Bell, Bell's is now part of the Diageo empire. It is a blend of grain whisky and a number of single malts. The basic Bell's eight-year-old is a reliable, slightly spicy young blend, while the Extra Special (with no age statement) is a little more complex. The 12-year-old is a truly excellent whisky with honey, malt, and smoke – a great buy.

BELL'S

J&B

C COLOUR Distinctive, pale lemon yellow; almost neutral.

A AROMA Delicate; malt and grain, with vanilla, spice, and toffee.

T TASTE Very smooth and sweet; fresh and light-bodied, with grain and malt.

J&B's 18th-century founder was Giacomo Justerini, an Italian wine merchant. The company was later bought by Alfred Brooks and is now owned by the Diageo group.

J&B Rare is a great whisky, originally developed for the US, but now a favourite everywhere. It is light, but deeply flavoured with malt, fruit, vanilla, and spice. Other J&Bs to try are Jet (a little sweeter than Rare) and Reserve, richer and smoother than Rare and blended from 15-year-old malt and grain whiskies.

WHITE HORSE

C COLOUR Bright medium gold through to dark gold with a lighter golden rim.

A AROMA Smoky and malty; vanilla, raisins, and a whiff of peat.

T TASTE Smooth; full-bodied; fruity, sweet; long, clean, lightly peaty finish.

Named in 1890 after a coaching inn that once lay just outside Edinburgh, White Horse is the top-selling whisky brand in Japan and is also big in the US and Brazil. It is part of the Diageo group.

The blend is made from eight-year-old spirits, and, along with many others, has traditionally contained the dry Islay malt Lagavulin. This is an appealing, rich, and complex blend, with a full body, and an abundance of smoke and peat. It also has a perfect balance of fruit and vanilla.

J&B

WHYTE & MACKAY

C COLOUR Bright gold through to mahogany for the older whiskies.

A AROMA Powerful and fruity, with nuts, dates, and honey.

T TASTE Very smooth; light-bodied with a round, mellow, nutty sweetness.

The standard Whyte & Mackay blend has been made to the same formula since 1844. It is a confident, powerful whisky, with strong fruits and nuts, and a balanced sweetness. The bright, golden 12-year-old is subtle and light, but has a powerful character, with a great harmony of wood, sherry, and malt. I love the 21-year-old, which is deep and rich, and tinged with citrus to balance its sweet sherry. The luxury blend is the incredibly complex 30-year-old – a perfect, slow-sipping, after-dinner Scotch.

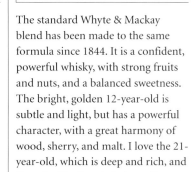

REP. OF IRELAND / N. IRELAND

Irish whiskey (note the spelling with an "e") is made slightly differently from Scotch: it uses a high proportion of raw, unmalted barley, and is usually distilled three times to Scotch's two. This results in a smoother taste and lighter coloration.

JAMESON

C COLOUR Light lemon gold through to dark amber for the "specials".

A AROMA Light and delicate: malt, sherry, and spice.

T TASTE Smooth, medium-bodied; wood, malt, vanilla, nuts, caramel.

Jameson dates back to 1780, but it was not sold in its own bottle, under its own name, until 1968. It is now part of the Pernod Ricard group and has greatly improved in quality over the last few years. For me, Jamesons are now great whiskeys.

The basic Jameson blend combines a number of 12-year-

JAMESON

old malt and grain whiskeys, matured in sherry casks.

The result is a mellow, sweet, and fruity whiskey, with a hint of spice. The luxurious Gold is darker, richer, and sweeter than the basic blend, with a delicate mix of oak, honey, and fruit; and the 1780 is a complex blend of sherry and spice – but very hard to find. Midleton Very Rare, also part of the Jameson range, is an exclusive, vintage blend, with nut, fruit, honey, and herb flavours.

THE PERFECT TOT
I could pour myself a Jameson over ice every day – it is excellent before, after, or even during a meal!

BUSHMILLS

C **COLOUR** Light gold through to darker amber for the aged versions.

A **AROMA** Distinctive; warm and fruity, with baked apple, sherry, and spice.

T **TASTE** Full-bodied, smooth, warming; sweetness and spice; dry finish.

Bushmills, in Northern Ireland, is the oldest distillery in the UK and one of the greatest names in Irish whiskey. Dating back to 1608, Bushmills was founded by Sir Thomas Phillips, who used the Bush River as the source of the peaty water needed for his brew. Triple distillation gives a clean, warm, and fresh feel to this excellent whiskey.

The Bushmills ten-year-old, matured in both Bourbon and sherry casks, is warm, malty,

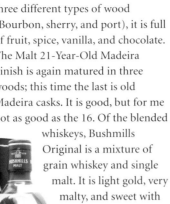
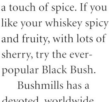
BUSHMILLS

and very satisfying. The 16-year-old Single Malt, on the other hand, is unusual, but I love it! Matured in three different types of wood (Bourbon, sherry, and port), it is full of fruit, spice, vanilla, and chocolate. The Malt 21-Year-Old Madeira Finish is again matured in three woods; this time the last is old Madeira casks. It is good, but for me not as good as the 16. Of the blended whiskeys, Bushmills Original is a mixture of grain whiskey and single malt. It is light gold, very malty, and sweet with a touch of spice. If you like your whiskey spicy and fruity, with lots of sherry, try the ever-popular Black Bush.

Bushmills has a devoted, worldwide fan base – some of its members will drink nothing else. Try it – it may very justifiably hook you, too.

COOLEY

C **COLOUR** Light, lemony gold through to light amber.

A **AROMA** Really complex; a harmony of fruit, peat, orange, and wood.

T **TASTE** Delicate; smooth; fruit, peat, sweet biscuits; great finish.

Cooley, launched only in the 1990s by John Teeling and his colleagues, is the only independent distiller in Ireland. Its aim is to revive and relaunch old names in Irish whiskey and launch some great new ones.

The Connemara Single Malt is the only peated Irish single malt. (The kilns are peat-fired.) It is like an Islay whisky – with attitude! I particularly love the 12-year-old version, which is already an award-winner, with a fantastic balance of fruit, sweetness, and peat. This is definitely one to look out for.

COOLEY

The Tyrconnell is a single malt with intense citrus-fruit characters, and honey and oak. If you are looking for a dry, tangy single malt with power and style, try Locke's Eight-Year-Old. For some refreshing tastes, and a great apéritif, try Greenore – a single-grain whiskey, with honey, oak, and nuts.

Of the blended whiskeys, Kilbeggan has sherry and fruit aromas, and smooth flavours of honey and oak, with a dry finish. A really satisfying after-dinner drink is Locke's Premium Blend, which is sweet, malty, smooth, and rich.

Finally, in 1994 Cooley's relaunched Millar's Special Reserve Irish Whiskey. This award-winning brand is a blend of grain and malt whiskeys that have been double-distilled and matured in oak Bourbon casks, making a full-bodied whiskey, with great harmony of grain, grapes, and wood.

REDBREAST

C **COLOUR** Dark gold through to light amber; darker than most Irish whiskeys.

A **AROMA** Fruit, sherry, oak, and spice, with a hint of citrus.

T **TASTE** Smooth; malt, caramel, grain, spice; a short, sweet, then dry finish.

Redbreast whiskeys are made at the Midleton Distillery in Cork, western Ireland, in a pot still (a traditional still shaped like a cooking pot, which gives fuller flavours to the spirit).

Sometimes called "Irish Bourbon", Redbreast is a distinctive 12-year-old whiskey that is fruity and similar to rye whiskey, but also heavily influenced by sherry and spice.

Redbreast also make a blended whiskey, containing both pot-still single malt and grain whiskeys. It is smooth and soft, with a great blend of vanilla and spice. I love it!

PADDY

C **COLOUR** Quite pale yellow, but light and bright.

A **AROMA** Light, subtle, and fruity, with a hint of orange.

T **TASTE** Caramel and vanilla, and a little spice; medium length.

Produced by the Irish Distillers' Group's Midleton Distillery in Cork (the mother-company is actually Pernod Ricard), Paddy is a blended whiskey with a big Irish following – both in Ireland itself and beyond. Once called the Cork Distilleries Co. Whiskey, Paddy was re-named in 1930 as a tribute to its top salesman Paddy Flaherty.

Paddy is quite a light whiskey with a warm, malty aroma, and a nutty, toasty taste. It is an honest blend, without pretensions to greatness, but true to the flavours of Ireland.

PADDY

TULLAMORE DEW

C **COLOUR** Light yellowish gold, typical of the Irish whiskeys.

A **AROMA** Balanced citrus fruits, spice, toffee, wood, and vanilla.

T **TASTE** Not too full; clean and crisp, with vanilla and citrus; medium finish.

Popular in Germany, Scandinavia, the US, and eastern Europe, Tullamore Dew produces a basic blend, which is quite lemony and spicy, but without any great depth or complexity; and an award-winning 12-year-old, which is similar to the basic blend, but much more complex. This is an altogether much more full and satisfying whiskey, especially for after-dinner drinking. In addition, there is the rather more gimmicky Tullamore Dew Heritage, which is an "historic" blend, linked to the Tullamore museum and heritage centre.

JOHN POWER & SONS

C **COLOUR** Intense deep gold with light brown tinges.

A **AROMA** Light and delicate, with malt, sherry, toffee, vanilla, and spice.

T **TASTE** Full-bodied, smooth, rich, and sweet, with a spicy finish.

John Power & Sons ("Powers"), part of Pernod Ricard, is the best-selling brand in Ireland. All of Powers' whiskeys, from the Gold Label upward, are triple-distilled and particularly smooth and full-bodied.

In an attempt to enhance the Gold Label's complexity, the company produces a 12-year-old – a blend of whiskeys aged between 12 and 23 years – but I still prefer the standard blend.

Try Powers mixed with boiling water, lemon, and brown sugar in a Hot Irish, or drink it in Irish coffee.

JOHN POWER & SONS

USA

Corn, rye, and sour mash whiskeys are made across the US, but the heart of whiskey really lies in Bourbon County, Kentucky. The county – and the Bourbon whiskey – are named after the French royal family in recognition of their support for American independence.

JACK DANIEL'S

C COLOUR Old gold through to light amber; intense.

A AROMA Very mellow; rye grain, smoke, dried apricot, liquorice, caramel, honey.

T TASTE Medium-bodied; rye, caramel, burnt toast; toffee and spice finish.

Jack Daniel began distilling his Tennessee whiskey in the 1860s, when he was only 13 years old. His distillery, in Lynchburg, southern central Tennessee, now produces a number of different whiskeys, mainly using the sour mash process, where previously fermented barley – which has lost much of its sweetness –

is added to the corn and rye. The whiskey is filtered through specially made charcoal (a process known as "mellowing") before maturing in new oak barrels. The unique charcoal-mellowing (which gives Jack Daniel's its own category as a Tennessee whiskey, rather than a Bourbon) results in a smooth, pure, and not over-sweet or over-rich spirit.

All Jack Daniel's whiskeys are made in the same way, but different maturation times and environments give different blends. The key brand is Jack Daniel's Old No. 7, otherwise known as

JACK DANIEL'S

Black Label. This is full, rich, and oily, with a charred sweetness, and a kick! It is not subtle, and you get a rough, warming sensation when you drink it. It makes a great pick-me-up, rather than an elegant digestif. Lighter is the Green Label, with a gentle start, but a hot and spicy finish.

Others in the range are Gentleman Jack Rare Whiskey – a much sweeter and softer premium single whiskey, aged for a minimum of four years; and Jack Daniel's Single Barrel, which is quite fruity and spicy, and also warming and satisfying. For the collector, in 2004 Jack Daniel's issued a 1904 brand to commemorate the centenary of the company's first gold medal. It comes in a large 1.75-litre (3½-pint) decanter!

HUMBLE BEGINNINGS

A statue of Jack Daniel now stands outside his original office – a humble building next to a limestone spring. Daniel chose this spot carefully: water from limestone caves is free from iron, which can cause off-flavours in whiskey. The spring is used to make Jack Daniel's to this day.

DICKEL

C COLOUR A darker whiskey; rich deep amber to copper.

A AROMA Aromatic; butterscotch, apple, honey, herbs, and cedar wood.

T TASTE Smooth, dry, fruity; vanilla; more corn than rye and barley; crisp finish.

Established in the mid-19th century, George Dickel's distillery was closed during Prohibition (1919–33) and didn't re-open until the 1950s. Following another period of closure, it was again re-opened, this time by Diageo. The distillery offers a delicious alternative to Jack Daniel's. (Although Dickel always insisted that his spirit was a whisky, like Scotch, not a whiskey!)

The two main brands are No.8 and No.12. The No.8 (40% ABV) is very well-balanced. The No.12 (45% ABV) is light, honeyed, and beautifully woody and herby.

WILD TURKEY

WILD TURKEY

C COLOUR Ranging from amber through to darker bronze.

A AROMA Complex, with wood, corn, coffee, caramel, toffee, and orange.

T TASTE Very full, rich, smooth; smoke, caramel, fruit, oak; long, sweet finish.

Wild Turkey is made by the Austin Nichols Company, now owned by Pernod Ricard. Some believe that Wild Turkey is the best Bourbon of all – and I know what they mean!

The whiskey is available in a number of blends, but the one I would go for is the eight-year-old, which is matured longer than most other Bourbons, making it smoother and richer, with complex aromas of fruit, flowers, and sweetness. The Russell's Reserve Aged 10 Years is also highly complex and well balanced – and definitely worth trying.

HEAVEN HILL

C COLOUR Bright gold to amber and bronze for the aged whiskeys.

A AROMA Complex; wood, leather, cinnamon, smoke, and caramel.

T TASTE Smooth, with nuts, fruit, pepper, herbs, spice, and honey.

Fire destroyed the original Heaven Hill distillery in 1996 – consuming 90,000 barrels of whiskey. The company now has a new, highly automated plant in Louisville, Kentucky, producing a range of reliable, good-quality Bourbons.

Heaven Hill's Evan Williams 7-Year-Old is named after Kentucky's first distiller, who set up his stills in 1783. This is the second-largest-selling Bourbon in the US, and is bright gold, with a great mixture of sweetness and smoke, and a spicy edge. There are also other versions of Evan Williams, comprising various Single Barrels from particular years, including the award-winning 1993.

HEAVEN HILL

Another award-winner, and a "must-try", is the Elijah Craig 12-Year-Old, named after a pastor who reputedly first charred the insides of oak barrels. It is a rich, floral, and perfectly balanced whiskey.

The Henry McKenna Single Barrel 10-Year-Old is a cask-strength Bourbon, and is very powerful, spicy, and complex, with a beautiful mingling of rye and coffee. There is also a regular Henry McKenna, which is six years old, and full of oak, vanilla, and spice. If you want something particularly sweet, try Heaven Hill's Old Fitzgerald; and for something especially dry and hot, drink Fighting Cock – an uncompromising Bourbon!

Heaven Hill also offers its own-brand Bourbon, bottled at various levels of alcohol and various ages, and most of these are very good.

MAKER'S MARK

C COLOUR Light gold through to darker amber for the Black and Gold brands.

A AROMA Rich, delicate; flowers, exotic fruits, honey, oak, and spice.

T TASTE Light, elegant; deep sweetness; nutty, chocolatey finish.

Since beginning in the 1940s, the Samuels family – owners and inventors of Maker's Mark – have tried to produce a Bourbon that is softer, gentler, and more delicate than the traditional Kentucky brew. So committed was Bill Samuels Sr. to this goal that in 1943, he burned the whiskey recipe that had been in his family for 170 years, so that he could start again with something better.

By combining maize (corn) and barley with winter wheat instead of rye, and "hand-making" the whiskey using traditional methods, even if

MAKER'S MARK

they take longer or are more costly, this small distillery (the smallest in the US) produces a distinctive, elegant, and sophisticated range of whiskeys, just as Samuels intended.

The basic Red Wax Seal (which has a buff label with black lettering) is 45% ABV and quite simply a beautiful Bourbon, with softness and complexity, particularly in its nutty sweetness. This whiskey also comes as the VIP brand, in a decanter and gift packaging.

The Black Wax Seal (black label) is 47.5% ABV and a rich, oily, deep, and complex Bourbon.

The Gold Seal (with a gold label) is a luxury Bourbon, and is even richer, smoother, and more complex again.

Overall, these are carefully made, top-quality Bourbons – American whiskeys definitely worth trying.

BUFFALO TRACE

C COLOUR Light bronze with streaks of gold at the rim.

A AROMA Complex and elegant; vanilla, herbs, oak, smoke, and honey.

T TASTE Brown sugar, spice, wood, leather, toffee, fruit; long, dry, finish.

Buffalo Trace is the modern name for the long-established Ancient Age. In an attempt to appeal to a younger market, the brand was re-named in 1999 after the distillery nearly closed. The new name refers to the fact that the distillery lies on a site where buffalo once crossed the Kentucky River.

Happily, the name is the only thing that has changed, and Buffalo Trace retains the high standard of the original whiskey. The basic Bourbon (45% ABV) has a great rye character, with a subtle sweetness and complex aromas and flavours.

BUFFALO TRACE

A number of other Bourbons are distilled at the site, some of which – such as George T. Stagg – set the very highest standards for US whiskeys, and are as good as any Scotch single malt. For a fantastic, full, herbaceous drink, try Eagle Rare; or for a younger drink in the classic Bourbon style, try W.L. Weller, a seven-year-old. Old Charter, also made at this site, is a luxury 13-year-old, golden, peppery whiskey. If you like "hot" whiskey, try eight-year-old Benchmark. One of the very best is multi-award-winning Blanton's. This is a dark, creamy, peppery Bourbon. However, if you are really lucky, you might still find a bottle of Ancient Age. For me the Ten-Year-Old is one of the great whiskeys of any type: it offers a perfect balance of fruit, spice, corn, rye, wood, and vanilla.

JIM BEAM

C COLOUR Medium gold to a darker, richer old gold.

A AROMA Elegant and light with wood, vanilla, and flowers.

T TASTE Mellow, rounded; smooth and spicy, with a light vanilla and oak finish.

Jim Beam Kentucky Straight Bourbon Whiskey is the best-known and biggest-selling Bourbon in the world. This success story began in the 18th century, when the Bohm family arrived in the US from Germany and changed their name to Beam. In 1795, Jacob Beam began distilling the first Beam whiskies. Passed from generation to generation of Beam sons, the distillery has closed only during the Prohibition era (1919–33). In 1935 – once Prohibition had ended – at the age of 70, Jim Beam (Jacob's great-grandson), rebuilt the distillery and gave the brand his name. During the 1950s, Jim Beam's grandson, F. Booker Noe Jr., launched Jim Beam whiskey onto the international stage.

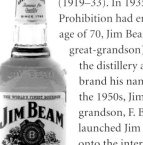

JIM BEAM
WHITE LABEL

The main Jim Beam brand is its White Label (40% ABV). This whiskey, which bursts with life and passion, is matured for a minimum of four years in new oak barrels, and is fruity, full, and spicy; it is also flowery and yet not too delicate; nor is it too complex. I always use Jim Beam White Label as a mixer in long drinks – it blends perfectly with other flavours.

Jim Beam Black Label is a bigger whiskey with a full body, great balance, big personality, and a well-deserved reputation. Also look out for the Green Label and Gold Label – these represent different strengths and ages. The Yellow Label is a rye whiskey (more than half the grain used to make the whiskey is rye), with a full body.

Like the other major Bourbon producers, Jim Beam also markets a number of other brands made in

JIM BEAM BOOKER'S

their distillery. Basil Hayden 8-Year-Old is light and clean, with lots of upfront rye. Try it if you prefer a whiskey that is not too powerful or complex. Baker's 7-Year-Old is more powerful, with more corn influence, deeper fruit, and also a distinct sweetness, and vanilla notes.

Jim Beam also makes a "Small Batch" selection of high-quality whiskeys. One of the best is Knob Creek 9-Year-Old, which is extremely complex, with a balanced sweetness of rich fruits, caramel, and toffee. Its richness is enhanced by wood and "burnt" flavours. I love it. Booker's 7-Year-Old is also an excellent whiskey: very powerful and high in alcohol, with delicious flavours of cherry, spice, toffee, chocolate, orange, and tobacco all swirling together in every glass. Delicious!

Jim Beam has also acquired the stocks of Old Grand-Dad, once a much-loved, very rich and dry Bourbon, sadly now out of business. Look out for it – no doubt Jim Beam will be issuing some in the future.

MIXING IT UP

JIM BEAM AND COLA The perfect "long" Bourbon! Place a few ice cubes in a tall glass and pour over one measure of Jim Beam White Label. Fill the glass to the top with cola, and serve immediately.

THE QUINTESSENTIAL BOURBON
When most people ask for a Bourbon, what they expect to receive (or at least what they expect to taste) is a Jim Beam.

JAPAN

The first Japanese whisky distillers were trained in Scotland, and Hokkaido, the northernmost Japanese Island, has a similar climate. The Japanese have a keen taste for whisky and now produce high-quality brands that are good enough to rival classic Scottish malts.

NIKKA

C COLOUR An extremely distinctive, vibrant copper.

A AROMA Rich and attractive; peaty with notes of sherry.

T TASTE Extremely full-bodied; peat, smoke, and a long, dry finish.

Established shortly after the Second World War, Nikka is the second-largest Japanese producer of whisky and is a subsidiary of the global Asahi Brewing Company.

Nikka produces a fantastic array of whiskies, many of which are high-quality single malts, and genuine rivals to Scotch.

The best-known brand is Yoichi. Its single-malt Ten-Year-Old has been rated one of the world's top whiskies, and is oily, peaty, fruity, and sweet, with perfect balance. Other Yoichi single malts are 12, 15, and 20 years old; but these and the single casks from particular years tend to be whiskies for the connoisseur, and can be hard to find outside Japan.

Nikka's respectable blended whiskies – which are worth a try – include Black Nikka, Black Nikka Special, and Super Nikka.

SUNTORY

SUNTORY

C COLOUR Dark, rich gold through to amber for the older versions.

A AROMA Light and delicate, with citrus, malt, and smoke.

T TASTE Medium-bodied with malt, oak, vanilla, and caramel.

Suntory is the largest Japanese producer of whisky, with 60 per cent of its domestic market.

The company's market-leading blend is Hibiki, a forceful and powerful drink, with firm malt and a sweet finish. The aged versions, including 17-, 21-, and 30-year-olds, are also excellent. Suntory Royal, a luxury brand available at 12 and 15 years old, has a fruity sweetness.

My favourite Suntory is the 12-Year-Old Single Malt, which is clean, fresh, and malty, with lovely hints of vanilla and fruit.

KARUIZAWA

C COLOUR Dark, rich gold through to amber for the older whiskies.

A AROMA Quite sweet and fruity; sherry, orange, and vanilla.

T TASTE Complex; smooth and silky with a great orange-and-chocolate finish.

Karuizawa offers a range of single malts and blended whiskies, which are extremely popular in Japan, but – sadly – can be hard to find globally.

The best single ("pure") malt is the 17-year-old, which is full and fruity, and excellently smooth. The balance and the overall quality of this whisky is second-to-none.

The most important of the company's blended whiskies is called the Master's Blend. This excellent whisky is vibrant, bright gold in colour, and quite sweet, with plenty of sugar and malt in the mix; it is full bodied, and totally satisfying. This is a great everyday, after-dinner whisky.

CANADA

Canada is a natural whisky country: cool, with plenty of grain and water, and a strong Scots heritage. Canadian whiskies are traditionally made from rye, and the country produces some of the finest spirits of this kind in the world.

SEAGRAM

C COLOUR Golden amber to light bronze; deep and attractive.

A AROMA Elegant, aromatic; lavender, violets, lemon, toffee, sweetcorn.

T TASTE Soft and smooth, with fruit, malt, oak, and vanilla.

Part of the global Diageo group, Seagram is one of two important producers of Canadian whisky (the other is Hiram Walker). The company's two flagship brands are Seagram's VO and the luxury Crown Royal. These are basically grain whiskies made in a single-column still.

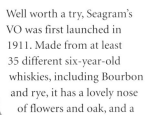

SEAGRAM

Well worth a try, Seagram's VO was first launched in 1911. Made from at least 35 different six-year-old whiskies, including Bourbon and rye, it has a lovely nose of flowers and oak, and a complex, delicate palate of fruit, grain, and corn.

The Crown Royal is a complex blend mainly of rye whiskies. It is rich and succulent, with a good balance between fruit and spice and a great finish of vanilla, corn, and oak.

Also worth trying is the fresh and complex Special Reserve.

CANADIAN CLUB

C COLOUR Dark gold for the younger versions through to darker amber.

A AROMA Delicate and smoky; rye, oak, creamy toffee, and malt.

T TASTE Soft, clean; rye, caramel; complex (sweet, dry, smoky), short finish.

First produced in 1884, Canadian Club is the flagship brand of the Hiram Walker Company, which is now part of Allied Domecq.

The standard blend is at least six years old, and has good balance between grain, fruit, and sweetness. The 12-Year-Old is gentle and soft, sweet and malty, and a complete contrast to the 100 Proof, which is powerful! For something closer to Cognac, try the Ten-Year-Old Reserve; for more fruit, try the ten-year-old Sherry Cask. All these whiskies are great after dinner.

FORTY CREEK

C COLOUR Medium gold through to lighter amber.

A AROMA Complex; vanilla, orange, and toffee, with hints of flowers and spice.

T TASTE Delicate, soft, and subtle, with honey and grainy dryness.

Forty Creek whisky is made by Kittling Ridge, founded in 1992. The company uses small pot stills (see p191), to produce separately a rye, a corn, and a malted-barley whisky. The spirits are aged individually in American oak, and only then blended and marketed as "Three Grain". The result shows a great balance of the different styles, and is fresh and dry as well as complex.

Another to try is the Barrel Select. Aged in sherry barrels, it is a richer, fruitier, smoother whisky. Drink it with a drop of water to bring out its complexity.

CANADIAN CLUB

AUSTRALIA

Most Australians drink imported whisky, but a small local industry exists in the cool climate of Tasmania. This is run on a part-time basis, and concentrates its efforts on good-quality single malts.

SULLIVAN'S COVE

- **C COLOUR** Rich, vintage gold through to light amber.
- **A AROMA** Essentially malt and vanilla, but also slightly herbaceous.
- **T TASTE** Lively and hot, with nuts and oak and a warm finish.

SULLIVAN'S COVE

The Tasmanian Distillery, makers of Sullivan's Cove, is situated near Hobart on the island of Tasmania, off the southeastern coast of Australia. As the coolest region in the country, Tasmania has the greatest potential to make excellent whisky. Unfortunately, the distillery has experienced several unsettling years, and has changed hands a number of times. This uncertainty has been reflected in its product, which over recent years has shown some unevenness in quality. The good news is that, in 2004, the company moved to a new distillery and seems more settled.

Sullivan Cove whiskies are produced using traditional methods and equipment. The Single Malt is available in regular strength, and also Cask Strength – this is a stronger, more complex whisky. It is a little more expensive than the single malt, and definitely worth a try.

SPAIN

Some regions of Spain are cool enough for making whisky, and produce well-balanced blends for the mass market.

DYC

- **C COLOUR** Bright, medium-gold, with orange highlights.
- **A AROMA** Lightly aromatic, with oak, vanilla, and malt.
- **T TASTE** Quite sweet and malty, with additional flavours of smoke and oak.

DYC (or Destilerías y Crianza del Whisky), one of the top 25 best-selling whisky brands in the world, makes blended whiskies that show a good balance of grain and malt, and a maltiness that always comes through with a light smoky touch. These are good-value whiskies. I like them best in mixes, particularly in the summer.

NEW ZEALAND

The last major producer of whisky in New Zealand, Wilson's, recently closed. I hope there will be a revival in the future.

MILFORD

- **C COLOUR** Pale straw yellow through to medium yellow-gold.
- **A AROMA** Quite strong, with peat and malt.
- **T TASTE** Full-bodied, with peat, salt, honey, and citrus.

Milford whiskies are in fact the remaining stocks of the Wilson Malt Extract Company, founded by Scottish settlers on South Island in 1926, but closed in 2002. Look out for the ten-year-old single malt, which is fresh and malty, with oak and chalk, and similar to single malts from Speyside, in Scotland.

AUSTRIA

Austria has the grain, water, and cool regions, as well as the skill in distilling, that are necessary to make great whisky.

WALDVIERTLER JH

- **C COLOUR** A dark gold, through to medium amber for the caramel version.
- **A AROMA** Complex; smoke and rye, with malt, fruit, and vanilla.
- **T TASTE** Quite oily, rich, and smooth; rye and malt; long, spicy, and sweet finish.

Produced since 1904, Waldviertler JH whiskies are frequent award-winners. There are five main types of Waldviertler. The basic and best-selling is 60-per-cent rye and 40-per-cent barley malt. This is quite sweet, but with a good balance of spice and oak. I especially like the rye–malt blend Roggenmaltz: it is complex and clean with great balance.

GERMANY

German whiskies are quite rare, especially outside Germany! But they are great as something new and may develop in the future.

BLAUE MAUS

- **C COLOUR** A fine, medium-amber, with golden tinges.
- **A AROMA** Rich and fruity, with vanilla, malt, and honey.
- **T TASTE** Quite oily, with a good balance of spice, peat, and sweetness.

Blaue Maus issued their first whisky in 1994. The two original brands were the malty and peaty Glen Blue and the clean, oaky Glen Mouse. Since then the company has issued the full-bodied Krottentaler (1994 vintage), the sweet and spicy Schwarzer Pirat (1994), and the light, sweet Spinnaker (1993), which has the best reputation.

SOUTH AFRICA

With British (including Scots) heritage in South Africa, you would expect the country to have a long tradition of whisky-making, but the warm climate and political issues restricted its growth. The ever-creative South Africans are now branching out into the field.

THREE SHIPS

- **C COLOUR** Deep amber colour; a darker copper for the ten-year-old.
- **A AROMA** Complex; peat and smoke, with wood and sherry.
- **T TASTE** Relatively smooth, with sherry, toffee, spice, and smoke.

Since its launch in 1977, Three Ships, based in the Western Cape, has grown to be the fourth biggest-selling whisky in South Africa.

One of Three Ships' most successful blends is its five-year-old. Made from a blend of South African grain whisky and imported Scotch single malt, this whisky offers the sharpness of the grain, offset by the softness of the peaty, smoky malt and, exceptionally, manages to find a balance between all its parts.

Recently the company launched its own Ten-Year-Old Single Malt, blended from only the highest-quality casks. The style is very similar to an Islay single malt (from Scotland) – beautifully smoky and peaty, with a long, warm finish – but its colour is much darker than the Islay whiskies, and richer, more like a Bourbon. This is one to watch.

THREE SHIPS

66 Elegant, subtle, and full of fun, rum is relaxation and enjoyment in a bottle – feel the spirit of the Caribbean in your glass. 99

RUM

INTRODUCING RUM

There is no better spirit to lift the mood than rum – it is like a drop of Caribbean sunshine. Made from a base of cane sugar and its by-products, rum is far more versatile than most people think: some styles are ideal for mixing in fruity cocktails, but others are really special, and should be treated with the same respect as a fine Cognac.

The origins of the modern word "rum" are rather obscure, but the name is thought to come from the 17th-century English slang term "rumbullion", meaning a "riotous good time". To me, this seems absolutely fitting for this party spirit! The historical home of rum is in the West Indies and Guyana, as well as other parts of South America. During the 18th and 19th centuries, Jamaica, Haiti, and Trinidad were the largest rum producers, closely followed by Cuba and Puerto Rico. In 1862 Facunado Bacardi established a distillery in Santiago, Cuba, and his light white and golden Cuban-style rums rose to stardom. Today, Bacardi is the biggest-selling international spirit brand (not just rum!) in the world.

HONEY *Golden rum has a slight honey-sweetness on the nose.*

MAKING RUM

Rum is a spirit distilled from sugar cane or molasses (the syrupy residue left over after sugar has been refined). To make the drink, yeast is added to a mixture of sugar cane or molasses and water, and fermentation begins. The fermented liquid, called the "wash", usually undergoes distillation several times in copper pot stills – just like those used to make brandy and whisky. The resulting spirit is clear; to produce golden or darker rums, it is aged in oak barrels, often those formerly used for Bourbon whiskey.

BARBADOS RUM PUNCH *This famous cocktail blends lime, sugar, water, and dark Barbadian rum.*

These barrels are charred on the insides, which adds a smoky depth to the end product. The rum matures quickly in the hot climate of the Caribbean and is usually left in the barrels for a relatively short period of between one and five years. Once fully matured, the rums are blended with rums of other ages until the producer achieves exactly the right flavour, colour, and texture for his product. If there is an age statement on the bottle of rum that you buy, it will normally refer to the youngest spirit in the blend.

White rums tend to be made slightly differently, in that they are usually distilled in patent stills, using continuous distillation. This process involves pumping the wash into one half of the still (actually a metal column) where it is vaporized, and then into another column where it is purified (a process known as rectification) to the right alcoholic strength. This is a continuous process and creates a cleaner, more neutral spirit.

STYLES OF RUM

There are four main styles of rum. The darkest is Jamaican or "Navy" rum, a heavy, concentrated drink made not only in Jamaica but also in Barbados and the British Virgin Islands. Since the middle of the 20th century, Jamaican rum has lost ground to lighter, more mixable styles. These "light and white" rums originate from Cuba, but are now also produced by the Cruzan company in the US Virgin Islands. Once distilled, these rums are filtered through charcoal and matured in uncharred oak barrels, which may impart a hint of colour, and character.

The third style of rum is Demerara, originating from Guyana and made from molasses. Not as dark as Jamaican rum, Demerara has a golden colour and a strong, fruity style. In the past, producers added caramel to boost colour and add a certain sweetness, but today, distillers are tending towards a less-sweet style. They have even launched superior-quality Demerara rums, some of which have been aged up to 15 years; the latter are among the finest rums on the market.

The final style is *rhum agricole*, a drink produced on the French-influenced islands, particularly Martinique. It is usually made by fermenting sugar-cane juice to give a fruity and distinctive spirit. Look out for AOC on the label, a guarantee of quality. Cane juice rum is also made in the British Virgin islands, Grenada, and Haiti. Brazil makes a near-rum, from cane juice and maize distillate, called cachaça. The biggest brand of cachaça sells a staggering 50 million cases a year.

RHUM AGRICOLE *At the Rhum de Bologne distillery in Baillif, Guadeloupe, the rum is made directly from sugar-cane juice, rather than from molasses, resulting in a lively drink.*

THE CARIBBEAN TIPPLE *You do not need to find a supermarket to buy rum in the Caribbean! The islands' foremost drink is easily found in local stores, such as this one in St Lucy, on Barbados.*

INTERNATIONAL

If politics had not intervened, we might well have known Bacardi as a Cuban rum, as this is its origin and its style. After the Cuban revolution the Bacardi company left the country, and today it has distilleries all over the world. Other popular rums are produced globally by big drinks companies, though they mainly originated in Jamaica.

BACARDI

C **COLOUR** Light and clear for the white rum; golden hues for the aged rum.

A **AROMA** Fresh and crisp; hints of peach, butterscotch, flowers, and citrus fruit.

T **TASTE** Dry and well-balanced; honey and apricot with a hint of spice.

Bacardi is one of the largest drinks companies in the world – its four distilleries provide more than 20 million cases each year.

The great Bacardi story began in 1862 when Don Facunado Bacardi, a Spanish emigrant to Cuba, used the Coffey still to create the world's first white rum. This still produces spirit by continuous distillation *(see p211)*, allowing lighter spirits to be produced than when using a traditional still. The inspiration for the Bacardi logo – the distinctive symbol of a bat – came from fruit bats in the roof of the distillery. Bats are said to bring good luck, health, and family unity.

Bacardi's flagship brand, and the original white rum, is Bacardi Superior. It is light, fresh, and fruity, with a subtle sweetness. One of the few rums to be asked for by name in bars worldwide, Bacardi is the classic mixer, especially with cola or fruit juice. Anyone can drink it, and almost everyone likes it.

Bacardi also produces aged rums, such as Bacardi Gold – a soft and honeyed, and slightly nutty rum. Use this as a mixer if you like your Bacardi slightly richer, or to give a little extra style to a daiquiri or other cocktail. Bacardi 8 is Bacardi's match

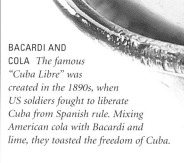

BACARDI AND COLA *The famous "Cuba Libre" was created in the 1890s, when US soldiers fought to liberate Cuba from Spanish rule. Mixing American cola with Bacardi and lime, they toasted the freedom of Cuba.*

for its great Cuban rival, Havana Club. Made from rums aged for at least eight years in mature oak casks, Bacardi 8 is more complex than other Bacardi rums. It is a dark gold colour, with rich flavours of nuts, spices, and wood, combined with bananas and apricot. It should be drunk without a mixer, but with plenty of ice.

In the early 1990s, Bacardi launched its now world-famous and highly successful Bacardi Breezer range, a mixture of light rum and fizzy fruit juices, in a wide variety of flavours. It also produces a range of flavoured rums, including Limon (citrus), O (Orange), and Cóco (Coconut), which are fruity and slightly spicy.

Bacardi rums are good value and widely available, and will make any party go with a bang!

BACARDI SUPERIOR

CAPTAIN MORGAN

C COLOUR Deep, dark amber through to gold, and clear for the light rums.

A AROMA Dark and rich; caramel, toffee, raisins, and chocolate.

T TASTE Soft and quite light on the palate, with a spicy finish.

Seagram & Sons formed the Captain Morgan Rum Company in 1944, but the heritage of the company dates back much further. It is named after Captain Henry Morgan, the daring British buccaneer who became Jamaican governor in the late 17th century. It is now available in almost every country of the world, and is one of Diageo's flagships.

Captain Morgan produces a range of rums in a variety of styles. The Black Label is a blend of rums, and has the dark toffee and raisin feel of the old Jamaica rums. It has

CAPTAIN MORGAN

a traditional style, and is full-bodied, smooth, and rich.

The Original Spiced Rum, made in Puerto Rico, was launched in 1983 as one of the first flavoured rums, and today is a big seller. It is a light rum blended with a range of spices and natural flavours, including vanilla and cinnamon. There is also a sweeter version, Silver Spiced, which is mainly sold in the US, and is great for mixing. Captain Morgan Private Stock is a stronger version of the spiced rum, with more body and character. It is designed to be sipped over ice rather than mixed to create long drinks. Parrot Bay is a flavoured Puerto Rican white rum, available in mango, pineapple, or coconut flavours. They are light, very sweet, and sticky!

Captain Morgan rums are reliable and widely available, and really are fun – a great introduction to rum.

LEMON HART

C COLOUR Light amber, ranging from completely clear to golden.

A AROMA Very fruity; notes of pineapple, vanilla, molasses, and banana.

T TASTE Medium-bodied with a good balance of fruit and sweetness.

Lemon Hart Jamaica Rum is a well-made product. Not too dark, it combines a cocktail of fruit flavours with a deep sweetness, a fine woody finish, and an elegant aroma. Lemuel Hart first created the blend in Cornwall in the southwest of England in 1804, making it not only one of the earliest Jamaica rums, but also one of the first to be supplied to the British Royal Navy.

Lemon Hart Demerara Rum is produced using a blend of rums from Guyana, and is lighter than the Jamaica Rum. It is not too complex but very satisfying, with a smooth, sweet finish. Both Lemon Hart rums can be drunk on their own, or mixed with cola or fruit juice.

MYERS

C COLOUR Rich, deep mahogany for the dark rum; clear for the white rum.

A AROMA Burned wood with a slightly smoky feel, and notes of molasses.

T TASTE Full-bodied and sweet with caramel and coconut.

Myers's Original Dark Rum is the descendent of a Jamaican brand originally launched in 1879. It is heavy, thick, and rich, with plenty of "burn" in the taste. Blended from nine different rums, Myers's Original has power and character. Myers also produces a Platinum white rum, and Myers's Legend – a 100% Jamaican pot-still rum. This is spicy and complex, with a great long finish. It is also very expensive!

MYERS

THE CARIBBEAN, SOUTH AND CENTRAL AMERICA

Early trade in rum was dominated by the Caribbean islands: Cuba, Jamaica, Barbados, and Trinidad all made their mark. Production spread south to the mainland, especially to Guyana with its Demerara rum.

WRAY & NEPHEW

C   **COLOUR** Clear and bright; colourless through to gold and dark amber.

A   **AROMA** Fruity and sweet; lime, molasses, banana, and nuts.

T   **TASTE** Grassy and sweet at the same time; nutty feel; fresh, long finish.

In the mid-19th century, Jamaican distiller John Wray joined forces with his nephew, Charles Ward, to create a highly prosperous rum business. At the start Wray & Nephew faced competition from Appleton's, another distillery on the island. However, in 1916 the company absorbed Appleton's to create what is now Jamaica's best-selling rum brand – 90 per cent of the rum consumed on the island is Wray & Nephew.

Wray's White Overproof Rum really is the definitive Jamaican white rum: it is complex, fruity, and nutty, with real class. Jamaicans say that, on the island, even non-drinkers have a bottle of Overproof in the house. Of the Appleton brands, the

WRAY & NEPHEW

flagship is the Appleton Estate V/X Jamaica Rum. This amber-coloured blend combines rums aged between five and ten years. It is full-bodied, soft, smooth, and complex, with excellent toffee, orange, apricot, and spice flavours.

If you want a good mixing rum, use Appleton Special Jamaica Rum, which is golden, medium-bodied, and sweet, light, and smoky. However, the absolute "must-try" is Appleton Estate Extra Jamaica Rum. A deep amber to copper colour, this is an elegant, smooth, and superb blend of rums aged up to 18 years. It has great complexity, with honey, fruit, spice, tobacco, and leather.

These are rums rich with the taste of Jamaica, and perfect for a party.

BRISTOL SPIRITS' CLASSIC RUMS

C   **COLOUR** Clear, through pale golden to darker amber.

A   **AROMA** Openly aromatic; vanilla, banana, pineapple, and grass.

T   **TASTE** Smooth, oily, and silky, with wood and spices.

Bristol Spirits, based in southwestern England, ships its rums in oak casks from distilleries across the Caribbean, and matures and bottles them in the UK (a technique known as "early landing"). In my view Bristol Spirits is the most exciting entry into the rum world since Bacardi. I am a fan of all of the rums on their "Classic Rum" list, which are delicate, elegant, and firm, with complex flavours.

Recently Bristol Spirits has been at the forefront of a move to

BRISTOL SPIRITS MONYMUSK

produce rum rather like single-malt whisky – using spirit from only one estate, or even from one particular pot still. This means that, like single malt, the rum is labelled with the name of the distillery where it has been produced, and its age. These innovative rums appear on the "Classic Rum" list, along with Bristol Spirits' other excellent products.

One of my favourite aged rums is the Gardel 10-Year-Old, from Guadeloupe, which is finished in Limousin oak casks (from France). This is a complex and aromatic rum, with toffee and flower flavours, and a rich woody and chocolatey palate.

One to drink with an espresso and a large cigar is the Long Pond 13-Year-Old. The Long Pond Distillery is in Jamaica, to the east of Montego Bay, and this distinctive, golden-amber rum brims with wood and fruit and has a great oily feel. On its own or after dinner you could try the Long Pond 16-Year-Old, which is

BRISTOL SPIRITS LONG POND

smooth, nutty, and woody, and, because it is finished in *oloroso* sherry oak casks, has a delicious extra, sherry richness.

Some of the very best Bristol Spirits' rums are those from Jamaica's Monymusk Distillery. Try the 23-year-old, with its great balance of flowers, wood, and citrus flavours; or the 25-year-old, aged in Bourbon casks, giving great depth, with hints of smoke and vanilla. This rum reminds me of a great single malt.

In order to provide an "entry" brand at an approachable price, Bristol Spirits now offers a product called The Caribbean Collection – a blend of golden Demerara rums, matured in England for an average of five years; and Guyana and Guadeloupe, an award-winning blend of young white rums – and a "must-try".

CADENHEAD'S

C   **COLOUR** Ranging from very pale straw through to light gold.

A   **AROMA** Often delicate and floral, with apple and raisins.

T   **TASTE** Light to medium-bodied, with smoke, oak, and fruit.

Cadenhead's is a Scottish firm sourcing its rums throughout the Caribbean. The company issues a range of Green Label rums, made by traditional methods. The Demerara 10-Year-Old is light, pale, and clean, while the Barbados 15-Year-Old has a great balance of sweetness, wood, and spice. The Cuban 5-Year-Old is light gold in colour, and fruity and fresh – a typical example of the Cuban style. Cadenhead's also produces a range of special dated rums, often up to 50 years old or more. These are darker amber and much more complex.

CADENHEAD'S GREEN LABEL

MOUNT GAY

C COLOUR Bright golden amber through to light brown.

A AROMA Floral, with vanilla, mint, apricot, banana, cherry, and nuts.

T TASTE Very soft and light-bodied, with smoke and oak.

Mount Gay is the leading rum from Barbados, and the company claims to be the oldest rum distillery in the world – the first written records of rum production on what is now the Mount Gay Estate date back to 1703. After centuries of weathering the storms of the Barbadian rum industry and continued steady growth, in 1989 the company became part of the global Rémy-Cointreau group, and its products are now available worldwide.

Mount Gay produces two flagship rums. The first,

MOUNT GAY

Mount Gay Eclipse, is a golden, delicate, light rum, with excellent balance. Flowery and creamy, this is one of my favourites for enjoying in the summer, in the garden. However, the second, Mount Gay Extra Old, is the company's real star. This blend of well-aged spirits has won so many awards that the company claims that it is "the best rum in the world".

And Extra Old really is a great rum: it is dark amber in colour and light-bodied, with tastes of oak, fruit, chocolate, and burned wood, all of which melt into an intensity of fruit and spice.

Other key products include Mount Gay Sugar Cane Brandy (actually a white rum), which in the US is called Sugar Cane Rum. This is perfect for parties: golden, sweet, smoky, and spicy, with a fruity freshness.

The White, White Overproof, Vanilla, and Mango rums are also great rums: delicate and good fun.

FOURSQUARE

C COLOUR Attractive bright amber with a golden rim.

A AROMA Brilliantly spicy: ginger, nutmeg, and cloves; herbs and orange.

T TASTE Dry; great balance of herbs, fruits, and spice.

Foursquare Spiced Rum is the flagship brand – and a classic rum – of R.L. Seale, a modern, dynamic company based in Barbados. Cinnamon, vanilla, and nutmeg are all blended at an early stage into the two-year-old spirit according to a formula handed down from generation to generation. The result is an excellent, award-winning, lively rum, with a strong but balanced spiciness. It is a worthy competitor to other spiced rums on the market.

FOURSQUARE

DOORLY'S

C COLOUR Very intense; a wonderfully rich, dark amber.

A AROMA Very complex and rich; honey and mango, with nuts and sherry.

T TASTE Elegant, soft, and smooth; raisins and vanilla, with a long, orange finish.

Founded in the 1920s, this is a Barbadian brand (recognized by the distinctive blue macaw on its logo) with a great range – starting with a basic rum in a plastic bottle for sale on the island! Part of the R.L. Seale company, and made at the Foursquare plantation, Doorly's has one flagship label: the XO. This is a blend of five rums with no age mark. The spirit is matured, and then second-matured in *oloroso* sherry oak casks, which gives an extra smoothness and a fuller flavour. You can use it as a mixer, but I think it is great to sip after dinner, too.

CARONI

C COLOUR Clear through to gold for the Felicite.

A AROMA Sweet, with molasses, lemon, lime, banana, and spice.

T TASTE Soft and delicate, with light spice, chocolate, and soft fruits.

Caroni is made by Rum Distillers of Trinidad and Tobago, a government-run company. Its products include the delicate and well-made Superb White Magic and the straw gold, light, fruity, and gently spicy Felicite Gold. Old Cask is the best of the heavier rums: ten years old, with lemon, spice, and coconut, it tastes smooth and chocolatey, with a fresh finish. Use the Stallion Punch in your cocktails (or punch) – it is one of the strongest rums made in Trinidad (75% ABV!), quite dry, and full of power.

ANGOSTURA

C COLOUR Clear, bright, and golden through to mahogany.

A AROMA Wonderfully fruity, with apple, caramel, vanilla, wood, and spice.

T TASTE Soft and mellow; subtle with spice, fruit, and a chocolate edge.

Most people associate Angostura with bitters (often used in cocktail-making), but this Trinidad-based company also makes rum. All of the rums in the range (white, gold, and dark) make good mixers. For a light, clean, citrusy white rum, try the Angostura three-year-old; or for a lighter gold rum, try the spicy 5-year-old Gold, which bursts with flavours of mango and banana. One of my favourite gold rums is the eight-year-old 1919. It is matured in Bourbon casks to give a delicious, well-balanced, fruity rum, that is good on its own.

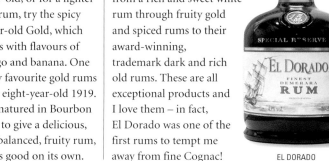

ANGOSTURA

EL DORADO

C COLOUR Ranging from clear and bright through gold to dark mahogany.

A AROMA Wonderfully complex; caramel, coffee, cigar box, spice, oak, and fruit.

T TASTE Smooth and soft; spice, rich oak, honey, nuts, and toffee.

El Dorado rum is produced and marketed by Demerara Distilleries, a company based in Guyana, which, over the past 300 years, has established a strong reputation for producing outstanding rum. The company offers an enormous range – from a rich and sweet white rum through fruity gold and spiced rums to their award-winning, trademark dark and rich old rums. These are all exceptional products and I love them – in fact, El Dorado was one of the first rums to tempt me away from fine Cognac!

One of my all-time favourites is the El Dorado 12-year-old (although the five-year-old is superb, too). The 12-year-old is a frequent award-winner: it is elegant and complex, with a fantastic balance between nuts, fruit, sweetness, and spice.

The 15-year-old Special Reserve is the finest rum in the range, and one of the best on the market. Dark, full, and complex, its sweetness and spice mixes brilliantly with citrus and oak. Perhaps not quite as good as the 15-year-old, but still excellent, the 21-year-old Special Reserve is reddish, dry, and woody, with tobacco and cigar-box aromas, and very smooth.

To celebrate the new millennium, the company introduced the 25-year-old in a limited edition of 3,000 decanters costing $200 each. If you love rum, and you have the money, you will not do better – this rum is simply divine.

EL DORADO

J.M.

C COLOUR Ranging from clear through to pale gold and light amber.

A AROMA Aromatic, highly complex; nuts, herbs, spice, exotic fruits, and citrus.

T TASTE Light, with an excellent balance between fruit, spice, and sweetness.

This is a very old house, its name derived from the initials of Jean-Marie Martin, who set up the distillery at the site on Martinique. The flagship is the Vieux Rhum – one of the best in the world – but there is also a highly respected white *rhum agricole*. The distillate is matured with passion for ten years in small barrels, previously used for Bourbon. This brings out the complex flavours and deep gold colour of the rum. Personally I would choose an old J.M. over an XO Cognac every time – try it with some dark chocolate and a small creamy cigar.

LA MAUNY

C COLOUR Medium golden yellow with orange to brown highlights.

A AROMA Rich and perfumed, with notes of bread, plum jam, and cooked fruits.

T TASTE Suave, smooth, and beautifully balanced with a long, clean finish.

LA MAUNY

This is one of the most consistent and successful of all the Caribbean distilleries, and is the best-selling rum on its home island of Martinique – a recommendation in itself.
All of the La Mauny rums are excellent value, but if at all possible, try the Rhum Vieux or ideally the 1995 – they are delicious. The rums are aged in small oak barrels from the Cognac region, which makes them slightly dryer than those of other distillers, and gives them notes of almond and hazelnut.

J BALLY

C COLOUR Dark amber for the aged rums; lighter for the younger rums.

A AROMA Toffee, nuts, oak, beeswax, and raisins; notes of wood for younger rums.

T TASTE Soft, delicate, creamy, and honeyed with a long, elegant finish.

J Bally is a *rhum agricole* from Martinique, based in the west-coast town of Carbet. The house founder, Jacques Bally, began making rum in 1917, establishing a very high quality by letting his rums age for a long period in oak casks. These are really special rums – delicious, subtle, and elegant, classy and pure, and without the sweetness of so many brands. J Bally is particularly known for its vintage rums. They are produced only in good years, and are sold with the vintage date on the label. But look out before you buy – some can be very expensive!

NEISSON

C COLOUR Bright, charming golden yellow with walnut tinges.

A AROMA Complex, with baked fruits, cocoa, vanilla, sweet spice, and liquorice.

T TASTE Subtle, oily, and round with dried fruit flavours; amazingly long finish.

J BALLY

This rum is relatively discreet on the palate, but is certainly worth having on your trolley of digestifs. It comes from one of the newest distilleries on Martinique, which has gained a stellar reputation since it was set up in the 1930s. Different *cuvées* are produced, including possibly the finest of all white rums. I particularly like the Extra Old 55 for its subtlety and elegance, or, for that very special occasion, the XO – a specially selected blend of the best vintages over the past 15 years.

SAINT JAMES

C COLOUR Gorgeous, deep gold yellow, with red-tile nuances.

A AROMA Notes of exotic fruit, toffee, cigars, flowers, and nutmeg.

T TASTE Smooth and elegant, with a long, complex finish.

I have a lot of respect for this classy and fine rum. It is a drink with a strong sense of identity – strong enough to compete with good Cognac when choosing a refined digestif. Complex and fresh, but with subtle aromas, Saint James is the true expression of what a rum should taste like, and thanks to its smooth and easy approach, it appeals to almost every palate.

Saint James hails from the west coast of the island of Martinique – a fragment of France dropped into the Caribbean – and its origins are rooted in French colonial history. The distillery was established back in the mid-18th century by a group

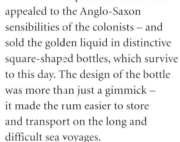

SAINT JAMES

of priests, led by Father Edmond Lefebure. The priests needed to support their charitable work at the St Pierre Hospital, and turned to rum production as a reliable source of income. At that time, the import of rum into France was prohibited, so Father Lefebure – who clearly had a talent for marketing – decided to sell his rum to the colonies of New England. He named his rum "Saint James" – a name that was easy to pronounce and that appealed to the Anglo-Saxon sensibilities of the colonists – and sold the golden liquid in distinctive square-shaped bottles, which survive to this day. The design of the bottle was more than just a gimmick – it made the rum easier to store and transport on the long and difficult sea voyages.

CULTURE AND TRADITION

A FINE HERITAGE Saint James is made from cane juice rather than molasses, and distilled in small alambic pot stills before storage in Limousin oak barrels for ageing. Saint James was one of the pioneers in the world of fine rums, and the distillery's standards are recognized by connoisseurs around the world: a museum of rum housed in a fine colonial mansion at the Saint James distillery *(below)* displays the centuries of hard work behind the brand and attracts thousands of visitors every year. Saint James is highly sought after and available only in small quantities outside the Caribbean.

STRAIGHT UP *Saint James is not a rum for mixing. Nurture and savour it like a good brandy and you will be well rewarded.*

CLÉMENT

C **COLOUR** Ranging from clear through to gold, amber, and copper.

A **AROMA** Toffee and ripe fruits, with smoke and vanilla.

T **TASTE** Gentle, smooth; well-made; clean and satisfying.

A premium rum, with a light, bright style, Clément is classic *rhum agricole* – traditional rum made from sugar-cane juice – at its best. There is an enormous range of Clément rums, ranging from a nutty white rum through to the golden Cuvée Charles Clément, with its delicious, lively sweetness. However, for me it is the rich, deep, and complex Rhum Vieux series that most rivals Cognac. Look out for the XO, and the vintages, which go all the way back to 1952.

CLÉMENT

TROIS RIVIÈRES

C **COLOUR** Clear and bright to light and darker gold, depending on the style.

A **AROMA** Perfumed and elegant, with distinctive fruit and flowers.

T **TASTE** Smooth and quite oily, but nevertheless dry; nutty finish.

Trois Rivières is a long-established Martinique distillery once owned by Martini & Rossi, but now part of the BBS Group, which also owns La Mauny rum. The best Trois Rivières is the award-winning White Rhum "50%", which is flowery and fragrant, with a good, fresh feel. In the hot Caribbean climate, one year's ageing is worth three years in, say, Scotland, so look out for the aged rums, some without dates and others, such as the 1996, aged for at least 6 years.

Trois Rivières also makes the good *rhums agricoles* Duquesne Rhum Blanc and Ambre.

DILLON

C **COLOUR** Clear through to golden amber and dark brown.

A **AROMA** Quite spicy, with a good harmony of citrus fruits and pear.

T **TASTE** Delicately crisp, fresh, and dry, with a firm finish.

Established on Martinique in 1857 and now owned by the French group Bardinet, the Dillon distillery produces two white rums, at 50% ABV and 55% ABV. The latter has a better reputation, but both make perfectly acceptable mixers. Dillon also produces a dark rum, and a Rhum Vieux (50% ABV), which is quite dry and not too rich. Overall the style of these rums is crisp, rather than warm and full – if you prefer a fresher style for your spirit, Dillon could be the rum for you.

RIVIÈRE DU MAT

C **COLOUR** Dark gold for the basic rum; darker amber for the aged versions.

A **AROMA** Quite sweet and light, with fruit, vanilla, and wood.

T **TASTE** Smooth and light, with a refreshing but sweet character.

Rivière du Mat is the largest distillery on Réunion, an island in the Indian Ocean and a former French colony, which first produced rum in 1704.

The basic Rivière du Mat is the Rhum Agricole de la Réunion, with variations such as Rhum Blanc, Rhum Paille ("straw"), and Rhum Traditionnel de la Réunion, which comes in versions of three, five, ten, and 15 years old. Rivière du Mat also markets the Mascarin brand. Mainly available locally or in France, these are certainly rums to watch out for.

DILLON

TORTUGA

C **COLOUR** Bright and clear; deep gold with yellowish tinges.

A **AROMA** Elegant, powerful; quince, crystallized fruits, and Oriental spices.

T **TASTE** Rich but savoury, with a soft texture and medium to long finish.

Based in the Cayman Islands and set up in 1984, the Tortuga Rum Company blends its rums from those of Jamaica and Barbados.

The original Tortuga rums are the Light and Gold – the Gold is oak-aged for longer to give it extra depth – but the range also includes an award-winning Dark Rum, and a host of flavoured rums, among them Banana, Spiced, and Coconut. The company is famous for its Tortuga Caribbean Rum Cake – delicious!

TORTUGA

HAVANA CLUB

C **COLOUR** Light straw gold through to coffee-amber and mahogany.

A **AROMA** Sweet and light; nuts, spice, tobacco, caramelized fruit.

T **TASTE** Soft and approachable, with vanilla, lush fruit, and chocolate.

Havana Club rum dates back to 1878 when Don Jose Archebala founded the distillery in Cárdenas, on the coast of Cuba. The Cuban party scene of the 1930s was great for Havana Club, but following the Cuban revolution of 1959, when the island's distilleries came under state control and the US imposed sanctions on imports from Cuba, sales of the rum fell into decline. Havana Club is now distributed around most of the world by Pernod Ricard. This has revived its fortunes and turned Havana Club into one of rum's market leaders.

The youngest Havana Club is Añejo Blanco. This is an aged white rum (although the age is unspecified), and is extremely fresh, with notes of cherry and chocolate. It makes a great mixer. In a Mojito cocktail (*see p378*) try the Añejo 3 Anos, which has a golden, nutty, and soft character.

The Añejo Especial is darker, older, and smokier, and is the perfect Cuba Libre mixer (with cola and lime wedges), but I prefer it straight with lots of ice. The flagship Añejo Reserva has a dark bottle and dark label, and is a darker rum, with coffee, chocolate, and spice. Full of flavour, it is great as a mixer or on its own.

Best of all, though, is the Añejo 7 Años, considered to be the pride of Cuban rum. This is dark, rich, and complex, and definitely one for after dinner, on its own, with a delicious "Bolivar" brand cigar.

HAVANA CLUB

BERMUDEZ

C **COLOUR** A dark, shimmering, vintage gold, through to a light amber.

A **AROMA** Sweet and attractive, with orange, burned fruit, wood, and nuts.

T **TASTE** Smooth, with toffee, nuts, and spice; well-balanced.

This distillery is not in Bermuda, as the name suggests, but the Dominican Republic, where it was established in 1852. Although not well known, the company is working hard to raise its profile around the world.

The distillery's rum is similar in style to Cuban rum. Well worth a try is the Don Armando. This rum is amber, quite complex and fruity, not too heavy, and pleasant on the palate. The 150 Aniversario is smoother still, and quite nutty and spicy in its flavours.

I really like these lively and fresh rums, and they are definitely good enough to drink straight, in a snifter, like a Cognac.

PUSSER'S

C COLOUR Dark amber to mahogany, with good intensity.

A AROMA Elegant and complex; flowers, prune, toffee, and caramel.

T TASTE Sweet but not cloying; fresh on the palate right up to its spicy finish.

Based in the British Virgin Islands, Pusser's takes its name from "purser", the officer who once distributed a daily tot of rum to the sailors of the Royal Navy. The navy rum ration was abolished in 1970, but in 1979, former US marine Charles Tobias obtained the rights and all the blending information for Pusser's Rum from the Admiralty, and formed Pusser's Ltd. Made to the award-winning traditional recipe, Pusser's is a blend of five West Indian rums, distilled in a pot still, rather like malt whisky.

PUSSER'S

BARBANCOURT

C COLOUR Pale to medium gold; intense and rich.

A AROMA Brilliantly complex; fruit, flowers, honey, spice, and earth.

T TASTE Elegant, perfectly balanced; soft and smooth, with a spicy or nutty finish.

This is a really special rum from Haiti. Made in the French style, like *rhum agricole* (from sugar-cane juice), but double-distilled like Cognac, Barbancourt produces rums that are soft and silky, with great flavour and balance. I love them!

The basic Three Star, aged for four years, is light and delicate, and good on its own, but fantastic as a mixer. Best of all is the Five Star 8-Year-Old Special Reserve. This is golden and complex, and well balanced, with sweetness, nuts, spice, and wood – great on its own after dinner.

ENGLISH HARBOUR

C COLOUR Clear; from gold through light copper to dark amber.

A AROMA Complex; a mix of oak, coconut, cherry, and smoke.

T TASTE Medium-bodied; great balance of spice, oak, and dried fruit; dry finish.

At home in Antigua this rum is known as Cavalier; for export it is English Harbour. The three-year-old white and golden rums are light and fresh, with a great balance of citrus and spicy oak. Perfect for mixing, these rums are really well made. The aged rums are excellent; the award-winning five-year-old is smooth and light-bodied, with great balance. It is good on its own, or as a mixer. After dinner try the excellent Extra Old – dark, dry, and fruity, with a perfect balance of spice, tobacco, and earth.

ENGLISH HARBOUR

FLOR DE CAÑA

C COLOUR Clear; crystal white through amber to dark, reddish bronze.

A AROMA Extremely fruity, with mango, apricot, strawberry, and oak.

T TASTE Soft, creamy, and smooth; well-balanced, with a long, woody finish.

These rums have been made in Nicaragua since 1937, and a slow ageing process gives them fine complexity. They are among my favourite rums of all.

The Extra Dry, four years old, is much more fruity and complex than most other white rums. Drink it with a dash of lime juice. Black Label (five years old) is the well-balanced, fruity, nutty, and woody flagship brand. I love the Grand Reserve (seven years old). It has oranges and caramel to the fore, with hints of pepper. First class!

SAN MIGUEL

C COLOUR Clear, through to dark gold for the aged rums.

A AROMA Attractive; fruit (pear, lemon, banana), with nuts and cocoa.

T TASTE Sweet, but also fresh and quite light and delicate.

San Miguel is the most important distillery in Ecuador. Unlike most other rums, which are aged in hot climates, those from San Miguel are matured in the cool air of the mountains, making the ageing process slower, producing rums of great complexity and quality. The Plata is the white (or "silver") rum, and is slightly citrusy, and dry and refreshing. It makes a great alternative to Bacardi. The Gold provides a mixer with a little more depth (especially of nuts and citrus). My favourite is the 5 Años. Light, bright, charming, soft, and easy to drink, this is a true rival to the Cuban style.

CACHAÇA

C COLOUR Clear spirit – distillation removes all traces of colour.

A AROMA Direct and uncomplicated; mainly sugar cane, earth, and lemon.

T TASTE Sweet and fiery, like a very young white rum.

Cachaça means "burning water" – which gives you some indication of what to expect from this unique spirit!

Brazil is the largest grower of sugar cane in the world. It produces most of the world's molasses – and it is molasses that makes most of the world's rum. However, Brazilian cachaça is made from fermented sugar-cane juice – rather like the French *rhum agricole* – sometimes with the addition of maize. Cachaça sold for international

CACHAÇA

consumption is around 40% ABV, and has distinct aromas and flavours of sugar cane.

Although there are an estimated 4,000 brands of cachaça in Brazil, the biggest of all (and the second-biggest spirit brand in the world) is 51. This brand comes in various versions, depending upon its region of origin. You may find Pirassununga 51, from the town of that name near Sao Paolo, or Caninha 51 from the south. The brand Pitú, now making its mark, is another to look out for.

Cachaça is becoming increasingly popular as an addition to fruit-flavoured cocktails, but I like it in the traditional way – in a Caipirinha.

MIXING IT UP

CACHAÇA AND COCKTAILS If cachaça is agreed to be the national spirit of Brazil, then the Caipirinha *(see p348)*, the traditional way to drink cachaça, is its national cocktail. A delicious mix of fresh lime juice and cachaça, the Caipirinha is the perfect refresher for a hot summer's day. For something even more fruity, try a Batida – a Brazilian fresh fruit cocktail made using cachaça. For a Passion Fruit batida, pour cachaça over crushed ice and top up with freshly squeezed passion fruit juice. Delicious!

PUERTO RICO

Puerto Rican rum is made primarily for the US market – relatively light and accessible with a slightly sweeter feel.

DON Q

C COLOUR Clear, through light gold to darker gold for the older rums.

A AROMA Spicy, with tobacco, chocolate, orange, and coconut.

T TASTE Sweet and chocolatey; soft, with toffee and oak; spicy finish.

Don Q is the flagship rum of Serrallés, a Puerto Rican company. The white rum Cristal and the Gold make fresh and fruity mixers. Añejo, a blend of five-year-olds, is dark gold, with fruit, spice, and chocolate – good for mixing or on its own. Best is the Grand Añejo, a complex and balanced blend of 12-year-olds.

NEW ZEALAND

The creative New Zealanders exploit the cool climate on the South Island to make some great spirits, including a fine rum.

ROARING FORTIES

C COLOUR Reddish mahogany through to light gold for the Overproof.

A AROMA Deep and complex; tobacco, molasses, spice, and charred fruit.

T TASTE Firm and smoky, with dark fruits, burnt wood, and chocolate.

Roaring Forties, on South Island, produces its rum using traditional methods, focusing on quality over quantity. The basic rum, at 40% ABV, is dark and rich, with dark fruit, oak, and smoke flavours. The Overproof is lighter in colour, young, and lively, but powerful. Try them for something new.

AUSTRALIA

Queensland has long been a major producer of sugar cane, so it is natural that it should also support a thriving rum industry; its favourite rum, Bundaberg or "Bundy" is popular worldwide. Rum made in Western Australia is becoming increasingly important, too.

ORD RIVER

C COLOUR Medium amber with light golden highlights.

A AROMA Young and fresh; sugar, oak, and earth, with caramel.

T TASTE Lively and fresh with good balance and a spicy finish.

Ord River is produced by the Kimberly Hoochery Distillery in Western Australia. The basic Ord River is a perfectly respectable brew, but if you want something powerful try the cask strength, which is 65% ABV or more. Canefire is the company's award-winning light rum. Definitely a brand to look out for.

INNER CIRCLE

C COLOUR Ranging from medium bright gold through to medium and dark amber.

A AROMA Very aromatic, with fruit, vanilla, and wood in great balance.

T TASTE Light bodied in the Cuban style; smooth and satisfying.

INNER CIRCLE

These are high-quality Australian rums with a growing reputation. The company is now owned by Olympic yachtsman Stuart Gilbert, who has rescued the brand following its withdrawal during the 1980s. The well-balanced Red Spot Original is the basic rum, and makes a very good mixer, but the star is the award-winning Green Spot Overproof, which is smooth and rich. For something really strong, try the Black Spot Full Strength – it is 75% ABV, so watch out!

BUNDABERG

C COLOUR Amber, with hints of orange and red.

A AROMA Light and bright; nutty, with notes of citrus and wood.

T TASTE Woody and quite warm, with a flowery, herby feel.

The Bundaberg Distilling Company, based in the small town of Bundaberg, in Queensland, began producing rum in 1888, but is now owned by global group Diageo. In 2004, the rum was voted Australia's number one spirit.

The basic Bundaberg is golden, with a warm and sharp taste. Young and lively, it makes an excellent mixer. The OP is a macho rum – quite hard and deliberately fiery and strong, which gives it character. The newest product is the Distiller's No. 3. Intended to be a more sophisticated rum, it is softer and gentler than the older products, and one to watch.

CREATING IDENTITY *Bundaberg rum is well-branded: the company introduced the square bottle and the distinctive "Bundy R." polar bear in 1961.*

MECHANICAL HARVESTING
Queensland has been producing sugar cane since the 19th century. Whereas hand-cutting is common in the Caribbean, in Australia farmers tend to use mechanical cutters, such as combine harvesters.

UNITED KINGDOM

Britain has long-established links with the Caribbean, and for many years provided by far the biggest market for rum. The system of "early landing" allows very young spirit to be exported from the Caribbean to Britain and slow-matured in its cool climate.

OVD

C COLOUR Very dark brown, with a traditional navy rum feel.

A AROMA Rich and aromatic, with charred ripe fruit, treacle, and wood.

T TASTE Medium-bodied; warm, with caramel and ripe fruits.

Amazing as it may seem, this is a Scottish rum. OVD stands for "Old Vatted Demerara", and it was first produced by George Morton, a broker from Montrose, in the 19th century. The company had been bought out by Diageo, but in 2002 Diageo sold it to the whisky

OVD

distiller William Grant. The rum is actually distilled and blended in Guyana and Trinidad, but bottled and marketed by OVD in Scotland. The Scottish connection is very important in terms of the rum's success – it is one of Scotland's top-selling brands.

OVD Demerara Rum is similar to traditional navy rum. The spirit is dark, heavy, and treacle-like, and is rich with flavours of caramel, and ripe or dried fruits – rather like the fortified wine of Madeira. This is a rum for a cosy winter evening by the fire.

LAMB'S

C COLOUR Very dark, rich brown with some tinges of red.

A AROMA Treacle, dark sugar, black fruits, and wood.

T TASTE Quite dry, with banana, caramel, nuts, and a spicy finish.

The Lamb's tradition dates back to 1849 when Alfred Lamb opened a wine-and-spirit business in London. Lamb imported his rum using the system of "early landing": the spirit was shipped from the Caribbean to the UK in oak barrels, while it was still young, and then left to mature in the cool cellars beneath the River Thames in London. The cooler conditions enabled the rum to mature more slowly and so develop fuller, deeper flavours than if it had been allowed to mature in the warmer Caribbean climate.

LAMB'S

Lamb's is marketed as a navy rum – a name that originates from the practice of the Royal Navy to give its sailors a daily ration of rum. The spirit the sailors drank was thick, dark, and sweet, and the term "navy rum" is now used to describe a traditional, heavy, dark style of rum.

Lamb's Navy Rum is made from a blend of 18 rums from Barbados, Guyana, Jamaica, and Trinidad. Aged in oak for up to four years, it is very much in the navy rum style, with a deep brown colour, dark fruits, lots of molasses, and a distinctive note of toffee. It has a deep, mellow flavour and a long finish. Overall, Lamb's Navy Rum is well-made and reliable; so, if you like traditional dark rum, look no further.

In some countries, such as Canada, you may find that a light, golden Lamb's rum, called Palm Breeze, is also available.

USA

In the days before political conflict, much of Cuba's lighter Havana-style rum was exported to the US; enterprising producers began to copy this style, making it in other parts of the Americas for sale in the US. Other rums are made in the US Virgin Islands.

MATUSALEM

C COLOUR Clear gold through to darker amber for the aged versions.

A AROMA Elegant; coconut, vanilla, pepper, caramel, and plum.

T TASTE Quite sweet; wood, vanilla, caramel, banana; spicy finish.

First produced in 1872 by two brothers and an associate who arrived in Cuba from Spain, Matusalem is a light Cuban-style rum. Its name (derived from a Spanish proverb) implies that the spirit is as old as the biblical character Methuselah, who lived for more than 950 years!

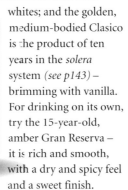

MATUSALEM

In the 1960s the company relocated to the US, but the brand was not revived until 2002; it is now manufactured in the Dominican Republic.

For your cocktails, the white rum Platino is fuller and richer than most whites; and the golden, medium-bodied Clasico is the product of ten years in the *solera* system *(see p143)* – brimming with vanilla. For drinking on its own, try the 15-year-old, amber Gran Reserva – it is rich and smooth, with a dry and spicy feel and a sweet finish.

CRUZAN

C COLOUR Clear gold through to amber, with good intensity.

A AROMA Very fruity and spicy; cinnamon, sherry, mint, and molasses.

T TASTE Sweet and well-balanced; good fruit and vanilla, with a fresh, dry finish.

St Croix in the US Virgin Islands once abounded with sugar and rum. Although most of the sugar has now gone, Cruzan rum continues to be a big success, imported to the US through its owners, Todhunter.

Cruzan is best known for its flavoured rum, but it also makes some very good "straight" rum, including light and dark two-year-olds, which both have an excellent balance of fruit and spice, and are perfect for cocktail-making. However, my

CRUZAN

favourite of the straight rums is the elegant, award-winning Diamond Rum. Oaky, soft, and gentle, it is a blend of five- to ten-year-old rums, and has a light amber colour and a medium body. The Single Barrel Estate Rum is an outstanding 12-year-old (and another award-winner) and great to drink on its own. The rum is deep and complex, with fine fruit flavours and delicious sweetness, balanced with a distinct spiciness and a dry finish.

No Cruzan entry would be complete without mentioning the company's fantastic range of light, refreshing fruit rums. Banana, Mango, Coconut, Orange, and Citrus rums are all available, but my particular favourites are the Vanilla and the Pineapple – great fun!

66 Icy, fresh, and very cool, vodka is the spirit of today – the world's most versatile and fashionable spirit. **99**

VODKA

INTRODUCING VODKA

Vodka – from the Russian word for "little water" – is the world's most popular spirit, due in part to its enormous versatility. Many people assume that all vodkas taste neutral and that there is little difference between brands, but even a quick delve into the offerings of eastern Europe reveals individual vodkas of distinct character and quality.

Vodka was most likely first distilled in 14th-century Russia, but only by the 16th century had the spirit begun to gain popularity throughout the country. In 1818 Peter Smirnoff opened a distillery in Moscow, an enterprise that became one of Russia's biggest in the period leading up to the Russian Revolution of 1917. (Smirnoff was eventually exiled to Paris, where he began his venture again.) Worldwide recognition for vodka, particularly in the UK and US, did not come until after World War II,

ANISEED *Vodka made from wheat carries aromas of aniseed.*

when soldiers who had served in eastern Europe returned home. Since the 1960s vodka has done nothing but soar in popularity; driven by sophisticated marketing, brands like Smirnoff, Absolut, Finlandia, and Grey Goose have established themselves as some of the most successful drinks on the planet.

MAKING VODKA

Vodka is most commonly made from potatoes, molasses, or grain – especially rye (mainly in Poland) and wheat (mainly Russia and Sweden), although barley is most widely used in Finland and maize in the US. There are also many other, more obscure base ingredients for vodka, such as beets, onions, and a whole variety of other plants. The base ingredient is cooked and mixed with water and yeast to begin fermentation and create a "wash". The wash is then distilled, sometimes in a pot still (a kettle-like structure), which allows the vodka to retain some of the character of its base ingredients, but more often in a patent still. The latter uses continuous distillation, a process that purifies the spirit in one go. Since 1780, many producers have also filtered the distillate through charcoal to remove any impurities that might be left after distillation.

BLACK GOLD *Ice-cold vodka is the classic partner for the finest beluga caviar – often called "black gold".*

Once the spirit is made it is diluted with water to adjust its alcoholic strength – usually down to 40% ABV. If the vodka is a flavoured style, the flavouring agents are added at this stage. The biggest-selling vodkas remain those that are largely clear and

---

DRINKING AND SERVING

DRINK PROFILE In the US and western Europe we are used to drinking vodka that is neutral in taste and aroma; but eastern Europe provides an array of vodkas that are quite different from one another.

C COLOUR Classic vodka is, of course, clear, colourless, and crystalline. Flavoured vodkas will reflect their additives, from pale yellow for lemon vodka to black for liquorice.

A AROMA Wheat vodkas often have distinct aromas of aniseed, and rye vodkas have a nutty sweetness. Other aromas are vanilla, flowers, citrus, and perhaps herbs and tobacco.

T TASTE Vodkas from Russia, Poland, and the Baltic states retain the flavours of their original grain, and new Western vodkas, such as Ketel One, are becoming more spicy and distinctive.

BUYING AND STORING Vodka is easy to produce and is not aged, so it tends to be the cheapest of the spirits. Be cautious about how you choose an expensive vodka – often price is a reflection of the quality of the packaging rather than the drink. Vodka does not improve in the bottle.

SERVING SUGGESTIONS Vodka is extremely flexible. Drink it with tonic as an apéritif, or in any number of cocktails. It has become fashionable to serve vodka frozen – which is great for a party. Vodka can be drunk neat (a good brand will make an excellent digestif), but it is less common to do so. When you do, use a shot glass.

FOOD COMPANIONS In Russia, chilled vodka is often served with *zakuski* – appetizers – such as slivers of smoked fish or spicy mushrooms.

unflavoured. However, many Polish vodkas, and some major worldwide brands, such as Absolut, provide a range of flavoured spirits. These might contain anything from herbs and spices, such as vanilla, through citrus and other fruits, to more unusual flavours such as cucumber! Although normally clear, these vodkas have a delicate flavour of the additive – lemon vodka is one of the most popular. Flavoured vodkas are well worth seeking out and can add a twist to a vodka cocktail.

THE VODKA WORLD

In the late-20th century, Russian vodkas (which for marketing purposes include vodkas from the former Soviet Union) have launched themselves on the world, and some – such as Stolichnaya – are now established greats.

In Poland, the former state monopoly Polmos, which took over all spirit distilleries during the communist era, has been broken up into many separate, independent vodka enterprises, which market a range of well-known brands such as Wyborowa, and also luxury and flavoured brands, such as Chopin, Polonaise, and Belvedere.

Sweden has given us Absolut vodka – a masterpiece of lifestyle advertising – which led the way for other sophisticated campaigns for vodka from elsewhere in the world, Finlandia from Finland being just one.

Although the US and other European countries are traditionally importers of vodka, their cool climates are perfect for vodka-making and we are now seeing a growth in other brands such as Ketel One (from Holland), Grey Goose (from France), and Skyy and Hangar One (from the US).

THE COSMOPOLITAN *Vodka, triple sec, and cranberry juice combine to make this classic vodka cocktail. The purity and clarity of vodka make it the most essential of all cocktail bases.*

THE ABSOLUT ICEBAR *Carved entirely from ice, the bar at the Nordic Hotel in Stockholm, Sweden, is a remarkable structure. The bar is the epitome of modern vodka culture, which has been inspired by the marketing genius of Absolut – a brand aimed at a new generation of vodka drinkers.*

POLAND

Vodka is produced in both grain- and potato-based varieties in Poland, which are graded by purity: *zwykly* (standard), *wyborowy* (premium), and *luksusowy* (deluxe). Richer and bolder in flavour than Western brands, Polish vodka has a unique complexity that is best appreciated without a mixer.

POTOCKI

POTOCKI

C COLOUR Clear, in a smart modern bottle with the distinctive cross.

A AROMA Subtle, with hints of rye bread and nuts.

T TASTE Complex and delicate, with nuts, rye, and a touch of sweetness.

The Potocki family have been making vodka for centuries, but their fame extends well beyond the distillation of spirit. Polish aristocrats, with estates at Lancut (southern Poland) and Antoniny (eastern Poland), the Potocki family once rubbed shoulders with the highest officials of Austria's Habsburg Empire – including Emperor Franz Josef. One of the family, Jozef Potocki, represented Poland at the Russian Parliament after 1905, and it is his signature that is embossed on each bottle of Potocki vodka.

The distillery at the Lancut estate produced vodkas, rums, and liqueurs from 1816 up to the Communist period (beginning in 1944). However, in 2002 Jan-Roman Potocki re-launched his family's vodka brand. He wanted to produce a high-quality vodka for the Western market, made using traditional techniques and little or no filtering to retain the natural flavours of the rye. He has succeeded: the new Potocki is already an award-winner.

Potocki is altogether much richer than Western vodkas. It has the distinctive aromas of rye bread and nuts, and its taste is velvety, smooth, and complex, with a slightly nutty feel.

I prefer to drink Potocki chilled (but not frozen) to bring out the complexity of the flavours. Try drinking it straight, as an accompaniment to foods such as caviar, smoked fish, or mildly sweet pastries.

LAND AND PRODUCTION

MAKING WÓDKA In Poland vodka (*wódka*) is made using grains (often rye or wheat) or potatoes. Whereas many countries launder out all the ingredients' residual flavours to create pure, flavourless alcohol, in Poland producers rectify their vodka to remove the unpleasant tastes of the by-products of fermentation, such as aldehydes, while retaining some sense of the spirit's original ingredients. The results tend to be richer on the palate.

ZYTNIA

C COLOUR Clear with a slight golden tinge, from the addition of apple brandy.

A AROMA Very attractive and unusual, with a sweet, toffee-apple nose.

T TASTE Velvety; good balance of grain and fruit; mineral and apple finish.

One of the best-selling Polish vodkas, Extra Zytnia is a rye vodka with a firmer flavour than most Western vodkas. However, it is special mostly because it contains a small amount of fruit juice and aged apple brandy, which gives this vodka a fruity nose and a slight tinge of gold.

Zytnia is owned by Polmos Bielsko (based in Silesia, western Poland), which works in partnership with Bacardi Martini – making this brand readily available throughout the world. Drink it straight, or add it to a cocktail for a little extra zing.

ULTIMAT

C COLOUR Clear, in a distinctive, vivid blue decanter.

A AROMA Elegant and complex, with a balance of earth and citrus.

T TASTE Oily and quite dry; medium body; baked bread, grain, and pepper.

Ultimat is an extremely special vodka – with a price tag to match. It is the first vodka to blend rye, wheat, and potato spirits in one drink. The rye gives complexity and flavour; the wheat, delicacy and subtlety; and the potatoes (which provide 70 per cent of the spirit in the blend), smoothness and body. Aimed mainly at US drinkers, Ultimat is marketed as the perfect vodka: smooth, with a fiery kick. It comes in a Polish-style decanter sealed with a cork – pure luxury.

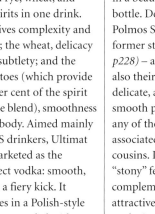

ULTIMAT

CHOPIN

C COLOUR Clear, in an elegant, tall, white, frosted bottle.

A AROMA Complex, with a balanced mix of flint and minerals.

T TASTE Oily; citrus, mint, and a touch of sweetness; potato and pepper finish.

Chopin is aimed at a new generation of vodka drinkers. It is classy, smart, and well marketed in a beautiful, elegant, white bottle. Deliberately created by Polmos Siedlce – one of the former state distilleries *(see p228)* – as a luxury brand, and also their flagship, this is a delicate, approachable, and smooth potato vodka, without any of the fire or rough edge associated with many of its cousins. It has an attractive "stony" feel, which is perfectly complemented by an equally attractive oily texture. This is a relaxing vodka to serve over ice and to sip gently.

LUKSUSOWA

C COLOUR Crystal clear, in a clear bottle with an icy feel.

A AROMA Strong pungent lemon and sugar (Citrus vodka).

T TASTE Oily; sweet, then drier lemony notes; long, dry finish (Citrus vodka).

Luksusowa, produced by the Polmos Poznan distillery, is an excellent potato vodka, worthy of its translated name "luxury". However, Luksusowa is best-known for excellent flavoured vodkas. Luksusowa Citrus has a beautifully integrated lemon character, which is firmer and stronger than many flavoured brands. The wild-berry vodka is flavoured with blackberries, cherries, raspberries, blueberries, and cranberries, all of them wonderfully evident in its aromas. If you find these too fruity to drink straight, try them in tonic or soda water.

LUKSUSOWA

WYBOROWA

C COLOUR Clear and very pure, in a clear bottle with a striking, striped label.

A AROMA Elegant, with rye, citrus, and minerals in perfect balance.

T TASTE Smooth, mellow, nutty; stony; a hint of toffee sweetness; smooth finish.

Wyborowa, meaning "choice", is one of the great brands of Polish vodka. A rye-grain vodka made originally by Polmos Poznan, a former state distillery (see p228), its production began more than 80 years ago. However, when Polmos Poznan went bankrupt in the 1990s, Pernod Ricard saved Wyborowa by buying it out. The new owners have shown great respect towards the long traditions of Wyborowa and have kept the product unchanged.

The rye-grain spirit is triple-distilled and then triple-filtered through charcoal. The resulting vodka is clean with a lemony zest. The rye is always there, but it does not dominate; and both the aromas and the taste are complex, with a great balance of nuttiness, spice, and sweetness. (Although never sugary – a simple sweet feel comes from the rye itself.) Like all great grain vodkas, it has a balanced bite. Overall this vodka is smooth and powerful – and a favourite with bartenders, who know it makes a great cocktail.

Wyborowa now also makes flavoured vodkas, which come in lemon, orange, pineapple, peach, melon, and pepper. Zubrówka (see p228), a herb-flavoured vodka, is also part of the Wyborowa family.

VODKA CLASSIC *If you like traditional, powerful Polish vodka, full of character, look no further than Wyborowa. Serve it over ice, with lime.*

BELVEDERE / LANCUT

C COLOUR Clear, in an elegant frosted bottle (Belvedere).

A AROMA Spice, citrus, caraway, herbs, grains, vanilla, and spirits.

T TASTE Silky and smooth, with a crisp freshness and a light finish.

During the Communist era, Polish vodkas were all made by the state distiller known as Polmos. In the 1990s, when Communism was overthrown, the new democratic government privatized the Polmos distilleries. Although the quality of vodka had generally been very high, some of these newly independent distilleries now produce truly excellent vodka – in fact, among the best in the world.

One of these is Polmos Belvedere, a premium vodka, made from rye

BELVEDERE

that is quadruple distilled. The result is an internationally successful vodka that is very clear, crisp, and fresh, with a great complexity.

Belvedere also makes a range of fruit vodkas, such as orange-flavoured Pomarancza. Like its brother, it is clean and refreshing (and not over-sweet), with a delicious orange finish – excellent! Cytrus is also very good, with a lemon flavour that is not overpowering.

Another Polmos brand to look out for is Lancut. Made from neutral grain spirits and artesian water, it is crystal clear with perfect balance – a vodka full of flavour but delicate and cool. The Lancut distillery also produces CK, which is a brilliant, spicy brew of cinnamon, toffee, and black pepper. This is definitely not a mixing vodka: sip it and savour it slowly – over ice.

THE STORY OF POLMOS In 1896 the Polish government first introduced a state monopoly for the production and sale of spirits, leading ultimately in 1924 to the creation of the state's Polish Spirits' Monopoly (Polmos). Essentially, the state had established the exclusive right to buy and sell the country's liquor. However, Communism was on borrowed time and after the emergence of many illegal unions, which protested heavily and often angrily for workers' rights, in 1980 workers formed the legal trade union, Solidarity, led by Lech Walesa. At the end of the 1980s Communism was overturned and Lech Walesa elected president. Eventually, Polmos would sell off its 25 distilleries, all of which became private enterprises, producing vodka in a new, democratic Poland.

ABSOLWENT

C COLOUR Clear, in traditional eastern European packaging.

A AROMA Quite aromatic; grain, minerals, and citrus in fine balance.

T TASTE Very full and powerful; smooth with a warm finish.

Absolwent is a traditional, pure-grain vodka and the flagship brand of the Polmos Bialystock distillery, in eastern Poland. The grain is carefully distilled and mildly filtered. There are about 80 different products in the Absolwent range, and Poles love them for their classic vodka attributes (they are full, warm, and uncompromising) and for their excellent value. Entirely unlike the neutral spirits of the West, this vodka will hold its own in any long drink, or give you an unforgettable experience as a straight short.

STARKA

C COLOUR Unusual dark golden amber, a result of oak-ageing.

A AROMA Complex and well-balanced; vanilla, fruit, and herbs.

T TASTE Rich and full of flavour; tannin, oak, and fruit; smooth with a long finish.

In both Russian and Polish, *starka* means "the old one", and starka vodka is not a brand or a distillery, but a type. The style has grown out of the tradition of "laying down" vodka spirit in wine casks to celebrate an event, such as the birth of a child.

The ageing in oak casks turns the spirit whisky-like, with a golden colour and great smoothness. There are several Polish brands, usually aged for at least five years. Look out for Polmos Krakowska or Polmos Szczecin.

STARKA

ZUBRÓWKA

C COLOUR Pale greeny yellow, with a blade of bison grass.

A AROMA Delicate, with grass, lavender, thyme, and flowers.

T TASTE Dry; light-bodied; herbs; citrus; slightly sweet.

Originating in the 17th century, Zubrówka is dry – and one of the greatest of all flavoured vodkas. Each bottle of Zubrowka contains a blade of European bison grass, which has a distinctive fragrance, and was once used to flavour tobacco, cakes, and beverages. The grass gives the vodka a greeny yellow colour, and a delicate herbal aroma – like freshly mown grass – bringing the vodka to life. This is really something special, and a "must-try" among vodkas.

ZUBRÓWKA

SOBIESKI

C COLOUR Clear, in a round, Polish-style bottle with a traditional feel.

A AROMA Complex and balanced, with minerals, citrus, and grain.

T TASTE Smooth, oily; great elegance and class; lemon, baked bread; spicy finish.

This award-winning rye vodka is named after the 17th-century King of Poland Jan Sobieski III. The vodka is distilled four times, making it exceptionally smooth.

This is a traditional vodka in all ways, from its packaging to its warm finish. The vodka is not over-filtered and purified as some modern versions can be, so it has some distinct, even powerful, rye flavours and a bit of a bite.

If you like your vodka to stand up for itself then this is definitely one to drink straight. However, I prefer Sobieski in a long drink, to give the flavour a chance to come through in a slightly cooler, more subtle way.

RUSSIA

After the fall of Communism, Russian vodkas firmly established themselves on the world market. A range of brands in export (*osobaya*) and strong (*krepkaya*) grades are now available in the West, including familiar favourites like Stolichnaya. Deluxe vodkas, such as Youri Dolgoruky, are multi-distilled and made to a high specification, and sell at a much higher price.

STOLICHNAYA

C   **COLOUR**   Clear, in the familiar clear bottle with a white, red, and gold label.

A   **AROMA**   Complex and elegant; vanilla, aniseed, and citrus.

T   **TASTE**   Quite oily; very smooth; medium-bodied; citrus, spice; long peppery finish.

The number of Russian vodkas for sale inside and outside the country is almost uncountable; but of them all, Stolichnaya is among the very best. Known to its many fans as Stoli, this vodka combines subtlety and complexity with power and taste – exactly as a good vodka should.

The word *stolichnaya* means "from the big city" and, true to its name, the vodka is made in Moscow, at Russia's oldest distillery. It is distilled from winter wheat, and made with natural glacier water. The spirit is filtered through charcoal, like most other vodkas, but then it is filtered again – twice through quartz and once through cloth. The result of this extra filtering is a superior, smooth, and clear vodka.

Stolichnaya has a strong aniseed and lemon aroma, with notes of sweetness. The vodka feels velvety on the palate, but always with a powerful, peppery edge. This is such a classy vodka that I often like to drink it straight – like the Russians themselves – but it also tastes good mixed with juice, tonic, or soda water, or as the base for a Black Russian cocktail *(see p366)*.

Stolichnaya also make a range of fruit-flavoured vodkas. All are clear and colourless spirits, but the fruit character of each is extremely distinctive. The dry and fruity Stoli Persik is peach vodka; Citros, very clean and fresh, is lemon; Strasberi is like strawberry sorbet, with a nutty, peppery character; Vanil (my favourite and great in a cocktail) is luscious and creamy with a feel of vanilla ice-cream, but not so sweet as to be cloying; Cranberi (one to try with turkey!) has a rich, sweet start, with a dry, red-berry finish; Ohranj is light and delicate, with just a hint of orange, and delicious over ice with soda water; and the Razberi (raspberry) is dry, ripe, and smooth.

LIKE ICE *Serve your Stolichnaya ice cold in a shot glass. Sip it to let its powerful flavours unravel on your palate.*

FLAGSHIP

- **C COLOUR** Clear, in a smart, clear bottle; label colour indicates the type.
- **A AROMA** Elegant, with grain, citrus, and spirit.
- **T TASTE** Full-bodied and smooth; with a dry and spicy feel.

Flagship is one of Russia's best vodkas, and experiencing rapid growth throughout Europe.

The company produces the Flagship Classic (blue label), Supreme Staff (white label; made with added oats to give it a velvety feel), and Night Landing (black label; lemon-flavoured), as well as nastoyskas (bitter vodkas), with herbs and spices. Each vodka is made with spring water, which helps to retain quality and softness, and is triple-distilled. The results are fresh and clean, and delicious neat or in cocktails.

FLAGSHIP

JEWEL OF RUSSIA

- **C COLOUR** Clear (also deep red for the Wild Bilberry fruit vodka).
- **A AROMA** Fruit, melon, minerals, and spice.
- **T TASTE** Very smooth and oily with a warm finish.

Jewel of Russia is made from rye and winter wheat to give fresh tastes and a smooth palate. The Classic is satisfying and creamy, with vanilla, nuts, and spice.

Try it straight or in a Martini. The company's most exclusive product is the Ultra. This special vodka undergoes extra filtering to make it especially crisp, as well as strong and complex, warm, and smooth.

Of the fruit vodkas try the Wild Bilberry Infusion. The berries blend perfectly and overall the vodka has great balance. Drink it over ice.

ALTAÏ

- **C COLOUR** Clear, with a deep blue label featuring the icy Altaï mountains.
- **A AROMA** Delicate, with aniseed, flowers, fruit, citrus, and minerals.
- **T TASTE** Rounded; medium-bodied; citrus, vanilla, pepper; elegant, smooth finish.

All vodkas like to be marketed as "icy", and Altaï vodka comes from one of the iciest parts of the world – at the foot of the Golden Mountains in the Altaï region of western Siberia.

Established in 1887, but now part of the Pernod Ricard drinks group, Altaï is an award-winning brand making waves on the international stage, especially in France. The vodka is exceptionally smooth, with strong wheat flavours. It is an excellent vodka to sip neat, deeply chilled, from a shot glass.

ALTAÏ

IKON

- **C COLOUR** Clear, in smart, modern pale blue-and-orange packaging.
- **A AROMA** Fresh, delicate, and pure; citrus, toffee, oranges, and flowers.
- **T TASTE** Medium-bodied; spice, minerals, vanilla; a citrus and pepper finish.

With a string of awards to its name, Ikon is not only one of the best vodkas in Russia, but also one that is really making its mark elsewhere in the world – particularly in the US.

First made in 1862, Ikon is a quadruple-distilled, premium-grain vodka. Fresh and delicate, it has the slightly oily, mineral feel that is typical of the Russian spirit. However, it is also really smooth, with no "burn" on the back of the throat as you drink. This is one of my favourites. Give it a try – I think you will love it.

YOURI DOLGORUKI

- **C COLOUR** Clear, in a modern-style, frosted glass bottle.
- **A AROMA** Subtle, with spice, citrus, grain, and a hint of chocolate.
- **T TASTE** Extremely full, mellow, and oily; firm texture; long, dry finish.

Youri Dolgoruki is one of the newest brands from the Cristall distillery. Once state-owned, but privatized at the end of the Soviet Union, Cristall now markets many vodkas throughout the world.

Luxurious, complex, and stylish, Youri Dolgoruki boasts Russian strength and oiliness with the subtle approach enjoyed by vodka drinkers elsewhere in the world. Cristall has an unrivalled reputation for excellence (it also produces Stolichnaya), and "Youri" is great mixed or straight.

SPUTNIK

- **C COLOUR** Colourless; pale yellow for Sputnik Gold.
- **A AROMA** Delicate and quite floral, with hints of grain.
- **T TASTE** Light and fresh, with a sweet note at the finish.

Recently launched in the UK, Sputnik is the flagship brand of Russian Vodka House, whose primary purpose is to market Russian vodka in the West. It is definitely one to watch.

Sputnik is a wheat vodka, made in Russia from an authentic recipe and then triple-distilled to 40% ABV. Every effort is made to filter out impurities and create a vodka with a fresh, clean feel. The company also produces Sputnik Gold. This has added honey and pepper, to give a richer and more mellow spirit.

SPUTNIK

BELARUS

Belarus was formerly a western region of the Soviet Union, but today enjoys a fruitful independence. Many vodkas from ex-Soviet states are sold as Russian but Belarus has already established a world-class brand with its own identity.

CHARODEI

- **C COLOUR** Clear, in a cool, opaque glass bottle with distinctive red lettering.
- **A AROMA** Very intense; citrus, grass, herbs, and grain.
- **T TASTE** Medium-bodied; soft and smooth, with a long, clean finish.

Although Charodei is a vodka in the Russian style, it is actually made in Minsk, now the capital of Belarus.

Named after a fictional Russian hero-wizard (rather like Merlin from Arthurian legend), Charodei is one of the best vodkas in the world. It is wonderfully smooth, without losing its firm character and distinctive herbal and citrus flavours. In fact it achieves the very thing to which all great vodkas aspire: strong, powerful flavour and a kick that does not sacrifice smooth coolness.

During its production, Charodei is filtered through a flint-like mineral known as Cremia, which allows the liquid to retain its taste. To make a bottle of Charodei takes a month – two weeks to filter the water, and another two for the spirit.

A superb, multi-award-winner, you could put this in a cocktail, but it is truly excellent on its own.

CHARODEI

FINLAND

Finnish vodka came of age with the launch of Finlandia in 1970. In recent years, products such as Pramia (a vodka-based fruit "breezer") have joined it on the world stage. Finnish vodkas use barley as a base.

FINLANDIA

C COLOUR Clear, in a distinctive, shaped bottle with an icy feel.

A AROMA Fresh and lively, with hints of lime and citrus.

T TASTE Elegant and bright, with a dry, nutty feel and a spicy bite at the finish.

Finlandia is a barley vodka made with pure glacial spring water. In 1971 this was the first vodka to be imported into the US on a large scale, and it is now the country's third-largest imported vodka, behind Absolut and Stolichnaya. Although the production of Finlandia is controlled by the

Finnish company Altia, the vodka is owned and distributed by Brown-Forman, which also owns Jack Daniel's whiskey and Southern Comfort; this makes it widely available throughout the world.

Made using water from a glacial spring, Finlandia is marketed as the spirit of pure, ice-age water. Unusually, the water is not filtered before it is used to break down the spirit – the company claims that filtration would only impair its purity. However, the distillery is

FINLANDIA

highly sophisticated: barley is distilled into grain spirits using a continuous distillation system. Rather than going through several separate distillations, Finlandia has only one, but it is long (around 50 hours) and has several stages. The result is an extremely clean, fresh vodka – a vodka as pure as the water that makes it. This purity is enhanced by chilling the vodka – try a shot straight from the freezer.

There are also three fruit vodkas in the Finlandia range: Cranberry, Lime, and Mango. Finlandia Cranberry is smooth, with a delicious nose of fresh fruit. I like to spice up my cocktails with this little addition of berries. Finlandia Lime has been infused with fresh lime fruits, and squeezed lime oil. It has a subtle citrus flavour with delicate sweet notes. The Mango infusion is exotic and sweet, and perfect over ice or in a cocktail.

KOSKENKORVA

C COLOUR Clear for the unflavoured vodka; black for the Salmiakki.

A AROMA Delicate and fairly neutral; grain and mineral hints.

T TASTE Very fresh and neutral, with grain and spirit to the fore.

Koskenkorva was first made in 1953 from potatoes, but is now made from barley. It is a little sweeter than Finlandia, Finland's other big brand, which is also slightly richer and more complex. Koskenkorva vodka

is easy to drink – either short or long. Koskenkorva also produce *Salmiakki Koskenkorva*. This is a black vodka, made by infusing salty black liquorice in the vodka spirit – its launch caused something of a Finnish sensation!

KOSKENKORVA

SWEDEN

Vodka has a long history in Sweden, where it was originally known as *Brannvin* ("burnt wine"). The Absolut brand has been particularly successful, thanks to superb marketing and design. The best Swedish vodkas are made from wheat, providing a clean, neutral character.

ABSOLUT

C COLOUR Clear, in the world-famous medicine-style bottle.

A AROMA Light, clean, and neutral; varies for the flavoured vodkas.

T TASTE Light-bodied, rich, and smooth, with notes of wheat.

Absolut is the world's third-largest vodka brand (and the number-one imported vodka in the US). Its mastermind was Lars Olsen Smith, who introduced continuous distillation to Sweden. (The spirit is distilled just once, but in several stages and over many hours, giving an especially pure, fresh taste.) In 1879 Smith launched his new

brand Absolut Rent Brannvin (Absolute Pure Vodka), a zesty, lighter spirit to challenge the state-monopoly vodkas. In 1979 the Swedish company Vin & Sprit launched Absolut in the US, then onto the world markets.

Absolut Vodka owes much of its success to perfect timing and excellent marketing. Launched when drinkers wanted something lighter than traditional, powerful vodkas, Absolut is a culture

ABSOLUT

as well as a drink. Its medicine-bottle shape even implies that drinking vodka might just be good for your health!

The vodka is made from wheat to give a good-quality spirit that is quite neutral and dry, but also characteristically clean and fresh.

In the 1990s, Absolut was faced with a new challenge from a new crop of super-premium vodkas with even more style and character. The best of these are Skyy from the US (*see p234*), Grey Goose from France (*see p233*), and Belvedere (*see p228*) and Chopin (*see p226*) from Poland. In the face of this competition, Absolut launched a range of flavoured vodkas, all of which are excellent (many bartenders swear by them for their cocktails). Try the aromatic and spicy Absolut Peppar, which has a peppery nose and finish; or Absolut Citron – flavoured mainly with lemon, but also with a hint of lime

and other citrus flavours, making it full and fresh. For something dark, deeply fruity, and sweet, try Absolut Kurant (black-currant); or try Absolut Mandrin for a sweet vodka flavoured with orange-dominated citrus fruits. Absolut Vanilla is the Chardonnay of vodkas, buttery and rich; while Absolut Raspberri has delicious red-fruit flavours without being too sweet.

In whatever way you take your Absolut (straight or in a cocktail), you are guaranteed a great vodka.

In 2004, V&S launched Level in the US, a super-premium vodka designed to compete at the luxury end of the market. Marketed in a taller, leaner, frosted version of the classic Absolut bottle, V&S claims that the double distillation process gives both a smoothness and a fruity, citrus edge to Level vodka. For a vodka to sip and savour on its own, why not give Level a try?

LEVEL

UK

Culturally, whisky and gin have deeper roots in Britain than vodka, although the rise of the cocktail has boosted vodka sales in the UK. The market is still dominated by the big international brands, but UK-made premium vodkas are also worth a try.

GRAFFITI

C COLOUR Clear; packaged in a smart, modern bottle.

A AROMA Delicate; nuts and aniseed, with hints of malt.

T TASTE Lively, fresh; full-bodied with a grainy character; dry finish.

For many years, vodka in the UK meant Smirnoff – for many drinkers, other brands were virtually unheard of. However, the popularity of vodka has led to the launch of more brands into the British market – including Graffiti, which hit the shelves in 2002.

GRAFFITI

Marketed as a premium vodka, Graffiti does not aim to be "firewater" – it is not a vodka that has to be tempered with cola or juice. Uniquely, Graffiti is made by distilling not only wheat, but also malted barley in patent stills. As vodkas go, it is especially smooth – rather like a whisky, but without the oak-ageing – and bright and lively, with the malt adding an attractive complexity. This is a vodka for everyday drinking, when you are looking for something light and fresh.

DENMARK

Denmark is best-known for the caraway-flavoured spirit aquavit, but it also makes good wheat vodkas, like those of Sweden.

DANZKA

C COLOUR Clear; in a distinctive aluminium container, rather than a bottle.

A AROMA Delicate, attractive, and subtle, with grain and faint herbs.

T TASTE Clean and pure; light and refreshing with a warm finish.

Danzka, produced by Danish Distillers, is a clear and clean wheat vodka. The unflavoured version is available at 40% or 50% ABV. The company also produces flavoured vodkas, including lemon, black-currant, and grapefruit, and the premium brand Fris, which is especially smooth.

ICELAND

Vodka is a relatively new product in Iceland. Based on barley grain, it resembles Finnish vodka brands in taste and style.

POLSTAR

C COLOUR Clear for the unflavoured vodkas; pale green for the Cucumber.

A AROMA Delicate; hints of aniseed, citrus; varied for the flavoured vodkas.

T TASTE Quite strong, creamy, and distinctive; hints of honey and orange.

Polstar is a grain vodka, triple-distilled, and blended with water drawn deep from within the volcanic rocks of Iceland. Polstar make a range of strengths, from 37.5% to 45% ABV, and flavoured vodkas. The most famous is Cucumber – just like a cucumber sandwich. You have to try it once!

HOLLAND

The Dutch have great distilling expertise, and they are now making a number of top-flight vodkas, such as Ketel One.

ROYALTY

C COLOUR Clear; presented in a smart, modern, blue bottle.

A AROMA Full and complex, with grain, toffee, and minerals.

T TASTE Rich, full, and elegant; with minerals and a touch of spice.

Royalty comes from Holland's Hooghoudt Distillers. It is made from wheat and filtered through charcoal five times to give a delicate smoothness, with a mineral feel and slight sweetness. It is bolder than many Polish vodkas, and firmer than "new" vodkas, such as Grey Goose. One of my favourites, Royalty makes perfect sipping over a little ice.

VOX

C COLOUR Clear, in an unusual and distinctive mottled glass bottle.

A AROMA Fresh and light with citrus, grass, liquorice, and herbs.

T TASTE Quite full-bodied with a smoky, spicy, peppery feel.

This wheat vodka has been a big success in the US and, although made in Holland, is owned by whiskey-maker Jim Beam. Vox is classy, modern, and smart, with quality and complexity. The aromas are light and delicate, and there is no burn on the throat when you drink it – this vodka is refreshing and cool all the way through.

Vox Raspberry is also clear, but the raspberry sweetens the spirit to make this flavoured version even smoother than the original.

These are great additions to the vodka market, and I love them!

KETEL ONE

C COLOUR Clear, in a distinctive retro-style, tall, glass "crock".

A AROMA Complex and well-balanced, with grain, citrus, and spice.

T TASTE Very full-bodied and powerful; oily and fulfilling; long, clean finish.

KETEL ONE

Launched in 1992 by the Dutch Nolet family, who have been making spirits for more than 300 years, Ketel One is a traditional-style grain vodka made in pot stills, and not by continuous distillation as with most vodkas (see p224). The result is a vodka with excellent balance and a fine, mineral taste. I am a big fan!

Launched in 2000, Ketel One Citroen is even better – complex, round, smooth, and clean on the palate. The citrus aromas are balanced with flowers, minerals, herbs, anise, and pepper.

BELGIUM

This small country is justly famous for its world-class beers, but there are also one or two Belgian vodkas worth trying.

VAN HOO

C COLOUR Clear, packaged in a sleek, tapered, royal-blue bottle.

A AROMA Complex; citrus, juniper, lime, mineral, and pepper.

T TASTE Quite full-bodied and oily; but also soft and quite approachable.

The oldest distillery in Belgium, Van Hoo has been producing spirits since 1740. It produces ultra-premium vodka made in the traditional manner – distilled four times and filtered through charcoal.

Although Van Hoo is quite strong (45% ABV) it is a well-balanced and sophisticated vodka, with a smooth feel and rich texture.

FRANCE

Vodka might be the last drink you would associate with France, but the north of the country has a long tradition of distilling grain spirits, and the French are second-to-none at blending and quality control. The excellent Grey Goose brand is now popular worldwide.

GREY GOOSE

C COLOUR Clear, in an opaque bottle with the emblem of flying grey geese.

A AROMA Attractive; gentle alcohol spirit, apple, pear, and honey.

T TASTE Silky and smooth: flowers, vanilla, and cream; soft finish.

Made in Cognac, France, Grey Goose was recently awarded a fantastic 96 points by the Beverage Tasting Industry – from me it gets 100 points every time! Since 1997 the American-owned company Sidney Frank have turned Grey Goose into the US's best-selling premium vodka.

GREY GOOSE

In June 2004, Sidney Frank sold the brand to Bacardi.

Grey Goose is made not from a single grain, but from a blend of corn, wheat, rye, and barley. It utilizes the expert blending skills of local Cognac-makers, and, like Cognac, is produced using the pot-still process (see p224). The spirit is filtered through limestone, giving it a freshness that balances the richness of the grain – perfect! Grey Goose comes in original and flavoured versions, and all are winners.

USA

US vodka is often quite neutral in taste, but in recent years characterful regional brands from California and Kentucky have made headway in the domestic market. Some brands like Teton use potatoes to make their vodka – a clear challenge to the Poles!

HANGAR ONE

C COLOUR Clear (the Straight); hints of colour for the fruit infusions.

A AROMA Distinctive; fine balance of citrus and grapey fruit aromas.

T TASTE Fantastically rich and complex; smooth and beautifully balanced.

Hangar One is named after the place where it all began – Hangar 1 at the Almeda Naval Air Station, San Francisco. Believing that skilled brandy-blenders could produce superior vodkas, Jorg Rupf, owner of St. George Spirits, and expert fruit-brandy maker Ansley Coale set about making a series of carefully crafted

pot-still grain vodkas flavoured with real fruit infusions. The unflavoured Straight contains vodka distilled from Viognier wine, and is smooth, with citric overtones. The Buddha's Hand Citron, Kaffir Lime, and Mandarin Blossom are all lush with distinct but delicate flavours of their fruits. Fraser River Raspberry is infused with raspberries, and following redistillation, raspberry juice is reintroduced to enhance the aromas.

HANGAR ONE

CHARBAY

C COLOUR Clear; subtle shades of colour for the fruit-flavoured vodkas.

A AROMA Very delicate and subtle; minerals; grainy aromas.

T TASTE Oily, rounded; minerals and grain; quite stony; slightly bitter finish.

Charbay vodka is made in Napa Valley, California, by the Domaine Charbay Winery and Distillery. This small producer makes its vodkas entirely from American grain, distilled to high levels of purity. There is little filtration, and the result is a rounded, clean spirit.

The company is famed for its flavoured vodkas, such as Blood Orange, Meyer Lemon, and Ruby Red Grapefruit. Distillation takes place only in the peak of the fruit's season to ensure that only the ripest fruit is infused into the spirit. The results are of superb quality.

CHARBAY

TETON GLACIER

C COLOUR Clear and pure, packaged in a smart, decanter-shaped bottle.

A AROMA Quite neutral aromas, with subtle hints of mineral.

T TASTE Fairly oily; medium-bodied; hints of vanilla and potato; clean, smooth.

Most people think of Poland when they think of potato vodka. However, the recent explosion of US interest in vodka has led to American distillers experimenting with making vodka from ingredients other than grain, and Teton Glacier is potato vodka from Idaho.

Teton Glacier is particularly clean and smooth, with the potato giving an unusual depth and complexity. It is much less harsh than many grain vodkas, but also not too aromatic, making it an excellent mixer, especially in a Martini.

RAIN

C COLOUR Crystal clear, and presented in a long-necked bottle.

A AROMA Delicate; sweet, sugary nose, with a touch of spice.

T TASTE Light- to medium-bodied; apple, toffee, nuts; warm finish.

Rain vodka is produced in Kentucky by the same company that makes the excellent Buffalo Trace Bourbon, and is the only vodka made exclusively from organic American grain.

The Rain Vodka distillery claims to be the oldest in the US, and its super-premium, high-quality vodka was first launched in 1997, after its creators realized that the vodka cocktails they were drinking one rainy night just did not taste as good as they should. The company ensures that it does everything it possibly can to keep the quality of the spirit as high as

RAIN

possible, and the production standards are second-to-none. The grain is mashed, cooked, cooled, and fermented (fermentation is set off using organic yeast cultivated by the Rain distillery), and then quadruple distilled to ensure that only the purest spirit makes it through to have its strength adjusted with natural limestone water. Filtration is not only through charcoal, like most other vodkas, but also through diamond dust!

The result is a pure vodka that is quite sweet and spicy, and extremely soft and smooth. It is beautifully presented in a sleek, elongated bottle, shaped like a drop of rain, and aimed at the new generation of vodka drinkers – Rain is a world away from the macho style of hard-hitting, fiery vodkas.

If you want something ultra-modern and ultra-cool, there is no question that Rain is the one for you.

SKYY VODKA

C COLOUR Clear, in the world-famous deep blue bottle.

A AROMA Quite neutral and delicate; grain and mineral hints.

T TASTE Light, fresh, and smooth, with a great balance of flavours.

US inventor Maurice Kanbar created Skyy Vodka in 1988 to be as clean and filtered as possible, and (according to the slogan) "hangover free".

Skyy is a grain vodka that has been triple-distilled and quadruple-filtered. It is deliberately neutral, making it approachable and smooth, without the rough power of traditional Polish or Russian vodkas. It is perfect for a long drink or a cocktail.

Skyy's flavoured vodkas are great – not overly complex, but fun. Among the best are the Melon – a blend of honeydew and cantaloupe melons, and watermelon, creating a delicious, refreshing vodka that reminds me of mixing drinks in the garden in summer; and the Berry – a blend of raspberry, blueberry, and blackberry, giving a deep fruity taste, perfect for mixing with lemonade or soda water. The Spiced, made with cinnamon, nutmeg, and cloves, is marketed as an alternative to spiced rum and definitely worth a try.

MIXING IT UP

PERFECT MARTINI To make a really good Martini you need a vodka that is pure, clean, and fresh – making the triple-distilled, four-times filtered Skyy absolutely perfect. Chill the vodka until it is frosty cold; mix and serve the cocktail in a Martini glass, with a green olive.

COBALT BLUE *Skyy vodka is now part of the Campari group and competes fiercely in the international market. Part of its successful marketing strategy is the stunning cobalt-blue bottle, introduced in 1993.*

CANADA

Canada makes more rye whiskey than vodka, but has developed some interesting brands. One uses water from melted icebergs!

PEARL

C COLOUR Clear, in a simple and elegant colourless bottle with a black label.

A AROMA Wheat and a hint of citrus and minerals.

T TASTE Light, fresh; rice and grain, with a cool, oily, and full finish.

Award-winning Pearl is made from Canadian wheat, blended with the pure water from Canada's Arctic north. Modern, clean, fresh, and lively, Pearl can be drunk straight, but is so cool that it can even be used in a Martini or Cosmopolitan.

ICEBERG

C COLOUR Clear, in icy blue-and-white packaging.

A AROMA Delicate, with grain, herbs, spice, and minerals.

T TASTE Very clean, and quite light-bodied, with a creamy, nutty feel.

Iceberg is a premium vodka made from iceberg water and grain spirit. After harvesting and purifying the ice, the water is blended with triple-distilled neutral grain spirit, to give a pure and smooth vodka with a hint of sweetness. Iceberg is not deeply complex, but I like its purity. Drunk icy cold, this is a refreshing vodka, and as it is quite light, it also responds well to freezing.

ICEBERG

NEW ZEALAND

The South Island of New Zealand can be very chilly, and this cool "spirit" infuses the fashionable 42 Below brand, evoking a landscape of mountains and glaciers. The canny marketing was guided by the drink's creator, an advertising executive with a passion for vodka.

42 BELOW

C COLOUR Clear, in a crystal-clear bottle with an ultra-modern feel.

A AROMA Very sweet and creamy, with icing sugar and spirit.

T TASTE Light- to medium-bodied; smooth; fruit, citrus; warm finish.

Although we normally think of vodka as coming from the northern hemisphere, particularly from Russia, Finland, and Sweden, 42 Below is made way down in the southern hemisphere (42 degrees below the equator) – on New Zealand's South Island, making it the most southerly vodka in the world. Smart and stylish, this is a modern, luxury brand aimed at a new generation of sophisticated vodka-drinkers, and designed to appeal to both men and women.

42 Below is quadruple-distilled and broken down with pure volcanic spring water. Although it is strong (42% ABV), it is wonderfully smooth and, to suit the palate of its customers, it is approachable, with a sweet edge, a fruity feel, and a tingly finish. Drink 42 Below vodka on its own, over ice.

42 BELOW

INTERNATIONAL

Since the 1940s, neutral, medium-strength vodka has become popular all over the world for cocktails and long drinks. Smirnoff dominates this lucrative market, despite the current trend for charismatic Russian styles and sleek, designer brands.

SMIRNOFF

C COLOUR Clear, in a traditional bottle; coloured labels indicate the style.

A AROMA Light, clean, and neutral, with tinges of mint and fresh herbs.

T TASTE Light-bodied; rich and smooth, with notes of wheat.

For many people, the great name of Smirnoff is synonymous with vodka. Smirnoff's origins lie in 19th-century Moscow when Piotr Arsenyevitch Smirnov founded a vodka distillery, using a continuous still and charcoal-filtration (see p224) to make a cleaner, lighter, more approachable spirit than other Russian offerings. The results were wildly successful. In the 1880s and 1890s, Smirnov won many awards for his vodka, and became known worldwide as a master-distiller. His fame was such that he was given the right to use the Russian state coat of arms on his bottles. However, after the Russian Revolution in 1917, one of Smirnov's sons, Vladimir, fled Russia and his family. He ended up in Paris, where he continued to distil the family vodka, but he gave it the French version of his name – Smirnoff.

In the 1930s, production of Smirnoff was moved to the US and the brand was sold to an American company – strictly making it an American vodka. In the 1940s, Smirnoff became famous as "white whiskey" and formed the basis of the Moscow Mule cocktail (a mix of Smirnoff, ginger beer, and lime juice). Since the 1960s, Smirnoff has become the biggest brand in both the US and the world, and is now owned by Diageo. Meanwhile, after several legal challenges, Smirnov and Smirnoff are now both on sale in Russia.

The Smirnoff style epitomises Western vodka: it is clean and light, in body and taste. (The company claims that it also light on hangovers!). Smirnoff Red Label is the straight vodka. At 37.5% or 40% ABV, this makes a reliable base for any cocktail or long drink. Smirnoff Blue Label is stronger, ranging from between 45% and 50% ABV. This is for vodka fans who like their drink to "hit" them. It is more complex than the Red Label, with citrus, pepper, and smoke flavours, and a silky finish. Smirnoff Black Label is a traditional vodka that remembers the brand's Russian roots. It is made using 19th-century techniques, including pot stills and charcoal filtration. This is a mellow vodka, with a stronger, more powerful flavour than its brothers.

Smirnoff introduced its first flavoured vodka – Citrus Twist – in 1999. The portfolio now also includes Raspberry, Orange, Green Apple, and Vanilla. All of these make great cocktails, but Vanilla is my favourite as it has more depth and complexity than the others.

Smirnoff does not pretend to be a collector's classic, but it is great value, unwaveringly reliable, and always available – in other words, it is a truly global product.

SMIRNOFF
RED LABEL

SMIRNOFF
BLACK LABEL

66 The most subtle and sophisticated of all the spirits. Equally loved by men and women, gin is the ultimately versatile cocktail ingredient. **99**

GIN

INTRODUCING GIN

Gin is a grain spirit flavoured with juniper berries and other botanicals – assorted herbs and spices. After years in the doldrums, the gin industry has recently undergone a fabulous revival. With the introduction of a host of new-generation gins and a renewed love of cocktails – especially the classic Martini – gin is definitely here to stay!

DRINKING AND SERVING

DRINK PROFILE With so many different gin products available, the variety of intriguing, welcoming aromas is almost too great to mention; but in terms of taste gin, by definition, must be dry.

C COLOUR Most London Dry gin is colourless; other styles may be pale yellow to slightly golden, either as a result of wood-ageing or the addition of flavourings, such as saffron.

A AROMA A complex mix of botanicals: juniper, ginger, nutmeg, and often lemon and other citrus fruits. Some gins are earthy, and many "new" gins, such as Bombay Sapphire, are spicy.

T TASTE Flavours should be fresh and stimulating and never sweet or cloying. The length should be clean and very long. Better-quality gins have a complex balance of herbs and citrus.

BUYING AND STORING The gin industry is extremely well organized and it is usually easy to find all the most popular brands in the supermarket, so that you can try them to discover which you like best. Gin does not age in the bottle, so there is no need to lay it down.

SERVING SUGGESTIONS Gin is strong and full of flavour, therefore it keeps its character probably better than any other spirit when mixed. Great gin mixers include orange juice, bitter lemon, sparkling lemonade, and cola (a favourite in Latin countries), but of course the best-loved is tonic.
 Cocktail lists brim with gin-based mixes – the Dry Gin Martini (see p376), Gibson (see p377), Tom Collins (see p343), Gin Fizz (see p342), and White Lady (see p344) are just a few of the classics. As gin is rarely drunk neat, there is no specific gin glass.

The word "gin" is an English contraction of *genever*, the Dutch word for juniper, which itself came from the French *genièvre*. The earliest gins originated from the practice of distilling surplus wine and grain, which was popular in the low countries (Holland and Flanders) during the 17th century. It is thought that English troops fighting in the Eighty Years' War (1568–1648) – the war against the Spanish to establish the Netherlands' independence – brought the spirit back to England, where its success story really begins.

JUNIPER BERRIES *The main flavouring in gin and genever is the highly aromatic berry of the evergreen juniper bush.*

THE RISE TO STARDOM

The popularity of gin received an enormous boost when, in 1689, Dutch-born William, Prince of Orange, and his English wife Mary became Protestant co-rulers of England. Soon after his accession, William declared war on Louis XIV of France. He actively discouraged the import of French brandy (as well as brandy from other Catholic European countries), and encouraged the production of spirits made from local grain. The result was an explosion of gin-drinking. In 1733, at the height of the gin craze, London was producing 53 litres (14 gallons) of gin a year for every resident!

PINK GIN *This mix of gin, water, and Angostura bitters has been a popular gin cocktail for more than a century.*

Between the 18th and 19th centuries, the British government established control over gin production, and the great gin houses began to market products of much higher quality – and price. Among these products are names still well known today – Booth, Burnett, Gordon, Tanqueray, Gilbey, and James Burrough's Beefeater. By the end of the 19th century, with the big firms making their gin mainly using grain spirit from Scottish whisky distilleries, the British took the drink with them to the far corners of their Empire. The drink also became well established in the US, and in countries such as Spain and their former colony, the Philippines.

GIN PRODUCTION *When gin is first released from the still (shown here) it is too high in alcohol for bottling. Its strength is adjusted to around 40% ABV by the addition of water.*

The 19th century saw the birth of many of the cocktails that we know today, and gin became the basis of many classic mixes, such as the Gin and Tonic (which offered a daily dose of quinine to ward off malaria for officials posted in the colonies), and the Pink Gin *(see p385)*, which became a staple for officers of the Royal Navy. Meanwhile, the Dutch used their trading skills and their own far-flung empire to promote their Genever. Rotterdam became a centre for distilleries, and firms such as Bols and De Kuyper established themselves firmly in the world market.

In the 20th century, Prohibition in the US (1920–1933) increased gin's popularity still further. It became the bootleg spirit of choice, because it was easy to make and required no ageing. Even after the end of Prohibition, gin was the dominant white spirit in the US until the rise of vodka in the 1960s.

MAKING GIN

The basic principle of gin production is to flavour a neutral grain spirit with botanicals – a range of plants, herbs, spices, and fruits that includes, but is no longer limited to, juniper berries. Most producers keep their recipes a secret, but these ingredients certainly include spices such as angelica root, cardamom, coriander, orris root, cassia bark, ginger, and nutmeg, as well as nuts and fruit-based ingredients such as almonds, and lemon and orange peel. The proportions of the botanicals are the determining factor in the character of the gin.

The traditional way to make the gin is to steep the botanicals in grain spirit; the mixture is re-distilled in a special "carterhead" still (similar to the copper pot stills used for whisky and brandy). However, some of today's producers use a faster process called "cold-compounding", where a highly concentrated mixture of botanicals is macerated in grain alcohol and distilled to give a spirit with an extremely strong flavour. This is then diluted with more neutral grain spirit to reach the required level of flavouring. Some of the most flavourful gins are made by vaporizing the spirit and allowing the vapour to pass through the botanicals to collect their characteristics. All gins are diluted with water before bottling.

The different processes and ingredients give distinct styles of gin. The most famous is probably London Dry. This style is dry, clean, and fresh, and is the standard gin product, accounting for most of the gin made in the world. Plymouth Gin is a variation on London Dry, but tends to be sweeter and more aromatic. Finally, Genever (or Jenever; mostly from Holland) comes in three sub-styles: Oude (old) Jenever is sweetened and has strong botanical flavours; Jonge (young) Jenever is more neutral and similar to London Dry; and Korenwijn Jenever, which is cask-aged. This is a premium product, and is extremely malty and full bodied.

GIN COCKTAILS *Some of the most famous cocktails in the world – including the classic Dry Martini – are based on gin. The best gin cocktails are made when both the gin and the glass are icy cold.*

INTERNATIONAL

The world's gin market is dominated by brands made in the London Dry style. The popularity of this style has spread far beyond its origins in England, and brands such as Gordon's, Tanqueray, and Beefeater are now made and enjoyed across the globe. New generation gins like Bombay Sapphire are catching up fast with the traditional giants.

GORDON'S

C COLOUR Crystal clear and bright, with a green or clear glass bottle.

A AROMA Fresh and aromatic; citrus, nutmeg, ginger, and coriander.

T TASTE Citrus, particularly lemon, and juniper; clean finish.

The beginnings of Gordon's gin lie with a Scot named Alexander Gordon, who capitalized on the government's drive to improve the quality of London's home-brewed spirits in the late-17th and the 18th centuries. His refined gin spirit, which he perfected in 1769, was instantly and hugely popular.

In 1898 Gordon's merged with another gin distillery, Tanqueray, and so dominated the UK's gin market. The company enjoyed steady expansion throughout the 20th century, and today they are both part of Diageo. Gordon's is now the second-biggest-selling gin in the

world, after the Philippine's Ginebra San Miguel; and it is the biggest-selling in the West.

The gin continues to be made to Alexander Gordon's 1769 recipe – a closely guarded secret, known only by 12 people in the world at any one time. We do know that the original recipe specified ginger, cassia oil, and nutmeg, as well as coriander seeds and juniper. Whatever other botanicals (herbs, spices, and fruit) go into the mix, Gordon's is an excellent gin, with a fresh, herby character and a lively finish.

In the UK Gordon's is marketed in its distinctive green-glass bottle (the only coloured-glass bottle that could be produced in bulk during the 19th century), whereas the Gordon's for export is bottled in clear glass. The two gins are not identical: the export gin is slightly stronger than the UK version (40% ABV, compared with 37.5% ABV), making it feel richer, more oily, and more complex.

For something with a citrusy, zesty kick, try Gordon's Distiller's Cut, which is the basic gin with added lemongrass and ginger. Over ice with tonic water, it makes a great apéritif. Or, for something more fruity, try the Sloe Gin (*see p287*).

Overall Gordon's is a no-frills spirit, but the best original gin of all.

MIXING IT UP

GIN, OR GORDON'S? Distilled three times for purity, Gordon's makes the perfect gin and tonic. Pour a measure of Gordon's into a tumbler, over ice. Fill to the top with tonic water, and add wedges of lemon or lime.

A WORLD OF GIN
Gordon's is made in the UK, Canada, the US, South America, and Jamaica – always to the same recipe.

BEEFEATER

C COLOUR Bright and clear in a colourless glass bottle.

A AROMA Complex, with coriander, orange, and angelica.

T TASTE Dry and citrusy, balanced by notes of caramel.

Pharmacist James Burrough created Beefeater gin in London in 1820, naming it after the guards of the Tower of London. Although Beefeater is still made in London, it is now part of the Allied Domecq group.

Beefeater is very fresh and dry, with a citrus edge and good balance. It is great in a gin and tonic. If you are going through Duty Free, try the Crown Jewel 50% Premium Gin – it has real punch!

BEEFEATER

GILBEY'S

C COLOUR Clear spirit in a clear glass bottle with a traditional feel.

A AROMA Spicy, with mature herbs and minerals.

T TASTE Medium-bodied; strongly flavoured; creamy, delicate texture.

The Gilbey brothers established their distilling business in the 1860s, in London. They created a light, dry gin which quickly became a worldwide best-seller, especially in the US (and now in the Philippines, India, Japan, Canada, and South Africa, too). Today, Gilbey's is owned by Diageo, and is distilled throughout the world.

Gilbey's Special Dry Gin is well made, with a light to medium texture. It has a strong flavour, so I prefer to use it in cocktails rather than drinking it straight or with tonic.

BOMBAY SAPPHIRE

C COLOUR Clear spirit in a distinctive translucent blue bottle.

A AROMA Complex and aromatic; juniper, eucalyptus, spice; floral and citrus notes.

T TASTE Refreshing, elegant, complex; lemon, spice, herbs; fresh finish.

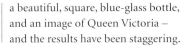

GILBEY'S

As Absolut is to vodka, so Bombay Sapphire is to gin – a marketing triumph, bringing gin into the 21st century.

In fact, the brain behind the two campaigns is the same: Michel Roux. In 1988 he developed the idea of a new-style gin, based on the successful Bombay Dry, but packaged in a new, cool bottle that would combine modern design with reminiscences of gin's British history. He gave us a beautiful, square, blue-glass bottle, and an image of Queen Victoria – and the results have been staggering.

Bombay Sapphire now forms part of the global Bacardi group.

It is not just the bottle that is special: Bombay Sapphire is an altogether great gin. It is made with at least ten botanicals (herbs, spices, and fruits), including almond oil, lemon peel, liquorice, and orris root. The botanicals are not boiled in the

BOMBAY SAPPHIRE

spirit, as with many other gins, but the pure spirit itself is vaporized and passed through the botanicals, allowing them to impart their fullest flavours. The result is especially complex, refreshing, and well-balanced, giving a gin that is full-bodied, yet cool; and powerful yet approachable.

I think Bombay Sapphire is too complex for a mixer – but as a gin to sip on its own, it beats the lot!

TANQUERAY

C COLOUR Clear spirit, in a distinctive round green bottle.

A AROMA Complex; with juniper and citrus most prominent.

T TASTE Very smooth, dry, and crisp; full juniper flavours; spicy finish.

Tanqueray is the Rolls-Royce of gins. In the middle of the 19th century Charles Tanqueray set out to produce a superior premium gin aimed at the most sophisticated drinkers. As the world has moved on, Tanqueray has gone from being the favourite gin of the British aristocracy to the gin of choice for Hollywood glitterati. Tanqueray is easily the biggest-selling gin in the US, with about 50 per cent of the market. It is now owned by the drinks company Diageo, which also owns Gordon's.

Tanqueray London Dry is distilled four times, with the spirit vaporized through the botanicals (to a secret recipe handed down by Charles Tanqueray) to give a pure but full-flavoured gin. The result is very dry, spicy, and strong (it is marketed at 47% ABV), and absolutely perfect for being turned into a Dry Martini.

In 2000, the company launched Tanqueray No.10. This gin is made using botanicals that have been picked by hand and infused into the spirit in their whole form. The idea is to give a superior gin with deeper, richer, and more complex flavours. And it succeeds. This award-winning gin is especially dry, citrusy, and oily, and yet it retains all the class we expect from Tanqueray. Try it in a Martini or other cocktails, but to fully appreciate its complexity, drink it chilled (from the refrigerator), on its own.

TANQUERAY

HENDRICK'S

C COLOUR Clear, in a stylish bottle made from black glass.

A AROMA Distinctive, with herbs, flowers, and cucumber.

T TASTE Smooth, well-balanced; unusual, but refreshing, dry cucumber flavours.

All gins have botanicals added to the raw spirit, usually in the form of juniper, citrus peel, and coriander and other herbs. However, Hendrick's, now made by William Grant and Sons (famous for their whisky), also contains rose petals, and, most extraordinary of all, cucumber. As its own advertising slogan says "It's not for everyone", but it has taken the US, and now the UK, by storm. Creamy, full-flavoured, and unusual, you have to taste it to truly understand it. I love it, and at more than 41% ABV, it is no weakling!

PLYMOUTH

C COLOUR Clear, in a translucent bottle with the Mayflower on the label.

A AROMA Elegant, with juniper, herbs (such as cardamom), and orangey notes.

T TASTE Distinctive, subtle, full-bodied; earth; forest roots; great balance.

This gin has been made in Plymouth, southern England, since the 18th century. However, the brand had been neglected until, in 1996, it was revived by private investors. It is now marketed through Vin & Sprit.

Plymouth produces great gin. Original Strength is strong, but subtle, spicy, and full bodied – and great with tonic. Navy Strength (57% ABV) manages to keep its balance, despite its powerful strength. In the summer try the Fruit Cup, a light mix of gin, vermouth, and herbs.

PLYMOUTH

CADENHEAD'S OLD RAJ

C COLOUR Yellowish green, in a retro-style square bottle.

A AROMA Very aromatic, with juniper, nuts, and pepper.

T TASTE Rounded, complete, characterful; spicy; crisp finish.

Best-known for its single malt whisky, Cadenhead's produces a fantastic gin called Old Raj. The gin is unusual in a number of ways. Most noticeably, the botanicals are steeped and distilled separately before being added to the neutral spirit; and the gin is not clear, but greeny yellow, owing to the addition of saffron. The result is a dry, peppery gin with a lovely body and a full finish. This is a special gin for sipping.

CADENHEAD'S OLD RAJ

BOMBAY DRY

C COLOUR A limpid spirit, in a clear traditional bottle.

A AROMA Highly aromatic; strong orange peel, juniper, and coriander.

T TASTE Complex, satisfying; smooth, spicy, and dry, with lemon notes.

Production of Bombay Dry began in the 1950s, but the brand did not really come into its own until the 1980s, when a new generation of gin-drinkers turned their backs on old-style, colonial gins. Bombay Dry is now part of Bacardi, but sadly it is available only in the US and Spain.

Bombay Dry is a spicy gin, and a perfect match for tonic. It is extremely refreshing with complex aromas of herbs and citrus fruits (especially orange and lemon). Chill the gin well, and then drink a Bombay Dry gin and tonic as a refreshing summer apéritif.

DARESBURY'S QUINTESSENTIAL

C COLOUR Clear and bright; in a slightly frosted glass bottle.

A AROMA Distinctive, with an excellent balance of herbs and minerals.

T TASTE Smooth, delicate; citrus, minerals; great balance.

Originally launched only in the US and Canada, Daresbury's Quintessential Dry Gin made such a hit that it is now available worldwide.

The "5" on the label refers to the fact that the gin is distilled five times using five botanicals – juniper, coriander, angelica (for dryness), cubebs (pepper), and lime oil. The result is a strong, fresh, and citrusy gin with excellent balance.

DARESBURY'S QUINTESSENTIAL

POLO CLUB

C COLOUR Clear, in a square glass bottle, with a "polo" theme.

A AROMA Quite aromatic, with juniper and citrus to the fore.

T TASTE Dry and complex, with spice and a refreshing finish.

Polo Club gin is made in Perthshire, Scotland, by Burn Stewart, part of the Angostura Group. The gin is marketed as a luxury product – in the past, the company has even tried to tie one of their products in with the Burberry fashion house.

Its presentation is very stylish, with a smart square bottle adorned with a horse's head and the Houses of Parliament.

Polo Club is a fine gin in the dry, spicy, and complex modern style. It is fairly strong at 43% ABV. I find that it makes an excellent Martini, and is generally a great mixer.

UNITED KINGDOM

England, and especially London, is the home of the modern gin style, and many of its great brands are now global products. As some of the traditional British gins have fallen from favour, new brands, often adopting a "retro" British Empire style, have taken their place.

SPAIN

Spain has the highest gin consumption per head of any country in the world. Its home-grown brands are very popular.

XORIGUER

C COLOUR Clear, in a green glass bottle based on stone gin crocks.

A AROMA Vibrant, appealing fruit, without being too obvious; subtle and classy.

T TASTE Dry, mild; orris root, citrus, and juniper; very refreshing.

GREENALL'S

C COLOUR Clear spirit, in a very pale green square bottle.

A AROMA Subtle and delicate, with herbs and lively spice.

T TASTE Very smooth and dry, with a long, satisfying finish.

Although it is now owned by the De Vere Group, Greenall's is still made to its 1761 family recipe, which includes almonds and cassia bark. The gin is classy, dry, and complex, and at 43% ABV, quite strong! The export version, Greenall's Special London Dry (at 48% ABV) is also excellent. Great gins from a small company.

BOOTH'S

C COLOUR Clear, in a square, colourless bottle with distinctive dimpled glass.

A AROMA Delicate and subtle, with molasses and spice.

T TASTE Light, not too complex; good flavour and slightly sweet.

In the 19th century Booth's became the largest distilling company in Britain, and its brands were hugely popular during the 1920s and 1930s. Now the only Booth's still on the market is High and Dry, a fresh, crisp, and spicy gin with a hint of sweetness at the finish. This is a fine and well-balanced gin – and is said to be the Queen's favourite!

LARIOS

C COLOUR Clear, in a white-glass bottle with a cheerful yellow label.

A AROMA Delicate, with juniper, citrus, and spice.

T TASTE Dry and fresh, with a slight cane-spirit taste at the finish.

The Larios family began making gin in 1933, and, offering quality and reliability, soon became Spain's market leaders. Larios gin is a very respectable copy of the London Dry style, and is perfectly good in a gin and tonic, or other long drink. Why not try it and see if you can tell the difference?

This is gin's rising star and my new favourite! The Pons' family's Xoriguer gin (pronounced "sho-ri-guer") is a Gin de Mahon, which can be made only on the Spanish island of Menorca using wine alcohol, rather than grain spirit. The gin is distilled to 38% ABV, and not watered down, keeping the juniper and herbs prominent. Xoriguer is mild, dry, and complex, with almond and caraway and a fresh finish. Drink it straight, with a slice of lemon.

XORIGUER

HOLLAND

Dutch gin often has a strong aroma of juniper, malt, and herbs. There are many local brands, as well as giants like Bols.

DE KUYPER

DE KUYPER

C COLOUR Light gold, yellow, or clear, in traditional bottles.

A AROMA Distinctive and clear, with malt, juniper, and herbs.

T TASTE Full-bodied and full-flavoured; malt.

De Kuyper's Oude Jenever is pale yellow and slightly sweetened, and has strong botanical flavours, with caramel and malt. Weaker Jonge Jenever is more neutral – closer to London Dry. Drink them on their own, without mixing.

BOLS

C COLOUR Clear, yellow, or golden, in traditional bottles or stone jars.

A AROMA Clean and distinctive, with malt, caramel, juniper, and herbs.

T TASTE Very strong; mellow and full-bodied.

Established in Amsterdam in 1572, Bols is the oldest distillery in the Netherlands. It is now part of the French Rémy-Cointreau group.

Bols makes a wide range of products, including all kinds of flavoured spirits and mixers. If you are looking for a straight but traditional Dutch gin, try the Oude Jenever, which has hints of sweetness, as well as being malty and complex. The Jonge Jenever is lighter and more delicate, and clear. Drink either of these chilled, on their own.

BOLS

The classic Corenwyn (meaning "grain brandy") is rich, select, and Bols' most traditional jenever (gin). It has a light gold colour, and is sold in an old-fashioned stone jar, with which Bols is often identified. Drink it as an apéritif, or you could even try it with seafood.

Most recently, Bols has introduced Damrak Amsterdam Gin, which is aimed at the new, modern generation of gin-drinkers. The gin is made using 17 botanicals (herbs, spices, and fruits) and is distilled five times, making it pure and fresh, but without losing its complexity. It makes an excellent mixer, and is a perfectly good alternative to the more established modern brands, such as Bombay Sapphire.

IRELAND

Ireland's Midleton distillery near Cork produces a fine, fruity, and citrusy gin, slightly sweeter than the traditional London Dry style.

CORK DRY

C COLOUR Clear and bright, in a clear glass bottle with a red label.

A AROMA Delicate and fruity, with prominent citrus.

T TASTE Pleasant, mellow; medium strength with a sweet, malty feel.

Cork Dry Gin is made to a 1793 recipe using Irish grain. More citrus fruit and less juniper are used in the blend than in London dry gin, making the style a little sweeter. At 38% ABV, it is also quite easy to drink. (The export version is stronger at 43% ABV.) I like to enjoy it chilled, on its own.

FRANCE

Northern France has a long tradition of making gin, focused in Flanders; it is being revived by new-style brands like Citadelle.

CITADELLE

C COLOUR Clear, in a round clear bottle with striking vivid-blue labelling.

A AROMA Fresh and vibrant, with notes of citrus and juniper.

T TASTE Full-bodied and complex, with herbs, spice, and a long finish.

Citadelle was relaunched in 1998 according to its original 1771 recipe, using 19 botanicals (herbs, spices, and fruits), and distilling the spirit four times in copper stills. The result is a superb, complex gin, in which juniper takes second place to the herbs. The gin keeps its character in a Martini or other long drink, and overall it feels great. I love it!

USA

The American thirst for cocktails makes this a huge market for fine gin. US-based producers help to meet the growing demand.

SEAGRAM'S

C COLOUR Clear and limpid, in a stylish mottled-glass bottle.

A AROMA Delicate and elegant, with juniper, citrus, and spice.

T TASTE Smooth, fresh; dominant citrus notes; spicy, lively, finish.

Seagram's is a huge brand in the US. Use it to make an excellent Martini – one that retains the fresh citrus character of the gin – or in a long drink. The Twisted range (slightly flavoured gin, with lime or grapefruit) is lively and fruity, and great for parties.

SEAGRAM'S

BOODLES

C COLOUR Crystal clear, in a transparent decanter-style bottle.

A AROMA Fragrant, with complex and stimulating spice and flowers.

T TASTE Superior and full-bodied; crisp and dry with a slightly oily finish.

Originally a 19th-century British brand, Boodles is now made by Pernod Ricard in the US and aimed at the American market, although it is popular around the world. Marketed as Boodles British Gin, it is offered as the superior partner to the regular Seagram's Extra Dry.

Boodles is an excellent gin and I am a big fan. It is clean, dry, and strong, yet subtly spicy and oily.

Some debate whether to drink Boodles or Bombay Dry (they are both excellent, on their own or mixed); Boodles is cheaper – but I'll leave it up to you to decide!

NEW ZEALAND

New Zealand produces its own gins using botanicals indigenous to the Southern Hemisphere – an exciting development.

SOUTH

SOUTH

C COLOUR Clear, in a tall, beautifully elegant bottle.

A AROMA Unusual, attractive; juniper, caramel; wet grass.

T TASTE Distinctive, smooth; slightly sweet; fruity finish.

South, made on the South Island, is an excellent gin in the London Dry style. However, its nine botanicals include some native to the Southern hemisphere, such as kawakawa leaves and manuka berries. These give the gin fresh aromas and a fruity, sweet taste. Brilliant!

TEQUILA
AND MEZCAL

66 Deeply embedded in the culture of Mexico, tequila and mezcal have a primitive character full of earth and fire. 99

INTRODUCING TEQUILA AND MEZCAL

When I think of a drink that sums up Mexico, one spirit springs to mind: tequila. Made from the "hearts" of the agave plant, it is often confused with mezcal, another agave spirit, but the two drinks differ both in flavour and in method of production.

Tequila and mezcal are closely related spirits. Tequila is distilled from the *piñas* (hearts) of the blue agave, which flourishes in the volcanic soil found in and around the plains of Jalisco, in Mexico; mezcal, by contrast, is made from wild varieties of the agave family found in the more southerly Oaxaca.

Both spirits are thought to derive from the undistilled drink *pulque*, which the early Aztecs are believed to have used in their rituals and ceremonies as a means of communicating with the gods. *Pulque* is still made today: it is a milky, slightly sour liquid that is about the same strength as wine, and frankly, it takes a little getting used to. For me, it is a far inferior drink to mezcal and tequila.

LIME *Citrus fruits fill the nose of young, fresh tequilas.*

ALL ABOUT TEQUILA

Tequila is named after a small town in the state of Jalisco: indeed, only spirit made in Jalisco and in four surrounding regions may be marketed as tequila. In the 19th century the spirit was known as *Aguardiente de Agave* (meaning "Agave brandy").

THE MEXICAN WAY *Guacamole and other tapas-like foods are often eaten alongside a glass of tequila.*

Even then, the companies of Jose Cuervo and of Sauza dominated the market, and when they began to ship barrels of the spirit to the US using the label "tequila", the name stuck. By the 1940s, when Cognac and whisky were hard to find in the US, tequila was in its heyday and had established itself as the basis of the famous Margarita cocktail (with Cointreau and lime juice; *see pp346–7*), and as a serious drink for before and after dinner. Today, tequila is shipped and drunk all over the world but, apart from in its home in Mexico, the US remains by far the spirit's biggest market.

To make tequila, the producers cultivate blue agave plants, which take between eight and 12 years to mature. The *piñas*, which contain a sweet, milky sap, are then cut from the plants and cooked in steam for around two days. Milling the cooked *piñas* extracts the sap, which is then mixed with water and fermented in oak vats.

The fermented liquid, or *mosto* (similar to the "wash" of whisky and vodka) is then at least double-distilled in copper pot stills to produce tequila. Before bottling, the spirit's strength is adjusted by the addition of water.

Tequila is classified by the amount of agave it contains and also by the length of its ageing process. *Blanco* or Silver tequila is unaged (although some may be rested for a month or so before bottling), which makes it fresh and spicy with a distinctive agave flavour. *Joven abocado* tequila is "young" and golden in colour – usually through the addition of caramel – and is more whisky-like than other styles of the spirit. *Reposado* describes tequila that has been rested in wood for up to one year. An *añejo* is an aged tequila that has been matured in wood for between one and five years. However, increasingly tequila is appearing as expensive luxury brands made from 100-per-cent blue agave (the spirit must contain at least 51 per cent to carry the name tequila) and aged for up to six years in wooden casks. These spirits are like Cognac – rich and smooth, with extra spice and earth.

ALL ABOUT MEZCAL

Mezcal is made in the south of Mexico from the local wild agave plants known as *maguey*. Although similar in style to tequila, and classified in similar ways, it has one important distinction that sets it apart from its cousin. Whereas in tequila-production the *piñas* are steamed to make it easier to extract the sap, in mezcal-production the *piñas* are baked or roasted over charcoal in special underground ovens for up to three days. This process gives the spirit a distinctive earthy smokiness that is not present in tequila. Some bottles of mezcal are instantly recognizable because they contain the "worm" or *gusano* – a grub that bores into the leaves of the agave plant. These mezcals are marketed as *mezcal con gusano* and are not for the faint-hearted!

TEQUILA SUNRISE *After the Margarita, the Tequila Sunrise is the most famous of all tequila cocktails. A long drink, best imbibed through a straw, it blends tequila with orange juice and grenadine.*

RAW MATERIALS *The* piñas, *the pineapple-shaped hearts of the blue agave plant, weigh up to around 90kg (200lbs) each, so it is common to see harvesters rolling them downhill toward the collection truck.*

MEXICO

Tequila is Mexico's national drink, with more than 200 million litres (52 million gallons) produced every year. About half is exported – most to the US – where tequila has become *the* happening party drink.

CUERVO RESERVA DE LA FAMILIA

CUERVO RESERVA DE LA FAMILIA

C **COLOUR** Medium to dark gold, imparted by the oak ageing.

A **AROMA** Rich and complex, with caramel, flowers, vanilla, and spice.

T **TASTE** Ultra-smooth and rich; sweet, nutty, and spicy, with a long finish.

To many people in the world, tequila means Jose Cuervo. With 40 per cent of the global market this long-established producer – now part of the global group Diageo – has a presence in almost every liquor store. The drink's story began in 1758, when the king of Spain gave a plot of land to Don José Antonio de Cuervo in return for running the parish church in the Mexican town of Tequila in the state of Jalisco. In 1795, his son was granted the first concession to produce tequila commercially. The original agave plants used to make the tequila were taken from the wild, but they were soon replaced with cultivated fields, and Cuervo began its spectacular rise to become the world's favourite tequila. The first recorded imports into the US were three barrels, sent to El Paso in 1873. The company won awards for its "Agave Brandy" at the Paris Exposition in 1889, and the World Fair in 1893, and many more into the 20th century.

Reserva de la Familia was launched in 1995 to celebrate Cuervo's 200th anniversary, and the company certainly pulls out all the stops for this special brand. Only a limited number of bottles of this 100-per-cent agave tequila are produced – each one hand-processed and numbered. And every year, the company commissions a Mexican artist to design the wooden box in which the bottle is packaged.

Reserva is a very special drink; keep it safely under lock and key so that no-one uses it by mistake for slammers! This is one to savour and enjoy on special occasions, like a classy Cognac.

LAND AND PRODUCTION

THE AGAVE RUSH The world's thirst for tequila has rocketed since the 1990s, and Mexico's agave growers are struggling to keep up with demand for the precious raw material. Today, more than 90,000 acres (36,000 hectares) of blue agave are cultivated in pastures, chiefly in the western state of Jalisco. The plant takes up to 10 years to mature, so growers have been unable to respond rapidly to the new fashion for tequila.

CUERVO CLASICO

C **COLOUR** Silver and clear; light, bright, and fresh.

A **AROMA** Fresh, spicy, and young; agave, citrus, and wood.

T **TASTE** Smoother than most silver tequilas; lively with a sweetish finish.

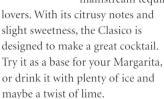

CUERVO CLASICO

The name Cuervo means "crow," and in the early days of tequila, when most customers could not read, the sign of the crow gave the drink a distinctive visual brand. But just like every other spirit, tequila has to move with the times to attract new markets. Cuervo has refreshed its range with this lively but basic tequila, presented in a fresh package.

Cuervo Clasico is a descendent of the old Cuervo Blanco tequila. Some people have always preferred the slightly more raw edge and richer agave flavour of the young blanco tequilas. But in order to make the brand less fiery and more palatable around the world, Cuervo has blended young silver tequila with oak barrel-mellowed tequilas. This gives a smooth, well-balanced silver spirit that is still sharp, fresh, and lively, but also a little more approachable.

Clasico was launched in 2003 to complement the company's huge-selling Especial. The silver Clasico was aimed at a new, younger market, while the Gold targeted mainstream tequila lovers. With its citrusy notes and slight sweetness, the Clasico is designed to make a great cocktail. Try it as a base for your Margarita, or drink it with plenty of ice and maybe a twist of lime.

CUERVO TRADICIONAL

C **COLOUR** Pale straw golden yellow, tinged with the sun.

A **AROMA** Quite delicate, with spicy agave, vanilla, and oak.

T **TASTE** Medium-bodied, with a dry, spicy feel and a warm finish.

Tradicional looks back with reverence to the first tequila produced by Cuervo in Mexico more than 200 years ago. The old-style bottle and label evoke the qualities of the past, and the black crow motif on the cap harks back to Cuervo's early history *(see left)*. But the references to the past are more than cosmetic. This tequila is made in the old style – from 100-per-cent blue agaves harvested at the peak of their maturity, and then baked in traditional stone and clay ovens. Carefully fermented and double distilled, the spirit is aged in white oak barrels to give the tequila a richer, more sophisticated flavour.

Tradicional is produced in strictly limited quantities. Each bottle is uniquely numbered, and this exclusivity has contributed to the brand's success – it is hugely popular both in Mexico and in the US.

This is another great tequila to enjoy straight and well chilled, perhaps with a sangrita (a Mexican fruit juice) on the side. You can, of course, use it in a Margarita too, where its richer flavours and fuller body will enhance the classic cocktail. I would choose to sip this tequila neat – slowly and deliberately, to enjoy its aroma, body, and taste, which are every bit as complex as those of a fine wine.

CUERVO TRADICIONAL

TOP SELLER *Cuervo Especial is currently sold in 80 countries around the world – and the list is still growing.*

CUERVO ESPECIAL

C COLOUR Light and attractive gold, imparted by short ageing in wood.

A AROMA Earth, spice, rich vanilla, caramel, and oak.

T TASTE Very smooth, with some sweetness, wood, and spice.

Especial is Cuervo's flagship brand and can be found in almost every bar and every supermarket in the world. Like most top global brands, it is not outstanding, but is marketed at a price anyone can afford, is reliable, and always "hits the spot". Especial is a *reposado* – "rested" for a few months in oak, to remove some of its fire and give it a little more body.

I sometimes drink this neat – it is good enough – but more usually I serve it with a mixer in a long drink, or in a Margarita. Especial has now lost some of its popularity to the "super tequila" premium brands, but for sheer availability and value for money it is hard to match, and will be with us for a long time yet.

SIERRA

C COLOUR Clear and transparent through to pale gold.

A AROMA Light and delicate, with spice, earth, and herbs.

T TASTE Medium-bodied, fresh, and lively, with a spicy finish.

Every tequila needs something to make it stand out from the crowd, especially on the shelves of a supermarket, and Sierra tequila has a little stroke of genius – a red or gold sombrero perched on the top of a crystal clear bottle. The brand is targeted at those of us who are not regular tequila-drinkers: the marketing slogan is "A wonderful drop, sombrero on top" – and the eye-catching hat on the lid reminds us to choose Sierra over other bottles.

SIERRA SILVER

Although the tequila in the bottles is Mexican, the Sierra operation is owned by a German company, NMK Schulz. The fastest-growing brand in Europe and distributed worldwide, Sierra holds the lion's share of the German market. It poses a real challenge to Cuervo.

Sierra Silver (with the red hat) is the more popular of Sierra's offerings, and is a great introduction to tequila if you have never tried it before. It is light, clear, and young, and ideal neat over ice or as a mixer in a tequila cocktail – try it in your Margarita. Sierra Gold (with a gold hat) is matured in oak casks, giving it a golden colour and gentle, rounded, fuller flavours. I like to drink this one neat with a slice of orange and a sprinkle of cinnamon; or it makes a great addition to a long cocktail, such as a Tequila Sunrise.

SAUZA BLANCO / EXTRA GOLD

C COLOUR Clear (Sauza Blanco); medium gold (Sauza Extra Gold).

A AROMA Delicately perfumed, with earth, vanilla, smoke, and caramel.

T TASTE Light, fresh, and spicy, through to smooth, with a warm finish.

Established in Tequila in 1873, Sauza has always prided itself on its quality, and it is now the flagship tequila of the global Allied Domecq group. It produces a large range of brands at the original La Perseverancia distillery.

Sauza Blanco is a good mixer – a light, bright, fresh tequila, with touches of earth and wood. For something smoother, great as a mixer or neat, try the Extra Gold, which is aged in white oak, and has aromas of herbs and vanilla.

SAUZA EXTRA GOLD

SAUZA 100 AÑOS

C COLOUR Dark old gold with amber highlights.

A AROMA Complex and sweet; fruit, citrus, smoke, and spice.

T TASTE Full-bodied, but smooth, with a warm earthy finish.

Meaning "100 years", 100 Años is a *reposado* tequila from the Sauza range. The spirit is "rested" in oak casks for one year to allow its kick to soften and its flavours to fill out. The result is a reliable, good-value tequila, with a dark golden colour, and a smoky, vanilla nose. This is not a tequila for special occasions, but it has a slightly sweet edge, and not too much spice and power, making it easy drinking in a cocktail or in the traditional manner – neat, with salt and lemon.

SAUZA HORNITOS

C COLOUR Pale straw yellow, in a clear bottle with a lime green label.

A AROMA Aromatic; vanilla, smoke, pepper, mint, and lime.

T TASTE Very warm and smooth; medium-bodied; earth, spice, and sweetness.

HORNITOS

This tequila has the perfect combination of being good-quality at a good price. A flagship brand of the Sauza range, Hornitos (meaning "oven") is made by baking the hearts of the agave plants, rather than steaming them. This gives the tequila a smoky aroma to accompany the attractive vanilla and earthy agave. Mild, with full, deep flavours, this is one of my favourites, and its light, peppery style makes it great for drinking neat.

SAUZA TRIADA

C COLOUR Deep sunset gold; presented in a small decanter.

A AROMA Rich and fruity, with spice, wood, and earth.

T TASTE Warm and gentle, with a soft, spicy, woody finish.

Triada falls into Sauza's luxury tequila category, and justifiably so – it is on another planet compared with many other tequilas! It is 100-per-cent agave, and undergoes a two-stage ageing process – it begins as a *reposado* (aged in oak for a few months), but then it becomes an *añejo* (aged) tequila by maturing in small, oak Bourbon barrels that have had the charring on the insides removed. (Charring gives a Bourbon its flavour.) This imparts an extra woodiness to the spirit. The two-tier ageing system is unique to Triada, and makes a perfectly balanced spirit to be drunk neat. But try not to look at the price tag before you buy – uniqueness is expensive!

SAUZA CONMEMORATIVO

C COLOUR Medium gold, imparted by the oak ageing process.

A AROMA Very elegant; with raisins, spice, vanilla, and earth.

T TASTE Complex, full-bodied, well-balanced, warming; fruit, caramel, oak.

One of the smoothest tequilas in the Sauza range, Conmemorativo is produced to rival Cognac, and so is definitely one for drinking on its own. This is an *añejo* tequila: 100-per-cent agave and aged in wood for at least three years. The ageing offers an extra layer of personality and complexity to the spirit. The spiciness of the agave is underlined by rich fruit, caramel, and notes of vanilla, all of which come from the oak barrels. The result is a perfectly balanced tequila with a warm, spicy finish.

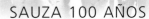

CONMEMORATIVO

SAUZA GALARDON

C COLOUR Pale golden amber, a mix of silver and darker gold.

A AROMA Delicate, elegant; vanilla, clove, caramel, cinnamon; a hint of smoke.

T TASTE Extremely smooth and rich; great balance and a tender finish.

This member of the Sauza range is a satisfying spirit, with a complex character and a smooth, silky texture. The word *galardon* means "highest prize" – and you can see why it was chosen to name this special tequila! Made from 100-per-cent agave, Galardon is marketed as a *gran reposado*: it is aged for a year in white oak barrels, which is not quite long enough to make it an *añejo*, but longer than most *reposados*. This gives a distinctive woody and spicy nose, and rich flavours with a hint of warm caramel on the finish.

SAUZA TRES GENERACIONES

C COLOUR Pale gold, in a rich, Cognac-style bottle.

A AROMA Quite floral, with a balance of earth and spice.

T TASTE Complex, smooth; butterscotch, oak, and pepper; clean finish.

Sauza added this luxury tequila to its range in 1996. It joins a new generation of high quality "super-tequilas", made with 100-per-cent agave, and under close government scrutiny to ensure that producers meet rigorous standards.

Tres Generaciones has been a great success and is one of the best-selling ultra-premium tequila brands in the world. It is aged in oak barrels for up to six years, making it rich and smooth – and, of course, it has a price tag to match. As a result this is definitely not a tequila for slamming! Treat it like a special Cognac – drink it neat and sip it slowly after dinner.

GRAN CENTENARIO

C COLOUR Clear to light and rich gold, in the elaborate "fallen angel" packaging.

A AROMA Intense and complex; earth, spice, caramel, fruit, and vanilla.

T TASTE Particularly smooth and rich; medium body; nuts, spice; sweet finish.

Gran Centenario produces good, modern tequilas to attract the new generation of tequila drinkers. The Plata is more complex than many other white tequilas, with more body and fruit, and is great for a more sophis-ticated mixer. The Reposado is well-balanced with a subtle fruitiness. Slightly oily, it is great over ice. The Añejo is aged in French oak barrels – and said to be watched over by angels as it matures! This is a soft, harmonious tequila, for drinking neat.

GRAN CENTENARIO

1800

C COLOUR Ranging from clear, through to dark gold and amber.

A AROMA Clean and crisp; orange, butterscotch, vanilla, and oak.

T TASTE Very modern, fresh, and lively; wood and spice, and a sweet finish.

Once a premium Cuervo brand, 1800 is now the flagship tequila of the Campari group. The award-winning Silver and Reposado are excellent – the former is delicate and smooth and was one of the first 100-per-cent agave silver tequilas; the latter has a great balance of citrus and spice. But the most successful 1800 is the amber Añejo. I am a big fan of this aged tequila, which is matured in charred French and US oak barrels. It is a real treat, with rich aromas of charred oak, and vanilla, nutmeg, and cloves, with layers of butterscotch and chocolate.

VIUDA DE ROMERO

C COLOUR Ranging from clear (Blanco) to pale copper (Reposado, Añejo).

A AROMA Traditional tequila; spicy, with cinnamon and toffee.

T TASTE Clean, smooth, and rich; velvety with a cinnamon finish.

Founded in 1852, this is Mexico's second-oldest tequila and is still made in Tequila itself, even though the brand is now owned by Pernod Ricard. Viuda de Romero makes a *blanco*, *reposado*, and *añejo*. The Reposado is especially good, with a full flavour and spicy finish. Try the Añejo in a quiet moment – it is aged in wood for at least two years, and so is extremely smooth, soft, and gentle.

VIUDA DE ROMERO

THE HEART OF THE AGAVE *After harvesting, the blue agave plants used to make tequila are stripped of their pointed leaves, leaving pineapple-like cores (called piñas), which are then processed at the tequila distillery.*

HERRADURA

C COLOUR Clear, through light to deep vintage gold.

A AROMA Earth and spice; grass, citrus, and herbs, with pepper.

T TASTE Smooth; subtle flavours; slightly sweet finish.

The well-respected distillery of Herradura ("horseshoe"), founded in 1870, has a long-standing reputation for producing quality spirits. For some, Herradura's tequila is the best of all.

The reputation is well-deserved; even the basic white tequila (Blanco 46) is made with 100-per-cent agave. This is one of my favourite whites. More complex than many others on the market, it is fresh and citrusy, with a herb and earth feel, and a note of sweetness – perfect over ice as an apéritif.

For something a little spicier, try the Suave Blanco instead. This is short-aged in white oak barrels, giving it a light yellow colour and a hint of pepper. As well as making a great apéritif, Suave is delicious in cocktails.

Herradura claims that its was the first ever *reposado* ("rested") tequila. The spirit stands for 11 months in oak, making a tequila that is citrusy and earthy on the nose, with smooth but strong flavours, a medium body, and a long, dry finish. It makes a really good tequila shot – strong enough to stamp its personality, but not so strong as to knock you out!

Herradura also produces an *añejo*, aged for two years in white oak, with a smooth, whisky-like feel. This, and the company's luxury Selección Suprema (aged for four years), should be drunk straight as a digestif – like a good Cognac.

HERRADURA

EL JIMADOR

C COLOUR Silver, through straw yellow to deep gold.

A AROMA Aromatic; herbs, agave, wood, and cinnamon.

T TASTE Complex and slightly oily, with spice, nuts, and vanilla; sweet finish.

Launched in the 1990s, El Jimador is owned by the great tequila House Herradura *(see left)*. El Jimador comes in three styles. The Blanco is young and fresh, and good for cocktail-making. The year-aged Añejo is a great digestif: smooth, full, fruity, and well balanced, with aromas of caramel and lanolin. The flagship is the Reposado, which is aged in oak for two months. Smoky and spicy with hints of cinnamon, this is Mexico's biggest-selling tequila and delicious as a mixer in a long drink.

CASA NOBLE

C COLOUR Silver through to dark gold for the Añejo.

A AROMA Delicate, with agave, spice, vanilla, and caramel.

T TASTE Quite full-bodied and smooth, with a long finish.

Casa Noble is pure luxury. Its products are 100-per-cent blue agave, and are marketed in beautiful decanters.

The award-winning Casa Noble Crystal is one of the best silver tequilas you will find. Fresh, spicy, and lively – but smooth – it is better than many aged tequilas. Drink it chilled over ice. The Reposado and Añejo are both aged in French oak, for one and five years respectively. They are exceptional and well worth a try – neat.

CASA NOBLE

DON JULIO

C COLOUR Silver through straw yellow to dark, vintage gold.

A AROMA Subtle and attractive; agave, caramel, and vanilla.

T TASTE Elegant, smooth, and silky, with honey, herbs, and chocolate.

Don Julio Gonzalez Estrada is one of tequila's most famous names. He began making quality spirit in 1942, and was one of the first producers to market aged tequila, launching one of the first *reposados* in the 1950s. He has two great brands, one of which takes his name (Don Julio), while the other is Tres Magueyes (also excellent). In 2003 Don Julio formed distribution partnerships with Mexican tequila-producer Cuervo and Diageo, which will make Don Julio tequila an international star.

Don Julio Blanco and Reposado are both fantastic tequilas, great over ice or in a cocktail. They both have the perfect balance of fruit, sugar, and spice; and a richness that is offset by a dry finish. The 1942 commemorates the opening of Don Julio's first distillery, and is a luxury sipping tequila, with sweet and ripe aromas of apple and oak, a smooth, rich taste, and a charming vanilla finish.

The star of the Don Julio brand is Real – and at around $400 a bottle, it is the most expensive tequila in the world. Created in 1996 to celebrate the company's 45 years in production, this is a blend of three- and five-year-old oak-aged tequilas. The result is exquisite. This is a sumptuous tequila with flavours of chocolate, caramel, and sweet agave – easily rivalling some of the world's best single malt whiskies. Savour every sip – slowly.

DON JULIO REPOSADO

CHINACO

C COLOUR Clear through to a glistening light gold.

A AROMA Peppery, fruity, and spicy; lime, pear, peach, apple, and quince.

T TASTE Elegant, complex; vanilla, spice, pepper; smooth finish.

Chinaco (named after landowners who fought to free Mexico in the 19th century), was the first distillery to launch an "ultra-premium" tequila, made from 100-per-cent agave. All but the Blanco (light, fresh, and great in a Margarita) are sipping tequilas. The Reposado is rested in oak for up to a year to give a fruity, satisfying spirit. The smooth Añejo (a serious competitor for Cognac) is aged for three years in large oak barrels, and is rich with vanilla and caramel. Best of all is the Emperador, aged for seven years – smooth, rich, and totally satisfying.

TWO FINGERS

C COLOUR Clear through to a sparkling pale straw gold.

A AROMA Distinctive; herbs and earth, with rich spice.

T TASTE Quite smooth and fruity, with a long, satisfying finish.

Two Fingers tequilas come in striking straight, black bottles – catchy packaging for tequilas with a catchy name. I think of this as "entry-level" tequila – a brand to try if you are new to the spirit, when you want good quality at a reasonable price. The Silver (young, fresh, and spicy) makes a great mixer; while the Gold, although also young, is softer, fruity, and herby, and can be enjoyed sipped over ice. Two Fingers does not produce classics, but for everyday drinking, these tequilas are just great.

TWO FINGERS

EL CONQUISTADOR

C COLOUR Clear through straw yellow to early-morning gold.

A AROMA Vanilla, cloves, earth, and citrus, with alcohol to the fore.

T TASTE Clean, crisp; medium- to full-bodied; smooth, sweet finish.

Marketed in the US by Heaven Hill Distilleries, which also imports the Two Fingers tequila brand *(see opposite)*, El Conquistador produces a range of tequilas made from 100-per-cent agave. They are beautifully presented in distinctive, hand-blown, tall bottles – the cobalt blue used for the Blanco is stunning.

In fact the Blanco is stunning in many ways. At 46% ABV, this is a strong silver tequila. Although strictly this spirit is "unaged", it does spend a short time

EL CONQUISTADOR
BLANCO

in oak barrels before bottling. The result is a clean, crisp, well-structured spirit, with peppery agave and a sweetish finish from the oak. I love to use it in my Margaritas.

The Reposado's flavours are similar to the Blanco's, but this tequila is rested in oak barrels for at least seven months before bottling, which makes it slightly richer, smoother, and sweeter, with vanilla aromas and citrus notes. It stands up well enough to be drunk alone, or otherwise makes a superior mixer.

One definitely to drink on its own is the Añejo. Oaked for at least 18 months, this premium tequila has a spicy, pungent nose and is moderately full-bodied and complex, with flavours of fig, lemons caramel, cloves, and minerals. Delicious!

EL CONQUISTADOR
REPOSADO

DEL MAGUEY

C COLOUR Clear and clean; or bright, sparkling silver.

A AROMA Distinctive, with leather, citrus, vanilla, spice, and smoke.

T TASTE Extremely smoky and warm; moderately smooth with a firm finish.

Del Maguey provides rare mezcals – spirits made by individual family producers in the state of Oaxaca, southern Mexico. The region's wild agave (*maguey* in the local dialect) is harvested at only two years old, left to dry for 15 days, and then re-planted in Oaxaca's outlying hills where it remains for a further five years or so, before being harvested again and used for distillation. Del Maguey mezcals are truly special spirits, produced in limited quantities and marketed by village and vintage. Rich, smooth, and complex, with spice and smoke, these are definitely for sipping.

MEZCAL AND THE WORM Theories abound as to the purpose of having a worm in a bottle of spirit. Some say that the worm (or *gusano*), which bores into the leaves of the agave plant, is a mark of the drink's authenticity. More interestingly, others say that it was once a priest's way of adding divinity to the drink; or that great heroes (and lovers!) are made of those with enough nerve to eat it. Still others say that it is simply a marketing gimmick, with little tradition at all.

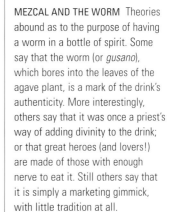

MONTE ALBAN

C COLOUR Light straw golden yellow, with a worm.

A AROMA Distinctive, with earth, spice, minerals, and smoke.

T TASTE Complex, powerful; unusual mix of dark chocolate, charcoal, and honey.

Dare you drink something with a worm in the bottle? And if you drink will you swallow the worm itself when the bottle is finished? Apparently, many people do!

Mezcal is a regionally produced spirit, specifically from the agave plants of the state of Oaxaca in southern Mexico. Although it says mezcal on the bottle, Monte Alban is really smooth and sophisticated, like a tequila. The spirit is extremely complex, with little sweetness but with plenty of wood, smoke, pepper, and bitter chocolate – this is a result of the agave being baked over charcoal, rather than steamed or boiled as it generally would be to make tequila.

The effect of the worm on the taste of the mezcal is disputed. Some claim that it adds character and sweetness to the spirit; others say that it makes no difference at all. I think that the only way to find out is by drinking it. So, do you dare?

A TASTE OF MEXICO *Monte Alban is the biggest-selling mezcal with a gusano – not actually a worm, but the larva of a Mexican night butterfly.*

66 A testament to human inventiveness!
A bewildering range of bases can be
transformed into subtle, beguiling drinks
to suit every palate. 99

OTHER SPIRITS

INTRODUCING OTHER SPIRITS

Far from being in any way second-class, the category of "other spirits" gives us some of the most complex and interesting spirits in the world – among them kirsch from cherries, Calvados from apples, and saké from rice.

Winemakers were the first to realize that the process of distillation could be applied to any number of raw materials – even those that appeared to be waste. Once their grapes are crushed and the juice extracted for the wine, winemakers are left with "pomace" – the grapes' skins, stalks, pips, and so on. Early producers soon latched on to the idea that they could distil these leftovers, thus minimizing the waste from the process of making wine. The new spirit became known as marc in France, grappa in Italy, and bagaceira in Portugal. Traditionally people drank it mixed with fruit juice or in coffee; nowadays, some of the better products are marketed as spirits for drinking on their own.

LIQUORICE ROOT *Boonekamp, a German bitter, is made using liquorice root and other herbs.*

NATURE'S SWEET GIFTS

Soon spirit producers realized that Nature herself provided a great variety of fruit other than grapes that might also be suitable for distillation. They used apples, peaches, apricots, blackberries, plums, cherries, pears, raspberries, and many more to create fruit eaux-de-vie – that is, fruit brandies. The best-known are Calvados, known as applejack in the US, which is distilled from fermented apple juice; Poire William, from the juice of the Williams pear; framboise, from raspberry; kirsch, from cherry; and slivovitz, from plum. Some brands of these drinks are extremely dry and complex, making them true rivals to Cognac and malt whisky.

RAW MATERIALS *We can use a vast array of fruits, herbs, and plants to create delicious spirits. From left to right, grape pomace is used to make grappa; peaches to make schnapps; caraway to flavour aquavit; and apples to make Calvados.*

SPIRITS FROM HERBS AND OTHER PLANTS

Drink-makers also realized that pretty much any plant matter could be macerated in alcohol (usually a basic grape spirit) and then distilled into a distinctive, new spirit with its own character and personality. The world-famous Greek Metaxa is based on grape brandy, but the brandy is flavoured with Muscat wine, anise, and other spices. The French drink Suze is essentially grape spirit that has been infused with gentian root and other herbs and then re-distilled. The Scandinavian spirit aquavit takes grain or potato spirit and blends it with a host of herbs too numerous to mention! Some of the most important spirits from nuts, herbs, and other plants are the "bitters", such as Fernet Branca, Campari, and Angostura, which were often developed for medicinal purposes, but are now famously delicious simply as alcoholic beverages.

SPIRITS FROM RICE

In Asia the practice of distilling spirit from rice dates back into time immemorial. The most important rice-based drinks are shochu and saké, both from Japan, and soju from Korea. Shochu and soju are distilled, like true spirits – you might think of them as rice vodkas; but saké is more difficult to classify. I have included it as a spirit because alcohol spirit is often mixed with the fermented rice drink; however, it is not distilled and its production techniques mean that it could arguably be considered a wine or a beer. Quite simply it is in a class of its own!

MAKING MARC *In France spirit made from grape pomace is known as marc. Most commonly the pomace is steam-heated to produce fumes which are collected, condensed, and distilled.*

SAKÉ PRODUCTION *The city of Kobe, in southern Japan, is one of the country's saké-making centres. Breweries line the streets, especially in the city's Nada district.*

MARC

When winemakers press grapes, a mixture of skins, pips, and stalks (known as *pomace*) is left behind by the process. This can be fermented and distilled into a rough brandy. In France this is known as marc, in Italy as grappa, and in Portugal as bagaceira.

GRAPPA

C **COLOUR** Ranging from clear through to light, and even dark, amber.

A **AROMA** Intense, fresh; grapes, citrus fruit; some have wood and smoke.

T **TASTE** Intensely grapey and oily, but balanced with a firm structure.

A hard-hitting pomace brandy, grappa was once intended simply to warm its drinkers against the cold Alpine winters of its historical home in northern Italy. Somewhat unfairly, over time grappa has gathered a bad reputation – with some likening it to petroleum, or calling it the "poor man's brandy". Although there are undoubtedly some grappas that might be hard to swallow, there are more, especially those from small, careful producers, that are excellent. And there is certainly nothing "poor" about it! A basic grappa might cost almost nothing, but an aged version, presented in a Venetian cut-glass bottle, could cost a small fortune.

The best grappa comes from the fresh, moist pomace of grapes that have not been crushed too heavily, thus leaving a fairly high sugar content. Red grapes tend to make the best grappas, and many higher-quality versions, some of which will give a vintage, are made from a single grape variety (look out for Barolo and Barbaresco from Italy, and red Zinfandel from the US). The best areas for grappa's production are the same as those for good Italian red wines –

GRAPPA JULIA

BENIAMINO MASCHIO GRAPPA

Piemonte (Piedmont), Trentino, Friuli, Lombardia, and the Veneto. Grappa can be aged for up to around ten years, often in wooden barrels made from oak, cherry, acacia, or chestnut.

Of the big producers, look for Nardini (the biggest), and Stock's Grappa Julia. Luxury brands come from Nonino and Jacopo Poli. There are hundreds of artisan producers, but especially try Beniamono Maschio from the Veneto, Bertagnolli from Trentino, and Marolo from Piemonte. One of my favourites is di Tignanello. Fantastic!

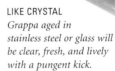
LIKE CRYSTAL
Grappa aged in stainless steel or glass will be clear, fresh, and lively with a pungent kick.

BAGACEIRA

C **COLOUR** Usually colourless, but versions aged in wood are very pale gold.

A **AROMA** Rich and fruity, with black fruits, grapes, and port.

T **TASTE** Rich, dry, and smooth, with finesse, full body, and a long finish.

Bagaceira is a Portuguese pomace brandy, rather like grappa. (In Spain a similar spirit is called *aguardiente de orujo*, but even in Spain itself this has only a small following.)

Dry and fruity, bagaceira is made using the residue of the grapes that have gone into Portugal's delicious Vinho Verde wine, grapes such as Alvarinho. After distillation the spirit is often aged in ex-port barrels, which gives bagaceira a certain richness. Look out for producers such as Avelada, Impoerio, Neto Costa, and Sao Domingo.

MARC

C **COLOUR** Clear through to light or dark amber when aged in oak.

A **AROMA** Aromatic; fruit and earth, quite often with an oily feel.

T **TASTE** Deeply fruity and grapey, and often warm and lively.

The most important marc-producing regions in France are Champagne, Burgundy, and Alsace. Marc de Champagne is the most aromatic and so has the best reputation. Some of the better-known marcs include Chateau d'Arlay, Marc d'Irouleguy Etienne Brana, and Marc du Chateau Rayas. Examples from very prestigious appellations, such as Montrachet and Chambertin, are worth trying – with a reputation to uphold, they make sure that their marcs are among the best available.

CHERRY

Almost any fruit can be fermented and distilled, but the best, such as cherries, are those that are not naturally over-sweet, and that have pips or stones that can add complexity to the final product.

KIRSCH

C **COLOUR** All the colour is distilled out – kirsch is clear, pure, and crystalline.

A **AROMA** Intense and attractive; cherry, with almond, stone, and minerals.

T **TASTE** Quite dry, with fresh, underripe cherry and almond, and a fresh finish.

Kirsch, or Kirschwasser ("cherry water"), makes a great alternative to Cognac at the end of a meal. First made in around 1650, when monks began to distil cherries for use as a medicine, kirsch is extremely pure and clear. Enjoy it as an after-dinner snifter, or use it to brighten up an espresso, or in a Black Forest gâteau.

KIRSCH

Kirsch is usually made from black cherries, which give a concentrated, rich flavour. However, it is not only the flesh of the cherries that is important, but the stones, too. These give kirsch its slaty, mineral notes, and lift it above being merely "another" fruit spirit.

There are many kirsch producers, particularly in France (concentrated around Alsace) and Germany, but brands most widely available internationally are Bols, De Kuyper, Etter, Meyer, and Dettling – all worth trying.

RASPBERRY

Raspberry is another fruit with a useful touch of acidity, which prevents its distilled spirit from becoming too sweet and cloying.

FRAMBOISE

C **COLOUR** Clear and pure – distillation removes all traces of red fruit.

A **AROMA** Intensely fruity and jammy; red fruits, especially raspberry.

T **TASTE** Fresh and lively; not too sweet, with a zesty finish.

Framboise (not to be confused with Framboise liqueur) is a raspberry brandy fermented from a mash of pure raspberries. Once distilled, the brandy is aged in glass. The result is fruity and intense, but with an attractive dryness. Drink it from a large, chilled glass, and swirl – to release its aromas – before you sip.

HIMBEERGEIST

C **COLOUR** Clear and pure, with no trace of the red of the raspberry.

A **AROMA** Very aromatic; jammy; raspberry and other red fruits.

T **TASTE** Rich and deeply fruity, but not overly sweet.

Himbeergeist is the raspberry brandy of Germany, equivalent to the French framboise, originating from the Black Forest in the southwest of the country.

Clear and fresh, but also full and fragrant, and quite high in alcohol, Himbeergeist is great on ice as an apéritif or at room temperature as an after-dinner drink. You could also use it to make a variation on a Kir (usually made with Crème de Cassis de Dijon), by placing a dash of Himbeergeist in a glass of dry white wine. Himbeergeist's main producer is Schladerer, part of NMK Schulz.

APPLE AND PEAR

Using apples and pears to make cider and perry is as old as civilization, and outstanding spirits can be derived from them too. Selected varieties of fruit and special processes give flavour, quality, and character to the distilled spirit.

POIRE WILLIAM

C **COLOUR** Most versions are clear, although some may be pale yellow-gold.

A **AROMA** Intensely fruity and beautifully balanced, with pear to the fore.

T **TASTE** Smooth, powerful, and full-bodied, with a long finish.

Poire William is a fruit brandy, or eau-de-vie. It is distilled from the aromatic and intense Williams pear, known in the US as the Bartlett pear after Enoch Bartlett of Massachusetts, who introduced it from Europe. The spirit is made all over the world, and, with the notable exceptions of Cognac, Armagnac, and Calvados (apple brandy), Poire

William is the most important fruit brandy in France. France produces about four million bottles each year, half of which leave the country for export – mainly to Italy, Germany, and the Benelux countries, and to Canada and the US.

MARIE BRIZARD POIRE WILLIAM

Poire William is made by a large number of small, traditional producers. It takes 8kg (62lbs) of Williams pears to make a one-litre bottle of spirit, making Poire William expensive to produce and buy. Once distilled, the spirit is aged for around five years, usually in glass containers, which keep the liquid

clear. The result is a spirit that is quite strong (around 45% ABV), and not overly sweet. Swiss versions may be more complex, as in Switzerland the spirit is often aged in wood, which also gives a pale golden or amber colour (like the pears themselves).

Overall Poire William has a great balance between deep fruitiness and freshness, which makes it especially delicious in the summer. Serve it chilled. Producers to look out for include: from France, Marie Brizard, Miclo, Massenez, and Meyer; from Germany, Schladerer (in Germany Poire William is known as Birnenwasser or William Birne); from Hungary, Zwack or Vilmos; and from the US, from Clear Creek or Koenig.

THE PEAR TRICK
To get the pear into the bottle, the empty bottle is attached to the tree as the pear is in bud. Then, the fruit simply grows inside.

Eau de vie de

Poire William

G. Miclo
Distillateur à Lapoutroie
Haut-Rhin-France

70 cl   43% vol.

Produce of France
114085

CALVADOS

C COLOUR Light, greeny gold, through to dark amber for the aged versions.

A AROMA Aromas of cider, cloves, wood, cinnamon, and raisins.

T TASTE Quite dry and smooth, with apple, and notes of vanilla and oak.

Calvados is a brandy distilled from a mash of cider apples, although in theory it can also be made from pears. Traditionally, the fermented mash is double-distilled and matured in oak casks for up to 25 years. It is named after the Norman *département* of Calvados (France), which itself was named after a Spanish galleon, *El Calvador*, wrecked on Normandy's rocky coast.

Apple brandy produced only in the French regions of Normandy, Brittany, and Maine can be called Calvados. The regions form part of the Appellation d'Origine Contrôlée (AOC) system that governs French wine production, and there are 11 AOCs producing Calvados. The best spirit is from the small heartland area of the Pays d'Auge.

Around 50 different varieties of apple may be used to make Calvados, giving plenty of variation in style – from sweeter and softer, to drier and more zesty. Most exported Calvados is six or seven years old, but you may find a "*vieux*" (old) Calvados, which will be smoother and richer, with better balance.

These older versions (more than six years old) are the ones to look out for. Try producers such as Busnel, Boulard, Coquerel, Chauffe Coeur, Dupont, Groult, Massenez, Morice, and Pere Magliore, and drink them straight – fine calvados is too good for mixing!

CALVADOS

WINTER DIGESTIF *My favourite way to drink a smooth Calvados is at room temperature, at the end of a meal, in winter.*

APPLEJACK

C **COLOUR** Clear through to pale gold if aged in oak barrels.

A **AROMA** Quite grapey and fruity, with hints of oak.

T **TASTE** Dry and complex, with a mellow smoothness, and a medium finish.

Applejack is an apple brandy from New England in the US. The spirit is made from the fermented mash of cider apples. In times gone by, applejack producers created the spirit by leaving containers of the fermented mixture outside in the frost. This separated the water from the alcohol by literally freezing it out, leaving a neat apple brandy. Needless to say the results were pretty impure and gave rise to the nickname "Jersey Lightning" – an almost lethal substance!

Modern production is closer to that of Calvados. Several varieties of apple are picked, usually at the peak of the apple harvest – a standard sized bottle at 40% ABV needs around 4.5kg (10lbs) of apples; stronger versions need more. The mash is fermented and then the spirit is double-distilled – in pot stills for the best versions – and aged in oak for about two years. The applejack may then be sold as a straight brandy, or mixed with a neutral spirit to be marketed as a lighter "blended applejack".

Look out for Laird's. This distillery, founded by a Scotsman in the 18th century, in Scobeyville, New Jersey, produces 1.5 million bottles of spirit a year, most of which is applejack. Clear Creek, based in Oregon, produce an Eau de Vie de Pomme, which is well-balanced and fruity, with a long finish and worth drinking straight. Otherwise, as a general rule I prefer to put applejack in a cocktail – it offers the mix a sour, citrus edge, and some bite.

APPLEJACK

PEACH AND APRICOT

Flavoured vodkas are often marketed as fashionably modern drinks, but in Germany and eastern Europe, fruit has long been used to make schnapps, or flavoured grain spirit. Peaches and apricots have an element of acidity which gives a better quality spirit.

PEACH SCHNAPPS

C **COLOUR** Any colour is distilled out to give a pure, crystal-clear liquid.

A **AROMA** Ripe, fruity peach, with a soft and attractive sweetness.

T **TASTE** Sweet and luxurious; peach overlaid with nuts and honey.

Strictly speaking, schnapps, which originates from northern Europe and Scandinavia (where it is known as *akvavit*), is a spirit distilled from grain or potatoes, and then flavoured with aniseed or caraway seeds. However, the term schnapps (from a Nordic word meaning "gulp", and referring to the idea that the drink should be taken down in one go) is now used to refer to any neutral grain spirit that has been infused with fruit – essentially making a fruit-flavoured spirit, similar to flavoured vodka, but much sweeter and more fruity.

Peach schnapps is a grain spirit in which the producer has steeped fully ripe peach fruits, including the stones (pits). In one way, a mouthful of peach schnapps is like a mouthful of lovely, fresh peach; but in another it is not! While the drink is so sweet and attractive that it can very easily lure you into drinking too much, at around 23% ABV, peach schnapps has quite a kick, and is definitely no soft drink or fruit juice. Be warned!

However, peach schnapps is a great drink for enjoying at any time, and it is absolutely perfect in the summer. My ideal method for serving it is to keep the spirit in the freezer, taking it out only to pour. The icy chill will bring out the lovely fruit flavours and balances the sweetness with a fresh, cold feel as it slips down. What could be more perfect for a summer party?

Of course, peach schnapps need not be drunk neat and schnapps begs to be added into a cocktail. Try it with soda water for a long, refreshing pick-me-up at the end of the day, or in fruit juice. (When peach schnapps is poured into orange juice the mix is known as a "Fuzzy Navel".) If you feel like spoiling yourself, add a shot into a glass of Champagne – making a peach schnapps Bellini.

A more unusual alternative, but one that works really well, is to drink peach schnapps neat as a dessert wine. The sweetness makes a good match for fruit ice creams or a fruit salad.

The two most important peach schnapps brands on the market are Archers, owned by Diageo, and sold mainly in the UK and elsewhere in Europe, and De Kuyper Peachtree, which is the main brand in the US. Both are excellent for drinking neat or in cocktails.

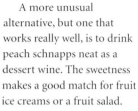

ARCHERS

KECSKEMÉT

C **COLOUR** Any colour is distilled away, leaving a beautifully clear spirit.

A **AROMA** Quite aromatic and well-balanced, with apricot and herbs.

T **TASTE** Dry, with fruit and spirit to the fore; quite lively; bright finish.

Kecskemét, or to give it the proper title Kecskeméti Barack Palinka, is an outstanding and distinctive Hungarian eau-de-vie. It is made using the *kajszi* variety of apricots, traditionally grown on the plains around the town of Kecskemét in central Hungary. Here, the perfect growing conditions create fruit that is so rich and flavourful that there is never any need to add sugar or alcohol to the mash after fermentation. Since Kecskemét was first made in 1920, the Hungarian company Zwack Unicum has become the world's leading producer. This spirit is dry and complex, and perfect on a warm evening.

LAND AND PRODUCTION

WHAT'S IN A NAME? The term "brandy" is often used loosely and interchangably with "eau-de-vie" to describe any spirit distilled from fermented fruit. Strictly speaking, however, the term brandy refers only to grape spirit. To add more confusion to the terminology, some cherry and apricot brandies are in fact liqueurs – that is, they are made from any spirit (even grain spirit) in which fruit is macerated. Kecskemét, from Hungary *(see right)*, is an example of a true eau-de-vie because it is made from apricots that are minced, fermented, and double-distilled.

PLUM

In central and eastern Europe plums are used as the basis of brandy, and they give a tangy, dry feel to the distilled spirit.

QUETSCH

C **COLOUR** Clear; any colour from the fruit is entirely removed by distillation.

A **AROMA** Complex and aromatic, with plum and nuts, especially almond.

T **TASTE** Quite dry, smooth, and warm, with a fine balance and a lively finish.

Quetsch is plum brandy from the mash of the black Switzen plum. After distillation, the spirit is aged for eight to ten years, and is fresh and dry. It works best in cocktails. (For a digestif, try Mirabelle plum brandy, made from yellow plums.)

SLIVOVITZ

C **COLOUR** Colourless through to light gold for versions that have been wood-aged.

A **AROMA** Aromatic and delicate, with plum and dried dark fruits.

T **TASTE** Very dry and quite intense, with a slightly bitter finish.

Slivovitz is an eastern European brandy made from dark blue Sljiva plums. Producers crush ripe plums and ferment the mash for about three months, before double-distilling and ageing in oak barrels. Fresh plums may be added to the maturing spirit to give more intense aromas and flavours.

Serve slivovitz well-chilled in a shot glass. Brands to look out for are Jelinek, Maraska, Zwack (which produces a kosher version), Koenig, and Clear Creek.

SLIVOVITZ

FIG

Figs are grown primarily in Muslim countries, where alcohol is prohibited. As a result, only a few fig-based spirits are available.

BOUKHA

C **COLOUR** Colourless – distillation removes all the colour of the figs.

A **AROMA** Delicate and intensely fruity, with sweet fruit and light molasses.

T **TASTE** Extremely dry; rounded and elegant, with a complex structure.

Boukha, a fig brandy, is the national drink of Tunisia. The best brands – look for Soleil or Bokobsa – are fresh and dry, and quite restrained and delicate (poor-quality boukha is a bit like fig syrup). Drink it ice cold as an apéritif; at room temperature as a digestif; or mixed with fruit juice for a refreshing and unusual long drink.

MAPLE

One variety of maple tree yields a sugary sap that is used to produce maple syrup. This syrup can be fermented and distilled.

FINE SÈVE

C **COLOUR** Clear through to very pale gold.

A **AROMA** An appealing mix of vanilla, maple, and honey.

T **TASTE** Delicate, with honey-and-vanilla sweetness.

Originating from Quebec, in Canada, Fine Sève is a smooth and rich brandy made from maple and honey. It is aged in oak casks and can be drunk straight or over ice. As a treat, I like to pour some over vanilla ice-cream.

FINE SÈVE

TI PLANT

Once used in Hawaiian medicines, ceremonies, and customs, the boiled roots of the ti plant are distilled into a spirit.

OKOLEHAO

C **COLOUR** Colourless, through to medium gold if aged in wood.

A **AROMA** Bright and appealing; herbs and fruits, with vanilla and honey.

T **TASTE** Quite lively, spicy, and earthy, with a warm feel.

Okolehao is the distilled spirit of a blend of tropical herbs and spices, and, most important of all, the Hawaiian ti plant – said to ward off evil and bring goodness and strength. The colourless version is a "pure" okolehao spirit, and the golden version has been either aged in Bourbon barrels or mixed with Bourbon whiskey.

BITTERS

Bitters are blends of herbs, roots, and spices with an alcohol base. They were popularized in the 19th century as health "elixirs".

FERNET BRANCA

C **COLOUR** Dark brown with orange tinges from the herb mixture.

A **AROMA** Very complex, with lots of herbs, especially fresh, grassy mint.

T **TASTE** Bitter and medicinal, with menthol and a dry, herb finish.

Fernet Branca is a bitter, aromatic Italian spirit made with a base of grape alcohol (like brandy) and more than 40 herbs and spices, including St John's wort, myrrh, rhubarb, camomile, cardamom, and saffron – although the precise recipe is a secret. In the mid-19th century a young Milanese woman, Maria Scala, developed the blend, and her husband Bernadino Branca founded a company for its manufacture in 1845. The company, Fratelli Branca, which is still overseen by the family, now produces Fernet Branca in Milan and sells it all over the western world.

The herbs and spices are mixed into a base of premium spirit, and aged in oak barrels for more than a year, creating a powerful brew at 42% ABV. The Italian way to drink Fernet Branca is as a digestif, served at room temperature in a shot glass, although many people now use the spirit in cocktails, dropped into coffee, or sometimes with cola or mineral water.

A special feature of Fernet Branca is that it is greatly prized as a hangover cure. Generally, I am sceptical about claims of miracle cures, but many of my friends

FERNET BRANCA

CROSSING THE OCEANS *This poster, from 1887, proudly boasts the already international success of Fernet Branca.*

swear by this one! Try the Corpse Reviver: 40ml (1½oz) brandy, 15ml (½oz) Fernet Branca, and 30ml (1oz) white Crème de Menthe, mixed with plenty of ice.

The company also makes a mint-flavoured version, Branca Menta. The menthol makes the spirit a more palatable straight digestif.

ANGOSTURA

C COLOUR A very dark and mysterious deep amber.

A AROMA Herbs, roots, molasses, and a balance of rum.

T TASTE Essentially bitter, but finely balanced with rum and herbs.

Angostura is a Trinidadian company producing "bitters" – a complex range of roots and herbs, in this case in a base of rum. In 1824, Dr. Johann Siegert, surgeon-general in Simon Bolivar's army against Spanish rule in Venezuela, developed aromatic bitters to a secret formula and used them to improve the well-being of the soldiers. These became known as Angostura bitters – after the town in Venezuela where Siegert was based.

ANGOSTURA

From the early 1800s onward, it was not unusual to find bitters in the guise of medicinal elixirs. However, soon people began drinking them like any other spirit, and in time the American Food and Drug Administration banned all reference to their medicinal qualities. Once bitters were purely in the alcoholic domain, US bartenders began using them in cocktails – the herbs and spices helped fuse together a cocktail's ingredients, and the alcohol (around 40% ABV in Angostura) added an extra kick. In the 1870s Carlos Siegert (Dr. Siegert's son) promoted his bitters in Europe, making them a hit there too. If you are serious about making cocktails, then a bottle of Angostura bitters is essential for your drinks cabinet.

SPICING UP YOUR GIN
Angostura was first exhibited in London in 1862, where testers raved about the new bitters as a perfect way to spice up the potentially bland flavour of gin.

CULTURE AND TRADITION

THE ANGOSTURA BANNER
Although the company is based in Trinidad, Angostura is sold around the world. The company's phenomenal success is down to its great marketing. In the cocktail heyday of the 1920s and 1930s, Angostura was merely one of a range of bitters used in mixed drinks – now it is often the only one.

APEROL

- **C** COLOUR Dark orange from the fruit – rather like darkened orange skins.
- **A** AROMA Complex and well-balanced, with herbs, orange, and spice.
- **T** TASTE Quite sweet, with a blend of orange, rhubarb, and herbs.

Aperol is a dark orange, Italian apéritif with a sweet-orange taste. It is made from a blend of spirits, along with rhubarb, gentian, and other roots and herbs – the precise formula has been kept a secret since 1919 – and has an alcohol content of only 11% ABV. It is made by Barbieri, part of the Campari group.

Although intended to be drunk straight, Aperol is enjoyed diluted with soda water by millions of Italians – a refreshing, long apéritif combination that I love – as well as in a range of cocktails.

APEROL

BOONEKAMP

- **C** COLOUR Dark orange-amber from the herbs and spices.
- **A** AROMA Aromatic, pungent; herbs, roots (especially liquorice), and spice.
- **T** TASTE Sweet liquorice, spice, and a warm, bitter finish.

Boonekamp is a traditional bitter, made in Germany from a mixture of herbs, roots, and spices. It was named after Herr Kamp, who invented the medicinal formula as "stomach drops" in 1815, then sold it to a Dutch firm who turned it into bitters with a strong alcoholic content (43–48% ABV).

In the great days of cocktail-making, Boonekamp would have been on every bartender's shelf. Now, however, it has lost much of its market share to Angostura.

SUZE

- **C** COLOUR Medium yellow – the influence of the gentian root.
- **A** AROMA Unusual, distinctive; gentian, with apricot, vanilla, citrus, and caramel.
- **T** TASTE Oily, round, and full; bitter-sweet with gentian, citrus, vanilla; long finish.

The creation of Parisian distiller Fernand Moureaux, Suze was launched in 1889 and is a complex blend of wild gentian roots and herbs that have been thoroughly macerated and distilled. It is quite oily and has a bitter-sweet character similar to Campari.

Suze is most widely available in France, where it is often drunk straight with ice, or diluted with tonic water or even blackcurrant cordial. If you have never tried it, then give it a go as an apéritif – like many others, you may love it.

SUZE

AVÈZE

- **C** COLOUR A light golden yellow, from the gentian root.
- **A** AROMA Aromatic and pungent, with herbs, spice, and earth.
- **T** TASTE Herbal, dry, and slightly bitter, but well-balanced.

Created in 1928, Avèze is the only apéritif made from the must of fresh gentian roots that have been macerated for nine months. (The roots come from the yellow gentian plant, found exclusively in central France.) This prolonged maceration results in an unusual, dry flavour, with a mildly bitter, herbal character.

You can drink Avèze as an apéritif either straight or with soda water. I sometimes have an Avèze "Kir" – I mix blackcurrant liqueur with Avèze, rather than dry white wine.

CAMPARI

- **C** COLOUR A wonderful, deep, red-pink – the result of added cochineal.
- **A** AROMA Elegant and distinctive – orange, fruit, and spice.
- **T** TASTE Refreshing, dry; bitter-sweet taste of orange and herbs; fresh finish.

Along with Angostura, Campari is probably the best-known bitter in the world. However, unlike Angostura, Campari is not a "medicinal" bitter, primarily for use in cocktails, but rather an apéritif – more often drunk with soda water or lemonade, than in a large mix of other drinks (although it unquestionably tastes great in cocktails).

Created in the 1860s, Campari is the quintessential taste of Italy. A master drink-maker and café-owner in the town of Novara, just outside Milan, Gaspare Campari brought

CAMPARI

together a formula of more than 60 herbs and plants to create his bitters. Following his marriage to a Milanese woman, Campari moved to Milan where he opened a popular café in the Galleria Vittorio Emmanuele, the city's most prestigious shopping mall. To capitalize on the reputation and popularity of Dutch cordials, Campari initially called his invention *Bitter all'uso d'Hollandia* (meaning "bitter as used in Holland"), although it had no connection with Holland at all. His campaign worked and the bitters quickly caught on with the Milanese customers. Soon, helped by the marketing genius of his son Davide, Gaspare Campari turned his drink into a global product. Now it is available in more than 190 countries worldwide, and part of the massive Campari Group, owners of Cinzano, Skyy Vodka, and Ouzo 12, along with many other famous brands.

Campari's precise formula is a closely guarded secret, but the drink is known to contain quinine, rhubarb, ginseng, bitter orange peel, and a host of aromatic herbs. These are combined and then macerated for two weeks in a blend of distilled water and alcohol. The resulting mixture is sweetened with sugar and tinted red with cochineal dye, and then the alcohol level is adjusted to 24% ABV.

The classic way to drink Campari is with soda water *(see box, below)*, but if you enjoy really bitter flavours, try drinking it straight, over ice – always before dinner, of course. When I am relaxing in the garden on a summer's day, and I need something really long and refreshing, I like to drink it with orange or grapefruit juice. For a summer party, Campari and vodka will certainly get things going!

CULTURE AND TRADITION

CAMPARI AND SODA In 1932 Gaspare Campari's son Davide introduced single-measure, pre-mixed bottles of CampariSoda, turning Campari and soda water into a classic combination. Hugely popular in Italy and in other parts of Europe, this mix can be quite dry, so many drinkers substitute lemonade for the soda water. The best way to appreciate Campari and soda is to chill the ingredients, and then mix them together in a chilled glass.

AQUAVIT

This unusual Scandinavian drink sits somewhere between vodka, gin, and whisky! Aquavit is made by adding herbs and spices to a spirit base. Its name is derived from *"aqua vitae"*, which means "water of life".

AQUAVIT

C **COLOUR** A distinctive pale gold colour, with bright yellow highlights.

A **AROMA** Complex, with notes of citrus, herbs, and caraway.

T **TASTE** Quite smooth and warm, with a herbal and spicy finish.

Scandinavia has been producing aquavit (or akvavit) for many centuries. It is made from either potato or grain spirit, usually flavoured with caraway, dill, aniseed, fennel, citrus-fruit peel, and herbs.

Danish aquavit (made from grain spirit) is considered to be the best, but there are many different varieties

AQUAVIT

from throughout Scandinavia, and it is simply a matter of trying them to find your favourite. The best-known brands and a good starting point, are Aalborg (from Denmark), Gamel of Linie (Norway), and O.P. Anderson (Sweden), but also look out for Gammal Norrlands (also from Sweden).

In Scandinavia aquavit is enjoyed with with herrings, gravadlax, or pickled duck or chicken, and spicy Asian dishes. I like to drink mine chilled and straight, just like vodka.

RICE AND GRAIN

Most of the rice used in making alcoholic drinks goes into the production of "rice wine" or saké. Japan, China, and Korea do not have a long tradition of making strong spirits, but they all now produce distilled spirits from rice and other grains.

SOJU

C **COLOUR** An icy clarity – similar to a good, clear vodka.

A **AROMA** Light and delicate, with a mellow, fruity feel.

T **TASTE** Fresh, light, and crisp, with a touch of sweetness and a smooth finish.

A traditional Korean spirit, similar to vodka, soju was originally a distilled form of sake (*see pp266–7*), but is now made from rice, barley, other grains, and sometimes sweet potatoes. It has a crisp, clean, and powerful palate. In Asia, soju is drunk straight or over ice, but in the West it is often blended with juice or other mixers.

MOU TAI CHIEW

C **COLOUR** Pure and clear – a result of distilling away the traces of grain.

A **AROMA** Rich and scented, with a good balance of alcohol spirit and grain.

T **TASTE** Full, warm, and rich, with a lively feel and a long finish.

Mou Tai Chiew is China's most famous distilled spirit, made from sorghum and barley. The grain mash is fermented eight times and distilled seven times, and the whole process can take anything up to five years to complete. The Chinese drink their liquor with food, but try it as a shot, or diluted with water, soda, or juice.

SHOCHU

C **COLOUR** Colourless; similar to vodka, especially purified shochu.

A **AROMA** Complex and delicate; melon, citrus fruits, and flowers.

T **TASTE** Smooth and fresh, and sometimes quite sweet; lively finish.

Shochu is a spirit produced almost throughout Japan, but originating in the Kagoshima district of Kyushu island, in the south. Although its exact origins are unknown, the spirit was mentioned in documents dating from as long ago as 1500AD, and it most likely came to Japan from China via Korea.

Shochu comes in two versions. The standard version, called *otsu-rui* or *honkaku*, is made from rice, sweet potatoes, rye, corn, or raw sugar, and is distilled in pot stills (stills shaped like old-fashioned kettles, with a

SANWA IICHIKO
SHOCHU

round bowl and a neck), which better reflect the aromas and flavours of the ingredients that have gone into the spirit. This makes *otsu-rui* best for drinking straight, with a dash of water, or over ice, rather as you might a malt whisky.

The other version of shochu is *ko-rui*. The main ingredient in *ko-rui* shochu is molasses, and the spirit is made using continuous distillation (the spirit is distilled several times in consecutive stages of the same process), leaving hardly any aroma at all. This makes *ko-rui* shochu particularly suitable for mixing, as it adds a fresh, clean bite to a cocktail, without tampering with the cocktail's flavour. The alcohol content of both types ranges from 20% ABV up to even 45% ABV, although most shochus are

TAKARA ZIPANG
SHOCHU

marketed at around a more reasonable 25% ABV.

In Japan, shochu is traditionally drunk mixed with hot or cold water, oolong tea, or a fruit juice, such as orange, peach, or grapefruit (*see right*). In addition, rather than drinking it aside from food, the Japanese often enjoy shochu as a perfect partner to spicy Asian cuisine.

The sheer number of different brands of shochu – altogether there are more than 3,000 available in Japan – is testament to its ongoing popularity among a new generation of younger drinkers, many of whom are women. Vending machines have even begun to sell pre-mixed, single-measure bottles of the spirit, and the desirability of some brands has elevated them to cult status: the Mao, Moriizo, and Murao brands – nicknamed "Kagoshima no 3M" – are particularly sought-after. On the world

market look out for examples from Tori Kai, Takara, and Sanwa, as well as shochus from the big brewers Suntory, Kirin, and Asahi.

The Japanese say that shochu is good for your health – but I have heard that one before!

MIXING IT UP

CITRUS SHOCHU In Japan it is normal practice to mix shochu with fruit juices for a refreshing drink with a kick. Put one measure of *ko-rui* shochu in a glass and top with chilled orange juice.

SAKÉ

C COLOUR Clear through to light golden, depending upon the style.

A AROMA Delicate and light; fruity and flowery, with a fresh character.

T TASTE Fresh and lively, with sometimes spicy, nutty, or sweet notes.

Saké tends to be a source of confusion for Western drinkers. Is it a wine, a beer, or even a spirit? Certainly, it seems to have characteristics associated with each. Although it is often described in terms applied to wine (dry or sweet, light or heavy), and is served like a wine, it is brewed like a beer. But it has a higher alcoholic strength (usually around 14 or 15% ABV) than either wine or beer, and so perhaps is closer to a spirit. And yet saké is not really like any other alcoholic drink at all. Made from rice and selected

HAKUTSURU SAKÉ

types of water, saké is produced using a unique process.

In Japan production of saké began in around 300BC, after the Japanese had established rice as their basic food crop. However, saké is not normally made from ordinary cooking rice. Rather, most saké comes from a special variety of rice called *sakamai*, which has an especially high level of starch stored within the grain.

This rice is "polished" (milled) before brewing to expose its concentrated starch centre. The polished rice is then steeped in water, steamed, and finally cooled ready for fermentation. A small amount of the steamed rice is separated out to encourage growth of *koji* (*Aspergillus oryzae*) – a beneficial mould, similar to the mould in blue cheese,

GEKKEIKAN SAKÉ

which breaks down the rice starch into glucose and then alcohol. Added yeast also performs this function, creating a process known as "parallel fermentation", unique to making saké. Fermentation takes about a month – much longer than that for beer or wine – after which the saké is aged for around six months. In some types of saké, alcohol spirit is added, not to add strength, but to dissolve any impurities.

Saké should be light and fresh, not rich and heavy, and its aromas and taste should be delicate and sensitive. All saké is pasteurized except for *nama-zake*, which has particularly bright, lively flavours, but needs to be refrigerated until you are ready to drink it.

There are four basic types of quality saké. *Junmai-shu*, made only from rice with no added alcohol, is usually quite full bodied. *Honjozo-shu*, made with a small amount of alcohol spirit, is light, dry, and fragrant. *Ginjo-shu* is very high quality, and made with highly polished rice. The more a grain of rice is polished, the less of it remains, but the more concentrated its starch content. It is deliberately fermented in cool conditions, making it complex, fruity, and especially delicate. *Daiginjo-shu*, made with an even higher grade of polished rice, is exceptionally fragrant and delicate. (The "*shu*" in these names merely denotes saké, and is often omitted in description.)

Together these four make up the highest classification of saké, called Special Designation Saké – or *tokutei meishoshu* – comprising around 20 per cent of the world's total saké production. "Normal" saké often contains large amounts of alcohol spirit, and is known as *futsu-shu*. Some of this is rough and harsh – but by no means all.

Saké is incredibly versatile. You can drink it cold, at around 5°C (40°F), or warm – up to about 55°C

FOOD MATCH

LIGHT FOODS The range of food partners for saké is vast, but as a general rule avoid matching saké with heavy meats or strong, spicy foods. Instead, saké makes the perfect accompaniment for light dishes, especially light fish and seafood, such as Japanese sushi, as well as salads.

(130°F), but not any warmer, otherwise you will destroy the flavours. Most of the better sakés are served at room temperature or chilled, which brings out their delicacy and subtlety. The drink is often used as an apéritif, but also makes a good accompaniment to certain foods (*see box, above*).

There are thousands of saké brands, and hundreds of producers. The biggest-selling brand in the world is Gekkeikan, which, along with two of the other biggest producers, Ozeki and Shochikubai, makes and markets saké in the US. Sakés from another large producer, Sawanotsuru, and from the Japanese beer company Asahi, are available in a number of Western supermarkets, as are quality brands, such as Hakutsura. Some of the most well-respected Japanese brands are Juyondai, Isojiman, Rikyubai, Kamoizum, Kaiun, and Otemon – but there are many more.

SAWANOTSURA SAKÉ

LAND AND PRODUCTION

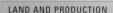

MAKING SAKÉ The rice-and-water mixture is fermented using the simultaneous action of yeast and *koji* – a mould cultivated on an extracted portion of the steamed rice. The picture *(right)* shows yeast and *koji* being mixed with rice at the Takahashi Saké Brewery in Nagaoka, Japan, at the beginning of this process. At the end, ageing takes place in small barrels *(below)*, but only for around six months: producers have to pay hefty taxes for storing saké that is otherwise ready for drinking.

CEREMONY AND SAKÉ *Here two traditional porcelain cups, known as* masu, *offer Hakutsuru saké – a medium-dry, light, and mellow brand of saké made using techniques that are 250 years old.*

LIQUEURS

SWEET REWARDS

Deliciously flavoured with ingredients from every corner of the world, liqueurs are sweetened spirits infused with almost any fruit, plant, or food you can think of – from cherries to chocolate.

HERBAL FLAVOURS *The earliest liqueurs used herbs, such as thyme* (top), *and spices, such as vanilla* (above), *to flavour spirits. Many liqueur recipes are centuries old and even now are closely guarded secrets.*

Sweet rewards indeed! I love the fact that a new fashion is emerging for diners to enjoy a liqueur digestif at the end of their meal. And with such a wonderful array of liqueurs on offer, there is something for everyone.

Historically, liqueurs were made and drunk for their medicinal properties, but by the beginning of the 20th century, certain towns and regions became famous for particular types of liqueur (curaçao from Amsterdam, anisette from Bordeaux, and so on). Liqueur production became integrated into the wider drinks industry, and the differences in styles were accentuated to create the diverse brands available today.

LIQUEUR STYLES

A liqueur is any flavoured spirit that has been sweetened. All kinds of flavourings can, and have, been used, but I like to think of three basic styles of liqueur: fruit-based drinks, made from berries, soft fruits, citrus fruits, and exotics; those made with vegetables, herbs, and spices; and those based on any number of other ingredients, such as eggs, chocolate, and coffee.

Fruit-based drinks make up the largest and most diverse group of liqueurs, ranging from the intense, concentrated dry fruit liqueurs, such

as triple sec (made from bitter oranges) through to light and sweet concoctions, such as cherry brandy. Not surprisingly, methods of production of these liqueurs vary enormously, too. The best examples are made by macerating the fruit and creating a sort of "must" – a liquid thick with the skins, stems, and flesh of the fruit, and often also its stones, kernels, or pips, which impart a complex, nutty flavour. Raw spirit is then added to the must, along with sweeteners and herbs, and the mixture is allowed to steep before filtering and bottling. Other liqueurs are produced by distilling the fermented fruit mash to create a genuine eau-de-vie (brandy), which is then sweetened and further flavoured with fruit, and diluted to the right strength with water. Some lower-end fruit liqueurs are made by the simple process of mixing fruit juice with spirit and then adding other flavouring ingredients.

Liqueurs made from a base of vegetables, herbs, and spices are the most obvious descendants of the original medicinal elixirs. Many are still made by monks according to ancient and closely guarded recipes, but the basic method of production is to steep the mélange of herbs, roots, and other plants in alcoholic spirit. This group of drinks includes the

SURPRISING INGREDIENTS *Amaretto liqueur has a distinctive almond flavour, but some of this nuttiness comes from apricot kernels.*

" The wonderful thing about liqueurs is their sheer variety, which is a tribute to hundreds of years of human inventiveness."

PERFECT ENDINGS *A glass of amaretto and a coffee is the perfect way to end a meal. The bitterness of the coffee is offset by amaretto's luscious sweetness.*

TIMELESS BENEDICTINE
First created at the abbey of Fécamp, northern France, in 1510, Benedictine is still made in the same town and uses the same secret recipe to this day.

famous monastic liqueurs of Chartreuse and Benedictine (both from France), as well as the herby Galliano (from Italy), vegetal Unicum (from Hungary), and fresh Licor 43 (from Spain). Crème de menthe also falls into this category; it is worth noting that the word "crème" does not mean that cream is added, but that the liqueur is made from only the named ingredient – in this case, mint. Several important liqueurs in this group are based on star anise and aniseed – two ingredients that taste similar, but are actually from different plants – along with a cocktail of other herbs and roots, especially liquorice. They vary in style and in the way they are produced, but they are all related and include Pernod, Pastis 51, Ricard, Sambuca, Raki, Anisette, Ouzo, and many other famous names.

The third group of liqueurs is based on nuts, beans (particularly coffee and cocoa beans), eggs, milk, and cream. This group includes some of the most luxurious and rich liqueurs of all – the wonderful amaretto, with its mixture of fruit and almonds, and Frangelico, almost as famous, but made using hazelnuts. It also includes some of the most popular and widely available of the liqueur brands: Malibu, which combines white rum and coconut, has introduced rum to a whole new generation of drinkers; and Baileys, a mixture of Irish whiskey, cream, and chocolate, which is the biggest-selling liqueur in the world. Spirits made using cream, chocolate, and coffee have proved irresistible to sweet-toothed, modern liqueur-drinkers, and there are some liqueurs that are almost entirely based on chocolate – Godiva and Godet have successfully managed to bottle Belgian chocolates; while Mozart, from Austria, tempers its chocolate sweetness by including fruit and herbs.

Among the traditional liqueurs in this category, three spring to mind for special mention. Advocaat, a Dutch liqueur based on eggs, has ongoing popularity; while Tia Maria and Kahlúa, which bring together a mix of coffee and rum, are enduringly successful drinks.

BOLS BANANA LIQUEUR

A HISTORY OF LIQUEURS

As early as 800BC the ancient Chinese were distilling spirits from fermented rice wine, and the ancient Egyptians and Greeks were known to be making spirits from grape wine by 400BC. It is safe to speculate that these ancient people would have macerated their spirits with fruit and spices to produce the earliest liqueurs.

However, it is only in Medieval Europe that we can trace the history of liqueurs with any certainty. Thirteenth-century monks, searching for the "elixir of eternal life", grew herbs and spices which, from ancient times, had been reputed to have medicinal properties. Finding a way to preserve these herbs so that they could be used to cure ailments all year round was crucial, and the monks soon realized that they could achieve this goal by steeping the herbs in alcohol. These infused "medicines" were the precursors to today's herb liqueurs.

As European sailors began making voyages to India, China, Indonesia, and the Americas, exciting new herbs, spices, and

CLASSIC LIQUEUR *This label, which first appeared on a bottle of the bitter-orange liqueur curaçao in the early 19th century, tempts the buyer with a vivid depiction of fresh, intense fruit.*

> " Sampling a great liqueur is much more than just having a drink. It is a ritual. Each glass is a gem of colour, clarity, and richness. "

fruits arrived on the continent. Crucially, the sailors also brought back with them cane sugar, and it did not take long before distillers realized that adding sugar to the medicinal infusions made them considerably more palatable.

As these exotic ingredients made their way to Europe along the new trade routes to the east and west, so the practice of distilling spirits from wine and grain also spread more widely across the continent, and became especially well developed in Holland. The Dutch were the first to preserve fruit in alcohol, and to carefully control its distillation, monitoring the sugar-content and quality of the final product. They succeeded in transforming rough, raw spirit into sweet, smooth, pleasant drinks – the forerunners of modern triple sec and curaçao.

New styles evolved, with monks and commercial houses alike experimenting with ingredients such as aniseed, mandarin oranges, and liquorice. The first new companies included Bols, founded in Holland in 1575, and Der Lachs, a German company, which began producing Danziger Goldwasser (an aniseed liqueur containing tiny flakes of gold) in 1598.

HONOURED IN GLASS *This window celebrates Benedictine's global success. Alexander Le Grand, who commercialized the liqueur in the 19th century, is shown holding the world.*

During the 18th century the name "elixir" became outmoded; by now many of the drinks were no longer medicinal, but fruit-based and made for enjoyment rather than cure. People began to use the word liqueur, from the Latin *liquefacere*, meaning "melt" or "dissolve". By the 19th century the drinks market was already boasting many of the names familiar to us today: Pimms, crème de menthe, curaçao, crème de cassis, advocaat, cherry brandy, and even some brand names such as Grand Marnier and Cointreau had come into existence. The liqueur was born.

LIQUEURS TODAY *Although at the start of the 20th century sales of liqueurs seemed to dip, renewed interest in cocktail-making and the increasing popularity of liqueurs as digestifs has led to a well-deserved revival.*

CHOOSING AND SERVING LIQUEURS

Many people still think of liqueurs as dainty drinks, to be sipped sedately by maiden aunts. Not so! Today, they have a younger appeal, and are just as likely to be drunk at parties in ice-filled glasses.

Rich, intense, and often sweet and thick, liqueurs are the most romantic and evocative of all drinks. I can't imagine Christmas without a glass of creamy advocaat, or walk past a Parisian café without being tempted by a fresh pastis, and I defy anyone to forget their first ever sip of Chartreuse! Some liqueurs will always be great apéritifs – consider crème de cassis mixed with white wine to make a Kir – while others, such as Grand Marnier or Drambuie, are for savouring after dinner. But others are more versatile than you can imagine, capable of being drunk straight, on the rocks, or with a variety of mixers in the most exotic cocktails. Indeed, it was the growth in popularity of cocktails in the Prohibition era in the US during the 1920s and 30s that really revived the fortunes of liqueurs. Liqueurs were used to

disguise both the taste and colour of poor-quality spirits, and their many flavours – from aniseed to chocolate, mint to spices, and flower essences to fruit – still provide the strongest taste elements in contemporary cocktails.

Liqueurs don't need to be mixed in cocktails to be party drinks – brands like Passoã, Malibu, Midori, and Soho are modern "feel-good" drinks designed to be enjoyed with friends. And while many liqueurs are drunk on their own, there are some aniseed-based drinks that work well with food, especially raki and ouzo, their strong flavours capable of standing up to rich Mediterranean dishes.

LIQUEUR GLASS *Also known as a cordial or pony glass, the classic stemmed liqueur glass is designed to hold about 30ml (1oz) of liquid.*

PARTY SHOTS *A tray of Baileys Irish Cream liqueur is readied for serving. Baileys is the world's best-selling liqueur, partly because of its great versatility. It can be served straight up, on the rocks, and in cocktails, and it blends well with dairy products, coffee, and fruit and nut flavours.*

BALLOON DISPLAY *Swirling a liqueur like crème de cassis in a brandy balloon, or snifter, helps show off its incredible viscosity.*

DIFFERENT WAYS TO ENJOY LIQUEURS

Liqueurs are nothing if not versatile. Not only are they made from an amazing range of ingredients in countless different styles, but they can also be enjoyed in all sorts of different ways. They can be served as apéritifs, either on their own or mixed with fruit juice or another drink. Liqueurs such as Benedictine can be taken after dinner in a traditional liqueur glass or mixed with ice or other ingredients, as in the classic blend of Benedictine and brandy. Mixed with fruit juices or other mixers, some liqueurs – notably Southern Comfort and Malibu – can be enjoyed as session drinks, while others are vital cocktail ingredients. Pictured here are some of my favourite serving suggestions, but my advice, as usual, is to be brave and experiment. It's part of the fun!

CHERRY BRANDY
On ice as an apéritif

AMARULA
At room temperature as a digestif

GALLIANO
On ice as a digestif

IZARRA
On crushed ice as a digestif

MALIBU
With orange juice and ice as an apéritif

BLUE CURAÇAO
With a submerged cherry in a cocktail

SERVING SUGGESTIONS

Sweet liqueurs are usually drunk as digestifs, but there are many drier varieties that have appeal throughout the day, for example Pernod and ouzo, which have a liquorice and herbal character. Raki can be very dry, and some of the complex herbal and vegetable liqueurs like Cynar and Jägermeister can be very dry indeed. Triple sec, curaçao, and other orange and citrus-based liqueurs are cut through with a citrus edge, which prevents them from being too cloying.

A general rule with liqueurs – as with wines – is that the sweeter the drink, the colder it should be served. Chilling the drink helps to check its sweetness, giving a more balanced drinking experience. I prefer to serve most liqueurs in a brandy balloon with plenty of crushed ice, rather than larger cubes. As the ice melts, it slightly dilutes the drink, reducing its intense flavours and so making it a little more approachable. There are of course exceptions: pastis should be served in its traditional, tapering, heavy-bottomed glass and sambuca in a shot glass.

BUYING LIQUEURS

Big brand liqueurs, such as Cointreau and Southern Comfort, are available in almost every supermarket in the world. Others are distributed widely in their country of origin, but less so elsewhere – a crème de menthe like Get 27 is much harder to find in the US than in France, though versions made by global companies like Bols and Marie Brizard will be easier to source. Regional or niche liqueurs like La Vieille Cure, tsipouro, or Nassau Royale can increasingly be bought through internet dealers.

KEEPING LIQUEURS

Keep liqueur bottles vertical, in a dark, cool cupboard. Most should last at least three years if unopened. Once opened, oxidation speeds up and will spoil the drink; try to finish the bottle within six months. Cream liqueurs and egg liqueurs are the exceptions; they should be refrigerated after opening and consumed within eight weeks.

TASTING AND ENJOYING LIQUEURS

The great diversity of ingredients and production methods means there are hundreds of different liqueur styles. For these luxury drinks, colour is just as big a part of the appeal as aroma and taste.

With so many flavours and such a diversity of character on offer, tasting liqueurs can be quite a dizzying experience! And although most liqueurs are not as strong as spirits (usually around 20% rather than 40% ABV) their sweet, smooth taste can disguise their alcohol content – so beware.

To get the most out of each drink, I pour about 30ml (1oz) of the liquid at room temperature into a brandy balloon; the narrow neck of this glass concentrates the aromas and helps to bring out the qualities of the liqueur's base spirit. The glass should be spotlessly clean; this will let you assess the drink's colour and its viscosity – visible as the "tears" running slowly down the sides of the glass.

TASTING TIPS *At a serious liqueur tasting, I would never expect ice in my glass, even with drinks that I would normally serve over ice.*

After pouring, wait for a minute to let the drink fully release its aromas. Gently swirl the glass and, keeping your nose at the rim of the glass, test the aroma. This should be elegant, delicate, and sympathetic to the style of the drink – fruit-based liqueurs, for example, should have an identifiably fruity nose, while that of a pastis should suggest aniseed and liquorice.

Next, take a sip of the liqueur and gently roll it around your mouth. The flavours should be rounded and complex; sweetness should be expected, but it should never dominate the drink. After you have swallowed the drink, you should be happy to have another glass – this will not be the case if the liqueur is over-sweet or out of balance.

TASTE COMPARISON

It is great fun to organise a liqueur tasting to compare drinks of one style – fruit liqueurs, or nut-based drinks, for example. Unless you're very brave, don't mix liqueur styles and don't try more than six drinks at one session. The taste of liqueurs can be very persistent, so rinse your mouth with cool water and cleanse your palate with a neutral biscuit after each drink. If possible, try to rest your palate for a few minutes before sampling the next liqueur – it will help keep your senses keen.

LIQUEURS IN THE KITCHEN

Liqueurs are enjoyed in their own right, but their sweet, powerful flavours have won them a place in the kitchen, too. Amaretto can be used to flavour cakes and is delicious poured over ice cream, crème de cassis blends well with chocolate in desserts, and Frangelico adds a pungent kick to a cheesecake. Liqueurs are used as a luxurious filling for chocolates and in the manufacture of premium jams – the alcohol is an effective preservative.

CRÊPE SUZETTE
Created by the French chef Escoffier, this dish consists of pancakes in orange sauce, flamed in Grand Marnier.

STEEPED FRUIT
Oranges steeped in curaçao, or pitted cherries in cherry brandy, are a treat on top of a scoop of ice cream.

COFFEE AND LIQUEUR
A strong coffee pairs perfectly with a luscious liqueur. Try tipping the liqueur into the coffee for added interest.

DRINK ANALYSIS

COLOUR

Liqueurs come in every colour of the rainbow! Some, such as Cointreau, are completely clear or neutral in colour while others are defined by their hue as much as anything else. Consider, for example, the bright yellow of advocaat, and the bright green of Midori and crème de menthe. Chartreuse Green and Chartreuse Yellow are actually named for their colour. Curaçao is manufactured in a range of colours, primarily so that it can be used to tint cocktails, even though the taste is the same across the spectrum.

Anise drinks change colour when water is added, becoming cloudy. The creamy liqueurs like Baileys or Amarula are opaque, while Benedictine is made attractive by its elegant clarity.

There are few rules when assessing the colour of a liqueur. As with spirits check the colour in bright daylight (but not direct sunlight) against a sheet of plain white paper; clear liqueurs should be perfectly clear, and have no haze. Liqueurs are often viscous, and cling to the glass, which serves to intensify the effect of their colour.

AROMA

Liqueurs typically carry a touch of sweetness in the nose, but their aromas are as varied as their tastes and colours, reflecting the ingredients used in their manufacture. Key aroma groups are: fruit, often rich and intense; citrus zest or peel, typical of triple sec; spice, sometimes sweet like cinnamon, but also bitter, as in the anise drinks and kümmel. Toasted nut aromas, particularly almond, are important, especially in the great Italian liqueurs like amaretto and Frangelico. Sweet toffee aromas are strong in Baileys and whisky-based liqueurs like Glen Mist. Alcohol spirit comes through in some of the traditional herbal liqueurs like Génépi, while some of the softer liqueurs like Galliano and Alchermes have notes of flowers. Coffee is dominant in Tia Maria and Kahlúa.

FRUIT
Cherries

ZEST
Orange zest

SPICE
Cinnamon

NUT
Almonds

SWEET
Toffee

SPIRIT
Distilled alcohol

FLOWERS
Rose

COFFEE
Coffee beans

TASTE

When tasting a good liqueur, its sweetness should not feel too sticky or "fatty" in the mouth, and the finish should be fresh – never tired or over-sweet. Beyond this, liqueurs as a group contain almost every taste on the planet! A good starting point when tasting is to identify opposing taste "categories", such as those shown on this taste wheel *(right)*, and picture where your spirit is located on the wheel. The notion of taste also encompasses the liqueur's body (full or light, smooth or firm) as well as its length (how the taste persists and develops after the drink is swallowed).

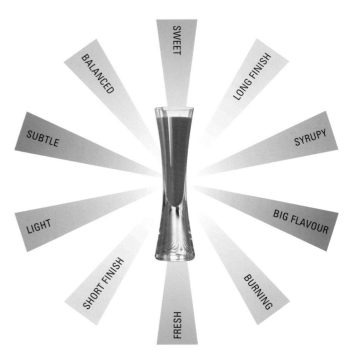

SWEET

BALANCED

LONG FINISH

SUBTLE

SYRUPY

LIGHT

BIG FLAVOUR

SHORT FINISH

BURNING

FRESH

66 Looking deceptively gentle in the glass, these drinks give a burst of juicy tanginess that is far more powerful than fresh fruit. Hefty, with a swaggering finish. Superb!**99**

FRUIT

INTRODUCING FRUIT LIQUEURS

While the monks of continental Europe were concentrating on concocting bitter-tasting herbal elixirs to ward off illness, the Dutch were creating some of the first delicious, sweet liqueurs made from fruit, particularly oranges.

During the 17th century, Amsterdam, the capital city of Holland, was a port alive with the bustle of ships bringing home exotic gifts from Dutch colonies around the world. One of these colonies, Curaçao, an island in the Caribbean, provided the Dutch sailors with a special type of bitter orange. On arriving in Holland, these oranges found their way into the hands of liqueur-makers, who began to use the fruit to flavour *brandewijn*, what we know as grape brandy. Once sweetened, the result was an orange liqueur known as curaçao, after the fruit's place of origin. This was one of the first fruit liqueurs ever to be made. Nowadays the term curaçao is often used generically to mean any type of orange liqueur that may or may not also be a triple sec (an orange liqueur that has been triple-distilled), and the liqueur is now made using bitter oranges from places other than the original island in the Caribbean.

PASSION FRUIT *This fruit flavours Maracujá, a liqueur from Madeira.*

THE FRUIT EXPLOSION

Soon the Dutch carried their new liqueur-making techniques to other parts of Europe, and liqueurs containing other fruits – from cherries to lychees – began to emerge. By the time Queen Victoria occupied the British throne in 1837, red-fruit liqueurs were *de rigueur* in English society, being particularly enjoyed by women, who drank them to help their digestion after the end of a meal – or so they claimed!

RAW MATERIALS *All manner of fruits are used in liqueur-making. From left to right: lemon flavours Parfait Amour; lychee, Soho; melon, Midori; and cherry, a whole array of liqueurs.*

In the 20th century, fruit liqueurs began to be known as fruit brandies, giving us the especially popular cherry brandy, apricot brandy, and peach brandy. Of course, because these drinks are not distilled directly from the fruit themselves, they are not true brandies, and in the US they are known as cordials to make the distinction clear.

After the orange, the cherry is perhaps the most important fruit used to make liqueur – kirsch, guignolet, and maraschino are all forms of cherry liqueur, but the term kirsch is also used for a spirit distilled from cherries *(see p259)*, so take care when buying. The most important berry fruits are blackberries, blackcurrants, and raspberries, with strawberries, cloudberries, and cranberries running a close second. However, the range of fruit is vast! Liqueurs are also made from plums, bilberries, rowanberries, apples, quinces, and tropical and exotic fruits, such as bananas and pineapples. In Japan, the ancient tradition of *reishu*, making melon liqueurs, is enjoying a revival. Other fruit liqueurs include kiwi, lychees, and passion fruit – and many more.

Some of these liqueurs are pure fruit, and others are made with plants and herbs, too. So, while Cointreau is made from oranges, it is also enriched with herbs.

COCKTAILS *Fruit liqueurs have found their home in cocktail-making. For example, the orange-flavoured liqueur triple sec is an essential ingredient (along with Cognac) in the Side Car (see p349).*

CHERRY BRANDY *For those with a sweet tooth, a good-quality cherry brandy is delicious over ice after dinner, as a digestif.*

CITRUS FRUITS

Some of the world's most successful and popular liqueurs are made from citrus fruits, particularly the bitter oranges of the Caribbean island Curaçao that are used to make triple sec. Cognac, which matches well with this fruit, is often used as the base, creating well-balanced and smooth liqueurs.

CURAÇAO

C **COLOUR** Originally clear, but also orange, blue, red, green, and brown.

A **AROMA** Aromatic, with a fine balance of orange, honey, and herbs.

T **TASTE** Extremely sweet flavours, with some citrus character.

Curaçao is an orange-flavoured liqueur made using orange peel. The peel is steeped in water and alcohol, distilled, and coloured according to type. Originally from the dried peel of bitter oranges found only on the Caribbean island of Curaçao, the term "curaçao" is now also applied to orange liqueurs made using fruit from elsewhere in the world.

The Dutch companies Bols and De Kuyper both make a famous blue curaçao; but orange (try the French Cusenier or Bardinet) and white (clear) curaçao are popular too. Senior's Curaçao of Curaçao comes from the island itself.

BLUE CURAÇAO

BURSTS OF COLOUR *All curaçao is essentially the same – the various colours are there simply to brighten up our cocktails.*

COINTREAU

C **COLOUR** Colourless, but becomes cloudy when chilled.

A **AROMA** Aromatic and delicate, with orange, vanilla, oak, and herbs.

T **TASTE** Mildly bitter, with a wonderful balance of orange and herbs.

Cointreau is a triple-sec liqueur, expertly created using the peel of bitter and sweet oranges. The famous brand name was popularized shortly before World War II in order to distinguish Cointreau from other triple secs – all of which were at that time known simply as Triple Sec.

However, although the company coined the name Cointreau relatively recently, the liqueur's origins are much older. During the 19th century Edouard Cointreau, the son of a confectioner from Angers, in the Loire region of France, travelled in the Caribbean and discovered the bitter oranges. His father, Edouard-Jean Cointreau, who was already experimenting with spirits made using different varieties of oranges and herbs at his distillery in Angers, used his son's discoveries to create the new, now world-famous, Cointreau liqueur.

Made to a secret recipe, and based on brandy, Cointreau is clear at room temperature, but turns cloudy when cooled or poured over ice. This change – a sign of authenticity – is caused by the oils breaking out of the blend at cold temperatures.

I just love Cointreau with nothing but plenty of ice as an apéritif; but I also like it at room temperature as a digestif. However you drink Cointreau – even if it is in a cocktail – you will never lose the distinctive flavours of this wonderful liqueur.

COINTREAU

GRAND MARNIER

C **COLOUR** Dark gold to light amber, presented in a "squat" bottle.

A **AROMA** Subtle, with a wonderful balance of orange, flowers, and herbs.

T **TASTE** Smooth and rich, with orange, Cognac, and a long, soft finish.

This orange liqueur, created in France in 1880 by the Marnier-Lapostelle company, and based on a balance of fine Cognac and bitter-orange peel, is perhaps the most famous in the world. Although Grand Marnier is similar to curaçao, it is essential to think of it as a "Cognac-plus", because the fine Cognac base is the secret of this liqueur's success.

The original Grand Marnier liqueur is marketed as Cordon Rouge. I simply cannot make up my mind whether I prefer it as an after-dinner drink, neat

GRAND MARNIER

ORANGE PEEL *Citrus bigaradia*, the family of bitter orange used to flavour Grand Marnier, is found primarily in the Caribbean. In order to achieve the maximum concentration of flavours in the peel, the oranges are picked while they are just underripe. The peel is separated from the pith, and dried, before being macerated in alcohol and distilled.

in a Cognac glass; as an apéritif with ice; or mixed in a cocktail!

In 1927 Grand Marnier issued its Cuvée du Centenaire to celebrate Marnier-Lapostelle's centenary. This is based on fine Cognacs up to 25 years old, and blended with oranges and herbs to produce a satisfying and exceptionally smooth liqueur. Fifty years later (on its 150th birthday), the company launched Cuvée Speciale Cent Cinquantenaire, made from a blend of rare Cognacs aged up to 50 years, and primarily from Grande Champagne, the best growing area for the grapes that make fine Cognac. It is rich with vanilla, oak, oranges, and herbs.

Some people say that liqueurs are going out of fashion. If you try Grand Marnier, you will think that these people are mad! This is an absolutely beautiful liqueur, and one of my all-time favourites.

TRIPLE SEC

C COLOUR Clear and pure – any orange colour is removed during distillation.

A AROMA Distinctive, with citrus, orange, herbs, and honey.

T TASTE Sweet and smooth, with orange and lemon to the fore.

Triple sec is an umbrella term for orange-flavoured liqueurs. Many are often known simply by their style or brand name – for example, Grand Marnier and Cointreau are essentially triple secs. The use of herbs and French brandy in some of these famous names generally means that they are slightly drier than the generic triple sec, which retains the sweetness of its original base spirit – rum. Some triple-sec brands are made on Curaçao, in the Caribbean, while others are made in France, Mexico, and the US.

The term "triple sec" does not mean that this liqueur is very dry (from the French word *sec*, meaning "dry"), but instead that during production the liqueur has been "triple-distilled", making it very clean, pure, strong (around 40% ABV), and sweet, but not cloying.

Apart from famous brands, there are many well-known generic versions of triple sec, with those from Holland being the most important (this reflects the country's historic links with Curaçao). The Dutch firms De Kuyper, Smeets, and Bols all produce fine triple secs; while French producers such as Marie Brizard and Leroux, and others such as Juarez and Hiram Walker, also make this excellent liqueur.

Triple sec is extremely versatile. I often drink it on ice before dinner, or at room temperature as a digestif. If you are mixing cocktails, you must have triple sec to hand!

TRIPLE SEC

VAN DER HUM

C COLOUR Deep golden yellow through to tangerine and amber.

A AROMA Fruity, herbal aromas of orange, brandy, and spice.

T TASTE Smooth, complex; fresh; herbs, spice, citrus fruits; a sweet finish.

Van der Hum is a South African liqueur that was created by early Dutch settlers who were trying to reproduce their favourite orange-flavoured liqueur Curaçao, but using South Africa's naartjies fruit, which is a citrus fruit similar to a tangerine. The result is a citrus-flavoured liqueur made from a blend of aged brandy, wine distillate, citrus-fruit peel, herbs, spices, seeds, and barks, which is sweetened with glucose and sugar-cane syrup. You will find good versions of Van der Hum liqueur from KWV and Bertrams.

VAN DER HUM

FILFAR

C COLOUR Clear, but with a luscious orange feel to the packaging.

A AROMA Complex, with orange, herbs, and sweet spice, especially cinnamon.

T TASTE Smooth and tangy; warming, with a long spicy finish.

Filfar is an orange liqueur from the island of Cyprus, said to have been first developed by monks. Producers use only Cypriot oranges to make the liqueur, which ages in oak casks for four months. The entire production process is completed by hand – from picking to bottle, making this very special indeed. Filfar is also great value for money, and while it may not have the subtlety and depth of Cointreau or Grand Marnier, it is extremely drinkable – try it in a cocktail or over ice as an apéritif.

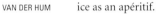

PARFAIT AMOUR

C COLOUR Mainly bright violet; some versions are closer to purple.

A AROMA Very aromatic and distinctive; rose, vanilla, almond, and citrus fruits.

T TASTE Exotic and sweet, with spicy orange and flowers.

Parfait amour (meaning "perfect love") is an exotic, sweet, citrus-based liqueur, with a heady aroma and flavoured with rose and vanilla. Some say that it will end lovers' quarrels, so try offering it to your lover – straight or in a cocktail – next time you have a row! Excellent producers include Bols, Joseph Carton, Bardinet, and Marie Brizard. The US version is quite different – it is darker in colour and blended from spirit, lemon, coriander, and sugar.

PARFAIT AMOUR

CEDRAT CORSE

C COLOUR Bright and charming, with a very pale, light lemon colour.

A AROMA Aromatic, with lemon zest; clean, with hints of the exotic.

T TASTE Suave, rich; beautifully balanced, with great intensity of flavours.

Cedrat is a type of citrus fruit similar to a lemon, originally from China or southeast Asia, but imported into Europe during Greco-Roman times. Now it grows beautifully on the French island of Corsica in the Mediterranean, and Cedrat Corse is something of a Corsican speciality.

The liqueur's appealing and distinctive bouquet (it was originally intended as a perfume!), vibrant lemon flavours, and moderate alcohol (30% ABV), make Cedrat Corse an ideal digestif – serve it at room temperature in a brandy snifter, and swirl it before you drink to make the most of its nose. It is sold in 50cl bottles – just perfect for an intimate dinner party.

MANDARINE NAPOLÉON

C COLOUR A sophisticated and elegant golden orange, with pink tinges.

A AROMA Fresh; mandarin and tangerine, with notes of herbs.

T TASTE Very fruity; full-bodied; tangerine, nutmeg, and cinnamon.

Mandarine Napoléon is an orange-flavoured liqueur made in Belgium by the Fourcroy Company, using mandarin oranges, Cognac, and 21 botanicals (herbs, plants, and spices used in the production of some spirits). In this case, the botanicals include green tea, clover, coriander, and cumin.

In the early years of the 19th century, Count François de Fourcroy, a French scientist, developed a recipe for a new liqueur and presented it to Napoleon. In his diary Fourcroy noted all the ingredients for his liqueur – especially mandarins, which in the early 1800s, were considered an exotic fruit with medicinal qualities. These qualities were of particular interest to Napoleon, hence the liqueur's name. The liqueur was manufactured commercially from 1892 onward.

Only fresh mandarin-orange-peel from Sicily is used to make Mandarine Napoléon. The spirit is then distilled three times to produce an intense tangerine essence, and a fairly high alcohol-content (40% ABV).

I particularly like the complexity of this liqueur. You can always taste the Cognac and the orange, but the range of herbs and spices is so broad that each sip finds something new. Try it neat after dinner (with or without ice), with orange juice as an apéritif, or in cocktails. Its sweet, spicy finish makes it a warming drink – perfect against a winter chill.

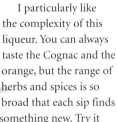
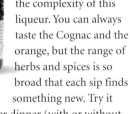
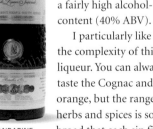

MANDARINE NAPOLÉON

CHERRIES AND BERRIES

One of the most popular liqueurs in the world is cherry "brandy", actually made by macerating cherries in pure spirit. Other berries, especially sour varieties, make equally good liqueurs of a similar style.

CHERRY BRANDY

C **COLOUR** Very bright, and typically transparent, light, cherry red.

A **AROMA** Highly aromatic: cherry, almond, flowers, and herbs.

T **TASTE** Dry, bitter-sweet, and complex, with cherry and herbs.

There is often a great deal of confusion over cherry brandy. This spirit is not true brandy, but a liqueur (sometimes you will see it marketed as "cherry brandy liqueur"). A true brandy is usually much higher in alcohol – around 40% ABV, compared with around 25% ABV for a liqueur – and is generally better for sipping neat or over ice (a liqueur is normally intended for mixing).

However, the real difference between a brandy and a liqueur lies in their production – a true brandy (or eau-de-vie) is distilled directly from the fruit itself, as with kirsch, while a liqueur, such as cherry brandy, is a flavoured

SWEET SIPPING *Cherry brandy tends to be very sweet, but if you have a sweet tooth, try it straight.*

spirit – the fruit (or other flavouring) is steeped in a base spirit to give flavour.

Cherry brandy is made by blending cherry mash (the type of cherries will depend upon the producer) with grape brandy, herbs,

and sugar and leaving it to steep in the spirit for several months. Then the liquid is run off and bottled, creating a sweet liqueur with a slightly bitter edge from the cherry skins.

Apart from the Danish producer Peter Heering, the Dutch drinks companies Bols and De Kuyper make the best-known brands of cherry brandy, but also look out for examples from Marie Brizard, Lejay Lagoute, and in the UK, brands such as Grants, and Lamb & Watt.

My particular favourites are Heering and De Kuyper. Heering Original Cherry Liqueur is made to the early-19th century recipe given to Peter Heering by Mrs Carstensen, the wife of Heering's mentor – a local grocer from Copenhagen. The

liqueur is made using the whole fruit – in this case Danish Steven's cherries, including the stones – giving a nutty, almondy feel. It matures in oak casks for three years, which adds to its complexity.

Like Heering's, De Kuyper's Cherry Brandy is more complex than other brands. It is made from a mixture of dark red cherries, crushed with their stones, and then blended in brandy and left to mature. A secret concoction of spice distillates also goes into the mix.

Cherry brandy is an absolute essential if you are making cocktails, such as the Singapore Sling *(see p342)*. However, if you enjoy sweet drinks, try one of the good brands over ice, or mixed with cola.

HEERING CHERRY LIQUEUR

LAND AND PRODUCTION

CHOOSING CHERRIES The kind of cherries chosen for a brandy will depend upon the particular producer, but the best cherry brandies are made with cherries that are sour, rather than sweet. Although these are inedible as fruit, their juice is rich and flavourful. One of the most popular varieties is the Morello cherry. This fruit is vibrant red deepening to mahogany as it ripens, and its juice is dark, yielding a unique, concentrated cherry flavour perfect for making a delicious cherry brandy.

MARASCHINO

C COLOUR Clear; bottles traditionally have a straw casing.

A AROMA Aromatic, with cherry, almond, flowers, and herbs.

T TASTE Dry, bitter-sweet and complex, with cherry and herbs.

Arguably the greatest of all the cherry liqueurs, Maraschino is a clear, concentrated drink from Venice, Italy. It is made from sour maraschino cherries, which are crushed and fermented along with their kernels. Sugar, flower-blossom extracts, and herbs are added, and the result is a deeply fruity, bitter-sweet, intense, and elegant liqueur – wonderful on its own, and also added to many dishes during cooking. Once you have tried this drink, you will not confuse it with sweet cherry brandies; Maraschino is dry and complex, the bitter cherries and nutty kernels giving it unexpected depth.

MARASCHINO

This liqueur was first made in the 18th century by Francesco Drioli in Zara (now Zadar), Croatia – a city which was then a possession of Venice. Drioli introduced the classic Maraschino bottle, with its straw casing, and, before the Second World War, his Maraschino was the height of fashion. After the war, Zara became part of Yugoslavia, and to safeguard production of the liqueur, thousands of cherry trees were planted in Italy along the slopes of the Po Valley.

One of the firms to survive the post-war disruption is Luxardo, which has been going strong since 1821. Luxardo ages its Maraschino in Finnish ash wood, adding extra complexity to the brew. Cucchi, De Kuyper, and Bols also make fine examples of this liqueur.

GUIGNOLET

C COLOUR Cherry red; retains its colour for months after opening if chilled.

A AROMA Quite full, with notes of ripe cherry, almond, and herbs.

T TASTE Very fruity; cherry sweet; warm and creamy finish.

Guignolet is the umbrella term for French cherry liqueurs, which tend to be richer, more elegant, and smoother than generic cherry brandy. Many of these cherry liqueurs are given extra finesse by the addition of a small amount of eau-de-vie – usually kirsch. Although this makes up only around 2 per cent of the total, it is enough to enhance the bouquet and intensify the flavour of the Guignolet, making it more delicate and – well, for me – much more interesting! Check the label carefully –

GUIGNOLET

a good French cherry liqueur will be called Guignolet-au-kirsch, and the best examples will most likely come from Burgundy.

The liqueur is the product of slow maceration of blends of sweet and bitter cherries (the most notable being the small black-heart cherry, called *guignes*, from which the drink gets its name). The liqueur typically displays the subtle aromas and flavours of the fruit itself, and of the kernels, skins, and stems. These contribute to Guignolet's nutty character and crucially add the tannins that strengthen the drink's structure.

I like this best as an apéritif, either well chilled on its own or on the rocks. It is also great mixed with a dry white wine as a fruity alternative to Kir, and it is, of course, a key ingredient of many cocktails, because it mixes so harmoniously with fruit juices.

AMOUR EN CAGE

C COLOUR Golden from the stones, rather than cherry red from the fruit.

A AROMA Highly aromatic with notes of cherry, almond, citrus, and herbs.

T TASTE Dry and delicate, with prominent cherry and citrus.

For me, this delicious cherry liqueur from Quebec in Canada is the essential winter drink. I love it on a cold afternoon by the fire with a plate of warm muffins, but it is just as good on the rocks before dinner. Amour en Cage (literally "caged love") is made from crushed and ground cherries steeped in alcohol. The result is a complex liqueur – not too sweet – with a lovely fruity nose and citrus notes that remind me of gooseberries.

AMOUR EN CAGE

JERZYNÓWKA

C COLOUR Very dark purple – close to a natural blackberry hue.

A AROMA Dense and intense blackberry fruit and alcohol spirit.

T TASTE Full and highly fruity flavour; sweet with a smooth finish.

The word Jerzynówka may be hard to say, but this Polish liqueur is easy to drink, and packs a real fruit punch. It is prepared by macerating fully ripe blackberries in brandy or spirit. Sometimes sugar is added, and more often than not, the aroma, taste, and body of the drink is improved by the addition of eau-de-vie. In Poland, it is mixed with honey and lemon, added to black tea, and drunk as a cure for the common cold! Other, similar drinks are sold as blackberry brandy but the spirit used along with the fruit is just as likely to be based on grain as on grapes. Some of the best-known and available brands are Baks, Leroux, and De Kuyper.

ECHTE KROATZBEERE

C COLOUR Dark and deep reddish blackberry purple.

A AROMA Very aromatic, with wild blackberry dominant.

T TASTE Not too sweet; excitingly fruity and complex.

Blackberry liqueurs are produced in many countries around the world, but my favourite is this special drink from Germany. Echte (which means "the real thing") Kroatzbeere is made only from wild berries, so along with its alcoholic kick, it delivers a powerful and seductive aroma of wild blackberries. Look out for the liqueur produced by Thienelt, which I consider to be one of the best. It can be enjoyed well chilled or over ice as a digestif, but it really comes into its own when teamed with sweet desserts. It is a brilliant partner for fruitcake or chocolate mousse; alternatively, pour it generously over ice cream for a fruity dessert that you will not forget in a hurry!

CHICOUTAI

C COLOUR Translucent dark golden amber, from the cloudberries.

A AROMA Quite aromatic, with hints of red fruits, vanilla, and honey.

T TASTE Sweet with a slightly bitter finish.

This extraordinary liqueur is made from wild fruits collected from one of the harshest environments in which plants grow – the northern extremes of Quebec, Canada. The fruit is the cloudberry – a relative of the raspberry – which, when steeped in alcohol produces this golden liqueur. Chicoutai is very sweet, with a strong taste and aroma. At only 25% ABV, this drink can be sipped over ice for a real taste of the north.

CHICOUTAI

MINAKI

C COLOUR Deep garnet red to blue, reflecting the dark berry skins.

A AROMA Full and lively, with strong notes of blueberry.

T TASTE Full-bodied, with jammy red fruit and a peppery finish.

Minaki is a blueberry liqueur from Quebec, Canada. Its name is derived from an Algonquin word meaning "land of blueberries", which is where a sip of this unusual liqueur will take you! Minaki is not over-sweet, and, at 18% ABV, not too strong to be enjoyed straight or over ice; I love it poured over crêpes. There is also a German version of this blueberry drink called Heidelbeere – look out for the Weis brand.

MINAKI

L'ORLÉANE

C COLOUR Very dark red and opaque; similar to blackcurrant.

A AROMA Rich and fruity; prominent blackcurrant and alcohol spirit.

T TASTE Full and fruity flavour, sweet and smooth to the finish.

The Île d'Orléans lies on the St Lawrence River, not far from the city of Quebec, Canada. In the early years it was called Nouvelle France, and it still retains a strong French influence, producing its own version of the Burgundian favourite, crème de cassis – this blackcurrant liqueur called L'Orléane.

The drink is made from very high-quality blackcurrants, which grow under near-perfect conditions on the island. The resulting crème de cassis is rich and, at 23% ABV can be served chilled on its own, or, of course, topped with dry white wine – the Canadian version of a Kir!

CHAMBORD

C COLOUR An elegant, rich, dark red liqueur in a regal package.

A AROMA Intense but pleasant notes of jammy fruits, especially raspberry.

T TASTE Thick and syrupy, with fruity and balanced sweetness.

The first thing you will notice about this drink is its outrageously stylish bottle – how French! But it is more than a just a marketing gimmick, because Chambord has genuine regal credentials. It was the favourite of French king Louis XIV and is still referred to as *La Liqueur Royale* 300 years after its formulation.

Chambord is made from black raspberries (*framboises noires*). The macerated fruit is infused with fine Cognac, red raspberries, currants,

CHAMBORD

and blackberry extracts. Towards the end of the production process, spices such as mace, cinnamon, ginger, cloves, and vanilla are added, along with several other herbs, orange, and lemon. The crucial addition, though, is acacia honey, added just before the entire mixture is aged in barrels.

The result is a creamy, rich, fruity, and deeply sweet liqueur. It is very delicate, elegant, and well balanced – character-istics that make it a premium liqueur.

At 17% ABV, Chambord is not strong, but its overwhelming sweetness means that it is best when mixed – in a Champagne or wine punch, for example. It also goes really well with desserts, especially dishes with berries. My favourite is to pour it over vanilla ice cream: it sticks to the ice cream and gives it a great colour.

DARK FRUIT LIQUEURS

C COLOUR Dark garnet red to light purple, depending on the fruit.

A AROMA Rich dark fruits, blackberry, raspberry, spice, and spirit.

T TASTE Elegant and deeply fruity; full bodied and not over-sweet.

France produces a wonderfully diverse range of deep, dark, and rich fruit liqueurs. At their best, these drinks are finely balanced; they are packed with the sweetness of the fruit, but retain a citrusy dryness so that they never become cloying. The three most notable of these liqueurs are crème de cassis, crème de mûre, and crème de framboise.

Crème de cassis is a speciality of the Burgundy region, and histor-ically the centre of production is Dijon. From as far back as the 16th century, monks in the Dijon region were producing blackberry liqueur

MARIE BRIZARD CRÈME DE CASSIS

for medicinal use, but in 1841, one M. Lagoute registered a commercial brand as crème de cassis.

It was, and still is, made from fresh blackcurrants – the best coming from the Côte de Nuits – macerated with brandy spirit and sugar. Today, crème de cassis is most often used in cocktails or as the basis for the apéritif Kir, when it is mixed with a dry white wine, ideally Aligoté.

There are some excellent brands that are widely available. Look out for Lagoute, Joseph Cartron, Bols, Mathilde, Marie Brizard, and Vedrenne Supercassis, in particular.

Crème de mûre is made from wild blackberries, macerated with brandy spirit and honey or sugar. This is another dark and fruity liqueur, with an almost overwhelming aroma of crushed,

fresh blackberry fruit. A sharp acidity cuts through the drink's sweetness, freshening its taste, but even so, this liqueur is very rich on its own. Try it over ice, or even better over ice cream! Fine brands include Massenez, Bols, Monin, Joseph Cartron, and Meyer.

Crème de framboise is made from raspberries, but should not be confused with Framboise eau-de-vie, which is much drier and far stronger, with roughly twice the content of alcohol. This sweet liqueur is much paler than crème de cassis, and has a very delicate and subtle taste. Ripe raspberries are very pronounced, along with a hint of spice. It can be drunk over ice, and is great with desserts. Good producers are Marie Brizard, Gabriel Boudier (Pernod Ricard), Meyer, Massenez, Sisca (Lejay), and Joseph Cartron.

CARTON CRÈME DE MÛRE

SLOE GIN

C COLOUR A rich, attractive, deep red; quite dense.

A AROMA Aromatic, with well-balanced fruit, herbs, and spirit.

T TASTE Very smooth, with rich fruit, and hints of sweet almond.

This rich, deep-red liqueur is made by steeping sloe berries in spirit (usually gin) and added sugar. Sloe berries are the small blue-black round fruit of the blackthorn bush – a relative of the plum. At 26% ABV, sloe gin is a lively drink, but is well balanced between fruity sweetness and bitterness, with almond notes from the fruit stones. I drink it neat as an after-dinner liqueur, with a piece of strong cheese; but it can also be chilled over ice, added to sparkling wine, or mixed with bitter lemon.

Look out for Plymouth Sloe Gin, where the base is the excellent Plymouth gin.

PEACH AND APRICOT

Winemakers in the warmer parts of Europe used to grow fruit trees in vineyards to divert insects away from the grapes. This, in turn, led to a tradition of using fruit to make distilled spirits and also liqueurs. This has continued in the modern era with the production and marketing of apricot brandy, and the sweetening of whiskey with peaches – most famously in Southern Comfort.

SOUTHERN COMFORT

C **COLOUR** Rich dark amber, in the instantly recognizable ribbed bottle.

A **AROMA** Rich and complex, with notes of peach, orange, and vanilla.

T **TASTE** Rich, but not over-sweet, with fruit, herbs, and a spirit finish.

This graceful, rich, peach-flavoured whiskey liqueur is the embodiment of the Deep South – like *Gone with the Wind* in a glass! The Bourbon-based drink was created in 1874 by a young barman, M.W. Heron of La Rue Bourbon in New Orleans, and it was aimed squarely at a new emerging market – sophisticated southern belles.

Heron's idea was to soften and sweeten harsh whiskeys of the time, which were typically served from the barrel, to create a more refined, feminine drink. The drink was originally named Cuffs & Buttons, but was rebranded Southern Comfort in 1885. In 1889 Heron moved to Memphis, Tennessee, and began producing Southern Comfort as a bottled liqueur. Nearly a century later, the company was taken over by the giant Brown Forman company and is now made in a number of locations, and distributed around the world.

Southern Comfort is a complex mixture of Bourbon whiskey, fruit, and herbs – so complex indeed that the producers claim that only eight people in the world know the exact formula! The spirit is blended with a wide range of fruit and herbs, including orange, vanilla, cinnamon, peach, and lemon, and then matured in oak barrels. The result is a drink that looks like whisky, has the depth, character, and quality of a Bourbon, but is more flexible and appealing than either, and can be teamed successfully with a wide range of mixers. This versatile liqueur is traditionally paired with lemonade, served on the rocks in a highball glass, but it is equally at home with cola, tonic, or citrus juices, such as lime and grapefruit, or in cocktails, such as the Amaretto Comfort *(see p364)*. I love it with a dry cranberry juice – perfect as a long, sundown drink.

Originally marketed as a drink for genteel ladies, Southern Comfort changed its image in the 1960s, when singer Janis Joplin adopted it as her favourite, often appearing on stage with a bottle in hand. Ever since, it has been associated with a spirit of rock-and-roll rebellion and today is just as likely to be enjoyed by young urbanites as southern belles. The producers have reduced its strength (to 35% ABV) to keep in tune with the younger market.

CLASSIC ADVERTISING
Southern Comfort has always had a strong brand identity: its famous label, showing a plantation house on the banks of the Mississippi, has been around since 1934.

OLD FAVOURITE *Southern Comfort is the best-known of all American liqueurs. It is incredibly versatile, mixing well in a range of cocktails.*

APRICOT BRANDY

C COLOUR Rich golden amber from the crushed fruit and stones.

A AROMA Mild and delicate, with apricot and almond to the fore.

T TASTE Light and clean taste, with apricot and almond.

Even if you do not like apricots, I recommend that you try this golden, light, and refreshing liqueur. It is very popular throughout the world, and for me this is one of the best of the fruit liqueurs, especially when served over crushed ice on a warm summer's evening.

Like cherry brandy, there tends to be some confusion over whether apricot brandy is actually a brandy or a liqueur. The answer lies in its production method – the process of macerating fruit with a spirit base, rather than distilling the fruit to produce a spirit, classifies it squarely as a liqueur.

To produce apricot brandy, ripe apricots are loaded into vats, where they are macerated with neutral grape (or sometimes grain) spirit for seven to eight weeks. The resulting blend of spirit and juice is then mixed with crystallised sugar to lower the alcohol

JOSEPH CARTRON
APRICOT BRANDY

content and further develop the fruit flavours. Herb essences are sometimes added to boost the taste, resulting in a light, fruity, and nutty liqueur, with an almond feel emerging from the crushed apricot kernels.

Apricot brandy is produced globally, but there are a few excellent brands to look out for. Bols makes a version as part of its wide fruit liqueur range that has a nice almond feel on top of the fruit. Joseph Cartron, a French producer, uses apricots from the Rhône Valley to make a deeply fruity version, while Marie Brizard's Apry is Cognac-based, and, to my palate, superior. One of the US brands – Jacquin's Apricot Flavored Brandy – at 33% ABV, is a little stronger than the competition.

Apricot and other fruit "brandies" have much in common with the crèmes *(see p287)*, both in the method of production and in their uses. They can be enjoyed neat, but are most often seen as key ingredients of cocktails.

APRICOT HARVEST *Fresh, high-quality apricots from South Africa and the Roussillon region of France go into every bottle of Marie Brizard's Apry apricot brandy – one of the best on the market.*

BOLS APRICOT
BRANDY

CRÈME DE PÊCHE DE VIGNE

C COLOUR An elegant light golden hue drawn from the peaches.

A AROMA Deeply fruity, with peach, almond, honey, and vanilla.

T TASTE Rich and satisfying, with the fruit sweetness balanced by a nutty flavour.

Crème de Pêche de Vigne de Bourgogne is so called because, in years gone by, peach trees were grown among the vineyards of Burgundy in France. The peaches were an effective defence against vine pests, which would attack the fruit trees in preference to the precious vines. Liqueur made from the fruit of the peach trees was a welcome bonus for the winemakers.

Today, the peaches are grown specially for use in the liqueur. The small, sweet, and succulent fruits mature at the end of summer, and are harvested in September.

The fruit is placed in large vats, and macerated in pure alcohol spirit for about three months. The result is a wonderful golden, fruity, nutty liqueur – not too sweet, and with great balance. At 18% ABV this drink is not excessively strong; it is subtle, gently perfumed, and not over-exuberant – rather like a Viognier wine *(see p48)*. It can be enjoyed neat, mixed with sparkling wine, or poured over a dessert, such as ice cream or fresh fruit salad.

MIXING IT UP

MORNING CHAMPAGNE A dash of apricot brandy topped up with Champagne and garnished with orange is a perfect fresh and fruity start to any big celebration.

EXOTIC FRUITS

Many fruit liqueurs have traditional roots. In Japan, for example, melon has been used for centuries to flavour spirits. Other exotic-fruit liqueurs are completely new, and you can now find drinks made from bananas, dates, passion fruit, kiwi fruit, and many others.

TAMARA

C COLOUR Light gold, developed from the infusion of honey and dates.

A AROMA Sweet, intense; an appealing combination of ripe fruit and vanilla.

T TASTE Extremely sweet and oily, with dates and vanilla, and a nutty feel.

Tamara (from *tamar*, the Hebrew world for date palm) is an Israeli date liqueur. The dates are macerated in neutral alcohol, which is then sweetened with sugar or honey. The result is sweet, but quite rich and complex, and around 20% ABV. Drink it in small amounts, on its own.

SAFARI

C COLOUR Dark yellow – slightly paler than the colour of orange juice.

A AROMA Bright and lively; lemon, lime, mango, papaya, passion fruit.

T TASTE Sweet, bright, and fruity; stimulating on the palate; sugary finish.

Safari is an exotic-fruit liqueur, which is not too powerful (20% ABV), and fresh enough to display its flavours of lemon, lime, and passion fruit. Try mixing it with orange juice or lemonade at a ratio of one part Safari to four parts mixer. If you have a really sweet tooth, you can try it neat or over ice.

PIMM'S

C COLOUR Dark, reddish brown, in the world-famous No.1 bottle.

A AROMA Aromatic and elegant, with fresh herbs and lots of fruit.

T TASTE Light and refreshing; gin, spices, and herbs; clean, fresh finish.

In the middle of the 19th century, James Pimm, a restaurateur in the City of London (the original London, traditionally housing the financial district) invented a new drink that mixed spirit (initially, and most famously, gin) with various herbs and spices, including quinine. The strong drink was then diluted with ginger ale to create something long and refreshing. In 1856 Pimm's new concoction had proved such a success that he began producing and bottling the stuff to sell to other restaurants and bars. This

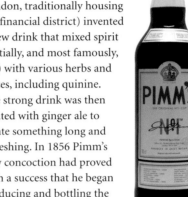

PIMM'S

was the beginning of Pimm's No.1 (the No. 1 comes from the number one cup – a tankard – in which Pimm served his drink).

Since Pimm's No.1, Pimm's No.2 (made with whisky), No.3 (brandy), No.4 (rum), and No.5 (rye whiskey) have come and gone and now only Pimm's No.6 – made with vodka – remains as a brother to the original drink. And whereas James Pimm's original brew was a shocking 40% ABV, the modern version is a much more reserved and refreshing 20% ABV, making it very easy to drink too much!

Combine one part Pimm's to four parts mixer (lemonade or orange juice work best), or make a punch – mixing Pimm's with lemonade and tossing in some cucumber, strawberries, and white fruit. There really is nothing better for a hot day in the garden.

LENA

C COLOUR Bright, glorious yellow – like a freshly ripened banana.

A AROMA Strong notes of banana, with a back-up of almonds and vanilla.

T TASTE Satisfying and not too rich; a fine balance of banana and vanilla.

Lena is the brand name for the banana liqueur marketed by the Japanese drinks' company Suntory.

All parts of the banana are macerated in spirit, which means that, although banana liqueur is sweet, it is not over-sweet and has a subtle taste – similar to crystallized bananas rather than fresh – with complex notes of almond and vanilla.

Bols, Leroux, and Marie Brizard all make banana liqueur, but Lena is usually the bartender's choice. It is great in tropical cocktails, mixed with spirits such as Malibu, helping to bring together all the flavours.

BOLS KIWI

C COLOUR Charming emerald green – just like the heart of the kiwi fruit.

A AROMA Unusual combination of the sweet aromas of kiwi fruit and citrus.

T TASTE Sweet and light-bodied, with delicious kiwi dominating.

The kiwi fruit, or Chinese gooseberry, has no great tradition in making alcoholic drinks. However, as it is a fruit that is tangy rather than sweet, kiwi has great potential to make a full-flavoured liqueur that is not cloying.

Bols Kiwi (also known as Kibowa) is bright emerald green, quite restrained in its aromas, and mild and refreshing to taste.

My mind is not yet made up about kiwi liqueur. I suggest giving it a try either neat over ice or in fruit juice or lemonade to see what you think.

BOLS KIWI

SOHO

C COLOUR Clear and bright, in a clear bottle with a bright red label.

A AROMA Quite aromatic with lychee; extremely floral.

T TASTE Slightly minty, with a long lychee finish.

Launched by Pernod Ricard in 1991, Soho is a liqueur made from the Chinese fruit lychee. Often used in Chinese cooking, the lychee is famous for being intensely sweet and fresh – and this is very much the appeal of this liqueur. Soho manages to freshen up even the zestiest orange juice, especially when both the juice and liqueur are ice cold. It is also great on its own over ice, and, of course, in an exotic-fruit cocktail. Look out for examples of lychee liqueur from the drinks' companies Bols and De Kuyper, too.

SOHO

MARACUJÁ

C COLOUR Bright golden yellow; also reddish-orange.

A AROMA Exotic; passion fruit and citrus; extremely full and fresh.

T TASTE Sweet, bright, and fruity, with a hint of tea as well as the passion fruit.

Maracujá (Portuguese for passion fruit), or Licor de Maracujá to give it its full name, is a sweet, fruity liqueur from the Atlantic islands of Madeira and the Azores.

Try drinking maracujá in a cocktail – I love it mixed with Champagne and gin, or with a light or white rum. Alternatively, add a measure to a tall glass of pineapple juice to make a long drink, or enjoy it really cold with crushed ice.

If you are unable to find a bottle made by the local producer Monin, Bols and De Kuyper make similar liqueurs, which include other fruits, and are red or reddish orange.

EXOTIC FRUITS *Lychees, kiwi, figs, bananas, dates, mangoes, pineapples, melons – the beauty of a liqueur is that virtually any fruit, no matter how exotic, can be steeped in spirit to create a little taste of paradise in a glass.*

PASSOÃ

C **COLOUR** Bright orange-red – the influence of the passion fruit.

A **AROMA** Delicate, fresh, and lively, with ripe fruits and citrus.

T **TASTE** Light, bright, fruity; sweet, with rich passion fruit and lemon.

Owned and marketed by the French drinks group Rémy Cointreau, Passoã is a passion-fruit-flavoured liqueur aimed at passionate young partygoers. The liqueur is sweet, fruity, and fun, and perfect for an exotic cocktail or for making into a long drink with fruit juice.

Passion fruit was first discovered by Europeans during the colonization of South America by Spanish missionaries in the 1500s. There is debate over how exactly the passion flower (which gives us the fruit) got its name. Some believe that it is a reference to the fruit's aphrodisiac qualities; other believe that it is a reference to Christ's Passion – the last hours of his life – because the thorns of the passion-flower bush are reminiscent of Christ's crown of thorns. Certainly, the flower is often used as a symbol of Christ's Passion in iconic display.

Passoã is a relatively young liqueur – it was launched in northern Europe only in 1986, but has already established a thriving reputation as an essential addition to the cocktail cabinet. The brand is now the second-most popular liqueur in Holland and third-most popular in Belgium.

At 20% ABV, Passoã is not too strong. Apart from doing its duty in cocktails, this exotic liqueur can be served on the rocks (its zest keeps its sweetness in check), or mixed with orange or grapefruit juice.

PASSOÃ

MIDORI

C **COLOUR** A vibrant and luscious bright green – like a juicy green melon.

A **AROMA** Clean and lively, with lots of melon and other sweet fruits.

T **TASTE** Extremely sweet, but also refreshing, with a warm finish.

Developed by the Japanese drinks company Suntory, Midori is a melon-flavoured liqueur now made in Mexico and aimed largely at the US market. However, to date its greatest success has been in Australia.

Launched in 1978, at New York's Studio 54 nightclub, Midori liqueur is marketed as a young person's party drink – bright, sweet, refreshing, and, at 21% ABV, not too heavy on alcohol. The base of the liqueur is neutral spirit, and it is flavoured with honeydew melon, which is pale green, and sweet and fresh. These qualities are highly recognizable in Midori, making it the perfect mixer for long, refreshing summer cocktails. Try it in The Universe – an award-winning cocktail that mixes Midori with vodka, lime juice, and pineapple juice. Many bartenders mix the liqueur with Baileys, Malibu, or sparkling apple juice – and also in a more "straight" version, just with lemonade. Generally, I would say that Midori is too sweet to drink on its own, but for something really long and refreshing on a hot summer's day – perhaps even at a beach party – try it with soda water, plenty of ice, and a twist of lemon to balance the sweetness.

Unmistakable for its bright green colour, Midori is definitely one for the cabinet – especially if you like your liqueurs refreshing and fruity, with lots of

MIDORI

flavours of the exotic.

66 Delicate, unique, and intense; these are exquisite drinks, many made to secret recipes handed down through generations, or kept within monastery walls. 99

VEGETABLE, HERB, AND SPICE

INTRODUCING VEGETABLE, HERB, AND SPICE LIQUEURS

In the Middle Ages, European monks tended gardens filled with health-giving vegetables, herbs, and spices. In order to preserve these "medicines" they steeped them in alcohol to create "elixirs of life" – the very earliest forms of liqueur.

DRINKING AND SERVING

DRINK PROFILE Plant-based liqueurs may be coloured by their base spirit (such as the amber of whisky or brandy), by the plant ingredients themselves, or by the addition of colouring.

All liqueurs are sweet, but in herbal liqueurs this is offset by the bitterness of the plants. In liqueurs based on many different ingredients, each sniff and sip can reveal something new; in liqueurs based on a single plant, such as crème de menthe, the aromas and taste of the herb or spice tend to be powerful. Plant-based liqueurs may be served as apéritifs (especially the anise liqueurs), as digestifs (such as Galliano), but most often in cocktails.

Although, like all good medicines, many of the early plant-based liqueurs were not terribly tasty, they were often extremely complex and rich, and as a result survive today in famous names such as Benedictine and Chartreuse. Once Europeans began to explore the Caribbean, bringing back with them sugar cane, a new era of the herbal liqueur began. Producers added sugar to their unpalatable elixirs, making them altogether more drinkable. From there it was only a matter of time before they stopped being "elixirs of life" altogether, and we started to enjoy them merely for pleasure.

LAVENDER *The Italian liqueur Galliano offers complex aromas of herbs, spices – and flowers, including lavender.*

A WORLD OF PLANTS – AND POSSIBILITY

Some herb or plant liqueurs, such as the Italian Galliano, are made using more than one hundred herbs, leaves, and roots, often from the far corners of the world; others, such as Crème de Menthe (mint liqueur, traditionally from France) and Xanath (a Mexican vanilla liqueur), are made from mainly one plant. Ginger "wines", such as Stone's (from England), also fall into this latter category, as does the artichoke-based Italian liqueur Cynar. Caraway seeds, mastic gum, and even pieces of gold have found their way into herbal liqueurs – the possibilities are endless.

RAW MATERIALS *Almost any plant can be used to flavour a liqueur. From left to right: star anise (used in pastis), peppermint (crème de menthe), ginger (ginger wine), and artichoke (Cynar).*

One plant, the star anise, has spawned a whole family of herb-based liqueurs, known as "anise" liqueurs and including the famous names of Pernod, pastis, sambuca, and ouzo. However, not all the liqueurs from this family are necessarily made using only star anise itself, and might also be flavoured with other members of the anise plant group, including fennel. Liquorice root also gives the distinctive anise aromas and taste, although this is a different plant altogether. Most interestingly, however, these drinks are the descendents of absinthe, which horrified people in 19th-century France because of its powerful, drug-like effects on drinkers. The liqueur contained wormwood bark, a known hallucinogen, which ultimately led to the banning of absinthe altogether. To overcome this, producers had to find an alternative that gave their liqueurs the same flavours as wormwood, but without its hallucinatory properties – namely, the star anise.

The category of vegetable, herb, and spice liqueurs offers some of the oldest and most complex liqueurs in the world. Not only that, many of them have fascinating stories to tell, too – from the scandal of absinthe hallucinogens to formulae that lay hidden for years in the personal diary of a single monk, as was the case for Benedictine.

COCKTAILS *The long cocktail Suissesse (see p349), is based on Pernod, an anise-flavoured liqueur, which goes cloudy when in contact with water. The cocktail also includes egg white, lemon juice, and soda water.*

FLAMING SAMBUCA *Sambuca is a powerful anise liqueur. Traditionally it is set alight and served with a solitary floating coffee bean, known as the "fly".*

STAR ANISE AND ANISEED

Although drinks of this type are often called "anise", they are not made just from aniseed, but from a wide range of herbs, roots, and spices. Their origins go back to the production of absinthe, but each product is slightly different, using its own balance of ingredients to achieve subtle variations in taste. Manufacturing techniques also vary, and they too influence the character of the liqueur.

PERNOD

C **COLOUR** Greeny yellow becoming lighter opaque cream when mixed with water.

A **AROMA** Distinctive; anise, liquorice, herbs, and sandalwood.

T **TASTE** Dry and tingling, with anise, cloves, and a lingering finish.

MILKY WHITE *The classic way to drink Pernod is to "louche" it – to add water and make it cloudy.*

Created by the Pernod family as an alternative to the banned absinthe, Pernod dates from 1920. The spirit uses all the same ingredients as absinthe (including fennel, nutmeg, hyssop, angelica, and other herbs and roots), but replaces the wormwood bark – said to be an hallucinogen – with star anise, the fruit of the Chinese Star Anise tree and not to be confused with aniseed, which is the flower of the Mediterranean anise plant.

Rather like a flavoured vodka, Pernod is made by distilling star anise and fennel to produce a liquid that is then blended with alcohol and the distillates of aromatic plants and liquorice, before being sweetened and coloured. Incidentally, many

people think that because Pernod and pastis *(see opposite)* both "louche" – go milky when mixed with water – they are the same drink. However, pastis is made by a different process – maceration of herbs, spices, and liquorice.

Dry, complex, and powerful (around 40% ABV), Pernod is dominated by its flavours of anise and herbs, even after water has been added. To make a classic apéritif, mix one part Pernod with five parts water, adding ice if you wish. Its herbal qualities also make Pernod a good digestif – just enjoy it whenever the mood takes you!

CULTURE AND TRADITION

ABSINTHE The ancestor of today's anise drinks is the legendary liqueur, absinthe. In 1792 a Frenchman, Dr Ordinaire, combined liquorice, wormwood bark, and other herbs with alcohol, and named his drink absinthe (from the botanical name for wormwood). Henry-Louis Pernod bought the recipe, and in 1797 began to produce the drink for sale. However, wormwood contains the hallucinogen thujone, and in 1908 absinthe was banned in Switzerland, and later in France, and then elsewhere. In response, Pernod dropped the wormwood, creating the drink we know today.

RICARD

C COLOUR Light golden brown, turning opaque cream when mixed with water.

A AROMA Delicate and floral, with aniseed, herbs, and liquorice.

T TASTE Dry, refreshing, and complex; herbs, aniseed, and liquorice.

Invented by French entrepreneur Paul Ricard in 1932, Ricard is an anise-based spirit that is dry, delicate, and floral, but also strong. It is now the number-one anise spirit in the world.

Ricard's full formula includes star anise, herbs, and liquorice (more dominant than in Pernod), which are macerated and then distilled. For the best results, louche the spirit with five parts water to one Ricard, then sit back and dream of France!

RICARD

PASTIS 51

C COLOUR Light golden brown, turning opaque white when you add water.

A AROMA Distinctive; aniseed, liquorice, herbs, and sandalwood.

T TASTE Clean and crisp, with aniseed and herbs, and a fresh finish.

Pastis 51 (the 51 refers to 1951, the year of its launch) is the second-best-selling spirit in France, but in its home region, around Marseilles and the Midi, it is the best!

Pastis 51 is made through the maceration of herbs and roots, especially star anise and liquorice, with the liquorice dominating. Although strong, it is drier than Pernod and does not have Pernod's greenish tinge.

Try Pastis 51 as an apéritif – drink it over ice, diluted with five parts water to one part spirit.

PASTIS

CASANIS

C COLOUR Opaque; pale creamy yellow, with a slight tinge of green.

A AROMA Delicate and typically "anise", with aniseed and herbs.

T TASTE Dry and light-bodied, with hints of flowers, anise, and liquorice.

Casanis is one of the favourite brands of anise spirit in Provence, in the south of France, although actually this drink originates from Corsica.

Made from both green and star anise, blended with herbs such as thyme and rosemary, Casanis is known for its aromatic and light character.

According to the traditional Provençal and Corsican styles for drinking pastis, the spirit must be neither drowned, nor drunk neat – to bring out its best flavours, mix one part Casanis to five parts water.

BERGER BLANC

C COLOUR Clear and pure, without the greeny yellow of more traditional pastis.

A AROMA Delicate, with aniseed and herbs in a fine balance.

T TASTE Dry and fresh, with hints of anise and liquorice.

Berger Blanc is a French anise apéritif drink, but produced with fewer botanicals (herbs and aromatic plants) than many of the other brands. As a result it is clear and pure, subtle and delicate, with a fine balance and a less obvious aniseed-and-liquorice character than most. It makes a great introduction if you have never tried pastis before.

Berger also makes a Berger Pastis, in the more traditional style, and with a small amount of sweet caramel. This is also worth trying as an alternative to the main brands.

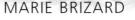

BERGER BLANC

MARIE BRIZARD

C COLOUR Clear and bright – rather than creamy yellow like other pastis drinks.

A AROMA Elegant and slightly medicinal; aniseed and spices.

T TASTE Extremely smooth and warming; aniseed and herbs; long, spicy finish.

Marie Brizard Anisette is the drink that launched the French company Marie Brizard. Marie herself was born in Bordeaux in 1714. In 1755 she nursed back to health a feverish French planter who had arrived in Bordeaux from the West Indies. In gratitude he gave her a secret formula for the production of anisette. That same year Marie and her nephew Jean-Baptiste Roger began the commercial production of the liqueur, founding not only their own great company, but the French drinks industry as we know it today.

The recipe for this special liqueur uses the sweet green anise (aniseed) fruit from southern Spain, and more than ten other plants, fruits, and spices. The aniseed is blended into a pure spirit base, giving a smoothness and richness absent in many other, more challenging anise drinks. The result is a full and rich set of flavours that are elegant and fresh on the palate and better enjoyed over ice, with or without a mixer, as an after-dinner drink rather than an apéritif. Be careful though! This liqueur makes extremely easy sipping, but at 25% ABV it is no weakling!

Marie Brizard also produces a Lemon Anisette, which combines the original aniseed drink with lemon juice, although presently this is available only in Spain.

MARIE BRIZARD

SAMBUCA

C COLOUR Clear; there are also versions that are black, blue, gold, green, and red.

A AROMA Delicate, with aniseed, elderberry, liquorice, and herbs.

T TASTE Balanced sweetness, the aromas filling out on the palate.

Sambuca is an anise- and elderberry-flavoured liqueur made in Italy. The use of elderberries separates sambuca from the other anise-based spirits from around the Mediterranean, including pastis and ouzo.

Sambuca is made by macerating anise, elderberries, liquorice, and other herbs and spices in alcohol spirit. The basic liqueur is clear (known as "white" sambuca), although it also comes in coloured versions, including one that is deep blue, but known as

SMEETS SAMBUCA

"black" sambuca. Its flavours are sweeter and richer than aniseed-flavoured apéritifs, lying somewhere between Pernod and the sweet, French anise liqueur known as anisette.

As a result there are several different ways to enjoy sambuca. Try it as an apéritif, diluted with water, or if you are really brave turn it into a traditional, Italian "Flaming Sambuca". Pour it into a shot glass, drop in three coffee beans (which float on the top and are known as the "flies"), and set it alight! Some foolhardy people take the liquid into their mouths, then light it, closing their mouths to quench the flames. However, I certainly do not recommend that you ever try this method.

There are thousands of sambuca producers for you to choose from. One of the

OPAL NERA SAMBUCA

biggest is Romana (owned by Diageo), which offers smooth, rich, and sweet sambucas in both clear and black versions. Other good brands are Smeets, Luxardo, Galliano, and the exceptional Molinari, which was created in 1944 by Angelo Molinari and is the only sambuca in Italy allowed to call itself "extra", as a mark of its high quality.

There is very little difference between white sambuca and the coloured versions, except for their appearance and the fact that the coloured versions may be a little sweeter. First produced in 1989, Opal Nera is the original brand of "black" sambuca. The opaque, black colour comes from the skins of elderberries, which also give a slight purplish tinge. It has a distinctly "dark", smooth taste, with lots of black liquorice, and a syrupy palate balanced by gentle citrus.

ANESONE

C COLOUR Clear and bright, with a medium viscosity.

A AROMA Aniseed, herbs, and spice – as you would expect from an aniseed spirit.

T TASTE Dry and full-bodied, with strong aniseed and herbal flavours.

Anesone (pronounced "an-nih-so-nih") is the Italian equivalent of French pastis or Greek ouzo. It is strong and dry, and makes an excellent apéritif when mixed with water and served as a long drink. The Italians also drink it as a shot in an espresso coffee at the end of a meal, or even neat as a straight digestif.

One of the most readily available brands outside Italy is Stock Anesone – from a company founded in 1884 by Italian Lionello Stock. This is full and rich and makes a good alternative to pastis.

ANESONE

MASTIC

C COLOUR Clear, sometimes with a slight tinge of opaque white.

A AROMA Delicate; herbs and flowers, especially aniseed and liquorice.

T TASTE Smooth, bringing the aromas on to the palate; warm finish.

Mastic, also known as mastika, masticha, mastikha, mastichato, and mastiha, is a sweet liqueur made from aniseed and the sap from the mastic (*letinsk*) tree. Most brands come from Greece, Turkey, Cyprus, and some of the Balkan countries, especially Bulgaria.

The mastic tree, which of course also produces chewing gum, is actually a member of the pistachio family; its Latin name is *Pistacia lentiscus*. Although the tree is grown in many countries of the world,

amazingly the liquorice-flavoured resin is found only on the Greek island of Chios, in the northeastern Aegean Sea. Both in Greece and the Middle East (the island lies just off the coast of Turkey), the resin is used as a spice, a medicine for stomach upsets, and in sutures, tooth-fillings, and perfumes. The resin is even said to absorb cholesterol!

The base of mastic liqueur is anise-flavoured spirit (ouzo in Greece), to which producers add a number of botanicals. Sometimes the resin itself is added with the botanicals early in the production process; alternatively, it is added to the distillate later. The resin's natural liquorice flavours mean that it blends easily with the spirit, while also adding body to make the ouzo (or other anise spirit) feel smoother and softer. The result is 21% ABV, and usually served over ice. One of the best-known producers is the Greek Mavrakis.

ARACK

C COLOUR Clear, but occasionally slightly opaque white as a result of impurities.

A AROMA Alcohol spirit, with aniseed, herbs, and molasses.

T TASTE Quite warm, even fiery; dry, with aniseed and herbs.

Arack (or arrack) is made in the Middle East and Asia, especially Sri Lanka and Indonesia. The name comes from the Arabic word for juice, and is applied to a variety of strong spirits made variously from rice, palm sap, raisins and other fruits, coconut, molasses, and sugar cane. The spirit is flavoured with herbs and spices, particularly anise. The quality and character of arack will depend upon its ingredients and its country of origin. The best examples tend to come from Indonesia.

ARACK

RAKI

C COLOUR Clear, turning cloudy when water is added.

A AROMA Grapey, pungent; aniseed, liquorice, and herbs.

T TASTE Dry and warming, sometimes with a kick; aniseed and herbs.

Raki is a Turkish anise spirit. The word *raki* originates from the Arabic word *araqI*, literally meaning "of liquor", and the spirit has a history that dates back 300 years. Different regions of Turkey distil the spirit from various different fruits, including figs and plums, and most commonly raisins. The pomace (the pulp of pips, skins, and stalks) of grapes may also be used. Modern producers making raki on a commercial scale often use *suma*, or concentrated grape distillate, rather than actual fruit. Of course,

RAKI

all producers, no matter how they get their base spirit, add aniseed to the mix at some point in the production process – sometimes at the beginning with the other botanicals (herbs, plants and spices), sometimes nearer the end.

The resulting spirit can be really strong, usually around 40–50% ABV, but sometimes up to 60% ABV. Its strength and the fact that it turns opaque white when added to water have given the spirit the Turkish nickname *aslan sütü*, the "lion's milk". Traditionally raki is drunk ice cold, mixed in equal amounts with water, to accompany light foods, such as salad, and also with fish, especially mullet and mackerel. Commercial brands include those from government-owned Tekel (look for Yeni Raki, Tekirdag, Altindag), Golden Horn, and Efe.

TSIPOURO

C COLOUR Clear, becoming cloudy white when mixed with water.

A AROMA Medicinal, with grapes, spirit, herbs, and aniseed.

T TASTE Extremely lively and warm, with aniseed and herbs.

Tsipouro is a truly authentic Greek spirit, sometimes known as *tsikoudia* in Crete. Distilled from grape pomace (the residue of wine production), tsipouro is a true eau-de-vie, or brandy. In many parts of Greece, producers add aniseed to sweeten and flavour the pomace spirit.

Far from being a boring, automated process, making tsipouro is a great family and community ritual in Greece. Called *rakizio*, the tsipouro-making festival begins when the grape-growers have pressed their

grapes and sent the juice to the wineries for fermentation into wine. When the juice is safely inside the fermentation vats, whole families arrive at the winery with their grape pomace. Together the local people distil the pomace, often through the night, and party while they wait; then everyone shares the results. It was only in the 1980s that the Greek government allowed the commercial sale of tsipouro (look for the brands of Tsantali and Vrissass). Until then, the spirit was kept wholly in the family.

Tsipouro is quite strong at around 36% ABV, and is usually served in shot glasses. For a longer drink, add water to produce a cloudy effect, just as you would with ouzo. The Greeks usually drink this spirit with *mezedes*, which are small, appetizer dishes, rather like Spanish tapas.

TSIPOURO

OUZO

C COLOUR Clear, but turns white when mixed with water.

A AROMA Pungent aromas of aniseed, black liquorice, and herbs.

T TASTE Dry, with strong aniseed, liquorice, and herbs.

Ouzo is probably the most famous Greek and Cypriot aniseed spirit, and is thought to have originated in central Asia, most likely as raki *(see above)*. The classic Greek ouzo is distilled from a combination of pressed grapes, berries, and herbs, including aniseed, liquorice, mint, wintergreen, fennel, and hazelnut.

Not all ouzo is made in the same way. Some producers use pot stills (copper stills shaped like enormous kettles) to redistil a base spirit with aniseed and other botanicals (herbs

OUZO 12

and plants used as flavourings in spirit); while others distil liquid flavoured with anise and fennel seed to make a kind of concentrate, and then dilute the flavour using plain alcohol spirit. To the uninitiated all ouzos might taste the same, but to the ouzo aficionado, they are all very different.

Some are moderately alcoholic at around 35% ABV; others go through the roof at strengths of up to 60% ABV! Most brands are around 40% ABV, with "luxury" versions coming in at between 46% and 48%. Flavours range from soft and dry, to rich and dry. All have dominant aniseed aromas.

There are quite literally hundreds of brands of ouzo altogether, most of them local to a particular island or region of Greece or Cyprus. One of the best-known brands is Barbayanni, which

OUZO BARBAYANNI

is made on the island of Lesbos, in the northeastern Aegean. First produced in 1860, Barbayanni ouzo comes in four different versions. The classic of the four is the blue label (46% ABV), which has a light, delicate taste. The strongest (48% ABV) is the Aphrodite, which has dry, ripe flavours. Other well-known ouzos include Ouzo 12, owned by the Campari Group, which was the first ouzo ever to be bottled and sold commercially. Nowadays this spicy, flavourful spirit is the biggest-selling brand of ouzo in the world.

One of the more interesting ouzo brands is Aphrodite. Not to be confused with the Barbayanni version, this ouzo is made in New Zealand and is as good as most of the main commercial, Greek brands. I think this ouzo from the southern hemisphere is definitely worth a try.

The traditional ways to serve ouzo are straight as an apéritif or mixed with a small amount of water in a shot glass. Mixing ouzo with water turns the spirit whitish and opaque, as the essential oils from the aniseed latch onto the water molecules. This process is known as louching.

> **FOOD MATCH**
>
> **SEAFOOD** Drinking ouzo with food is an accepted part of Greek culture. The spirit is particularly good with seafood, especially octopus and squid, as well as whitebait and other *mezedes* (Greek appetizers).

CACTUS

Cactus liqueurs are usually made with an agave spirit base, which is blended with fruit juice and other natural sweeteners.

AGAVERO

C COLOUR Dark gold, from the blend of tequila and herbs.

A AROMA A fine mix of earth, spice, vanilla, and caramel.

T TASTE Rich and smooth, with a herbal sweetness.

Agavero is blend of young and aged tequila macerated with the damiana herb, indigenous to the mountains of Jalisco, near Tequila. The liqueur is luscious and easy to sip, with the spicy tequila balanced by a rich vanilla sweetness from the herbs and the ageing process.

TEQUILA ROSE

C COLOUR Bright pink, obscured by a very dark bottle.

A AROMA Sweet, with strawberry, vanilla, and earthy spirit.

T TASTE Sweet and luscious; strawberry and sugar, and a hint of medicine.

TEQUILA ROSE

Tequila Rose is an up-and-coming liqueur made in Mexico and distributed in the US by the McCormick Company. It is made from tequila blended with strawberries and cream.

If you are a fan of Baileys Irish Cream, but you also enjoy something with a bit of kick, Tequila Rose has a tang to set off its creaminess – although it is unquestionably very sweet. At 17% ABV, it is also not too strong. Try it with ice or in a cocktail.

ARTICHOKE

The artichoke is a complex plant, and contains cynarin, a substance that stimulates the taste buds responsible for detecting sweet flavours. This makes liqueurs produced from this vegetable ideal as dry apéritifs.

CYNAR

C COLOUR Dark red and quite viscous, with a greeny-brown tinge.

A AROMA Distinctive, and quite pungent, with earth and vegetables.

T TASTE Quite bitter and dry, with a distinct vegetal feel.

The special Italian liqueur Cynar – owned by Campari – is the only internationally marketed liqueur using globe artichokes as the primary ingredient. The name Cynar comes from the plant's botanical name *Cynara scolymus*, a member of the thistle family native to central and western parts of the Mediterranean.

CYNAR

The first recorded edible form of the globe artichoke dates from 1400 in Italy, but the plant is now grown throughout the milder climates of Europe (notably in France and other Mediterranean countries), and along the coast of California.

Delicate and nut-like in flavour, artichokes are interesting, but not sweet, and Cynar is characterized by its bitterness. Expect a moderately dry, vegetable-like palate and drink it with ice, soda water, or lemonade, or even in a cocktail.

CUMIN AND CARAWAY

Caraway and cumin are highly aromatic plants that are closely related – some languages even refer to them by the same name. The seeds of both are used to make the liqueur kümmel, although the majority of brands contain only caraway.

KÜMMEL

C COLOUR Clear and fresh; distilled to purity like vodka.

A AROMA Very distinctive; nutty, with herbs, spice, and minerals.

T TASTE Dry, with caraway, aniseed, and exotic spice; refreshing.

Kümmel is the generic name for caraway-seed liqueur. The digestive benefits of caraway have been known for centuries, and in 1575 Lucas Bols began making a caraway-seed liqueur in Amsterdam, Holland. Production soon spread across eastern Europe and into Russia, making famous brands such as

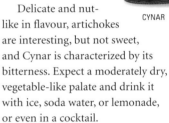

KÜMMEL

Wolfschmidt and Mentzendorff, which still produce kümmel today.

Overall, kümmel is distinctive and refreshing, with a nutty, spicy character. At around 40% ABV, it is strong, and makes an ideal apéritif, after-dinner liqueur, or cocktail. I like it to drink it straight from the freezer, like vodka.

Try the traditional brands, especially Wolfschmidt, made in Latvia but to an original Danish recipe, which has flavours of aniseed and caraway. Also look out for the smooth German Gilka Kaiser.

VANILLA

Both the Maya and the Aztecs used seed pods from the vanilla plant to flavour *chacau haa* – a special drink prepared with water, cocoa beans, and spices. It is still drunk in southern Mexico, Guatemala, and Belize, and has led to a tradition of making vanilla-based liqueurs.

XANATH

C COLOUR Dark brown; presented in a decanter based on a Mexican pyramid.

A AROMA Very aromatic, with vanilla, spice, herbs, and molasses.

T TASTE Sweet and complex; rich and satisfying; sweet, vanilla finish.

A popular Mexican liqueur, made in the Veracruz region of east-central Mexico, Xanath was first produced in 1949 by Italian immigrants, who made it using rum and extract of vanilla. The name Xanath means "vanilla flower" in the language of the Totonac, the region's indigenous peoples, who are believed to have

XANATH

first discovered vanilla and used it for flavouring. The Gaya family, who own and produce Xanath, grow their own vanilla beans and use only natural ingredients.

The spirit of Mexico is essential to the marketing of this liqueur, which comes in a bottle shaped like a Mexican pyramid. At 19% ABV, Xanath is not too strong, and is extremely flexible in its drinking. It can be served straight, at room temperature or over ice; in coffee; or blended with other spirits. Alternatively, try it poured over ice cream.

HONEY

Honey is one of the oldest substances to be used as the basis of an alcoholic drink. Many ancient societies made mead, or its equivalent, by fermenting honey in water, and today's more sophisticated liqueurs developed from this centuries-old tradition.

KRUPNIK

C COLOUR Elegant dark gold, rather like clear honey.

A AROMA Delicate but spicy, with honey and herbs and a great balance.

T TASTE Smooth; good balance of honey, spice, herbs, and spirit; warming.

Krupnik (pronounced "kroop-NEEK") is a Polish honey liqueur, first written about in the 1300s and still popular today, holding more than ten per cent of the entire Polish liqueur market.

Krupnik is made using natural honey, from wild bees, and exotic spices. It has a distinctive, sweet taste, a spicy bouquet, and a strong, warming effect. In Poland during the summer, krupnik is drunk chilled with ice; in the winter it is warmed up – delicious!

Look out for krupnik from the Starogard Distilleries of Gdansk. You may also see a Lithuanian honey vodka called Krupnikas, which is sweeter and is made with fewer herbs; or honey vodka from the Polish Polmos distilleries. This is smooth and tasty, and not over-sweet, with a herby character.

KRUPNIK

HYDROMEL

C COLOUR Dark honey gold with highlights of yellow.

A AROMA Distinctively sweet and delicate; mainly honey and herbs.

T TASTE Delicate and sweet, with honey and vanilla, and a soft finish.

Hydromel ("honey and water") is one of the oldest alcoholic drinks in the world, dating at least as far back as Ancient Greece. The drink is made by diluting different kinds of honey in water and fermenting the mixture with various yeasts. The end product is dry, semi-sweet, or sweet, depending on how much honey is used in the original blend.

Drink hydromel chilled as an apéritif, or as a digestif with cheese; in cocktails; or with fruit juice. Sweet versions are best with desserts. Finally, beware – hydromel is easy to drink, and may knock you off your feet!

OTHER PLANTS AND HERBS

Many drinks that we now call liqueurs were originally made as medicines, often by monks. Most had a spirit base, to which a mixture of herbs, spices, and roots were added. Today's herbal liqueurs are often close relatives of these "elixirs".

GALLIANO

C COLOUR Pale amber yellow, packaged in a tall, elegant bottle.

A AROMA Complex; herbs, flowers, anise, liquorice, and vanilla.

T TASTE Distinctive; sweet and smooth with herbs and flowers.

Tuscan distiller Arturo Vaccari first created Galliano in 1896 and named it after Giuseppe Galliano, a major in the Italian army during the Italian–Abyssinian conflict of the late-19th century. With a minimal force behind him, Galliano died heroically at the Battle of Adua in Abyssinia in the same year that Vaccari created his new drink.

The liqueur – now owned and marketed by the Rémy Cointreau group – is made at Salara, just north of Milan. It is light amber-yellow in colour, and has a distinctive herbal and peppermint aroma, and a spicy, sweet flavour. During production, the liqueur is stored for up to six months in glass tanks to allow the complex mix of herbs, flowers, anise, liquorice, and spirit to blend together perfectly. Its "inverted-cone" bottle has been the same since 1896.

Most suitable as a mixer, Galliano's biggest claim to fame is the Harvey Wallbanger (a mixture of vodka, orange juice, and Galliano), but it can also be drunk straight over ice as an apéritif, or in a shot glass at room temperature as a digestif.

ENDLESS FLAVOURS *Galliano is a complex blend of more than 25 herbs and spices, including vanilla, star anise, and mint. As a result it makes interesting drinking – with something new coming to the fore with every sip.*

ALCHERMES

C COLOUR Light, bright red, created by the addition of cochineal dye.

A AROMA Flowers – especially jasmine and rose – and vanilla.

T TASTE Quite spicy, as well as sweet and floral.

Made in Florence, although brought to Italy from Spain, Alchermes is a complex liqueur made with spirit, sugar, rose water, jasmine, orange peel, and vanilla, as well as with spices including cinnamon, coriander, cloves, nutmeg, aniseed, and cardamom. Its name comes from the Spanish word *alquermes* meaning "ladybird" – a reference to the drink's red colour. Considered too sweet for modern tastes, the liqueur is popular in cooking, which uses the spices and colour to great effect.

LICOR 43

C COLOUR Light, vibrant gold, with bright sparkling highlights.

A AROMA Fresh and aromatic, with herbs, vanilla, and fruit; refreshing.

T TASTE Bright, fresh, and lively, with spice, citrus, and vanilla.

Licor 43 comes from Cartagena, Murcia, on the southeastern coast of Spain, and since 1924 has been made by the Diego Zamora company. The recipe for Licor 43 is said to have been directly inherited from the ancient city of Carthage – in the region that is now Tunisia – and at least 2,500 years old!

The herbs give Licor 43 a fresh, complex taste, with strong notes of vanilla. It is sweet, but not cloying, and a big hit as an ingredient in the Spanish punch Sangria.

LICOR 43

LA VIEILLE CURE

C COLOUR Pale; golden, greeny yellow – a result of the mixture of infused herbs.

A AROMA Medicinal and herbal; extremely complex, with notes of vanilla.

T TASTE Beautifully balanced, with herbs and Cognac; sweet and smooth.

The Abbey of Cenon, in the Gironde, southwestern France, first produced La Vieille Cure in the Middle Ages, although commercial production did not begin until after the French Revolution, and all production ceased in 1986. Nevertheless, bottles occasionally come up for sale. The secret recipe involves macerating up to 50 roots and herbs, including juniper, myrrh, angelica, cardamom, tea, and honey, in Armagnac and Cognac. To me this is one of the best herbal liqueurs ever produced.

BENEDICTINE D.O.M.

C COLOUR Distinctive, vintage, golden yellow, with glints of orange.

A AROMA Elegant and well-balanced, with citrus fruits and spice.

T TASTE Rich, smooth, and elegant, with spice, honey, and citrus.

Benedictine D.O.M. – the initials stand for *Deo Optimo Maximo*, meaning "To God, most good, most great" – is a world-famous herbal liqueur made to a recipe dating from 1510. Venetian monk Don Bernardo Vincelli developed the liqueur as a means of combating malaria around the Benedictine abbey at Fécamp, on the north coast of France. He used a formula that included 27 herbs and spices from all around the world, many of which he probably brought with him from Venice, at that time the gateway to the spice centres of Arabia and the East. Drinkers found that not only did the liqueur protect them against malaria, but also helped to "cure" rheumatism – although probably the alcohol simply dulled the pain! Soon the drink became highly popular among the monks and locals alike and became known as *Benedictine ad majorem dei gloriam* – "Benedictine for the greater glory of God."

At the end of the 18th century, during the French Revolution, the monastery was dissolved, and production of the liqueur ceased. However, in 1791 a distinguished Fécamp local bought the 16th-century manuscript containing the original formula. The recipe went unnoticed and the manuscript passed down through the generations of this man's family until, in 1863, it came into the hands of Alexandre Le Grand, a wine merchant and one of the man's descendants.

BENEDICTINE

GOLDWASSER

C COLOUR Bright yellow, with a hint of orange – and flakes of real gold!

A AROMA Delicate and attractive, with herbs and spice.

T TASTE Quite full and distinctive; fresh and complex, with anise to the fore.

First produced in the 17th century, in what is now Gdansk, in Poland, Goldwasser (or Zlota Woda in Polish, both meaning "gold water") is a herbal, spicy liqueur made from distilled spirits flavoured with oils and spices, including anise, angelica, gentian, and juniper. However, the real attraction is that floating in it are thin flakes of 23 carat gold! Over ice Goldwasser makes an unusual apéritif, or you can drink it in coffee.

GOLDWASSER

L'ARQUEBUSE DE L'HERMITAGE

C COLOUR An extremely pale greeny yellow, from the herbs and plants.

A AROMA Distinctly medicinal aromas, with a range of floral and herbal notes.

T TASTE Quite grassy, with flowers, herbs, and spirit in fine balance.

What a strange name for a liqueur! The plants used to make this drink once treated the wounds caused by an *arquebuse* – an early type of rifle. In 1857 Brother Emmanuel, a Marist monk, developed the formula for l'Arquebuse de l'Hermitage, which included the maceration and distillation of 33 different herbs and plants, including camomile, artemisia, lime blossom, and marjoram, all of which have therapeutic characteristics. The liqueur is hard to find now, especially outside France, but a good producer is Cherry-Rocher.

B AND B

C COLOUR Deep amber orange – slightly darker than Benedictine.

A AROMA Attractive and pungent, with spice, vanilla, and herbs.

T TASTE Medium-bodied; smooth; spice, honey, and citrus; slightly sweet finish.

B and B is a blend of Benedictine and brandy – the brainchild of a 1930s barman in New York's "Club 21", who decided to mix these two drinks, both of which were by then firm favourites in cocktail lounges everywhere. It is now produced by the Benedictine company.

B and B is drier than Benedictine alone, with a little more body and more kick. Treat it as an alternative to a fine Cognac – one with a touch of sweetness in its perfume – and drink it as a digestif from a brandy balloon. I love it!

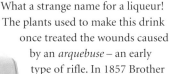

B AND B

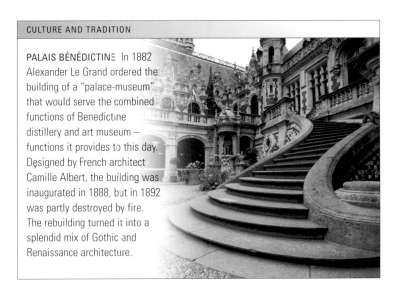

PALAIS BÉNÉDICTINE In 1882
Alexander Le Grand ordered the
building of a "palace-museum"
that would serve the combined
functions of Benedictine
distillery and art museum –
functions it provides to this day.
Designed by French architect
Camille Albert, the building was
inaugurated in 1888, but in 1892
was partly destroyed by fire.
The rebuilding turned it into a
splendid mix of Gothic and
Renaissance architecture.

Le Grand decided to produce the
liqueur commercially, marketing
it as Benedictine D.O.M. By 1873
Benedictine had become a big hit,
and in 1876 Le Grand established
the Benedictine SA company, which
makes the liqueur in Fécamp to this
day, now selling it all over the world.

Benedictine's 27 herbs and spices
include some that are sweet-tasting,
such as vanilla and coriander; bitter,
such as myrrh; and peppery and
hot, such as cardamom and
cinnamon. The result is complex,
satisfying, and completely unique –
the drink is citrusy and spicy, with
a sweetness that is not overpowering,
and a rich herbal quality that still
allows the fruit to shine through.
The finish seems endlessly long,
and is wonderfully warming.

This liqueur is extremely
versatile and can be drunk in a
number of ways. My favourite is to
drink it in the evening (I think it is
too powerful and rich for the
afternoon), in a large Cognac glass
with ice. I like to enjoy it just for
itself – or perhaps with something
light to nibble, such as a few olives,
but probably not as an apéritif.
Others like it as an after-dinner
digestif, and it is often used by
bartenders for adding a little
herbiness to cocktails.

A CABINET ESSENTIAL
*However you drink your
Benedictine – over ice with
a light evening snack, or
straight at the end of an
evening meal – this liqueur
is a timeless classic.*

ELIXIR DE SPA / ELIXIR D'ANVERS

C **COLOUR** Light greenish yellow, reflecting the herb ingredients.

A **AROMA** Aromatic, with a fascinating mixture of herbs and flowers.

T **TASTE** Full-flavoured and soft, and bittersweet at the finish.

To many Belgians, Elixir d'Anvers (Anvers is the French spelling of Antwerp, a city in northern Belgium) brings back memories of childhood – a visit to a grandparent would often come with the possibility of a tiny sip of the liqueur. For the older generations, Elixir d'Anvers presented the perfect remedy for all manner of ailments, especially stomachaches.

First produced in 1863 by the Antwerp-based company de Beukelaer, from a blend of 32 plants and

ELIXIR D'ANVERS

herbs, Elixir d'Anvers continues to be made using traditional methods. Production takes five months, over the course of which the liqueur is macerated, distilled, and then matured in old oak casks to allow its flavours to develop. The result is yellow, bittersweet, and herbal, with a fine, full flavour. It is quite strong at 40% ABV.

Elixir de Spa is another sweetish tonic liqueur, this time made in Spa, east-central Belgium. First produced in the 17th century to a Medieval formula, the liqueur is made using 40 different herbs and spices from the area around Spa. It is similar to Elixir d'Anvers in that it is said to have medicinal properties, and is also full bodied and quite herbal. In 1956 de Beukelaer, makers of Elixir d'Anvers, purchased Elixir de Spa, thus bringing the two liqueurs together under one roof.

IZARRA

C **COLOUR** Green or yellow, depending on the formula of plants and herbs.

A **AROMA** Elegant and complex, with herbs, almond, and peppermint.

T **TASTE** Well-balanced and smooth, with Armagnac and herbs, and a spicy finish.

This French liqueur originates from the Pyrenees, the range of mountains in the south of the country that separates France from Spain. Izarra is Basque (the local language) for "star" – and a star it is! It is thought that monks first developed the formula of herbs and spices that go into Izarra in 1835, although the liqueur was not made commercially until the end of the 19th century. The brand is now made and owned by drinks company Rémy Cointreau.

Izarra is made from a base of Armagnac, then

IZARRA

flavoured with plants and herbs native to the Pyrenees. There are two versions of Izarra: green and yellow. The recipes are kept secret, but we do know that the yellow liqueur contains 32 plants, and the green 48. There is reportedly very little crossover between the two sets of ingredients, giving the two versions of the liqueur distinct characters. Yellow Izarra is smooth, with a slight flavour of bitter almonds. The influence of saffron is evident in both the colour and the aroma. The green version has notes of peppermint. Both are quite potent: 40% ABV for the yellow and 48% ABV for the green.

In my opinion, these are both excellent liqueurs. They are not in the same classic league as the more famous Chartreuse (*see opposite*), but they make very good alternatives and represent great value for money.

GÉNÉPI

C **COLOUR** Three versions: clear (white), pale, greenish yellow, and light gold.

A **AROMA** Distinctly herbal and floral; well-balanced sweetness.

T **TASTE** Quite grassy with some bitter notes; flowers and herbs.

Génépi is an aromatic herb of the Artemisia family, which also includes wormwood, the hallucinogenic ingredient that led to the banning of absinthe in France – and elsewhere – in the 19th century. The liqueur (also known as Génépy des Alpes) has powerful aromas and flavours of grass and herbs. At around 40% ABV it is quite strong. There are several types of Génépi, but the most delicate is the *blanc* (white). Drink this liqueur straight in a shot glass or mixed with a little water, like a pastis.

GÉNÉPI

AIGUEBELLE

C **COLOUR** Green or yellow, depending on the version.

A **AROMA** Medicinal, with a range of herbs and flowers.

T **TASTE** Quite powerful, with a fine balance of herbs and spice.

In 1137 Trappist monks founded the Abbey of Notre Dame d'Aiguebelle in the hills near Montelimar, in the lower Rhône Valley, southern France. Here, Brother Jean developed a formula for a herbal liqueur, but it was not until 1815, when Swiss monks took over the abbey, that commercial production of the liqueur began. A range of scented Provençal herbs are macerated in spirit to give both a stronger, drier, green liqueur and a softer, sweeter, yellow version. Sip either version of Aiguebelle gently, on its own over ice.

VERVEINE DU VELAY

C **COLOUR** Green or yellow, depending on the precise formula of herbs.

A **AROMA** Fairly aromatic, with herbs, especially juniper, citrus, and flowers.

T **TASTE** Quite bittersweet and complex, with a smooth feel.

This French liqueur is made by infusing verveine (or vervain) – a lemon-flavoured herb, juniper, honey, and other herbs in brandy.

First produced in 1859, in Velay, in the Auvergne, southwest France, Verveine du Velay was developed by a herbalist named Joseph Rumillet-Cartier. However, since 1886 it has been exclusively made and marketed by Pagès, a French drinks company.

The verveine herb has long been regarded as having magical properties, especially as a restorative or aphrodisiac (the Romans called it "Venus grass", after the goddess of love). However, the liqueur is a blend of 32 herbs altogether, of which verveine is just one.

Verveine du Velay comes in a green version, which is 55% ABV, and powerful but fresh, and a yellow version, which is 40% ABV, and is finer and softer. There is also an Extra, which is made with Cognac, and available at five or ten years old. These are all fine liqueurs. They are delicately scented, and perfect neat, on the rocks, or in a cocktail.

VERVEINE DU VELAY *This classic ad pays homage to the liqueur's home, Le Puy en Velay, once a major religious centre.*

CHARTREUSE

C COLOUR A distinctive green or a greeny-yellow depending on the version.

A AROMA Powerful, with herbs and flowers; medicinal.

T TASTE Distinctive; full but light; sweetness balanced by bitter herbs.

St Bruno founded the Carthusian Order of monks almost 1,000 years ago, at Chartreuse, near Grenoble in the French Alps. The order was already more than 500 years old when, in 1605, the monks received a gift from the Marshall of Artillery of King Henry IV of France. This gift was a manuscript entitled *An Elixir of Long Life*, and it contained the recipe for a liqueur that would eventually (more than 130 years later; *see box, below*) become the world-famous Elixir Végétal that we know today.

Chartreuse liqueurs are made from a base of grape brandy and approximately 130 botanicals – herbs, plants, roots, leaves, and other vegetation. The botanicals are soaked in the alcohol, and then distilled and mixed with honey and sugar-syrup before being put into large oak casks to mature.

The original Chartreuse Elixir is exceptionally strong – 71% ABV! – and is not sold in France as an alcoholic beverage, but rather as a digestive tonic to be taken on a sugar cube or in an infusion. Instead, the world of liqueurs has been given Green Chartreuse, first produced in 1764 by Brother Antoine, who had also been the first to perfect the Elixir. Adapted from the Elixir's recipe, Green Chartreuse is

YELLOW CHARTREUSE

diluted to 55% ABV and is a pale, refreshing green colour. The colour is entirely natural – a genuine result of the plants that have been used to make the liqueur. The flavours are strong, with powerful herbs, spices, and fruits – including aniseed, menthol, and citrus – but the texture is light. In addition, any sweetness from the sugar syrup is balanced by the bitterness of the herbs, which results in a perfect bittersweet harmony.

In the late 1830s Brother Bruno Jacques adapted the Elixir's recipe again to produce the less powerful (40% ABV) Yellow Chartreuse. This version is actually bright greeny-yellow in colour, and is lighter and smoother than its green brother, with a buttery finish. Like Green Chartreuse, it is coloured

GREEN CHARTREUSE

entirely by the plants and flowers that are used to make it.

Both Green and Yellow Chartreuse also come in versions known as V.E.P. (*Vieillissement Exceptionnellement Prolongé*, meaning "exceptionally long-aged"). These are herbal liqueurs at their finest – like the very best wines of Bordeaux as compared with a simple Vin de Table (table wine). The long-ageing in oak casks (for at least eight years) gives a delicacy and finesse that, I promise you, is unrivalled in any other liqueur in the world.

The best way to drink all forms of Chartreuse is cold, with plenty of ice, to bring out the complexity of the flavours. Although Chartreuse liqueurs are traditionally thought of as after-dinner drinks, you could also try them mixed with soda water in a long drink, drunk before dinner as an apéritif. Wonderful!

ELIXIR VÉGÉTAL DE LA GRANDE-CHARTREUSE

CULTURE AND TRADITION

CHARTREUSE THROUGH TIME It took 32 years for the Carthusian monks to decipher Marshall d'Estrée's formula for the "elixir of life". In 1737 a monk named Brother Antoine perfected the formula and named it Elixir Végétal de la Grande-Chartreuse. Both this and the later Green Chartreuse were hugely successful, leading to the need for a new distillery, at Fourvoirie in

southeast France. From here, in 1838, the monks launched the sweeter, milder Yellow Chartreuse.

However, things have not always been easy for Chartreuse. Various events such as the French Revolution, the confiscation of the monastery, and the loss of the formula broke the chain of production in the early years. In 1903 Chartreuse monks were exiled from France and began production of their liqueur in Spain. However, the French government prohibited the use of the name Chartreuse for any liqueur other than that produced in France, and it was not until 1929 that the monks, once again on French soil, won back the name of Chartreuse. In 1935 a landslide destroyed the distillery in Fourvoirie, forcing production to move to nearby Voirin, where all Chartreuse is distilled today. However, in a perfect ending, the 130 botanicals have found their home back at the Monastery de la Grande-Chartreuse, where they are stored and blended before making the short journey to Voirin.

SECRET FORMULA *The recipe of herbs, plants, and other botanicals used in Chartreuse is a closely guarded secret, known to only three monks at any time.*

BOTTLING CHARTREUSE *This photograph, taken in the 1950s, shows the bottling factory at Voirin, close to the original monastery of Grande-Chartreuse.*

GET 27 AND 31

C COLOUR Get 27 is green, while Get 31 is white.

A AROMA Very crisp, fresh, and lively, with peppermint and spirit.

T TASTE Rich, moderately sweet and smooth; soft with a delicate mint taste.

In 1796 Jean and Pierre Get (pronounced "jet"), heirs to one of the largest French distilleries, aimed to create the ultimate crème de menthe (mint liqueur). They combined alcohol with strong mint and marketed it as Get Peppermint, but the brand, which is 27% ABV, quickly became known as Get 27. This gentle, green crème de menthe is wonderful over a mountain of crushed ice, and it adds a bright, minty flavour to apéritifs, cocktails, and other mixed drinks. The success of Get 27 has since led to the creation of Get 31. This is white and a little stronger (31% ABV), spicier, and livelier than the 27.

CRÈME DE MENTHE

C COLOUR Distinctive bright green or bright, clear, white.

A AROMA Aromatic; fresh and clean, with mint to the fore.

T TASTE Sweet, soft, and minty, with a fresh finish.

Crème de menthe is one of the oldest herbal liqueurs, owing to mint's renown as an aid to digestion. To flavour the liqueur producers most often use the oil of peppermint, which is related to sweet garden mint. The result is sweet and aromatic, and usually drunk in a long drink or cocktails. There is no great difference in flavour between the two colours of crème de menthe, but the striking green is more popular in cocktails. Some of the best brands are Marie Brizard, Cusenier, Bols, and Smeets.

CRÈME DE MENTHE

ESCORIAL GRÜN

C COLOUR Subtle green; a product of the range of herbs and spices.

A AROMA Medicinal, with spice and herbs to the fore.

T TASTE Slightly sweet, but also with bitter notes of mint and spice.

Developed by monks, Escorial Grün is a German liqueur based on a secret recipe and was first sold commercially in 1910.

Like many herbal liqueurs, Escorial Grün is a complex mix of citrus fruits, with herbs, spices, flowers, and the barks of different trees. The plants give the liqueur its special flavour, with noticeable mint and some spice, and its subtle green colour. At 56% ABV, this liqueur is really strong, but I still prefer it undiluted, although with plenty of ice.

TRAPPISTINE

C COLOUR Pale, greeny yellow as a result of the herb-and-brandy infusion.

A AROMA Aromatic and herbal, with brandy and mint in excellent balance.

T TASTE Quite bittersweet, with the herbs balancing the sweet brandy.

Trappist monks in Normandy first developed the formula for this herbal liqueur in around 1670, although now it is made at the abbey of Grace-Dieu in the Doubs region of east-central France. Trappistine is based on a mixture of Armagnac and fresh herbs from the local mountains. It is quite strong and the formula itself – which remains a secret – must be quite complex to give such a wide range of herbs and roots in the aromas and flavours. These are needed, though, to offset the sweetness of the brandy. A very well-balanced liqueur with a minty feel, it is delicious on its own, or over ice to bring out its complexity.

JÄGERMEISTER

C COLOUR Extremely dark reddish brown, coloured by roots and herbs.

A AROMA Strong and distinctive; herbs and earth; medicinal.

T TASTE Full-bodied and really chewy, with a dense herbal taste.

A herbal liqueur from Germany, Jägermeister was first produced in 1935 to an age-old formula that combines 56 different herbs, spices, and fruits, macerated in neutral spirit. Despite its powerful flavours, Jägermeister has become one of the bestselling imported liqueurs in the US.

The word Jägermeister means "master of the hunt", and the liqueur is named in homage to the patron saint of hunters. At the death of his wife, a young, noble hero named Hubertus became

a recluse. One day, while he was out in the forest hunting for food, he came across a great stag with the cross of Christ's crucifixion floating between its antlers. Hubertus took this as a sign from God, gave all his wealth to the poor, and entered a monastery. After his death he became the patron saint of hunters.

Jägermeister's flavour is really quite strong – even formidable. The herbs, spices, and fruits used to make it come from all parts of the world, and include bitter oranges, cinnamon, ginger root, red sandalwood, and blueberries. The liqueur has a firm structure, but it is also very flexible. Try it ice cold in a shot glass as a beer "chaser" or in the popular long drink known as the Jäger Bomb – a glass of an energy drink, such as Red Bull, topped with Jägermeister.

This is one you will either love or hate – give it a try and see.

JÄGERMEISTER

STONE'S GREEN GINGER WINE

C COLOUR Rich, dark gold; the "green" is only in the colour of the bottle.

A AROMA Ginger and orange citrus, with sherry notes.

T TASTE Bright and fresh ginger; well-rounded; long, warming, tingling finish.

This classic British drink – also popular in Australia and the Caribbean – dates back more than two centuries. In the 18th century a London company known as the Finsbury Distillery began to make ginger wine. The drink was so popular with London businessmen that it became the only wine label in the world ever to carry the City of London Coat of Arms.

In the mid-19th century, London grocer Joseph Stone began to market the wine, putting his own name on the label. This is perhaps one of

the earliest examples of "own-brand" retailing! Nevertheless, the name stuck and Stone's Green Ginger Wine was born.

Stone's is made from the raisins of Muscat grapes, imported from Cyprus, Greece, and Turkey. The raisin wine is fortified and then ground ginger is steeped in it for several weeks before filtering and bottling. The result is dark golden in colour and extremely warming and satisfying – making it perfect for drinking on winter nights.

At 13.5% ABV, Stone's is quite light in alcohol for a liqueur, so it mixes easily with spirits. I like to drink it with whisky – mix one part whisky to two parts Stone's. If you want to stretch it out, you could serve the wine in one of many ways – as an apéritif in a long drink with soda water, as a mixer in a brandy cocktail, or with sparkling wine, lemonade, or even with coffee!

STONE'S GREEN GINGER WINE

STREGA

C COLOUR Pale and neutral; transparent saffron yellow.

A AROMA Aromatic, with herbs and flowers in fine balance.

T TASTE Soft, smooth; bittersweet with herbs and vanilla; warm finish.

Strega is Italian for "witch", and legend has it that witches disguised as maidens first made this liqueur in the city of Benevento, between Rome and Naples. It is said that when two people drink Strega together, they are united for ever. Made and marketed by the Alberti company since 1860, this excellent liqueur contains around 70 herbs and roots – including saffron, which gives the yellow colour – and is aged in oak casks, which impart vanilla. Drink it straight or over ice.

STREGA

CALISAY

C COLOUR Clear, and also orange or lemon-yellow for the flavoured versions.

A AROMA Aromatic and medicinal, with herbs, flowers, and citrus.

T TASTE Full-bodied, smooth, and syrupy, with herbs, grass, and citrus.

Calisay is a speciality of Catalonia in northeastern Spain. Thought to date back to the Middle Ages, it is neutral brandy flavoured with a range of mountain herbs, but particularly the bark of the quinquina tree. This bark gives us quinine, which was once used to ward off malaria, and it gives the liqueur a distinctive, medicinal taste. Although Calisay is traditionally a straight digestif, try it over ice and mixed with fruit, such as slices of lemon or orange, or with Maraschino cherries. You can also buy flavoured lemon and orange versions.

UNICUM

C COLOUR Dark opaque brown, with yellow highlights.

A AROMA Medicinal and herbal, with orange, anise, and almond.

T TASTE Bittersweet, with spice and herbs, especially liquorice; long finish.

In 1790 Jozsef Zwack, court physician to the Habsburg Emperor Joseph II, created Unicum, now a world-famous Hungarian liqueur and the flagship product of the Zwack drinks company. Made to a secret recipe, award-winning Unicum contains more than 40 different herbs and spices, which together give the liqueur its deep complexity in both aroma and flavour. This is a flexible liqueur – try it before or after meals, with or without ice. Or, for an authentic taste of Hungary, steep prunes in the spirit overnight (or longer) and serve them alongside the drink as a digestif.

ST HUBERTUS

C COLOUR Light, golden amber; the influence of the oranges.

A AROMA Distinctive and elegant, with orange and herbs.

T TASTE Quite mellow and subtle; orange, balanced with herbs.

First introduced in the latter years of the 19th century, and named after the patron saint of hunters, St Hubertus is a traditional Hungarian liqueur made from a blend of oranges and herbs. One of the most widely available brands is Zwack, the drinks company that also produces Unicum *(see left)*. In 2004, Zwack introduced St Hubertus 33, which is darker and richer than the original liqueur, and is made using a wider variety of herbs. It is primarily promoted as a cocktail mixer, and as such is aimed at the younger market. The original makes a pleasant digestif.

SECRET INGREDIENTS
Many herbal liqueurs are made to complex formulae that have been kept secret for hundreds of years.

CENTERBE

C COLOUR Electric green, from the blend of spirit, plants, and herbs.

A AROMA Aromatic and distinctive, with peppermint and herbs.

T TASTE Strong, but also smooth and gentle, with a bitter taste.

Centerbe – meaning "100 herbs" – comes from the Abruzzo region of eastern-central Italy. Its origins lie in a 15th-century medicinal elixir known as *Terriaca Universale*, which was made from 99 different plants. It is said that Brother San Silvestre, a local monk, added the one extra herb to create Centerbe. Italians tend to drink Centerbe as a digestif, but it is also good in cocktails, where its strong taste holds its own against the other ingredients. The liqueur comes in various strengths, but is usually around 35% ABV. For a good brand, try Benefort.

WHISKY-BASED LIQUEURS

The Holy Grail of whisky makers is to devise a liqueur that broadens the spirit's appeal. Some of these recipes are old, like Drambuie, but those that mix whisky and cream are modern developments. Most whisky-based liqueurs are weaker than the original spirit.

DRAMBUIE

C **COLOUR** Reddish-brown and golden, similar to aged malt whisky.

A **AROMA** Rich whisky aromas – malt and peat – with distinctive heather.

T **TASTE** Silky smooth, with earth, spice, and citrus fruit; refreshing on the palate.

The word Drambuie comes from the Gaelic *an dram buidheach*, meaning "the drink that satisfies" – and not a truer word has been spoken of a liqueur! Originally from the island of Skye (northwestern Scotland), it is now made down in West Lothian (southeastern Scotland). Drambuie made its first commercial appearance in 1909, produced by Malcolm MacKinnon, who had inherited the secret recipe through the generations from his ancestor John MacKinnon. John had acquired it from Bonnie Prince Charlie *(see box, below)* in the 18th century.

Drambuie is a blend of fine malt whisky, honey, and herbs, making it sweet, smooth, and warming. Unlike many liqueurs, Drambuie is strong – 40% ABV.

This is the drink that you want around you at Christmas, or any other special occasion, when you need something a little unusual and especially warming after dinner. If you like to enjoy a digestif, but prefer whisky to Cognac, then Drambuie is the perfect compromise.

Look out for the luxury, expensive blend Drambuie Black Ribbon, which is made using aged single malts; and also the recently launched Drambuie Cream (marketed as Sylk in the US) – which uses the traditional Drambuie formula and adds cream. Always serve this version over ice; while the original Drambuie is great with or without.

DRAMBUIE

HIGHLAND HEATHER *The strong flavours of the whisky are balanced by the soft sweetness of heather honey in Drambuie. This liqueur holds the essential flavours of the Highlands in one glass.*

GLAYVA

C COLOUR Light amber and clear, similar to malt whisky.

A AROMA A lovely balance of whisky, honey, herbs, and spice.

T TASTE Rich, full-bodied; sweet; whisky, orange, and herbs; a warm finish.

Glayva liqueur, while not as famous as Drambuie and a little sweeter, has an established reputation among whisky-drinkers for being more complex in its flavours – a result of the 26 herbs and spices that go into the blend.

Ronald Morrison, from a family of Scottish distillers and the owner of a liqueur firm in the port of Leith, near Edinburgh, created the liqueur in the years after World War II. Together with his associate George Petrie,

GLAYVA

Morrison took some fine Scottish whisky and combined it with some of the herbs, fruits, and spices that were coming in on the ships arriving at the port – oranges from Spain, and herbs from India and the Caribbean. Once he had perfected his blend, Morrison named it Glayva, derived from the Gaelic phrase *gle mhath* meaning very good, which is said to be the spontaneous comment of the liqueur's first tasters. Since 1993, Glayva has been owned by whisky distillers Whyte and Mackay.

The liqueur is rich, full-bodied, and sweet, with a slight orange or tangerine feel. The whiskies in the blend are 12 years old, and the result is slightly less strong than Drambuie at 35% ABV.

You can drink Glayva straight or in cocktails, but the best way is with ice; as with whisky the flavours unfold as the ice melts into the spirit.

LOCHAN ORA

C COLOUR Dark amber – similar to a deep, blended whisky.

A AROMA A rich whisky nose; herbs; well-balanced malt and earthiness.

T TASTE Smooth and full-bodied; fine balance of honey, herbs, and whisky.

This luxury whisky liqueur is made by Pernod Ricard entirely from Chivas Brothers' aged whiskies. However, unlike Chivas whisky, Lochan Ora can be hard to find. Like its rivals Drambuie and Glayva, Lochan Ora offers a complex combination of honey and herbs on a base of strong, rich Scotch. The result is 35% ABV, and is sweet, full, and warming. Drink it straight, on ice; or in the winter try it gently warmed over a candle flame.

LOCHAN ORA

GLEN MIST

C COLOUR An extremely attractive light amber, with golden highlights.

A AROMA A swirling blend of whisky, honey, herbs, and spice.

T TASTE Drier than other whisky liqueurs; finely balanced with a warm finish.

Invented by Hector MacDonald shortly before World War II, this is a relatively young whisky liqueur.

Glen Mist is made from high-quality Scotch, and honey and herbs. The liqueur is matured in whisky casks for several months, which helps to balance the flavours of the whisky and herbs, and to temper the sweetness of the honey – making this liqueur relatively dry. At 40% ABV, Glen Mist is a full-strength liqueur, and best sipped gently on its own, with or without ice.

IRISH MIST

C COLOUR Medium bronze to copper – rather like a dark Scotch whisky.

A AROMA Whiskey, caramel, sweet fruit, and honey in good balance.

T TASTE Medium to full-bodied; baked fruit; spice; sweet, warm finish.

Irish Mist is the Irish equivalent of Glen Mist (*see above*). During World War II, when the ingredients needed to produce Glen Mist were hard to find in wartime Scotland, the liqueur's producers transferred production to the Tullamore distillery in neutral Ireland. Instead of using Scotch in the blend, they used Irish whiskey. In 1963, with the war long over, Glen Mist returned to Scotland, but production of the Irish liqueur continued under a new name – Irish Mist. This liqueur soon established a reputation all of

IRISH MIST

its own and found itself being enjoyed all over the world. The brand is now owned and marketed by the C & C Group.

Irish Mist uses the same general formula as Drambuie and Glen Mist – blending whiskey with honey and herbs to give sweetness and complexity. If you find Irish whiskey too harsh or strong, then try Irish Mist as an alternative (and delicious) after-dinner digestive. However, it is so warming and comforting that my favourite way to drink it is straight, with no ice, by the fireside on cold winter nights – the honey and herbs mix perfectly with the Irish whiskey to give you a special, contented glow. If you are feeling really indulgent, try it in an "Irish Mist" coffee, or dispense with the coffee altogether and simply warm up the liqueur and put a big dollop of thick cream on top – a fantastic combination!

RUM-BASED LIQUEURS

Rum is traditionally mixed in a long drink, usually with fruit juice or cola, so few liqueurs exist. There are one or two, however, which blend herbs and spices with a basic rum. This is not to be confused with spiced rum, which is a distinct style of its own.

RUMONA

C COLOUR Bright golden amber, like a light Cuban rum.

A AROMA Rich aromas of rum, butterscotch, and molasses.

T TASTE Sweet and smooth, with a warm, spicy, honey taste.

Rum-based liqueurs are quite rare, but one of the best is Rumona, made in Jamaica by Wray and Nephew. Rumona is a sweet blend of rum, honey, herbs, and spices, giving full, complex flavours of butterscotch and honey. Drink it on a hot evening with plenty of ice and a twist of lemon – ideally overlooking the twinkling Caribbean Sea!

NASSAU ROYALE

C COLOUR Light golden amber, similar to golden Cuban rum.

A AROMA Complex; orange, vanilla, coffee, and rum.

T TASTE Elegant and quite sweet; citrus fruit, molasses, and vanilla.

This liqueur, from the Bahamas, has a distinctive orange-citrus character combined with hints of vanilla and coffee. At 35% ABV, it is quite powerful. As it is based on sugar-cane spirit and has a strong citrus feel, Nassau Royale makes a great alternative to triple sec, especially in cocktails. If you see a bottle, this is definitely one to try.

66 These are the drinks to choose if you're after a liquid dessert, or crying out for that heartwarming after-dinner glow. Toasty, nutty, smooth, and effortlessly drinkable.99

NUT, BEAN, MILK, AND EGG

INTRODUCING NUT, BEAN, MILK, AND EGG LIQUEURS

If you have a sweet tooth, then this is the liqueur category for you. Fun and luscious, these are the liqueurs of pure indulgence, from the velvet sweetness of a warming amaretto to rich chocolate liqueurs, and the fresh, party spirit of Malibu.

DRINKING AND SERVING

DRINK PROFILE Coffee and most nut liqueurs are amber-brown in colour; coconut liqueurs are usually clear or white. Chocolate liqueurs will reflect the colour of the kind of chocolate (white, milk, or dark) from which they are made.

All the liqueurs in this category will give sweet, rich aromas, with accents of their ingredients. They are smooth, full, and silky, with the notable exception of the coconut liqueurs, which are sweet and fresh. Coconut liqueurs make excellent mixers in long drinks, but most of the other liqueurs in this category are perfect over ice at the end of a meal; or, for the coffee liqueurs, added as a dash in coffee.

RAW MATERIALS *From left to right, here are some of the ingredients used to flavour this category of liqueurs: coconut (used in Malibu and others), almond (in amaretto), egg (in advocaat), and coffee (in Tia Maria, Kahlúa, and so on).*

Once the tradition of fermenting all manner of plants and fruits had been established, it did not take long before liqueur-makers began experimenting with nuts, and then dairy products. What soon became clear was that almost anything could be used to flavour a liqueur, and slowly but surely the range of commercial liqueurs grew to give us the immense array that we have today.

NUTS AND BEANS

One of the best things about the use of nuts in liqueurs is that they balance the sweetness, especially when the liqueur also contains fruit, and give a deep complexity to the liqueur's aromas and flavours. One of the most attractive liqueurs in the world, the Italian amaretto, is made using almonds and apricots and achieves this balance beautifully. Other Italian liqueurs, such as Pisa (made with hazelnuts and almonds) and Frangelico (made with hazelnuts, berries, and herbs) have a rich, smooth, nutty style.

There are, of course, many different types of nut, and a completely different style of liqueur is found in Malibu, Cocoribe, and their many imitators. In these liqueurs light, white rum is mixed with coconut to give a young, fresh, and sweet feel – these are much more likely to be enjoyed at a beach party than over ice after dinner.

FUDGE *The rich, toffee-sweetness of Baileys Irish Cream offers a wonderful fudge aroma.*

Chocolate and coffee have long been perfect partners for spirits. The liqueurs of Mozart and Godiva blend all kinds of chocolate (white, milk, and dark) with spirits such as brandy and fruit eaux-de-vie, while the wonderful, but unusual, Sabra from Israel blends chocolate with the distillate of a cactus plant. Coffee liqueurs, such as Tia Maria and Kahlúa, tend to be coffee beans infused in a base of rum. In some brands herbs are added too; in others the coffee is enough.

EGGS AND CREAM

It may seem odd to use egg yolks in liqueurs, but advocaat, first developed by Dutch colonists in South Africa, has been around for centuries. Meanwhile the use of cream in liqueurs goes from strength to strength, led by the unparalleled success of Baileys Irish Cream, a delicious, smooth blend of cream, chocolate, and Irish whiskey.

AMARULA *This cream liqueur comes from South Africa, and is flavoured using the sweet fruit of the indigenous marula tree.*

ALMOND AND HAZELNUT

The attraction of using nuts in a liqueur is their elegant bitterness, which offsets the sweetness of fruit. This creates a fine balance, which is the hallmark of a great drink. The monks of Italy were expert at achieving this balance, especially in the excellent Frangelico.

LIQUID LOVE *Drink amaretto on its own or on the rocks; or put a drop in your coffee. Even better – on a cold evening relax with an amaretto hot chocolate. Simply divine!*

AMARETTO

C COLOUR A rich, beautiful, and distinctive orange-red to light brown.

A AROMA Elegant and unique, with almond, fruit, and herbs.

T TASTE Full-bodied; sweet but well balanced; almond, apricot, marzipan.

Amaretto comes from a long tradition of blending together apricots and almonds in a bitter-sweet drink (just thinking about it makes my mouth water!), and is cloaked in the mystery of love. It is said that in 1525 the artist Bernadino Luini arrived in Saronno, northwest of Milan, to paint an "Adoration of the Magi" in the church of Santa Maria delle Grazie. Luini modelled his Virgin on a beautiful, local innkeeper. The two fell in love, but the innkeeper was in mourning for her husband and the love remained unrequited. Instead, the innkeeper made Luini a gift – amaretto liqueur.

There are many brands of amaretto on the market – the original and one of the best is Disaronno, said to be made to the innkeeper's recipe. Good brands – look out also for Luxardo – are made with fine-quality spirit, and whole apricots and almonds; the cheaper or imitation brands, which are best avoided, are made with basic spirit, apricot essence, and almond kernels.

LUXARDO AMARETTO

PISA

C COLOUR Medium golden amber – in a "leaning" bottle, like the tower!

A AROMA Spicy, and nutty, especially with marzipan and almond.

T TASTE Nutty (almond and hazelnut); a sweet feel, and smooth, velvety texture.

For centuries the Italians have been gathering nuts around the town of Pisa and turning them into liqueur. Whereas many nut liqueurs can be one-dimensional, the official Pisa has a fine, delicate balance of almond and hazelnut, keeping it spicy and toasty, with a light sweetness, velvety texture, and marzipan hints in the gentle finish.

Warming and comforting, this is a liqueur to curl up with in the winter. Try it straight in a brandy ballon, or add a dash to your coffee or hot cocoa.

FRANGELICO

C COLOUR Light amber in a waisted bottle, tied with a cord.

A AROMA Aromatic; fresh, interesting; hazelnut, flowers, herbs, and vanilla.

T TASTE Strong and full-bodied, nutty and warming, with a vanilla sweetness.

This liqueur takes its name from Fra Angelico (brother Angelico) a 17th-century hermit-monk living in the hills of Piemonte (Piedmont) in northern Italy. It is said that this monk created the liqueur when he began to infuse wild hazelnuts and other natural flavourings, mainly herbs and plants from the forest around him, in fine alcohol.

Now Frangelico is owned by the C & C Group, which produces the liqueur on a large scale by roasting the

FRANGELICO

hazelnuts, macerating them in water and spirit, then distilling the result. Once the hazelnut distillate has been made, the producers add cocoa, coffee, vanilla, rhubarb, and sweet-orange flowers, and then the mixture is left to mature in oak casks.

The result is a wonderfully complex, award-winning liqueur, which is sold and appreciated around the world. At 24% ABV, it is moderately strong. You can

drink it straight, with or without ice, but it is especially good to accompany coffee – or tea – at the end of a meal, or in hot chocolate for an indulgent nightcap. Bartenders recognize its great worth as a mixer in cocktails, especially if they contain brandy or vodka. Finally, if you are ever on your own in the middle of winter, and you have a cold, there are only two things that you need – a bottle of Cognac and a bottle of Frangelico!

MIXING IT UP

FRANGELICO AND MILK
There are only a few liqueurs that taste really good with dairy products, and Frangelico is one of them. Gently warm some milk in a pan – so that it is quite warm, but not boiling. Pour it into a warmed glass and add a measure of Frangelico. Sip it and savour it as a perfect nightcap.

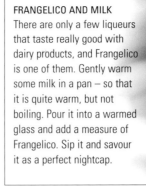

COCONUT

Although coconut milk can be fermented, it does not produce an attractive spirit, and coconut is best used as a sweetener for rum. This is something of a magic formula, which has brought rum to a completely new market, including younger women.

MALIBU

C COLOUR Crystal clear – like the white rum that is its base.

A AROMA Light and fresh, with sweet coconut milk and vanilla.

T TASTE Sweet; light- to medium-bodied; coconut, almond, coffee, and white rum.

It is probably true to say that Malibu has created more rum-drinkers than any other rum-based spirit. People who would not normally dream of drinking rum love this sweet and attractive coconut liqueur.

The tradition of spicing up rum with other flavours is as old as the spirit itself. Fruit or spices added to rum temper the spirit's harshness

and, beginning in the 1980s with Four Square Spiced Rum, flavoured rums have now hit the big-time.

Made in Scotland by Allied Domecq, Malibu is a white,

MALIBU

Barbadian rum with added coconut. Although sweet, Malibu is quite refreshing, and because it is aged for up to two years in oak barrels, it is complex, with nuts, coffee, and vanilla. You can drink it with lots of ice, or in a long drink with cola or fruit juice (try grapefruit or pineapple). There are many Malibu copies out there, but few are as good. For me it is worth the extra to buy the original.

COCORIBE

C COLOUR Opaque white – the influence of the coconut.

A AROMA Light and fresh, with coconut milk, herbs, and vanilla.

T TASTE Light- to medium-bodied; sweet and lively, with coconut and white rum.

The success of Malibu has spawned a great many imitators, some of them extremely good, and some not so good! The US-based company Cocoribe produces an excellent coconut rum. Like Malibu, this is a blend of light, white rum, coconut milk, and herbs, and packaged in a light and refreshing style.

While Malibu is usually made using rum from Barbados, and sometimes Jamaica, Cocoribe imports the rum into the US from the US Virgin Islands. The result is a liqueur that is 21% ABV (the same as Malibu), and excellent in long drinks with fruit juices or cola, but unlike Malibu it also mixes well in cocktails.

LAND AND PRODUCTION

THE COCONUT PALM One of the most important crops in the tropics, the coconut palm grows up to 25m (80ft) tall, with a slender trunk and feathered leaves. The coconuts themselves, which can take up to a year to ripen, have a hard outer husk, and contain a delicate-flavoured white flesh, as well as liquid, known as coconut milk.

COFFEE

Coffee liqueurs are made using a rum base, which is softened and sweetened with coffee and sugar. These liqueurs are very appealing as an after-dinner drink, as they combine two fine tastes. The best strike the perfect balance between sweetness and strength.

TIA MARIA

C COLOUR Deep tawny amber, in the famous tapered bottle.

A AROMA Pungent; elegant aromas of sugar cane, caramel, and coffee.

T TASTE Well-balanced; medium-bodied; coffee and vanilla; sweet.

TIA MARIA

One of the most important coffee liqueurs in the world, Tia Maria is made in Jamaica using coffee beans harvested from the foothills of Jamaica's Blue Mountains. The coffee is mixed with water, vanillin, citric acid, and strong cane spirit. The mixture is then filtered and added to a vat of liquid sugar. The result, which is a little over 32% ABV, is known as Tia Maria concentrate, and is shipped worldwide for secondary processing and bottling. The finished product is 26% ABV, and has flavours of sweet coffee, vanilla, and rum.

Tia Maria is now owned by Allied Domecq, but its origins are said to date from some 300 years ago, when Jamaica was in the midst of 17th-century colonial wars. A Spanish noblewoman was forced to flee her home and, in the haste of escape, her maid only had time to grab her mistress's small treasure box, containing a pair of black pearl earrings and a family recipe for a special liqueur. After a successful escape, the grateful noblewoman named the liqueur after her maid, Tia Maria.

MIXING IT UP

TIA MARIA AND COLA Tia Maria is so delicious that I like to drink it just as it is. However, for something long and refreshing, try it with cola and ice. Or, for a treat at the end of a meal, add some to your coffee.

BOLIVAR

C COLOUR Deep tawny brown, a result of the infusion of coffee.

A AROMA Attractive and appealing, with caramel, vanilla, and coffee.

T TASTE Medium-bodied and moderately sweet, with coffee and vanilla.

Bolivar is a Canadian coffee liqueur, made by the Kittling Ridge Winery and Distillery near Niagara, Ontario. Kittling Ridge is an experienced, top-quality wine producer, renowned for its excellent ice wine. The company imports the coffee for its liqueur from South America, which it mixes with alcohol spirit and sugar syrup.

Overall the result is a well-balanced liqueur that is not quite as rich or sweet as the more famous brands of Kahlúa and Tia Maria, although at 26% ABV it is roughly the same strength. If you like coffee liqueur, then I think that this is certainly worth trying.

KAHLÚA

C COLOUR Deep brown, similar to dark, freshly ground coffee.

A AROMA Lovely bouquet of coffee and molasses, with a tinge of fruit.

T TASTE Sweet, with dark coffee and chocolate, and a slightly bitter finish.

This coffee-flavoured liqueur is made in Mexico using a blend of Arabica coffee beans, spices, pure alcohol spirit, sugar syrup, and delicious rum. Kahlúa and Tia Maria are both owned by Allied Domecq, and both are the market-leaders – often swapping first and second places – with Kahlúa having the edge as the leading imported brand of coffee liqueur in the US. In taste they are really quite similar, but Kahlúa is slightly sweeter than Tia Maria, and not quite as dark.

A beautifully well-balanced liqueur, Kahlúa has all the coffee flavour you would expect, in harmony with the sweetness of fine molasses, and a touch of bitterness – rather like a cup of good-quality coffee, especially if you are drinking the coffee and eating a piece of excellent bitter chocolate. However, don't be fooled by these comforting flavours – at 27% ABV, Kahlúa is quite powerful!

Allied Domecq has capitalized on Kahlúa's excellence as a mixer by marketing it in the US in bottles of ready-made cocktails – known as Kahlúa Ready to Drink – which include Kahlúa Mudslide (with Irish cream liqueur, vodka, and cream), Kahlúa B52 (with Irish cream liqueur and triple sec), and Kahlúa and Milk. Generally Kahlúa is a wonderful mixer for all the major spirits, and one of my favourite ways to drink it is simply to pour some into a shot of vodka – and relax.

KAHLÚA

CHOCOLATE

Belgium and Austria have a fine tradition of making quality chocolate, so it is logical for them to use their expertise to make chocolate liqueurs. These can be very sweet, so some brands add fruit for a little acidity, making wonderfully smooth and luscious drinks.

GODIVA

C COLOUR Dark or light brown, or creamy white depending upon the blend.

A AROMA Soft; honey, chocolate; coffee in the cappuccino blend.

T TASTE Rich and sweet; luscious chocolate with a touch of spirit.

Godiva chocolate liqueur is made by the prestigious Godiva chocolate company. Chocolatier Joseph Draps founded his company in Brussels in 1926, naming it in honour of Lady Godiva, who famously rode unclothed through the streets of Coventry, England, to convince her husband that he should lower the local taxes.

The original Godiva liqueur is made using dark chocolate blended into a base spirit. It is rich and velvety on the palate. Try it over ice, on ice cream, or in the Godiva Chocolate Martini – mixed with vodka. The White Chocolate Liqueur is just as silky. The company recommends it with peppermint schapps. The newest product is Godiva Cappuccino, which mixes coffee, cream, and chocolate. This is one to be sipped on the rocks.

GODIVA

MOZART

C COLOUR Light brown (Original); dark brown (Black); opaque white (White).

A AROMA Intense chocolate, with notes of fruit and vanilla.

T TASTE Rich, creamy, and full-bodied; intense sweetness; slightly bitter edge.

In 1981 the Austrian drinks company H.C. Konig, based in Salzburg, launched its first sumptuous chocolate liqueur and named it after Salzburg's most famous son, Wolfgang Amadeus Mozart. The company's aim was to blend the finest chocolate with fruit distillates such as kirsch (cherry brandy, usually from France or Germany), nougat, herbs, and vanilla. The company uses no artificial flavourings or colourings.

MOZART WHITE

MOZART ORIGINAL

There are presently three versions of Mozart, all of which are more complex than the usual chocolate liqueurs – the intense sweetness of Mozart's chocolate is offset with lively fruit flavours, and the vanilla brings the liqueur an extra depth. The Original is made with milk chocolate, Black with unsweetened dark chocolate, and White with white chocolate and cream. Original and White are rich, sweet, and creamy; while the Black is deeper and darker, with notes of liquorice and caramel, and a bittersweet finish. All three are bottled at a moderate 20% ABV. As there are no artificial preservatives in any of the Mozart liqueurs, they have a limited shelf life. To protect the liqueurs before opening, the company wraps the Original and White bottles in gold or white paper respectively, which shields the contents from the degenerating effects of sunlight. The Black version comes in a black bottle, which has the same effect. In their sealed bottles, the liqueurs have a shelf life of up to two years, but once opened should be kept in the refrigerator and consumed within six months.

Try the Original with triple sec, or added to iced coffee. The Black is delicious on the rocks or sipped through "floated" cream; and the white makes a great cocktail with mint schnapps and vodka.

SABRA

C COLOUR Dark orange to amber, and quite opaque.

A AROMA Distinctive, with citrus, bitter orange, cocoa, and earthy spirit.

T TASTE Rich, bittersweet chocolate with orange; smooth and warming.

Sabra, from Israel, brings together the extraordinary combination of cactus and chocolate in a blend that I think works really well. The producers distil the juice of the Sabra cactus, blend it with chocolate and orange peel, and macerate and age the mix in wooden barrels. The result is an excellent, fairly strong (30% ABV), bittersweet liqueur that tastes like rich, orange-flavoured chocolate. You can drink Sabra straight, but it is best either chilled, when it becomes thicker, or gently heated as a wonderful winter-warmer.

GODET

C COLOUR A dense, opaque white, presented in a luxury decanter.

A AROMA Delicious hints of cream, chocolate, vanilla, and honey.

T TASTE Extremely sweet; good balance of nougat, brandy, and chocolate; warm.

Belgium has a reputation for making high-quality chocolate presented in the most luxurious packaging. Godet is a liquid version! This white chocolate liqueur is made by blending white chocolate with cask-aged brandy. The result is rich, luscious, and sweet, with a dense texture. It is just like drinking liquid white chocolate.

If you do not have a sweet tooth, you may find it too syrupy, and some find that the brandy does not entirely integrate into the liqueur. However, for those who love this drink, the only problem to avoid is drinking too much – at only 15% ABV, Godet is light, which can easily lead to one too many!

CHOCOHOLIC'S DREAM *Only the best-quality chocolate goes into good chocolate liqueur. The results give exquisite chocolate flavours without even having to chew!*

EGGS, MILK, AND CREAM

Liqueurs made with eggs, milk, and cream are very approachable – the perfect non-drinker's drinks! This style has its origins in "Irish coffee", a 20th-century cocktail that combines coffee with whiskey, cream, and sugar. Eggs are used in liqueurs to add richness.

ADVOCAAT

C COLOUR Bright, creamy, pale yellow; extremely thick and opaque.

A AROMA Very distinctive; with vanilla, spirit, and egg.

T TASTE Thick, rich, and creamy; sweet with a luscious feel.

At its most basic, advocaat is a thick liqueur made by mixing the yolks of newly laid eggs with grain spirit or brandy. Some versions are more complex, with ingredients such as kirsch, vanilla, or citrus peel.

The classic Dutch version is so thick it can be eaten with a spoon! It also contains egg white, and the traditional way to serve it is in a wide glass with whipped cream and with cocoa powder sprinkled on top. The more familiar export version is still creamy, but uses only egg yolks and is thinner. It is particularly suited to cocktail-making.

The best-known advocaats are the Dutch brands Warninks (by De Kuyper), Cooyman's, and Bols. There are also some fine advocaats made in Germany, Belgium, Poland (notably Stawski), and Australia (try Continental).

ADVOCAAT

AMARULA

C COLOUR Light chocolate brown – a mix of the fruit and the cream.

A AROMA Sweet and attractive; cream, citrus, vanilla, and ripe fruit.

T TASTE Smooth, chocolatey, creamy; medium body; long, cool finish.

Launched in 1989, Amarula is a South African cream liqueur made with the exotic fruits of the African marula tree – known locally as the "elephant tree" in recognition of the large numbers of elephants that gather under its branches to taste its ripening fruit. This special tree grows only in sub-equatorial Africa and its fruits, highly prized among the local people and wildlife alike, are light yellow in colour, and similar in size and shape to a medium plum, with a large, oil-rich stone. Locally the marula fruit is believed to have aphrodisiac properties.

AMARULA

The fruits are harvested and pitted and then the pulpy flesh (packed with vitamin C) is fermented – a process that begins with the addition of yeast, rather like wine. Distillation occurs in copper pot stills, which allow the flavours of the fruit to develop fully. Once distilled, the spirit is matured in small oak casks for two years, before being enriched with marula extract and blended with fresh cream.

The result is a rich, soft, and creamy liqueur – and, as you might expect, it has a slightly fruity edge. At 17% ABV, it is not too strong, but is both stylish and relaxing. Serve this liqueur well-chilled or with crushed ice to bring out the fruit flavours. Unopened, Amarula will stay fresh for more than a year; but once you have opened it, store a bottle of Amarula in the refrigerator and drink the contents within a month.

BAILEYS

C COLOUR A light, milky, rich beige; quite opaque.

A AROMA Extremely attractive; whiskey, nougat, fudge, nuts, toast, and vanilla.

T TASTE Smooth and creamy; quite sweet with nuts, brown spice, and whiskey.

Baileys Original Irish Cream is the biggest-selling liqueur brand in the world, and a household name in most of Europe, Australia, America – and far beyond! It is a delicious, complex, and approachable liqueur; drinkable on its own, but also great as a mixer. Launched in 1974, by the R. and A. Bailey distillery in Dublin which still makes the liqueur, Baileys is now owned and distributed by Diageo.

Baileys' origins lie in attempts to bottle the delicious flavours of Irish coffee. As a result, you might expect it to be a coffee liqueur, but Baileys is actually a blend of triple-distilled Irish pot-still whiskey, cream, eggs – and chocolate. The result is smooth and wonderfully creamy (it takes 40,000 cows to produce enough milk for one day's production of Baileys). And since it is only 17% ABV, it is especially appealing if you are not looking for something particularly strong. In fact, Baileys is often claimed to be the perfect drink for non-drinkers! My only problem with it is that I drink it too quickly!

Although they say there is no need to refrigerate Baileys after opening, I think it is best to do so. Unfortunately, in my house a bottle does not last long enough to worry about deterioration!

There are now many imitators of Baileys, some, of course, better than others. Other good Irish cream liqueurs come from Carolans, Bushmills, St Brendan's, and Brady's.

BAILEYS

BOTTLED SILK My favourite way to drink Baileys is in a rocks glass or a brandy snifter, with lots of large ice cubes – crushed ice dilutes the silky liquid too quickly.

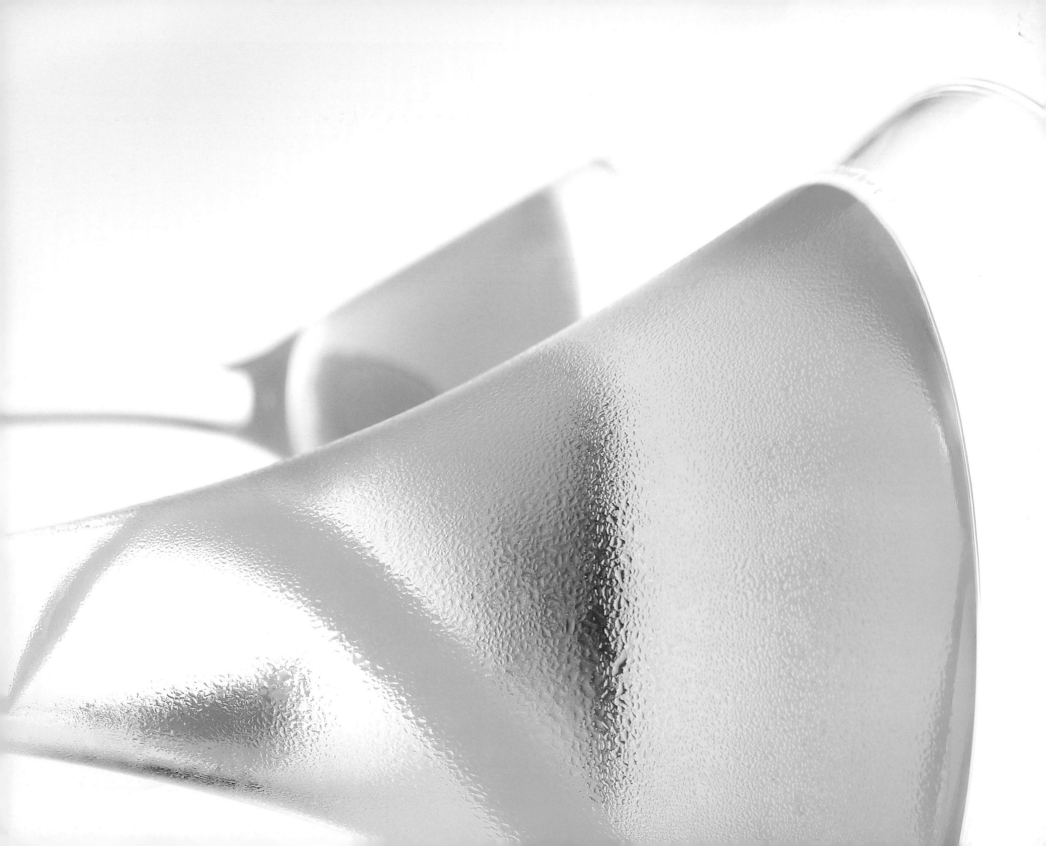

COCKTAILS

MYTH AND MIXOLOGY

The cocktail ranks among the most special – even romantic – of all drinks. Conjured up by bartending wizardry, these are the drinks of moonlit cityscapes and beaches at sunset.

CLASSIC COOLER *The Mint Julep was once made using peach brandy and Cognac. However, the more popular American version is a mix of Bourbon, sugar syrup, soda water, and fresh mint.*

There is a certain mystique about the cocktail – a lofty sophistication that can make ordering one seem a little foreign or even intimidating. However, there is nothing intimidating about drinks such as sangria (a mixture of red wine and spirits), or simple mixes such as a vodka and orange (known in the cocktail world as a Screwdriver). Cocktails are for everyone.

Making a great cocktail is just like finding the perfect combination of food and wine – it all depends upon the marriage of flavours. Essentially, a cocktail is simply a drink made up of a minimum of two ingredients – one of which is the "base" and the other the "modifying agent". The base is usually one, although occasionally more than one, major spirit, such as gin, vodka, or whisky, and it is this spirit that gives the drink its fundamental character.

Although subsidiary to the base, the modifying agent or agents will give the cocktail its uniqueness – its own distinct personality. There is an enormous range of modifying agents, including fruit juices, especially tomato, lemon, orange, and lime; myriad liqueurs; aromatic vermouths and amères, such as Dubonnet and Noilly Prat; bitters, such as Angostura; and "smoothing" agents, such as eggs, milk, and cream.

THE BELLINI COCKTAIL *This mix, a sumptuous blend of peach purée and sparkling wine, was invented in 1948 at Harry's Bar in Venice – one of the most important cocktail bars of all time.*

However, there is also one other aspect that makes a cocktail a cocktail. Not only should cocktails taste good, but they must look good too. Colour is the most important element of the cocktail's aesthetic, so once the basic mix has been made, bartenders may add colouring agents to give a cocktail an irresistible appearance (in terms of flavour these additions should be the least influential). For example, grenadine will give a dash of red; blue curaçao, a hint of blue; and Galliano, a splash of orange.

There are so many permutations of base, modifier, and colouring that the result is a virtually infinite variety of cocktail recipes for us to enjoy, from classics such as the Whisky Sour and the Bellini to modern delights such as the Tequila Sunrise.

COCKTAILS THROUGH TIME

The history of the cocktail begins with the history of the base spirits. Distilled alcoholic drinks evolved during the Middle Ages giving us our modern distinctions between brandy, whisky, vodka, and gin. The 14th and 15th centuries brought new additions to the spirit world – Caribbean rum, from sugar cane or molasses (the material

" Mixology is a craft and an art form, but most of all it is great fun. Experiment, invent, and enjoy – and never be afraid to try something new. "

TOOLS OF THE TRADE
Cocktail-makers need gadgets! Among the most important are the shaker, bar spoon, strainer, citrus juicer, and measure.

THE FIRST COCKTAIL BARS
One of the great pioneering cocktail bars, Hoffman House in New York was a lavish venue famed for serving mixed drinks during the 1870s. Drinkers would stand at the mahogany bar and order their mixes from bartenders specially trained in the fine art of cocktail-making. These men in smart white uniforms were some of the world's first mixologists.

THE FIRST COCKTAIL *The Sazerac is often hailed as the world's first cocktail. Created in the 1830s in New Orleans by Antoine Péychaud, it is a mix of Bourbon and bitters.*

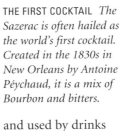

left over from sugar production); and tequila, from the Mexican blue agave plant.

In both Europe and the New World, the 18th and 19th centuries saw people experimenting with the addition of plants, herbs, and spices to spirit bases to produce medicines, and eventually to find new and attractive products for the drinks market. The result was the emergence of many of the liqueurs, bitters, and other aromatic, alcoholic drinks that would soon provide the cocktail's raw materials.

In 1806 an American publication called *Balance and Columbian Repository* first used the word "cocktail" to describe a mixed drink (in this case a spirit mixed with bitters). However, it seems likely that the origin of the word is French, perhaps from *coquetier*, a two-sided "eggcup" used for mixing small portions of ingredients,

and used by drinks inventors such as Antoine Péychaud, creator of Péychaud's bitters, in the early 19th century.

As US industry expanded during the 19th century, both the production and the marketing of alcoholic drinks became big business. At the same time the country saw the emergence of new bars, such as the huge Hoffman House in New York, where quality of service and the variety of drinks available began to make preparing and serving drinks an art in itself. By the end of the century, bartenders' manuals were publicizing the new mixology techniques, and some of the most famous cocktails that we know today – among them the Martini, Old Fashioned, Manhattan, and Whisky Sour – established themselves as firm favourites.

During the 1920s Prohibition prevented the consumption of alcohol in the US. However, this gave rise to an illicit drinking culture, which further encouraged the mixing of drinks, not only to disguise the look of an alcoholic drink, making it appear harmless, but most often to mask the inferior quality of "bootleg" (illegally brewed) spirits. In 1933 the Prohibition laws were fully repealed, and movie stars and other celebrities were seen with cocktails in hand. Vodka, rum, and tequila all became acceptable in the mainstream drinks cabinet, and whisky, gin, and brandy all found new partners in the cocktail glass.

However, with the onset of World War II the cocktail's popularity fell into decline. During the war ingredients were too scarce for use in alcoholic drinks, and after the war the marketing of "ready-made" products for food, clothing, and every other aspect of life meant that the new generation had no time for the elaborate ritual of customized cocktail-making – they preferred ready-mix!

" The success of a cocktail lies in the use of the best and freshest ingredients, and in the attention to detail during the making of it. "

ALL ABOUT IMAGE *Companies such as Martini often try to link their products to classic cocktails. This poster shows Martini being used to make a Manhattan (vermouth, whisky, and bitters).*

CHANGING FORTUNES *In the 1930s, Hollywood popularized the cocktail, but by the time Joan Fontaine and Harry Belafonte starred in* Island in the Sun *in 1957, the "Rock-and-Roll" generation had turned its back on cocktails.*

Happily, though, in the late 1980s and the 1990s a new generation of drinkers grew tired of standardized products, and the cocktail found its revival. Venues such as New York's Rainbow Room (at the top of the Rockefeller Center) and London's Sanderson became the new centres for a modern cocktail culture. The cocktail was back!

ENJOYING COCKTAILS

Quite simply, there are cocktails for every mood and occasion. Some, such as the Whisky Sour, are distinctly dry and tangy, making them perfect pick-me-ups or apéritifs; while others, such as the Irish Coffee, are sweet and rich, making them wonderful after a meal. Fresh, dry cocktails, such as the Tom Collins (with gin and lemon juice), and smooth mixes, such as the Bloody Mary (vodka, tomato juice, and spice), are perfect for any time.

Fruit-based and wine-based cocktails fall into two main camps. For before dinner, nothing beats a Kir, Bellini, or Champagne Cocktail; while for anytime drinking, the mixture of spirit and fruit juice in cocktails such as the Harvey Wallbanger and Tequila Sunrise creates a delicious, longer drink.

However, for me the very best thing about cocktails is experimenting. For that bit of extra personality, take a classic, add an ingredient that you love, and make the mix your own. Perfect!

MAKING COCKTAILS *It is said that a sign of a great shaken cocktail is a bartender with a tired arm! The result, however, seems effortless as it slips easily into the glass.*

THE BASICS

There are four simple things to bear in mind when mixing a cocktail. First, the quality of the ingredients; second, the mixing equipment; third, the mixing technique; and, finally, the presentation.

FRESH INGREDIENTS *Rather than mixing your cocktails using ready-prepared juice, use fresh juice extracted from ripe fruits. The result will not only taste better, it will look better, too.*

The first and most important rule about cocktail-making is that if you want a great cocktail you have to use the best ingredients – and that means everything from the "base" ingredient to the garnish. Before you mix, look at the spirit or wine base that you are intending to use. Do you have the best that you can find or afford? Or, are you keeping the good Champagne or the best brands of Cognac or gin for drinking on their own? Inferior-quality ingredients will show up in the final mix – so indulge yourself with the best whenever you can.

JUICY FRESHNESS

This "best" rule is particularly important for fruit ingredients. Try not to be tempted into mixing cocktails using long-life fruit juice, or the juice or purée extracted from tinned fruit. The difference in quality is vast – think of the difference between fresh, ripe raspberries and those from a tin! Tinned fruit

GREAT INGREDIENTS *In making cocktails you will get out what you put in. For guaranteed success, always aim to use the best-quality ingredients.*

particularly is often soft and over-sweet, and is probably stored in sugar syrup. This will artificially sweeten your cocktail, upsetting the delicate balance of flavours. (The same goes for ready-made purées, which also often have added sugar.) Extracting your own juice, or making your own purée in a liquidizer, may be a little more time-consuming – and a little more expensive – but the results will be worth it.

Of course, you may not always be able to find fresh fruit. If you have to use ready-prepared juice, avoid that made from industrial concentrate. Go to the chiller cabinets in the store and look for signs that the juice has been freshly squeezed.

CRUSHED ICE OR CUBES?

In mixology, ice does more than chill; the water influences the strength of the cocktail. Used in a shaker, crushed ice melts too quickly and dilutes the mix, so save it for the glass or blender. Ice cubes, on the other hand, are perfect for shaking; they chill the mix without diluting the drink too much.

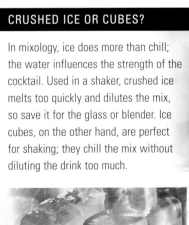

THE RIGHT EQUIPMENT *Building up your "cocktail kit" is part of the fun of making cocktails. Make sure the kit is kept clean and dry when not in use.*

GOOD TECHNIQUE *Making a cocktail is a great bit of theatre. Practise the techniques often, pay attention to detail, and never rush.*

IMMACULATE PRESENTATION *A cocktail should please the eye as well as the tastebuds. Make sure that your glasses are sparkling and your garnishes fresh.*

COOL AS ICE

It is plain to see how the freshest fruit and the best alcoholic ingredients will make the best cocktails, but do not overlook the quality of the ice. Water has flavour, too, and once the ice has melted, it will dilute the ingredients in the cocktail and add an extra dimension to the taste. Make your ice with fresh, filtered or bottled water with as few additives as possible. In addition, use ice that has been recently frozen – the ice can pick up flavours from other products in the freezer. Also think about the size of your ice. Large cubes will melt slowly; crushed ice quickly. If the cocktail needs to be diluted, use crushed; for chilling only, use cubes. You can make crushed ice using a crusher, or by placing the cubes in a clean tea towel and hitting the bundle against a wall or with a rolling pin.

Finally, never re-use a shaker without first cleaning out the old ice – even if you are making the same cocktail again – as the residue will affect the flavour of the new batch.

FRESH MIX *Freshly made "sweet-and-sour" (or "sour mix") is so much better than ready-made versions. For every 30ml (1oz) of fresh lemon or lime juice mix in a dash of sugar syrup.*

SWEET AND SOUR

Some cocktails, such as the classic Margarita *(see p346)*, call for using an ingredient known as "sweet-and-sour" or sometimes as "sour mix". This is a blend of freshly

DAIRY PRODUCTS *Many cocktails use dairy products, especially eggs and cream, in order to produce a smooth, soft texture in the final mix. When choosing dairy products for a cocktail, use the same rules as if you were going to eat them – they should be as fresh as possible.*

squeezed lemon juice (lemon sour) or lime juice (lime sour) and sugar syrup. Sweet-and-sour is available ready-made, but the home-made alternative is much better. *(See caption on p327 for the recipe.)*

Similarly, sugar syrup itself is available commercially, but it is easy to make your own. Using a saucepan, mix one part hot water with two parts granulated sugar (measuring cups are good for this – one cup of water to two cups of sugar works well). Gently bring the mixture to the boil, stirring as you go. Once the mixture begins to bubble, turn the heat down to a gentle simmer, taking care not to let the mixture caramelize (turn brown). The result should be viscous, but not too thick. Once you have achieved the right consistency, take the syrup off the heat and leave it to cool. You can store it in a sealed container in the refrigerator for approximately two months. An alternative method is to half fill a jam jar with hot water and then fill to the top with caster sugar. Put the lid on the jar and shake it until the sugar has dissolved. Although this is quicker, there is a danger that you will have residual sugar crystals in the mix, so follow the longer method if you have time.

USING DAIRY

There should never been any question about the freshness of any dairy ingredients in your cocktails – not only so that you achieve just the right flavour and texture, but to prevent stomach upsets, too. Eggs can make cocktails wonderfully smooth and silky, but they can also be harmful. The salmonella bacteria is stored in the uncooked, unpasteurized white of an egg and is most concentrated just

USING EGG WHITE

Egg white is flavourless, but gives cocktails a creamy texture. Here's how to separate the white from the yolk.

SEPARATING AN EGG
1 Choose farm-fresh eggs that wobble if you roll them along a flat surface (a sign of freshness).
2 Break the egg carefully into either a strainer (a) or a funnel (b), over a clean, dry mixing glass; take care not to allow any shell fragments to pass through.
3 Using a clean whisk, whip the white until frothy.

1 Use fresh eggs

2a Separate using a strainer

2b Separate using a funnel

3 Whisk the white

JUST A DASH *A few drops of ingredients such as Worcestershire sauce or Angostura bitters gives a mix a burst of flavour.*

underneath the shell. Buy only the best-quality eggs (organic, free-range eggs will give the best flavour), and make sure that you use them well before the sell-by date. Even if the eggs are within the sell-by date, smell them first to make sure that they are fresh. Take care to ensure that no eggshell finds its way into the mix – apart from the bacteria, you do not want a piece of shell lodged in a guest's throat!

Cocktails use both double and single cream to add texture and flavour. An alternative to single cream would be a "light" cream: mix single cream 50/50 with some whole milk.

COCKTAIL LAYERING

Some cocktail ingredients have greater density than others, and lighter ingredients can be layered on top of heavier ones for dramatic effect. This table gives you an idea of the relative density of some of the most popular cocktail ingredients. *(For the layering technique itself, see box on p365.)*

DRINK	DENSITY	COLOUR
Southern Comfort	0.97	Amber
Water	1.00	Clear
Grand Marnier	1.04	Clear
Brandy	1.04	Amber
Irish Cream	1.05	Coffee-cream
Campari	1.06	Red
Sambuca	1.08	Clear
Triple sec	1.09	Clear
Amaretto	1.10	Light brown
Galliano	1.11	Golden yellow
Crème de menthe	1.12	Green
Kahlúa	1.15	Dark brown
Grenadine	1.18	Red

ADDING FLAVOUR AND COLOUR

Most specific flavourings – and colourings – are added to cocktails as a "dash". When a recipe asks for a "dash" of something, a few drops of the ingredient will suffice. For example, a Bloody Mary can easily become too spicy in flavour and muddy in colour with too much Worcestershire sauce. When adding bitters, such as Angostura or Péychaud's, it is worth remembering that these are concentrates and selected for their powerful flavours – just a hint is enough for them to work their magic.

Syrups will not only add flavour, but often colour, too. One of the most well-used is grenadine – sugar syrup flavoured with pomegranate – which gives a cocktail a wonderful splash of red and is most famously used in the Tequila Sunrise *(see p374)*.

Colours are used to their best effect in layered cocktails, such as the B-52 (Kahlúa, Baileys, and Grand Marnier; *pictured above and on p365*) and the Mud Slide (vodka, Kahlúa, and Dooley's; *see p368*).

SUBTLE FLAVOUR *Coating (or conditioning) the inside of a glass can add a slight hint of flavour to a cocktail. Tip the conditioning agent – usually liqueur, bitters, or flavoured syrup – out of the glass before pouring in the cocktail mix.*

FRUIT FINISH *A slice of kiwi fruit makes an exotic and colourful garnish for a cocktail. Don't be tempted, however, to use kiwi fruit in blended cocktails: the black seeds give a slightly bitter taste when crushed.*

TOOLS AND EQUIPMENT

Mixing a cocktail is partly a science – the chemistry of the ingredients in the glass. And, like all good scientists, mixologists need a certain amount of kit to get the best results.

Mixing the perfect cocktail is very difficult – in some cases impossible – using conventional kitchen equipment. Dedicated kit makes life a lot easier, but don't panic – it is not expensive, and can be bought from most good department stores.

All the cocktail recipes in this book include an equipment list to guide you on the items you will need, and perhaps the most crucial of these is the glass. Every cocktail needs to be presented in a glass that shows off its colours to their best advantage and releases its flavours in the right way. For example, the wide-rimmed Margarita glass releases aromas quickly, leaving enjoyment mostly down to the tastebuds; in contrast, the hurricane glass concentrates the aromas. Size is the most important thing – never "lose" a short cocktail such as a Martini by serving it in huge glass. Use clean, unblemished glasses and handle them by the base or stem. This prevents fingermarks on the side of the glass and stops the drink from warming up as it is handled. Some drinks require a chilled glass. Leave the glass in the freezer or filled with ice and topped with water for ten minutes or so before mixing.

BLENDED COCKTAILS
A blender is essential to make a perfect Banana Daiquiri, with a smooth, luscious texture (see p347).

THE GLASSES *There are eight basic glasses for serving cocktails. You need not be too strict about which you use, as long as you adhere to the rule that you should find a glass appropriate to the cocktail's size.*

CHAMPAGNE FLUTE

HURRICANE GLASS

MARGARITA GLASS

MARTINI GLASS

TODDY GLASS

HIGHBALL GLASS

SHOT GLASS

TUMBLER

COCKTAIL TOOLS

Cocktail tools are part of the fun of cocktail-making, but they can also be the key to your success. Most importantly, your tools will help you to measure the ingredients properly. Without this you risk losing the delicate balance of flavours in the cocktail. Try not to neglect your cocktail kit. Any dirt or residue in your equipment could affect the flavour of the mix, so to give yourself the best chance of the perfect cocktail every time, clean and dry all your tools thoroughly between cocktails, as well as when the party is over.

BOSTON SHAKER

The Boston shaker is my preferred style of cocktail shaker, and I recommend that you make the shaken cocktails in this book using one as it enables you to watch the cocktail as it mixes. It is made up of two parts: a glass tumbler, which fits snugly into a larger metal container, forming a seal. You can also use the glass independently as a mixing glass.

EURO SHAKER

The Euro shaker is easier to use than the Boston shaker as it has a proper cap to seal it, making the act of shaking very safe. You are unable to watch the cocktail as it mixes, but once the sides of the shaker are ice-cold, the mix is ready for pouring. These shakers often have in-built strainers, so you would not need to buy a separate one.

JIGGERS

Jiggers are measuring "thimbles", and usually come in measures equal to 1 US fluid ounce (30ml), 1½ fluid ounces (45ml), and 2 fluid ounces (60ml). They make easy work of measuring the cocktail ingredients precisely, so I recommend that you invest in some. Precision is the key to making sure that your cocktails are perfectly balanced.

STRAINER

If you are using a Boston shaker, or other shaker without an in-built strainer, this is an essential piece of kit. There are two main types of strainer, the Hawthorne (shown here) and the Julep, which has holes but no spring. I recommend the Hawthorne because the spring and the tabs allow the strainer to be rested easily on the shaker or mixing glass.

BLENDER

Some cocktails – especially those made with whole fruit – need to be blended. When you are blending with ice, use only crushed ice as cubes can damage the blender's blades. Pour the liquid ingredients in first and then add the ice; this way the ice has as little chance to melt as possible before mixing. Begin on the slowest setting and build up to the fastest.

JUICE SQUEEZER

Find a squeezer that is big enough to take a grapefruit and use ripe, thin-skinned fruit. Gently turn the fruit, using moderate pressure, until it is not-quite spent.

REAMER

This useful, hand-held tool makes a good alternative to a squeezer for extracting the juice of lemons, limes, and oranges. Find one with a comfortable handle.

ZESTER

The zest of citrus fruit – particularly lemon, lime, and orange – is used to flavour certain cocktails. Take care to slice only the skin and not the pith, which can be bitter.

KNIVES

Knives must be razor-sharp. Use a small paring knife for garnishes from smaller fruit, and a chef's knife for cutting larger fruit, such as pineapples.

BAR SPOON

The length of the bar spoon enables you to stir all the way to the bottom of a long cocktail. The twisted stem may be used for layering ingredients (see p365).

MUDDLING STICK

The muddler is used to crush fruits in a glass. Find one in a natural wood or else the alcohol will strip the varnish. Take care not to press too hard on the glass.

POURER

Use a pourer to measure ingredients by timing your pour; a slow count of three gives 45ml (1½oz) of fluid. However, it does take practice to perfect!

IN THE MIX

Making a cocktail is a bit like cooking. You can slavishly follow a recipe, but if you learn a few basic principles, you'll be free to adapt, experiment, and create your own masterpieces.

There are more cocktails on Earth than you could drink in a lifetime. Alongside the classic mixes – the Martinis, sours, daiquiris, and their like – are the younger upstarts, like the Zombie and Cosmopolitan, which you will find in any cocktail bar worth its salt. But cocktails are constantly evolving, guided by fashion and driven by the drinks industry, which employs expert bartenders to create new mixes to showcase its spirits and liqueurs.

Just as with cooking, there are no strict rules about mixing cocktails. But keeping in mind a few general principles will help you avoid disaster, and guide you to create drinks that have good balance and structure, and which will bring a smile to your face. First of all, try not to drink the ingredients as you mix. Cocktail-making is much easier when sober! Second, always measure the ingredients as accurately as possible (see box, opposite), and note down what you use when experimenting. As a general rule, avoid using more than five different liquid ingredients, and stick with one spirit base – mixing lots of ingredients will almost certainly result

FINAL TOUCH *A fresh garnish – some lemon rind, a salted rim, or even a green olive – makes a cocktail come alive, adding visual flair as well as flavour.*

STIRRED COCKTAILS

This classic method is used to make refreshing cocktails, such as this Bruised Apple – a cool blend of Zubrówka vodka, apple purée, and apple syrup, poured over Chambord (see p367).

CREATING A STIRRED COCKTAIL

1 Fill a mixing glass – here the glass part of a Boston shaker – with ice, turning the ice with a bar spoon to chill the glass.

2 Use a strainer to remove any excess water from the melting ice cubes, to avoid diluting the cocktail.

3 Pour in the ingredients in their correct measures.

4 Stir the cocktail until it is perfectly chilled, when condensation forms on the outside of the glass.

5 Strain the mixture into a chilled glass. To make the Bruised Apple, the mix is layered on top of Chambord.

6 Finish off with your chosen garnish (see p336).

1 Fill a mixing glass with ice

EASY MEASURES *Accurate measurement of ingredients is the key to the balance and structure – and ultimately the success – of your cocktail.*

3 Add ingredients

4 Stir the cocktail

in a nasty clash of flavours. I have said this before but it is worth saying again: the better the ingredients, the better the cocktail. Use freshly squeezed fruit juices whenever possible, and buy spirits and liqueurs that you would happily drink on their own, rather than economy brands.

SHAKEN OR STIRRED?

There are four basic techniques for mixing a drink – stirring, shaking, blending, and building – all of which are explained on these pages. The technique you use depends on the different ingredients that make up the recipe. For example, cocktails that contain eggs (preferably free-range and organic), fresh fruit juices, cream, and sugar should always be shaken over ice; the ice will help to break up the egg

MEASURING INGREDIENTS

QUANTITY COUNTS Traditionally, bartenders tend to work in fluid ounces (oz) rather than millilitres (ml); 1 US fluid ounce is equivalent to 30ml. Many cocktails are based on 1½oz of spirit – here are three quick ways of measuring that quantity.

SPEED POURER Insert a pourer into the neck of the bottle. Fully invert the bottle and slowly count to three.

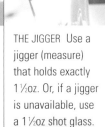

TABLESPOON If you do not have access to professional bar tools, use 3 tablespoons for an approximate 1½oz measure.

THE JIGGER Use a jigger (measure) that holds exactly 1½oz. Or, if a jigger is unavailable, use a 1½oz shot glass.

2 Strain off excess water

5 Strain into a chilled cocktail glass

6 Add garnish and serve

(by cutting through it) and create consistency in the cocktail. Drinks containing citrus fruit, such as the Angel (Grand Marnier, white rum, and lemon, orange, and cranberry juice; *see p375*) are best shaken, because shaking creates a slightly fizzy texture, which suits the zesty flavours. On the other hand, drinks containing only spirits, such as the Manhattan (whisky, sweet vermouth, and Angostura bitters; *see p383*) are better stirred to give a soft, silky texture. A "built" cocktail, such as the Negroni (gin, red vermouth, and Campari; *see p349*), is also a stirred cocktail – only this time the ingredients are poured directly into the serving glass, rather than being poured into a mixing glass, stirred, and then strained into the glass for serving.

There are other considerations to bear in mind when deciding whether to shake or stir. If your cocktail is particularly strong and would benefit from a little dilution, vigorous shaking helps because it melts the the ice into the mix. Shaking also chills a drink more thoroughly than stirring. Cocktails that should be crystal clear, such as the Dry Gin Martini *(see p376)*, are better stirred than shaken, because shaking introduces tiny bubbles that cloud the mix. Elegant cocktails designed to be sipped slowly are usually better stirred, because stirring combines the ingredients without "muddying" their flavours. Shaking, however, cannot be matched for its dramatic impact. Watching a well-schooled bartender in action is a form of visual poetry – and one that you can achieve at home with a little practice.

SHAKEN COCKTAILS

Shaking a cocktail fully combines the ingredients and chills the mix. Here, a Raspberry Crush (gin, Chambord, lime juice, and sugar syrup) is made in a Boston shaker.

CREATING A SHAKEN COCKTAIL
1 Fill the glass part of the shaker two-thirds full with largeish ice cubes. (For a fruit-juice-based mix, pour in the juice first.)
2 Add the ingredients carefully – always using a measure – into the glass part of the shaker.
3 Fit the shaker together, tap the glass to seal it, and shake. Grip with both hands and keep the metal part at the bottom (though an occasional turn helps to combine the drink).
4 Tap the shaker at the top, then the sides, to release the seal.
5 Pour the mix through a strainer into the glass.
6 Top with the garnish – presentation is part of the fun!

1 Fill the shaker with ice

4 Tap the shaker to release the seal

3 Shake to mix

When shaking a cocktail, measure the ingredients accurately. If you are using a Boston shaker, pour them into the glass (not metal) part of the shaker. If your cocktail includes fruit juice, pour in the juice before the ice (to avoid dilution), otherwise put the ice in first. Use large ice cubes (not crushed ice) to avoid diluting the drink.

Shake gently and steadily – the action should be lively, but not frantic. When the mixture contains eggs, shake a little more firmly because the viscosity of the egg makes it harder to combine. If you are using a Boston shaker, keep the glass part at the top when shaking; if your hand slips there is a better chance that the cocktail will end up in the larger metal part, rather than all over your guests! Shake until the cocktail is slightly fizzy and thoroughly cold.

BLENDED COCKTAILS

The aim with blended cocktails is to create a mix that has a fine, smooth finish. Most blended cocktails are mixed with ice. Always use crushed ice rather than ice cubes, to avoid damaging the blender. Place all the ingredients in the blender first and the ice last, to minimize the chance of the ice melting before you begin. Start mixing using the slowest speed on your blender and build up to the fastest. When the mix is completely smooth, pour it slowly and carefully into the glass and top with your chosen garnish. Making blended cocktails makes brilliant theatre – do it in front of your friends!

2 Add the ingredients

5 Pour over crushed ice

6 Add garnish and serve

PRESENTATION

If mixing a cocktail is science in a glass, then presenting it is an art. The ultimate cocktail should bring gasps of delight before you – or your guests – have taken even a single sip.

EXOTIC GARNISHES *While you are out gathering your cocktail ingredients, scour the exotic fruit section of the supermarket for some unusual garnishes, such as the vibrant yellow star fruit.*

Some cocktails look good the instant you mix them – for example, the lavish Tequila Sunrise *(see p374)* with its burnt orange colour and splash of red grenadine, or the sophisticated Bellini *(see p381)*, with its delicate bubbles and colour of inviting peach, are beautiful as they are – all they need is the right glass. However, most mixes need an all-important finishing touch – a garnish.

Most garnishes are made from pieces of fruit, such as lemons, limes, pineapples, oranges, and cherries, although herbs (especially mint), celery, and olives are popular too. The basic rule is to garnish using a fruit, herb, or other item appropriate to the content of the drink. So for a cocktail with a strong citrus element, such as the Gin Fizz *(see p342)*, garnish with a slice of citrus fruit; for the more savoury cocktails, such as the Bloody Mary *(see p358)*, use a herb or a stick of celery (which doubles as a swizzle stick).

Make sure that you use only the freshest fruits, herbs, and vegetables. With citrus fruit, especially, try to choose fruit that has a good, firm skin – a slice of thin, weak skinned lemon will look limp and apologetic on the rim of the glass. And remember, garnishing is all about style, so think about how you use things: use cherries, olives, and small berry fruit such as redcurrants individually or in small bunches; and cut pineapple wedges by slicing the whole fruit across the middle (rather than top to bottom), and cutting wedges from the circular slice.

Like most things to do with cocktails, garnishing has its own terminology. For example, fruit (especially citrus fruit) may be cut into a wheel (a whole, circular slice of fruit), a slice (wheel that has

COCKTAIL GARNISHES

Always take care with your garnishes. It may be the last part of preparing the cocktail, and you may be anxious to serve your friends or join in the fun, but remember that the garnish will be the first thing that your guests will notice – and first impressions count.

The following are some of the most popular cocktail garnishes. However, never be afraid to experiment. For simple and sophisticated cocktails, such as the Martini, keep the garnishes simple and sophisticated, too; but for beach-party mixes, such as the Piña Colada, have some fun!

CITRUS ZEST TWISTS

A twist is a thin slice of zest (use a sharp paring knife or a zester) from an orange, lemon, or lime. It looks great with one end draped over the rim of the glass, the other winding its way through the drink. It also adds a hint of flavour.

LEMON AND LIME WEDGES

To cut a citrus wedge, cut off the ends, then cut lengthways down the middle of the fruit. Cut each half lengthways into three (to give six equal wedges). Remove any pips. Place a wedge on the rim of the glass or in the drink.

MINT AND OTHER HERBS

Mint is one of the most refreshing garnishes of all, and essential for the Mint Julep *(see p378)*. Use fresh mint with small, firm leaves. Other herbs often used for garnish are sage, vervain, basil, and lemon balm.

CHERRIES

Most cherry garnishes call for Maraschino cherries (Marasca cherries preserved in liqueur), or less-sweet fresh cherries. They can be speared on a cocktail stick and placed across the glass, or dropped into the cocktail.

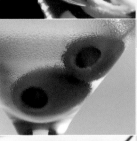

OLIVES

Never garnish using olives that have been preserved in oil – instead use fresh olives or those that have been stored in brine (but wash the salt off them first). Drop an olive into the glass, or spear one or two on a cocktail stick.

FRESH FRUIT

Mother Nature has provided a host of garnishes in the form of fresh fruit. Try redcurrants, blackcurrants, strawberries, or raspberries – or any combination of them on a cocktail stick. Always wash the fruit first.

been cut in half), a wedge (a thick slice taken length-ways), a twist (a long, thin piece of zest), or a spiral (a tightly curled zest). The term "split" refers to the small incision you make in the flesh of your garnish in order to be able to attach it to the rim of the glass.

HOSTING A COCKTAIL PARTY

Nothing will impress your guests more than serving up freshly prepared cocktails, perfectly garnished. So, to host the perfect cocktail party, first keep the cocktail menu short. Two or three different mixes are plenty, especially if one of them can be pre-mixed. For example, you could make up jugs of the Rum Punch *(see p361)*; or of the alcoholic part of the Long Island Iced Tea *(see p378)*, so that all you have to do at the party is pour it into an ice-filled glass and top with cola. Always prepare the garnish before you begin mixing the actual cocktail (although bear in mind that if left too long fruit will brown). The aim should be to serve with a confident flourish, without frantically reaching for a paring knife!

GLASS RIMMING

One of the most impressive presentations is the cocktail glass rimmed with salt (in the case of the Margarita) or sugar. The crystals also add an extra taste-dimension as you sip.

RIMMING A GLASS

1 Cut a thick wedge of lime and gently and evenly rub it around the rim of the glass.
2 Roll the outer rim of the glass over a saucer of salt crystals (or sugar, depending upon what your cocktail needs).
3 Run the lime wedge around the inside of the glass to remove any stray crystals that might otherwise fall into the drink.

2 Roll the rim over a saucer of salt

WITH A TWIST *A lime twist is a perfect garnish for the Margarita. Cut off the ends of the lime, then hold it upright and, using a channel knife, which has a small hole at the end that cuts a groove in the fruit, cut from the top down for about 1cm (½in). Turn the knife sharply left or right and cut round and down the rest of the fruit. The result should be a tight spiral.*

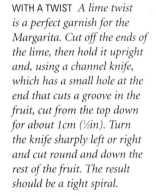

1 Rub a wedge of lime around the rim of the glass

3 Remove stray crystals from the inside of the glass

SOUR AND TANGY

66 After a hard day by the pool, kick off your evening with one of these appetizing, sophisticated, classic cocktails. **99**

INTRODUCING SOUR AND TANGY COCKTAILS

The classic sour, tangy cocktail blends a spirit base with a zesty, dry fruit juice. These are pick-me-up cocktails, perfect for getting everyone in the mood for a party.

DRINK PROFILE The overall look of these cocktails should be fresh, clear, and bright. Aromas should be clean and citrusy, with a lively, youthful feel, and the taste should be sharp and stimulating. The idea is to drink a sour and tangy cocktail to liven you up for the evening, or to let your body know that it is almost time for dinner (they make excellent apéritifs). There should be a good balance between the alcohol spirit and the fruit juice – they should enhance the character of each other, rather than either one overpowering the other. Some of these cocktails, such as the Side Car, have a touch of sweetness to balance the overall zest.

The origins of the sour and tangy cocktail may well date back to the early sailors of the Royal Navy, who were given lime juice as a prevention against scurvy, a disease caused by a lack of vitamin C. To make the fruit's sharp taste more palatable, the sailors mixed the juice with their standard-issue rum or gin. Today, this style of cocktail brims with classics, including the Whisky Sour (whisky, egg white, sugar syrup, and lemon), Tom Collins (gin, lemon, sugar, and soda water), and Margarita (tequila, triple sec, and lime juice). To make the perfect sour, tangy cocktail, be sure to measure the lime or lemon juice precisely. The balance is a delicate one; too much or too little "tang" will spoil the result.

SIDE CAR *A simple but delicious mix of brandy, triple sec, and lemon juice makes this classic cocktail.*

SOUR AND TANGY COCKTAILS

The base ingredient of each sour, tangy cocktail will influence the balance of the citrus zest. For something tangy with a sweet edge, try cocktails with a base of rum; for something tangy and dry, go with a gin base. Use this table to help you find cocktails with flavours that fire your senses.

WHISKY SOUR

PISCO SOUR

CAIPIRINHA

BASE	COCKTAIL	OTHER INGREDIENTS
GIN	Gin Fizz *(see p342)*	Lemon juice, sugar syrup, soda water
	Singapore Sling *(see p342)*	Cherry brandy, Benedictine, Cointreau, Angostura bitters, pineapple juice, lime juice, grenadine, soda water
	Tom Collins *(see p343)*	Lemon juice, sugar syrup, soda water
	Red Lion *(see p344)*	Grand Marnier, grenadine, lemon juice, orange juice
	Maiden's Prayer *(see p344)*	Triple sec, lemon juice, orange juice
	White Lady *(see p344)*	Cointreau, lemon juice, egg white
	Blue Devil *(see p347)*	Blue curaçao, lemon juice, maraschino liqueur
	Bronx *(see p349)*	Sweet red vermouth, dry vermouth, orange juice
	French Sherbet *(see p349)*	Cointreau, orange juice, lime juice

BASE	COCKTAIL	OTHER INGREDIENTS
GIN (CONT.)	Negroni (see p349)	Sweet red vermouth, Campari
	Trinity (see p349)	Sweet vermouth, dry vermouth
	Rose (see p350)	Lime, vermouth, apricot brandy, lime juice, grenadine
	Zaza (see p350)	Dubonnet vermouth, orange peel
	Rickey (see p352)	Lime juice, sugar syrup, soda water
WHISKY	Affinity (see p344)	Sweet vermouth, dry vermouth, Angostura bitters
	Apple Jim (see p347)	Apple sour
	Napoleon (see p349)	Mandarine Napoléon, lemon juice, orange juice
	Rob Roy (see p350)	Sweet vermouth, Angostura bitters
	Whisky Sour (see p351)	Lemon juice, sugar syrup, egg white
	Boxer (see p352)	Dry vermouth, grapefruit juice
VODKA	Kamikaze (see p349)	Cointreau, lime juice
	Cosmopolitan (see p353)	Triple sec, lime juice, cranberry juice
	Aloe Vera (see p344)	Midori, sweet-and-sour mix, lime cordial, soda water
	Absolut Trouble (see p347)	Grand Marnier, orange juice, grenadine
RUM	Presidente (see p345)	Dubonnet, grenadine, lime juice, curaçao
	Banana Daiquiri (see p347)	Banana, lemon juice, crème de banane
	Caipirinha (see p348)	Lime, sugar
	Adam and Eve (see p352)	Apple sour, dry vermouth, Campari
BRANDY	Honeymoon (see p342)	Benedictine, triple sec, lemon juice
	Side Car (see p349)	Triple sec, lemon juice
	Pisco Sour (see p350)	Lemon juice, sugar syrup, egg white, Angostura bitters
	Between the Sheets (see p352)	Cointreau, white rum, lime juice
TEQUILA	Matador (see p344)	Triple sec, apple juice
	Margarita (see p346)	Lime, salt, triple sec, lime juice
	Parked Car (see p350)	Campari, Cointreau, egg white
	Alligator (see p352)	Pisang Ambon liqueur, pineapple sour, lemon sour
CAMPARI	Tampico (see p342)	Cointreau, lemon or lime juice, tonic water
	El Greco (see p350)	Bitter lemon
PERNOD	Suissesse (see p349)	Lemon juice, egg white, soda water
	Après Midori (see p352)	Midori, lime juice
CHAMPAGNE	Alfonso (see p348)	Sugar cube, Angostura bitters, Dubonnet vermouth
	Black Velvet (see p352)	Dark Irish stout

TOM COLLINS

COSMOPOLITAN

MARGARITA

MATADOR

PRESIDENTE

DRINK ANYTIME

These are great cocktails to drink when you are feeling hot and bothered after a hard day, or simply feel like a pick-me-up. Many well-known cocktails are ideal for this; citrus and fruit flavours work particularly well, as they balance the sweetness of a liqueur or spirit base with zesty freshness. The result is a drink that is lively and stimulating but not too heavy and filling.

GIN FIZZ

■ INGREDIENTS
Lemon wedge ▪ 60ml (2oz) gin ▪ 40ml (1⅓oz) freshly squeezed lemon juice ▪ sugar syrup to taste ▪ soda water

■ EQUIPMENT
Tumbler or small highball glass ▪ shaker ▪ strainer ▪ knife ▪ stirring spoon

This popular cocktail has appeared on bar lists since the mid-19th century. Try using Plymouth gin to add complexity. Gin Fizz is perfect as a summer-afternoon freshener.

METHOD Rub the lemon wedge around the rim of the glass. Fill the shaker with ice, and pour in the gin, lemon juice, and sugar syrup. Shake. Strain into the glass, top with soda (use a new bottle – fizziness is key), and stir. Decorate with an orange slice and a cherry.

GIN FIZZ

SILVER FIZZ

■ INGREDIENTS
60ml (2oz) gin ▪ 60ml (2oz) lemon juice ▪ sugar syrup to taste ▪ chilled soda water ▪ white of 1 egg

■ EQUIPMENT
Shaker ▪ strainer ▪ highball glass ▪ stirring spoon

This is a frothy version of the Gin Fizz, thanks to the egg white. Many people love it – but it's not for me! If you add the yolk too, it becomes a Golden Fizz.

METHOD Put all the ingredients except the soda in the shaker. Shake for 20 seconds, then strain into the highball glass. Top with soda; stir, and serve with a lemon wheel, or two lemon slices, and a straw.

SILVER FIZZ

TAMPICO

■ INGREDIENTS
30ml (1oz) Cointreau ▪ 45ml (1½oz) Campari ▪ 30ml (1oz) lemon or lime juice ▪ tonic water

■ EQUIPMENT
Shaker ▪ strainer ▪ highball glass

The combination of sweet Cointreau, bitter Campari, and refreshing tonic makes this cocktail deliciously complex. It is an ideal apéritif, or holiday charmer.

I prefer lime to lemon in my Tampico – its sharpness is slightly softer. All the liquid ingredients should be well chilled to help hold the cocktail's flavours together.

METHOD Fill the shaker with ice and pour in all the ingredients except the tonic. Shake well. Strain into an ice-filled highball. Top with tonic.

TAMPICO

HONEYMOON

■ INGREDIENTS
20ml (⅔oz) apple brandy ▪ 20ml (⅔oz) Benedictine ▪ 1 tsp triple sec (ideally Cointreau) ▪ juice of ½ lemon, plus extra lemon for zest

■ EQUIPMENT
Shaker ▪ strainer ▪ chilled Martini glass

This is an unforgettable cocktail! For the best results use Cointreau and VSOP Calvados (apple brandy). A chilled glass keeps the flavours fresh. It is light amber in colour.

METHOD Pour all the ingredients into a shaker filled with ice. Shake well and strain into the glass. Peel a zest of lemon, and squeeze it into the cocktail to release its oils, then drop the zest into the glass.

SINGAPORE SLING

■ INGREDIENTS
30ml (1oz) London Dry gin ▪ 15ml (½oz) cherry brandy ▪ 1½ tsp Benedictine ▪ 1½ tsp Cointreau ▪ dash Angostura bitters ▪ 120ml (4oz) pineapple juice ▪ 15ml (½oz) fresh lime juice ▪ 10ml (⅓oz) grenadine ▪ soda water

■ EQUIPMENT
Shaker ▪ strainer ▪ highball glass

A fantastic, timeless classic, and easy to drink at any time of day. I love it!

METHOD Place all the ingredients except the soda into a shaker filled with ice. Shake energetically, then strain into an ice-filled glass. Top with soda and decorate with a slice of lemon. (If you like, add a Maraschino cherry, too.)

SINGAPORE SLING

TOM COLLINS *This is a long and refreshing gin cocktail, with a delicate sweetness to balance its lemony zest. It is perfect on hot summer days.*

TOM COLLINS

■ INGREDIENTS

60ml (2oz) London Dry gin ▪ 30ml (1oz) freshly squeezed lemon juice ▪ 1tsp sugar syrup ▪ 90ml (3oz) soda water

■ EQUIPMENT

Shaker ▪ highball glass ▪ strainer ▪ stirring spoon

This classic cocktail is thought to date from the early 19th century. Although no-one knows its exact origins, we do know that it was first mixed by a bartender named Collins at the famous Limmer's hotel in London. The original recipe used Genever – a Dutch juniper-berry spirit, similar to gin. Eventually the Genever was replaced by the slightly sweeter London Dry gin called "Old Tom" – and the Tom Collins was born.

Actually, the name Collins is now used to refer to many other cocktails with a blend of soda water, sugar syrup, lemon juice, and spirit. In the US the John Collins is made using Bourbon whiskey in place of the gin, and other Collins drinks are made using brandy, rum, or Scotch.

Overall, I really like this cocktail. It is refreshing and stylish, elegant and full of flavours: ideal around the pool!

METHOD Half fill the shaker with ice. Pour in the gin, lemon juice, and sugar syrup. Shake well. Strain into an ice-filled highball, and carefully add the soda water. Stir gently to retain the bubbles. Garnish with a Maraschino cherry dropped into the glass, and a slice of lemon either dropped in or positioned on the rim.

ALOE VERA

■ **INGREDIENTS**
40ml (1⅓oz) lemon-infused vodka, such as Absolut Citron ■
30ml (1oz) Midori melon liqueur ■
40ml (1⅓oz) sweet-and-sour mix ■
20ml (⅔oz) Rose's lime cordial ■
soda water to fill

■ **EQUIPMENT**
Highball glass ■ stirring spoon

A beautiful ocean green, this party cocktail is long and light, with a good vodka kick.

METHOD Fill the glass with ice, pour in everything except the soda, and stir well. Fill with soda. Serve with a thin slice of lime, and a straw if you wish.

ALOE VERA

RED LION

■ **INGREDIENTS**
30ml (1oz) gin ■ 30ml (1oz) Grand Marnier ■ dash grenadine ■ 15ml (½oz) freshly squeezed lemon juice ■
15ml (½oz) freshly squeezed orange juice, plus extra orange for zest

■ **EQUIPMENT**
Shaker ■ strainer ■ chilled Martini glass ■ lighter

Booth's Gin created this mix in the 1930s. Its orange flavours are underlined by a lemony bite.

METHOD Fill the shaker with ice. Add the liquid ingredients, shake well, and strain into the glass. Cut a thin piece of orange zest and hold it over the glass. Squeeze it to release the oils, setting them alight as you do so (see p353). If you wish, drop the peel into the glass to garnish.

RED LION

MATADOR

■ **INGREDIENTS**
30ml (1oz) gold tequila ■ 10ml (½oz) triple sec (or Cointreau) ■ 20ml (⅔oz) freshly pressed apple juice

■ **EQUIPMENT**
Shaker ■ strainer ■ Martini glass

If you like a Margarita (see p346), then you will love the Matador too! Thanks to the refreshing touch of apple, this cocktail is just as special as the Margarita, but even easier to drink. The apple juice and the orange tang of Cointreau, teamed with the sweeter flavours of golden tequila, can fool you into thinking this is a soft drink. Be warned – it is not! For me the best way to enjoy the Matador is on a hot, summery day with friends, or perhaps relaxing on a terrace with your favourite book. This is a happy cocktail for happy times, and will always put you (and your guests) in a wonderful frame of mind.

METHOD Fill the shaker with ice and pour in all the ingredients. Shake the contents well and strain into the glass. Garnish with an orange peel, and serve with a small straw if you wish.

AFFINITY

■ **INGREDIENTS**
30ml (1oz) blended Scotch whisky ■ 30ml (1oz) sweet vermouth ■ 30ml (1oz) dry vermouth ■ dash Angostura bitters ■ 1 lemon

■ **EQUIPMENT**
Mixing glass ■ stirring spoon ■ strainer ■ Martini glass

A classic cocktail, especially popular in the 1920s, the amber-coloured Affinity is simple but characterful, and light and refreshing. It makes a great apéritif or mood-booster.

Try to use a good-quality blended whisky, so that the malty flavours persist without any harshness.

METHOD Pour the sweet and dry vermouths, whisky, and bitters into the mixing glass with ice and stir well. Strain into the Martini glass. Slice a twist of lemon zest and squeeze its oils into the mix. Place the zest in the glass as garnish.

MAIDEN'S PRAYER

■ **INGREDIENTS**
30ml (1oz) gin ■ 30ml (1oz) triple sec ■ 20ml (⅔oz) freshly squeezed lemon juice ■ ½ tsp orange juice

■ **EQUIPMENT**
Shaker ■ strainer ■ chilled Martini glass

The Maiden's Prayer is a more straightforward version of the Red Lion (above). Lemony-mango in colour, it has a well-balanced sweetness and a fresh finish. Wonderfully easy to drink, it is an instant mood-lifter. Make sure that the juice in this cocktail is from fruit in prime condition, and that it is freshly squeezed.

METHOD Pour all the ingredients into an ice-filled shaker. Shake well and strain into the glass.

WHITE LADY

■ **INGREDIENTS**
30ml (1oz) gin ■ 15ml (½oz) Cointreau ■ 30ml (1oz) freshly squeezed lemon juice ■ 1 tsp egg white

■ **EQUIPMENT**
Shaker ■ strainer ■ chilled Martini glass

US bartender Harry MacElhone created this classic cocktail in 1919. To make the most of its fresh, zesty nature, chill the ingredients before you begin. Turn the White Lady blue by using blue curaçao rather than Cointreau. I find this a bit sweet – but the intense colour is unbeatable!

METHOD Place some ice and all the ingredients in the shaker. Shake well and strain into the glass. Drop in a cherry to decorate if you wish.

WHITE LADY

BARTENDER'S TIP

Always try to squeeze your own juice from the freshest fruit available.

METHOD To juice by hand, run the fruit under warm water and cut it in half. Roll it over a hard surface and then squeeze into a container. When using an extractor (below), take care not to squeeze too hard, otherwise the pith will make the juice bitter.

Juicing citrus fruit

PRESIDENTE *Drop in a Maraschino cherry to garnish the Presidente. If you are feeling creative you could add a twist of orange peel too.*

MATADOR *With its apple and orange flavours, this light and refreshing cocktail is perfect for enjoying with friends.*

PRESIDENTE

■ **INGREDIENTS**
45ml (1½oz) Bacardi white rum ■ 20ml (⅔oz) Dubonnet vermouth ■ dash grenadine ■ dash fresh lime juice ■ 1 tsp curaçao (optional)

■ **EQUIPMENT**
Shaker and strainer, or mixing glass and stirring spoon ■ chilled Martini glass

The perfect holiday mix – not too powerful, but tasty. Dubonnet gives a slight sweetness; but you could use dry Martini, in which case add a dash of sweet Martini too. The curaçao is optional: the cocktail may be sweet enough for you without it.

METHOD The quick method is to stir: put all the ingredients in a mixing glass, stir well, and transfer to the Martini glass. If you shake all the ingredients with ice (and then strain into the glass), you will chill them thoroughly and prevent any burning sensation from the alcohol.

MARGARITA

■ **INGREDIENTS**
Slice of lime ▪ fine salt ▪ 45ml (1½oz) white tequila ▪ 15ml (½oz) triple sec ▪ 30ml (1oz) freshly squeezed lime juice

■ **EQUIPMENT**
Frosted Martini or Margarita glass ▪ saucer ▪ shaker ▪ strainer

This is perhaps the most famous party cocktail of all, and probably the best tequila cocktail ever made.

Appealing, fresh, and vibrant, the Margarita is perfectly balanced. The taste of the tequila is tempered by the other ingredients, so that the hit is not of alcohol, but of something much more delicious and complex. The effect is boosted by the salt on the rim of the glass, which reinforces the flavours of the cocktail as you

sip, and takes away the sharpness of the lime, leaving only a thirst-quenching citrus taste. Some people use egg white in their Margarita – but not me!

There are now many variations on the Margarita. For example, you can turn the mix an exotic blue by using blue curaçao rather than triple sec; or you can create colourful fruity versions, such as the Mango Margarita (with mango purée), Raspberry Margarita (with muddled fresh raspberries), and the Peach Margarita (with peach purée); or make longer versions, such as the Frozen Margarita with handfuls of crushed ice and sugar syrup, served in a hurricane glass.

METHOD First you need to "salt" the glass. Gently and evenly rub a thin slice of lime around the glass's rim. Lightly roll the rim in a saucer of salt. Turn the glass upright and set aside to dry while you pour all the cocktail ingredients into an ice-filled shaker. Shake them well and strain into the glass. Although the salted rim is the main garnish, I like to decorate with a twist of lime, too.

APPLE JIM

- **INGREDIENTS**
  50ml (1⅔oz) Jim Beam Bourbon
  whiskey ▪ 30ml (1oz) apple sour

- **EQUIPMENT**
  Tumbler ▪ bar spoon

Known as the green Bourbon whiskey drink (from the colour of the apple sour), the Apple Jim is traditionally enjoyed on St Patrick's Day (March 17) by Irish-Americans. The ideal party drink, this cocktail looks stunning, and is both refreshing and thirst-quenching.

METHOD Fill the glass with ice cubes and pour in the apple sour. Gently pour in the Bourbon over the back or bowl of the spoon to give two layers of colour (*see p365*). Drop in a lemon zest to garnish.

APPLE JIM

ABSOLUT TROUBLE

- **INGREDIENTS**
  40ml (1⅓oz) Absolut Citron vodka
  ▪ 20ml (⅔oz) Grand Marnier
  ▪ 60–80ml (2–2⅔oz) orange juice
  ▪ dash grenadine

- **EQUIPMENT**
  Shaker ▪ strainer ▪ tumbler

This easy-drinking, pink-coloured cocktail relies on lemon vodka – my favourite of all the flavoured vodkas. Here, the vodka enhances the drink's aromatic, citrus qualities. Its kick comes in only at the end, offsetting the sweetness of the grenadine.

METHOD Fill the shaker with ice and add all the ingredients. Shake well and strain carefully into an ice-filled tumbler. Garnish with a slice of lemon on the rim.

BLUE DEVIL

- **INGREDIENTS**
  30ml (1oz) gin ▪ ½ tsp blue curaçao
  ▪ freshly squeezed juice of half a
  lemon ▪ 10ml (⅓oz) Maraschino
  cherry liqueur

- **EQUIPMENT**
  Shaker ▪ strainer ▪ Martini glass

This is a cocktail for cold evenings when you need something comforting. Exotic Pacific blue in colour, the Blue Devil has a refreshing, aromatic character and is best made with the more complex Plymouth gin.

METHOD Fill the shaker with ice and pour in all the ingredients. Shake well and strain into the glass. Garnish with a red Maraschino cherry on a stick, and slice of tangy blood orange.

BANANA DAIQUIRI

- **INGREDIENTS**
  2 tbsp crushed ice ▪ half a banana
  ▪ 15ml (½oz) freshly squeezed lemon
  or lime juice ▪ 60ml (2oz) white rum
  ▪ 15ml (½oz) crème de banane

- **EQUIPMENT**
  Blender ▪ shaker ▪ strainer
  ▪ Martini glass

In this exotic Daiquiri, the strong banana flavours are underlined by zesty lemon. For variety and extra richness, you could add a dash of coconut milk, too.

METHOD Blend the crushed ice, banana, and lemon or lime juice. Put the mixture into the shaker with some ice cubes, as well as the rum and the banana liqueur. Shake and strain into the glass. Garnish with banana.

BANANA DAIQUIRI

MARGARITA *The best Margaritas are made using good-quality white tequila, and ideally Cointreau in place of the generic triple sec.*

CULTURE AND TRADITION

MARGARITA TALES There are many stories about the origins of the Margarita. In one, bartender Pancho Morales, at the Tommy's Place bar in Juarez, Mexico, was asked by a customer to mix a "Magnolia". Pancho could not remember any of the ingredients for the Magnolia except Cointreau, and so improvised by adding lime juice and tequila. He named his new mix after another flower – the Margarita, a daisy.

DRINK BEFORE DINNER

When guests have arrived for dinner but the food is still a little way off, why not serve them a sour and tangy cocktail? The style is zesty, funky, and refreshing, and should stimulate the appetite – these are drinks for when you want things to go with a swing. With a range of enticing flavours and colours and delicious complexity, one of this kind of cocktail is often not enough.

CAIPIRINHA

■ **INGREDIENTS**
1 small lime ▪ 2 tsp caster sugar, or 20ml (⅔oz) sugar syrup ▪ 60ml (2oz) cachaça sugar-cane spirit

■ **EQUIPMENT**
Muddler ▪ tumbler ▪ stirring spoon

ALFONSO

■ **INGREDIENTS**
1 white sugar cube ▪ 3 or 4 drops Angostura bitters ▪ 30ml (1oz) Dubonnet vermouth ▪ dry Champagne or sparkling wine

■ **EQUIPMENT**
Champagne flute

This amber-coloured party mix is not as popular as the Champagne Cocktail (see p379), but is better suited to afternoon drinking; its rich flavours include the sweet touch of

Dubonnet. The cocktail is named after King Alfonso XIII of Spain, who first tasted it while he was exiled in France in 1841.

METHOD Put the sugar cube in the glass and pour the bitters on top. Add the Dubonnet and top with Champagne, pouring really slowly as the sugar will cause the wine to froth. If you have a few glasses to serve, pour a little Champagne into each and then come back to fill them one by one.

CAIPIRINHA

The Caipirinha (which literally translated means "peasant drink", a reference to its origins as a favourite among Brazilian farmers) is crisp and funky. Cachaça, the drink's main ingredient, is a light, rum-like spirit, distilled directly from sugar-cane juice, and considered by many as the national drink of Brazil.

In the Caipirinha the sugar cuts through the sharpness of the lime, and the cachaça adds a little sweetness and gives a decent kick at

the finish, reinforcing the flavours of lime on the palate. The result is fresh and thirst-quenching, and so perfect on summer afternoons. I love it!

If you do not have cachaça, you can make an alternative version of this mix using light, white rum.

METHOD Cut the lime into eight wedges and place them in the glass. Gently muddle the wedges to extract the juice from the flesh and the oil from the skin. Add the sugar and muddle until the crystals have been dissolved into the lime juice. (If you are using sugar syrup, you just need to make sure that the drink is well mixed.) Add in some ice, pour in the cachaça, and stir well.

THE BRAZILIAN COCKTAIL *The immense statue of Christ that towers over Rio de Janeiro is for many the ultimate image of Brazil. The ultimate cocktail is the Caipirinha, made using Brazil's national spirit, cachaça.*

BRONX

■ INGREDIENTS
30ml (1oz) gin ▪ 15ml (½oz) sweet, red vermouth ▪ 15ml (½oz) dry vermouth ▪ 15ml (½oz) freshly squeezed orange juice

■ EQUIPMENT
Shaker ▪ strainer ▪ Martini glass

Created in 1906 by Johnny Solon, the bartender at New York's Waldorf-Astoria hotel, the famous Bronx cocktail has a well-balanced sweetness and nuttiness, making it a perfect apéritif. For a slightly less herby version, try it with lemon vodka instead of gin.

METHOD Place some ice cubes in the shaker, then add the other ingredients and shake well. Strain into a Martini glass.

BRONX

FRENCH SHERBET

■ INGREDIENTS
10ml (⅓oz) Plymouth gin ▪ 10ml (⅓oz) Cointreau ▪ 10ml (⅓oz) freshly squeezed orange juice ▪ 10ml (⅓oz) freshly squeezed lime juice

■ EQUIPMENT
Shaker ▪ strainer ▪ chilled Martini glass ▪ lighter

Orange juice mixed with dry gin makes this orange-coloured cocktail a great apéritif; the tangy lime brings freshness. To add a touch of bitterness, flame an orange zest (see p353) to extract its oils before dropping it into the glass.

METHOD Fill the shaker with ice. Pour in all the ingredients. Shake, and strain into the glass. Garnish with a twist of orange zest.

KAMIKAZE

■ INGREDIENTS
30ml (1oz) Cointreau ▪ 60ml (2oz) vodka ▪ 30ml (1oz) freshly squeezed lime juice

■ EQUIPMENT
Shaker ▪ strainer ▪ chilled tumbler

Packed with zest and fruity freshness, this is a well-balanced, cream-coloured cocktail. You could try replacing the vodka with white tequila or even white rum. The result may not be as crisp and tangy, but it will still be excellent.

METHOD Fill your shaker with ice cubes. Add the ingredients. Shake well, and strain into the glass. If you like, you can garnish with a zest of lime.

NEGRONI

■ INGREDIENTS
30ml (1oz) gin ▪ 30ml (1oz) sweet, red vermouth ▪ 30ml (1oz) Campari ▪ soda water (for long version only)

■ EQUIPMENT
Chilled Martini glass, or chilled highball glass for the long version ▪ stirring spoon

The Negroni was first mixed in the 1920s at the Casoni bar in Florence, Italy. It is my favourite summer cocktail.

METHOD For the short version pour all the ingredients into a Martini glass and stir. Garnish with a lemon zest. In the long version pour all the ingredients except the soda into a highball, then top with the soda, and stir.

NEGRONI

NAPOLEON

■ INGREDIENTS
30ml (1oz) Scotch whisky ▪ 20ml (⅔oz) Mandarine Napoléon ▪ 20ml (⅔oz) lemon juice ▪ 40ml (1⅓oz) orange juice

■ EQUIPMENT
Mixing glass ▪ stirring spoon ▪ strainer ▪ chilled highball glass

This is an exotic cocktail, dense with sharp citrus flavours. The Mandarine Napoléon liqueur carries the scent of mandarin peel, which fuses perfectly with the mellow whisky base.

METHOD Fill the mixing glass with ice and add all the ingredients. Stir until condensation appears on the outside of the glass. Strain into the highball, and garnish with mint.

NAPOLEON

TRINITY

■ INGREDIENTS
20ml (⅔oz) dry vermouth ▪ 20ml (⅔oz) sweet vermouth ▪ 20ml (⅔oz) gin

■ EQUIPMENT
Mixing glass ▪ stirring spoon ▪ strainer ▪ chilled Martini glass, or tumbler if preferred

The pink-coloured Trinity is relatively light in alcohol and perfect for whetting your appetite – especially if you are a fan of vermouth. Although the mix traditionally comes in a Martini glass, I like it on the rocks in a tumbler. If you add some orange juice, you can turn the Trinity into a Bronx (see above).

METHOD Fill the mixing glass with ice and add all the ingredients. Stir well and strain into the Martini glass.

SUISSESSE

■ INGREDIENTS
60ml (2oz) Pernod ▪ 30ml (1oz) freshly squeezed lemon juice ▪ half the white of one egg ▪ soda water to fill

■ EQUIPMENT
Shaker ▪ strainer ▪ tumbler

This a long, Mediterranean-style drink. The egg white softens both the sharpness of the lemon and the aniseed of the Pernod, while the soda water enhances the cocktail's fresh character (although you can use still water if you prefer).

METHOD Fill the shaker with ice and add all the ingredients. Shake for ten seconds and strain into the tumbler filled with ice. Top with soda water. Garnish with half a slice of lemon dropped into the drink.

SIDE CAR

■ INGREDIENTS
30ml (1oz) brandy ▪ 15ml (½oz) triple sec ▪ freshly squeezed juice from one quarter of a lemon

■ EQUIPMENT
Shaker ▪ strainer ▪ chilled Martini glass

Bartender Harry MacElhone created this dry, complex cocktail in the 1920s at Harry's New York Bar in Paris. The name recalls a certain customer who arrived at the bar in a motorcycle side car. For the best results use Cointreau rather than generic triple sec, and a dry Cognac. It is crucial that the cocktail is ice cold.

METHOD Fill the shaker with ice and add the ingredients. Shake well and strain into the glass.

SIDE CAR

PARKED CAR

- **INGREDIENTS**
  30ml (1oz) Campari ▪ 30ml (1oz)
  white tequila ▪ 15ml (½oz) Cointreau
  ▪ white of one egg

- **EQUIPMENT**
  Shaker ▪ strainer ▪ chilled
  Martini glass

The instantly loveable Parked Car makes a superb party drink. It is highly alcoholic, but also full of flavour with a slightly sweet tinge, making it really easy – perhaps a little too easy – to sip. Part of its appeal is its colour – a wonderfully dainty pink.

METHOD Fill your shaker with ice and pour in all the ingredients. Shake vigorously for ten seconds to ensure that the egg white has properly combined with everything else in the mix. Strain into the chilled Martini glass.

EL GRECO

- **INGREDIENTS**
  30ml (1oz) Campari ▪ 30–50ml
  (1–1⅗oz) Schweppes bitter lemon

- **EQUIPMENT**
  Mixing glass ▪ stirring spoon
  ▪ chilled Martini glass

This is a cocktail for hot afternoons. The Campari is refreshingly bitter, and the bubbles of the bitter lemon enhance the astringent style of the drink. The El Greco is usually served in a Martini glass, but I also like it over ice in a highball, drunk through a straw.

METHOD Place the ingredients in a mixing glass with ice. Stir and strain into the Martini glass. Garnish with a slice of lemon on the rim.

EL GRECO

PISCO SOUR

- **INGREDIENTS**
  60ml (2oz) pisco brandy ▪ 30ml (1oz)
  fresh lemon juice ▪ sugar syrup
  ▪ half the white of one egg ▪ few
  drops Angostura bitters (optional)

- **EQUIPMENT**
  Shaker ▪ strainer ▪ chilled
  Martini glass

Pisco is grape brandy made in Chile and Peru. It is spicy and earthy, and slightly sweet, with undertones of honey and sugar.

An ideal pick-me-up and apéritif, the Pisco Sour is widely regarded as the national cocktail of Peru. Add more or less sugar syrup depending upon how sour you want the mix to be, but take care not to drown out the sourness altogether – it is essential for whetting the appetite. Basically, if you like the Caipirinha (see p348), you will love the Pisco Sour!

METHOD Fill your shaker with ice and add all the ingredients, except the bitters (if you are using them). Shake really well to ensure that the egg white is fully blended in. Strain into the glass. For added complexity, sprinkle a few drops of Angostura bitters on the top.

ROB ROY

- **INGREDIENTS**
  60ml (2oz) blended Scotch whisky
  ▪ 30ml (1oz) sweet vermouth (chilled)
  ▪ 2 dashes Angostura bitters

- **EQUIPMENT**
  Mixing glass ▪ stirring spoon
  ▪ strainer ▪ tumbler or Martini glass

Created during the 1940s, the Rob Roy has a delicate, pleasant texture, with dominant whisky flavours.

You can turn the Rob Roy into a Green Briar by replacing the Angostura bitters with a dash of orange bitters and a splash of Cointreau.

METHOD Pour all the ingredients into a mixing glass and stir. Strain the mix into your chosen serving glass. Garnish with half a slice of lime on the rim, or a Maraschino cherry.

ROB ROY

ROSE

- **INGREDIENTS**
  Wedge of lime ▪ 15ml (½oz) dry
  vermouth ▪ 30ml (1oz) gin ▪ 15ml
  (½oz) apricot brandy ▪ 15ml (½oz)
  fresh lime juice ▪ 1 tsp grenadine

- **EQUIPMENT**
  Martini glass ▪ saucer of caster
  sugar ▪ shaker ▪ strainer

This is a powerful and intensely flavoured cocktail – and not for the fainthearted. Enjoy it on a cold evening before sitting down to dinner with friends.

METHOD Gently rub a thin slice of lime around the rim of the glass. Dip the rim in caster sugar. Chill the glass for an hour or so. Fill the shaker with ice and pour in all the ingredients. Shake well and strain into the glass.

ZAZA

- **INGREDIENTS**
  45ml (1½oz) gin ▪ 20ml (⅔oz)
  Dubonnet vermouth
  ▪ twist of orange peel

- **EQUIPMENT**
  Mixing glass ▪ stirring
  spoon ▪ strainer
  ▪ chilled tumbler
  ▪ lighter

Although it may be hard to imagine how gin and Dubonnet can combine into something really palatable, this is a delicious cocktail and superb as a lunchtime apéritif. The orange peel (which is flamed to release its oils into the mix) reinforces the character of the rich, spicy, red-wine Dubonnet, while the botanical flavours of the gin break through. For the best results use Plymouth gin. If you have a really sweet tooth, you can replace the Dubonnet with Martini Rosso.

METHOD Fill the mixing glass with ice and pour in the liquid ingredients. Stir well and strain into a tumbler containing a few cubes of ice. Hold the orange peel over the glass and, using the lighter, flame the peel so the orange oils drip into the mix (see p353). Drop the peel into the glass as garnish. Alternatively, serve it in a Martini glass, without the ice.

ZAZA

WHISKY SOUR

■ **INGREDIENTS**
60ml (2oz) whisky ▪ juice of half a lemon ▪ ½ tsp sugar syrup ▪ white of one egg

■ **EQUIPMENT**
Shaker ▪ strainer ▪ frosted Martini glass

Any type of whisky can be used to make the Whisky Sour, but my favourite is Canadian Club, which is smooth enough to balance out the kick from the lemon.

METHOD Fill the shaker with ice and pour in all the ingredients. Shake vigorously to ensure that the egg white is well integrated. Strain into the frosted Martini glass.

WHISKY SOUR *One or two leaves of mint make the perfect garnish for this frothy cocktail, thought to date from the 1850s.*

PISCO SOUR *I love just a few drops of Angostura bitters on top of the froth of this refreshing cocktail – they add an extra dimension as you sip.*

ADAM AND EVE

■ **INGREDIENTS**
20ml (⅔oz) Havana Club Añejo Blanco rum ▪ 20ml (⅔oz) apple sour ▪ 20ml (⅔oz) Martini Bianco dry vermouth ▪ 1 tsp Campari

■ **EQUIPMENT**
Shaker ▪ strainer ▪ Martini glass

This appealing cocktail is a lovely pinky golden colour. The contrast of the sweetness of the rum and apple against the bitter bite of the vermouth and Campari make it ideal for awakening your appetite.

METHOD Fill the shaker with ice and pour in the ingredients. Shake well and strain into the glass. Decorate with a slice of lime on the rim, or gently squeezed and dropped into the mix.

ALLIGATOR

■ **INGREDIENTS**
30ml (1oz) tequila ▪ 20ml (⅔oz) Pisang Ambon banana or other fruit liqueur ▪ dash pineapple sour ▪ dash lemon sour

■ **EQUIPMENT**
Shaker ▪ strainer ▪ tumbler

Exotic and vibrant, the Alligator is a summer-holiday cocktail with a full spectrum of flavours: it takes you all the way from sweet, through sour, to sharp. It has a long, fruity finish and can easily be mistaken for a soft drink!

METHOD Fill the shaker with ice and pour in the ingredients. Shake well and strain into the glass. Garnish with a wheel of lime on the rim.

ALLIGATOR

APRÈS MIDORI

■ **INGREDIENTS**
30ml (1oz) Pernod ▪ 30ml (1oz) Midori melon liqueur ▪ 30ml (1oz) freshly squeezed lime juice ▪ crushed ice

■ **EQUIPMENT**
Mixing glass ▪ stirring spoon ▪ strainer ▪ tumbler

This cocktail has a great balance of sweet and sour flavours, and an aniseed-laced finish, which comes from the Pernod. Many people make it in a shaker, but I like using a mixing glass to watch the colours change as the ingredients combine.

METHOD Fill the mixing glass with ice cubes and add the ingredients. Stir well. Strain into a tumbler containing crushed ice. Garnish with a sprig of mint.

APRÈS MIDORI

BOXER

■ **INGREDIENTS**
30ml (1oz) blended Scotch whisky ▪ 30ml (1oz) dry vermouth ▪ 30ml (1oz) freshly squeezed grapefruit juice

■ **EQUIPMENT**
Mixing glass ▪ stirring spoon ▪ strainer ▪ tumbler

Use a good blended whisky for this cocktail – try Famous Grouse, which is elegant but not overly aromatic. I favour Noilly Prat for the vermouth – its nuttiness combines well with the grapefruit. The resulting cocktail is an opaque, pale-brown colour, and refreshing to drink.

METHOD Fill the mixing glass with ice. Pour in the ingredients. Stir and strain into the tumbler.

BETWEEN THE SHEETS

■ **INGREDIENTS**
20ml (⅔oz) good quality brandy ▪ 20ml (⅔oz) Cointreau ▪ 20ml (⅔oz) white rum ▪ splash of freshly squeezed lime juice

■ **EQUIPMENT**
Shaker ▪ strainer ▪ Martini glass

First created in the 1930s by Harry MacElhone, the famous bartender who set up Harry's New York Bar in Paris, this cocktail is based on the Side Car (see p349). The drink was an instant success in the post-prohibition era and even now offers guaranteed pleasure.

Expect sweetness from the Cointreau and a vibrant kick from the lime juice. The delicate balance of these sensations makes this cocktail perfect for

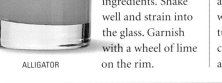

stimulating your appetite before dinner. For the best results use a good-quality brandy such as a VS or VSOP Cognac, or even an Armagnac. My personal preference is for a Cognac, because Armagnac tends to be a little too firm for cocktail-making: it almost gets in the way, making it harder for the flavours to combine seamlessly.

For a longer drink you can pour the mix into a tumbler filled with ice cubes rather than a Martini glass – but for me the Martini glass is best because it gives the cocktail an greater feeling of delicacy.

METHOD Fill the shaker with ice cubes. Pour in all the ingredients and shake well. Strain into the Martini glass. Garnish with a zest of lemon hanging over the rim of the glass – utterly irresistible!

BETWEEN THE SHEETS

BARTENDER'S TIP

Frosting a glass keeps the contents icy cold and adds to the visual glamour of the cocktail.

METHOD Place the glass in the freezer for 20 to 30 minutes, and remove only when you are ready to fill it. Hold the glass by the stem to avoid fingerprints.

Frosting the glass

RICKEY

■ **INGREDIENTS**
60ml (2oz) Plymouth gin ▪ 15ml (½oz) freshly squeezed lime juice ▪ 1½ tsp sugar syrup ▪ soda water to fill

■ **EQUIPMENT**
Shaker ▪ strainer ▪ highball glass ▪ stirring spoon

First made for Colonel Joe Rickey in the early 1900s in Washington DC, the Rickey is often confused with the Tom Collins (see p343). The cocktails look the same (both are clear), but the main difference is that the Rickey is made using lime rather than lemon, giving it an even tangier taste. For something lighter, try replacing the gin with vodka.

METHOD Fill the shaker with ice and pour in all the ingredients except the soda water. Shake well and strain into an ice-filled glass. Top with soda and stir gently. Garnish with a lime twist.

DRINK AFTER DINNER

A light, tangy cocktail can often be the ideal way to end a meal, especially a long lunch. The best cocktails of this kind have a dry, cutting edge, backed with something a little more substantial. Clean and full of flavour, they make the perfect finale to an enjoyable dinner or any gastronomic occasion.

BLACK VELVET

■ INGREDIENTS
75ml (2½oz) dark Irish stout
■ Champagne to fill

■ EQUIPMENT
Bottle opener ■ Champagne flute
■ stirring spoon

This smooth cocktail was invented at London's Brook's Club in 1861 to mark the death of Queen Victoria's husband Prince Albert. Members felt that drinking straight Champagne was frivolous, but the mixture of

Champagne and Irish stout produced something more sombre. Despite its dark colour, this cocktail is quite fresh with the zesty Champagne cutting through the meaty stout. If you do not want to use Champagne, a good Spanish Cava also works very well.

BLACK VELVET

METHOD Pour the stout gently into the glass ensuring there is as little "head" (froth) as possible. Pour in the Champagne and stir lightly.

COSMOPOLITAN

■ INGREDIENTS
30ml (1oz) premium brand vodka
■ 15ml (½oz) triple sec ■ 15ml (½oz) freshly squeezed lime juice ■ 15ml (½oz) cranberry juice

■ EQUIPMENT
Shaker ■ strainer ■ chilled Martini glass

The Cosmopolitan, created in the US in the 1980s but now found on bar lists all over the world, is probably one of the most fashionable cocktails of the present day.

In my view its popularity is very well-deserved – if I had to choose one cocktail to take with me to a desert island, the Cosmopolitan might very well be it! I love the complexity of its flavours and its crisp and refreshing texture, as well as the nuances of

COSMOPOLITAN

orange from the triple sec (use Cointreau for the best results), which gently cut through the red fruit of the cranberry, and the fresh lime.

Take care when you measure the cranberry – too much will not only disrupt the Cosmopolitan's flavour, but also its lovely soft pink colour.

For a slightly sweeter variation you could use a white rum, such as Bacardi, in place of the vodka; alternatively, on a really hot day try using lemon-flavoured vodka for the extra freshness.

METHOD Pour all the ingredients into an ice-filled shaker and shake well for a few seconds – between four and six seconds is ideal because you are trying to chill the ingredients without diluting the subtlety of their flavours. Strain into the Martini glass. If you wish, you can garnish by dropping into the glass a flamed peel of orange or lime.

BARTENDER'S TIP

Flaming a zest of citrus fruit helps to release its pungent oils into a cocktail. It adds an extra layer of flavour, and also creates a dramatic bartending effect. Take care with naked flames!

METHOD Take a thick-skinned orange, lemon, or lime and cut a deep slice of peel. Using a lighter, warm the peel (be careful not to burn your fingers) over the cocktail, squeezing gently to release the oils in a flaming jet. Before drinking, cover the glass to extinguish any residual flames.

Cutting a zest

Flaming the oils

66 Warming, velvety, and soft, these indulgent cocktails offer intense flavours and total comfort for the soul. 99

SWEET, RICH, AND CREAMY

INTRODUCING SWEET, RICH, AND CREAMY COCKTAILS

Sweet and creamy cocktails are the most seductive of all. Rich in flavours but velvety smooth in texture, these are the cocktails to fire all your senses.

DRINK PROFILE The colours of these cocktails could fill the entire spectrum, but the aesthetic that most of them share is opaqueness. This category also gives us layered cocktails – where ingredients are separated, one on top of the other, in the glass. Aromas should be sweet and attractive, without too much spirit. If you find that alcohol is the dominant aroma, you may have made the cocktail too strong. This type of cocktail tends to have intense flavours, often of sweetness. However, any sweetness should be offset with a hint of spirit, or a refreshing coolness. The palate should be smooth and soft, with a lingering finish.

Many sweet, creamy cocktails gain silkiness through the addition of dairy products. Among the classics in this group are the Irish Coffee (Irish whiskey, coffee, and cream) and Egg Nog (brandy, rum, milk, and egg yolk). However, dairy is not a pre-requisite: other classics such as the Bloody Mary (vodka, tomato juice, and spices) appear here too. When dairy is involved be sure to use only the freshest ingredients, and take care to shake or blend the cocktail so that it is fully combined – only then will you achieve the perfect texture. Energetic shaking with ice will also cool the cocktail properly; chilling is essential to balance out the sweetness so that the mix never feels sickly.

BRANDY ALEXANDER *An opulent blend of brandy, crème de cacao, and cream, topped with grated nutmeg.*

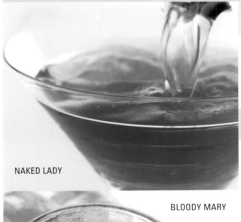

NAKED LADY

BLOODY MARY

SWEET, RICH, AND CREAMY COCKTAILS

The cocktails in this section are the natural choice for people with a sweet tooth. However, a sweet, creamy cocktail with a whisky or brandy base will tend to be slightly drier than one based, say, on rum. Use this table to guide your choices according to your mood and preference.

BASE	COCKTAIL	OTHER INGREDIENTS
VODKA	Bloody Mary (see p358)	Tomato juice, lemon, Worcestershire sauce, Tabasco sauce
	Back on Track (see p360)	Blueberry liqueur, Pisang Ambon
	Sex on the Beach (see p360)	Peach schnapps, raspberry liqueur, pineapple juice, cranberry juice
	Absolut Me (see p361)	Crème de banane, cream, grenadine, orange juice
	Chi Chi (see p362)	Malibu
	Melancholy Martini (see p362)	Midori, Cointreau, Malibu, pineapple juice, cream, lime juice
	Vanilla Coin (see p363)	Cointreau, ginger ale
	Colorado Boulevard (see p363)	Kahlúa, milk, mineral water
	Swamp Thing (see p363)	Irish Cream liqueur, cola
	ASAP (see p365)	Crème de cacao, cream

BASE	COCKTAIL	OTHER INGREDIENTS
VODKA (CONT.)	Climax *(see p366)*	Amaretto, crème de cacao, triple sec, crème de banane, cream
	Black Russian *(see p366)*	Kahlúa
	Godmother *(see p367)*	Amaretto
	Bruised Apple *(see p367)*	Puréed apple, apple syrup, raspberry liqueur
	Mud Slide *(see p368)*	Kahlúa, toffee cream liqueur
	Multiple Orgasm *(see p368)*	Crème de cacao, amaretto, triple sec, cream
	Snowball *(see p368)*	Lemonade, advocaat
WHISKY	Nabo *(see p358)*	Worcestershire sauce, tomato juice
	42nd Street *(see p361)*	Grand Marnier, Cointreau, dry vermouth
	Bourbon Rose *(see p362)*	Triple sec, orange juice, grenadine
	Alcazar *(see p364)*	Benedictine, cream
	After Eight *(see p366)*	Crème de cacao, crème de menthe, espresso coffee, milk
	Godfather *(see p367)*	Amaretto
	Rusty Nail *(see p368)*	Drambuie
	Irish Coffee *(see p368)*	Brown sugar, strong coffee, cream
RUM	Naked Lady *(see p358)*	Apricot brandy, lemon juice, grenadine, egg white
	Piña Colada *(see p360)*	Malibu, pineapple juice
	Rum Punch *(see p361)*	Lime juice, sugar syrup, soda water or still mineral water
	Top Notch *(see p361)*	Midori, Frangelico, peach schnapps, Malibu, orange juice, cream
BRANDY	Port Flip *(see p362)*	Ruby port, egg yolk, caster sugar
	Brandy Alexander *(see p363)*	Crème de cacao, double cream or crème fraîche, nutmeg
	Banana Bliss *(see p363)*	Crème de banane
	Egg Nog *(see p367)*	Dark rum, sugar syrup, egg yolk
	Stinger *(see p368)*	Crème de menthe
IRISH CREAM LIQUEUR	B-52 *(see p365)*	Kahlua, Grand Marnier
	Belfast Brownie *(see p365)*	Crème de cacao, curaçao, candied orange peel, cream
	BMW *(see p366)*	Malibu, whisky
	Dramatic Martini *(see p366)*	Tuaca Italian liqueur, Grand Marnier, milk
SOUTHERN COMFORT	Alabama Slammer *(see p364)*	Sloe gin, amaretto, orange juice
	Amaretto Comfort *(see p364)*	Amaretto
CHAMPAGNE	Mimosa *(see p360)*	Orange juice, curaçao
	Ritz Fizz *(see p361)*	Amaretto, blue curaçao, lemon juice
TEQUILA	White Bull *(see p366)*	Kahlúa, double cream

ALCAZAR

EGG NOG

IRISH COFFEE

ALABAMA SLAMMER

DRINK ANYTIME

When you need to chase away chills, or are generally in need of comfort, these are the cocktails to turn to. Although they are frequently served very cold, the spice and the rich texture has a pleasant warming effect. The ingredients that go into these drinks may seem unconventional at first sight, but don't let that put you off, as these cocktails have real personality.

BLOODY MARY

■ INGREDIENTS
45ml (1½oz) vodka ▪ 120ml (4oz) tomato juice ▪ freshly squeezed juice of half a lemon ▪ 2 drops Worcestershire sauce ▪ dash Tabasco sauce ▪ salt and pepper ▪ ½ tsp horseradish (optional)

■ EQUIPMENT
Shaker ▪ strainer ▪ highball glass

One of the most famous energy-boosting cocktails of all, the Bloody Mary originates from Harry's New York Bar in

BLOODY MARY

Paris, where it was first mixed in 1921 by bartender "Pete" Petoit. He supposedly named it after Mary Tudor – the Catholic daughter of King Henry VIII of England – who during her five years as queen killed off most of her significant Protestant adversaries, earning her the title "Bloody Mary".

METHOD Place some ice cubes in the shaker and add all the ingredients. Shake gently and strain into an ice-filled glass. Alternatively, roll the mix (*see below*). Decorate with a stick of celery.

BARTENDER'S TIP

Cocktails that contain tomato juice, such as the Bloody Mary, may become too frothy when they are shaken, and this can spoil the thick, rich texture that is so fundamental to the drink. To avoid this, try mixing them using the "rolling" technique.

METHOD You will need two mixing glasses. Pour all the ingredients into one of the glasses, then very gently pour the mixture back and forth between the glasses until it is well-combined – around four or five times. Transfer to the serving glass.

Tip from one glass to another | Continue rolling until fully mixed

NAKED LADY

■ INGREDIENTS
30ml (1oz) white rum ▪ 30ml (1oz) apricot brandy ▪ 30ml (1oz) freshly squeezed lemon juice ▪ 2 dashes grenadine ▪ white of one egg

■ EQUIPMENT
Shaker ▪ strainer ▪ chilled Martini glass

This funky, tasty, and vibrant cocktail has a silky-soft and delicate feel, making it great before or after dinner. I recommend using Bacardi rum in the mix because it has a light texture; it is not overpowering and so will not upset the cocktail's balance. It is also important to use a good-quality apricot brandy – try to find one where the flesh of the fruit has been macerated with the kernels. This gives a nuttiness to the final spirit, which in the Naked Lady cocktail comes through as a light almond finish.

NABO

■ INGREDIENTS
60ml (2oz) blended Scotch whisky ▪ dash Worcestershire sauce ▪ tomato juice to fill

■ EQUIPMENT
Highball glass ▪ stirring spoon

The Nabo (a name taken from the Norwegian word meaning "neighbour") is a warming cocktail, and especially great for sipping with friends on a cold Scandinavian evening. For the best results use a good blended whisky, such as Famous Grouse, or for something sweeter try using a good Bourbon.

METHOD Fill the highball with ice and add the whisky and Worcestershire sauce. Top up with tomato juice and stir. Garnish with fresh basil and serve with a straw.

NABO

If you have a sweet tooth, add a dash of sweet vermouth to the blend to lend a little extra texture.

METHOD Fill the shaker with ice and add all the ingredients. Shake energetically for ten seconds to make sure that the egg white is integrated into the blend. Strain into the glass.

BULLSHOT

■ INGREDIENTS
30ml (1oz) vodka ▪ 60ml (2oz) cold, clear beef stock ▪ 15ml (½oz) freshly squeezed lemon juice ▪ 1 or 2 dashes Worcestershire sauce ▪ 4–6 drops Tabasco sauce ▪ pinch celery salt ▪ black pepper to taste

■ EQUIPMENT
Shaker ▪ strainer ▪ highball glass

Reputed to be an instant hangover cure, this dark brown cocktail may not look or sound attractive, but it is great if you want a savoury mix that is light in alcohol. In winter, serve it hot.

METHOD Fill the shaker with ice and add all the ingredients except the pepper. Shake well and strain into the highball filled with ice. Add some pepper to taste.

NAKED LADY *No one is sure how the Naked Lady got its name, but perhaps it comes from the cocktail's pink colour and its soft, delicate texture.*

MIMOSA

■ INGREDIENTS

30ml (1oz) freshly squeezed orange juice ▪ 10ml (⅓oz) curaçao ▪ dry Champagne or good-quality sparkling wine to fill

■ EQUIPMENT

Champagne flute ▪ stirring spoon

Named after a tropical shrub with yellow blooms, this cocktail was created at the Ritz Hotel, Paris, in 1925. It is light and fresh. For the best results find the sweetest oranges possible for the juice.

METHOD Pour the orange juice into the flute, add the curaçao and stir well. Steadily pour in the Champagne, running it down the inside of the glass. Garnish with a small wedge of orange.

MIMOSA

FUZZY NAVEL

■ INGREDIENTS

90ml (3oz) peach schnapps liqueur ▪ 90ml (3oz) freshly squeezed orange juice

■ EQUIPMENT

Highball glass ▪ stirring spoon

Do not expect great complexity from the Fuzzy Navel. Bright orange, this is an uncomplicated, fun cocktail to be enjoyed at a beach or pool party on a balmy summer night. A dash of soda water makes it more suitable for the afternoon, while a shot of vodka will give an extra kick. (If you do this, serve it without ice in a Martini glass.)

METHOD Fill the highball with ice, pour in the peach schnapps and then the orange juice. Stir. Garnish with a slice of orange, or peach, on the rim.

BACK ON TRACK

■ INGREDIENTS

30ml (1oz) vodka ▪ 20ml (⅔oz) blueberry liqueur ▪ 20ml (⅔oz) Pisang Ambon banana or other fruit liqueur

■ EQUIPMENT

Chilled shot glass ▪ teaspoon

It may take a while to perfect the green and dark red layers of this cocktail, but the practise is worth it! Use vodka that has been stored in the freezer – it will be ice cold, but not solid – to help keep the flavours fresh. Drink it through a straw without stirring.

METHOD Pour the vodka into the glass. Then, in turn, pour in the blueberry liqueur and Pisang Ambon over the back or bowl of the spoon, so that they create layers (see p365).

SEX ON THE BEACH

■ INGREDIENTS

30ml (1oz) vodka ▪ 30ml (1oz) peach schnapps ▪ 30ml (1oz) Chambord raspberry liqueur ▪ 60ml (2oz) freshly pressed pineapple juice ▪ dash cranberry juice

■ EQUIPMENT

Shaker ▪ strainer ▪ highball glass

This is a juicy, full-flavoured cocktail. If you do not have Chambord, any raspberry liqueur will do. You could also replace the peach schnapps with Midori (melon liqueur).

METHOD Fill the shaker with ice, pour in all the ingredients, and shake well. Strain into an ice-filled highball. Garnish with a wedge of lime.

SEX ON THE BEACH

PIÑA COLADA

■ INGREDIENTS

30ml (1oz) white rum ▪ 15ml (½oz) Malibu coconut rum liqueur ▪ 60ml (2oz) freshly pressed pineapple juice

■ EQUIPMENT

Shaker ▪ strainer ▪ highball glass

Created in the 1950s in Puerto Rico, this is surely the most famous rum cocktail ever made. Easy-to-drink, smooth, and appealing, the Piña Colada is perfect for the summer, when it should be served well chilled, or for around the fire in the winter, when it need not be chilled so thoroughly.

Unlike many other cocktails, the Piña Colada is white. If, like me, you are not a fan of mixes that look like

PIÑA COLADA

a glass of milk, add a measure of dark rum, which will give a slightly golden colour to the finished blend.

Fresh, sweet pineapple is essential if you are pressing your own juice (doing so will always give the best results), but you could blend a few slices of tinned pineapple if you prefer – about three slices will give you enough juice.

METHOD Fill the shaker with ice. Add all the ingredients and shake well. Strain into a highball glass. Garnish with a slice of orange on the rim, and serve with a straw.

An alternative method to make this cocktail is to blend all the ingredients, including the unpressed pineapple slices, in a blender with some crushed ice. However, I prefer the shaker method as the ice has less opportunity to dilute the other ingredients.

MULLED WINE The practice of warming wine, cider, or mead, with spices and fruit to ward off the winter chill has been around for centuries. Mulled wine (a term in use since at least the 17th century) is made by mixing red wine with spices, such as cinnamon, cloves, and nutmeg, and fresh oranges, then warming the mix on the hob.

(Warming was once achieved by heating a poker in the fire and stirring it through the liquid.) Don't allow the wine to boil – if the alcohol evaporates, the wine will not be able to balance the rich flavours of the spices. Almost any wine can be used, but I would choose an inexpensive, full-bodied, unaged red, such as a decent Merlot.

DRINK BEFORE DINNER

You should drink these cocktails when you want to boost your energy and feel ready for anything. They are normally either spicy or slightly bitter, and the best are beautifully balanced and delicate – but don't drink too many as you may find they take they edge off your appetite. Many have a high liqueur and spirit content, so they can be quite potent and should be drunk with a little caution.

RUM PUNCH

■ INGREDIENTS

30ml (1oz) freshly squeezed lime juice ■ 60ml (2oz) sugar syrup ■ 90ml (3oz) golden rum ■ 120ml (4oz) soda water or still mineral water

■ EQUIPMENT

Highball or punch glass ■ bar spoon

Rum punch is Jamaica's answer to Puerto Rico's Piña Colada, although it offers completely different taste sensations. My measurements above are enough for one glass, but Rum

Punch is really a pre-dinner, party drink and one that you will want to make in a jug. Mix a batch according to the rhyme: "One part sour [lime], two parts sweet [sugar], three parts strong [rum], four parts weak [water]" and you can't go wrong!

I love the way the sourness of the lime cuts through the rum to give a refreshing drink that is wonderful for awakening the appetite.

METHOD Put some ice in the glass (or jug) and pour in all the ingredients except the water. Stir well and top with the water or soda. Garnish with a twist of lime, or grated nutmeg.

TASTE OF THE EXOTIC
Tropical cocktails call for elaborate garnishes – have some fun!

42ND STREET

■ INGREDIENTS

40ml (1½oz) Bourbon whiskey ■ 10ml (⅓oz) Grand Marnier ■ 10ml (⅓oz) Cointreau ■ 10ml (⅓oz) dry vermouth

■ EQUIPMENT

Mixing glass ■ stirring spoon ■ frosted Martini glass ■ strainer

This is the perfect Martini cocktail for Bourbon-lovers: it has all the rich, grain flavours of Bourbon with a touch of orange from the liqueurs, and then dried nuts from the vermouth in the finish. Its warm, amber hue and silky palate make it a truly perfect winter apéritif.

METHOD Place a few ice cubes in the mixing glass and pour in the ingredients. Stir well and strain into the Martini glass.

RITZ FIZZ

■ INGREDIENTS

Dash amaretto liqueur ■ dash blue curaçao ■ dash freshly squeezed lemon juice ■ dry Champagne or good-quality dry sparkling wine to fill

■ EQUIPMENT

Chilled Champagne flute ■ stirring spoon

This fabulous blue-coloured cocktail offers an amazing combination of almond from the amaretto, orange from the curaçao, and a kick of lemon – all topped off with exquisite Champagne bubbles. If you do not want to use Champagne, good-quality Cava is an excellent substitute.

METHOD Pour the amaretto, curaçao, and lemon juice into the glass. Stir gently, then slowly pour in the Champagne to fill. Garnish with lemon balm.

RITZ FIZZ

TOP NOTCH

■ INGREDIENTS

15ml (½oz) Havana Club light rum ■ 30ml (1oz) Midori melon liqueur ■ 15ml (½oz) Frangelico herb liqueur ■ 15ml (½oz) peach schnapps liqueur ■ 15ml (½oz) Malibu coconut rum liqueur ■ 30ml (1oz) freshly squeezed orange juice ■ 30ml (1oz) double cream

■ EQUIPMENT

Shaker ■ strainer ■ chilled tumbler

The host of herb and fruit flavours and the citrus of the orange balance the rich texture of this sweet cocktail. For the best results use blood (red) oranges, which are more tangy than regular oranges.

METHOD Fill the shaker with ice, add the ingredients, and strain into the glass. Garnish with a slice of kiwi fruit.

ABSOLUT ME

■ INGREDIENTS

45ml (1½oz) Absolut Kurant vodka ■ 20ml (⅔oz) crème de banane ■ 20ml (⅔oz) single cream ■ dash grenadine ■ dash freshly squeezed orange juice

■ EQUIPMENT

Shaker ■ strainer ■ highball glass

I love this mix as a winter apéritif. It is a drink to sip slowly – you need time to enjoy its complex, fresh flavours.

If, like me, you prefer your cocktails less creamy, use only a dash of cream.

METHOD Fill the shaker with ice and pour in all the ingredients. Shake vigorously and strain into the glass. Garnish with orange; serve with a straw.

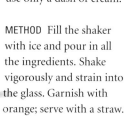

ABSOLUT ME

PORT FLIP

- **INGREDIENTS**
  30ml (1oz) brandy ▪ 90ml (3oz) ruby port ▪ yolk of one egg ▪ 1 tsp caster sugar

- **EQUIPMENT**
  Shaker ▪ strainer ▪ Martini glass

I am not a fan of raw egg, but I love this cocktail for its perfect balance of sweetness and alcohol. The result should be red-brown in colour, but is slightly paler if you use the white of the egg too. (This also gives a lighter texture.)

METHOD Place some ice in the shaker and pour in the ingredients. Shake for 12–14 seconds to fully integrate the egg. Strain into the glass and decorate with grated nutmeg.

CHI CHI

- **INGREDIENTS**
  40ml (1⅓oz) vodka ▪ 20ml (⅔oz) Malibu coconut rum liqueur ▪ 1 slice fresh pineapple

- **EQUIPMENT**
  Blender ▪ strainer ▪ hurricane or highball glass

This cocktail is so sweet that you can hardly taste the alcohol. Like the Piña Colada (see p360), which is made using rum not vodka, there is great harmony between the coconut of the Malibu and the pineapple.

METHOD Whizz one cup of ice with the other ingredients in a blender until smooth. Strain into an ice-filled glass. Garnish with pineapple and a cherry.

CHI CHI

BOURBON ROSE

- **INGREDIENTS**
  45ml (1½oz) Bourbon whiskey ▪ 30ml (1oz) triple sec ▪ 120ml (4oz) freshly squeezed orange juice ▪ 1 tsp grenadine

- **EQUIPMENT**
  Shaker ▪ strainer ▪ highball glass

The character of the Bourbon is the driving force behind this attractive, sunset-orange cocktail. Nevertheless, the triple sec and fresh orange juice provide plenty of zest, and the grenadine a slight sweetness.

METHOD Fill the shaker with ice and pour in all of the ingredients except the grenadine. Shake and strain into the ice-filled glass, then pour in the grenadine.

MELLOW YELLOW BIRD

- **INGREDIENTS**
  20ml (⅔oz) white or golden rum ▪ 20ml (⅔oz) Galliano liqueur ▪ 20ml (⅔oz) Cointreau ▪ freshly pressed pineapple juice ▪ freshly squeezed orange juice ▪ dash freshly squeezed lime juice

- **EQUIPMENT**
  Shaker ▪ strainer ▪ highball glass ▪ stirring spoon

Serve this mix well-chilled to make the most of its fresh flavours. White rum gives a drier drink; golden, sweeter.

METHOD Fill the shaker with ice. Add the rum, Galliano, and Cointreau. Strain into the glass and top with equal amounts of pineapple and orange juice. Add the lime, and stir. Garnish with mint.

MELLOW YELLOW BIRD

MELANCHOLY MARTINI

- **INGREDIENTS**
  30ml (1oz) Absolut vodka ▪ 30ml (1oz) Midori melon liqueur ▪ 15ml (½oz) Cointreau ▪ 15ml (½oz) Malibu coconut rum liqueur ▪ 30ml (1oz) freshly pressed pineapple juice ▪ 20ml (⅔oz) double cream ▪ 1½ tsp freshly squeezed lime juice

- **EQUIPMENT**
  Shaker ▪ strainer ▪ chilled Martini glass

Created in 2002 at the Ocean Bar in Edinburgh, Scotland, this is the cocktail to help you drown your sorrows! Its multiple flavours give a fine balance of sweetness, richness, and zest all winning through to make a fruity apéritif.

METHOD Fill the shaker with ice and pour in all the ingredients. Shake vigorously and strain into the glass. Serve with a wedge of pineapple.

CULTURE AND TRADITION

THE FAMOUS FACES OF COCKTAILS The cocktail owes much to the movies, and especially to 1930s and 1940s Hollywood glitterati. Cary Grant (shown here with Sylvia Sidney in 1934), Dorothy Parker, Spencer Tracy, and Errol Flynn are just a few famous names renowned for their love of cocktails. Many were often found in the company of novelist Ernest Hemingway – the greatest celebrity cocktail-drinker of all time.

DRINK AFTER DINNER

These cocktails are particularly fine during the winter season. They are intense, rich, and comforting, and some are very good at helping the digestion. With elements of spice and dairy richness, you can rely on these to make you feel a whole lot better on a cold, blustery day!

VANILLA COIN

■ **INGREDIENTS**
30ml (1oz) vanilla-flavoured vodka ▪ 30ml (1oz) Cointreau ▪ ginger ale to fill

■ **EQUIPMENT**
Highball glass ▪ stirring spoon

The structure of this cocktail is held together by the vanilla vodka, so try to get a really good brand – for the best results I like to use Absolut Vanilla. The subtle flavours of orange from the Cointreau and

vanilla from the vodka melt together to make the mix simply irresistible, and perfect for after dinner – or even after lunch! This mix is quite sweet, so if you prefer something drier, try using Canada Dry ginger ale.

VANILLA COIN

METHOD Place as much ice into the highball as you can. Add the vanilla vodka and then the Cointreau. Top with ginger ale. Stir gently and garnish with lemon balm.

BRANDY ALEXANDER

■ **INGREDIENTS**
20ml (⅔oz) brandy ▪ 20ml (⅔oz) brown crème de cacao ▪ 45ml (1½oz) double cream, or crème fraîche ▪ 1 tsp grated nutmeg

■ **EQUIPMENT**
Shaker ▪ strainer ▪ chilled Martini glass ▪ grater

The elegant Brandy Alexander reminds me of Baileys Irish Cream, without as much cream, but with the same delicious combination of chocolate and toffee-sweetness; it is perfect for after dinner.

The key to making a good Brandy Alexander is to ensure that all of the ingredients are well chilled before you begin; keep them in the fridge overnight if you can. The

BRANDY ALEXANDER

alternative of crème fraîche over double cream is simply a matter of taste – and calories! Crème fraîche is slightly less sweet and better for your waistline.

Of course there is now a whole family of Alexander cocktails. To make a Gin Alexander replace the brandy with gin and use white crème de cacao. For Alexander's Sister (with either brandy or gin) substitute green crème de menthe for the crème de cacao; use blue curaçao to create Alexander's Brother.

METHOD Fill the shaker with ice and add all the ingredients except the nutmeg. Shake for around 12 seconds to ensure that the cream is well integrated. Strain into the glass and dust a layer of grated nutmeg over the surface of the drink. Serve with a small straw if you wish.

COLORADO BOULEVARD

■ **INGREDIENTS**
20ml (⅔oz) vodka ▪ 20ml (⅔oz) Kahlúa coffee liqueur ▪ 20ml (⅔oz) fresh milk ▪ 20ml (⅔oz) still mineral water

■ **EQUIPMENT**
Shaker ▪ strainer ▪ chilled Martini glass

Strange as it seems, water is a crucial part of this cocktail, because it makes it light and unusually easy to drink. For the ultimate digestif combination, sip it after dinner with a small cigar. The mix is a milky-coffee colour.

METHOD Fill the shaker with ice and add all the ingredients. Shake well and then strain into a Martini glass containing a solitary cube of ice.

SWAMP THING

■ **INGREDIENTS**
30ml (1oz) vodka ▪ 15ml (½oz) Baileys Irish Cream liqueur, or other cream liqueur of your choice ▪ cola to fill

■ **EQUIPMENT**
Shaker ▪ strainer ▪ highball glass

Although the appearance of this cocktail might be offputtingly muddy, the Swamp Thing is truly amazing. It has a well balanced texture, combining smooth cream liqueur with a gentle fizz of cola. Its cosy, comforting flavours are dominated by toffee and vanilla.

METHOD Fill the shaker with ice and add the vodka and the cream liqueur. Shake and strain into an ice-filled highball. Top with cola. Garnish with a physalis, and serve with a stirrer.

SWAMP THING

BARTENDER'S TIP

The Brandy Alexander is odd because its garnish – a dusting of nutmeg – is not purely decorative, but actually adds a layer of flavour. More often, dusting – with grated nutmeg or cocoa powder – is just for visual appeal. As a general rule when dusting, remember that less is more!

METHOD Place the nutmeg in the bottom of a nutmeg grinder. Position the grinder over the cocktail and make one or two turns to leave a light sprinkling on the surface. If you do not have a grinder, use a small handheld grater; one or two strokes with the nutmeg should suffice.

Fill the nutmeg grinder   **Grind over the cocktail**

ALABAMA SLAMMER

- **INGREDIENTS**
  45ml (1½oz) Southern Comfort
  ▪ 45ml (1½oz) sloe gin ▪ 45ml (1½oz)
  amaretto liqueur ▪ 45ml (1½oz)
  freshly squeezed orange juice

- **EQUIPMENT**
  Mixing glass ▪ stirring spoon
  ▪ strainer ▪ Martini glass

With such an array of liqueurs in
the mix, it is no wonder that this
is a sweet and very rich cocktail.
However, the sweetness is well
balanced by the strong alcohol
content and a citrusy edge from
the orange juice.

METHOD Fill the mixing glass with
ice and pour in all the ingredients.
Stir until condensation appears on
the outside of the glass, as this
indicates that the contents are well
chilled. Strain into the Martini glass.

AMARETTO COMFORT

- **INGREDIENTS**
  20ml (⅔oz) Southern Comfort
  ▪ 20ml (⅔oz) amaretto liqueur

- **EQUIPMENT**
  Tumbler ▪ stirring spoon

This cocktail is sweet, soft, and
delicate. The mix effortlessly
combines the peach, plants, and
spices of the Southern Comfort,
with the apricot and almond of the
amaretto. If you do not have a sweet
tooth, I recommend dropping
a couple of ice cubes into the glass
to take the edge off the sweetness
and reinforce the flavours. This
cocktail is so easy to make that it is
perfect for impressing your guests
at the end of a dinner party.

METHOD Pour both ingredients
straight into the tumbler and stir
gently. Serve without garnish.

ALABAMA SLAMMER
*Despite the name, I do not
recommend "slamming" this
cocktail – it is too rich for
downing in one; sip it slowly.*

ALCAZAR

- **INGREDIENTS**
  30ml (1oz) Canadian Club whisky
  ▪ 10ml (⅓oz) Benedictine ▪ 20ml
  (⅔oz) single cream

- **EQUIPMENT**
  Tumbler ▪ bar spoon

This is the ideal after-dinner
cocktail, with a perfect balance of
flavours. The Alcazar offers smoky,
caramel sweetness from the whisky,
and herbs from the Benedictine; and
any harshness is softened by the
cream. If you prefer your mixes
even creamier, use double cream
instead of single.

METHOD Place a few cubes of ice in
the glass. Pour in the whisky and
Benedictine and stir. Place the tip
of the bar spoon in the liquid and
gently pour over the cream to create
a layer. Alternatively, dispense with
the layering and simply stir all the
ingredients together.

ALCAZAR *This
cocktail is much less
sweet and rich than
many others, making
it a great digestif.*

B-52

■ INGREDIENTS
20ml (⅔oz) Kahlúa coffee liqueur
■ 20ml (⅔oz) chilled Baileys Irish
Cream liqueur ■ 20ml (⅔oz)
Grand Marnier

■ EQUIPMENT
Shot glass or tumbler ■ bar spoon

This cocktail, named after the
American B-52 bombers, is the
original layered cocktail. Its three
distinct layers not only taste great,
but look great too! This is my perfect
Christmas cocktail, for drinking in
front of a roaring fire.

METHOD Pour the Kahlúa into
the glass. Rest the tip of the
bar spoon against the inside
of the glass, back or bowl
uppermost. Slowly pour the
Baileys and then the Grand
Marnier over the spoon to
create the layers.

BARTENDER'S TIP

When the ingredients of a cocktail
have different densities, the cocktail
can be layered – with each liquid
sitting on top of another. Pour in the
heaviest liquid (usually syrup) first
and the lightest (usually spirit) last.
(Liqueurs will fall between the two.)

METHOD The easiest method is
to pour the liquids one by one over
either side of a large teaspoon held
in the glass. If you have a bar spoon,
hold the flat end of the spoon in the
glass with the tip just touching the
uppermost liquid, then pour.

Layering with a bar spoon   A completed, layered B-52

AMARETTO COMFORT
*If you find this cocktail
too sweet to drink
straight, add a couple
of ice cubes to the glass.*

ASAP

■ INGREDIENTS
30ml (1oz) white crème de cacao
■ 20ml (⅔oz) Absolut Mandarin vodka
■ double cream

■ EQUIPMENT
Mixing glass ■ stirring spoon
■ chilled Martini glass ■ whisk

Drink this before bed and I promise
you a peaceful night's
sleep! This is a rich,
warming cocktail for
the end of the day. The
mandarin of the vodka
gives a pleasant citrus finish,
and the colour is a delicate pale
gold, topped with white.

METHOD Fill the mixing glass with
ice and pour in everything except
the cream. Stir well and strain into
the Martini glass. Top with
lightly whisked cream.
Garnish with a little grated
bitter chocolate.

BELFAST BROWNIE

■ INGREDIENTS
20ml (⅔oz) Irish cream liqueur
■ 20ml (⅔oz) brown crème de cacao
■ 20ml (⅔oz) curaçao ■ 4 pieces
candied orange peel ■ 2 tbsp
single cream

■ EQUIPMENT
Blender ■ strainer
■ chilled Martini glass

This warm and
creamy cocktail
reminds me of orange-
flavoured chocolate. It is
heaven for anyone with a
sweet tooth. Serve it really well
chilled to bring out the full
complexity of the flavours.

METHOD Mix all the ingredients
in the blender and then strain
into the chilled Martini
glass. If you prefer, you
could serve it over ice
in a tumbler.

BELFAST BROWNIE

AFTER EIGHT

■ INGREDIENTS
30ml (1oz) white crème de cacao
■ 30ml (1oz) white crème de menthe
■ 30ml (1oz) whisky (of any kind)
■ 1 small cup espresso coffee or
strong filter coffee ■ warm milk to fill

■ EQUIPMENT
Shaker ■ stirring spoon ■ toddy
or hurricane glass

This cocktail has all the
pleasure of after-dinner
mints, but in a glass. The
whisky cuts through the
creamy texture to give a
good balance to the
mix. If you have a sweet
tooth, add a spoon of sugar.

METHOD Pour the liqueurs and
the whisky into the shaker.
Shake well. Add the coffee,
and pour the mixture into
the glass. Stir in warm milk.

AFTER EIGHT

BANANA BLISS

■ INGREDIENTS
30ml (1oz) brandy ■ 30ml (1oz)
crème de banane

■ EQUIPMENT
Mixing glass ■ stirring spoon
■ strainer ■ chilled Martini glass

This is a tonic among cocktails –
a sunset-yellow energizer
to pick you up at the end
of a meal. The brandy
cuts through the sweet,
creamy texture of the
banana liqueur to give
long-lasting enjoyment.
Any VS-quality Cognac
will be sufficient.

METHOD Fill the mixing glass
with ice cubes and pour in the
ingredients. Stir well and
strain into the glass.
There is no need to
decorate this drink.

BMW

■ INGREDIENTS
30ml (1oz) Baileys Irish Cream liqueur
■ 30ml (1oz) Malibu coconut rum
liqueur ■ 30ml (1oz) whisky

■ EQUIPMENT
Shaker ■ strainer ■ tumbler

The BMW (the name comes from
the initials of the ingredients, rather
than from the German car-maker)
is quite strong but easy to
drink. Its mellow, creamy
texture is perfect to round
off a meal.

METHOD Fill a shaker
with ice and pour in all
the ingredients. Shake,
and then strain into an
ice-filled glass. Garnish
with a sprig of mint.
You could also serve the
BMW in a Martini glass,
but without ice cubes.

BMW

CLIMAX

■ INGREDIENTS
15ml (½oz) amaretto liqueur
■ 15ml (½oz) white crème de cacao
■ 15ml (½oz) triple sec ■ 15ml (½oz)
vodka ■ 15ml (½oz) crème de banane
■ 30ml (1oz) single cream

■ EQUIPMENT
Shaker ■ strainer
■ chilled Martini glass

This is an awesome
cocktail with lots of
rich flavour and a
smooth texture. Enjoy
it slowly as an after-
dinner treat on a cold
autumn evening.

METHOD Fill the shaker
with ice and pour in all
the ingredients. Shake
vigorously, then strain
into the Martini glass.
Serve with a straw.

BLACK RUSSIAN

■ INGREDIENTS
45ml (1½oz) vodka ■ 30ml (1oz)
Kahlúa coffee liqueur

■ EQUIPMENT
Tumbler ■ stirring spoon

In the early 1950s Gustave Tops,
barman at the Hotel Metropole in
Brussels, Belgium, first mixed the
Black Russian for Perle Mesta, the
US Ambassador to Luxembourg at
the time. The drink is a classic to this
day. I particularly love the way the
vodka supports the coffee and
chocolate flavours of
the Kahlúa.

METHOD Place some
ice in the glass, and
pour in all the
ingredients. Stir, and
garnish with a cherry
on a cocktail stick.

BLACK RUSSIAN

WHITE RUSSIAN

■ INGREDIENTS
30ml (1oz) vodka ■ 15ml (½oz) Kahlúa
coffee liqueur ■ double cream to top

■ EQUIPMENT
Tumbler ■ bar spoon ■ whisk

This variation of the famous Black
Russian also dates from the 1950s.
The cream adds to the velvety
texture of the Kahlúa making a
rich, creamy-white cocktail with
a refreshing, clean vodka finish
(use Absolut for the best results).

METHOD Place some ice
in a tumbler and add
both the vodka and
Kahlúa. Stir for ten
seconds. Lightly whip
the cream in a separate
container, and then
using the back or bowl
of the bar spoon layer
the whisked cream on
top. Serve with a straw.

WHITE BULL

■ INGREDIENTS
30ml (1oz) white tequila
■ 30ml (1oz) Kahlúa coffee liqueur
■ double cream to top

■ EQUIPMENT
Chilled Martini glass ■ whisk
■ bar spoon

This variation on the classic White
Russian has a beautiful
combination of
flavours: coffee from
the Kahlúa and spice
from the tequila. For
the best results chill the
ingredients before mixing.

METHOD Pour the tequila and then
the Kahlúa into the glass. Lightly
whip the cream, then using the
back or bowl of the bar spoon,
carefully create a layer of cream
on top of the cocktail.

WHITE BULL

DRAMATIC MARTINI

■ INGREDIENTS
30ml (1oz) Tuaca liqueur ■ 30ml (1oz)
Grand Marnier ■ 30ml (1oz) Baileys
Irish Cream liqueur ■ 30ml (1oz) milk

■ EQUIPMENT
Shaker ■ strainer
■ chilled Martini glass

Tuaca is an Italian brandy-based
liqueur with sweet
flavours of vanilla
and orange. I
particularly love the
Dramatic Martini for
its combination of orange
and herbs, and the hint of
hazelnut from the Baileys.
Delicious! This cocktail is the
colour of milky coffee.

METHOD Fill the shaker with ice
and add all the ingredients. Shake,
and then strain into the
glass. Garnish with a
dusting of nutmeg.

EGG NOG

- **INGREDIENTS**
  90ml (3oz) good quality brandy
  - 90ml (3oz) dark rum ■ 165ml
  (5½oz) fresh milk ■ dash sugar syrup
  - yolk of one egg

- **EQUIPMENT**
  Shaker ■ strainer ■ highball glass
  - stirring spoon

This amazing mix is a classic Christmas treat. For a less alcoholic version you could drop the rum or brandy according to your own preference. Traditionally, Egg Nog is made using cold milk, but you can turn it into Hot Egg Nog by warming the milk before mixing.

METHOD Fill the shaker with ice and add the brandy, rum, egg yolk, and sugar syrup. Shake vigorously and strain into the glass. Pour in the cold milk and stir. Garnish with a light dusting of nutmeg.

CULTURE AND TRADITION

EGG NOG Although the origins of Egg Nog are not clear, it is likely to have derived from the English drink "posset", a mixture of sherry and milk served in a "noggin", a small, wooden mug. By the 19th century Egg Nog as we know it had become a favourite Christmas drink on both sides of the Atlantic.

GEORGE WASHINGTON *The first US president's own powerful Egg Nog recipe used whisky, rum, and sherry.*

GODFATHER

- **INGREDIENTS**
  30ml (1oz) Bourbon whiskey
  - 30ml (1oz) amaretto liqueur

- **EQUIPMENT**
  Tumbler ■ stirring spoon

As its name suggests, this is the definitive Italian-American cocktail! Although the textures of US Bourbon and Italian amaretto are quite different, in this mix they complement each other perfectly; the result is a big, strong cocktail, with a small, citrus kick. I think it is best-suited for drinking late at night.

METHOD Pour the Bourbon and amaretto into the glass and stir. Add three or four ice cubes and serve with slices of star fruit or lime.

GODFATHER

GODMOTHER

- **INGREDIENTS**
  30ml (1oz) vodka ■ 30ml (1oz) amaretto liqueur

- **EQUIPMENT**
  Tumbler ■ stirring spoon

If you like amaretto then you are guaranteed to love this pale-amber cocktail: the toffee and vanilla of the liqueur are reinforced by the vodka's alcohol (use a good brand such as Absolut or Skyy). If you want to take the edge off the sweetness, you could reduce the amaretto to 20ml (⅔oz) and increase the vodka to 40ml (1⅓oz) to compensate.

METHOD Place four ice cubes in the glass. Add the vodka and amaretto. Stir. Decorate with a dusting of cocoa powder and a zest of orange if you wish.

GOLDEN CADILLAC

- **INGREDIENTS**
  30ml (1oz) Galliano liqueur
  - 60ml (2oz) white crème de cacao
  - 30ml (1oz) single cream

- **EQUIPMENT**
  Shaker ■ strainer ■ chilled Martini glass

This 1960s American cocktail is one of the most successful after-dinner drinks of all. It has a warm, off-white colour with hints of yellow, and is creamy but delicate. The chocolate liqueur just takes the edge off the Galliano's powerful herbs, to make a really complex mix.

METHOD Fill the shaker with ice and pour in all the ingredients. Shake vigorously and strain into the glass. Serve with a small straw.

BRUISED APPLE

- **INGREDIENTS**
  30ml (1oz) Zubrówka vodka
  - 30ml (1oz) puréed apple
  - dash apple syrup ■ dash Chambord raspberry liqueur

- **EQUIPMENT**
  Mixing glass ■ bar spoon ■ strainer

This is a great party cocktail combining apple freshness with a good vodka "kick".

METHOD Fill the mixing glass with ice. Add the vodka, apple purée, and syrup. Stir. Put the Chambord into the Martini glass. Strain the vodka mixture down the spiral handle of the bar spoon and into the Martini glass so that it "floats" on the Chambord. Garnish with a lime wheel.

BRUISED APPLE

GRASSHOPPER

■ **INGREDIENTS**
30ml (1oz) green crème de menthe ▪ 30ml (1oz) white crème de cacao ▪ 30ml single cream

■ **EQUIPMENT**
Shaker ▪ strainer ▪ chilled Martini glass

Named the Grasshopper after its pastel green colour, this cocktail is like mint chocolate in a glass. Serve it well chilled to get the freshest flavours out of the mint.

METHOD Fill the shaker with ice cubes and pour in all the ingredients. Shake vigorously for ten seconds to thoroughly chill the contents, and strain into the glass. To garnish, grate a little bitter chocolate on the top.

RUSTY NAIL

■ **INGREDIENTS**
60ml (2oz) blended Scotch whisky ▪ 30ml (1oz) Drambuie

■ **EQUIPMENT**
Tumbler ▪ stirring spoon

This cocktail has been a hit since its creation in Scotland in the 1950s. I like it on the rocks; but you could drink it without ice at room temperature, in which case it will feel richer and more alcoholic. I use Famous Grouse for the whisky as it is well balanced but not too flavoursome.

METHOD Fill the glass with ice, add all of the ingredients, and stir. Garnish with a lemon rind in the glass (squeeze its oils into the drink first for extra complexity) and add a cherry.

RUSTY NAIL

IRISH COFFEE

■ **INGREDIENTS**
2 tsp brown sugar ▪ 60ml (2oz) Bushmills Irish whiskey ▪ 150–180ml (5–6oz) hot, strong, black coffee ▪ Double cream to top

■ **EQUIPMENT**
Toddy glass (or wine glass with firm walls) ▪ bar spoon

What better way to end a meal than with this classic cocktail? In 1942 a bartender at what is now Shannon Airport (then it was known as Foynes Airport), in the Republic of Ireland, created the Irish Coffee. However, his classic concoction lay largely undiscovered until 1947, when a US journalist returning home tried the special coffee and thought it so delicious that he took the recipe back to San Francisco, from where word spread. Stick to the recipe for this drink – never be tempted to use longlife cream.

METHOD First, warm the glass: fill it with hot water, leave for two minutes, then tip the water out. Pour in the sugar and whiskey, followed by the coffee. Stir. Using the back or bowl of a bar spoon, float the cream on top.

MIXING IT UP

THE COFFEE-LIQUEUR FAMILY
Coffee mixes well with spirits and liqueurs other than Irish whiskey. Here are some ideas:

CAFÉ AMORE
Amaretto and brandy
CALYPSO COFFEE
rum and Kahlúa
JAMAICAN COFFEE
rum and Tia Maria
KIOKE COFFEE
brandy and Kahlúa
MEXICAN COFFEE
tequila and Kahlúa
PRESIDENT'S COFFEE
cherry brandy
ROYALE
Cognac

MUD SLIDE

■ **INGREDIENTS**
30ml (1oz) vodka ▪ 30ml (1oz) Kahlúa coffee liqueur ▪ 30ml (1oz) Dooley's toffee cream liqueur

■ **EQUIPMENT**
Chilled shot glass ▪ bar spoon

This delicious cocktail looks like a million dollars, and tastes like five million! Delicate, rich, and warming, it has amazing length and is perfect for cold winter nights around the fire. For the best results use Absolut vodka, and if you are unable to find Dooley's liqueur, replace it with Baileys Irish Cream.

METHOD Using the back or bowl of the spoon layer the ingredients into the shot glass in the following order: Kahlúa, then Dooley's, and finally the vodka.

MUD SLIDE

MULTIPLE ORGASM

■ **INGREDIENTS**
15ml (½oz) white crème de cacao ▪ 15ml (½oz) amaretto liqueur ▪ 15ml (½oz) triple sec ▪ 15ml (½oz) vodka ▪ 30ml (1oz) single cream

■ **EQUIPMENT**
Shaker ▪ strainer ▪ chilled glass

The complexity and intensity of the flavours in this cocktail are almost overwhelming! The neutral vodka provides the backbone for the perfectly balanced cocoa, almond, sweet apricot, and orange of the liqueurs. It is simply spectacular!

METHOD Fill the shaker half full with ice. Add all of the ingredients and shake well for ten seconds. Strain into the glass.

MULTIPLE ORGASM

STINGER

■ **INGREDIENTS**
40ml (1⅓oz) Cognac ▪ 20ml (⅔oz) white crème de menthe

■ **EQUIPMENT**
Mixing glass ▪ stirring spoon ▪ strainer ▪ chilled Martini glass

This golden cocktail was first mixed in the 1920s and was hugely popular in the US during Prohibition (1920–1933), because the taste of mint masked the rough flavours of bootleg liquor. For me it makes a perfect digestif, combining the warmth of Cognac with the freshness of mint.

METHOD Fill the mixing glass with ice and pour in the ingredients. Stir for ten seconds and strain into the glass.

SNOWBALL

■ **INGREDIENTS**
30ml (1oz) vodka ▪ sparkling lemonade (such as Sprite or 7 Up) as necessary ▪ 30ml (1oz) advocaat liqueur

■ **EQUIPMENT**
Tumbler or highball glass ▪ stirring spoon

The rich Snowball is a revolutionary cocktail. First created in the early 20th century, it marks the transition between simple, long drinks, such as whisky and soda, and "punch"-style drinks, which mix several spirits into longer cocktails.

METHOD Pour the vodka into the glass and add lemonade to two-thirds of the way up. Add a few ice cubes and then pour in the advocaat. Stir.

SNOWBALL

IRISH COFFEE *For the perfect cream top, dip the tip of a bar spoon into the coffee and pour the cream over it. Alternatively, hold a teaspoon, either way up, over the coffee and slowly let the cream flow over it.*

" A wonderful marriage of zesty fruits and spirit, with a great alcohol balance. The perfect thirst quenchers for warm summer evenings. "

DRY, FRUITY, AND FRESH

INTRODUCING DRY, FRUITY, AND FRESH COCKTAILS

These are cocktails to drink at the end of the day to help you unwind. They have the power to refresh you, as well as prepare you for dinner, or cool you down on a hot day.

BRAMBLE *Gin and crème de mûre form this refreshing cooler.*

DRINKING AND SERVING

DRINK PROFILE The key look for these cocktails is fresh and appealing. Many are clear, or nearly clear, with just a hint of colour from vermouth, bitters, or fruit juice in the mix. Garnishes may help to highlight any subtleties in hue, and the ingredients should be well chilled, so that a slight frosting of condensation appears on the outside of the glass. Aromas should be fruity and fresh, and not too strong or overpowering – they should invite you to drink and savour. Dry, fruity, and fresh cocktails are sophisticated drinks to be sipped slowly – they are dry, even extremely dry, and are definitely not for downing in one go.

Dry, with the added complexity of fruit, these cocktails are essentially apéritifs. The group includes some of the most popular of all cocktails – including the Martini (gin and vermouth), Manhattan (Bourbon, vermouth, and bitters), Bellini (peach juice and sparkling wine), Screwdriver (vodka and orange juice), and Kir Royal (blackcurrant liqueur and Champagne).

The aim of the fruit in many of these cocktails is not to sweeten the drink, but to make the cocktail fresh. One of the most important aspects about this group of cocktails is temperature – ice-cold is key. Not only does this bring out the complexity in the flavours, but it heightens both the dryness and freshness of the cocktail. As a rule of thumb, chill the ingredients thoroughly before you mix.

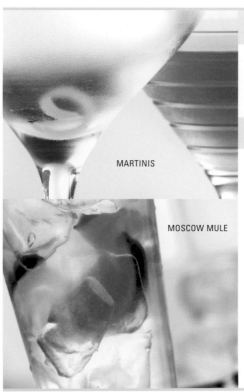

MARTINIS

MOSCOW MULE

DRY, FRUITY, AND FRESH COCKTAILS

Dry and fruity cocktails are probably those that will appeal to the broadest range of drinkers – they are to the world of cocktails as Chardonnay is to the world of wine. Use this table to find your perfect mix – a dry, fruity, and fresh cocktail made with your favourite base spirit.

BASE	COCKTAIL	OTHER INGREDIENTS
GIN	Alcudia *(see p374)*	Galliano, crème de banane, grapefruit juice
	Gimlet *(see p375)*	Lime juice
	Strawberry Martini *(see p376)*	Strawberries, sugar syrup, black pepper
	Italian Martini *(see p376)*	Dry vermouth, Galliano liqueur
	Classic Dry Gin Martini *(see p376)*	Dry vermouth
	Ballantine's *(see p381)*	Dry vermouth, orange bitters, Pernod
	Bramble *(see p381)*	Lime juice, sugar syrup, crème de mûre
	Macca *(see p381)*	Dry vermouth, sweet vermouth, crème de cassis, soda water
	Dubonnet Cocktail *(see p381)*	Dubonnet, Angostura bitters
	A1 *(see p383)*	Grand Marnier, lemon juice, grenadine

BASE	COCKTAIL	OTHER INGREDIENTS
GIN (CONT.)	Pink Lady *(see p384)*	Grenadine, egg white, lemon juice, sugar syrup
	Pink Gin *(see p385)*	Angostura bitters
RUM	Melon Daiquiri *(see p375)*	Lime juice, sugar syrup, Midori
	Angel *(see p375)*	Grand Marnier, lemon juice, orange juice, cranberry juice
	Mojito *(see p378)*	Mint leaves, lime juice, sugar, soda water
	Long Island Iced Tea *(see p378)*	Gin, vodka, tequila, lime juice, cola
	Planter's Punch *(see p378)*	Lime juice, sugar syrup, grenadine, Angostura bitters, soda water
	Blue Hawaiian *(see p381)*	Blue curaçao, pineapple juice, cream of coconut
	Rum Swizzle *(see p384)*	Lime juice, caster sugar, Angostura bitters, soda water
	Mai Tai *(see p384)*	Lime juice, Grand Marnier, almond syrup, sugar syrup
	Zombie *(see p384)*	Cherry brandy, pineapple juice, orange juice, lime juice, papaya juice, almond syrup
VODKA	Screwdriver *(see p374)*	Orange juice
	Sea Breeze *(see p374)*	Cranberry juice, grapefruit juice
	747 *(see p375)*	Lime cordial, cranberry juice, lemonade
	Madras *(see p375)*	Cranberry juice, orange juice
	Moscow Mule *(see p378)*	Lime juice, ginger ale
	Showbiz *(see p380)*	Crème de cassis, grapefruit juice
	Babar *(see p384)*	Passoã, guanabana juice, cranberry juice, lemonade
CHAMPAGNE	Buck's Fizz *(see p374)*	Orange juice
	Champagne Cocktail *(see p379)*	Sugar lump, Angostura bitters, brandy
	Kir Royal *(see p380)*	Crème de cassis
	Pick Me Up *(see p380)*	Brandy, orange juice, grenadine
	Bolli Stolli *(see p380)*	Vodka
	Bellini *(see p381)*	White peach juice
WHISKY	Mint Julep *(see p378)*	Sugar syrup, sprigs of mint
	Old Fashioned *(see p378)*	Angostura bitters, sugar cube, soda water
	Quicky *(see p381)*	Rum, triple sec
	Manhattan *(see p383)*	Sweet vermouth, Angostura bitters
	Brooklyn *(see p383)*	Sweet red vermouth, Campari
BRANDY	Champs-Elysées *(see p380)*	Green Chartreuse, lemon juice, Angostura bitters
	Biarritz *(see p384)*	Grand Marnier, lemon juice, egg white, Angostura bitters
	Jack Rose *(see p384)*	Lime juice, grenadine
PIMM'S	Pimm's No.1 Cup *(see p382)*	Lime juice, ginger ale

CHAMPAGNE COCKTAIL

PIMM'S

PINK GIN

MANHATTAN

DRINK ANYTIME

This group includes some of the world's most famous cocktails. They are popular and approachable, with heaps of fruit and a slightly exotic character, and they make ideal summer coolers. Note that the colder the cocktail, the earlier in the day you can enjoy it!

BUCK'S FIZZ

BUCK'S FIZZ

■ **INGREDIENTS**
60ml (2oz) freshly squeezed orange juice ▪ 90ml (3oz) dry Champagne or good-quality sparkling wine

■ **EQUIPMENT**
Strainer ▪ chilled Champagne flute

This cheerful party drink was first mixed in 1921 by a certain Mr McGarry, a bartender at the Buck's Club in London. Personally, I like a glass of Buck's Fizz with breakfast on the morning of a lazy Sunday or special occasion – what better way to

begin a birthday or anniversary than with this vibrant, fruity, and fizzy energy-booster?

Although Buck's Fizz is traditionally made with Champagne, a good sparkling wine, such as high quality Cava from northeast Spain, can work equally well. If you want to get the best from the zesty orange, it is crucial that the glass is well chilled.

METHOD Pour the orange juice into the glass through the strainer to remove any pieces of orange flesh. Gently pour in the Champagne to fill. Garnish with a mint sprig.

SCREWDRIVER

■ **INGREDIENTS**
60ml (2oz) vodka ▪ freshly squeezed orange juice to fill

■ **EQUIPMENT**
Shaker ▪ strainer ▪ highball glass

In the 1950s US oilmen in the Arabian desert used screwdrivers to stir their vodka-orange mixes, giving this cocktail its name. I like to use Smirnoff vodka – its peppery notes go well with orange. For extra citrus try adding a dash of Cointreau.

METHOD Place ice in the shaker. Pour in the juice and vodka; shake. Strain into a highball containing some ice. Garnish with a slice of orange and cherry.

SCREWDRIVER

GARIBALDI

■ **INGREDIENTS**
30ml (1oz) Campari ▪ 75ml (2½oz) freshly squeezed orange juice

■ **EQUIPMENT**
Tumbler ▪ stirring spoon

I just love this cocktail! Although it is sometimes known as the Campari Orange, I prefer the name that commemorates the Italian hero General Giuseppe Garibaldi, whose army wore distinctive red scarves – like the sunset-red of this mix.

The fresh orange and bitter Campari make this a perfect refresher or apéritif.

METHOD Place two or three ice cubes in the highball glass. Pour in the Campari and then the orange juice. Stir. Decorate with a slice of orange on the rim.

SEA BREEZE

■ **INGREDIENTS**
60ml (2oz) vodka ▪ 120ml (4oz) cranberry juice ▪ 60ml (2oz) freshly squeezed grapefruit juice

■ **EQUIPMENT**
Shaker ▪ strainer ▪ highball glass

The Sea Breeze is thought to have been first mixed in the 1920s in New York, but its present popularity owes much to Absolut, which – since the 1990s – has promoted its brand as the perfect Sea Breeze vodka. I absolutely agree: this vodka's gentle sweetness is a great match for the tangy cranberry and grapefruit juices.

METHOD Fill the shaker with ice, and pour in the ingredients. Shake well and strain into the glass.

SEA BREEZE

TEQUILA SUNRISE

■ **INGREDIENTS**
60ml (2oz) tequila ▪ freshly squeezed orange juice to fill ▪ dash grenadine

■ **EQUIPMENT**
Highball glass ▪ stirring spoon

The Tequila Sunrise is a classic holiday cocktail. It is thought to have been created in the 1950s in Mexico as a mix to welcome tourists to the holiday hotspots of Acapulco and Cancún. However, a more interesting story is that a certain wayward bartender, caught by his boss drinking behind the bar in the early hours of the morning, excused his presence by saying that he was trying to create a cocktail that reminded him of the

TEQUILA SUNRISE

sunrise: of course, for the sake of authenticity, he had to perfect the drink as the dawn broke!

Whatever its origins, this is a wonderful, vibrant, and refreshing cocktail that looks and tastes great. It makes excellent summer drinking, especially at a party. But beware! The sweet grenadine masks the strong alcohol of the tequila and it can be very easy to drink one too many.

METHOD Place two ice cubes in the highball. Pour in the tequila and the orange juice and then stir well for a few seconds. Add the dash of grenadine. Wait a few moments before serving the cocktail; the syrup sinks to the bottom of the glass, giving a beautiful sunrise effect. (Once the grenadine is in, do not stir again.) Decorate the glass with slices of orange and star fruit, and add a Maraschino cherry.

ALCUDIA

■ **INGREDIENTS**
30ml (1oz) gin ▪ 15ml (½oz) Galliano liqueur ▪ 15ml (½oz) crème de banane ▪ dash freshly squeezed grapefruit juice

■ **EQUIPMENT**
Shaker ▪ strainer ▪ chilled Martini glass

Such a mixture of flavours – the sweetness of Galliano, freshness of gin, richness of banana, and sourness of grapefruit – may appear over-complex, but it works brilliantly, bringing several layers of flavour to the palate in this opaque cocktail. However, to make the most of the citrus, and to keep control of the sweetness, ensure that the mix is served well chilled.

METHOD Fill the shaker with ice and pour in all the ingredients. Shake vigorously and strain into the Martini glass. Serve ungarnished.

747

■ **INGREDIENTS**
30ml (1oz) vodka ▪ Rose's lime cordial and cranberry juice in equal measures, to taste ▪ sparkling lemonade (Sprite or 7 Up)

■ **EQUIPMENT**
Highball glass ▪ stirring spoon

This elegant, long drink is light and refreshing, with subtle aromas. For the best results use Absolut or Finlandia vodka. If you prefer your mixes drier rather than sweeter, you could use soda water instead of lemonade.

METHOD Fill the highball with ice and pour in the ingredients, beginning with the vodka and ending with the lemonade. Stir gently and serve with a straw.

747

MELON DAIQUIRI

■ **INGREDIENTS**
60ml (2oz) white rum ▪ 45ml (1½oz) freshly squeezed lime juice ▪ 15ml (½oz) sugar syrup ▪ 15ml (½oz) Midori melon liqueur

■ **EQUIPMENT**
Shaker ▪ strainer ▪ chilled Martini glass

This version of the famous Daiquiri (created in 1896 by US engineer Jennings Cox) is an exotic cocktail, perfect for summer parties. It has a wonderful, springtime-green hue from the Midori.

METHOD Place some ice cubes in the shaker and add the ingredients. Shake well for ten seconds to fully cool the contents. Strain into the glass. Garnish with a wedge of lime on the rim.

GIMLET

■ **INGREDIENTS**
60ml (2oz) Plymouth gin ▪ 30ml (1oz) freshly squeezed lime juice

■ **EQUIPMENT**
Shaker ▪ strainer ▪ chilled Martini glass

This classic, pale-yellow, gin cocktail takes its name from the small tool once used on board naval vessels to tap spirit barrels. I think it is best with Plymouth gin, which is more perfumed and earthy than London Dry. An alternative is the Vodka Gimlet – simply replace the gin with vodka.

METHOD Fill the shaker with ice and add all the ingredients. Shake, then strain into the glass. Decorate with a wedge of lime and a cherry.

ANGEL

■ **INGREDIENTS**
15ml (½oz) Grand Marnier ▪ 15ml (½oz) white rum ▪ dash freshly squeezed lemon juice ▪ 15ml (½oz) freshly squeezed orange juice ▪ 15ml (½oz) cranberry juice ▪ 2 tsp egg white (optional)

■ **EQUIPMENT**
Shaker ▪ strainer ▪ Martini glass

Created in the 1940s, this cocktail is both intense and subtle. Its flavours are dominated by the orange of the Grand Marnier and the citrus, but are softened by the egg white, which also gives it a creamy feel.

METHOD Fill the shaker with ice and add all the ingredients. Shake well and strain into the glass. Garnish with fresh berries.

ANGEL

MADRAS

■ **INGREDIENTS**
60ml (2oz) Absolut vodka ▪ 60ml (2oz) cranberry juice ▪ 60ml (2oz) freshly squeezed orange juice

■ **EQUIPMENT**
Shaker ▪ strainer ▪ highball glass

This variation of the classic Sea Breeze, which uses orange juice rather than grapefruit (*see opposite*), offers a light touch of sweetness to balance the citrus of the orange. Serve the cocktail well chilled to get the most from its appealing fruitiness. I prefer to use blood oranges rather than ordinary ones – they give the cocktail just that little extra layer of complexity.

METHOD Fill the shaker with ice and pour in all the ingredients. Shake very briefly and then strain into a highball containing just one ice cube. Place a slice of orange in the glass and serve with a straw.

CULTURE AND TRADITION

NON-ALCOHOLIC COCKTAILS
Nicknamed "mocktails", these make delicious alternatives for non-drinkers – and especially for children. Try the Lemon Squash: add the juice of half a lemon and a dash of sugar syrup to a glass, and top it up with still mineral water; or the Shirley Temple (named after the 1930s child star) – a large dash of grenadine topped with ginger ale in an ice-filled highball.

LEMON SQUASH

SHIRLEY TEMPLE

SHIRLEY TEMPLE *The child actress is said to have drunk a mix of ginger ale and grenadine at her movie premières.*

STRAWBERRY GIN MARTINI

■ INGREDIENTS
Five ripe strawberries, crushed
■ 75ml (2½oz) London Dry gin
■ 15ml (½oz) sugar syrup
■ two pinches black pepper

■ EQUIPMENT
Shaker ■ strainer ■ chilled
Martini glass

This version of the Martini rivals some of the greatest classic cocktails – the strawberry and gin are great in combination, as the zestiness of the gin picks up the sweetness of the fruit. If you prefer drier-style cocktails, replace the gin with vodka.

METHOD Put the crushed strawberries in the bottom of the shaker. Fill the shaker with ice, and add the rest of the ingredients. Shake well and strain into the glass. Garnish with a strawberry on the rim of the glass if you wish.

ITALIAN MARTINI

■ INGREDIENTS
15ml (½oz) dry vermouth ■ 15ml (½oz) Galliano liqueur ■ 45ml (1½oz) London Dry gin

■ EQUIPMENT
Mixing glass ■ stirring spoon
■ strainer ■ chilled Martini glass

The Italian Martini (made Italian by the addition of Galliano liqueur) does not have the subtlety of the original Martini. Instead, it is an upfront mix, perfect as a dinner apéritif. Use Noilly Prat or Martini Extra Dry vermouth.

METHOD Fill the mixing glass with ice. Add the vermouth, Galliano, and gin, stirring well to thoroughly chill the ingredients. Strain into the Martini glass. Garnish with a lemon zest twist dropped into the glass.

CLASSIC DRY GIN MARTINI

■ INGREDIENTS
45ml (1½oz) London Dry gin
■ 15ml (½oz) dry vermouth

■ EQUIPMENT
Mixing glass ■ stirring spoon
■ strainer ■ chilled Martini glass

This is possibly the most famous and sophisticated cocktail ever mixed. There are many stories about its exact origins, but many authorities believe that it was first made in 1911 at New York's Knickerbocker Hotel by a bartender called Martini.

There are two important elements in mixing the perfect Dry Martini. First, the ingredients must be ice cold. The best way to achieve this is to stir them with ice a little longer than you might any other cocktail. Second, the ingredients must be as dry as possible. For the best results, I recommend you use Noilly Prat or Martini Extra Dry vermouth. If you shake the Dry Martini rather than stir, the mix is known as a Bradford.

METHOD Fill the mixing glass with ice. Add the vermouth. Stir well and strain away the liquid, leaving only the flavoured ice. Pour in the gin, stir, and strain into the Martini glass; garnish by dropping in a green olive.

STRAWBERRY GIN MARTINI
Straining out the flesh of the strawberries to leave only the juice produces a beautiful pink cocktail, with a soft hint of the delicious fruit.

ITALIAN MARTINI *A Tuscan distiller created Galliano liqueur at the end of the 19th century. It adds a honey and peppermint edge to the Martini, and a subtle hint of yellow.*

VANILLA VODKATINI (VANILLATINI)

■ **INGREDIENTS**
60ml (2oz) vanilla-flavoured vodka ■ dash dry vermouth

■ **EQUIPMENT**
Mixing glass ■ stirring spoon ■ strainer ■ chilled Martini glass

When you ask for a Martini in the US – and increasingly worldwide, too – chances are it will be made with vodka rather than gin. Technically, this drink should not be called a Martini, but a Vodkatini. But let's not split hairs! When made with vanilla-flavoured vodka, a Vodkatini becomes a Vanillatini. I like this elegant cocktail with home-made vanilla-infused vodka, but Absolut Vanilla also works well.

METHOD Fill the mixing glass with ice and pour in the vermouth. Stir well and strain away the liquid. Pour in the vodka and stir again. Strain into the Martini glass. Garnish with a twist of lemon peel and perhaps a vanilla pod.

VANILLA VODKATINI

GIBSON

■ **INGREDIENTS**
45ml (1½oz) Plymouth gin ■ 15ml (½oz) dry vermouth ■ two white cocktail onions

■ **EQUIPMENT**
Mixing glass ■ stirring spoon ■ strainer ■ chilled Martini glass

There are many variations of the classic Dry Martini, and this mix was created in the 1940s for Charles Dana Gibson, a US illustrator, and presumably a ladies' man too – the two cocktail onions are said to represent the breasts of his female admirers! As far as the mix goes, the onions take the biting edge off the gin and add their own layer of complexity.

METHOD Place some ice in the mixing glass and pour in the vermouth. Stir and strain away the liquid. Pour in the gin and stir again. Strain into the Martini glass containing the two onions on a cocktail stick.

GIBSON

PARADISE (MARTINI)

■ **INGREDIENTS**
60ml (2oz) Plymouth gin ■ 30ml (1oz) apricot brandy liqueur ■ 30ml (1oz) freshly squeezed orange juice

■ **EQUIPMENT**
Shaker ■ strainer ■ chilled Martini glass

Thought to have been first mixed in the UK in the 1920s, this is a fruity cocktail with great harmony of flavours. Take care to mix according to the precise measurements, otherwise the marriage of flavours can go awry. This drink is quick and easy to make – especially if you leave out the garnish – so perfect for parties.

METHOD Place some ice cubes in the shaker and pour in all the ingredients. Shake for about six seconds and strain into the chilled Martini glass. Garnish with a flamed orange peel and a few leaves of lemon balm.

CLASSIC DRY GIN MARTINI *For me, the perfect garnish for the original Martini is a green olive, not a lemon twist. The olive lets the mix retain the peppery bite of the gin, while a lemon twist adds a certain sweetness.*

MINT JULEP

■ **INGREDIENTS**
40ml (1⅓oz) Bourbon whiskey ■ dash sugar syrup ■ 3 sprigs mint

■ **EQUIPMENT**
Highball glass ■ muddling stick ■ stirring spoon

The Mint Julep has risen to fame as the traditional cocktail of the Kentucky Derby horse race, held in Kentucky, in the southern US, each May. There are many variations of the basic mix, but the key is to serve it cold and fresh.

METHOD Muddle the sugar syrup and mint in the glass (*see p348*). Add the Bourbon and some ice. Stir well, and serve immediately. Garnish with a sprig of mint.

MINT JULEP

MOJITO

■ **INGREDIENTS**
4 leaves fresh mint ■ freshly squeezed juice of half a lime ■ 2 tsps sugar ■ 45ml (1½oz) Bacardi white rum ■ 210ml (7oz) soda water

■ **EQUIPMENT**
Highball glass ■ muddler ■ stirring spoon

This Cuban classic, thought to have been created at Sloppy Joe's bar in Havana in the 1900s, was a favourite of the writer Ernest Hemingway. Tall, cool, fresh, and minty, the key to this drink is the partnership between the rum and the lime tang. Wonderful!

METHOD Muddle the mint leaves in the highball; add the juice and sugar, and lots of crushed ice. Pour in the rum. Stir well and top with soda. Garnish with a wedge of lime and a sprig of mint.

OLD FASHIONED

■ **INGREDIENTS**
5 or 6 drops Angostura bitters ■ one sugar cube ■ dash soda water ■ 80ml (2⅔oz) Bourbon whiskey

■ **EQUIPMENT**
Tumbler ■ stirring spoon

The first mention of this cocktail is in the *Old Waldorf-Astoria Bar Book* of 1931, where it is listed as being invented by a certain Colonel James E. Pepper. Dry, light, and refreshing, with a lovely amber colour, this is one for Bourbon-lovers. However, you can use rye whiskey or blended Scotch if you prefer.

METHOD Place the sugar in the glass and soak it with the drops of Angostura bitters. Just cover the cube with soda water, allow it to dissolve, then add ice and Bourbon. Stir well. Garnish with a slice of lemon and cherry on a stick.

MOSCOW MULE

■ **INGREDIENTS**
60ml (2oz) vodka ■ 45ml (1½oz) freshly squeezed lime juice ■ ginger ale to fill

■ **EQUIPMENT**
Highball glass ■ stirring spoon

Created in New York in 1941 by the then head of Smirnoff vodka, this great cocktail is long, fresh, and spicy. Use a strong ginger ale, such as Reed's, rather than Canada Dry.

METHOD Fill the glass with ice, add the vodka and lime, and stir. Top with the ginger ale. Garnish with a wheel of lemon on the rim.

MOSCOW MULE

LONG ISLAND ICED TEA

■ **INGREDIENTS**
10ml (⅓oz) white rum ■ 10ml (⅓oz) gin ■ 10ml (⅓oz) vodka ■ 10ml (⅓oz) Cointreau ■ 10ml (⅓oz) tequila ■ freshly squeezed juice of one lime ■ chilled cola to fill

■ **EQUIPMENT**
Highball glass ■ stirring spoon

This is the ultimate party cocktail, though a few too many could make for a stormy night! Despite its name, this cocktail does not contain tea. Every bartender has their own twist on the recipe – some take out the tequila, but double the quantity of vodka; some do the opposite. Whatever the precise mix, the flavours that come through are of the

LONG ISLAND
ICED TEA

exotic orange from the Cointreau and the citrus characters of the gin and lime juice; the other ingredients provide a mellow alcoholic backdrop.

Although the exact provenance of the Long Island Iced Tea is unclear, it is likely that the cocktail was first created in the days of the Prohibition era (1920–33) in the US, when bartenders at the speakeasies (illegal drinking dens) disguised their alcoholic mixes by adding cola to bootleg spirits, with the aim of making the drink look like a simple, harmless iced tea.

METHOD Pour all the spirits and the lime juice into the highball glass and stir well. Fill with ice cubes and stir well again, and then top with chilled cola. Garnish the cocktail with wedges of lime inside the glass, and perhaps a wheel of lime on the rim of the glass. I like to serve it with a straw.

PLANTER'S PUNCH

■ **INGREDIENTS**
45ml (1½oz) Myers' dark rum ■ 15ml (½oz) freshly squeezed lime juice ■ 30ml (1oz) sugar syrup ■ dash grenadine ■ few drops Angostura bitters ■ soda water to fill

■ **EQUIPMENT**
Shaker ■ strainer ■ highball glass

Created in 1879 to celebrate the opening of Myers' rum distillery in Jamaica, this delicious, deep orangey-red cocktail is able to balance the strong flavours of dark rum with sweetness from the sugar and grenadine, herbiness from the bitters, and citrus from the lime.

METHOD Fill the shaker with ice and pour in all the ingredients except the soda. Shake well and strain into an ice-filled highball glass. Top with soda water, and garnish with a sprig of mint in the glass and a slice of orange on the rim.

DRINK BEFORE DINNER

The style of these cocktails is very light, fresh, lemony, and aromatic. They should have a gently lingering finish with a slightly bitter touch to make you feel ready for your meal. For this reason, many cocktails of this type feature Champagne or other sparkling wine as a dry, effervescent base, with sweet liqueurs rounding off the flavour.

CHAMPAGNE COCKTAIL

■ **INGREDIENTS**
One sugar lump ▪ 4 or 5 drops Angostura bitters ▪ 30ml (1oz) brandy ▪ dry Champagne to fill

■ **EQUIPMENT**
Chilled Champagne flute

We can trace the recipe of this all-time classic cocktail back to 1862, when it first appeared in Jerry Thomas's book *How to Mix Drinks*.

This is a really easy cocktail to mix because you need no equipment other than the glass. For the best results find a really dry Champagne, such as Piper-Heidsieck Brut or Laurent Perrier Ultra Brut, and a good Cognac of VS-quality or better.

METHOD Place the sugar cube in the glass and soak it with the drops of Angostura bitters. Add the brandy and slowly pour in the Champagne to fill. Garnish with an orange wheel on the rim of the glass if you wish.

CHAMPAGNE COCKTAIL
As you sip this classic cocktail, the closer you get to the sugar cube at the bottom, the sweeter the mix becomes.

KIR ROYALE

■ **INGREDIENTS**
10ml (⅓oz) crème de cassis
■ dry Champagne or good-quality
sparkling wine to fill

■ **EQUIPMENT**
Chilled Champagne flute

This traditional French
cocktail is loved by
everyone who takes a sip.
Take care not to add too
much crème de cassis
(blackcurrant liqueur);
it is there only to take
the biting edge off the
Champagne. Raspberry
liqueur, in place of blackcurrant, makes a Kir Imperial.

METHOD Pour the liqueur into
the glass and then top up gently
with the Champagne.

KIR ROYALE

PICK ME UP

■ **INGREDIENTS**
30ml (1oz) brandy ■ 20ml (⅔oz)
freshly squeezed orange juice ■ 10ml
(⅓oz) grenadine ■ dry Champagne or
good-quality sparkling wine to fill

■ **EQUIPMENT**
Chilled Champagne flute ■ bar spoon

The use of grenadine and orange
juice makes this a sweet, amber-red
version of the Champagne cocktail
(see p379). It is so fruity and easy
to drink that the brandy is almost
unnoticeable on the palate. The key
to success is to chill the ingredients
well before mixing.

METHOD Pour the brandy, orange
juice, and grenadine into the flute.
Stir well and fill with Champagne.
Alternatively, stir the non-sparkling
ingredients in a mixing glass with
one cube of ice, strain them into the
flute, and top with the Champagne.

SHOWBIZ

■ **INGREDIENTS**
50ml (1⅔oz) vodka ■ 30ml (1oz) crème
de cassis ■ 50ml (1⅔oz) freshly
squeezed grapefruit juice

■ **EQUIPMENT**
Shaker ■ strainer
■ chilled Martini glass

This cocktail offers
sweet cassis, citrus bite,
and a vodka kick –
perfect! I like to use Absolut
for the vodka – its combination of citrus and sweetness
perfectly complements the
other flavours in the mix.
The result should be a
red-brown colour.

METHOD Fill the shaker with ice
and pour in the ingredients. Shake
well and strain into the glass.
Garnish with two black-
currants inside the glass.

BOLLI STOLLI

■ **INGREDIENTS**
30ml (1oz) chilled Stolichnaya Cristall
vodka ■ chilled Bollinger Special
Cuvée Brut Champagne to fill

■ **EQUIPMENT**
Champagne flute

The combination of great
Champagne and great vodka
can only make a great
cocktail! This is a feel-good
mix – the cocktail of Wall
Street brokers, celebrating a
good day on the stock market.
The Bolli Stolli is not overly
aromatic so serve it ice cold to
enhance the freshness.

METHOD Pour the vodka into the
glass and slowly fill with Bollinger.
Garnish with a twist of orange zest
and some lemon-balm leaves.

BOLLI STOLLI

SLOPPY JOE'S BAR, HAVANA One of the best-known cocktail
bars in the world, Sloppy Joe's in Havana became famous
during the 1930s as a popular haunt for US soldiers stationed
in Cuba. It was founded by José Abéal, who arrived in Cuba
from Spain in 1904. In 1918, after 14 years as a bartender in

Cuba and the US, José bought a grocery store in Havana.
Friends commented on the poor hygiene standards in
the shop, earning José the nickname Sloppy Joe. Soon
groceries gave way to the famous bar, which had its heyday
in the 1950s, when Havana was America's playground.

CHAMPS-ELYSÉES

■ **INGREDIENTS**
30ml (1oz) Cognac ■ 15ml (½oz)
Green Chartreuse liqueur ■ 30ml
(1oz) freshly squeezed lemon juice
■ 2 dashes Angostura bitters

■ **EQUIPMENT**
Mixing glass ■ bar spoon ■ strainer
■ chilled Martini glass

Green Chartreuse is a herbal liqueur
that was created by 18th-century
French monks and became famed
for its curative properties. What
better excuse for mixing this lovely
cocktail, named after the famous
Parisian boulevard? I love its
complexity, which gives a fine
balance of rich, sweet Cognac and
citrus, and herbs at the finish.

METHOD Fill the mixing glass
with crushed ice and pour in the
ingredients. Stir, and strain into the
glass. Alternatively mix the drink in
a brandy glass and serve over ice.

BELLINI

■ INGREDIENTS
1 fresh white peach ■ 60ml (2oz)
chilled Champagne, or Prosecco
Italian sparkling wine

■ EQUIPMENT
Knife ■ blender ■ chilled
Champagne flute
■ bar spoon

Created in 1948 by Giuseppe
Cipriani at Harry's Bar in
Venice, this is a vibrant and
luxurious cocktail.

METHOD Peel and stone
the peach, and blend it
with crushed ice and a little
Champagne until smooth. Put
30ml (1oz) of the mixture into the
flute and pour in Champagne to
fill, stirring gently as you do so.
Garnish with a slice of peach.

BELLINI

QUICKY

■ INGREDIENTS
30ml (1oz) Bourbon whiskey ■ 30ml
(1oz) rum ■ dash triple sec

■ EQUIPMENT
Tumbler ■ bar spoon

Exactly as its name suggests,
this is a quick and easy
cocktail, perfect for whipping
up at the shortest notice.
It has power and alcoholic
strength with a citrus
character and smooth finish.
I recommend serving it with
ice to prevent it from feeling
too alcoholic or heavy. As you
might expect, it has a warm,
amber colour.

METHOD If you are using ice,
place a few cubes in the bottom of
the glass. Pour in the ingredients
and give them a quick stir.
Serve ungarnished.

AMERICANO

■ INGREDIENTS
30ml (1oz) sweet, red vermouth
(Martini Rosso) ■ 30ml (1oz)
Campari ■ soda water to fill

■ EQUIPMENT
Highball glass ■ bar spoon

In the early 1900s this
Italian cocktail was known as
the Milano-Torino, because
Campari comes from Milan,
and Martini from Turin. Its
name changed in 1917, when
US soldiers fighting in World
War I arrived in Italy and loved
the mix. It has great intensity of
fruit, with a hint of bitterness that
is perfect for whetting the appetite.
This is an ideal drink for a hot
summer afternoon.

METHOD Fill the glass with ice. Pour
in the vermouth and Campari.
Top with soda and stir.

AMERICANO

BALLANTINE'S

■ INGREDIENTS
20ml (⅔oz) Plymouth gin ■ 20ml (⅔oz)
dry vermouth ■ 2 dashes orange
bitters ■ dash Pernod

■ EQUIPMENT
Shaker ■ strainer ■ frosted
Martini glass

This is a perfect
apéritif – fresh
with a touch
of bitterness.
I recommend
serving it well-chilled
to enhance the aniseed
and nutty flavours of
the Pernod.

METHOD Fill the shaker with
ice, then pour in all the
ingredients and shake well.
Strain into the glass.

BRAMBLE

■ INGREDIENTS
45ml (1½oz) gin ■ 20ml (⅔oz) freshly
squeezed lime juice ■ 20ml (⅔oz)
sugar syrup ■ 20ml (⅔oz) crème de
mûre (blackberry liqueur)

■ EQUIPMENT
Shaker ■ strainer ■ tumbler

Created in the 1980s by the British
bartender Dick Bradsell, this cocktail
is now ranked among the classics.
It is great as an apéritif.

METHOD Fill the
shaker with ice and
pour in all the
ingredients except the
crème de mûre. Shake
well and strain into a
glass near-filled with
crushed ice. Pour in the
liqueur so that it flows
through the ice. Garnish
with two blackberries and
a slice of lemon.

BRAMBLE

MACCA

■ INGREDIENTS
20ml (⅔oz) dry gin ■ 20ml (⅔oz) dry
vermouth ■ 20ml (⅔oz) sweet
vermouth ■ dash crème de cassis
■ soda water to fill

■ EQUIPMENT
Mixing glass ■ bar spoon
■ highball glass

This is a pink cocktail, perfect for
summer drinking. If you prefer your
cocktails to be on the dry
side rather than
sweeter, use only
the dry vermouth;
or replace the crème
de cassis with crème de
mûre, which tends to be
less sugary.

METHOD Pour all the
ingredients except the soda
into the mixing glass. Stir.
Pour into a highball filled
with ice and top with soda.

DUBONNET
COCKTAIL

■ INGREDIENTS
40ml (1½oz) Dubonnet vermouth
■ 40ml (1½oz) gin ■ dash
Angostura bitters

■ EQUIPMENT
Mixing glass ■ bar spoon
■ strainer ■ chilled
Martini glass

This is a classic, pre-dinner
cocktail with a charming pink
colour. The citrus and juniper
flavours of the gin reinforce
the complex herbs and fruit
of the Dubonnet vermouth
in a neat combination of
delightful flavours.

METHOD Fill the mixing
glass with ice and add the
vermouth, gin, and bitters.
Stir well and strain into the
Martini glass. Garnish with
a thin twist of lemon peel.

BLUE HAWAIIAN

■ INGREDIENTS
30ml (1oz) white rum ■ 30ml (1oz)
blue curaçao ■ 60ml (2oz) freshly
pressed pineapple juice ■ 30ml (1oz)
cream of coconut

■ EQUIPMENT
Blender ■ strainer ■ highball glass

This beautiful ocean-
blue cocktail makes your
mouth water before it
even reaches your lips! It
brims with exotic fruits
and has just a subtle hint
of coconut. Wonderful!

METHOD Put some ice in
your blender and pour
in the rum, curaçao,
cream of coconut, and
pineapple juice. Whizz
until smooth. Strain into
a highball, garnish with
a cherry on a stick, and

BLUE HAWAIIAN

serve with a straw.

PIMM'S NO.1 CUP

■ **INGREDIENTS**
90ml (3oz) Pimm's No.1 ■ 1½ tsp
freshly squeezed lime juice
■ ginger ale to fill

■ **EQUIPMENT**
Highball glass ■ stirring spoon

In 1823, a London restaurant owner and businessman named James Pimm needed a drink to offer his customers that matched perfectly with the oysters he was serving. Before long he came up with a recipe of herbs, spices, and fruit, steeped in gin, and mixed with quinine. He made the drink long by mixing his new liqueur with ginger ale, and served it in a tankard known as the "number-one cup" giving the cocktail its name. Pimm's customers loved it and in 1840 Pimm launched his No.1 commercially.

Pimm's is now owned by the drinks company Diageo, but the liquid is still made to James Pimm's original recipe – a recipe known only to the top six people in the firm.

Since the original No.1, several other "numbers" have been produced, including the now obsolete No.2 (made using Scotch whisky), No.4 (rum), and No.5 (rye whiskey). Diageo has recently revived the No.3 (made with brandy), marketing it as Pimm's Winter, and it continues to market the No.6 (made with vodka).

Although the Pimm's No.1 Cup is the most famous of the Pimm's cocktails, there are many others. The Pimm's Classic uses lemonade in place of ginger ale

PIMM'S NO.1 *By 1856 James Pimm was selling his original Pimm's No.1 to bars and clubs all over Great Britain.*

PIMM'S CLASSIC *If you have a sweet tooth, substitute the ginger ale in the Pimm's Cup with lemonade to make the Pimm's Classic. Either is perfect at a summer barbecue.*

(or a combination of both); while more exciting and sophisticated is the Pimm's Cocktail. This mix combines two shots of Pimm's No.1 with an extra dash of Plymouth gin, lemon juice, and sugar syrup. This is topped with dry Champagne (or good-quality, dry sparkling wine) and served in a chilled Martini glass. What could be more perfect for a summer garden party with friends? Alternatively, you could dispense with the extras and simply serve a measure of Pimm's in a flute and top with Champagne. Delicious!

METHOD Pour the ingredients into an ice-filled highball. Stir. Garnish with a vibrant array of berries, such as strawberries, raspberries, and blackberries, a few thin slices of cucumber, and half a slice each of orange and lemon, all placed inside the glass. Decorate with a sprig of mint on the top.

CULTURE AND TRADITION

QUINTESSENTIALLY ENGLISH First mixed by James Pimm in the 1820s, some believe the Pimm's No.1 Cup to be the first English cocktail. Whether or not this is true, the mix is associated with England's traditional summer events, especially those that fall in June and early July: the racing at Royal Ascot, the rowing regatta at Henley in Oxfordshire, and, most typically of all, the Lawn Tennis Championships at Wimbledon.

ANYONE FOR TENNIS? *Over 23,000 litres (40,000 pints) of Pimm's cocktails are sold at Wimbledon during the two weeks of the Championships.*

MANHATTAN

■ **INGREDIENTS**
60ml (2oz) Canadian rye whisky or Bourbon whiskey ▪ 30ml (1oz) sweet vermouth ▪ a few drops of Angostura bitters

■ **EQUIPMENT**
Mixing glass ▪ stirring spoon ▪ strainer ▪ Martini glass

This classic New York Martini is said to date from 1874. Variations include the Dry Manhattan made with dry vermouth; the Harvard, made with brandy rather than whisky; and the Star, which replaces the whisky with applejack (apple brandy).

METHOD Fill the mixing glass with ice, and add the ingredients. Stir gently and strain into the glass. Garnish with orange zest and a cherry.

MANHATTAN

BROOKLYN

■ **INGREDIENTS**
15ml (½oz) rye whiskey ▪ 15ml (½oz) sweet, red vermouth ▪ 15ml (½oz) Campari

■ **EQUIPMENT**
Mixing glass ▪ stirring spoon ▪ strainer ▪ tumbler

This trendy New York cocktail has something for both ends of a meal: the Campari and vermouth (for the best results use Martini Rosso) make it a great apéritif, while the whiskey makes it a good digestif. Use Canadian Rye whisky if a US rye proves elusive.

METHOD Place some ice in the mixing glass. Pour in all of the ingredients. Stir and strain into the tumbler.

A1

■ **INGREDIENTS**
30ml (1oz) gin ▪ 15ml (½oz) Grand Marnier ▪ 10ml (½oz) freshly squeezed lemon juice ▪ dash grenadine

■ **EQUIPMENT**
Shaker ▪ strainer ▪ Martini glass

This cocktail includes two of my favourite liquids – Grand Marnier and grenadine. I particularly love the way their sweetness contrasts with the sourness of the lemon in this mix. Overall, the A1 makes a refreshing summer apéritif, perfect for enjoying in the garden.

METHOD Fill the shaker with ice and pour in the ingredients. Shake well and strain into the glass. Garnish with a sprig of mint or lemon balm.

A1

BIARRITZ

■ INGREDIENTS
60ml (2oz) Rémy-Martin Cognac ■ 30ml (1oz) Grand Marnier ■ 15ml (½oz) freshly squeezed lemon juice ■ half the white of 1 egg ■ 3 dashes Angostura bitters

■ EQUIPMENT
Shaker ■ strainer ■ tumbler

This cocktail is basically a brandy sour (like the Whisky Sour; p351), with an extra layer of complexity added by the Grand Marnier. The citrus of the lemon juice and the bitterness of the Angostura make it a perfect apéritif.

METHOD Fill the shaker with ice and pour in the ingredients. Shake vigorously and strain into the ice-filled tumbler. Serve with half a slice of orange on the rim.

BABAR

■ INGREDIENTS
30ml (1oz) vodka ■ 10ml (⅓oz) Passoã passion-fruit liqueur ■ 30ml (1oz) guanabana juice ■ 20ml (⅔oz) cranberry juice ■ sparkling lemonade (such as Sprite or 7 Up)

■ EQUIPMENT
Highball ■ stirring spoon

This exotic fruit cocktail makes easy afternoon drinking. It is best made with the juice of the tropical guanabana (custard apple) fruit; if you cannot find this, use guava juice instead.

METHOD Half fill the glass with ice. Pour in the vodka, liqueur, and juices. Stir and top with the lemonade. Garnish with a mint leaf.

BABAR

RUM SWIZZLE

■ INGREDIENTS
60ml (2oz) white rum ■ 15ml (½oz) freshly squeezed lime juice ■ 1 tsp caster sugar ■ 2 dashes Angostura bitters ■ 90ml (3oz) soda water

■ EQUIPMENT
Shaker ■ strainer ■ tumbler

This perfect beach cocktail is long and tangy and carries a great herbal kick from the bitters. Pale pinky-beige in colour, it is just as refreshing but not quite as strong as a Rum Punch (see p361).

METHOD Pour the rum, lime juice, sugar, and bitters into an ice-filled shaker. Strain into a tumbler half filled with crushed ice. Top with soda water. Serve with a swizzle stick.

ALFIE

■ INGREDIENTS
50ml (1½oz) lemon-flavoured vodka ■ 10ml (⅓oz) Cointreau ■ 10ml (⅓oz) freshly pressed pineapple juice

■ EQUIPMENT
Shaker ■ strainer ■ frosted Martini glass

The Alfie is a finely balanced and refreshing mix, with a multitude of exotic and citrus flavours. Lemon vodka is the dominant taste, so try to use a good brand. (I always favour Absolut Citron.)

METHOD Half fill the shaker with ice. Pour in the ingredients, shake well, and strain into a Martini glass. Garnish with a few lemon balm leaves if you wish.

ALFIE

MAI TAI

■ INGREDIENTS
60ml (2oz) Appleton Estate V/X aged rum ■ 30ml (1oz) freshly squeezed lime juice ■ 15ml (½oz) Grand Marnier ■ 15ml (½oz) almond syrup ■ 1½ tsp sugar syrup

■ EQUIPMENT
Shaker ■ strainer ■ tumbler

In this classic cocktail, the almond syrup marries beautifully with the sweet, toffee flavours of the rum, while the citrus of the Grand Marnier provides intensity.

METHOD Fill the shaker with ice, add the ingredients, and shake well. Strain into the glass filled with ice. Garnish with slices of pineapple and kiwi.

MAI TAI

JACK ROSE

■ INGREDIENTS
45ml (1½oz) apple brandy ■ 10ml (⅓oz) freshly squeezed lime juice ■ dash grenadine

■ EQUIPMENT
Shaker ■ strainer ■ chilled Martini glass

This is one of my favourite apple-brandy cocktails. I like to use Calvados (French apple brandy), but applejack (from the US) would do just as well, although the result may be a little lighter. Overall this great-tasting, pink cocktail is fun and refreshing – and also wonderfully simple to make.

METHOD Fill the shaker with ice and add the ingredients. Shake well and strain into the glass. Drop in a zest of lime to garnish.

PINK LADY

■ INGREDIENTS
45ml (1½oz) Plymouth gin ■ dash grenadine ■ white of one egg ■ 20ml (⅔oz) freshly squeezed lemon juice ■ dash sugar syrup

■ EQUIPMENT
Shaker ■ strainer ■ chilled Martini glass

A sweeter version of the Gin Fizz (see p342), this cocktail is smooth, vibrant, and ideal for anyone who likes gin. The egg white gives a creamy and luscious feel to the mix that can mask its alcoholic content. The drink is a delicate, opaque pink colour.

METHOD Fill the shaker with ice cubes and pour in all the ingredients. Shake vigorously and strain into the glass. Drop a Maraschino cherry into the glass to garnish.

ZOMBIE

■ INGREDIENTS
20ml (⅔oz) white rum ■ 20ml (⅔oz) golden rum ■ 20ml (⅔oz) dark rum ■ 10ml (⅓oz) cherry brandy ■ 10ml (⅓oz) freshly pressed pineapple juice ■ 30ml (1oz) freshly squeezed orange juice ■ 10ml (⅓oz) freshly squeezed lime juice ■ 20ml (⅔oz) papaya juice ■ dash almond syrup ■ dash 151-proof Demerara rum

■ EQUIPMENT
Shaker ■ strainer ■ highball glass ■ stirring spoon

This cocktail was created in Hollywood in 1934.

METHOD Fill the shaker with ice. Pour in all the ingredients except the 151-proof rum. Shake; strain into an ice-filled highball. Pour in the rum; stir. Garnish with lemon balm and a straw.

ZOMBIE

PINK GIN *The "pink" in this cocktail comes from Angostura Bitters, which are swirled around the glass before gin is added.*

PINK GIN

■ INGREDIENTS
2 dashes Angostura bitters
■ 50ml (1⅔oz) Plymouth gin

■ EQUIPMENT
Chilled Martini glass ■ mixing glass
■ stirring spoon ■ strainer

Light and refreshing, the Pink Gin is to cocktails what Sauvignon Blanc is to wine. The origin of this cocktail lies with the English Navy: sailors drank gin to fortify themselves against sea life and took the bitters to cure their stomach upsets. Before long they married the two ingredients.

Place the gin in the freezer for 24 hours before making the cocktail to ensure that it is ice cold.

METHOD Pour the bitters into the Martini glass and "turn" the glass to coat (condition) the inside. Put ice in the mixing glass and pour in the gin. Stir well. Strain into the Martini glass. Garnish with lemon zest.

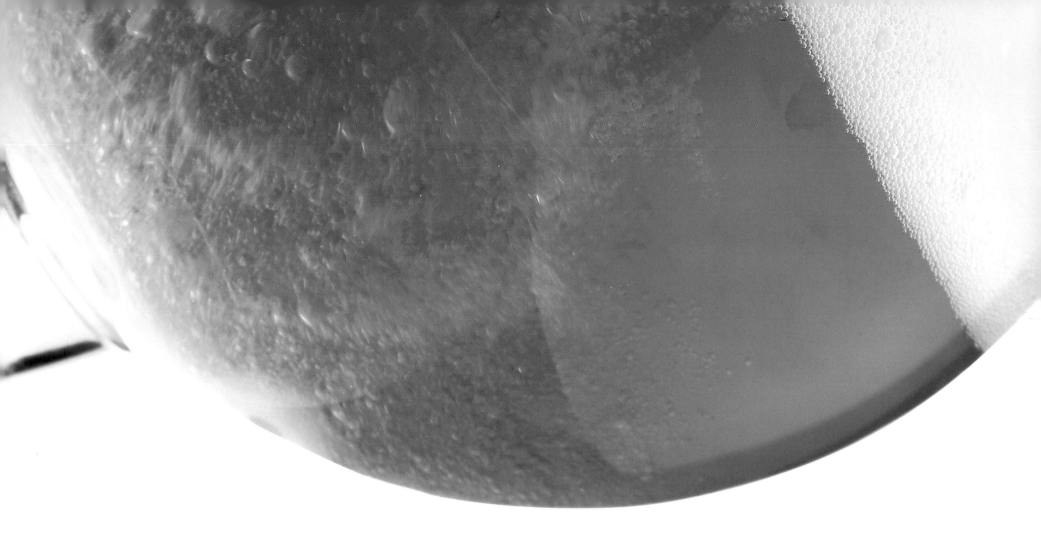

BEER

GRAIN TO GLASS

Wherever you go in the world, you will find a local beer, but few people appreciate the sheer diversity of brews on offer. It is time to savour and celebrate this great drink!

LEADING LAGER *Most of the beer sold worldwide is lager – a golden, clear style originating from Pilsen in Bohemia, now part of the Czech Republic.*

When you say "a beer", what image comes into your mind? Most likely, a light, golden yellow, frothy drink poured from a glass bottle or a tap; cold, fresh, and fizzy in a tall condensation-covered glass, it is ready to quench your thirst and cool you down. You are probably not thinking of a dark, mysterious, smoky brew, of a brown ale served in a brandy glass, or of a cherry-red fruit cup that has all the qualities of Champagne. Our perception today is shaped by the dominance, in recent decades, of the Pilsner style of lager – a style that dates back to just the mid-19th century. But for thousands of years before that, beer meant a dark, warm, and almost flat ale, not in any way like today's frothy lager!

As recently as 150 years ago, almost every town and village had its own beer. Good, bad, or indifferent, it was the "local" drink – as much a part of the region's character as its dialect, cuisine, and customs. In the following decades, new brewing and distribution technologies allowed relatively few producers to scale-up production and dominate not only regional, but also national, and international markets. These new brewing giants made their fortunes, often at the expense of the quality and diversity of the product. The reaction to this was fierce! In a number of countries, the "real ale" movement took off, and in Britain, Belgium, and the US, small-scale micro-breweries started producing a much wider range of styles, and lavishing real care and attention on their products, valuing pride over profit. This movement has been such a success that the global companies have been forced to pay attention; the result is a renaissance of interest in beer, and there has never been a better time to be a beer drinker.

A HISTORY OF BEER

The oldest reliable records of brewing date back about 5,000 years to the Sumerians, who inhabited the fertile region between the Tigris and Euphrates Rivers, an area that forms part of modern Iraq. Sumerian pictographs show bread being baked, crumbled into water to form a mash, and then made into a drink which is recorded as making one feel "exhilarated, wonderful, and blissful". The Chinese, and the native peoples of Africa and America were also making beer in these early times, also using crude forms of bread as the basis of the brew.

The Egyptians, Greeks, and Romans certainly developed the brewing tradition, but

LOCAL BREW *This fine ale from a small producer in the Pacific Northwest of the US typifies the attention to detail and tradition of the new micro-breweries.*

> " There has never been a better time to be a beer drinker. We can all rediscover the local beers and seasonal brews that our grandparents enjoyed. "

GRAIN HARVEST *Barley is grown for beer production in temperate parts of the world, such as Britain, Germany, Belgium, the Czech Republic, and parts of the US.*

" Beer is the ultimate democratic drink. When you down a glass you are taking part in a tradition that goes back at least 5,000 years. "

INDUSTRIAL BREWERY, 1953 *This barrel storage depot shows the huge scale of the Ind Coope & Allsopp's brewery in Burton-on-Trent, England. Modern breweries tend to be more compact, and use high technology to maximize productivity.*

beer took second place to wine around the Mediterranean at that time. It was not until the fall of the Roman Empire and the triumph of the "barbarians" in the 5th century that beer established a central place in the culture of drinking.

In the early civilizations, beer-making had been a woman's work, but during the Dark Ages, after the fall of Rome, the job was taken over by the European monastic orders. Monks made beer partly because poor sanitation meant that beer was far safer to drink than water, and partly because the sale of ale to travellers provided a steady income for the monasteries. Also, beer was permitted during times of fast because it was not considered a "food"; the canny monks knew it to be both nutritious and tasty, and some monastic records show that beer consumption in fast periods was more than five litres a day, per head!

The classic image of the jolly, red-nosed friar comes from the times when many monasteries had their own pubs, but with the rise of the Protestant Church, and a more austere regime in the Catholic Church, brewing moved into the towns, and kings and governments began to regulate and tax the beer trade.

GUINNESS ADVERTISING *The classic Irish stout, Guinness, was once marketed for its health benefits. The company no longer makes this claim, though recent research shows that a drop of the "black stuff" may actually be good for the heart.*

German Beer Purity Law in 1516. This decree established for the first time that only barley, hops, and pure water could be used to brew beer. Distinct brewing centres grew up – Munich, Hamburg, Bremen, Berlin, and some of the Flemish towns becoming important centres.

By the 19th century, inventions like the steam engine and refrigeration allowed the production of beer on an industrial scale. The role of yeast in fermentation began to be understood on a scientific level, which meant that the flavour and character of the resulting beer could be controlled from the outset, and pasteurization meant that the product could be stored and transported over long distances without deteriorating – one of the biggest steps forward in brewing history.

BREWING ADVANCES

The quality of beer certainly improved in the later Middle Ages. Hops began to be used, both to make the beer more refreshing and to act as a natural preservative. Better storage techniques emerged, and distinct regional styles began to develop. Germany led the way with the introduction of strict and detailed rules for quality, when the Duke of Bavaria, Wilhelm IV, proclaimed the

WHAT IS BEER?

Everyone knows that wine is made from grapes, but what goes in to a glass of beer? The answer is grain – usually barley or wheat, but sometimes other cereals, such as oats and rye. Extra flavour and character come from the

FRUIT BEERS *Mort Subite Kriek is a bright red Belgian fruit beer made with cherries. Fruit beers like this are refreshing, and not too strong – perfect as apéritifs.*

addition of hops, spices, and herbs; and the qualities of the water and yeast used for fermentation provide an extra dimension to the flavour of the finished product. Beer typically has a strength of around 5% ABV (although there are both weaker and much stronger brews) and, as a very general rule, is produced where wine is not. You can, for example, draw a line between Northern Europe, producing mainly beer, and Southern Europe, which is devoted to the production of wines.

Making beer involves two separate processes – malting and brewing. At the maltings, grain, usually barley, is steeped in water for around two days to trigger germination; as the grain germinates, the starch that it contains starts to break down into sugars. The germinated grain, or malt, is then dried and roasted in a kiln – a process that both stops further growth and adds flavour to the resulting beer. At the brewery, the dried malt is milled into a coarse "flour" and mashed with hot water, forming a sugary solution called the wort. The wort is filtered and then hops are added to give the beer a bitter freshness; sometimes spices and fruit are added for variety and style. The mixture is treated with steam to prevent the growth of bacteria and to extract the aromatic flavours from the hops; only now is the liquid ready for fermentation. Historically, brewers relied on wild, airborne yeasts to ferment the liquid, but today yeasts are carefully selected and cultured by biotechnologists to optimize efficiency and flavour. Traditional ales are produced by a fermentation that lasts about six days at 16°C (60.8°F), and the yeasts used float on top of the brew. In contrast, lagers are made using strains of yeast that sink to the bottom of the brew. Lager yeasts ferment at 10°C (50°F), and much more slowly, taking up to three weeks. After fermentation, the beer is piped

BREW HOUSES *Giant companies, such as Asahi in Japan* (below) *have dominated the world of beer over the past decades; small concerns, like the tiny Portland brewery in Oregon, US* (left) *are setting a higher standard for all brewing companies.*

COPPER KETTLES *The sweet wort is boiled by steam in giant kettles, known in the brewing trade as "coppers", though today many are made from stainless steel. Those used at the Coors brewery (pictured) are made of the traditional copper.*

" Pouring a beer is like putting out a welcome mat. There is no more sociable drink than beer. "

THISTLE GLASS *Many beers have their own dedicated glass. In keeping with Scottish tradition, Gordon Highland Ale from Edinburgh – a reddish-brown beer with a thick head – should be served in a thistle-shaped glass.*

into wooden casks or (more usually) metal tanks for conditioning, in which the yeast left in the brew ferments any remaining sugar. Carbon dioxide gas released in this secondary fermentation gives the beer its sparkle, and enhances its flavour. Lagers are conditioned for much longer than ales – several months in some cases (the word "lager" is derived from a German word meaning "to store") – and at much lower temperatures, which helps to remove proteins that would otherwise cloud the liquid.

BEER STYLES

The style of a beer depends on a whole host of variables: the type of grain, hops, and yeast used; the balance between the different ingredients, including the water; the process itself, including maturation; and the skill and preference of the brewer. It is useful to differentiate the top-fermented beers – ales, stouts, porters, and wheat beers – from the bottom-fermented lagers, but many people and organizations classify beers according to

OKTOBERFEST *Beer is the most social and seasonal of all drinks. Every year, thousands of beer enthusiasts gather at the Oktoberfest Beer Festival in Munich, Germany, to sample brews, many of which are made specially for the occasion.*

narrower technical style and place of origin (see tables, pp396–9). I have opted, in this book, to group beers together according to their taste and their "feel" because I want to choose the right beer to quench my thirst, to fire up my taste buds, or to give me that warm fireside sensation.

ENJOYING BEER

Many people think of beer as a "session drink" to be enjoyed in a bar or pub, with friends. Beer will always be a sociable drink, but the recent proliferation of new styles means that specialist beers can be matched with food, drunk as apéritifs, or savoured after dinner. For example, stout is great with shellfish, and some of the Belgian brown or amber ales are wonderful with lamb. Fruit beers and chocolate stouts are perfect with desserts, and the best barley wines can be nurtured like Cognac.

The choice and quality of beer is better now than ever before – specialist beer retailers have hundreds of brands on offer, and even your local supermarket will stock a good range of styles. Franchising of production means that traditional beers from one part of the world are often made internationally; and while there may be arguments about whether they are "the real thing", the diversity that results means that there is no longer a good excuse to ignore beer as a serious drink.

DRINKING UP *The image of beer is changing. Exciting beer styles and innovative marketing appeal to a younger generation of consumers, used to the diversity and sophistication of wine. But for me, there is still nowhere better to enjoy a beer than in a warm, wood-panelled pub!*

THE WORLD OF BEER

Beer is made and drunk in every corner of the world, but its spiritual heartland is western and central Europe. Famous brands drive a huge global industry, while micro-breweries help to keep beer's wonderful heritage and diversity alive.

MEXICO

Mexico is most famous for its tequila and mezcal, but the country is also a great maker and consumer of beer. The Corona brand became a cult favourite in the US and Europe, and since then beers such as Sol and Dos Equis have achieved a similar status. Mexican beers are light and thirst quenching.

UNITED STATES

As you might expect, the US is home to some of the largest brewers in the world, such as Anheuser Busch (makers of Budweiser) and Miller. The US is the second largest producer of beer after China, and most of its production is drunk at home rather than exported. In recent years, the micro-brewery movement has gained popularity in America, and small producers now make many fine beers by traditional methods. These include revivals of long-forgotten European styles, typically with an innovative, exciting twist.

NORTH AMERICA

CARIBBEAN

CENTRAL AMERICA

SOUTH AMERICA

BELGIUM

From medieval times, Belgium has been at the epicentre of beer production. Its beers – of which there are at least 300 distinct styles – offer unmatched variety, imagination, and quality. The country's lagers are widely exported, but the real treasures of Belgium are its native brews – its Champagne-like lambics, some flavoured with fruits, its wheat beers, sour red and brown beers, strong ales from Trappist monasteries, as well as its strong golden brews, to name just a few. The Belgians are just as passionate about beer as the French are about wine, and even a modest café will hold a selection of exciting brews – some so unusual that you may not recognize them as beer!

UNITED KINGDOM

The UK is famous for its top-fermented ales, especially India Pale Ale (IPA) and bitter. There are brewers throughout the country, from great old firms like Fuller's and Young's in the heart of London, to independent micro-breweries as far afield as northern Scotland. Some British pubs serve traditional beers directly from the cask, which allows secondary fermentation to take place while they are on sale, and many British ales display their best flavours at room temperature. Rich in tradition and variety, Britain's brewing is world-class.

CZECH REPUBLIC

This country is where the first Pilsner lagers were made, in the town of Plzen (Pilsen). This light, refreshing style of beer is today one of the most popular in the world. Premium Czech lagers, such as Urquell, Kozel, and Gambrinus, are of a very high standard and are becoming much more widely available.

EUROPE

ASIA

MIDDLE EAST

TROPIC OF
CANCER

AFRICA

EQUATOR

JAPAN

Japanese beer-making is dominated by the huge Kirin and Asahi breweries, which make a dizzying range of products from Pilsners to stouts. There is also an increasing number of local micro-breweries, which make specialist beers by traditional methods, including classic Belgian and German styles.

OCEANIA

TROPIC OF
CAPRICORN

GERMANY

Germany has a distinguished beer-making heritage, and no other country has so many breweries per head of population. There are well over 1,000 – a third of the world's total – and half of these are in Bavaria. The quality of German beer is strictly regulated, and is generally of a very high standard. There is an enormous range of German styles, from light, dry, Pilsner and wheat beers through to dark, heavy Bocks and smoked ales. One of the joys of visiting Germany is sampling the huge range of local varieties as you travel.

AUSTRALIA

AUSTRALIA

Australian beer-making is dominated by two big producers: Carlton and United Breweries (CUB), and Lion Nathan, who make Fosters and XXXX Gold respectively. There are also some fine traditional brewers such as Cooper's, whose top-fermented ales evolved from British beers in the country's colonial past.

WORLD BEER STYLES

With new beer brands launched almost every day, understanding the huge diversity of beers on the market might seem a daunting task. The best way to explore this great drink is to think in terms of beer styles, rather than brands. A style is simply a label that describes a beer's character and sometimes its origin too. The style tells you about the ingredients and processes used to make the beer, and gives strong clues about how the beer will look, smell, and taste. The following tables list the main world beer styles, from the lightest lagers to the darkest stouts, telling you their origin, how they should be served, and – most importantly – pointing you to good examples of these beers contained in the pages of this book. Enjoy!

BEER STYLE	DESCRIPTION	EXAMPLES	COUNTRY	SERVING
Kölsch	This very pale, golden yellow beer is top fermented and cold conditioned, making it more like an ale than a lager, which it resembles visually. Smooth and crisp with a light body, this beer displays a subdued maltiness. Fragrant floral hops and slightly sweet fruit flavours combine to great effect in this thirst quencher. Usually 4.0–5.0% ABV.	Früh Kölsch (p415) Dom Kölsch (p415) Gilden Kölsch (p415) Küppers Kölsch (p415)	Germany	Serve in a tall, narrow Stange glass with large head at 9°C (48°F)
Pilsner	The beer – which most people simply call "lager" – is bottom fermented and cold conditioned. The finest examples may be conditioned for several months to allow the flavour to develop fully. These are pale golden beers with crisp, flowery hop and biscuit-like aromas; the flavour is predominantly a clean light malt with a drying hop bitterness. Usually 5.0–5.5% ABV.	Budvar (p422) Pilsner Urquell (p421) Beck's (p411) Jever (p434) Bitburger Pils (p433) Stiegl Pils (p426) Christoffel Blond (p417)	Czech Republic Germany Austria Netherlands	Serve in a Pilsner glass with a frothy head at 5–7°C (41–45°F)
Saison	This is one of the most hoppy of all Belgian beer styles, and originates from the province of Hainault. It is typically golden yellow and highly carbonated; the flavours combine fruit with a peppery spice, which is also strongly evident in the aroma. The dryness and mild acidity make it a refreshing beer. Usually 5.5–8.5% ABV.	Saison Dupont (p439) Saison de Silly (p439) Saison de Pipaix (p439) Moinette Biologique (p439) Ommegang Hennepin (p441)	Belgium USA	Serve in an oversize wine glass or tulip glass with a big, rocky head at 8–10°C (46–50°F)
Weissbier	This Bavarian speciality is brewed with at least 50 per cent malted wheat. Yeast and proteins from the wheat remain in suspension when the beer is poured, making the beer cloudy. The yeast used helps to create the (false) impression that the beer contains cloves and bananas. These beers are light golden yellow and amazingly refreshing. Usually 5.0–5.6% ABV.	Mahr's Weisse (p424) Maisel's Weisse (p424) Huber Weisse (p424) Schneider Weisse (p423) Karg Weisse (p424) Pyramid Hefeweizen (p428)	Germany USA	Serve in a Weissbier glass with a big, billowing head at 7–9°C (45–48°F)

BEER STYLE	DESCRIPTION	EXAMPLES	COUNTRY	SERVING
Witbier	The beer is brewed with around 40 per cent unmalted wheat and is flavoured with coriander, cinnamon, curaçao, orange peel, and other spices. Pale and cloudy, this is an immensely refreshing and increasingly popular brew. Once almost extinct, this beer style was revived in 1966 by Belgian brewer Pierre Celis. Usually 4.5–5.5% ABV.	Hoegaarden Witbier (p426) Dentergems Wit (p427) Gulpener Korenwolf (p427) Allagash White (p428) Blanche de Chambly (p428) Hitachino Nest White Ale (p428)	Belgium Netherlands USA Canada Japan Italy	Serve in a tumbler with a thick head at 7–9°C (45–48°F)
Gueuze	Tart, very dry, and complex, Gueuze is unique in the beer world. Originating from south and west of Brussels, Belgium, the beer is brewed from at least 30 per cent unmalted wheat, using aged hops. Fermentation is by wild airborne yeasts. The beer that results (lambic) is then blended with young beer to produce Gueuze. Usually 5.0–8.0% ABV.	Hanssens Oude Gueuze (p439) Girardin Gueuze (p439)	Belgium Germany England	Serve in a flute or tapering glass with a thick, mousse-like head at 11–13°C (52–55°F)
Tripel	These very strong Blonde beers originated in Belgium but have been widely copied, especially in the US. Candy sugar is used in the brewing process which helps to achieve the high alcohol content. The vibrant fruity flavours are balanced with spicy hops, disguising the potency of these highly drinkable beers. Usually 8.0–12.0% ABV.	Tripel Karmeliet (p466) Chimay Tripel (Blanche) (p438) Victory Golden Monkey (p468)	Belgium USA	Serve in a goblet or tulip glass with a big, dense head at 8–10°C (46–50°F)
India Pale Ale	These beers (IPAs) were designed for shipping to British troops in India over 200 years ago. To ensure they would last the long voyage, the strength of the beer was increased and extra hops added for their preservative properties. However, British IPAs are significantly less hoppy than their American counterparts. Usually 5.0–6.5% ABV.	Worthington White Shield (p435) Victory Hop Devil (p440) Dogfish Head 90 minute IPA (p478)	UK USA	Serve in a pint glass with a medium, persistent head at 10–13°C (50–55°F)
Bière de Garde	These farmhouse beers of northern France cross style guidelines – some are clearly ales while others are brewed with lager yeasts. What brings them together are their common fruity malt accents, their distinct caramel notes, and spicy hops. Often highly carbonated, these beers are sometimes bottled like Champagne. Usually 6.5–8.5% ABV.	Ch'ti Ambrée (p463) Jenlain Ambrée (p463) Trois Monts (p463)	France	Serve in a tulip glass with a large head at 11–13°C (52–55°F)
Pale Ale	Ranging in colour from pale golden yellow to amber, these beers are often the bottled versions of cask conditioned bitters. A balanced mix of fruity, earthy, biscuity malts and floral bitter hops make them richly satisfying. Modern versions are increasingly pale; Belgian versions tend to have greater hop bitterness, often with a resinous character. Usually 4.0–5.5% ABV.	Timothy Taylor's Landlord (p435) Caledonian Golden Promise (p417) Young's Special London Ale (p435) Harviestoun Bitter & Twisted (p435) De Ranke XX Bitter (p439) Orval (p438)	UK Belgium	Serve in a pint glass with a low head at 10–13°C (50–55°F)

BEER STYLE	DESCRIPTION	EXAMPLES	COUNTRY	SERVING
American Pale Ale	These beers are everything that British Pale Ales start out to be, but with added hops, alcohol, and crispness. The accent of the American style is firmly towards the hop; the generous use of hop varieties such as Cascades imparts a fragrant, assertive burst of citric flavours, giving the impression of a clean taste. Usually 5.0–7.0% ABV.	Sierra Nevada Pale Ale *(p440)* Anchor Liberty Ale *(p441)* Smuttynose Shoals Pale Ale *(p440)* Little Creatures Pale Ale *(p429)*	USA Australia	Serve in a pint glass with a tight white or off-white head at 9–11°C (48–52°F)
Fruit Lambic	Dry, with occasionally intense fruit flavours, lambic beers are fermented by wild yeasts. Fruits are traditionally added to the beer after fermentation. Local Belgian Shaarbeek Cherries were the first to be used, but they have been joined by an array of other fruits to make these marvellously appetizing beers. Usually 5.0–7.0% ABV.	Drei Fonteinen Kriek *(p476)* Belle-Vue Kriek *(p476)* Cantillon Vigneronne *(p475)* Cantillon Rose de Gambrinus *(p439)* Cantillon St Lamvinus *(p475)*	Belgium	Serve in a flute with a big head at 8–10°C (46–50°F)
Altbier	Alt, which means "old" in German, is a top-fermented beer that is cold conditioned in the same way as Kölsch. The rich warm amber to brown colour comes from the use of Vienna and Munich malts. The taste is mildly hoppy and well balanced, with soft caramel malt and traces of burnt sugar and fruit. Usually around 4.5% ABV.	Uerige Alt *(p433)* Diebels Alt *(p433)* Schumacher Alt *(p433)*	Germany	Serve in a straight-sided glass with about 2.5cm (1in) of head at around 9°C (48°F)
Belgian Brown Ale	There are many Belgian Brown Ales with distinctive characters, ranging from the slightly oversweet to the faintly sour. They are all brimming with dark caramelized fruit and raisin flavours, and display a mild hop background. In colour they typically range from deep amber to chocolate brown. Usually 5.0–7.5% ABV.	Haacht Gildenbier *(p475)* Liefmans Goudenband *(p474)* Kasteel Bier Bruin *(p476)*	Belgium	Serve in an oversized wine glass with a thick head at 9–11°C (48–52°F)
Belgian Strong Dark Ale	The higher alcohol content of these beers brings added complexity to their flavours, with some chocolate notes in evidence along with spicy fruits. Often there is a "medicinal" element to the overall taste. The use of hops is restrained, allowing the darker malts to dominate these smooth, rich beers. Usually 8.0–12.0% ABV.	Westvleteren 8 *(p464)* De Dolle Oerbier *(p475)* Chimay Grande Réserve *(p466)* Abbaye des Rocs *(p464)* McChouffe *(p467)* Gouden Carolus *(p466)*	Belgium	Serve in a Goblet with a thick creamy head at 9–11°C (48–52°F)
Smoked Beer	A speciality of Franconia and especially Bamberg in Germany, this robust style of beer has influenced brewers around the world to experiment with the use of smoked malts. The degree of smokiness ranges from the subtle to the aggressive. Many beer styles have been smoked, including Weissbiers. Usually 4.5–7.0% ABV.	Schlenkerla Rauchbier *(p480)* Rauchenfelser Steinbier *(p481)* Moku Moku Smoked Ale *(p479)* Alaskan Smoked Porter *(p477)*	Germany Japan USA	Serve in a Stein or a Stange glass with a large, creamy head. at 10–12°C (50–54°F)

BEER STYLE	DESCRIPTION	EXAMPLES	COUNTRY	SERVING
Quadrupel	Originating in The Netherlands, this style has been adopted as a Belgian speciality. Rich, warming, and very strong, these beers have a fruity, almost vinous character, with bitter dark chocolate notes, caramel, and spices all melding together. These beers should be sipped slowly to allow their flavours to develop fully. Usually 8.0–12.5% ABV.	Westvleteren 12 (p464) St Bernardus 12 (p466) Rochefort 10 (p465)	Netherlands Belgium	Serve in a goblet with a thick, tight head at 11–13°C (52–55°F)
Barley Wine	Years ago, these strong beers were available only in the winter months – their rich, warming flavours were seen as the perfect antidote to the cold weather. These beers range from amber to deep russet in colour and their fruity malts are balanced by bittering spicy hops. Their great viscosity may be visible as "legs" in the glass. Usually 9.0–12.0% ABV.	Robinson's Old Tom (p461) Rogue Old Crustacean (p469) Anchor Old Foghorn (p469) Sierra Nevada Bigfoot (p469) Hair of The Dog Fred (p469)	UK USA	Served in a snifter or oversize wine glass with a low head at 11–13°C (52–55°F)
Weizenbock / Dunkel-weisse	These variations on the Weissbier style are achieved by the judicious use of small amounts of darker malts in the brew. The beers are mellower in flavour than Weissbier, yet still retain the characteristic banana and clove flavours. They are considerably darker in colour and have an added complexity of flavour. Usually 5.0–9.0% ABV.	Schneider Aventinus (p450) Hacker Pschorr Dunkel Weisse (p450)	Germany	Served in a Weissbier glass with a billowing, large head at 7–9°C (45–48°F)
Old Ale	These traditional beers are aged at the brewery after fermentation, and may be blended with young brews. They are full of rich malt flavours and usually restrained hop bitterness, and have a full body. Often these beers can be cellared for many years, during which the complexity of flavours will develop further. Usually 6.5–12.0% ABV.	Fuller's Vintage Ale (p460) Theakston Old Peculier (p461) Gales Prize Old Ale (p461) Thomas Hardy's Ale (p462) Greene King Strong Suffolk Ale (p461)	UK	Serve in a snifter or oversize wine glass with a tight head at 11–13°C (52–55°F)
Porter	Originally a blend of stale and new beers, modern porters are brewed using pale malts with the addition of various darker malts ranging from crystal to black. These additional malts not only deepen the colour, which may be close to black, but also produce complex flavours with dark chocolate notes and smooth fruitiness. A meal in a glass. Usually 4.0–7.0% ABV.	Eastwood & Sanders 1872 Porter (p448) Samuel Smith's Taddy Porter (p448) Porterhouse Plain Porter (p446) Sinebrychoff Porter (p450) Zywiec Porter (p451)	UK Ireland Baltic States USA Finland Poland	Serve in a pint glass with a tight, creamy, off-white or coffee-coloured head at 10–12°C (50–54°F)
Stout	The beer style that most people have sampled as Guinness. A jet-black body is topped with a tight, creamy head. Stouts gain their bitterness not only from the hops but also from the inclusion of roasted unmalted barley, which gives a burnt, dry flavour. Once the province of Ireland and the UK, stouts are now produced worldwide. Usually 4.0–7.0% ABV.	Guinness Foreign Extra Stout (p463) Samuel Smith's Imperial Stout (p447) Hop Back Entire Stout (p449) Rogue Shakespeare Stout (p452) Brooklyn Black Chocolate Stout (p451)	Ireland UK USA	Serve in a pint glass with a thick, tight, white, head at 10–12°C (50–54°F)

CHOOSING, BUYING, AND STORING BEER

Breweries and beer brands have proliferated over the past 20 years and it would take a lifetime to sample them all! But don't feel overwhelmed – a few simple tips will guide you to some great brews.

VARIETY CASE A reasonable range of beers is available from most supermarkets and liquor stores, but I always buy from specialist retailers, who hold a far wider selection of fresher, well-kept beers. Most will sell you a mixed case of 12 bottles selected by their own expert buyers – an excellent introduction to beer.

When you ask for "a beer" in a bar or restaurant, you are entering into a lottery. Most likely, you will be served a cold, gassy, and rather bland lager-style beer, which might slake your thirst, but will do little to excite your taste buds. The key to buying beer is to explore the pages of this book and get familiar with the main styles – to know what to expect from a wheat beer, a Czech Pilsner, an IPA, or a stout, for example – and to recognize the key producers from

around the world. Just as with wines, good producers tend to make good beers across the style range, and a little knowledge will give you a lot more confidence to experiment with different beers.

Surprisingly, buying beer has more pitfalls than buying either wine or spirits because beer is the most perishable of all drinks. Most major brands, including virtually all lagers, are matured at the brewery, filtered, pasteurized, and carbonated before being poured into bottles or cans (or metal kegs for supply to bars). Although these drinks are designed to last as long as possible (up to a year), they do not benefit at all from ageing in the bottle, can, or keg, and should be drunk as soon as possible after purchase. Try to buy beer that has been refrigerated, and always check the expiry date to ensure you are

THE BEER CALENDAR

In the days before pasteurization, beer was a highly seasonal drink. Autumn was the key season for production, and the year's most warming ales were ready for Christmas; other ales were made specially for summer, ready to refresh and quench the thirst. Specialist seasonal ales, made using traditional techniques, have been reintroduced by today's breweries, and many are very special indeed!

getting the "youngest" possible bottles. At home, store your beer upright in a cool, dark spot; beer is made with hops, which are sensitive to light, and prolonged exposure can give the brew a really nasty animal aroma. Always handle the beer gently; agitation speeds up chemical reactions within the bottle, which may change the flavour.

As your taste and interest in beer develop, you may be tempted to try some bottle-conditioned beers; these drinks, which tend to be made by specialist brewers, should be treated a little differently because they are not filtered or pasteurized, but instead have sugar or yeast added just before bottling. Secondary fermentation takes place within the bottle, giving them a gentle, natural carbonation; complex flavours may develop in these beers over months, or even years, so they can be cellared like good wines.

AGED BEERS *Most beers are pasteurized, but some are "alive", and continue to ferment and improve in the bottle for up to five years. Belgian Chimay Grand Reserve, Hair of the Dog Fred from the US, and Gales Prize Old Ale, a barley wine from the UK, are good examples of beers that benefit from ageing.*

REAL ALES

Cask-conditioned beer, or "real ale" as it is known in England, is different again. This traditional pub drink is made by primary fermentation at the brewery, followed by secondary fermentation in the barrel. The barrels, which in the UK hold up to 160 litres (36 gallons) of beer, are delivered to the pub cellar and allowed to settle and clear for a few days before serving. Real ale is usually made using only natural ingredients, and should be pumped from the barrel using a hand pump (rather than pressure from canisters of carbon dioxide gas, as with other keg beers); this introduces tiny bubbles of nitrogen from the air into the beer, giving it a smooth, sometimes "creamy" texture.

The quality of a real ale depends on the skill of the brewer, as well as the expertise of the pub cellarman and landlord. For this reason, real ales are hard to mass produce or franchise; they are idiosyncratic, a bit temperamental, but really worth exploring – a true reflection of the English!

MICRO MAKERS *The micro-brewery movement has been a huge success: using traditional methods and quality ingredients, enthusiastic brewers have developed and marketed highly innovative local beers.*

PRODUCTION LINE *Beers are big business. Brands and styles that originate in one country are often produced in breweries around the world for local distribution. These "localized" beers can be quite different to their parents.*

ON TAP *Draught beer has a special appeal – partly because a pub's atmosphere can never be bottled!*

TASTING AND APPRECIATING BEER

Every style of beer has its own character, and even within each style, there is great variety to be discovered. Tasting beer demands as much discipline as tasting wine, and brings great rewards.

I really like tasting beer, not least because it must be swallowed (rather than spat out like wine) to fully assess its hoppy bitterness! There are a few essentials to bear in mind. First, the glass: this should be squeaky clean, and well rinsed, because any oil or detergent present will "kill" the head of the beer.

I like to use a tulip-shaped glass or a brandy balloon to taste all beers, but others would disagree, choosing the "correct" glass for each style. Second, fill the glass to no more than one-third capacity, and ensure that the beer is at its correct serving temperature *(see pp396–9)*; if the beer is too cold, your taste buds will be anaesthetized!

It is interesting to taste about a dozen beers in one session, comparing beers from within one style – pale ales, for example – and tasting from lightest to darkest. I always rinse my glass in pure water between beers, and munch on a cracker and a little dry cheese to neutralize my palate.

HOW TO TASTE BEER

1 Examine the colour against a sheet of white paper. Is the beer cloudy? Most should be clear, but some, like the wheat beers, are cloudy.

2 Agitate the beer; this helps to release aromas.

3 Test the aromas by holding your nose just at the rim of the glass. Are the aromas fresh? Are they balanced or does one ingredient dominate? Do they make you want to drink the beer?

4 Take a small sip and savour the taste. Roll it around your mouth before swallowing. How does the beer feel in your mouth? What are the qualities of the flavour? Take another sip and repeat.

5 Record your observations. It is interesting to compare your notes with previous tastings.

1 Check the colour in natural light (not direct sunlight)   **2** Gently agitate the beer by swirling the glass

3 Smell the aroma in the glass   **4** Taste the beer   **5** Record the flavour in a notebook

DRINK ANALYSIS

COLOUR

Most lagers are a light, bright, fizzy golden yellow, but beer can also be amber, copper, rust, red, brown, black – even pink. If the beer has been filtered at the brewery and you notice cloudiness, it has probably spoiled, or has been served far too cold. Unfiltered or wheat beers, by contrast, are often naturally cloudy.

Darker colour usually, but not always, indicates a stronger flavour, but there may be considerable variation in colour within one style of beer. The colour of the beer should be appropriate to the style. Take a good look at the head on the beer: if this disappears abruptly or "fizzes", then the beer is probably low in malt content, has probably been loaded with carbon dioxide, and is likely to taste sour. A malty beer, by contrast, will have a head that lasts for at least one minute

AROMA

The head of a beer helps to release its aromas, so always sniff the drink soon after pouring. The essential aromas of a beer are the sweet, earthy malt and the grassy, citrus, and sometimes antiseptic hops. On top of that, you may find yeast, herbs, or plants, spice, smoke, flowers, fruit, grass or straw, wood or vegetables, among other aromas – a few of which are presented here.

SWEET
Dark chocolate

FRUIT
Cherries

FLOWERS
Heather

ROASTED
Roasted nuts

SPICE
Liquorice

HERBS AND GRASS
Straw

WOODY
Barrel

VEGETABLES
Asparagus

YEAST
Fresh bread

SMOKE
Charcoal

TASTE

As with aromas, the two basic tastes of beer are sweet, rich malt, and dry, refreshing, bitter hops. These tastes should be in good balance, with no residual sugary sweetness. The basic taste may be modified in countless ways by the influence of yeast, water, and other additives. A good starting point is to identify opposing taste categories, such as those shown on this taste wheel *(right)*, and picture where your beer is located on the wheel. The notion of taste also encompasses the beer's body (creamy or light) as well as its length (how the taste persists).

MALTY

CREAMY

AROMATIC

FLAT

SHORT FINISH

STRONG

LOW ALCOHOL

LONG FINISH

FIZZY

NEUTRAL

HOPPY

LIGHT

SERVING BEER

Beer is a drink to celebrate with or to quench your thirst; it can be taken before food, with food, or as food; in short, there is a beer for every situation, and how it is served is key to its enjoyment.

Each beer has its time, its place, and its own particular demands. For sultry summer evenings, it is hard to beat a cold lager, but when I am out sharing a few glasses with friends at my local bar or pub, I find it too gassy, and prefer a Belgian Ale or an English Pale Ale. If I need a real freshener, I like a sour red ale, and when I feel battered by life, give me a stout or a powerful barley wine. Whatever the beer, it is

essential to serve it at the right temperature *(see tables, pp396–9)*, never over-chilled. I generally keep my beers in the cellar; if refrigerated, I let them warm up for a quarter of an hour or so.

Pouring the perfect beer takes a little practice *(see below)*. Most beers are clear, but some (especially wheat beers) contain sediment – the yeasty residue of secondary fermentation. I like to pour these beers slowly into the glass in front of a light, so that I keep the sediment in the bottle, but some people like to mix the yeast with the beer (B vitamins in the yeast help prevent hangovers, and give the beer more body). For a cloudy drink, pour about two thirds of the beer into a glass, then gently swirl the remainder in the bottle to resuspend the yeast, and pour.

POURING A BEER

1 Check that the glass is spotlessly clean and free of grease and detergent. Open the bottle without agitating the beer.

2 Tilt the glass to about 45° and pour about half of the beer carefully down the side of the glass. At this stage it should have little or no head.

3 Straighten the glass to about 15°, pouring slowly into the centre of the glass. At this point, the head should start to appear.

4 Bring the glass fully upright and continue pouring into the centre until the foam nears the top of the glass. When pouring an ale, aim for a "one finger" depth of foam.

5 Taste and enjoy the beer.

1 Check the glass for cleanliness
2 Hold the glass at 45° and pour

3 Pour into the centre of the glass

4 Bring the glass upright

5 ...then enjoy

MATCHING FOOD AND BEER

Up to 100 years ago, beer was routinely served with food, and this tradition is being revived by today's micro-breweries, which often have attached restaurants. Here are a just a few ways to partner food and beer – the key is to experiment!

FOOD STYLE	BEER PARTNER
Cheese	Match mild, creamy cheeses with wheat beers; mature hard cheeses like cheddar with pale ales; and strong blue cheese with barley wines.
Salad	Match the beer with the dressing: with a vinaigrette, try a sour Belgian brown ale or a fresh Saison beer. For a mayo dressing try wheat beer.
Chicken	Roast chicken works well with amber beers, where the caramel of the malt complements the flavours from the skin.
Seafood	Pale beers, wheat beers, Pilsners, and Kölsch work with delicate fish; try fish and chips with an English Pale Ale, and oysters with stout.
Red meat	Hearty beers, brown ales, and porters work with most roast meats. For stronger meats, especially game, try an Old Ale.
Barbecues	Robust, slightly acidic beers that stand up to smoky, caramelized flavours include brown ales, bière de garde, and Rauchbier.
Thai food	Wheat beers, with their floral, citric, and spicy flavours, are a perfect match to fragrant Thai cuisine. American Pale Ales are an alternative.
Mexican food	Beers with a spicy hop character, such as IPAs, Saisons, and some of the darker lagers, will be quite at home with bold Mexican flavours.

WHEAT BEER

PILSNER

STOUT

ALE

HEAD SIZES *The foam on top of a freshly poured beer forms as bubbles of carbon dioxide rise through the liquid and become coated with proteins derived from malted barley. The size of the head can be varied by changing the speed of pouring, and so depends in part on local custom. Wheat beers and Pilsners should be served with a full, frothy head; stouts and ales have a medium head, which sometimes lasts right to the bottom of the glass.*

GLASS SELECTION *Each style of beer has its own glass shape to enhance the drinking experience.*

WEISSBIER GLASS

PILSNER GLASS

TALL, STRAIGHT KÖLSCH OR LAGER GLASS

GOBLET FOR BELGIAN ALE

TULIP-SHAPED GLASS FOR BIÈRE DE GARDE

ALE TANKARD

BOCK SNIFTER

PINT GLASS FOR ALE

66 This is what I expect when I ask for "a beer" – a drink that hits the spot with a cool, bright, and refreshing taste. 99

LIGHT AND REFRESHING

INTRODUCING LIGHT AND REFRESHING BEERS

From world-famous brands to some special local brews, light and refreshing beers are crisp, clean, and consistent. These are fun beers for drinking with friends, and your choice of favourite may have as much to do with the branding as with the flavour.

These beers are essentially Pilsner-style lagers, which means they are bottom-fermented in the brewing process and "lagered" – stored in cool conditions – and normally pasteurized. The resulting brew is light, golden, and refreshing. It is also very stable and serviceable – ideal for mass production and global distribution. These beers generally have little depth or complexity, but are extremely fit for their purpose.

The nature of the aroma is not important for these beers, which are usually bought to drink on their own as session or party beers, and are most often drunk when very cold. Refreshment is the most significant feature, which means a dry finish. But balance is vital: too dry, and there is no pleasure; too sweet, and it becomes cloying and undrinkable in any quantity. Consistency is key to their success. If you buy a can of Carlsberg or a bottle of Beck's, you expect to find exactly the same beer in Iceland or South Africa, New York or Hong Kong. The brewers know that availability of their beer is vital in keeping up demand; for most of these beers, like Heineken, Budweiser, or Stella Artois, the market is the world. For others, like Tsingtao, Efes, or Tusker, the market is regional, though even very localized brands can develop global ambitions under international ownership.

CINNAMON *Flavours of spice abound in sophisticated light and refreshing beers, such as De Koninck and Christoffel.*

POINTS OF DIFFERENCE

Most of these beers are quite similar, and, it may be argued, almost interchangeable. Could you really tell your Amstel from your Grolsch, or your Kronenbourg from your San Miguel, if you didn't know which one you were drinking? Some of these beers, like the American Budweiser, are made slightly sweeter for their core US market; while the Cologne and Munich beers, and Belgian regional beers like Jupiler, are more complex to reflect the palates of their home markets. Overall, though, these brands are standardized for the world market – straight down the middle!

SALTED SNACKS *Cashew nuts and other nibbles, such as peanuts and crisps, are perfect with light beers.*

DRINKING AND SERVING

DRINK PROFILE The essential colour for these beers is gold. The aromas are linked more to yeast and hops than to malt and fruit, but the taste is the key: light, fizzy, dry, and, above all, refreshing.

C COLOUR These lagers are mostly a similar dark yellow to light gold, although some are a little darker. Most have little head to speak of, and there is no yeast sediment to worry about.

A AROMA Most of these beers have very delicate, floral, and even neutral aromas. Some of the more elegant versions, such as the Kölsch style from Cologne, are more aromatic.

T TASTE The general feel is a gentle balance between light malt sweetness and hop dryness, or even spiciness. Most important is a dry and refreshing finish, leaving you wanting more.

BUYING AND STORING These beers are mainly Pilsner-style lagers, and most of them are international products, available in many countries. It is not necessary to store or "lay down" these beers; most are pasteurized, and will not improve over time. The fresher the better!

SERVING SUGGESTIONS The essential thing is to serve them very cold, never more than 9°C (48°F). Whether you serve this type of beer straight from the can or bottle, or pour it into a glass, is really a matter of culture and personal taste.

FOOD COMPANIONS These beers are best as an appetite-building apéritif with a few snacks or nibbles. If you drink them with food, it is only to wash it down and refresh the palate; neither the beer nor the food is particularly enhanced.

INTERNATIONAL

These light, refreshing, fizzy, and reliable beers include some of the biggest-selling worldwide brands. Wherever you are in the world, if you buy one of these beers, you can be confident that you know exactly what you are getting.

BUDWEISER

C COLOUR Pale gold, with a short-lived, bubbly head.

A AROMA Almost neutral, with only a delicate hint of hops.

T TASTE Light and mild; crisp and clean, with a slightly sweetish or fruity finish.

The biggest-selling beer in the world, Budweiser is produced by the brewing giant Anheuser Busch. This beer is made with rice as well as several types of hop, and it is clarified in tanks with beech chips. In some parts of Europe, it is known as Bud, due to a dispute over the name "Budweiser" *(see p422)*.

MILLER GENUINE DRAFT

C COLOUR Medium gold, with a bubbly, white head with medium retention.

A AROMA Delicate, sweet, and petrolly, with light hop aromas.

T TASTE Quite sweet overall, with a medium, refreshing finish.

Miller is the second-largest brewer in the US. This beer is made by the cold filtration process, which removes the need to pasteurize. It is geared to the American market, and is a little too sweet for many Europeans, I suspect. Despite the name, it is only sold in bottles.

SAN MIGUEL

C COLOUR Pale amber to dark gold, a good, full, frothy head.

A AROMA Quite strong for a lager, with hops and fruit.

T TASTE Fairly dry, with hops and malt, and a rich finish.

San Miguel is a long-established and very large company based in the Philippines. Their award-winning Pilsner-style lager is also brewed by a number of different breweries around the world, including in Spain and Indonesia. For a mass-market beer, San Miguel has established something of a reputation. The Philippine, Indonesian, and Spanish versions are all slightly different, but overall this beer is fruitier than other global lagers, and is a fairly rich and satisfying brew, with a firm hoppy flavour.

BIRRA MORETTI

C COLOUR Light gold, with a good, full, white head.

A AROMA Flowery and delicate, with notes of light hops and yeast.

T TASTE Full flavour, with malt and a dry finish.

The Moretti brewery was founded in Udine, Italy, in 1869, and established a fine reputation, always linked to its trademark of a mustachioed man blowing the froth off his beer. Moretti is now part of Heineken, but intervention by the Italian government has enabled the Udine brewery to make its traditional Moretti independently under the Castello name. The regular Heineken Moretti is a mainstream light lager, with a crisp feel and no great depth – a thirst-quencher on a hot day. This is a regular supermarket beer in Italy.

BIRRA MORETTI

PERONI NASTRO AZZURRO

C COLOUR Pale straw, with a very small and wispy white head.

A AROMA Subtle, almost neutral, delicate aromas, with yeast and hops.

T TASTE Bright and refreshing, with a bittersweet finish.

The Peroni family founded their brewery near Milan in 1846. Peroni's flagship brand is Nastro Azzurro (blue stripe). This is a premium lager at 5.2% ABV. It is light, bright, and fizzy, and similar in style to Stella Artois. In 1996 Peroni introduced a new Gran Riserva beer to celebrate its 150th anniversary. At 6.6% ABV, this is stronger, and quite rich and complex for a lager.

Nastro Azzurro is perfect with pasta for a summer lunchtime. For me it is one of the best Italian beers, and a match for German brews.

GROLSCH

C COLOUR A richer gold than many lagers, with a thick, foamy, white head.

A AROMA Delicate and fresh, with grass, hops, and a hint of citrus.

T TASTE Light, with refreshing citrus, and a bittersweet hop and malt finish.

Thanks to excellent marketing, Grolsch is very well known around the world, but until recent years this was quite a small brewery. It is named after the small town of Grolle (now Groenlo) in eastern Holland, where it was established in 1615. Grolsch beers are normally unpasteurized, apart from the canned version, and they have a hoppy aroma and a light, yeasty feel. They are moderately strong at 5% ABV. Grolsch also makes a number of variations, such as the dry Mei Bok and the richer Amber.

GROLSCH

HEINEKEN

C COLOUR Light gold, with a fairly long-lasting head with average lacing.

A AROMA Light hop scent and a gentle, grassy feel.

T TASTE Smooth and firm, with a hop feel and a lively finish.

The Heineken story starts in 1864, when Gerard Heineken bought a brewery in Amsterdam, which itself had been making beer since 1592. The company expanded continuously, and Heineken is now a truly global beer, massively exported and also brewed around the world, including in China and Russia. The basic Pilsner is lighter than a typical German version, but still has quite a bit of substance. It is bright, fresh, and full-bodied, with a sparkling and fizzy character – just right as a summer beer.

AMSTEL

C COLOUR Pale straw, with a white head that fades, leaving foam and good lace.

A AROMA Delicate and neutral, with a hint of hops.

T TASTE Slightly bitter, with a medium-length, dry finish.

Although a long-established name in the Netherlands, Amstel is now a second-string brand for Heineken. The brewery, named after Amsterdam's river, was taken over in the 1960s, and closed in the 1980s. So when you buy an Amstel you are really buying a Heineken. Amstel is still a global brand, and is positioned as the standard beer to Heineken's more premium product. At 4.1% ABV, Amstel is lower in alcohol, and is a neutral, slightly bitter Pilsner. It is promoted in draught as a light, daily drinking beer for all occasions.

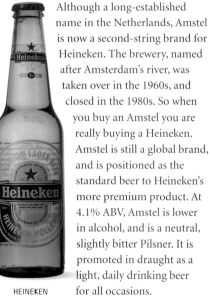

HEINEKEN

MALTED BREW *Stella Artois is brewed using malted barley and Bohemian Saaz hops. This bottom-fermented Pilsner is best served cold at 4–6°C (39–43°F).*

STELLA ARTOIS

C COLOUR Light gold, with a medium to full, white head.

A AROMA Quite delicate and almost neutral, with light hops.

T TASTE Light, with a sweet, citrusy feel and a slightly bitter finish.

Stella Artois, from Belgium, is a classic global brew – not too strong, not too much aroma, and a reliable, well-balanced taste. It is one of the world's top five biggest-selling beer brands, and one of the flagships of the giant InBev company (formerly Interbrew), along with Beck's, Bass, Brahma (South America), Leffe, Hoegaarden, and many more!

The story of Stella Artois goes back to 1466, when the Den Hoorn brewery was opened in the Belgian university town of Leuven (Louvain), to the east of Brussels. The brewery was built on the site of a natural spring, which gave a unique character to its beers. In 1708, Sebastian Artois was appointed master brewer, and nine years later he bought the company and gave it his name.

The old brewery was destroyed by artillery shells during the First World War; its replacement launched Stella Artois in 1926, using the original water source. First produced as a special Christmas beer, the new brew proved a great success, and its fame grew steadily.

In 1987, the Artois Brewery merged with the Jean-Theodore Piedboeuf Brewery to form Interbrew. Under the auspices of this major brewing conglomerate, Stella Artois was developed into a truly worldwide product with a "stellar" reputation!

The basic Stella is a 5.2% ABV Pilsner-style lager. It has a distinctive taste and a crisp, slightly bitter hoppy finish, with just that extra bit of character to distinguish it from other mass-produced beers, without losing the overall blandness essential for the global market.

To me, Stella Artois is one of the best, most complex, and most appealing of the international beer brands.

STELLA ARTOIS

KRONENBOURG

C COLOUR Pale straw, with a thin white head that disappears slowly.

A AROMA Delicate and quite neutral, with a touch of yeasty hops.

T TASTE Fresh and bright; slightly hoppy; well-balanced, with a subtle bitterness.

This lager – France's most popular brand – began life in Strasbourg's Cronenbourg district in 1664. Today, the brewer – Brasseries Kronenbourg – is part of the Scottish & Newcastle group.

The regular Kronenbourg brew is light and neutral, but well balanced. At 5.2% ABV, it is a good quality drinking beer. The premium 1664 brand (or *soixante-quatre*, as it it known) dates from 1952, and at 5.9% ABV is stronger and more complex. It is also dryer, but with a balanced sweetness and a hoppy feel. The slightly sweet finish hints at honey and fruit.

BECK'S

C COLOUR Medium straw, with a medium, white, foamy, quickly dissipating head.

A AROMA Light and delicate, with hints of malt and hops.

T TASTE Crisp and dry, with a neutral feel and a fresh finish.

Beck's has always been an innovative brewer, and its flagship Pilsner, at 5%, is quite dry for a world beer, with more depth and style. It is not as rich as many German beers, but very satisfying.

The Kaiserbrauerei Beck & May began brewing in Bremen in 1873, and it has now been absorbed into the InBev group. Beck's is Germany's leading export beer, and the brand is expanding in China as well as in the West. It currently accounts for 80% of German beer exports to the US.

BECK'S

CARLSBERG

C COLOUR Pale yellow straw, with a small, puffy, white head.

A AROMA Delicate and light, with hops and yeast in good balance.

T TASTE Clean and soft, with a fine head and a slightly sweet feel.

The Carlsberg company dominates the Danish beer market, and also owns its former rival, Tuborg. It was founded in 1847 by Jacob Jacobsen, at Valby, near Copenhagen. He named the company after his son, Carl, and the hill (berg) on which the brewery was built. From the start, Carlsberg concentrated on producing Bavarian-style lager, and experimented with new brewing processes. Carlsberg is now a famous global brand.

The basic Carlsberg Pilsner is 5.5% ABV, and a fine example of a drinkable world beer: not too distinctive, but reliable. It has a slightly sweet, hoppy finish.

KEO

C COLOUR Pale straw; bubbly, short-lived head, replaced by a thin veil of lace.

A AROMA Fresh and lively aromas, with malt and a slight note of honey.

T TASTE Quite sweet and full-bodied; a malty, resin flavour; slightly sweet finish.

Keo is part of the state-owned brewery on the island of Cyprus. The brewery motto is "Be Happy and Drink Well" – what a wonderful sentiment!

Keo is quite neutral on the nose, but has lots of flavour and character, with a slightly sweet and lemony feel. The hops are also evident. At 4.5% ABV, it is not especially strong, but it has a distinctive taste – Pilsner, with a little bit of Greek magic added! This is one of those beers that seems to taste better the colder it is served.

KEO

SPORTS PROMOTION Global brands need widespread and constant media exposure to maintain their market share. Beer companies have been quick to realize that sports sponsorship is a great way of achieving this and raising public awareness of their products. Apart from linking their brands to exciting, glamourous, high-profile events, they also feel, rightly or wrongly, that long-term sponsorship of a particular sport or competition can help to increase public goodwill towards their brand. Stella Artois, for example, has sponsored the tennis championships at the Queen's Club in London since 1979, while Budweiser (the US brand) has a long association with FIFA, football's ruling body, and the football World Cup.

EFES

C COLOUR Medium gold, with a good-sized bubbly, frothy head.

A AROMA Quite strong, firm aromas, with hops and yeast in evidence.

T TASTE Fairly sweet and full-bodied, with a distinctly hoppy finish.

Named after the ancient Roman city of Ephesus, Efes is Turkey's biggest beer producer. Although a Muslim country, Turkey tolerates alcohol, and the many thousands of Turkish workers throughout the rest of Europe are a ready export market for Efes' portfolio of beers. Recently, the company has expanded into Eastern Europe, setting up plants in Romania and Russia.

Efes is a Pilsner, and generally rather similar to Beck's, but with a stronger aroma and a sweeter taste. It is a bottom-fermented beer brewed with golden barley, high quality malt, and Hallertau hops. Efes is easy to drink, foamy, and bright, with an alcohol content of 5% ABV.

MYTHOS

C COLOUR Medium golden yellow, with a small head.

A AROMA Not too attractive; quite spicy and hoppy, with citrus and yeast.

T TASTE Clean, slightly malty flavour, with a dryish, metallic-and-lemon finish.

Mythos is brewed by Northern Greece Breweries, now part of Scottish & Newcastle. Introduced in 1997, Mythos has about ten per cent of Greece's steadily growing beer market. Western drinkers may feel that the aroma and taste of this Pilsner need polishing, but the colour and fizz are good, and it is quite creamy for an everyday lager. Mythos is best for hot afternoons by the beach, rather than for evening sipping.

MYTHOS

ASAHI

C **COLOUR** Pale yellow, with a short-lived, bubbly head.

A **AROMA** Distinctive; quite malty with a suggestion of rice and grain.

T **TASTE** Dry and light, with a touch of malt and hops and a short, dry finish.

Asahi is Japan's second-biggest brewing group, but remained a small brewery up to 1987, when the launch of its flagship Asahi Super Dry tripled its market share in seven years.

Asahi makes a wide range of beers, from a number of different raw materials, including rice. The rice-and-hop Super Dry is a pale lager, similar to a US Budweiser, but slightly drier. Its light aromas and taste are a perfect match for both spicy-hot and delicate Asian foods, and the short finish is good with sushi, as it cleans the palate.

KIRIN

C **COLOUR** Pale straw yellow, with a tight, white, fairly long-lasting head.

A **AROMA** Delicate and distinctive; hints of barley and rice.

T **TASTE** Light and dry, with a full body and crisp hop finish.

The Japanese giant! Kirin, founded in 1869 in Yokohama, is by far the largest Japanese brewery, and accounts for around half of the country's total production.

The flagship Kirin Beer is an everyday drinking beer, made with spring water, rice, barley malt, maize, and hops. It is light and refreshing, with a good dry balance, and moderately strong at 4.9% ABV. Kirin is best served *very* cold, in my view. The premium brew is Ichiban, which is slightly stronger and richer.

KIRIN

SINGHA

C **COLOUR** Light bright gold, with a big, fizzy head with little retention.

A **AROMA** Fresh and delicate aromas, with hops and a citrus feel.

T **TASTE** Malty sweetness, bitterness, and a fine dry finish; excellent balance.

Of all the world's Pilsner-style beers, to me this is one of the very best. Singha – named after the famous mythical Thai creature that resembles a lion – is produced in Thailand at a brewery established in the 1930s, and that has a strong German influence.

This is a powerful beer, at 6% ABV, and has a great balance between sweetness and dryness. It is a lovely light gold, and the flavour is sweet and fruity, but at the same time with a bitter edge, and a terrific dry finish. A must to try with spicy food, which it matches brilliantly!

SINGHA

HITE

C **COLOUR** Pale bright yellow, with a bright white, frothy head.

A **AROMA** Softly scented, with hints of hops and barley malt.

T **TASTE** Smooth and light, with a lively feel and a dry finish.

Hite stands for Humanity, Innovation, Trust, and Excellence.

It is the biggest brewer in Korea, which is something of a closed market for beer. If it was more open, I think local beers like this would improve with the competition! This lager is quite light and refreshing, but not as smooth and balanced as Western or Australian beer. It is also not too strong at 4.5% ABV, and is a bit like an Asian version of Budweiser.

Prime, an all-malt beer, is brewed in accordance with German regulations.

COBRA

C **COLOUR** Light bright yellow, with a tidy, white head.

A **AROMA** Gentle, with hints of hops, yeast, and corn.

T **TASTE** Smooth and light, with a refreshing feel and a peppery finish.

COBRA

The Indian beer from Bangalore, but brewed in Bedford in the UK and Poland! This pioneering Indian–British Pilsner was first introduced in 1989. It was founded by an Indian Army general's son, Karan Bilimoria, who discovered an interest in beer during childhood days in the officers' mess. Bilimoria studied at Cambridge University and became an accountant with the company of Ernst and Young, but soon left to realize his dream of developing a Pilsner that would go well with spicy Indian food, and suit both lager drinkers and more traditional British ale fans. He employed a Czech-trained master brewer, and built his market around the Indian restaurants in the UK, literally selling the beer by the case out of the back of his car.

This is a delicate brew made from barley, malt, maize, and hops. It is moderately strong at 5% ABV, with a light, malty, fairly aromatic, semi-sweet feel, and is an excellent match for Indian food. Sure, any lager would "do the trick" with spicy food or curry, but this, along with Singha *(see above)*, definitely works the best.

CULTURE AND TRADITION

BEER AND CURRY Indian beers, such as Cobra, have experienced a surge in popularity worldwide, mirroring the growing taste for the Indian cuisine they were designed to complement. Key to their success is the affinity between light Pilsner-style beers, especially those with a little malty sweetness, and spicy food. As well as calming the sensation of strong chilli, these light beers leave the palate clean – a great benefit when enjoying a mix of flavours in spicy Indian dishes, such as *sag aloo*, *niramish*, and *dhal*.

TUSKER

C **COLOUR** Pale yellow, with a light, white, foamy head.

A **AROMA** Quite hoppy, with grass and yeast in the distinctive mix.

T **TASTE** Creamy and dry, with a clean and slightly bitter finish.

"Kenya my country – Tusker my beer!" goes the slogan of this Kenyan lager, named after the African bull elephant, which appears on both the label and the cap. Legend has it that an elephant trampled to death one of the English brothers who founded the brewery back in 1922. (It was not until 1960 that the first African sat on the board of directors.)

Tusker is the flagship brand, and has established a very good reputation as one of the very best African beers. It is a creamy Pilsner with a dry yet fruity taste: light, clean, crisp, and clear. The traditional way to drink it in Kenya is with open spit-roasted meat called *nyama choma*. Sounds wonderful!

RED STRIPE

C COLOUR Pale gold, with a short-lived, foamy head that lightly laces.

A AROMA Hop and grain aromas, balanced with a little sweet malt.

T TASTE Strong and full-bodied, with hop bitterness and a slightly sweet finish.

Jamaica's favourite! This lager was originally made by the family firm of Desnoes and Geddes, established in 1918 in Kingston, Jamaica. It is very popular throughout the Caribbean, and worldwide among Afro-Caribbean beer drinkers. So much so, that it is now also brewed in the UK.

The original Red Stripe is quite strong-tasting with a good balance between sweetness and bitterness. The UK version has less character, in my opinion – best for a hot day to get at least a bit of the Jamaican atmosphere.

TSINGTAO

C COLOUR Light gold, with a light and bubbly head with almost no retention.

A AROMA Fresh and distinctive, with hops, herbs, and rice.

T TASTE Slightly bitter, with malt, grassy hops, corn, and a touch of vanilla.

TSINGTAO

Tsingtao is one of China's best-known beers around the world, and a cut above many lagers brewed with rice. It is quite strong, at 5% ABV, and has a complex set of aromas – hops, herbs, and even onions. For me, it is at its best served cold, but not ice cold, with spicy food.

Tsingtao is made across China, but the original brewery was in Qingdao, the old name for Tsingtao. Because of the number of breweries, there is inevitably some variation in taste and quality.

CORONA

C COLOUR Pale golden yellow, with a short-lived head and no lacing.

A AROMA Delicate, almost neutral, with a hint of malt.

T TASTE Crisp and refreshing, with not too much fizz and a slightly sweet finish.

At various times, Mexico's Corona has become the height of fashion in San Francisco, London, and New York, and the idea of sticking a piece of lime in the neck of the bottle was exported back into Mexico from the US – the Mexicans had never heard of it!

This is a fine everyday drinking beer, made using maize, rice, and hops. Light, bright, and best drunk very cold, Corona is not a great one for flavour, but is very refreshing with a wedge of lemon – or even better, lime – pushed into the bottle.

CASTLEMAINE XXXX

C COLOUR Medium gold, with a fairly creamy head.

A AROMA Mild, with corn and malt in a fine balance.

T TASTE Medium-dry and light-bodied, with some sweetness on the finish.

One for a hot afternoon! Although described in Australia as a bitter ale, Castlemaine XXXX is a lager brewed with whole hops. The brewery began life in the town of Castlemaine, Victoria, where the Fitzgerald brothers established the business in 1859. They later relocated to Brisbane, and XXXX, introduced in 1924, has become the definitive Queensland favourite.

At 4.8% ABV, this is not particularly strong; it is a mild, everyday beer that does not strive for any great depth or power.

CASTLEMAINE

FOSTER'S

C COLOUR Straw yellow, with a long-lasting, full, and frothy head.

A AROMA Quite fruity and light, with hops to the fore.

T TASTE Good balance, and a full, sweetish flavour.

To many people, Foster's is Australia. Originally founded in Melbourne in 1888 by two American brothers, Foster's was the first to import lager-making equipment into Australia, at a time when most Australians drank traditional English ales. After a year, the Foster brothers sold the brewery and returned to America; Fosters went on to become a global brand.

This refreshing lager has had its share of critics for being bland and mass-produced, but for an everyday beer, Foster's has a much better reputation than most. It is creamy, fruity, and well-balanced, and is very good when served in a very cold bottle. It is also sold in cans, and takes well to draught.

BAR CULTURE *Crisp, refreshing lager-style beers are perfect served well-chilled on draught and have become the definitive after-work bar drink for a hot summer's day.*

NEW ZEALAND

Like Australia, New Zealand began with a British brewing tradition, and lager was not introduced until 1900, and only then in the warmer North Island areas around Auckland. In the colder South Island, traditional "warm ales" ruled well into the late 20th century.

STEINLAGER

C COLOUR Pale gold, with a good, frothy but short-lived head.

A AROMA Aromatic, but well-balanced, with an acidic hop feel.

T TASTE Particularly dry and fresh, and even slightly bitter.

In 1917, the temperance movement persuaded the government of New Zealand to introduce a 6 o'clock closing time for pubs and bars, which lasted until 1967 – those poor New Zealanders!

The effect of this ruling was to threaten the very existence of the country's beer industry, and many New Zealand breweries either went to the wall or were forced to merge in order to head off the threat through economies of scale. Lion Nathan – formed by the merger of several small breweries – was one of the survivors.

In 1958, Lion Nathan launched a premium lager called Steinecker, named after the German brewing machinery used in its manufacture. With the beer growing in popularity both at home and abroad, Heineken mounted a legal challenge over the name. It was rechristened Steinlager in 1962 to provide greater clarity between brands.

Steer clear of this medium-strength brew (5% ABV) if you prefer fruity beers, but those who like dry lager will love it! I particularly enjoy this beer because of its complexity and weight, but it is also refreshing and aromatic, and great to awaken your appetite.

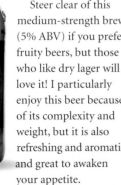

STEINLAGER

PREMIUM LAGER *This crisp lager has a grassy note and a clean, hoppy bitterness. The original brown bottle was changed to green in the 1970s to bring it into line with other premium brands.*

GERMANY

About 150 years ago, Germany was not a country, but a collection of states. Many states had a traditional style of beer, and some are still produced today, including Kölsch, from Cologne, and Münchner, from Munich.

FRÜH KÖLSCH

C COLOUR Pale lemony gold, with a firm, long-lasting, frothy head.

A AROMA Faint fruity aromas of flowers and strawberry.

T TASTE Dry and beautifully balanced, with firm, creamy malt and a dry finish.

The term Kölsch can only be applied to beers brewed in Köln (Cologne), and Früh Kölsch is one of the finest examples of the genre.

Früh Kölsch may look like a lager, but it is really an ale, and made using *obergärige* (top-fermenting) yeast. This brew was originally made on the premises at the famous Cologne

FRÜH KÖLSCH

tavern of P. J. Früh, before production was moved to larger facilities in the 1980s. It is now bottled and sold around the world.

Früh Kölsch is an outstanding light-bodied beer of 4.8% ABV. It is made from pale malt (and sometimes wheat) and hops. This is one of my favourite of all German beers; it is dry but fruity, delicate yet complex, and malty – all at the same time! I often recommend this beer with food, an as alternative to wine. Try it with *choucroute* (sauerkraut) – a surprisingly good combination.

DOM KÖLSCH

C COLOUR Light gold, with a small, firm head of bright white foam.

A AROMA Clean and fresh, with delicate hops and yeast.

T TASTE Malty and slightly sweet, with a dry citrus finish.

Kölsch is a survivor of the pre-lager brewing tradition of northern Germany. As well as having to be brewed in metropolitan Cologne, all Kölsch beers are top-fermented, pale in colour, hop-accented, and filtered. Dom ("Cathedral") Kölsch embodies the best Kölsch attributes – it is aromatic, sparkling, and refreshing. This beer is moderately strong, at 4.8% ABV, and smooth on the palate, with a very clean, fresh feel. It has an enticing bright-gold colour, a delicate hoppy aroma, and a dry, citrusy taste.

Sampling Dom Kölsch in its home city is imperative for any visitor to Cologne; and if you are fortunate enough to find it on sale in your own locality, don't waste the opportunity!

FOOD MATCH

MIXED SUMMER SALAD The light character of many Kölsch beers makes them well-suited to meals outdoors in the summer sunshine, especially dressed mixed salads and light picnic food. Kölsches have a reputation as being stomach-settlers, so they can also be served as pre-dinner apéritifs.

GILDEN KÖLSCH

C COLOUR Pale straw gold, with a large fluffy white head.

A AROMA Light, flowery, and very appealing, with hops and yeast.

T TASTE Bright, fruity, and fizzy, with a dry and slightly bitter finish.

This is another fine example of the Kölsch style, made by the Gilden brewery, which is now part of the Brau und Brunnen Group. The term "Gilden" refers back to the time of the Brewers' Guild, and this beer has a long and distinguished history.

Gilden Kölsch is made in the traditional style, and is moderately strong at 4.8% ABV. It has a flowery aroma and a medium gold colour. It is soft to the palate, with a fairly neutral flavour. There is a hint of fruit, but overall the feeling is dry, clean, and refreshing.

GILDEN KÖLSCH

KÜPPER'S KÖLSCH

C COLOUR Dark straw gold, darker than most beers in the style.

A AROMA Light scents of malt and fruit, especially apple.

T TASTE Quite smooth and dry, with a fruity citrusy feel.

The excellent Küpper's brewery was founded in the early 1800s in Düsseldorf by Gustav Küpper.

For many years it produced lager, and only began making Kölsch during the 1960s, when the firm relocated to Cologne.

Like the Gilden brewery, Küpper's has now been absorbed into Brau und Brunnen, the vast nationwide brewing conglomerate.

Unlike many Kölsch beers, which are draught-only and not bottled, Küpper's is widely available outside the Rhineland region, and actively marketed abroad.

KÜPPER'S KÖLSCH

With an ABV of 4.8%, Küpper's is a reasonably good Kölsch, with the combination of ale and lager characteristics that is typical of the style.

Küpper's is not quite as subtle as the very best of the Kölsch beers, but its fruity character comes through in the aromas (it has a nose reminiscent of dry cider) and flavours. The beer is never too sweet, with an overall dry and citrusy feel, but it is quite gassy, and this fizziness can sometimes inhibit the taste.

While it is certainly not the king of Kölsches, I have always found it eminently drinkable, and it is far better than many other beers on the market. Its export presence means that it will be the first "port of call" for many outside of Germany who want to sample this type of beer.

SPATEN MÜNCHNER HELL

C COLOUR Pale golden straw, with a large, white head with good retention.

A AROMA Distinctive, with herby hops, new-mown hay, and nettles.

T TASTE Quite malty and slightly sweet, with a dry, hoppy, nutty finish.

Spaten ("Spade") is one of the best and oldest breweries in Munich, dating from 1397. In the 1830s it became one of the first to perfect the modern method of making lager. (Yeast from Spaten was sent to Denmark to make the first Carlsberg lager.)

Spaten's standard lager is Münchner Hell, a moderately strong beer (4.8% ABV). Not too heavy, it has a lovely herby, hoppy taste and a fresh dry finish. I recommended it – especially for drinking on a warm, sunny afternoon!

SPATEN MÜNCHNER HELL

BELGIUM

The Belgians can justly lay claim to being the greatest brewing country in the world, producing superb beers in nearly every style. Their light, bright Pilsner lagers are outstanding for their delicate complexity and flavour-packed freshness.

MAES PILS

C COLOUR Medium gold, with a frothy, white head.

A AROMA Delicate and neutral, with a hint of flowers and hops.

T TASTE Very full-flavoured, with hops and a slight malty bitterness.

This is not a deep and profound beer, but it goes brilliantly well with a fine plate of Ostend or Bruges steak and chips! Maes Pils is a classic Pilsner, not too strong at 4.9% ABV, and light, with a slightly dry hint of hops in the aroma and taste. The aroma is delicate and flowery, not strong or yeasty.

DE KONINCK

C COLOUR Medium amber, with a full, firm, and frothy head.

A AROMA Rich, with hops and a hint of caramel.

T TASTE Creamy head; malty and spicy; yeast and grass; dry finish.

Antwerp's local brew is most usually served on draught in a *bolleken* (little ball), its special glass. It is quite dark in colour, with a great head and complex flavours of cinnamon spice and caramel. This is a lovely, refreshing beer – one for the evening rather than a hot afternoon.

DE KONINCK

JUPILER

C COLOUR Light gold, with a small, short-lived, frothy head.

A AROMA Complex bouquet, with well-balanced malt, fruit, and hops.

T TASTE Smooth and dry, with just a touch of bitterness.

Belgium's bestseller – a not-so-simple everyday beer, and deliciously refreshing! The Belgians certainly know their beer, and they make some of the best in the world, often in tiny quantities in micro-breweries. But for everyday drinking, this is their favourite brand. The beer is named after the town of Jupille, near Liege. The brewery was founded in 1853, and is now part of the giant InBev group, along with the world-famous Stella Artois brand.

Jupiler has a golden yellow colour, and is quite strong at 5.2% ABV. This is a really well-balanced beer, with a compact white head, complex bouquet, and great dry flavour. The hoppy dryness is overlain with a fresh, citrusy feel. You might expect simplicity, but you will be surprised at the smoothness of this beer. It is also excellent value. Some good beers are really expensive, but Jupiler is well-promoted by the InBev group, so there is never any difficulty in finding it at a good price.

It is often compared with its globe-conquering partner, Stella, and many beer drinkers find that they prefer it. If you consider yourself a lager drinker, and are in Belgium, you must give this a try!

JUPILER

AUSTRIA

Austria makes some fine light lagers, mainly in the German style, but often a little more fruity and traditional. The Czech's genius for light beers has also informed Austria's brewing traditions: Pilsner was invented by the Czechs, who were under Austrian rule at the time.

KAPSREITER LANDBIER HELL

C COLOUR Light golden yellow, with a full, frothy, white head.

A AROMA Very aromatic, with yeast and slightly bitter hops.

T TASTE Particularly smooth, with a fruity, hoppy flavour and a slightly bitter finish.

A very pleasant, straightforward, and well-made lager, presented in a traditional swingtop bottle. It is popular in Austria at lunchtime, as it is not too strong at 4.4% ABV. There is a touch of spice in the taste and the overall mildness of the fizz allows the well-balanced flavours to come through.

TRUMER PILS

C COLOUR Golden yellow, with a medium, bubbly, frothy head.

A AROMA Fresh and lively aromas, with hops, grass, and citrus.

T TASTE Very dry; mildly bitter, with a dry hoppy finish.

This is the flagship brand of the Josef Sigl brewery, which has been in operation since 1601. It is not too strong, at 4.9% ABV, and has quite a herby, hoppy feel; nor is it too fizzy. The aroma is its least attractive feature, but persevere and wait for the taste. It is normal to serve this beer in a long, tall glass, and it is best enjoyed on a warm afternoon.

FINLAND

Finland has some very traditional, almost medieval beers, but for everyday drinking, government legislation has meant that only two large companies control beer production. This limits the number of brands available from this country.

LAPIN KULTA

C COLOUR Golden yellow, with a medium to full, short-lived head.

A AROMA Very distinctive, with rich malt and yeasty hops.

T TASTE Rounded; full-bodied; good bittersweet balance and dry finish.

The beer from the Arctic Circle – well, almost! The Hartwall company controls more than half of Finnish beer production, and has a number of breweries, but the most northerly is at Tornio, right at the top of the Gulf of Bothnia, and only a few miles short of the Arctic Circle. This is where they make their flagship Pilsner, Lapin Kulta (Lapp gold) using water from rivers originating in Lapland (not, as some people say, fjords – they are in Norway!).

This is a very well made and distinctive lager, much better than many of the mass-produced brands. It has an attractive hop and malt aroma, and the taste is well balanced – a little sweet, but with a dry, tangy, citrusy finish. It is also quite strong at 5.2% ABV. This excellent beer is quite malty for a lager, and I would especially recommend drinking it in winter, by the fire.

LAPIN KULTA

UK

The British Isles are home to a huge variety of quality beers, particularly ales and bitters. The lighter brews make excellent summer drinking as they are hugely refreshing but retain a full, satisfying flavour.

OAKHAM JHB

C COLOUR Clear, bright gold, with a full, frothy head.

A AROMA Complex and attractive; fresh hop, hay, fruit, and citrus.

T TASTE Light and refreshing, with citrus fruitiness and a smooth dry bitter finish.

This is unmissable! Bright, fresh, fruity, and citrusy, with a great balance, a lovely head, and great taste – Oakham JHB is simply one of the very best.

Oakham Ales began in October 1993, when ex-insurance man John Wood decided to make use of his 20 years of experience as a home brewer and try his hand in the commercial world of brewing. Although he sold the business in 1995, production of some of Wood's excellent beers continues. The best for me is this Jeffrey Hudson Bitter (JHB), named after Sir Jeffrey Hudson – a royalist and courtier to King Charles I. It was originally brewed as a cask ale, and the bottled beer is stronger at 4.2% ABV (rather than the cask's 3.8%). JHB is this brewery's most famous and successful product, and has deservedly won a number of awards in competitions.

OAKHAM JHB

CALEDONIAN GOLDEN PROMISE

C COLOUR Light gold, with a short-lived, frothy head.

A AROMA Delicate and flowery, with watery hops and a hint of citrus.

T TASTE Quite dry, slightly bitter; woody, hoppy; citrus finish.

Caledonian is a fine traditional Scottish brewery based in Edinburgh, where they use copper vessels to make their beer. The brewery has branched out into the organic market with Golden Promise, a quality pale ale named after Scotland's traditional variety of barley. This is quite strong, at 5% ABV, and it tastes a bit like a Pilsner – not particularly intense, but great if you really want organic.

CALEDONIAN GOLDEN PROMISE

YOUNG'S ELYSIUM

C COLOUR Pale light gold, with a full but short-lived head.

A AROMA Attractive, delicate, with elder-flower and malt.

T TASTE Light and bright, with malt and a citrus finish.

Young's Brewery was first established in 1581, in Wandsworth, south London. Although now not controlled by the Young family, it has secured its position as a top brewer with a fine range of beers.

Elysium was originally released in 2002 as Golden Jubilee. This is a well-balanced beer, and although Young's have used elderflower for that "summer feel", a smooth, slightly caramel malt is the dominant feature. It is not too strong, at 4% ABV. Maybe not the beer of the gods, but a nice one for a summer's day!

NETHERLANDS

Holland's beer output is dominated by Heineken, but there are many smaller breweries that produce fine Pilsners, and there has been a heartening return to traditional values in recent years. Dutch beers are similar to German brews, but usually a little sweeter.

CHRISTOFFEL BLOND

C COLOUR Light bright gold; large, frothy, white head, which soon turns to lace.

A AROMA Distinctive, with hops, pine, and spice in great balance.

T TASTE Full of vitality, with hops, loads of flavour, and a bitter finish.

This really excellent Pilsner is made by a new-generation brewery, only established in 1986. Founder Leo Brand set up his business in the former coal-mining town of Roermond, Holland, not far from the German border, and named it after the town's patron saint. It is only a small brewery, although larger now than the original brewery situated behind a house in the town.

Christoffel Blond is made from 100-per-cent malt and hops, bottom-fermented, unfiltered, and unpasteurized. This beer has a beautiful bright golden colour, a really spicy and hoppy aroma, and a great, fresh, lively taste with a pleasantly bitter finish. It is relatively powerful at 6% ABV. The beer was originally known as Christoffel Bier, but changed its name to Blond after another brew, Christoffel Robertus, was added to the range.

Christoffel Blond is thought by its fans to be one of the best beers in the world, and I could hardly disagree. Don't miss this one if you want a taste of Pilsner at its best.

JAPAN

Japan is a great maker and consumer of beer. A number of micro-breweries specialize in emulating European styles, including light, refreshing German lagers. These beers often retain their classic character but feature uniquely Japanese innovations.

OTARU HELLES

C COLOUR Light gold, with a medium, lightly frothy, bubbly head.

A AROMA Unusual aromas of flowers and hops, with a Japanese feel.

T TASTE Well-balanced, with malt and a slightly bitter hop finish.

Germany comes to Japan! Since the law was changed in 1994 to allow small breweries to operate, Japanese enthusiasts have set up hundreds of small breweries and brewpubs, making their own distinctive beers. This beer is made in a brewpub in the Japanese port of Otaru, near Sapporo, on Hokkaido, Japan's most northerly – and coldest – island. The brewery is in a converted warehouse and is the brainchild of local businessman Akio Shoji. On a visit to Europe, Shoji was impressed by the way that every village in Bavaria seems to have its own brewery, and he wanted to emulate that model.

Otaru Helles was created at Otaru Beer by German brewer Johannes Braun. It is very much in the German Hell style of light beer, or Pilsner, using German malts and hops. This is really unusual, as you get a quality German lager with a Japanese feel. It has a great head, and a malty but dry taste, and is presented in an old-fashioned, oriental bottle, with a swingtop cap – excellent! The brewery also produces Dunkel dark beer and special seasonal brews.

THIRST
QUENCHERS

" Armed with an exciting, tangy, citrus edge, these beers are perfect for that special drink at the end of a long hot day. "

INTRODUCING THIRST-QUENCHING BEERS

For a perfect balance between fascinating flavours and sheer refreshment, try a thirst quencher. Styles vary from the classic Pilsners through to light and then dark wheat beers. Seek them out wherever you go, in Europe and beyond.

Thirst-quenching beers are usually bottom-fermented Pilsners, although some are top-fermented and bottle-conditioned, which means that fermentation continues in the bottle (see p401). These beers are cloudy, and sometimes very fizzy. All are more sophisticated than the light, refreshing lagers, and they often have a fine and frothy, pure white head.

Many of the thirst quenchers are Belgian Witbiers or German Weissbiers, which not only refers to their pale colour, but indicates that they are made using wheat. The wheat content provides an extra refreshing dryness, like an apple fresh from the tree, and the wheat and the hops should be the determining character. Some of these beers have oranges and other citrus elements added, or herbs and spices, creating appetizing aromas that marry wonderfully with dry fruitiness from the wheat. An unusual aroma also typical of a wheat beer is bubblegum, a kind of candy sweetness that comes from the yeast.

DISTINCTIVE NOSE *Schneider Weisse wheat beer has a hallmark aroma of nutmeg.*

DRINKING AND SERVING

DRINK PROFILE These beers offer far more aroma and depth of flavour than light, refreshing beers, but the taste should still be refreshing, whatever the particular style.

C COLOUR Colours range from very light yellow for Pilsners or German and Belgian wheat beers, through to amber or brown for dark wheat beers or some Belgian styles.

A AROMA With wheat beers, the aromas are usually yeasty, grassy, or citrusy, and often very attractive. The addition of orange, lemon, or coriander also enhances the aromas.

T TASTE There will be a big difference in flavour between a Belgian Witbier such as Hoegaarden and a pale ale like the Australian Coopers, but both should leave you satisfied and refreshed.

BUYING AND STORING Some of these beers are readily available global brands; for others try specialist shops or the Internet. There is no need to store these beers, as most do not improve with age, and they may actually deteriorate.

SERVING SUGGESTIONS To bring out the aromas and flavours, serve at 9–12°C (48–54°F). It is best to pour these beers slowly into a glass, to bring out the fine head. Where a beer is naturally fermenting in the bottle, care needs to be taken not to shake up the bottle and disturb the yeast, as most people prefer their beer to be as clear as possible.

FOOD COMPANIONS Most of these beers are best as an apéritif, with a few nuts, crisps, or nibbles, but some are good enough to accompany fresh fish, such as cod or sole, or food like pizza.

DOVER SOLE *Delicate white fish goes with Berliner Weisse beers as happily as with a glass of dry white wine.*

A GLOBAL STYLE

The thirst-quenching Pilsners include some of the world's best, especially those from the Czech Republic, where the style originated in the town of Pilsen with the creation of Pilsner Urquell. This style was then copied, first by other Czechs, then in Germany and Austria, and onwards around the world. Global brands of light, refreshing beers, such as Beck's, Budweiser, and Carlsberg, are all derived from this style, but lack the original intensity and hoppy dryness that makes a real thirst quencher.

Some of these beers are known worldwide, including Budvar, Hoegaarden, and Schneider Weisse. Others are more local or regional, such as Berliner Kindl Weisse or the Austrian Raschofer Zwicklbier. Most people try the local beers when they visit a new city. Look out for them when you do, and try the local food partners, such as bread and sausage with Unertl in Munich.

CZECH REPUBLIC

Pilsner will always be linked to the Czechs, who invented this classic, and now world-famous, style of light beer. The best Czech Pilsners, including such brands as Pilsner Urquell, strike a perfect balance between refreshing dryness and full-bodied flavour.

PILSNER URQUELL

C **COLOUR** Straw yellow, with a fine, full, and long-lasting head.

A **AROMA** Delicate and elegant, with flowers, spice, and hops.

T **TASTE** Intense, with dry, bitter hops, a hint of malty sweetness, and honey.

The original – and the best? The term *Urquell* means "original source", and it is claimed that Pilsner Urquell was the first Pilsner lager, brewed in the town of Pilsen, in what is now the Czech Republic.

The Pilsner style originated in 1842, when a group of brewers came together to found the Citizens' Brewery. They called in the German brewmaster Josef Grolle, who brought with him the German bottom-fermenting techniques. These had been used in Germany to make dark beer, but the Czechs used different ingredients, such as Saaz hops, to make a new, light-straw style. The Czechs took the opportunity to show off their new, golden product in glass drinking containers, rather than the traditional tankards and steins – and Pilsner was born!

When you try Pilsner Urquell, you just know it is the original. This beer is a lovely deep golden colour, with a fine head. It is full-bodied, and wonderfully bittersweet. A must for the lager-lover, I am a big fan of Pilsner Urquell – it is fine, elegant, and very stylish.

PILSNER URQUELL

PERFECT PRESENTATION
Pilsner Urquell should always be served in a pilsner glass – the tall, inverted cone shape not only shows the golden liquid off to best effect, but also helps to sustain the bubbles.

BUDVAR

C COLOUR Light gold, with a fluffy, white foam head that disappears quickly.

A AROMA Delicate and balanced, with hops and hints of vanilla.

T TASTE Soft, smooth, and bitterish; grassy hops, vanilla, and a slightly bitter finish.

The world-famous Budvar Brewery was established in the Czech town of Ceské Budejovice (Budweis in German) in 1895, using water from its own underground lake. Brewing in the area, which dates back to at least the 13th century, combined the best of both German and Czech traditions, establishing very high standards and an international reputation.

There has been an intense battle over the name Budweiser (which is German for "from Budweis") between the Czech government and the American brewer Anheuser Busch, which produces Budweiser lager *(see p409)*. While the Czech government claims that only the Budvar brand can rightly be called Budweiser, Anheuser Busch argues that it was the first to patent the name.

Under the current stand-off, Budweiser Budvar has to be sold under the name Crystal in the US, while the American Budweiser has to be sold as Bud in a number of European countries. In the UK, both beers can be sold alongside each other under the same name.

The US-Czech conflict over the name Budweiser has really come about because Budvar is so good! This superb pilsner lager is simply one of the world's best. At 5% ABV, Budvar has a rich flavour with a distinctly hoppy feel, and has a full head with a vanilla

BUDVAR

(see p409)

LAND AND PRODUCTION

MAKING BUDVAR Budweiser Budvar is produced from finest Saaz hops, Moravian malt, and pure water drawn from the brewery's own wells, which are more than 300m (1,000ft) deep. A 90-day maturation process and a 700-year long brewing tradition ensure a high-quality premium lager.

sweetness. I think it is best enjoyed very cold – what better to quench the thirst on a hot summer day!

Budvar also makes a Super Strong lager of 7.6% ABV. This is darker, and has more of a malty feel than the regular brew.

NÁCHOD

C COLOUR An attractive, medium-to-dark amber, with a yellow head.

A AROMA Intense and balanced, with yeast, cream, and hops.

T TASTE Rich, with nutty hops and malt, fruit notes, and a complex finish.

The independent brewery Náchod specializes in making strong beers.

Náchod's Primátor 15° brew, 6% ABV, is amber-coloured with a very rich aroma and a creamy yellow head. The taste is full, with a definite nutty feel, and it finishes in a swirl of bitter and sweet flavours.

Top of the Náchod range, in terms of alcohol content, is Primátor 24°, which claims to be the strongest lager brewed in the Czech Republic, with a daunting ABV of 10%! It is chestnut-coloured, with a dark fruit aroma, and a fruity, liquorice feel.

These are dark, rich, powerful lagers that keep their balance surprisingly well.

KOZEL

C COLOUR Golden yellow, with a thick white head that settles to a thin lace.

A AROMA Fresh and lively, with hops and honey in evidence.

T TASTE Fruity and light bodied; quite sweet and malty, with a citrus tang.

The Czech Republic's Kozel brewery, in Velké Popovice, makes inexpensive lager designed as an alternative to higher-priced, higher-profile beers such as Budvar and Urquell.

Kozel's golden pilsners have a white head and a hoppy, honeyed aroma. On the palate there is crisp, clean malt, a lemony tang, and a firm but rounded dryness. Kozel Pale is the weakest, at 4% ABV; the darker Kozel Premium, the flagship beer, is 5% ABV.

KOZEL

GAMBRINUS PILSNER

C COLOUR Light gold, with a large, soapy white head.

A AROMA Delicate and balanced, with spice and hops.

T TASTE Creamy, malty taste, with a minty hop finish.

The name Gambrinus is a corruption of Jan Primus, Duke of Brabant, nicknamed the "patron of beer". The Gambrinus brewery was founded around 1870 by a group of businessmen, one of whom was Emil Skoda, who later moved into the manufacture of cars.

Gambrinus has always been a competitor of Pilsner Urquell, and once shared a brewery with its rival. It is not as classy a brew as Urquell, but is nevertheless a fine thirst quencher, and also fairly strong at 5% ABV.

GAMBRINUS PILSNER

STAROPRAMEN

C COLOUR Light gold, with a fluffy, quite short-lived head.

A AROMA Rich, but well-balanced with hops and malt, and a slight smokiness.

T TASTE Very rounded, with a firm malty taste, a hint of vanilla, and a dry finish.

The name Staropramen means "old water source". The brewery, which dates from 1869 and is situated in the centre of Prague, still uses traditional methods, using water taken direct from the Moldau River. Sales of beer began in 1871, with the first batch being anointed by a local priest!

Staropramen's Lager 10 (ABV 4.2%) is quite light and pale, while its Lager 12 is a premium, golden, and very full-bodied beer of 5% ABV, with a natural "bite". There is also a fine, mellow, dark beer which is full-bodied, extremely soft, and smooth.

Being a quality Czech brew, Staropramen is always compared with Budvar, Urquell, and Gambrinus, and each beer has its own band of ardent admirers. Whatever the verdict, even to be mentioned in the same breath as such highly rated names proves that Staropramen is an excellent beer. It has great balance, and a slightly smoky aroma, rather like burnt hops. The flavour is very full, and the malt is finely balanced by a dry hoppiness.

Staropramen is now part of the Bass Group (which itself comes under the umbrella of brewery giant InBev); consequently, you may find that the beer you buy is not necessarily brewed in the Czech Republic, but made under licence elsewhere. Not surprisingly, most devotees of Staropramen prefer the original Czech version.

STAROPRAMEN

GERMANY

Germany produces a refreshing pale beer known as Weissbier, which uses wheat as a key ingredient. Munich is one of the centres of this style, and the great Schneider Weisse and other brands are made there for the royal Hofbräuhaus. A richer variation of Weissbier is the oddly named "dark white beer", and there is also an interesting Berlin style, which is less well known and rather sour.

SCHNEIDER WEISSE

C **COLOUR** Dark gold or light copper, with a firm, full, and lasting head.

A **AROMA** Very distinctive, with fruit and spice, including banana and nutmeg.

T **TASTE** Creamy and full-flavoured, with fruit, nuts, and a sweetish finish.

In 1850, George Schneider was asked by King Max II of Bavaria to begin brewing wheat beers for the royal Munich Hofbräuhaus, establishing Schneider as the largest commercial wheat brewer in southern Germany.

After making beer for the royal family for some years, the firm went into production on its own in 1872, and rapidly established a reputation for fine wheat beers. Misfortune struck in 1944, when the brewery was destroyed by bombing, so production was moved from the centre of Munich to Kelheim, on the Danube near Regensburg. It is still a family business, run by the sixth generation of Schneider brewers.

The star beer is Schneider Weisse (which, despite the name, it is not a white beer, but a wheat beer). Its exact method of production is a closely guarded family secret, committed to writing by George Schneider in 1864 and passed down from father to son ever since. Bavarian barley and wheat malts are blended with darker Vienna malts to give the beer a distinctive coppery-gold look.

Schneider Weisse is quite strong, at 5.5% ABV, and has a rich, fruity, and spicy aroma. It is fairly full bodied, with a fruity, nutty taste. The unusual bubblegum-like finish comes from the top-fermenting yeast strain, and can be experienced in some other wheat beers.

Schneider also make a creamy, dark, chocolaty wheat beer called Aventinus (see p450). Both this and the Weisse are excellent wheat beers from a great Bavarian brewing dynasty. You can expect a complex, luxurious feel, and a full palate. I recommend both!

WHEAT BREW *Schneider Weisse is one of the classic wheat beers. Although its recipe is secret, most Bavarian wheat beers use at least 50 per cent wheat in the mash.*

ERDINGER WEISSBIER DUNKEL

C **COLOUR** Pale golden yellow, with a full, firm, and long-lived head.

A **AROMA** Grassy hops, with spice and a touch of bubblegum.

T **TASTE** Fresh and fruity, with a bitter-sweet bubblegum and hop feel.

Erdinger is Germany's biggest brewer of wheat beers. One of its best is the Dunkel dark beer. This is a relatively recent (1991) addition to the range, brewed using both pale and dark wheat and barley malts. The result is a fine beer with a light, spicy, chocolaty nose, and a silky palate of caramel and milk chocolate, with a smoky hint. This beer is quite strong at 5.6% ABV, but the strength does not take away the flavour.

ERDINGER WEISSBIER DUNKEL

MAHR'S WEISSE

C **COLOUR** Attractive apricot; slightly opaque or cloudy.

A **AROMA** Quite sweet, with orange, banana, malt, and grapefruit.

T **TASTE** Fruity, with grapefruit, orange, and malt; quite earthy; warm finish.

This fine German wheat beer is produced by Mahr's brewery in Bamberg. The aromas are very complex, as is often the case with wheat beers. You can smell the wheat, the malt, and the yeast, but also banana, lemon, and orange. This beer also has a notable natural fizziness, which it keeps very well.

The flavours are very full and complex – sharply sweet wheat, banana, clove, and some citrus notes, with coriander, pepper, and cloves, all adding up to a lovely harmony of flavour. Perfect on a warm, sunny day, outdoors with nothing to do.

MAISEL'S WEISSE

C **COLOUR** Pale golden yellow, with a lasting head.

A **AROMA** Fruity and spicy, with cinnamon spice and banana.

T **TASTE** Very refreshing, with citrus peel, sweet overtones, and a dry finish.

Maisel's is based in Bayreuth, famous as the site of the Wagner opera festival. From a range of fine beers, the basic Weisse comes in Original and a filtered, more commercial Kristallklar (crystal clear) version. The aromas are very fruity and spicy, and the beer itself is a great mixture of wheaty and fruity sweetness offset with a dry and lemony finish. This beer is quite strong at 5.2% ABV, and I prefer it just that little bit warmer than ice cold, to bring out the flavours.

MAISEL'S WEISSE

GÖLLER WEISSE

C **COLOUR** Amber and cloudy, with a full and frothy head.

A **AROMA** Delicate aromas of malt and slight citrus notes.

T **TASTE** Mild, fruity, and lively, with a full flavour and a fresh finish.

The family-owned Göller brewery was established as long ago as 1514, and they have continued to make fine beer, particularly wheat beers. The regular brew, Steinhauer Weisse, is amber in colour, with a fine frothy head, malty aroma, and a soft, smooth, and fruity feel. It is not too strong at 4.9% ABV.

The original wheat beer, and still the best-regarded, is Freyungs Weissbier, named after the original location of the brewery. This is stronger, at 5.2% ABV, fresh and lively, with a good head produced by natural bottle fermentation.

HUBER WEISSE

C **COLOUR** Dark brown with ruby highlights, and a small brown head.

A **AROMA** Sweet and quite rich, with malt, and a hint of molasses.

T **TASTE** Creamy, like a sweet light stout, with a mildly dry, grassy finish.

The Hofbräuhaus Freising in Munich dates back to 1160 and claims to be Germany's oldest brewery, although this claim is challenged by Weihenstephaner *(see opposite)*. The brewery is best known for its range of wheat beers, and Huber Weisse is an excellent example of the style. This beer is pale orange-brown in colour and slightly opaque. It has a delicate and fruity aroma, with a suggestion of banana typical of some wheat beers. Overall, Huber Weisse is quite well balanced, and clean and dry.

UNERTL WEISSE

C **COLOUR** Light tan or toffee, and slightly hazy.

A **AROMA** Fruity, with sweet apple, banana, and smoky chocolate hints.

T **TASTE** Juicy, with a rich, fruity character and a dry finish.

This is one of a range of five lesser-known, but notably good, Bavarian wheat beers produced by the Unertl family at their brewery in Haag, south of Munich.

Unertl Weisse is made in the darker, richer style; it is a deeply intense brew with plenty of sediment and a good, thick head. Although the beer is basically dry, it has real richness. It is moderately strong at 4.8% ABV, and a very satisfying drink. It is traditional to drink this with bread and sausage, or, if you really want some sinful calories, pork dripping.

UNERTL WEISSE

KARG WEISSE

C **COLOUR** Medium brown to light tan, and quite cloudy.

A **AROMA** Spicy and fruity, with attractive hints of smoke.

T **TASTE** Rich, fruity, and creamy, with a bittersweet smoky feel.

The Karg brewery is a small family-owned brewery located in the lakeside town of Murnau am Staffelsee, south of Munich, not far from the Austrian border. Karg brews some of the finest wheat beer in Bavaria and typifies the Bavarian style. Karg Weisse has a fair amount of sediment, and is quite cloudy, with a deep but not actually dark colour. The head is moderate, not overblown, and this is a rich, creamy beer, with plenty of exuberant life, and quite strong at 5% ABV.

KARG WEISSE

KÖNIG LUDWIG WEISSBIER

C **COLOUR** Pale golden yellow and cloudy, with a fine-bubbled and lasting head.

A **AROMA** Fruity and spicy, with notes of citrus and cloves.

T **TASTE** Smooth and light-bodied, with vanilla, bubblegum, and a citrus finish.

This beer is named after "mad" King Ludwig II, a member of the Wittelsbach family, which held the monopoly for wheat beer brewing in Bavaria for 200 years. It is now brewed by his great grandson, Crown Prince Luitpold, at the Kaltenberg Castle at Geltendorf.

The prince specializes in dark beers, but also makes a light-bodied, golden Weissbier, with a refreshing citrus feel. It is quite strong at 5.5% ABV, and responds really well to the addition of a slice of lemon. In my opinion, this is one of the best Weissbiers – look out for it!

BERLINER KINDL WEISSE

C COLOUR Pale-straw; versions with added syrup are a range of bright hues.

A AROMA Quite sour; hint of yeast and baked bread – not unlike Champagne.

T TASTE Sharp, with smooth honey notes; woody and vegetal; long citrus finish.

Kindl is based in Berlin, and famous for making the city's great wheat beers, dubbed the "Champagne of the north" by Napoleon's troops. It is one of the two big Berlin breweries, along with its rival Schultheiss.

The style of Weissbier in north Germany is different from that in Bavaria. The beer is not so rich, with a slightly watery feel, and is also not so strong. This is an unusual and very special brew, part of

BERLINER KINDL WEISSE

a tradition of old Berlin that is now in decline. The beer is made deliberately sour, in the same manner as Belgian lambic beers, and I am sure it will appeal to fans of those Belgian brews.

Kindl Weisse is brewed using soft water, 70 per cent barley malt, and 30 per cent wheat malt. But it also has something special: it undergoes a secondary fermentation in the bottle, like Champagne. After storage and filtration, the beer is bottled with a dose of yeast, but only comes out at 2.5% ABV. A very refreshing beer, this is treated by the locals as more of a soft drink, like a fizzy lemonade, and is served at outdoor venues in the summer. Few Berliners would drink the beer on its own – it is regarded as too sour without a dash of *Himbeer* (raspberry) or *Waldmeister* (woodruff) syrup. Woodruff is a

sweet-scented herb with aromatic leaves that are also used to flavour liqueurs and in perfumery. Different versions of the beer are available; some are ready-mixed *mit Schuss* – with the sweet syrup added – and these can be strange colours for beers, including a lurid bright green. However, in my opinion, it is worth being brave – at least once! – and sampling the beer on its own to experience the tart, citrus flavour

with none of the heaviness that the sweet syrups add.

Although unusual and very difficult to get hold of outside Berlin, these beers are a superbly refreshing taste of brewing history, and well worth the trouble of seeking them out.

Kindl also makes a dark "black" beer, which has very different flavours, including dark chocolate and liquorice.

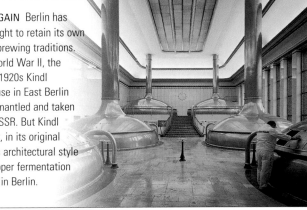

LAND AND PRODUCTION

BORN AGAIN Berlin has had to fight to retain its own special brewing traditions. After World War II, the original 1920s Kindl brewhouse in East Berlin was dismantled and taken to the USSR. But Kindl rebuilt it, in its original Bauhaus architectural style with copper fermentation vessels, in Berlin.

SCHULTHEISS BERLINER WEISSE

C COLOUR Pale golden yellow, with a short-lived, frothy head.

A AROMA Light, delicate, and flowery, like a dry Chardonnay wine.

T TASTE Complex, with a fruity, vegetable, and citrus feel; dry and refreshing.

Like Kindl's Weisse, this is light at just 3.3% ABV. It really sparkles in the glass, and has a wonderful range of complex aromas and tastes; part fruit, part dryness, and part citrus, it has an overall tangy and pungent feel.

Berliners drink it with syrup, although I like it on its own, served not too cold, to bring out the great flavours. Try it with food, as an alternative to a dry white wine – it tastes great, and it's fun!

SCHULTHEISS BERLINER WEISSE

WEIHENSTEPHANER KRISTALL WEISSBIER

C COLOUR Lovely bright gold, with a fine, full, and frothy head.

A AROMA Bright, fresh, and spicy, with vanilla and bubblegum.

T TASTE Well-balanced and rich; mango and banana; fine hop finish.

It is thought that the Weihenstephaner (sacred Stephen) brewery at Freising is the world's oldest, going back to the 8th century AD. This beer is one of the best regarded of the south German thirst quenchers. It is fizzy, fresh, bright, and lively, and reasonably strong at 5.4% ABV. The texture is light compared with most other Weissbiers, and the fruit and vanilla are in fine balance, without ever becoming too sweet. The aim of this beer is to be refreshing, and to me it couldn't be more so.

PAULANER HEFE-WEISSBIER NATURTRÜB

C COLOUR Very dark old gold; good, very long-lasting head.

A AROMA Delicate aromas of spice, especially cloves; honey and fruit.

T TASTE Peach, strawberry, banana, vanilla, and malt.

I love this one, and you will too! The Paulaner Hefe-Weissbier Naturtrüb is a really special beer with an incredibly mellow and soft flavour, as the harshness of wheat gives way to vanilla and banana tones, with lots of other fruity and malty sub-tastes. At 5.5% ABV, it is quite strong, but this is well balanced by the intensity of the flavours. Do not drink this beer too cold, to ensure that these flavours come out.

PAULANER HEFE-WEISSBIER NATURTRÜB

PYRASER WEISSE

C COLOUR Bright medium straw, with a lightly cloudy texture.

A AROMA Gentle, with wheat and apple in good balance.

T TASTE Quite fruity, with a tangy sweetness and a dry citrus finish.

The region of Franconia, in Bavaria in southern Germany, has its own distinct identity and traditions, and is known for its large concentration of traditional craft brewers and distinctive local styles. This particular beer comes from the small town of Pyras. This is a very traditional Bavarian wheat beer, with sediment and the characteristic aromas and flavours of the style, packaged in a traditional screw-top bottle and quite strong at 5.2%. It is never going to be a world-beater, but it is a fine example of the traditional Weissbier style, and well worth trying.

AUSTRIA

There are a growing number of local craft brewers in Austria that specialize in making organic, additive-free beers. Austria's historical links with the Czech Republic mean that their light, dry beers have a Pilsner feel.

STIEGL PILS

C COLOUR Pale golden yellow, with a full, fluffy, white head.

A AROMA Grains, bready malts, and a little hop spiciness.

T TASTE Quite sweet for lager; with hops, and a malty feel for the traditional brews.

Stiegl, founded in 1492, is Austria's largest private brewery, and is a specialist in producing unfiltered, natural beers. The company also produces a wide range of fine, popular beers in the Pilsner style, including an attractive regular Pils for everyday drinking. The special brands include Goldbräu, a malty

STIEGL PILS

Vollbier, which has been a great success, and Paracelsus Naturtrüb, a traditional, unfiltered version of Goldbräu. In the past, this used to be a sweet, dark lager, but the company has updated the concept in line with modern tastes, so that it is now a light golden colour. However, Paracelsus still retains its traditional deep malt character. The flavour is like a weak Märzen style, or a malty Pils. This is an unusual beer. On the one hand you expect a Pilsner; on the other hand, it is unfiltered and quite traditional in style. It could only be Austrian!

ZIPFER KELLERBIER

C COLOUR Straw yellow, with a medium-sized, short-lived head, and little lacing.

A AROMA Malt and hops, with a slight hint of citrus.

T TASTE Sweetish malt, with a slightly bitter finish.

The Zipfer brewery is named after the Austrian town of Zipf, in which it has been in operation since 1858. The brewery is now part of the Brau Union Group.

Zipfer is the Austrian beer with the most distinctive hoppy style. Although this Pilsner is quite strong at 5.4% ABV, it is designed to be an everyday drinking lager. It is quite light, with a touch of citrus, and when drunk very cold as an apéritif is refreshing and reliable. This Pilsner is ideal with food, when it is best served not too cold. Don't expect Zipfer to change your life, but for a good-value quaffing beer, it is certainly worth a try.

ST GEORGEN WEISSE

C COLOUR Light gold, with the cloudy character of unfiltered ales.

A AROMA Delicate, with wheat and hops and a little citrus.

T TASTE Slightly bitterish feel, with yeast and notes of bubblegum.

The St Georgen micro-brewery in the town of Murau was only established in 1998. It is run by two experienced brewmasters, Hans and Thomas Seidl. The brewery uses a combination of traditional methods and high technology to make quality beers, and this wheat beer is no exception. It is strong at 5.2% ABV, and made in the traditional, unfiltered style. Cloudy gold in colour, it has sweetish fruity aromas and a lightly bitter taste balanced by the yeasty sweetness.

St Georgen also makes a full-flavoured Pilsner beer in both filtered and unfiltered versions.

BELGIUM

One of the great producers of wheat beer is Hoegaarden, a small town whose name is known all over the world. This refreshing style came into being because of the abundance of wheat in the region.

HOEGAARDEN WITBIER

C COLOUR Light bright gold, and hazy, with a thick, frothy head.

A AROMA Unusual, with perfume of orange, apple, spice, and herbs.

T TASTE Essentially a sweetish taste, with honey, fruit, and malt.

This widely known beer is one of my favourites, for its quality and finesse. The town of Hoegaarden lies to the east of Brussels, and was once the centre of a thriving wheat beer industry, fuelled by the local wheat fields. As lager became the dominant brew in Belgium (and throughout Europe), the industry closed down,

HOEGAARDEN WITBIER

with the last brewery going out of business in the mid-1950s.

In the 1960s, Pierre Celis led a revival of the wheat beer style, and his successful beer was later acquired by the InBev group. Hoegaarden is now popular around the world and InBev makes this beer in a number of locations under contract, so you may need to make sure that what you are drinking is as good as the Belgian original. Be sure to taste an imported bottle of the "real thing".

Hoegaarden is quite strong, at 5% ABV, and is full of character and style. The nose is citrusy and rich, with apple, cinnamon, and

coriander coming through. It has a large, frothy head and a light, refreshing palate with very little bitterness or hop content. You can taste the oranges, which give a hint of bitterness but don't swamp the beer flavours.

This is a great beer, complex, vibrant, appealing, and refreshing, and well worth a try. Some people like to add a slice of lemon, or even orange, to make the flavour more complex, with an extra fruit lift. But to me, with an excellent

beer like this, it is best to drink it without any additions, at least until you make up your mind whether you are a fan or not.

Hoegaarden also makes special versions of the beer, including Grand Cru, which is much stronger, at 8.7% ABV, with a darker colour and fuller flavour (see p467). At 5.6% ABV, Hoegaarden Speciale is slightly stronger than the normal brew, and is maltier, more citrus-flavoured, and slightly sweeter. It is only brewed in autumn and winter and sold from September to February.

CULTURE AND TRADITION

SPICE ROUTE The secret of the fragrant, spicy style of Hoegaarden is the addition of coriander seeds and dried Curaçao orange peel in the brewing process. Although originally meant for the local market, the style took off and is now much emulated.

DENTERGEMS WIT

C COLOUR Light straw colour, and hazy, with a great frothy head.

A AROMA Delicate, with wheat, spice, yeast, and citrus.

T TASTE Smooth and refreshing, with a clean, malty taste and a fruity finish.

This wheat beer was launched in 1980 by the Riva brewery, a family-owned business based in the town of Dentergem, Flanders, as a rival to the successful Hoegaarden Witbier *(see opposite)*. The Riva brewery is an ambitious, modern company, although its origins as Brouwerij de Splenter (the name of the owning family) go back to 1896. In the wake of the success of Dentergems, it is also making its mark with quality beers such as Lucifer, a strong Belgian pale ale, and Vondel. It also owns the

highly rated Liefmans brewery. The Riva group is also responsible for the production of Straffe Hendrik.

Dentergems Wit, like its rival, is a lovely, complex beer, with a fine mixture of fruit, spice, and malt. It is a little more in the German style of wheat beers than the beers made by Hoegaarden, so expect a flavour that is more delicate and slightly less openly fruity.

Dentergems is quite strong at 5% ABV, with a lovely bright, white, creamy head. It has a spicy and light malt nose, with coriander, cinnamon, vanilla, and a hint of apple. It is smooth, refreshing, clean, and lightly malty, with a citrusy finish. You will find hints of a range of spices and fruits, along with a fine malt base, making it a really well-balanced beer.

For maximum enjoyment drink this very cold on a hot day – you'll never find a more refreshing beer!

DENTERGEMS WIT

BLANCHE DE BRUXELLES

C COLOUR Straw yellow and clear, unlike most wheat beers.

A AROMA Fruity and distinctive, with flowers, orange, and grapefruit.

T TASTE Dry and creamy; fruity wheat, coriander, and spicy orange.

This is a great Belgian white ale, made by the Lefebvre brewery, famous for its Floreffe abbey ale. This a bit different from most wheat beers, in that it is not cloudy at all if poured carefully. It is very bright and citrusy on the nose, with orange, grapefruit, and honeysuckle, and there is a herby, coriander, and rosemary feel to the taste. To me this is one of the spiciest and most aromatic wheat beers in Belgium, and great with food. It is sold as Manneken Pis in some markets.

WATOU WITBIER

C COLOUR Elegant pale lemon, with a hazy texture.

A AROMA Light and delicate, with yeast and spice.

T TASTE Very clean; good balance of bitter and sweet; short dry finish.

The Van Eecke Brewery in Watou produces this very delicate version of the Witbier style. This beer has a cloudy body that contains noticeable small pieces of yeast. The fizz is very natural and long-lasting and the aroma is very complex. The beer can vary, sometimes with more coriander and citrus, other times more neutral. The taste is also complex – an initially sweet and citrusy feel gives way to dryness. Quite an unusual beer – not the best balanced of all, but a genuine, natural product.

WATOU WITBIER

TITJE BLANCHE

C COLOUR Attractive pale bright gold, and a cloudy texture.

A AROMA Light and gentle, with yeast, orange, hops, and spice.

T TASTE Delicate, with orange, coriander, wheat, malt, and hops.

The Silly brewery is a fast-growing, dynamic operation, and it remains a family firm. It is based in the village of the same name (taken from its local stream, the Sylle) although the brewery was first known as Cense de la Tour. It has its roots in the 19th century, when local beer-makers, in the Hainault region, south of Brussels, brewed barley and hops. In 1975, the brewery bought Double Enghien, a beer well known in Belgium, and in 1990 it started producing Titje, a wheat beer.

This beer is a very light and delicate brew, with excellent orange and coriander notes. It is best served very cold, at 4–6°C (39–43°F), and is extremely refreshing.

FRANCE

Almost all French beer is made in Alsace-Lorraine and Flanders, but France has now joined the micro-brewery movement and producers are springing up in regions not commonly associated with beer-making. This has led to a new generation of exciting styles.

OC'ALE BIÈRE BLANCHE

C COLOUR Light amber, and cloudy, with a short-lived, full head.

A AROMA Quite sweet but balanced, with yeast and baked bread.

T TASTE Very smooth; delicately sweet; malt, yeast, citrus, and a dryish finish.

A very special and unusual French beer, and definitely one to savour. Jack Scourmont brews this wheat beer in Languedoc, southwestern France. Most people think of French beer as coming from the great brewing region of Alsace, but other regions also have their brewing traditions in this diverse nation.

Oc'Ale Bière Blanche has a very full head, which dissipates after a few seconds. Listen for the natural yeasty "pop" when you open the splendid half-litre swingtop bottle, and pour it carefully.

The aromas are quite delicate, without the very strong citrus-lemon notes of some wheat beers. The taste is quite mild and gently sweet, with hints of yeast and only the very smallest citrus feel. This beer is quite strong, at 6% ABV, but it doesn't seem it. Although the overall feel is sweetish and quite rich, the finish also has a bitter element, which creeps up on you as you drink. This is a lovely surprise from what you may have been thinking is an over-sweet beer – it is too good for that.

HOLLAND

Better-known for Pilsners, the Dutch also have a wheat beer tradition, though less extensive than that of the Belgians.

GULPENER KORENWOLF

C COLOUR Light gold, and hazy, with a small head, and only medium fizz.

A AROMA Complex, with yeast, fruit, vanilla, and spice.

T TASTE Very smooth; light-bodied; not too sweet, with elderflower and citrus.

Korenwolf (corn wolf) is Limburg dialect for the hamsters that inhabit the wheat fields in the area, and also feature on the label of the swingtop bottle! This subtly refreshing beer has a fresh and fruity nose, and is quite dry and light for a wheat beer – very different from some rich German and Belgian versions.

RUSSIA

In Russia, many former state breweries have expanded their scope and are launching new beers on to the world market.

BALTIKA NUMBER 8

C COLOUR Pale, golden yellow; cloudy, with a good head.

A AROMA Warm and attractive, with malt, fruit, and spice.

T TASTE Good balance between sweet and dry; hints of orange citrus; soft finish.

Number 8 is a wheat beer of 5% ABV from St. Petersburg's Baltika Brewery. It has a good, if short-lived, head and a yeasty, citrus-tinged aroma. The warm alcohol feel is offset by a tangy, spicy, dry bitterness, and the finish is pleasantly sweet. For the uninitiated, Number 8 makes a fine introduction to the world of Russian beer.

JAPAN

Beer is ever-popular in Japan, and the Japanese like to combine their traditional varieties with imported Western styles.

HITACHINO NEST WHITE ALE

C COLOUR Light gold; appealing and bright, with a frothy, pure-white head.

A AROMA Yeasty, with orange citrus, apricot, coriander, and nutmeg.

T TASTE Mild and refreshing, with a dry citrus finish.

In 1996, after 173 years making saké, the Kiuchi brewery began producing beer. The flagship brew is White Ale, a wheat beer flavoured with nutmeg, coriander, and orange juice and peel. The taste is similar to a Belgian ale, but sufficiently different to give it its own unique, refreshing character.

CANADA

The strong French influence in Canada extends to an appreciation of Belgian beers, which have been widely copied.

BLANCHE DE CHAMBLY

C COLOUR Pale golden yellow; cloudy, with a pure-white head.

A AROMA Elegant and attractive, with maple syrup, cloves, and coriander.

T TASTE Quite sweet, with intense fruit flavours.

Blanche de Chambly is a Canadian wheat beer produced by Unibroue, a micro-brewery based in the Montreal suburb of Chambly. The company wanted to make a Belgian-style wheat beer with spices, very much in the style of Hoegaarden, so took advice from the Riva Brewery of Belgium. The result is a very pale beer with a snow-white head and an ABV of 5%. The spice flavours are somewhat fainter than in Hoegaarden but, otherwise, there is little difference between the two.

Blanche de Chambly is only part-filtered, and the yeast in suspension gives the beer a cloudy appearance that tends to hide its true Champagne-yellow colour. Recognizably Belgian in style, Blanche de Chambly is more subtle and not as full-flavoured as a genuine Belgian brew.

While not exactly overflowing with character, Blanche de Chambly nevertheless makes a perfect afternoon beer. It can also go well with seafood, poultry, salads, and crudités.

BLANCHE DE CHAMBLY

USA

The explosion of the micro-brewery movement in the US has led to the revival of a whole range of long-forgotten styles.

PYRAMID HEFEWEIZEN

C COLOUR Pale golden yellow, with a good, white head.

A AROMA Elegant aromas of yeast, fruit, citrus, and coriander.

T TASTE Slightly oily texture, with a good, firm, fizzy-hop flavour.

Hefeweizen is a German-style wheat beer produced by Pyramid, an exciting brewer with bases near Seattle and San Francisco. This strong-tasting beer has a good but rapidly diminishing head, a complex aroma, and an ABV of 5%.

ALLAGASH WHITE

C COLOUR Pale golden yellow, with a thick, full, white head.

A AROMA Light and gentle, with orange, hops, and coriander.

T TASTE Delicate and crisp-tasting, with bright citrus and coriander.

The Allagash brewery in Portland, Maine, makes Belgian-style beer. The first of its six beers, Allagash White, was introduced in 1995 to great acclaim.

This classic wheat beer is cloudy, pale gold, and very approachable. The yeast is blended with coriander and bitter oranges to give an appealing and sophisticated aroma. Allagash White is refreshing and light, and quite strong at 5.5% ABV. Be warned: this beer is so drinkable that you can easily have one too many!

ALLAGASH WHITE

AUSTRALIA

Australia is a strong brewing nation. Along with great lagers, there are fine English-style ales with roots in the colonial past.

COOPER'S SPARKLING ALE

C COLOUR Medium gold; sometimes cloudy from the bottle conditioning.

A AROMA Very full and fruity, with apple, banana, and pear.

T TASTE Refreshing, with fruit, malt, great balance, and a dry finish.

Cooper's Sparkling Ale is quite strong, at 5.8% ABV, and slightly cloudy. When poured carefully, at not too low a temperature, the result is a complex and fresh-tasting ale, with an excellent balance of fruitiness and dryness, and a great finish – one of the world's classic beers!

COOPER'S PALE ALE

C COLOUR Pale yellow, with a full and long-lasting head.

A AROMA Very distinctive; yeasty, with banana and a herby, seaweed note.

T TASTE Light-bodied, with malt and hops; a traditional medium-dry feel.

Expect plenty of sediment with this fine, traditional-style Australian pale ale, so pour carefully! Cooper's Pale Ale has a marvellously thick, long-lasting head and a full set of aromas, including a distinct salty tang. It is not too strong, at 4.5% ABV, and is lighter than Cooper's Sparkling Ale.

This beer is at its best when drunk cold, almost lager-style, rather than at the warmer temperature at which British-style pale ale is often served.

COOPER'S PALE ALE

AUSSIE BREW *Little Creatures Pale Ale is currently one of the best Australian beers around. It is quite sweet and malty, with a hint of earthy woodiness.*

LITTLE CREATURES PALE ALE

C COLOUR Pale amber, and appealing, with a clean, white, foamy head.

A AROMA Delicate and aromatic, with flowers, orange, and lychee.

T TASTE Fresh and crisp, with a bright citrus feel and hop flavour.

This pale ale, produced by the Little Creatures Brewing Company in Fremantle, Western Australia, is made using specialty Australian malts combined with imported US Cascade and Chinook hop flowers. This gives the beer great balance and a very distinctive character.

Little Creatures Pale Ale is bottle-conditioned, which means that yeast (the "little creatures"!) is added to the beer during the bottling process to initiate secondary fermentation.

This moderately strong beer (5% ABV) has a light amber colour, and a good head. It has a fruity, flowery hop aroma, and a zesty citrus flavour. The finish is dry and bitter.

Little Creatures Pale Ale is a lovely little beer from a really big country!

FOOD MATCH

THAI FOOD The citrusy character of Little Creatures Pale Ale, from the hop varieties used *(see above)*, makes it well-suited to Thai dishes, which are often flavoured with lime.

66 Just as sophisticated as a Martini, these beers are dry and appetizing – just what you need before enjoying your meal. 99

APPETIZERS

INTRODUCING APPETIZER BEERS

Like the fresh acidity of a light apéritif wine, the dry, hoppy character in beer has the magic key to unlock your appetite. These appetizer beers place the emphasis on hops; drink them any time, but be prepared for your stomach to rumble!

The essential requirement of appetizer beers is that they should be dry and hoppy, rather than rich and malty. With the hops to the fore, these beers have an attractive flowery or grassy aroma, and leave a dry feeling and a clear palate at the finish, so your appetite is whetted and you are ready to eat. A whole range of different styles fill this brief excellently. Some are clear and others cloudy, such as amber and orange pale ales and bitters, and there are even some very dark but still hop-dominated beers. Some, like Chimay, are presented in a Champagne-style bottle, which adds to their appeal. With others, such as

FRUIT AROMA *Oranges, apples, and pears fill out the appetizing, spicy hop aroma of Duvel.*

German Altbiers, their appetizing qualities come as a surprise because the initial taste is malty and sweet, and the hops only come through later. Appetizer beers can be light or very strong, it really doesn't matter so long as they meet the need!

DRY BUT DIFFERENT

Although these beers have been grouped together because they play a similar role, they can be quite different. There are the Pilsner lagers from Belgium, the Czech Republic, Germany, and further afield in the USA. There are IPAs, again from the US, but also Fuller's Summer Ale and Coniston Bluebird from their traditional home in England, where the style was developed to create a beer that would keep when exported around the Empire. There are Belgian golden ales, such as Duvel, and the driest of the Belgian Trappist beers, like Orval and Chimay. Belgium has yet more to offer with its lively and distinctive Saison summer ales and the Gueuze style that blends young and old lambics to create a fresh, tart, apple-and-citrus

HORS D'OEUVRES *Dry, hoppy beers are perfect with light appetizers, such as scallops, before a meal.*

flavour. Particular types of hop, malt, and yeast are used to find the required taste, and often these recipes are closely guarded secrets, perhaps handed down within a family or a monastery over centuries. Each beer is unique, but still has that essential hoppy character or hint of dry sourness that stimulates the appetite.

DRINKING AND SERVING

DRINK PROFILE The whole point of an appetizer is that it leaves you wanting more, so these beers tend to be dominated by the dry hops rather than the rich malts, both in the aroma and the taste.

C COLOUR Pilsner lagers will be the typical golden yellow. Other beers in this group range from amber or orange to very dark. Normally, these beers have a fine white head.

A AROMA The hops typically give flowery and grassy aromas. These beers should feel fresh on the nose, with an appetizing suggestion of dryness, rather than sweetness or richness.

T TASTE The taste of these beers should lead you to want another beer or, more respectably, to move on to your meal! The flavour should be dry, hoppy, and fresh, particularly at the finish.

BUYING AND STORING Some of these beers, like Duvel or Young's Special London Ale, are very well known and quite easy to buy. Others, like Brooklyn Lager or the Belgian Saison beers, are more local or regional, and more difficult to find. These beers are best drunk when fresh, so should not be stored.

SERVING SUGGESTIONS These are appetizers, so they should look good, and be presented at 9–12°C (48–54°F) in a nice glass, with the head sitting firmly on top of the beer. They are suitable for introducing either lunch or dinner.

FOOD COMPANIONS As appetizers, these beers will normally be drunk with small snacks, tapas, or hors d'oeuvres before the main meal, but they are often good enough to stretch to fish and light pasta dishes, or even cold meats and sausages.

GERMANY

Germany makes fine Pilsners, but also produces really dry, appetizing beers characterized by their hoppy bitterness. Brands like Radeburger and Jever are classic examples of this clean, crisp style.

BITBURGER

BITBURGER PILS

C COLOUR Light golden yellow, with a light, white, frothy head.

A AROMA Aromatic, with grassy hops and a vanilla sweetness.

T TASTE Very light bodied and clean, with a soft feel and a dry finish.

This brewery is situated in the Pfalz area of the German Rhineland, and although established since 1817, its claim to fame is that it was the first brewery outside Pilsen, in what is now the Czech Republic, to have used the term Pilsner, in 1883. The technological breakthrough was the building of a new cooled cellar that created the necessary conditions to use bottom-fermenting yeasts. Despite a challenge from the Pilsen brewery, the company, run by the Simon family, stuck to its guns, and won a court battle in 1913 to be allowed to use the term Simonbräu-Deutsch-Pilsner. This effectively liberated the term Pilsner from its geographical origin, establishing Pils as the universal term for German-style, bottom-fermented lagers.

The company has continued to make its excellent lagers, and has also made great efforts to distribute its beers around Germany and beyond. Over the years it has had great success, and is now the second-bestseller in Germany.

Bitburger Premium Pils is a classic German lager. It is not too strong, at 4.6% ABV, and is unpasteurized. It is a straw-coloured beer with a fine frothy head, and an aroma of hops and vanilla. On the palate it is dry and bitter with some slightly smoky hop flavours and a touch of soft malt. The finish is delicately dry. Overall, this beer is particularly elegant and rounded for a lager, and makes a very refreshing and satisfying drink.

Bitburger is aimed at a mass market, but is definitely a cut above many of the global brands. If you want to venture into a better quality lager – drier, more complex – then this is a great one to try.

WIDE DISTRIBUTION *Bitburger Premium Pils is available at many traditional German Bierstuben, or pubs.*

RADEBURGER PILS

C COLOUR Attractive lemony yellow, with a long-lasting head.

A AROMA Fresh, with earthy hops, citrus, malt, and grape.

T TASTE Quite light-bodied, with vanilla balanced by hoppy dryness.

This old brewery in eastern Germany, near Dresden, once supplied the king of Saxony with his beer. It dates from 1872, and, having survived the isolation of the Communist years in East Germany, it is now making its mark once again. This Pilsner is very bright, lively, and refreshing, with a strong, long-lasting head and a malty, grapy lager aroma with a citrus hint. The flavour is bitter and very fresh, with a little hop character, a hint of vanilla, and a pleasantly bitter finish. This is a great apéritif or session lager.

SCHUMACHER ALT

C COLOUR Reddish brown, with a good frothy white head.

A AROMA Quite sweet but balanced aromas of malt and hops.

T TASTE Rich and sweet, with malt, caramel, vanilla, nuts, and fruit.

Schumacher is a family-owned brewery based in Düsseldorf. Although made in the dark, rich style of Altbier, this reddish-brown and moderately strong (4.6% ABV) brew is slightly lighter and drier than most others. Both the aromas and the taste are very malty and sweet, with a little bit of dry sourness in the middle that makes it work well as an appetizer beer. It is clean, smooth, and well made. Schumacher Alt also goes really well with *Sauerbraten*, a traditional Rhineland dish of marinated beef – delicious!

SCHUMACHER ALT

DIEBELS ALT

C COLOUR Dark copper, with light orange tinges and a long-lasting head.

A AROMA Spicy hop, with malt, nuts, mocha, and fruit.

T TASTE Well balanced between sweet and dry, with a spicy hop finish.

Diebels is the biggest producer of Altbier, based at Issum, near the Dutch border. This brewery was established in 1878, and is still a family firm. This fine beer is a dark copper colour with a dense off-white head that dissipates slowly. The aromas are full and dense with caramel malt, spicy hops, and an ample nut character. The flavour is sweetish and there is a great touch of flowery, dry hop bitterness on the finish. One of my favourite ways to drink this Altbier is with grilled meats, and especially bratwurst.

UERIGE ALT

C COLOUR Light orangey copper, with a rich, long-lasting, off-white head.

A AROMA Bright and fresh hops, with caramel and spice notes.

T TASTE Clean, firm caramel malt, with a dry undertone and bitter finish.

This is a classic of the Düsseldorf Altbiers, brewed at the famous old brewpub Zum Uerige. The aromas are complex. On the surface, they are mainly fresh, yeasty hops, but deeper down you find malt, caramel, and spices. It is medium-bodied and very silky and smooth. The initial taste is extremely dry, with nutty, caramel flavours. Later, the fruit comes through, with a caramel, malty sweetness, then a fresh, stimulating, and pleasantly bitter finish. This is great with Rhineland cold meats, sausages, and marinated cheese.

UERIGE ALT

JEVER PILSENER

C COLOUR Light bright yellow, with a full and lasting white head.

A AROMA Bright and earthy, with grassy hops and malt.

T TASTE Very crisp, dry, and fresh, with a stimulating bitter finish.

Jever is a small town in Friesland, in the far northwest of Germany, on the coast opposite the Frisian Islands, with Denmark to the north and the Dutch border to the south. The people of Friesland are proudly independent – indeed they were the first nation to recognize American independence in 1776! This remote region was made famous by Erskine Childers in the adventure *The Riddle of the Sands*, but it is also an area famous for its dry, refreshing beers and strong, tasty food. The label on a bottle of Jever Pilsener says Friesisch Herb, which proclaims that the beer is brewed in Friesland.

The Jever Brewery was founded in 1848, and established itself with its excellent quality Pilsners, which soon became well known throughout Germany. After several owners, it is now part of the Brau und Brunnen group. Although Jever is a traditional company, it has a very modern brewing facility, and the water for the beer is drawn directly from a well on the site. The brewers at Jever are very proud of their water, claiming that because it is so soft and pure they can add more hops to the brew.

It is sometimes said that the further north you go in Germany, the drier the beer tastes. Well, you cannot go much further north than this, and Jever Pilsener is often described as the driest beer in Germany – so case proven, I think!

This Pilsner is moderately strong, at 4.9% ABV. It has a distinct earthy and grassy aroma, and a lovely full white head. The palate is very smooth but it tastes bone-dry from the first sip. It is full of hops and has a grapefruity, citrus tang. The bitterness continues to develop in the finish, with just a hint of sweet vanilla to counterbalance it.

This is a very fine beer, basically very dry, but well balanced. If you like Pilsner, and you like your beer dry, then try this one – you will be in beer heaven.

JEVER

BITTER BUT HONEST
Jever Pilsener matches the character of its Friesland origins with its dry, uncompromising, and direct flavour.

SMOKED SALMON The pungently smoky, yet sea-fresh and salty flavours of smoked salmon are a perfect complement to the emphatically dry, refreshing style of Jever Pilsener. A typical meal in Friesland pairs a variety of smoked products, such as fish or pork, with a simple loaf of bread and cheese.

UK

Britain is the home of dry, hoppy ale, including the famous India Pale Ale (IPA), originally made so it would continue to ferment and stay fresh on long sea journeys to India. Some brands date back to the 19th century, while others are the product of modern micro-breweries.

WORTHINGTON WHITE SHIELD

C COLOUR Medium orange-amber, possibly cloudy from sediment.

A AROMA Hops and fruit, with just a hint of sulphur.

T TASTE Lovely balance between apple fruit and bitter hops.

Not just a beer, but a ritual! For many years, Worthington White Shield was the only naturally fermenting, bottle-conditioned pale ale for sale in most British pubs, and its devotees would find a special pleasure in carefully pouring the ale to avoid the cloudiness of the yeast.

It is a beautifully rounded beer with a full malty palate, powerfully bitter, with a long, complex finish.

After a battle between the Bass brewing group – which wanted to discontinue production – and the lovers of this ale, production was finally moved to the Museum Brewing Company in Burton on Trent. If you can find this wonderful traditional beer, store it carefully; if it is too cold, the yeast will become inactive and fermentation will stop.

WORTHINGTON
WHITE SHIELD

YOUNG'S SPECIAL LONDON ALE

C COLOUR Light amber, with a bubbly short-lived head.

A AROMA Complex, with yeast, fruit, citrus, and spice in fine balance.

T TASTE Smooth and creamy, with spicy and flowery hops and a peppery finish.

This bright, hoppy ale was originally produced for the Belgian market by Young's Brewery, to show what a traditional English ale was like. The brewery's efforts have resulted in a wonderfully complex and interesting brew, with aromas of hops and touches of red fruit and even bananas; creamy and smooth, yet dry, with a spicy, lemony, peppery finish.

It is quite strong at 6.4% ABV, so look out. This beer shouldn't be served too cold, a gentle chill will do – plus a nice plateful of sausage and chips.

TIMOTHY TAYLOR'S LANDLORD

C COLOUR Light amber, with an excellent rich-textured head.

A AROMA Distinct firm hops and zesty citrus fruits.

T TASTE Fairly bitter, with subtle malt and hops and a dry finish.

Originally made to cleanse the throats of thirsty miners from the nearby coalfields, this is a fine, strong, Yorkshire-style pale ale, best drunk not too cold. The aromas are built around hops, with a slight citrus feel. The taste has a superb balance of hops, malt, citrus, sweetness, and dryness. The cask version was chosen as the 1999 Champion Beer of Britain by the Campaign for Real Ale (CAMRA), and most people prefer it to the bottled version. So do I, but here, essentially, is the true taste of old-fashioned bottled bitter.

HARVIESTOUN BITTER & TWISTED

C COLOUR Attractive pale gold with orange tinges; short-lived head.

A AROMA Quite full and rich, with grassy hops and citrus.

T TASTE Clean malt; dry lemon citrus feel; long bitterish finish.

Harviestoun is a village brewery based in an old stone dairy at Dollar, Scotland. Its cask version of Bitter & Twisted was CAMRA's 2003 Champion Beer of Britain. The name of this beer implies a twist of lemon, but the lemony feel comes from late hopping, and the particular hop varieties used. So you will find a citrus character in both the aroma and flavour. This is a beer you'll either love or hate!

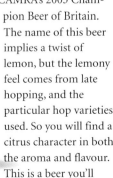

HARVIESTOUN
BITTER & TWISTED

CONISTON BLUEBIRD

C COLOUR Light amber brown, with a medium head.

A AROMA Barley malt and grassy hops in an excellent balance.

T TASTE Not too fizzy; quite dry and fruity, and light-bodied.

The Coniston Brewing Company was started in 1995 by two enthusiasts, Ian Bradley and Rob Irwin, who built it on the site of an old pigsty in Coniston, in the English Lake District. Also available as an award-winning cask version, this bottle-conditioned (*see p.401*) beer is distributed by Brakspear Brewery. Coniston Bluebird is not too powerful at 3.6% ABV, and is neither too sweet nor dry, while the gentle fizz allows the fruity flavours to come through.

CONISTON
BLUEBIRD

MEANTIME AMBA PALE ALE

C COLOUR Light amber and bright, with a good intensity.

A AROMA Delicate and light, with grassy hops, yeast, and malt.

T TASTE Soft malt base, with a subtle sweetness and a spicy finish.

The goal of the Meantime Brewing Company, in Greenwich, London, is to create an image of beer similar to that enjoyed by wine. It produces some unusual beers, including strawberry- and chocolate-flavoured brews *(see p448)*. Amba Pale Ale is an organic, English-style pale ale, with a malted barley sweetness and a fresh spicy finish. It is moderately strong at 4.9% ABV. This beer is excellent with pasta, pizza, or steak-and-kidney pie, and should be served lightly chilled.

DURHAM MAGUS

C COLOUR Very pale gold; unusual for an English ale.

A AROMA Delicate, with grassy hops and a lemon citrus feel.

T TASTE Quite bitter; good malt and hop balance and lemony notes.

DURHAM MAGUS

The Durham Brewery, based in the northeast of England, uses traditional skills to make a wide range of specialist beers, while retaining the traditional character of English ales.

The award-winning Magus is the brewery's best-selling beer. It is not very strong, at 3.8% ABV, and is really quite pale for an English ale. The Slovenian and Czech hops give it a slight lagerish feel, and make it really refreshing - you can easily drink too many!

FULLER'S SUMMER ALE

C COLOUR Very pale gold, with deeper orange tinges.

A AROMA Distinctive; grassy hops and a sweet note of vanilla.

T TASTE Dry and very light-bodied, with a fresh citrusy feel.

Fuller's regularly brews ales to match the seasons, but Summer Ale is a relatively new one from the London brewery. It is a pale golden beer, with a thick, lager-like head. The aromas are fresh and grassy, with a hint of vanilla. This beer is designed to refresh, so you have a light-bodied, bright, and not-too-dry feel to the taste. The flavours are not too strong, and nor is the beer at 3.9% ABV. I love sipping this beer from its lovely big glass bottle. This is definitely one for the garden on a hot day.

FULLER'S SUMMER ALE

HOP BACK SUMMER LIGHTNING

C COLOUR Bright medium gold, with a slight amber tinge.

A AROMA Delicate, with hops and a lemon citrus character.

T TASTE Full-bodied; dry and very refreshing; spicy citrus feel.

Most people love this beer, but some find it a little too citrusy. Summer Lightning is an award-winning bottle-conditioned summer beer with a large, bubbly head. This attractive summer ale was originally made for a beer festival, but was so successful that it went into production as a bottled beer. The aromas are light, with hops and citrus, and the taste is definitely refreshing, with a dry, lemony feel, and hardly any sweetness. It is quite strong for a summertime drink at 5% ABV.

HOP BACK SUMMER LIGHTNING

BELGIUM

Belgium is the home of Trappist beers, made exclusively by monks at one time. These fine beers are rich, dry, and fruity, and make a great apéritif. There are also tripel beers made with barley, wheat, and oats, and seasonal ales, which are rich, dry, and strong.

DUVEL

C COLOUR Light golden yellow, with a steady, pure white head.

A AROMA Very aromatic, with vanilla, spicy hops, apple, pear, and orange.

T TASTE Dry, creamy, and smooth, with citrus, vanilla, malt; complex finish.

This refreshing, dry, Belgian golden ale is made by the family firm of Moortgat, at Breendonck, between Brussels and Antwerp. The firm originally brewed Scottish-style dark ale, beginning in 1923, which was described as "a Devil of an ale". Duvel – pronounced "doov'l" – is a Flemish corruption of the word devil. In 1968 the company decided to move to making golden ale, with great success. The yeast still comes from McEwan's of Scotland, but lighter hops are used to make the golden ale.

This beer really is something special. It is a bottle-conditioned ale, although it can easily be mistaken for a lager. Because it is not too dry or bitter, it is extremely drinkable and approachable, but at a powerful 8.5% ABV, it is also highly dangerous! Duvel is a beautiful pale golden yellow, and the bottle fermentation gives it a thick, bubbly head. It has a nose rich in vanilla, with some hop, fruit, and spice content. The taste is brilliantly complex, with spice, fruit, and alcohol present all at once. The finish leaves you with a great feeling, and wanting more.

One of the special features of Duvel is that it works very well both cold, as an apéritif, or at room temperature, as an after-dinner beer. I personally prefer drinking it with cheese, nuts, or good, fresh, crusty bread.

This beer has many fans, and some of them claim it as the greatest beer in the world. It is certainly true that, for a beer this strong, it is surprisingly easy to drink, and the strength can dangerously creep up on you. Its colour makes it look like an ordinary lager, but it is much richer and more complex than that. Duvel is quite easy to obtain around the world, and is not an expensive, specialist beer. You must try it – and see if you agree with the fans that say this is the world's greatest beer.

DUVEL

CULTURE AND TRADITION

CAFÉ CULTURE The streets of Antwerp in Belgium are lined with cafés dedicated to the country's famous beers. Moortgat's brewery, which makes Duvel, made its name in the town after World War I, when the government banned the sale of hard liquor in cafés, and strong beers took its place.

POTENT BREW *The popular Duvel has the look of a light, refreshing lager, but is in fact a top-fermented ale, with a powerful 8.5% ABV.*

ORVAL

C COLOUR Dark and deeply intense old gold, with orange tinges.

A AROMA Complex and earthy, with yeast, citrus fruit, apple, and pear.

T TASTE Very dry and light-bodied, with fruit, spice, and a long finish.

The monastery at Orval makes only one beer – but what a beer! Trappist beers are mostly rich, complex, and spicy brews. The famous Orval is bottle-fermented, and can be cloudy. It is also strong, at 6.2% ABV, and is the only fully dry beer of all the Trappist brews.

Throughout the long history of Orval, there has probably always been a brewery at the monastery. But in the modern era, the brewery is operated as a separate company within the monastery and employs expert lay-people. The beer that

ORVAL

is sold today has its origins in the 1930s, when a German master brewer called Pappenheimer developed a production process that emphasized the hoppy characters.

The colour is a rich deep gold, and both the nose and the flavours are very complex, with great yeasty, acidic, hoppy, and citrusy notes throughout. The apple character gives a feel not far from a strong, rich cider. The head is large – and it lasts for ever! Despite the complexity, the beer is light, lively, and foamy, with an intense hoppy bitterness and fruity notes of grapefruit, lemon, and orange peel, and a spicy hint of cinnamon or nutmeg. Both the aroma and the taste can be suggestive of whisky.

This is a great, distinctive, ultra-dry, and complex beer. If you want to try a Trappist ale, start with this, with some dry biscuits and cheese, and you will never look back.

CULTURE AND TRADITION

SILENCE IS GOLDEN Orval is one of the best and most famous beers made by Trappist monks. The Orval monastery is in the Belgian Ardennes and is named after Vallée d'Or (valley of gold). The monks have occupied the site since 1070. The current complex of buildings dates from the

1920s and stands beside the ruins of the earlier monastery, destroyed during the Napoleonic period. Only beers produced by the silent orders – five in Belgium and one in Holland – can be called Trappist. Beer was originally produced for its nourishing properties. It was called "liquid bread" and was an important part of the monks' diet.

CHIMAY

C COLOUR Deep, rich, and shining gold through to dark amber-brown.

A AROMA Elegant, with malt, orange citrus, and spicy juniper.

T TASTE Quite dry, with deep and complex flavours of malt, orange, and herbs.

Chimay produces premium beers that are elegant, tasty, full of life and character – I love them!

Chimay has been known, since its foundation in 1862, for its rich, dark Trappist abbey beers. But in the 1960s it introduced a drier, lighter beer, making the third of the now famous Chimay "Tripel" range.

This lighter, drier beer is called Chimay Blanche, and it can be recognized by its white or pale cap. It has also been produced as Cinq Cents in a Champagne-style bottle to celebrate the 500th anniversary of the nearby town of Chimay. Chimay Blanche is a strong beer, at 8% ABV, and is very fresh, dry, and citrusy,

with great orange and herb flavours.

The Grande Reserve, or blue cap, is the deepest and richest of the Chimay beers, and is very strong at 9% ABV. It is produced in vintages of five years old and beyond, and has aromas and flavours of dark fruit, liquorice, and chocolate. The older vintages are much sought after, and treated as if they were port. They are wonderful with Roquefort cheese (see also p466).

CHIMAY

Première, or red cap, is the weakest of the three at 7% ABV, and is a rich, red-brown ale, with a fruity, spicy flavour. Despite being so overtly fruity, it is still dry. This beer is wonderful with the monastery's own Chimay cheese.

DELIRIUM TREMENS

C COLOUR Light, bright, and attractive; deeply elegant gold.

A AROMA Complex, with warm spice, sweet malt, and apple.

T TASTE Quite sweet and smooth; malt, wood, orange fruit; gently spicy finish.

This strong, triple-fermented ale is made by the Huyghe Brewery, and is aptly named, as it is sweet, attractive, and very easy to drink, and also really strong at 9% ABV. There is a light, frothy head, and a malty, spicy aroma. The texture is smooth, with spicy malt and orangey sweetness. This is not meant to be a classic, but a fun beer. Maybe the strength is overrated: when I tried it, I wasn't seeing pink elephants, except for the ones on the label, of course – and the one running across the kitchen floor!

PALM SPECIALE

C COLOUR Bright and intense; rich, dark-golden orange.

A AROMA Full and quite pungent, with yeast and orange citrus notes.

T TASTE Deep toasty malt sweetness, balanced by grassy hops.

PALM SPECIALE

The biggest-selling Belgian ale – and the Belgians know their beer. This company can trace its origins back to a local farm producer in 1597, and the family-run brewery itself dates from 1747. Its beer is moderately strong at 5% ABV, but it has an unusual earthy and pungent aroma, which some drinkers find unpleasant. The taste, however, is excellent – sweet at first, but developing into a more complex and dry hoppy feel. Not a world-class beer, but still very interesting, and one to try for something unusual.

CANTILLON ROSE DE GAMBRINUS

C COLOUR Beautiful deep pink, like rosé Champagne.

A AROMA Very fruity; raspberry and cherry with vanilla.

T TASTE Delicious balance of fruit and acidity; long finish.

Is it beer or Champagne? This is something different, special, and one of the world's great beers! The Cantillon brewery, in the heart of Brussels, is the foremost producer of lambic wheat beer, and also specializes in fruit beers. Rose de Gambrinus is named after Jan Primus, the 13th century duke of Brabant. It is beautifully fruity, with a wonderful balanced sweetness. What a great opener for a party!

CANTILLON ROSE DE GAMBRINUS

DE RANKE XX BITTER

C COLOUR Yellow-orange, with a hazy look when poured.

A AROMA Distinctly hoppy and tangy, with pineapple, sugar, and black pepper.

T TASTE Very bitter, clean malt flavour; liquorice and dill; sweetish finish.

If you like a good Belgian pale ale, in a different style from the English IPA, then you will really like this one. Expect a strong, dry, spicy brew, with a medium body but a full flavour. It is very strong at 6.2% ABV, and lively, with a full and long-lasting head. The aromas are quite citrusy and spicy, giving hints of the dry bitterness to come. The flavour is really dominated by the hops, which make this ale very dry indeed. This is a great apéritif, and you will feel very hungry after a couple of these, thanks to its appealing bitterness.

HANSSENS OUDE GUEUZE

C COLOUR Light and elegant; rusty amber brown.

A AROMA Quite dry and sour, with earth and a spicy feel.

T TASTE Lemon, apple, rhubarb; malt sweetness; spicy finish.

When young and old lambic beers are blended and bottled together, the mixture develops into a sweet-sour beer called Gueuze, which has more life than the original lambic. Hanssens Oude Gueuze comes in a corked bottle, which, on opening, produces a decent, bubbly head and an orangey-amber beer. The aroma is quite earthy and even dank. It is fairly strong at 6% ABV, and has a fine balance between the tart apple and citrus fruit, and sweetness.

HANSSENS OUDE GUEUZE

GIRARDIN GUEUZE

C COLOUR Dark yellow straw, with a hazy character.

A AROMA Pungent; citrus, with apple and new-mown hay.

T TASTE Dry and acidic; pineapple, lemon, grapefruit; fresh, long finish.

Girardin is a small, traditional farm brewery at St Ulricks Kapelle, which mainly uses its own wheat supplies to make lambic beer, Kriek (cherry beer), and Gueuze. This beer is conditioned in the bottle. It is a great example of the Gueuze style of blended lambic beer, even though it is not as well-known as some. This fantastic beer is dry and acidic with bags of citrus and apple fruit and fresh woody flavours, plus some spicy hints. Some wine drinkers say that beer can't be sophisticated, but this beer would convince them otherwise – I'm a great fan.

MOINETTE BIOLOGIQUE

C COLOUR Pale gold colour, with a yellowish tinge.

A AROMA Complex, with coriander, cinnamon, vanilla, pepper, fig, toffee.

T TASTE Light-bodied and smooth with a spicy, malty finish.

The Dupont brewery, in the Belgian province of Hainault, has been a family firm since it was purchased in 1920. Its reputation is based on traditional beers. Moinette Biologique is an unfiltered, organic ale with a lumpy, head and a pleasing, pale golden colour. The complex aromas are very fruity and spicy, and the taste is smooth with a lively, spicy finish. Moinette Biologique is strong at 7.5% ABV, and has won a number of awards.

MOINETTE BIOLOGIQUE

SAISON DUPONT

C COLOUR Pale straw with orange tinges, and quite hazy.

A AROMA Very fruity, with orange, vanilla, spice, and tobacco.

T TASTE Full-bodied, firm and dry, with a slightly bitter lemon feel.

The most famous beer from the Dupont brewery is this bottle-conditioned ale. In Belgium, the word "*saison*" only refers to one season – summer. But "summer ale" to the Belgians is no lightweight quaffing beer: it is rich and strong at 6.5% ABV. Saison Dupont is made using a long tradition of brewing, allegedly going back to the monks in the district. This beer has a fine creamy head and fruit aromas. It is full-bodied, with fruit, especially lemon, offsetting the sweetness. The finish is very citrusy, slightly bitter, and leaves a sparkling sensation on the tongue.

SAISON DE SILLY

C COLOUR Dark orange-bronze, and normally cloudy when poured.

A AROMA Sweet and very fruity with cherry and toffee.

T TASTE Soft and malty; cherry, caramel, and apple; acidic feel; sweetish finish.

Belgian Saison beers are always summer ales, but are often quite strong and intense. Brewery de Silly is a well-regarded Hainault brewer making a range of beers since 1950. This is a distinctive beer. It is dark and cloudy, with a caramel or honey sweetness balanced by woody hops. The head is quite short-lived, and the overall feeling from the beer is one of sweet caramel, balanced by an apple and hop bitterness. It is not too strong at 5% ABV, with a full body and an interesting flavour. I think this is one you'll either love or hate!

SAISON DE PIPAIX

SAISON DE PIPAIX

C COLOUR Bright and clear honey gold, with orange highlights.

A AROMA Pleasant, sweet, and tart, with zesty citrus.

T TASTE Smooth and full-bodied, with a quite dry and citrus taste.

A former schoolteacher, Jean-Louis Dits, revived an old steam-powered brewery and now produces the beer in a working museum at Pipaix, not far from Leuze. Saison de Pipaix is brewed according to an original recipe from 1785 using malt, hops, ginger, orange, pepper, and coriander. It is quite strong (6% ABV), and has a large head that disappears quickly. It is a honey-orange colour with an acidic aroma, and is not very fizzy. This is an unusual, quite herby beer that is full-bodied with a rich, malty, and dry citrus taste.

USA

American ales are dominated by hops rather than malt. As a result they are rich and very dry and make great appetizers. Some breweries also make fine top-fermenting pale ales in English and Belgian styles.

VICTORY HOP DEVIL

VICTORY HOP DEVIL

C COLOUR A pleasant deep amber, with orange highlights.

A AROMA Full and intense, with hops, lemon, and orange.

T TASTE Sharply bitter; zingy, peppery, orange and malt tones; long dry finish.

Victory Brewing was established in 1996 in Downingtown, near Philadelphia, by two enthusiasts, Ron Barchet and Bill Covaleski. Their brewpub produces a range of beers, but its flagship product is the IPA, Hop Devil.

The brewers were trained in Holland and Germany, but this beer is much more in the English–American pale ale style. It is quite strong at 6.4% ABV, with a big head and a huge aroma. Although there is a hint of caramel richness in the flavour, the true character of the beer is the dryness from the intense hops – truly a hop devil! The finish is something special. It is very long, and begins as dry and spicy, but is soon covered in a soft maltiness.

This is a full-flavoured, peppery beer, which I recommend trying with spicy Asian foods. It will always hold its own.

ROGUE BRUTAL BITTER

C COLOUR Deep orange to light-brown amber colour.

A AROMA Full, with hops and citrus, particularly grapefruit.

T TASTE Sharply bitter, with a hop and grapefruit feel, balanced with malt.

Rogue Ales, named after the local Rogue River, was established in 1988 in Newport, Oregon, a small coastal fishing town. It produces a dizzying array of beers, and I think that Brutal Bitter is one of the best. The feel is very dry, hoppy, and citrusy, and the dryness is quite well balanced so that it is much more than just a "hop monster". It is also quite strong at 6.5% ABV.

Brutal by name, but the balance of flavours saves it from being only that.

SIERRA NEVADA CELEBRATION ALE

C COLOUR Deep orange with light to medium amber highlights.

A AROMA Full and distinctive, with hops and grapefruit citrus.

T TASTE Sharply bitter, with a hop, dark chocolate, and citrus feel; dry finish.

One of the most famous of the American micro-breweries. Celebration is a rich, strong, IPA-style beer, usually produced at 6% ABV, but the alcohol content can vary. This beer is very aromatic and lively, with plenty of hop character, but also complex aromas and flavours of lemon and unsweetened dark chocolate. The brewery sometimes uses different varieties of hop, so the character of the beer subtly changes from year to year – but it is always excellent.

SIERRA NEVADA
CELEBRATION ALE

SIERRA NEVADA PALE ALE

C COLOUR Bright medium gold, verging on orangey amber.

A AROMA Elegant, with distinct malt, apple, and citrus notes.

T TASTE Fruity and flowery, with orange, grapefruit, and a strong hop character.

Sierra Nevada Brewing is one of the best-regarded American micro-breweries. It was established in 1981, and founder Ken Grossman opened a purpose-built, state-of-the-art brewery in 1989, in Chico, California, replacing the former set-up in a converted dairy.

Sierra Nevada Pale Ale has won a string of awards. It is reasonably strong at 5.6% ABV and not too different from a traditional English IPA – but just different enough to be interesting. The beer is a golden colour with a light, bubbly, short-lived head. It has a citrusy hop nose, with apple and cinnamon notes. It is quite bitter and very hoppy, but the fruit soon comes through, with orange, lime, and grapefruit.

It is clean and refreshing, disguises its strength well, and is a good summer-afternoon beer. This is a beer of character and class. While it is delicious cold, it improves if warmed from fridge temperature, as this brings out the best of the hop character. The best serving temperature is 14–17°C (57–63°F) – just like a red wine.

Some drinkers say that Sierra Nevada Pale Ale is one of those beers that is much better on draught, rather than from the bottle. I am not convinced – but you will have to decide. To me, this is one of the very finest beers available in a bottle. It will appeal particularly to lovers of the classic IPA style, but with a delicious character all of its own.

MCNEILL'S DEAD HORSE IPA

C COLOUR Beautiful deep orange, with attractive crimson notes.

A AROMA Full and malty, with earth and floral and grassy hops.

T TASTE Malty, creamy, quite sweet; caramel and citrus; dry, woody finish.

One of the best-known beers from this Vermont micro-brewery. Dead Horse is a strong IPA at 5.8% ABV, with an unusual earthy aroma that could be off-putting. The beer has a good full head, and a full malty and hoppy flavour.

Dead Horse IPA is made with Kent hops, and is very much in the English style, with added richness. It is often quite cloudy, and bottles vary from being very fizzy to nearly flat. This is a great strong ale.

MCNEILL'S DEAD HORSE IPA

SMUTTYNOSE SHOALS PALE ALE

C COLOUR Attractive copper, with transparent bronze highlights.

A AROMA Elegant and complex, with yeast, earth, grassy hops, and citrus.

T TASTE Medium-bodied, with a firm hop dryness, tangy fruit, and malt.

Smuttynose is one of the many micro-breweries on the northeast coast of the US, in this case in Portsmouth, New Hampshire. It was established in 1994 and is named after Smuttynose Island, an Atlantic shoal just off the coast, which has a history of pirates and murderers.

Their beer has been called the closest thing to an English ale in an American bottled beer, and has won prizes in the UK. It is quite dark, with a strong hop influence and tangy citrus fruit. There is a great balance between malty sweetness and dryness – it is very hard to find a better one, and I am a great fan, along with the competition judges!

ANCHOR LIBERTY ALE

C **COLOUR** Deep old gold to a classic light brown IPA colour.

A **AROMA** Distinctive; hops and fruit, especially pineapple.

T **TASTE** Dry and fresh; hops, citrus, pineapple; malty vanilla sweetness.

Anchor Brewing is a San Francisco legend, famous for its Steam Beer. Liberty Ale was first issued in 1975 to commemorate the 200th anniversary of Paul Revere's ride to mobilize the American revolutionaries against the British. It is strong at 6% ABV, golden-coloured, and has fine aromas. It has a great bittersweet and fruity balance and a wonderfully long malt finish. This is a true American classic, possibly the best of all. I really love this beer with Cajun and Thai food.

BROOKLYN LAGER

C **COLOUR** Light bright amber; more orange brown than most lagers.

A **AROMA** Quite rich, with caramel, malt, and hops.

T **TASTE** Full-bodied, with malt, caramel, and citrus notes.

BROOKLYN LAGER

There are still some great breweries in the centre of London in the UK, such as Fuller's and Young's, but the once-great New York brewing area of Brooklyn closed the doors on its last traditional brewery in the 1970s. Brewing in the district was revived in 1988 with the establishment of the Brooklyn Brewery, set up by a banker and an Associated Press correspondent who were both beer enthusiasts. The company very quickly made a hit with its Black Chocolate Stout, and began producing other beers, including wheat beers and a fine lager.

Brooklyn Lager is quite strong at 5.1% ABV, and is classed as an amber lager, all-malt and brewed to an old recipe. It is an award-winner, and is the brewery's flagship brew. The aroma is quite rich, with roast malt, caramel, and hops. When you drink this beer, it is refreshing and lively and there are faint citrus notes. The sweetness comes from malt and caramel, which are quite dominant, and the finish is fairly dry.

Although this is called a lager, it is not what you would expect. It is really more like an American brown ale or even an English old ale, and is very pleasant and drinkable. So long as you know what you are choosing, you will really enjoy this beer. In my opinion, it is great with – or after – dinner.

OMMEGANG HENNEPIN

C **COLOUR** Light orange; a rich, deep, and attractive hue.

A **AROMA** Hops and fruit, especially orange and grapefruit.

T **TASTE** Subtle and well-balanced, with citrusy orange and complex spice.

OMMEGANG HENNEPIN

The name of this New York State brewery refers to a traditional parade in Brussels, and the brewery is Belgian–American, with some of the big Belgian brewing families supporting it. Not surprisingly, it is already a big hit! Hennepin is a bottle-conditioned ale similar to a Belgian Saison, and strong at 7.5% ABV. It has a great full head, and is very complex, with a great orangey and spicy feel. It is also really strong and satisfying.

STAR BARS
The TV comedy Cheers *made the conversation-friendly Boston bar famous, and this bar in the city emulates the style of the show.*

SAMUEL ADAMS LAGER

C **COLOUR** Deep old gold; darker than the usual lager colour.

A **AROMA** Strong flowery hops and earthy malt.

T **TASTE** Quite bittersweet; vegetable, orange, malt, and hops; bitter finish.

SAMUEL ADAMS LAGER

The Boston Beer Company is one of America's best-known micro-breweries, so much so that some purists now consider it a mainstream commercial brewery. Such is the price of success! The flagship Samuel Adams Lager (named after one of the patriots of the American revolution, who was also a brewer) is a rich beer for a lager, maybe somewhere between a lager and a pale ale. It has a creamy head and is much better than the usual mass-produced lagers, with a really long finish – give it a try.

DARK AND CREAMY

66 Wonderfully smooth stouts and porters to restore your confidence and lift your mood. So good you could eat them! 99

INTRODUCING DARK AND CREAMY BEERS

Always smooth and satisfying, there are so many dark styles to savour beyond the world-famous Guinness. Never drink these beers straight from the bottle! One of their main attractions is the rich, dark body in the glass and the full, creamy head.

DRINKING AND SERVING

DRINK PROFILE Satisfying stouts and porters make a long-lasting creamy drink. They are a world away from fizzy lagers yet are often no higher in alcohol, despite the full body and dark colour.

C COLOUR By definition, these beers are a dark colour – black, brown, or red – from the roasted malt, and range from deeply opaque to partially clear. The head is dark cream or light tan.

A AROMA The roasted malt gives aromas of bitter chocolate, ground coffee, and dark fruits, such as plum, prune, or blackcurrant. Some beers have hints of spice, wood, or earth.

T TASTE The taste should be full, creamy, and smooth, and rich and satisfying, whether it is a bone-dry Irish stout like Guinness Original or a sweet porter or milk stout like Mackeson.

BUYING AND STORING You will find a variety of stouts and even porters in supermarkets, beer shops, and bars, and you will need to try a range to find your favourites. Some dark and creamy beers are pasteurized, and others not. Generally there is no need to store them.

SERVING SUGGESTIONS Although some stouts are served cold, serving stouts and porters at around 13°C (55°F) really brings out the flavours. Dark lagers and mild beers can be served a little cooler.

FOOD COMPANIONS The best partner for these dark beers is shellfish. Doppelbocks go well with strongly flavoured food, such as heavy sausage, cold meats, and cheese. Some sweet stouts work very well with creamy desserts. Chocolate stout is perfect with – you guessed it – chocolate cake.

This group of beers contains the widest range of tastes: but essentially, these beers are dominated by malt rather than hops. The roasting of the malt is important to the colour, aromas, and flavours, and the combination of malty richness and fizz gives the creamy feel. These beers can be fairly strong in alcohol, but they are generally not the strongest. Their apparent strength comes from the fullness of their body, so much so that they are sometimes termed "restoratives", and in the past have been used as food substitutes and health tonics.

COFFEE BEANS *Aromas such as coffee develop from the roasted malts used in stouts.*

AROUND THE WORLD

Although these are all dark beers, there is a wide variety of style and character. At one extreme they can be absolutely black, like Anchor Porter or Deschutes Obsidian, while German Doppelbocks are brown with red or amber highlights. Porter tends to be lighter and fresher than stout, and the dry Irish style of stout is only one end of a spectrum that goes all the way to the richest, sweetest versions like the Jamaican Dragon Stout. The sweetness comes from the malt, and dryness from the hops. Often, these beers have a peppery feel to them. One particular style is chocolate stout, which owes its taste not to the addition of chocolate, but to a special type of malt. The German dark beers like Doppelbock and old brown lagers are different again, while Hacker-Pschorr Dunkel Weisse is a dark wheat beer from Munich. The essential element is that they are dark, quite full, and have a malty feel.

CONTRASTING FLAVOURS *Salty shellfish are a perfect foil for the peppery feel of a dark stout or porter.*

Major brands like Guinness are of course available around the world, but many, like the British Black Sheep Riggwelter, are more closely tied to their home region. The UK, Ireland, and the Baltic states are the old strongholds of stouts and porters, but the US has established a vigorous new tradition, with breweries from coast to coast – Anchor, Brooklyn, Rogue, Sierra Nevada, Victory – vying to be the best.

IRELAND

The Irish took an old London porter and made it into a world-famous product: Guinness. The style is very dry and dark due to the use of roasted barley malt, and so full that it was once promoted as a food. Other brands offer variations on the theme.

GUINNESS

C COLOUR Very deep opaque black, with a dark-cream head.

A AROMA Elegant; burnt malt, spice, liquorice, and black coffee.

T TASTE Very dry with a smooth creamy texture, and smoky barley and hops.

The names of Guinness and Ireland are linked forever, but the famous stout was originally developed in London! Arthur Guinness inherited £100 from his father and started a small brewery in the village of Leixlip in Kildare. In 1759 he rented a brewery in Dublin, making ale and porter, but in 1799 decided to concentrate only on porter.

At that time, porter was a London style and Guinness employed a London brewer who made two types, X and XX, with the latter being called Extra Stout Porter. The use of roasted barley gave the special flavour that made the beer world famous. Later, Porter was removed from the name, and we were left with Guinness Extra Stout.

Guinness is made by different Guinness-owned breweries around the world. There are special editions for particular markets, and a draught version, which is very different from the bottled beer. There are many

GUINNESS

stories about the difference between various types of Guinness, including the view that it is better in Ireland than in the rest of the world.

Traditional Guinness did not travel well, so the modern pasteurized brew that was made in London for many years was different from an unpasteurized version. However, stories of the brew being made from the water of the River Liffey are part of Irish folklore.

The original, standard strength, bottled stout is very black, with a creamy head that lasts to the end. Its aromas are delicate and include the famous burnt malt from the roasted barley. It is very dry and bitter, in a treacly manner, and smooth and rich. The finish is also dry, malty, and long. It is a great, filling, satisfying drink, and very good with food. One of my favourite partners is bacon and eggs – try it!

ORIGINAL STYLE Since it first began to advertise in 1929, Guinness has had an idiosyncratic poster style that has built affection for the product. It started with memorable phrases like "Guinness is good for you" and "Guinness for strength", linked to eyecatching and amusing images, such as a man pulling a horse in a cart. Later, Guinness introduced the much-loved toucan.

There's nothing like a GUINNESS

WINDOW OF OPPORTUNITY
Traditional Irish pubs, with their colourful shop-front exteriors, reputedly offer the chance to taste the best Guinness in the world.

MURPHY'S IRISH STOUT

C COLOUR Deep black; opaque and bright, with a steady, firm cream head.

A AROMA Burnt malt, with spice and a hint of peat.

T TASTE Smooth and very creamy; malty sweetness and a smoky, bitter finish.

Murphy's was first established in 1856, on a site near Cork dedicated to the Virgin Mary. After some unsuccessful partnership ventures with other breweries, Murphy's is now part of the Heineken Empire, and is sold around the world.

Murphy's Irish Stout looks like Guinness, but it is generally lighter, smokier, and not quite so unforgivingly dry as its rival. It also has a sweetness (absent from Guinness) that leads some drinkers to question whether Murphy's should be called a dry stout at all.

At 4% ABV, Murphy's is a black beer of moderate strength. It is sold as a "bottled draught", and has a creamy, off-white, and long-lasting head, produced in part by a floating nitrogen gas capsule inside the bottle. The texture is luscious and smooth, with a slight malty sweetness and a smoky, bitter finish. The canned version, made in London, uses the same widget as the bottle, so the taste and texture are very similar. Unlike some beers, Murphy's does not change its character in the can!

I think it is better to serve Murphy's colder than you would Guinness, ideally at the same temperature as lager, and it goes really well with seafood dishes – especially Irish oysters!

MURPHY'S IRISH STOUT

PORTERHOUSE 4X WRASSLERS STOUT

C COLOUR Deep reddish-brown and very dark, almost black.

A AROMA Delicate and light, with hints of burnt malt and dark fruits.

T TASTE Rich and creamy; roasted malt, chocolate and fruit, with a bitter finish.

Produced by Dublin's Porterhouse brewpub, Porterhouse 4X Wrasslers Stout is based on a recipe used at Deasy's brewery in West Cork in the early 1900s. With an ABV of 5%, this dark-brown stout is smooth, creamy, and rich in flavour, with hints of roasted malt, dark chocolate, fruit, and coffee. The finish is bitter but stimulating.

A growing army of fans claim that this is the best of all the Irish stouts.

PORTERHOUSE 4X WRASSLERS STOUT

BEAMISH IRISH STOUT

C COLOUR Deep black and intense, with a dark cream head.

A AROMA Slight aroma of burnt malt, hops, and yeast.

T TASTE Roasted barley, chocolate, wood, and nuts, with a faintly metallic note.

Although not as well known as its competitors, Guinness and Murphy's, Beamish Irish Stout has a long history.

William Beamish was a Scots-Irish protestant landowner who became involved with brewing in 1792. In partnership with William Crawford, Beamish purchased an old brewery in Cork. The business flourished, and by 1805 Beamish and Crawford were turning out more than 100,000 barrels of beer each year, making them the largest brewers in Ireland – bigger

BEAMISH IRISH STOUT

PORTERHOUSE PLAIN PORTER

C COLOUR Very dark ruby, almost black; dark cream head.

A AROMA Light and delicate, with malt and dark fruits.

T TASTE Smooth, light texture; malt, fruit, and a dry, bitterish finish.

Plain Porter has won many plaudits and awards for Dublin's Porterhouse brewpub. Based on London porter, this creamy-headed beer (4.3% ABV) is brewed with malt, pale malt, roasted barley, and three different varieties of hop. It has a light body for a porter, but the flavours are full, and the finish is pleasantly bitter.

Plain Porter goes down especially well with an Irish whiskey chaser.

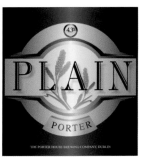

PORTERHOUSE PLAIN PORTER

even than Guinness. By the 20th century, the company's fortunes had declined, and it is now part of the Scottish & Newcastle Group.

Beamish Irish Stout is the only beer of its kind to be brewed exclusively in Ireland. It is moderately strong, having an ABV of 4.2%, and is deep black in colour. The head is full, rich, and creamy, but the aroma is surprisingly faint and delicate, with just a hint of malt and hops. The texture of Beamish is even smoother than that of Guinness, and the flavours are very complex. Striking a perfect balance, Beamish is neither too dry nor particularly sweet, with more of a woody, nutty, and unsweetened chocolate or peppery feel. The finish is dry and satisfyingly long-lasting.

Beamish is an absolute "must-try" beer for anyone with a taste for Irish stouts.

CARLOW O'HARA'S STOUT

C COLOUR Very dark brown, but looks black upon first sight.

A AROMA Roasted barley with a nutty, smoky, liquorice feel.

T TASTE Very dry, with roasted malt and a lively, bitterish finish.

The Carlow Brewing Company is devoted to brewing Celtic-style beers using traditional methods.

The flagship brew is O'Hara's Stout, a bottle-conditioned beer of 4.3% ABV, with a good roasted barley aroma and a fine rich head. It is light-bodied for a stout, and its finish is slightly citrusy and bitter. The overall feel is of a "young" stout, with a yeasty freshness rather than the richness of a more mature brew.

DARK CHOCOLATE Porters and stouts are perfect with dark chocolate due to their chocolaty flavours, which result from kilning the malt at high temperature. They are ideal partners for chocolate desserts, which can overpower even robust wines.

It is an excellent beer to drink on its own, but also makes the perfect accompaniment to virtually any seafood dish, particularly shellfish such as mussels, clams, or scallops. One of my favourite ways to enjoy this beer is to have a few glasses with a huge bowl of moules marinières!

UK

Porter was traditionally an English style, and many of these fine dark and creamy beers are still produced. The sweet or "milk" stout also retains a following. Some of the more traditional producers add oatmeal to the brewing process, as well as roasted barley.

SAMUEL SMITH'S IMPERIAL STOUT

C **COLOUR** A very dark chocolate brown, but looks black.

A **AROMA** Roasted barley, dark fruits, such as prune and plum, and sweet spice.

T **TASTE** Rich and heavy; treacly roasted malt, chocolate, fruit, and a dry finish.

INTENSE FLAVOURS
Samuel Smith's Imperial Stout is so rich that it has been described as "liquid Christmas pudding"! Some people even treat it as a liqueur and serve it in a brandy snifter at room temperature.

Founded in 1758, Samuel Smith's in Tadcaster, on the River Wharfe in the north of England, is Yorkshire's oldest brewery. The survival of this small, highly regarded establishment helped to promote the micro-brewery and traditional brewing movement, which has taken off in many parts of the world and has greatly added to quality and choice.

The original Russian Imperial Stout was brewed in the UK for export to the Czarist court. Because it had to be carried across the icy Baltic, it was brewed with a high alcohol content to prevent it from freezing; the modern version, launched in the 1980s, retains this characteristic with an ABV of 7%.

With a colour of dark chocolate and aromas of dark fruit and heavily roasted barley, Imperial Stout has a very deep, rich taste – not too sweet, but fruity, spicy, and creamy, and the strong alcohol is never far away!

You can drink this with a range of rich foods, including Stilton and walnuts, steak au poivre, caviar, oysters, and dark chocolate desserts. It can also easily match a fine cigar. This is a beer for extremists – very rich and very special!

SAMUEL SMITH'S OATMEAL STOUT

C COLOUR Very dark brown, almost black, with a light brown frothy head.

A AROMA Bright and fresh, with hops, dark fruits, sherry, and flowers.

T TASTE Rich, treacly, and smooth, but clean, with a fresh dry finish.

Oatmeal was first added to beers at a time when there was a desire for beers to be "nutritious", and the style was revived by Smith's in the 1980s. This is a classic stout – although it has a sweet feel, it becomes drier as you drink it, but then fades back to a sweeter, malty, slightly nutty flavour right at the finish. It is less heavy than many stouts, but full of flavour. This beer is as good as red wine, and it is great with food, especially seafood or roast beef and Yorkshire pudding.

SAMUEL SMITH'S
OATMEAL STOUT

SAMUEL SMITH'S TADDY PORTER

C COLOUR Very dark reddy brown, with a dark cream, frothy head.

A AROMA Treacly, with dry roast malt, hops, and caramel.

T TASTE Smooth and delicious, and not too heavy; roast malt and chocolate.

"Taddy", of course, refers to Tadcaster, Yorkshire, where the Samuel Smith brewery is located. Porter is a traditional London style that went out of fashion in the mid-20th century and merged into the more popular stout. Smith's has revived the style, which is generally slightly lighter and drier than stout. This beer is very attractive because it is easy to drink – not too heavy or filling – and also very warming. Drink it with a steak pie to shake off the cold in the winter.

EASTWOOD & SANDERS 1872 PORTER

C COLOUR Black and opaque, with a dark coffee-cream head.

A AROMA Complex, with roasted barley, dark fruits, and dark chocolate.

T TASTE Full-bodied, rich, and smooth; sweetness balanced by a dry hop finish.

A beer from true real-ale enthusiasts! Eastwood & Sanders is an English micro-brewery formed only in 2002 in Halifax, Yorkshire, by two locally well-known and well-respected brewers – John Eastwood and Dave Sanders. They were strongly supported by the Halifax and Calderdale Campaign for Real Ale (CAMRA) branch. John Eastwood left in November 2002, leaving Dave Sanders as sole brewer.

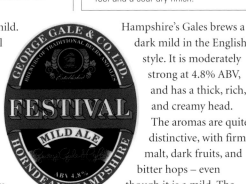

EASTWOOD & SANDERS
1872 PORTER

As well as the regular portfolio of beers, there are seasonal or monthly one-off special brews, including KSA, a Kölsch-style beer.

The 1872 is an American porter, quite strong at 6.5% ABV. It is a very deep black, with a dark, creamy head. The aromas are also very dark, rich, and fruity, with black fruits, burnt malt, and roasted barley. This beer is full bodied, with complex flavours, and sweetness and appealing bitterness swirling round to a mellow finish.

While porter is traditionally paired with steak, or with steak-and-kidney pie, its deep maltiness is an equally perfect match for the flavours of grilled mushrooms. You might also want to match the creaminess of this porter's chocolate and caramel malts with desserts, especially those made with chocolate.

MEANTIME CHOCOLATE BEER

C COLOUR Very dark and opaque with dark reddish highlights.

A AROMA Deep roasted malt, caramel, and chocolate.

T TASTE Quite dry, bitter and light-bodied, but very smooth.

The Meantime Brewery has really thrown down the gauntlet with this one! Although it is called Chocolate Beer, it is not really made from dissolved chocolate, but from very dark roasted malt which gives an aroma and taste similar to cooking chocolate. It is moderately strong at 4.9% ABV, and without the chocolate feel, it is really a regular lager. So although it has chocolate and caramel flavours, it is not too sweet. Very interesting, and well worth trying – it is one you will love or hate.

MEANTIME
CHOCOLATE BEER

MOOREHOUSE'S BLACK CAT

C COLOUR Deep dark brown, with a brownish-white, thick head.

A AROMA Gentle, with hints of roasted malt and dark fruits.

T TASTE Quite heavy and full-bodied, with a malty sweetness.

Moorhouse's brewery is located in the old cotton-milling town of Burnley, Lancashire. This old-established firm for years made bitter hop-flavoured soft drinks, switching to beer in the late 1970s. Since the 1980s, under new ownership, Moorhouse's has made a range of cask-conditioned draught ales.

It is best known for its Pendle Witches Brew ale. However, Moorhouse's also makes a dark mild, Black Cat, which is rapidly establishing a reputation on the back of the revival of interest in mild ale. The

term "mild" refers to the absence of hop bitterness. This style reached the peak of its popularity in the late 19th and early 20th centuries. It was popular with working men: cheap, filling, and not too strong. This beer has won a number of awards, including the Campaign for Real Ale (CAMRA) Champion Mild in 1998 and Supreme Champion Beer of Britain in 2000.

This is a very dark mild. The head is not too full and the aromas are very delicate – hardly there at all – but hint at burnt malt. What you will notice most is how heavy and full this beer is, almost a stout. The taste is richly roasted barley with a treacly sweetness and a liquorice-spicy finish. It is not at all strong at 3.4% ABV, but feels stronger because of the body. You might crave a little more bitterness – but that's mild ale for you.

GALES FESTIVAL MILD

C COLOUR Dark reddish-brown colour with rich ruby highlights.

A AROMA Rich; malt and burnt toast with dark fruits.

T TASTE Dry and toasty, with a smooth feel and a sour-dry finish.

Hampshire's Gales brews a dark mild in the English style. It is moderately strong at 4.8% ABV, and has a thick, rich, and creamy head. The aromas are quite distinctive, with firm malt, dark fruits, and bitter hops – even though it is a mild. The flavour conjures up black fruits, figs, and liquorice, with a gently bitter finish – it is certainly not sweet. Drink it at cool room temperature, with traditional British foods like pickles, fish and chips, or steak-and-kidney pie.

GALES FESTIVAL MILD

HOP BACK ENTIRE STOUT

C COLOUR Dark brown with hints of purple, and a light-tan head.

A AROMA Malt and hops, with hints of dark chocolate.

T TASTE Dry and lightly bitter, balanced by chocolaty malt.

The Hop Back Brewery has its origins in Salisbury, in the south of England, where in the 1980s John and Julie Gilbert were running the Wyndham Arms pub. They made their first beer, GFB (Gilbert's First Brew), in 1986, and soon began winning prizes at beer fairs. The brewery proper was established in 1992 at Downton and has won a reputation for fine ales, as well as growing considerably over the years. The Hop Back Brewery also owns a small but expanding estate of pubs around the south of England. Summer Lightning (*see p436*) is

perhaps its most famous brew, but this is something quite different – you could call it Summer Lightning's winter alter-ego. Entire Stout is Hop Back's version of a dark, porter-like brew, very similar to the dry, Irish stout traditionally epitomized by Guinness.

It is made mainly with pale malt, but also contains a small amount of chocolate malt, which gives it an extra darkness and depth. Yet it is not too strong at just 4.5% ABV.

This stout is not jet black, but dark brown with glints of purple, and a khaki-coloured head. You can sense the chocolate in the aromas, but the main experience of this beer when tasted is its malty and hoppy dryness, along with a smoke-and-cocoa finish. It is not over-heavy, and I find it really delicious with a beef or lamb stew.

HOP BACK ENTIRE STOUT

MACKESON STOUT

C COLOUR Deep, dark opaque black, with a khaki-tan frothy head.

A AROMA Cream, coffee, and rich, dark fruits.

T TASTE Light but very full-tasting; smooth and very sweet and creamy.

The favourite of the snug bar. During the mid part of the 20th century, Mackeson stout became one of the best known stouts in the world, and was one of the staples of the traditional English pub, and especially enjoyed by women.

Mackeson was first brewed in 1907 in Hythe, Kent, in southeastern England. Like oatmeal stout, it established itself as part-beer, part-tonic, and was promoted as "milk stout" because it contained lactose, or milk sugar. This

sugar does not ferment, so the beer is sweet and low in alcohol, at only 3% ABV. The term milk stout was banned in 1946, but there is still a milk churn on the label! It is now owned by Interbrew, a subsidiary of the giant InBev group, who also own Beck's and Stella Artois.

Do not underestimate this beautiful beer from a bygone age; it is still available, and you should try it. This stout is pasteurized but unfiltered, so it has plenty of aromas and taste. It is very dark in colour with a rich head, and notes of coffee and fruit. The flavours are a swirl of milk, dark fruits, bitter chocolate, and Turkish coffee, and the finish is as smooth as a Baileys cream liqueur. And if you have never tried Mackeson stout with oysters, you simply haven't lived. This is a great, sweet and rich stout, and is definitely not to be sniffed at.

MACKESON STOUT

BROUGHTON SCOTTISH OATMEAL STOUT

C COLOUR Deep black, with a dark-gold frothy head.

A AROMA Roasted barley, but also spicy pepper and ginger hints.

T TASTE Smooth and very creamy, but quite peaty, fresh, and dry.

"Beers with character" is the slogan of this small brewery, established in 1980 by David Younger, a descendant of the George Younger brewing family. This is a fine, well-balanced, and refreshing oatmeal stout, with a lively and satisfying taste, and a bitter chocolate and liquorice feel coming only right at the finish. It is quite delicate for a stout – some drinkers think it is not full or robust enough – and the peaty character makes it very nice with seafood.

BROUGHTON SCOTTISH OATMEAL STOUT

BLACK SHEEP RIGGWELTER

C COLOUR Deep ruby-red bronze, and a full cream-coloured head.

A AROMA Fine, with oak, toffee, dark chocolate, and coffee.

T TASTE Full malty flavour; liquorice, nuts, bitter dark chocolate, and smoke.

The Black Sheep Brewery was established in the early 1990s by Paul Theakston, of the famous brewing family, whose brewery is at Masham, near Ripon in North Yorkshire. When Scottish & Newcastle took over Theakston's, Paul decided to set up on his own as a rival not far from the Theakston's brewery, and used the name Black Sheep to reflect his new pariah status in the family.

Sheep have always been central to the North Yorkshire economy, and this fine dark ale is named after

a Riggwelter, Yorkshire dialect for a sheep which has fallen over and cannot get up. When you drink this potent ale, make sure that the same does not happen to you; it is fairly strong at 5.7% ABV, and it is very approachable and drinkable, which increases its potential to make a Riggwelter of you, too!

This beer is very much a traditional English ale, although it almost has the character of a stout or a porter. The aromas are complex, with fruity and malty-toffee notes to make your mouth water. The taste is also very complex, with the firm, burnt maltiness balanced by the hops and overlain with a bitter hoppy and chocolaty feel. The finish is also malty, but with an attractive smoky edge to it.

Black Sheep Riggwelter is one of my all-time favourites – a really special beer with a great character. Don't miss this if ever you get a chance to taste it.

ST PETER'S CREAM STOUT

C COLOUR Very dark brown to black, with a coffee-cream head.

A AROMA Roasted barley, with hints of bitter chocolate and malt.

T TASTE Smooth, rich, and creamy, with a bittersweet finish.

St Peter's Hall is a 13th-century manor house in Suffolk, in the east of England. Its newish micro-brewery has established a reputation for high technology, excellent marketing, and fine beers. The Cream Stout is quite strong at 6.5% ABV, and is very dark, with unsweetened chocolate and black fruit aromas. It uses a blend of local barley malts for a firm body and a balanced bittersweet taste. This beer was a gold medal winner at the International Beer Competition 2003 and 2004. One to watch!

ST PETER'S CREAM STOUT

FINLAND

This style is the main rival to the lagers made by Hartwall, Finland's dominant brewer, and is actually an old regional recipe.

SINEBRYCHOFF PORTER

C COLOUR Very dark black; dense and opaque.

A AROMA Complex and attractive, with dark fruits, coffee, cocoa, and wood.

T TASTE Very dry and quite oily; burnt malt, dark chocolate; tasty bitter finish.

The brewery dates back to 1819 and this porter is one of its oldest brews, reintroduced for the 1952 Helsinki Olympics. Also often labelled Koff, Sinebrychoff is made in the Guinness style, very dry and very dark. It is also very strong, at 7.2% ABV, and warm and filling.

OPTIMATOR

C COLOUR Deep and dark brown with orange hints; dense, lasting tan head.

A AROMA Very fruity and spicy, with figs, dried fruit, raisins, currants, and ginger.

T TASTE Extremely full; caramel, malt, toffee apple; bittersweet finish.

One of the flagships of the great Spaten brewery in Munich, which was founded in 1397, and is now known as Spaten-Franziskaner-Bräu, Optimator is an example of the

FOOD MATCH

OYSTERS The savoury, briny flavour of oysters is a perfect foil for rich, dark porters and the fuller-bodied stouts. Oysters were staples of working men's bars throughout the 17th and 18th centuries, as common as peanuts today. Whether raw or in stews or pies, oysters still taste wonderful with these dark beers – a fine reminder of times past.

GERMANY

Some of the greatest German beers are not light lagers, but deep, dark, and powerful beers called Bocks and Doppelbocks. These are made mainly in Bavaria, in the south of the country, and are very warming. Drinks to be savoured after a long winter walk!

SCHNEIDER AVENTINUS

C COLOUR Deep brown with strong red highlights.

A AROMA Grassy hay with hints of molasses and banana.

T TASTE Rich, fruity, and very warming, with prunes, raisins, and liquorice.

Schneider of Bavaria specializes in making wheat beer, but this is no ordinary version. At 8% ABV, it is an example of a Weizenbock – a strong wheat beer. It is particularly dark and rich, and has a large, cream-coloured head, which lasts only a short time. The aromas are typical of a wheat beer, but it is in the flavours that the true character of this excellent beer begins to shine. There is a hint of bitterness and the alcohol comes through, not dominating, but giving a true warming feeling. There is also a spicy feel, especially cloves, and chocolate and bananas. The finish is sweet and satisfying. This is a wonderful beer; perfect on its own, and also terrific with spicy Asian or Indian foods.

SCHNEIDER
AVENTINUS

Doppelbock style. It is very strong at 8% ABV, with a heavy, full-bodied character to match. This is not a beer I take lightly!

Optimator has complex and fruity aromas, which include deep roasted malt. It is very filling, and has quite a sweet flavour, but it is not thin and sugary. You hardly notice the balancing hops, but they are there.

This beer goes very well with any full and hearty food, such as steak or pie, but is best after dinner. If you are prepared for the strength and fullness, you can drink it at any time.

HACKER-PSCHORR DUNKEL WEISSE

C COLOUR Yellowish-brown, with a finely beaded, frothy head.

A AROMA Traces of burnt malt, banana, cloves, and yeast.

T TASTE Quite malty, with notes of dark unsweetened chocolate and vanilla.

The origins of the Hacker-Pschorr brewery in Munich can be traced as far back as 1417, and it is most famous for its Oktoberfest Märzen.

This particular brew is a lovely, well-balanced example of the dark wheat beer style. Quite strong at 5.2% ABV, it has a good, full, off-white head that lasts. The aromas are dominated by the yeast, but there is also banana and spice – especially cloves – and the aromas are light and appealing. The flavours are also well balanced, with the malt, chocolate, and dark fruit offset by the lightness of the wheat. This beer is great on its own or after dinner, even with a dessert.

MAXIMATOR

C COLOUR Attractive medium brown with orange highlights.

A AROMA Sweet malt, with grapefruit, citrus, cinnamon, and hops.

T TASTE Fresh and lively, with malt, caramel, and citrus.

The Augustiner brewery is one of the great breweries of Munich, and one of the most popular locally. Maximator is a Doppelbock, an example of the dark brown, very strong beer typical of Bavaria. This one is 7.5% ABV and, like all Doppelbocks, is very full, creamy, and satisfying, with flavours of sweet, dark, toasted malt, figs, dark fruits, such as raisins and prunes, and dark molasses. The finish is quite dry with a malty feel. Beers of this style go well with strong-flavoured food, such as heavy sausage or strong cheese and cold meats.

LATVIA

The Baltic porter style is not black but dark ruby or garnet red, topped with a large, frothy, cream-coloured head.

ALDARIS PORTERIS

C COLOUR Not jet black like some porters, but more a very dark ruby.

A AROMA Well-balanced, with malt, vanilla, raisins, and sweet molasses.

T TASTE Creamy, with smoky malt, black cherry, and liquorice.

I hear that this drink is a great favourite with the women of Latvia, to keep them warm in the winter evenings – now *that* I can understand! The beer boasts a large, frothy, creamy head, and is strong, at 6.8% ABV, and very warming. The sweet aromas are quite delicate and it has a great flavour of malt and dark fruit, and a dry, spicy finish.

POLAND

Poland's brewing industry was established when the country was part of the Austrian Habsburg empire. Baltic porter is bottom-fermented, with a very full and powerful flavour. It also tends to be somewhat stronger than other beers in this style.

ZYWIEC PORTER

C COLOUR Rich and deep mahogany, with ruby tinges.

A AROMA Distinctive, with hops, smoky malt, and coffee.

T TASTE Rounded and powerful, with roasted coffee and dark fruits.

Poland's most famous brewery makes a range of fine beers. This porter is very strong at 9.3% ABV, with little head to speak of and a complex aroma of roasted malt and tar, coffee, and prunes. The flavour is very full and powerful, with a hoppy, dry, and bitterish balance. Very satisfying – a great Baltic experience.

DOJLIDY POLSKI PORTER

C COLOUR Dark reddish-brown, with a creamy beige, long-lasting head.

A AROMA Brown sugar and molasses, with the alcohol quite prominent.

T TASTE Full and warming; molasses, burnt sugar, dark fruits, ground coffee.

One of the features of this beer is that the flavours ripen as it warms up, so it really does get better as you drink it – it is not just a feeling! This is a very strong, dark beer, at 9% ABV, and is rich and satisfying, with a bittersweet finish with a strong chocolate character.

CZECH REPUBLIC

Although the Czechs are famous for their golden lagers, they also make some fine dark beers in the Bock, or dark, lager style.

HEROLD BLACK BEER

C COLOUR Very dark ruby red, almost black at first sight.

A AROMA Elegant and well balanced between malt, hops, and yeast.

T TASTE Rich and malty; hints of dark chocolate, vanilla, and soft fruit.

The Herold brewery south of Prague, based in a castle at Breznice, is one of the oldest in the Czech Republic. Founded in 1720, it has had a long and turbulent history, at one time brewing at full capacity, then closed down by the government and turned into a brewing research institute. Since 1990, however, it has been back in beer production. It is best known for re-introducing wheat beers to the Czech public, after years of absence.

This beer is in the old style of black lager which, as Schwarzbier, is also found in the eastern part of Germany. Despite the name, it is not quite black, but very deep red. This beer has a fine head, and a gentle and well-balanced aroma, predominantly of malt. It is reasonably strong at 5.2% ABV, and there is not as much sweetness as you might expect – after all, this is a lager! You can taste a slight bitterness, balanced by the malt and fruit. The finish is very refreshing.

This is a great beer, and dark lagers are an intriguing style when we are so used to the straw-coloured variety.

HEROLD
BLACK BEER

USA

The explosion of local micro-breweries in the US has led to a bewildering array of styles. Stout and porter are becoming some of the most successful and established, even though they are the complete opposite of mainstream American lagers.

BROOKLYN BLACK CHOCOLATE STOUT

C COLOUR Dark and deep black, with a light-tan head.

A AROMA Rich unsweetened chocolate and toasty malt.

T TASTE Full-bodied, smooth, and creamy; rich dark chocolate, liquorice, and malt.

The Brooklyn Brewery (see p441) is one of the few inner-city breweries left in New York, and its beers are popular in the city's bars and clubs. This chocolate stout is the head brewer's own favourite. It is produced only in the winter season, and dated (for example, 2004–05). It is very strong, at 8.25% ABV, and an opaque black colour. The fantastic chocolate aromas and flavours (the unsweetened sort that used to be sold in the days before everything was sweetened) are not brought about through the addition of chocolate, but through the use of dark, "chocolate" malts.

This beer is wonderfully full-bodied, with dark malt, an attractive bitterness, and a quite dry and bitter finish. You need to drink this in the winter by the fire or in a nice warm pub. It is best to sip it, and don't order too many!

BROOKLYN BLACK
CHOCOLATE STOUT

VICTORY STORM KING STOUT

C COLOUR Deep opaque brown-black, with a thick creamy head.

A AROMA Quite floral and fruity, with lemon citrus and malt.

T TASTE Rich and full-flavoured; hops, mildly burnt malt, and chocolate notes.

This one will save you doing the cooking! The Victory brewery near Philadelphia, Pennsylvania, has established a fine reputation, combining technical expertise gained in Germany with a spirit of adventure and experimentation. Its excellent beers include Prima Pils, St Victorious Dopplebock, and especially the Hop Devil IPA (see p440). It also produces this fine rich stout, Storm King.

This beer has been called "a meal in a bottle", and it is very full-flavoured and powerful at 9.1% ABV – so not to be trifled with! The colour of this beer is very dark brown, almost black, with a creamy head that lasts only a short time. For such a powerful beer, the aromas are quite delicate, with flowers, dark fruits, and citrus all showing through, which is a lovely surprise. However, it is really true to form in the flavours, with the hops quite dominant and the malt not overdone, and the body is wonderfully full and rich. There are also citrus and chocolate notes in the taste, and a fine, gently bitter finish.

I really like this stout because it has a touch of delicacy. Although it is strong and full, it also has a lighter feel than many stouts, and is well worth a taste. It is produced through the autumn and winter months, from October to March, in both bottled and draught versions.

VICTORY STORM
KING STOUT

ROGUE SHAKESPEARE

C COLOUR Deep opaque brown to black, with a light-tan head.

A AROMA Dark grassy hops and malt, with fruity notes.

T TASTE Very rich and treacly; distinct bittersweet balance; dry hoppy finish.

The Rogue Brewery in Newport, Oregon, is a vociferous campaigner for the merits of small-scale breweries, and claims to make "products for the beer connoisseur, the entrepreneur, and the revolutionist". It gives all its beers a "rogueish" feel, with brilliant label design showing various characters linked to the name of the beers. It also has a rogueish attitude to naming and branding its beers, and it can be very confusing to find the same, or very similar, beers with completely different names. For example, Shakespeare Stout is also bottled in Japan and sold there as

Brown Bear. Rogue also makes a number of other stouts, including the Imperial Stout and Chocolate Stout. Nevertheless, the brilliant marketing of brands like Brutal Bitter *(see p440)* has extended its influence from its home in the far northwest of the US across the whole of America and beyond.

As part of its manifesto, the brewery declares that its beers aim to "have a standard about them that makes them not for everyone. If a beer is not all these things, then it shouldn't be made at all". So, does Rogue Shakespeare Stout measure up to the billing?

This is a fairly powerful brew at 6.1% ABV. It is heavy and full-bodied, and although it looks dark brown in the bottle, it is absolutely

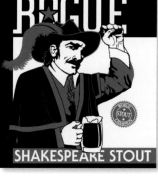

ROGUE SHAKESPEARE STOUT

jet black in the glass, and has a medium, light-tan head. You will find aromas of dark fruits, burnt malt, hops, and even chocolate. However, it is the flavour of Rogue Shakespeare Stout that really makes its mark. The first taste is sweet, rich, and treacly, but this very soon changes to an intense bitterness, even to the point of feeling a little sour. The flavours are complex, with the burnt malt vying with hops and dark fruits, such as raisins, along with nuts. It is quite smooth and creamy, and has a dry finish.

Unlike some brews, this one is just as good in the bottle as in the cask. Indeed, after a bottle or two of Rogue Shakespeare, you may find yourself happily discussing its merits with the Bard on the label!

SIERRA NEVADA STOUT

C COLOUR Deep opaque black, with a light-tan head.

A AROMA Full; dark hops and burnt malt, with citrus notes.

T TASTE Very rich and full-bodied; cocoa, coffee, and malt, and a bitterish finish.

The Sierra Nevada Brewery in Chico, California, has established itself as the most famous of the new generation of breweries. It has made its name with its wonderful Celebration Ale *(see p440)* and its Sierra Nevada Porter *(see p454)*, thought by many to be the best American porter of all. Its stout is no weakling, and is very full bodied and strong at 6.6% ABV. To me, this beer does not quite reach the levels of Sierra Nevada's other brews, but it is still very good, and great with rich, meaty food or shellfish.

SIERRA NEVADA STOUT

HEAVYWEIGHT PERKUNO'S HAMMER IMPERIAL

C COLOUR Deep, opaque brown-black with dark ruby or crimson highlights.

A AROMA Dark chocolate and rich, with deep hops.

T TASTE Powerful, smooth; sweet malts, dark chocolate, coffee; hop bitterness.

This is a very unusual beer – it is a Baltic porter, similar to those beers brewed in Latvia or Poland, but it is actually made by the Heavyweight Brewing Company in New Jersey. Heavyweight is a micro-brewery owned and run by husband-and-wife beer enthusiasts Tom Baker and Peggy Zwerver, who already had long experience of home brewing and then of other micro-breweries. The brewery was established in 1999, and is dedicated to making unusual and

traditional beers, particularly in darker, heavier styles.

Baker takes the view that these beers are excellent all year round, so why should they only be seasonal winter brews? All their bottled beers are conditioned with yeasts, so watch out for the sediment when you pour.

Perkuno's Hammer is named after the god Perkuno, a Baltic version of Thor, the god of thunder. The style is somewhere between a German Doppelbock and an Imperial stout, and is very strong at 8.3% ABV. It is very dark brown, almost black, with deep reddish highlights sparkling off the beer, and has a good, light-tan head. Although this beer is very powerful, it still manages to be smooth and creamy, with a great balance between sweet, dark, chocolaty malt and a pleasant bitter balance from the hops.

To me this is a fantastic porter. You can't go wrong with this brew in either tap or bottle form, and it is one of the best I have ever had. You won't want to drink too many, but this really is a "must-try"!

ANCHOR PORTER

C COLOUR Deep opaque black, with a very dark reddish hue.

A AROMA Malty, with chocolate, coffee, and dark fruits, balanced with hops.

T TASTE Great balance of sweet malt, chocolate, coffee, hops; very long finish.

This is a really distinctive brew, and there is much discussion as to whether it should be called a porter or a stout. You would expect a porter to be lighter and brighter than a stout, without the "meal in a bottle" body or bitter dryness that you might associate with a stout. Anchor insists that this beer is a porter, but the richness of its body and its full character

ANCHOR PORTER

make it very close to a stout. I think it is on the border between the two.

The beer is very dark, essentially black, with a dark-red note and a cappuccino-coloured head that lingers for some time. It has a wonderful aroma, dominated by the sweetness of malt, dark fruits, dark chocolate, and even raspberries. The flavours are

brilliantly balanced, beginning with malt and coffee, followed by herbs and spices, then chocolate, and a gentle hop bitterness to give the balance and save it from being too sweet. The body is also rich and creamy. But it is the finish that is really special. It is very pleasant; a mixture of all the fine flavours in the beer, and it lasts forever.

This is a great porter – and a great stout! It reminds me of the Finnish Sinebrychoff Porter *(see p450)* or Mackeson Stout *(see p449)*. It is very strong at 6.3% ABV, although the fine balance of flavours keeps the alcohol in line, and you can easily drink too many. It is equally a very good beer to sip gently at bedtime.

Wherever you place it, you will love this beer partnered with a good rich, meaty dish or some fine seafood. But don't expect to stay awake for too long!

BORDERLINE CASE *The richness of body and full character make Anchor Porter very close to a stout, and drinkers continually debate which it is.*

PAPER CITY RILEY'S STOUT

C COLOUR Deep black with tinges of amber, and a light-tan head.

A AROMA Well-balanced, with sweet malt, chocolate, and floral notes.

T TASTE Solid and full-bodied, with chocolate, coffee, and burnt roast malt.

Paper City Brewery in Holyoke, Massachusetts, produces a range of individual and seasonal ales, often with an Irish connection. Its Riley's Stout is no exception, being made in the dry Irish style. It is very black, with a cappuccino head that disappears quite quickly. The flavours are smoky, crisp, and dry. The body is much lighter than many stouts and even porters, making this beer very drinkable.

DESCHUTES OBSIDIAN

C COLOUR The deepest, darkest, richest, and most opaque black.

A AROMA Intense, with smoky burnt malt, unsweetened chocolate, and dark fruit.

T TASTE Very full-bodied, but really smooth; good bitter–sweet balance.

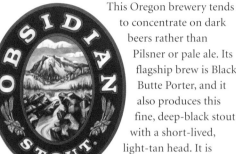

DESCHUTES OBSIDIAN

This Oregon brewery tends to concentrate on dark beers rather than Pilsner or pale ale. Its flagship brew is Black Butte Porter, and it also produces this fine, deep-black stout, with a short-lived, light-tan head. It is quite strong at 6.7% ABV, but the alcohol does not dominate, and the texture is very smooth. This is a little more full than a Guinness, but not over the top – I find it easy to drink and thoroughly enjoyable.

SIERRA NEVADA PORTER

C COLOUR Very dark brown, with a light-tan, fluffy head.

A AROMA Quite smoky and malty, with ground coffee and chocolate.

T TASTE Fruity, with hops, coffee, chocolate – all in great balance.

Sierra Nevada Brewing, based in Chico, California, claims that its Sierra Nevada Porter is one of the best in the country – if not the world. This is a tough challenge to meet; there are some great rivals around, especially Anchor Porter *(see p453)*. It has made a good start, however, with first place in the California Brewers Festival (Robust Porter; 2000) and the Colorado State Fair (Porter; 1996).

Sierra Nevada Porter is dark and rich, a delicious, medium-bodied ale, and moderately strong at 5.6% ABV. Unlike some porters, it should not be confused with a stout, as the

style is just what you should expect from a porter: not too over-powering in terms of body and strength, and thoroughly approachable.

This beer is very dark brown with a head that stays with you quite well. The aroma is of roasted malt, chocolate, and black fruits, and the flavours have an excellent

SIERRA NEVADA PORTER

balance of chocolate, malt, coffee, and caramel. The hops are there but they do not dominate and spoil the show with bitterness.

Sierra Nevada Porter is exactly what I think of when I think "American porter", and to me the best thing about it is that it is really approachable and drinkable – a pleasure, not a battle. But is it better than Anchor Porter? I'll leave that decision up to you.

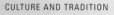

CULTURE AND TRADITION

FUNCTION OR FASHION? Stout was originally a hearty working-man's drink, and has also been promoted as a nutritious tonic, especially for breast-feeding mothers. Through much of the late 20th century, it languished unloved by a younger generation hooked on crisp, sparkling lager. But it turned the corner, with thanks due in part to the promotional efforts of Guinness *(see p445)* to redefine stout as a fashionable session beer, and in part to the spread of Irish-themed pubs, with stout as their signature drink. Drinkers around the world now have a passion for stout as a modern drink.

AUSTRALIA

A historical connection to British brewing still exists in Australia and means the country produces some excellent traditional ales. This fine stout is very much a product of that long-standing relationship.

COOPERS BEST EXTRA STOUT

C COLOUR Very deep, rich, and opaque black, with a light-tan head.

A AROMA Dark-roasted malt, coffee, charred wood, and burnt sugar.

T TASTE Quite oily in texture, with a woody, bitterish, and dry character.

Coopers of Adelaide is justly proud of its traditional approach to brewing. Its Best Extra Stout is brewed naturally, using a top-fermentation method *(see p391)*, with no additives or preservatives. The result is a beer with a rich, dark texture from roasted black malt. Special Old Stout is a deeper, thicker

version which is held back for six months before release to increase the complexity.

Coopers is quite strong at 6.3% ABV (6.8% for the Old Stout). The flavour is quite dry and lightly bitter, with a

COOPERS BEST EXTRA STOUT

roasted, smoky, dark fruity mix, but it develops more dark-roasted coffee flavours as it warms, with hints of black liquorice and milk chocolate. Special Old Stout has a very long and satisfying finish, and is a real treat at cool room temperature with some fine fresh seafood. Overall, these are very tasty and warming beers.

CREAMY DESSERTS Stout is the perfect partner for creamy puddings, and can even be used in dishes such as Zabaglione, or just poured over ice-cream. For best results choose a beer that is sweeter than the dessert – try Jamaica's Dragon Stout in particular. All stouts, dry or sweet, go well with chocolate.

JAMAICA

Jamaica was once part of the British Empire, and this surprisingly warming beer is a link to the island's colonial past.

DRAGON STOUT

C **COLOUR** Very dark brown, almost black, with a light-tan head.

A **AROMA** Molasses, cocoa, cane sugar, prunes, and malt.

T **TASTE** Very sweet and malty, with smoke, molasses, and toffee.

There are two words to describe Jamaica's own stout – sweet and strong (it is 7.5% ABV)! Brewed by Desnoes and Geddes of Red Stripe (*see p413*) fame, this popular beer has been dubbed an "alcopop". It is similar to a milk stout like Mackeson (*see p449*) and goes really well with good quality chocolate ice-cream.

SRI LANKA

Stout arrived in Sri Lanka during British rule and the Sri Lankans developed local varieties of this full-bodied, classic style.

LION STOUT

C **COLOUR** Very dark brown-black and opaque, with a light-tan head.

A **AROMA** Quite fresh, with porty alcohol spirit, red fruit, and molasses.

T **TASTE** Dry and velvety; unsweetened chocolate, treacle, and coffee.

Perhaps it was the British influence on Sri Lanka, when (as Ceylon) it was part of the British Empire, that led to this country's fondness for stout – and this affinity has remained. Lion Stout is made near the holy city of Kandy by the Ceylon/Lion Brewery. In its home region,

75 per cent of the brewery's sales are for stout rather than lager – quite a statistic, considering the warm, humid climate.

This beer is a very dark brown to black, with a fairly short-lived head. The aromas are not as dark as you might expect, and have quite a bit of red fruit and port in them. Perhaps the porty element is not surprising as the beer is strong, at 8% ABV. The texture is thick and velvety, with a treacly and malty feel, and some nice nut and chocolate flavours in the mix. The finish is attractively bitter, with a good malt feel to it. Although the idea may seem odd, Lion Stout is a great partner for Asian cuisine. If you prefer your stout on its own, this is one for steady but slow drinking. However you choose to try it, I think you'll agree with me that this is the best beer from Sri Lanka.

LION STOUT

JAPAN

Although most Japanese beers are in the lager style, the Japanese like a wide range of beers, including darker varieties.

ASAHI STOUT

C **COLOUR** Deep opaque black, with a cappuccino-coloured head.

A **AROMA** Fairly delicate, with roasted malt and an earthy feel.

T **TASTE** Very full-bodied and dry, with liquorice and smoke.

Asahi's flagship beer is the crisp, clean Super Dry (*see p412*), but like most Japanese brewers, the company produces a fine range of beers, including Black Beer, Z, Double Yeasts, and more. It also makes this excellent, richly roasted, top-fermented, traditional stout, designed to be very much in the British and Irish tradition.

This is a very rich and dark brew, jet black, with a firm, impenetrable density, and a light-tan head, which is not particularly long lasting. The aromas are not overpowering, but along with the malt you also encounter a quite yeasty, earthy feel from the particular yeasts used in the brewing process. The texture is very full, and the beer is strong at 8% ABV. Its taste is basically dry, but with smoke, tar, and liquorice all present.

This is a beer for winter evenings, to be supped alongside a rich, meaty stew, or with a meal of seafood. Alternatively, it would go down well after dinner on its own, or as a nightcap. Due to its strength, it is not really one for long drinking sessions – unless you're superhuman! Stick to Super Dry for that.

ASAHI STOUT

OKHOTSK MILD STOUT

C **COLOUR** Deep opaque brown-black, with a light-tan head.

A **AROMA** Elegant and not too over-powering, with hops and earthiness.

T **TASTE** Medium-bodied, with a roasted malt feel; very smooth and drinkable.

Although this may sound like a Russian beer, it is actually Japanese. The Sea of Okhotsk lies off the far north of Japan, with Siberia on one side and the Japanese island of Hokkaido on the other. This beer is made at a brewpub in the town of Kitami, located in quite a remote part of the island. Its full name is the Okhotsk Beer Factory, but there is nothing mass-produced about the brews from this outfit, despite the fact that the mighty Sapporo brewery,

which is based on the same island, helped finance the venture.

The "factory", which opened in 1995, produces various individual beers, including a peaty Black Beer and a creamy Bitter Pils. This beer is called Mild Stout to distinguish it from the heavy and very dry Irish-style stouts. Personally, I would call this more of a porter or milk stout, as it is certainly not excessively dry.

Okhotsk Mild Stout is a very dark brown, with a moderate head. It has quite delicate aromas that remind me of the roasted malt, but they are not too much to the fore. When you first drink this beer, it comes as something of a shock to discover that it is quite sweet, but with a strength of only 5% ABV and a smooth body, there is always room for one more!

OKHOTSK MILD STOUT

RICH AND WARMING

66 Real winter beers, full of rich malt and fine dry hops to give you that lovely, warm, fireside feeling.**99**

INTRODUCING RICH AND WARMING BEERS

It is almost worth enduring harsh winter weather just for these fabulous beers, many of them powerful brews to sip gently by the fireside. The beer may be cool in the glass, but that warming sensation will go all the way to your toes!

DRINKING AND SERVING

DRINK PROFILE Many of these beers are rich in flavour and strength, and some need to be treated like a wine. The flavours of these beers should be balanced, with an overall warming feeling.

C COLOUR Beers in this group can be anything from deep orange to dark brown or black. The ales have a fine head but the barley wines, orange in colour, have little or no head.

A AROMA Many of these beers have rich aromas, particularly of malt, orange, and red and black fruits, with spices and herbs in the Trappist beers. Some have sherry and port aromas.

T TASTE Warming flavours can be achieved with the balance of malts, fruits, and herbs, but more often it is the strength of the alcohol that comes through.

BUYING AND STORING These beers are more expensive than most, and can be difficult to obtain. Many of the barley wines and some special ales are designed to improve when cellared, usually up to about five years.

SERVING SUGGESTIONS Because of the strength of many of these beers, they are designed to be sipped rather than quaffed, and should be served in a snifter or other small glass. While the Bock beers can be served cool, the ales should be served at around 13°C (55°F). Some can be treated like a liqueur, to be sipped after a meal.

FOOD COMPANIONS The ales match winter dishes, like roast beef and pork sausages. Some of the richer beers and barley wines go with cheese, and the sweeter ones can be drunk with dessert.

The richness of this group of warming beers comes from the concentration of the barley malt, which intensifies both the sweetness and the alcohol. It can also be a product of fruit, herbs, and spices added to the brew. The warming sensation is primarily a result of the strong alcohol, and usually shows itself at the finish. The secret of a good beer is to balance the alcoholic strength with the flavours, and then balance these between sweetness and dryness – not easy to achieve! These beers are mainly winter warmers, and cover a broad range of styles: brown or orange old ales like Fuller's ESB; German Bocks; dark brown or black spiced ales, and stouts; lighter, golden Belgian tripel beers like Hoegaarden Grand Cru; and barley wines, which are not wines at all but rich, fruity beers.

DARK CHOCOLATE *Caramel and nougat flavours combine with rich chocolate in Westvleteren 8.*

STRENGTH AND AGE

Although the boundaries are vague, it is generally accepted that old ales are slightly weaker, and can be sold on draught, but that barley wine is stronger and sold in the bottle. There is also a warming Scottish ale style exemplified by Traquair House Ale.

COMFORT FOOD *Rich ales like Adnams Broadside go well with jacket potatoes.*

The German and Belgian styles are rich combinations of malt, fruit, hops, herbs, and spices. The most famous Belgian style is Trappist or abbey ale, the product of centuries of brewing in the monasteries. American micro-breweries, such as Victory and Anchor, are also making fine warming old ales and barley wine-style brews, which are gaining in reputation.

Some of these beers can improve over several years, like Chimay Grande Réserve or Hair of the Dog Fred, developing mellow and complex, and often winey or porty, aromas and flavours. It is not uncommon for them to be sold with a vintage date, as they are brewed once per year, like Fuller's Vintage Ale or the legendary Thomas Hardy's Ale, which it is claimed can improve for 25 years.

UK

Rich, warming ales are one of the greatest British brewing traditions. These strong ales are the opposite of lagers – deep, strong, and served at room temperature. The classic British beer in this style is barley wine.

HARVEY'S IMPERIAL RUSSIAN STOUT

C COLOUR Very thick, dark black, with little or no head.

A AROMA Dark fruits, unsweetened chocolate, and strong port.

T TASTE Thick, oily, and sweet, with figs and dark fruit; long chocolate finish.

Harvey's Brewery in Sussex, England, began operation in 1790. It remains an independent, family company, and is well-known for a number of excellent beers, including the Imperial Russian Stout. This stout recreates a 1912 Imperial Russian Stout, first brewed by Albert le Coq at Tartu, in what is now Estonia. In honour of the original brewer, the beer is also called Ale à le Coq, or Le Coq Imperial Double Stout.

This is quite a beer – extremely dark and thick, with no head, it has been compared with used motor oil, and has a vinous character, more like a port than a beer. Drinkers often think they have been given a corked or flat bottle – yet to fans it is to die for! At 9% ABV, it is very strong, and has deep, dark fruit aromas, such as prunes, and chocolate, with a port or Madeira feel. The flavours are incredibly rich, with toffee, molasses, coffee, and again, unsweetened dark chocolate. This also appears in the extremely long and spicy finish, to round off an amazing experience.

If you want a dark, rich, after-dinner beer and a deeply satisfying experience, then I think you can't do much better than this.

VINTAGE BREW *Harvey's Imperial Russian Stout is brewed on a seasonal basis, with the particular vintage shown on the label.*

FULLER'S ESB

C **COLOUR** Deep rich orange, with a fine, full, cream-coloured head.

A **AROMA** Great balance of malt, hops, and sweet orange citrus.

T **TASTE** Very rounded, with fine malt, grassy hops, and a spicy citrus finish.

FULLER'S ESB

Fuller's "Extra Special Bitter" was launched in 1969 as Winter Bitter, and renamed ESB in 1971. It has become a flagship brew around the world, and ESB is now used to denote a particular style of beer: strong, quite dark, with a firm, malty, and fruity feel. Fuller's ESB is typical, and probably the best of the style, with great balance. The bottled version, ESB Export, is almost as good as the draught. The original ESB, Fuller's is a beer not to be missed!

FULLER'S GOLDEN PRIDE

C **COLOUR** Very deep and dark gold or mid-brown.

A **AROMA** Rich and vinous, with orange citrus and dark fruit.

T **TASTE** Strong and sweet, with caramel, toffee, orange, and hops.

Although this is called a strong ale by the brewer, most people would agree that it is really a barley wine, and, at 8.5% ABV, is not to be trifled with. Its aromas give away its nature; they are rather like a sherry, with darker fruits in the background. The taste is immediately strong and sweet, but with balancing flavours of orange, that stay for the finish, and fine fresh hops. You have been warned – this is a beer only for gentle sipping.

FULLER'S
GOLDEN PRIDE

FULLER'S 1845

C **COLOUR** Orange-brown, with a fine, full, cream-coloured head.

A **AROMA** Intense treacly malt, with toffee sweetness and spice.

T **TASTE** Essentially bitter, balanced by rich malt, citrus, and hops.

Fuller's Brewery, not far from the centre of London, has managed to combine the brewing of traditional ales with high quality and a world-wide reputation: something that only a very few brewers have managed to achieve. This lovely beer was launched in 1995 to celebrate the company's 150th anniversary, and, in both 1998 and 2003 in the UK, was chosen as the Campaign for Real Ale (CAMRA)/Guardian newspaper's champion bottle-conditioned ale.

Fuller's 1845 is a strong ale at 6.3% ABV, and, because it is bottled with live yeast, it will improve for several months in the bottle. It looks attractive, with a fine, deep, orange-brown body and a lovely, rich, creamy head. The aromas are wonderfully rich and intense, with a sweet, treacly note overlain with flowers and citrus. The flavours are also in great balance, with the bitter feel combined with nuts, citrus, dark fruits, and firm malt. The finish is nutty, citrusy, and very fresh.

FULLER'S 1845

Fuller's 1845 has been called "the Châteauneuf-du-Pape of beers", and I think it is a great end-of-the-evening tipple. But take care; this is also a dangerous beer – you can easily drink too many without realizing until it is too late!

QUALITY FOCUS Fuller's Brewery has achieved a world-wide reputation for its excellent beers. Key to the success of such an ambitious operation is rigorous quality control to maintain standards and ensure that every one of a wide range of beers consistently displays its true character. Along with regular sampling, laboratory analysis is employed to check for contaminating bacteria and to monitor the yeasts.

FULLER'S VINTAGE ALE

C **COLOUR** Very deep and attractive golden orange-brown.

A **AROMA** Complex, with black fruits, liquorice, molasses, and nuts.

T **TASTE** Very firm malts, with dark fruits, toffee, cinnamon, and cloves.

Fuller's makes this special beer in limited quantities, and with each bottle individually numbered. It will keep for five or more years and there will be sediment in the bottle. The 2004 vintage is orange-brown, with a full, off-white head. The aromas are wonderfully complex, with sweet malt, toffee, fruit, nuts, and port wine. Over a firm foundation of malt, you can taste liquorice, nuts, and spice. This is a very strong ale at 8.5% ABV, but it is light and creamy, with a lovely warming finish.

LEES HARVEST ALE

C **COLOUR** Deep rich orange, with a fine dark-cream head.

A **AROMA** Rich, fruity, and vinous, with hops, figs, prunes, and dates.

T **TASTE** Very full but dry flavours of malt, hops, and herbs, with a spicy hop finish.

LEES HARVEST ALE

This special beer is made by the venerable John Willie Lees Brewery in Greater Manchester, which has a reputation for fine quality, dry ales. Produced each year at the end of November, using the season's hops, it is an amazing combination of a really strong brew – a mighty 11.5% ABV – with an excellent balance of flavours. It can improve in the bottle over a few years. The best thing is the way flavours keep developing as you drink, from sweet and fruity to dry and spicy, and everything in between.

ADNAMS BROADSIDE

C **COLOUR** Deep amber-red, with an off-white head.

A **AROMA** Quite strong and malty, with hops less prominent.

T **TASTE** Bitter and malty, and quite treacly, with dark fruit and a dry finish.

A fantastic example of English beer at its best! This is one of my all-time favourites, from the Suffolk brewery that rode to fame on the real ale revival of the 1980s. It is quite dark, and strong at 6.3% ABV. The taste has a perfect balance between dark fruit, malt, and a hoppy dryness. Overall, a great warming beer, and an ideal pub pint, lunchtime or evening.

ADNAMS BROADSIDE

ROBINSON'S OLD TOM

C COLOUR Very dark walnut brown and opaque, with a light-tan head.

A AROMA Quite malty, with chocolate, dark fruits, and molasses.

T TASTE Rich and malty, with caramel, prunes, dates, and chocolate.

Old Tom was first brewed by this Stockport-based firm as long ago as 1899, and is allegedly named after the brewery cat. This barley wine (or you could call it an old ale) is very dark and opaque, and very strong at 8.5% ABV. It is an all-malt beer, and quite sweet and rich, although the finish is dry. Maybe it is not the world's best barley wine, but it is a great one to ease someone into the style, without bombarding them with hops and alcohol.

ROBINSON'S
OLD TOM

THEAKSTON OLD PECULIER

C COLOUR Very deep dark brown, with a full and long-lasting head.

A AROMA Mainly peppery hops, but with yeast and a sherry feel.

T TASTE Quite sweet and treacly; chocolate and dark fruits; dry finish.

If any beer typified the real ale revival in the 1980s, it was this one.
It is the opposite of mass-market fizzy lager in every way: dark, thick, and traditionally packaged, with a soft and oily feel.
Yet the once tiny and independent Theakston's Brewery at Masham, North Yorkshire, made a great hit with a new generation looking for something different – even a bit peculiar! Theakston's has now been absorbed into the modern brewing industry as part of Scottish

and Newcastle, but Old Peculier goes on, and retains its medieval spelling.

This is a genuine example of old ale, rather than a barley wine. It is moderately strong at 5.6%, and easily managed in a full pint. It is dark brown with a full, frothy head. The aromas are quite lively, with that rich sherry or winey feel that comes with an old ale. The flavours are essentially sweet and rich, with burnt malt and chocolate, and a treacly, fruity feel.

Why is this beer so popular? You could argue that it is not the best-crafted beer in the world, but it is very satisfying and very tasty. There is also a certain frisson from the persistent myth that this beer really is a bit "peculiar" – and can give you hallucinations if you are not careful. Who could resist trying it once they know that?

THEAKSTON
OLD PECULIER

TRAQUAIR HOUSE ALE

C COLOUR Very deep ruby red, with a thin and short-lived head.

A AROMA Quite sweet and malty, with a hoppy, earthy, and woody feel.

T TASTE Distinctive, with malt, wood, nuts, and earth, and a dry finish.

The brewery at Traquair Castle, near Edinburgh, Scotland, closed to domestic beer-production around 1800. But in 1965, Peter Maxwell Stuart revived it, and began producing beer using traditional methods.
Traquair House Ale is dark, and a strong ale at 7.2% ABV. There is not much of a head, but very attractive nutty and woody aromas. The flavour is more complex, malty and again influenced by wood, with bitter chocolate, and a peaty, malt-whisky note. Excellent as an after-dinner beer. One of Scotland's finest!

MARSTON'S OWD RODGER

C COLOUR Very dark brown with deep purple highlights.

A AROMA Malty nose, with treacle, liquorice, and dark fruits.

T TASTE Very rich and sweet, with a fruity feel and a spicy finish.

Although called an old ale, this is really a barley wine, and a very good one. It comes from Marston, Thompson, and Evershed, the last independent brewer in the great brewing town of Burton on Trent.
Very strong at 7.6% ABV, and so dark brown it is nearly purple in colour, Owd Rodger is as warming as you could want a winter ale to be. Compare it with Theakston Old Peculier *(see above)*, as it has a similar feel. This is a great beer to have with a hot dessert, especially Christmas pudding.

MARSTON'S
OWD RODGER

YOUNG'S WINTER WARMER

C COLOUR Very dark brown with ruby tinges.

A AROMA Warm and sweet, with some hints of port.

T TASTE Quite full, smooth, and generous, with malt, hops, and a chocolaty finish.

Winter Warmer is a great example of a traditional English winter ale. This beer is moderately strong at 5% ABV, and very dark in the glass. The aromas – like everything about this beer – are warm, with a biscuity sweetness. You will find rich, smooth, rounded chocolate malt flavours, and the beer is quite light on hops. The finish is malty and chocolaty, but with enough dryness to be extremely pleasant and drinkable, perhaps by the fire with a nice meat pie or a jacket potato.

GALES PRIZE OLD ALE

C COLOUR Very deep dark red, with almost no foam or carbonation.

A AROMA Brilliantly balanced, with hops, dark fruits, and apple.

T TASTE Very full and very dry, with a rich fruity finish.

You might expect this beer to be sweet, but if you do, you are in for a surprise. Gales' version of a barley wine is very strong at 9% ABV. The aromas are quite distinctive, with a fruity or sweet-sherry feel, even a suggestion of sweetish cider. It is very rich, with strong caramel, walnut, and cherries. But then there is a bitter explosion, followed by fruit and Cognac at the finish. If you want a really strong, unusual, and warming beer, perfect for sipping after dinner, then Gales Prize Old Ale is it.

GREENE KING STRONG SUFFOLK

C COLOUR Very deep dark brown, with slight ruby tinges.

A AROMA Quite malty, with dark fruit and caramel.

T TASTE Rich and woody; sweet malt and dark fruits balanced by peppery hops.

An old ale with a difference! This is a blend of two ales: Old 5X – which is brewed to the maximum strength possible (around 12% ABV) and left to mature in oak vats for a minimum of two years – and BPA, a dark, full-bodied, freshly brewed beer, which is added just before bottling. The result is a unique beer – strong, at 6% ABV, and dark, fruity, and oaky. I think Greene King Strong Suffolk Ale is great on its own, or you could also try it with pickles and a blue cheese, such as Stilton.

GREENE KING
STRONG SUFFOLK ALE

THOMAS HARDY'S ALE

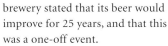

C COLOUR Wonderfully deep tawny brown, with a small, short-lived head.

A AROMA Very full malt, dark fruits, plums, dates, and raisins, with sweet spice.

T TASTE Intensely heavy, with dark malts, rich fruit, and sherry.

The world-famous English writer Thomas Hardy lived in the West Country town of Dorchester in the late 19th and early 20th centuries. He was a beer fan, and knew the local brewing families. In 1968, in commemoration of the 40th anniversary of the writer's death, the local brewery Eldridge Pope was asked by the Thomas Hardy Society to make a special beer to be launched at that summer's Thomas Hardy Festival. The brewery stated that its beer would improve for 25 years, and that this was a one-off event.

However, interest was so great that brewing continued. Each bottle was labelled with its vintage, allowing drinkers to compare vintages, and collectors began to pay large amounts for good older vintages – just like wine! The beer is still made to this day, but now by O'Hanlon's Brewery in Devon.

Thomas Hardy Ale is so rich, it can be talked about in the same way as a heavy red or even a fortified wine. It is 12% ABV, and over the years the beer changes from a rich, fruity, and lively ale when young to a deep, mellow, vinous drink with fantastic complexity when old. The dilemma is, do you enjoy this wonderful beer now, or do you store it, knowing that it will get better over the years?

THOMAS
HARDY'S ALE

IRELAND

Guinness is a familiar drink in today's market, but it also has a long historical connection with the British Empire. Special varieties of stout were made to suit conditions in hot countries and to withstand transport by sea.

GUINNESS FOREIGN EXTRA STOUT

GUINNESS FOREIGN EXTRA STOUT

C COLOUR Very dark brown-black – almost completely opaque.

A AROMA Thick, rich, and treacly malt, balanced with fresh hops.

T TASTE Rich and bitter, but also sweetish burnt malt, with a bitter finish.

Guinness's Foreign Extra Stout was originally made for export to the British colonies. It is a bottle-conditioned beer with an alcohol content of 7.5% ABV, designed to survive long sea voyages. It is now made in various locations around the world, so there is inevitable variation. The Nigerian version is especially different, with sorghum included instead of barley, and a lighter mouthfeel, and it is so good that Guinness is considering importing it back into Ireland! The basic Foreign Extra Stout is a classic Irish bitter stout: very dark, with rich aromas of malt and hops, and a bitter, dark flavour – intensely warming and satisfying. It is great with oysters, or with a winter evening meal.

AUSTRIA

Austria does not have a great tradition of making dark beers, but those that they do make are brewed with classic Austrian skill.

SAMICHLAUS

C COLOUR Dark reddish-brown, with little or no head.

A AROMA Dark malt, molasses, honey, caramel, and toasted rye bread.

T TASTE Very smooth and warming; full malt, caramel, and honey sweetness.

One of the world's strongest beers, at 14% ABV, this renowned Christmas ale (Samichlaus is Santa Claus) was reintroduced in 2000 by the Austrian brewer Eggenberger. It is matured for an entire year before release and resembles a light brandy, with very rich aromas, massively malty flavours, and no hop dryness.

FRANCE

Northern France has borders with Belgium, and brewing styles in the border region have been influenced by this close relationship. One of the classic varieties from the area is ambrée beer. It is strong and rich, and similar in character to the Belgian monastic beers.

TROIS MONTS

C COLOUR Very bright golden yellow, with a creamy, long-lasting head.

A AROMA Fresh, with grassy hops, spice, and yeast, in fine balance.

T TASTE Bright and hoppy, with a starchy fruit feeling and a warming finish.

This strong (8.5% ABV) beer from northeastern France is made by the Saint Sylvestre Brewery. Trois Monts refers to three small but distinctive hills rising out of the flat Flanders landscape. Unusually, it looks like a cooling lager, but is much more complex, and much more warming, quite like a good Belgian Trappist brew, and is perfect with lamb.

CH'TI AMBRÉE

C COLOUR Dark orange amber, with a smooth but short-lived head.

A AROMA Fresh, with hops, vanilla, and yeast, balanced by quite vinous fruit.

T TASTE Fairly fruity, with sherry, malt, and wood, and a tangy finish.

Ch'ti is Picardy dialect for a northerner – a native of this mining country near the Belgian border in northeastern France. The aromas of this beer are complex, with hops and vanilla, quite like a German Altbier. It is rich and smooth to taste, with hints of butterscotch, caramel, and malt, and a fruity, sherryish feel. The finish is fairly tangy and spicy.

JENLAIN AMBRÉE

C COLOUR Dark rich orange, with a fine head.

A AROMA Quite malty, with a good balance of spices.

T TASTE Rich and warming, with apple fruit and a sweet malty finish.

This attractive beer is made by the Duyck brewery at Jenlain, very close to the French–Belgian border. This is an all-malt bière de garde, strong at 6.5% ABV, and presented in a tall Champagne-style bottle with a wired cork. Jenlain has malty aromas, as the beer is not made with hops. It is very warming to the taste, with malt and an apple, Calvados, or Armagnac feel. Sweetness is present, but does not overpower. You might compare this to a strong brown ale, or even an old ale like Theakston Old Peculier *(see p461)*. It is normally drunk at cool room temperature, about 12°C (54°F), but some like it colder. Either way, it is wonderful with lamb in any form.

NETHERLANDS

There is only a small market for darker beers in the Netherlands, but some new micro-breweries now make these richer brews.

'T IJ COLUMBUS

C COLOUR Dark amber, with a long-lasting, light-tan head.

A AROMA Fairly hoppy, with a good citrus balance.

T TASTE Fine malt and hops, with lemony citrus and a dry finish.

From a spectacular brewhouse on the Amsterdam waterfront, topped by a windmill, this is a lovely strong ale (9% ABV). It is smooth and warming, but also bright and fresh, with an attractive dryness from the hops and the citrus notes. The hops have a vanilla character, leading to a satisfying and complex finish.

BELGIUM

The Trappist or monastic style of rich, dark beers is one of the great brewing traditions, and includes some of the finest beers in the world. Some are still made by monks, others by commercial breweries using ancient monastic formulas.

WESTVLETEREN 8

C COLOUR Dark brown, with an off-white head.

A AROMA Very fruity, with lemon and grapefruit citrus, melon, and herbs.

T TASTE Smooth and malty; chocolate, nougat, and caramel; spicy finish.

This beer is a product of the monastery of St Sixtus in the town of Westvleteren. It is the smallest of the Trappist breweries, located close to Ypres, near the famous World War I battleground. The monastery's own Westvleteren beers should not be confused with those now known as St Bernardus (*see p466*). After World War II, the monks licenced similar products to be made by a local brewery under the name of St Sixtus. In 1992 this arrangement came to an end, and since then St Sixtus beers have been marketed under the St Bernardus name.

The monastery's own beers, by contrast, do not have labels on the bottles, and are identified by their crown caps – the caps are coloured according to the type of beer. Their range includes the blue cap, called Westvleteren 8 or Extra 8, named for its strength (8% ABV);

the Westvleteren Blond, which has a green cap and is weaker, at 5.8% ABV; and Westvleteren 12 (*see below*), which has a yellow cap.

Westvleteren 8 is made by traditional methods and has complex and rich aromas of fruit, especially citrus, and herbs. In the mouth the beer is very smooth and full bodied, with fantastic depth and complexity, a deep, smoky maltiness, and flavours of chocolate and herbs. The finish is quite peppery, with a great warming sensation.

This beer can be difficult to find, and being sought-after, can sometimes be very expensive. Never-theless, if you like the Trappist style of beer, I think that Westvleteren 8 is one of the very best. It is wonderful with soft cheese, and even matches sweet puddings or cake.

WESTVLETEREN 8

WESTVLETEREN 12

C COLOUR Very dark brown-black, with virtually no head.

A AROMA Distinctly malty, with a winey feel, also yeast, wood, and dark fruits.

T TASTE Smooth, silky, rich; dark fruits, marzipan, nuts, spice; vinous finish.

This is the strongest beer produced by the St Sixtus monastery at Westvleteren (*see above*). Like their other beers, this has no label, but is identified by its yellow cap, and its number 12, which refers to its strength of 12% ABV.

Westvleteren 12 is a very dark beer, and when you pour it into a glass, there is almost no head. Its aromas are very full, with the dark malt enriched with dark fruits and a woody, winey feel, which is rather like a port-wood whisky. Although this beer is very strong, the alcohol does not overpower the flavour. The beer keeps a smooth and luscious feel, with a great complexity of flavours, especially

fruit, nuts, and spice. The finish is a fabulous blend of malt and spice.

The overall experience is very warming and satisfying, and although you can't really drink many of these, I couldn't think of anything better than sipping a Westvleteren 12 to sustain a hardworking monk at the end of a day of monastic duties!

FOOD MATCH

FRUIT CAKE Luxurious fruit cakes are a traditional product of Trappist monasteries, along with beers. The strong, warming beers are ideal partners for desserts and cake.

ABBAYE DES ROCS

C COLOUR Dark ruby-red brown, with a small, short-lived head.

A AROMA Elegant and rich; with wood, earth, spice, and sweet fruit.

T TASTE Infinitely complex; spicy, sweet, malty; fruity and woody; warming finish.

Abbaye des Rocs is a farm brewery in Montignies-sur-Roc, in the Belgian province of Luxembourg. It was established by a former tax inspector who was also a beer enthusiast. Although this is a commercial brewery, it just so happens to be on the site of an old monastery, and has established a reputation for fine beers in the style of monastery beers since its establishment in 1979.

Abbaye des Rocs was the first beer produced by the brewery. It is very dark and strong at 9% ABV. The head is fairly small and turns to

lace quite quickly. The first thing that hits you when you take a sip of this interesting beer is that the aromas and flavours are outstanding and amazingly complex! In this one beer you can taste fruit, spices, wood, whisky, tobacco, sherry, sweet malt, bitter hops – and more. One minute you are drinking a sweet beer, full of great red and black fruits, and the next you have a spicy, hoppy, and refreshing drink that makes you beg for more.

The brewery has this as their flagship, and no wonder. If you want to taste the best of the abbey-style beers, then go for this one. I would recommend Abbaye des Rocs with some strong cheese – perfection!

Other beers from this brewery include Blanche de Honelles, a strong, charac-terful wheat beer, and Montagnarde, named for the people of the region. This is as strong as Abbaye des Rocs, but with more emphasis on bitterness.

ABBAYE DES ROCS

ROCHEFORT 10

C **COLOUR** Very dark brown, with a good-sized, off-white head.

A **AROMA** Distinctive, with rich malts, dark fruits, and chocolate.

T **TASTE** Full-bodied and smooth, with chocolate, spice, and dark fruit.

Quenching the thirst and enriching the soul! Rochefort is the least known and most secretive of the Trappist monasteries, located in the heart of the Ardennes forest at the Abbaye de St-Remy, near the town of Rochefort. The monastery dates from the early 1200s and the first brewery on the site dates from as long ago as 1595.

Rochefort 10 is the strongest of the monastery's three beers at 11.3% ABV. This is a beer to savour, but is perfectly balanced and not so heavy as to make it difficult to enjoy. It is very dark – almost black – and cloudy. The aromas are very complex, with malt, chocolate, cocoa, damson, prunes, raisins, and a general berry–fruity and porty feel. The flavours come through very clearly, and include a hint of smoke, like an Islay whisky. Perfect with a winter meal, or Roquefort cheese.

PERFECT 10 *Dark chocolate aromas and flavours combine with spice, marzipan, and black fruits in the perfectly balanced Rochefort 10.*

TRIPEL KARMELIET

C COLOUR Bright translucent golden orange, with a full, frothy head.

A AROMA Spicy, with vanilla, cloves, cinnamon, coriander, and bubblegum.

T TASTE Citrusy, with lemon, lime, and pineapple, but also quite sweet.

Although this is a modern beer, introduced in 1997, the formula was originally created by Carmelite monks in 1679. The name Tripel refers to the three grains used in making the beer – wheat, barley, and oats. The beer is lively, with a good head and bright spicy aromas. The overall taste is sweet and citrusy, but there are also strong hints of spice and red fruit, and the finish is dry. This is a strong beer, at 8% ABV, but is very refreshing, especially if you serve it cold.

TRIPEL KARMELIET

CHIMAY GRANDE RÉSERVE

C COLOUR Very dark orange-brown, with a large, foamy, cream head, fading to lace.

A AROMA Elegant, with sweet fruit, malt, spice, and just a hint of caramel.

T TASTE Well-balanced, with a malty sweetness, spice, fruit, and hops.

Grande Réserve is the strongest (9% ABV) of the beers produced by the Trappist monastery of Notre Dame at Scourmont, near Chimay. Such an expensive and luxurious beer is normally laid down for some years to allow the full porty flavour to develop. Any time you open the bottle, though, you will find a great balance of flavours, with the sherry or port feel balanced by a fresh finish. This classic, exclusive beer is perfect with rich cheeses like Roquefort.

HOLY ORDERS *Trappist monks have been brewing on site at the Abbaye de Notre-Dame de Scourmont since 1862.*

ST BERNARDUS 12

C COLOUR Dark orange-brown, and quite cloudy in texture.

A AROMA Fragrant, with chocolate, raisins, and freshly baked bread.

T TASTE Not too sweet, with fruity raisins, plum, banana, and pineapple.

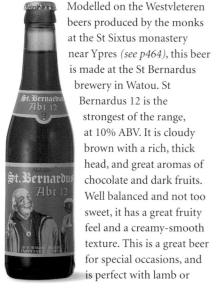

Modelled on the Westvleteren beers produced by the monks at the St Sixtus monastery near Ypres *(see p464)*, this beer is made at the St Bernardus brewery in Watou. St Bernardus 12 is the strongest of the range, at 10% ABV. It is cloudy brown with a rich, thick head, and great aromas of chocolate and dark fruits. Well balanced and not too sweet, it has a great fruity feel and a creamy-smooth texture. This is a great beer for special occasions, and is perfect with lamb or rich, soft cheese.

ST BERNARDUS 12

GOUDEN CAROLUS

C COLOUR Rich dark red, with a full light-orange head.

A AROMA Rich and fruity, with port wine and spice.

T TASTE Complex, with orange, passion fruit, toffee, and a spicy finish.

Gouden Carolus (Golden Charles) is named after a golden coin of the Holy Roman Emperor Charles V (1500–1558), who grew up in Mechelen, where the Anker Brewery is based. This is a rich, fruity, and distinctive Flemish brown ale, deep red with a good full head. The essential feeling of this beer is sweetness, with a port or sweet-sherry character, and notes of orange. The finish is still quite spicy and fresh, and I recommend this as a lovely after-dinner beer, especially with dessert, or even chocolate.

GOUDEN CAROLUS

LEFFE RADIEUSE

C COLOUR Dark orangey-brown, with a frothy, short-lived head.

A AROMA Fruity, with cherry, treacly malt, and grassy hops.

T TASTE Full-bodied and porty, with dark fruits and a peppery finish.

Now part of the multinational InBev group (formerly Interbrew) – owners of global beer brands such as Beck's, Stella Artois, Hoegaarden, and many others – Leffe is becoming a brand known around the world. The original beer came from the Norbertine Abbey of Notre Dame de Leffe, near Namur. The monastery had not made beer since the 18th century, but in the 1950s the abbot licensed a brewer to make beer based on its original formulas.

Since then, Leffe has gone from strength to strength, and a range of beers is now made and distributed around the world. Leffe Radieuse – meaning "halo" – is the strongest of the Leffe range, at 8.2% ABV.

Leffe Radieuse is a dark, rich beer with a short-lived head. The aromas are rich, malty, and treacly, with lots of dark fruit and a sweet-sherry feel. The beer is very full and firm, with a fine complexity of flavours. It begins as quite sweet and richly fruity, but ends with a spicy, peppery, and warm finish.

I would compare this beer to an English barley wine – it is very filling, warming, and satisfying, and you shouldn't drink too many of them! I think this beer works best as an after-dinner tipple. Treat it like a Cognac or Armagnac – go slowly, and savour.

LEFFE RADIEUSE

McCHOUFFE

C COLOUR Dark brown, with a firm, long-lasting head.

A AROMA Excellent balance of fruit and hops, and a woody, earthy, smoky feel.

T TASTE Very fruity and down to earth, with dark fruits and firm malt.

This sounds like a Scottish ale, although the Achouffe Brewery is in fact based on a farm in the Ardennes region of Belgium. The makers of this beer bill it as "the Skotch from the Ardennes", being very careful to avoid lawsuits by inserting a "k" in place of the "c"!

Achouffe was established, in the early 1980s, by two brothers-in-law who first broke into the Canadian market, then opened a pub alongside the brewery. They began to win prizes for their beer – gold at Eurobières, Strasbourg, in 1999, in the

MCCHOUFFE

abbey-style class, and silver in Australia in 2002. Achouffe has now established a reputation as a fine regional brewer, and its symbol of a bearded gnome printed on to designer bottles is a familiar sight.

McChouffe is a dark ale on the Scottish model: strong (8.5% ABV), spicy, bottle-fermented, unfiltered, unpasteurized, and without any additives. The brewery uses its own spring water to make its beer. It has a good-sized, firm, bubbly, and long-lived head, while its aromas are fruity, woody, and smoky, with a real forest-undergrowth character. The flavours have a great balance of dark and citrus fruits and sweeter malt, with the warming alcohol strength coming through for the finish.

This is a wonderfully warming and satisfying beer, and my favourite time to drink it is with a plate of roast beef – excellent!

HOEGAARDEN GRAND CRU

C COLOUR Dark golden amber, and a little cloudy.

A AROMA Lightly fruity, balanced by a spicy feel.

T TASTE Refreshing and complex flavours of spice, citrus fruit, and pineapple.

Hoegaarden was originally established as a local Belgian producer of wheat beers, and drove the renaissance of the style from the 1960s onwards. This brewer has since developed a wider reputation and has expanded its range, and it is now one of the flagship brands of the InBev group. This base has given Hoegaarden the opportunity to extend its reach and penetrate new markets, so that it is now available in many outlets in numerous different countries.

Hoegaarden Grand Cru is a step up from the more widely

HOEGAARDEN GRAND CRU

available Hoegaarden wheat beer (*see p426*), and is much more of a specialist beer, although it bears a strong family resemblance to the lighter version. The style is that of a Belgian tripel, made with barley malt, yeast, coriander, and orange peel. The result is a full-bodied and complex beer with a fruity and quite sweet taste.

Hoegaarden Grand Cru is very strong at 8.7% ABV, and is hazy, with a good, full head. It has a suite of very distinctive aromas, with plenty of citrus fruit and spice. Coriander and orange are very noticeable in the flavour, but you will also find pineapple, vanilla, and a tingling spicy finish.

Hoegaarden Grand Cru has a great balance, and a lovely smooth texture. To me, it is ideal as an apéritif or for drinking in small quantities.

DE DOLLE STILLE NACHT

C COLOUR Medium-orange amber, with a fine-bubbled, white long-lasting head.

A AROMA Distinctive, with plum, apple, lemon, cinnamon, and cloves.

T TASTE Smooth and creamy; sweet caramel and malt; apple and citrus.

"The Mad Brewers" – this nickname was attached to three brothers who, in 1980, rescued an old brewery in Esen, in West Flanders. Their De Dolle brewery (*Dolle* is Flemish for mad) now produces a range of seasonal ales.

Stille Nacht is a bottle-conditioned Christmas ale, and is very strong at 8% ABV. It has a very fruity and spicy aroma, and a good citrus feel. The sweetness on the palate is balanced by apple, cherry, citrus, and a spicy and warming feeling at the finish. I think the best time to drink a glass of Stille Nacht is after a heavy Christmas meal, just before you drop off to sleep.

CANADA

Micro-breweries in Canada, particularly in Quebec, are taking the Belgian style of warming ale and making it their own. This movement is led by Unibroue, which makes a bewildering range of fine ales, some of which are as good as the best Belgian beers.

TROIS PISTOLES

C COLOUR Dark, dusky mahogany-black, with a cloudy texture.

A AROMA Very dark and fruity, with malt, nuts, fruit, and chocolate.

T TASTE Rich and full; malt and chocolate sweetness; bitter hops at the finish.

Unibroue is the largest micro-brewery in Quebec, and was established in 1991 at Chambly, near Montreal. Initially, the brewery was advised by Belgian brewing experts, as it particularly wanted to make beer in the Belgian style. Their Blanche de Chambly, a hazy, spice-and-hop-seasoned wheat beer, and Maudite, a strong, dark, orange ale designed to

improve with age, have been particularly successful.

Trois Pistoles was launched in 1997. It is a dark, bottle-conditioned ale, and very strong, at 9% ABV. It is an altogether very dramatic beer, beginning with the imposing black bottle and the mysterious label of three towers pointing towards a winged horse.

This beer is very dark brown in colour. It is produced by fermentation in the bottle, which creates a hazy, cloudy texture. The aromas are rich and complex, with malt, chocolate, sweet biscuits, and fruit in a fine balance. The texture is

TROIS PISTOLES

rich and smooth, and the initial taste is quite sweet, with toffee, malt, and rum desserts all coming to mind. By the finish, though, the citrus character and the dryness of the hops come through, and you are ultimately left with a refreshing and quite vinous feel.

Trois Pistoles can be drunk before or after a meal, and is excellent with pasta as well as game and wild fowl. It can also partner desserts like chocolate mousse and fruit salad, and is strong enough to be served in smaller portions out of a port snifter. Like a port, this beer will improve with age in the bottle, for five or six years.

This is an unusual brew from an innovative and fairly new brewery, and one you should not miss. The beer may be sweetly attractive, but don't be fooled: take the dark, foreboding towers on the label as a warning sign – this beer really packs a punch!

USA

Some of the best beers produced by the new American micro-breweries are in the traditional British warm ale and barley wine styles. These breweries are varying the basic type with enthusiasm and creativity, adding new ingredients and taking the industry forward.

VICTORY GOLDEN MONKEY

C **COLOUR** Light gold, slightly cloudy, with a firm white head.

A **AROMA** Sweet malt, vanilla, coriander, and overall a yeasty feel.

T **TASTE** Light-bodied, with bittersweet herbs, citrus, and spice.

This award-winning tripel, made by Victory Brewing, in Pennsylvania, is a Belgian ale, made with German malts and Belgian yeast, giving it the feel of a Weissbier. When you pour the beer into a glass, you see a golden, quite cloudy texture, often with bits of the yeast sediment, and with a few slightly orangey highlights. The aromas are attractive, with yeast, and notes of citrus and spice. The flavours, at first, are quite sweet, with vanilla, banana, honey, and sweet cinnamon. Later, it becomes much more dry and herbal, and this slightly spicy feel remains at the finish. It is firm in the mouth, and quite warming – a hint of its alcohol content, a full 9.5% ABV. Overall, this is a beautifully balanced beer. Try it with cold meats or salads.

VICTORY GOLDEN MONKEY

GLOWING WITH PRIDE *Victory Brewing is justly proud of Golden Monkey, a great rival for even the best Belgian tripels.*

ANCHOR OLD FOGHORN

C COLOUR Chestnut-brown, with a red tinge, and a dark-cream head.

A AROMA Rich and sweet; hops, fruitcake, apricot, and sherry.

T TASTE Quite smooth rich hop and malt whisky; fruity finish.

Anchor Brewing has established itself as a permanent fixture in the San Francisco area of California, with its flagship Steam Beer, a cross between a lager and an ale, and named because its high level of carbon dioxide led to "steam" – actually gas – escaping from the barrels. It also makes Liberty Ale *(see p441)* and the great Anchor Porter *(see p453)* – another cross, this time between a porter and a stout. Anchor prides itself on combining very traditional brewing methods, using 100-per-cent malt, and advanced modern techniques to

ANCHOR OLD FOGHORN

assure quality and maintain the beers in optimum condition until they are sold to the consumer.

This is a very old brewery, first established in 1896, and saved from closure in 1965 by Fritz Maytag. He ran the brewery so effectively that by the 1970s it became a leader in the micro-brew movement. Back in 1975, when the micro-breweries were just taking off in the US, Anchor pioneered the introduction of a barley wine, Old Foghorn. If there was any beer that was the opposite of the light, weak, and over-fizzed lagers that were then almost totally dominating the American beer scene, then this was it!

Old Foghorn is billed as a barley wine-style ale, and is very strong at 8.7% ABV, or even 9.4% ABV in some versions. It is a dark chestnut

in colour, and clear, as it is not bottle-conditioned. The overwhelming feeling of the aromas is sweet fruit and sherry, but there is also a strong hop presence; as with all American barley wines, it is made with a good proportion of hops.

The flavours are strongly fruity, which they need to be to balance the fiery alcohol. You can taste the marzipan and the caramel, but towards the end the hops start to make themselves known, and the finish is quite dry and refreshing.

Naturally, you cannot drink more than one or two of these. Some drinkers prefer it as an after-dinner drink, like a liqueur, without food, or even as a nightcap. Others like to drink it with some very strong cheese. Whatever you do, take care with this powerful brew.

HAIR OF THE DOG FRED

C COLOUR Bright golden orange, with a good strong head.

A AROMA Dominated by hops; also malt, citrus, and sweet spice.

T TASTE Very full and rich, with orange and sherry, and a hoppy, earthy finish.

HAIR OF THE DOG FRED

"Faithful, loyal, pure, wet nose" runs the slogan of Hair of the Dog, a tiny micro-brewery in Portland, Oregon. It was established in 1994, and specializes in bottle-conditioned beers that are designed to improve with age. Fred is named after Fred Eckhardt, a Portland-based brewer and beer writer, and it is an amazing beer. It is brewed with ten different hop varieties, to a strength of 10%, or sometimes 11% ABV. The taste and the alcohol feel are very full, and the finish is warming – a bit like a whisky. I like to drink this as an after-dinner treat.

ALLAGASH GRAND CRU

C COLOUR Golden orange; cloudy with a creamy, off-white head.

A AROMA Gentle, with malt, orange citrus, nuts, yeast, and sherry.

T TASTE Sweet fruit, such as apricot, and coriander spice.

The Allagash Brewing Company of Portland, Maine, produces mostly Belgian styles, and Grand Cru is its version of a Belgian strong pale ale. It is bottled with a small amount of yeast, enabling it to continue to mature and soften in the bottle. This is a strong beer at 7.8% ABV, and it is a cloudy orange-brown from the bottle-conditioning.

The aromas are complex, and the body is quite light, with a great balance of sweet fruit, citrus, and spice. I like to drink this with pâté, sausages, or lamb.

ROGUE OLD CRUSTACEAN

C COLOUR Dark reddy brown, with a thin, but long-lasting, creamy head.

A AROMA Intense dark fruits, chocolate, floral hops, and orange citrus.

T TASTE Full-flavoured sweetness, then citrus, hops, herbs, and spice.

The Cognac of beers! This is the claim made by the Rogue Brewery of Newport, Oregon, for Old Crustacean, their version of an English-style barley wine. Barley wines are made to be stored and improved with age, and Rogue makes this beer with the intention that it should not be drunk for at least one year, although many fans prefer to keep it longer – up to about five years, and some for ten years and more.

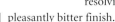

ROGUE OLD CRUSTACEAN

The key style is warming, with winter in mind, high in alcohol, robust, malty, and dark. Like all bottle-conditioned *(see p401)* barley wines, there will be some variation in both strength and flavour from the different batches and the ageing process.

Rogue Old Crustacean is cloudy brown, unfiltered, and unfined, and very strong at around 10.5% ABV. The aromas are a complex mixture of fruit, chocolate, and citrus, with hops in the background. The flavours are intensely powerful, with malt, hops, fruit, spices, and citrus all swirling together, finally resolving into a pleasantly bitter finish.

This is best as an after-dinner beer or a nightcap. You may have difficulty drinking more than one or two, unless you are a real old hand!

SIERRA NEVADA BIGFOOT

C COLOUR Deeply attractive red, with little or no head.

A AROMA Grassy hops, caramel, flowers, and pine trees.

T TASTE Deeply intense, with rich malt, dark fruits, and a hoppy spiciness.

Bigfoot is named after the mythical creature said to live in the forests of the Sierra Nevada mountains, and it is the brewery's version of barley wine. This is one of the best American barley wines, if not the best. The texture is very full, but the powerful malt, fruit, and hop flavours are not swamped by the strong alcohol (9.6% ABV). This beer is not over-sweet, and makes a wonderful, warming nightcap.

SIERRA NEVADA BIGFOOT

SPECIALITY

66 Every season, every occasion, and every hour of the day has a beer to match. Look here for some truly remarkable styles.99

INTRODUCING SPECIALITY BEERS

When is a beer more than a beer? When it is brimming with fruits and herbs, barrel-aged like a wine, or beechwood-smoked like a German sausage. Speciality beers pulsate with new and intriguing aromas and flavours that you simply have to try.

DRINKING AND SERVING

DRINK PROFILE The styles vary enormously, but the key is the combination of the basic beer with the extra ingredient. Does it add to the aroma, taste, and enjoyment, or is it just a novelty?

C COLOUR These beers have the widest range of all, from bright red through to black. The fruit beers reflect the colour of their fruit, and some are made almost clear to resemble Champagne.

A AROMA Malt and hops, of course, but also the aromas of the special ingredients – heather, flowers, herbs, spices, grapes, cherries, smoke… the list is almost infinite.

T TASTE The best, like Kriek cherry beers, or the German Rauchenfelser Steinbier, made with hot rocks, are really special, but some others are less successful. You need to try them to see.

BUYING AND STORING The Belgian Kriek beers are quite easy to obtain, as are some of the German smoked beers. Others are less easy, and may even be a local novelty. Others, like the Christmas ales, are marketed at a particular time of the year. Some will improve with age.

SERVING SUGGESTIONS Serve fruit beers and "wine" styles in appropriate glasses, and quite cold. Smoked beers can be treated as normal German strong beers, while herbal brews should be served cool, not cold, in a relatively small glass.

FOOD COMPANIONS The smoked beers are wonderful companions for German smoked sausage and any food cooked on the barbecue. Fruit beers are great with desserts, while some of the "wine" beers work quite well with lamb.

Brewers of speciality beers adapt traditional beer-making recipes to make beer that is different or unusual, or simply to enhance it. This may include adding extra ingredients to the mix during the brewing process, and is sometimes part of a historic tradition, like the Bamberg smoked beers from Franconia in Germany or juniper-infused Finnish Sahti. Others have been developed in an attempt to revive a long-dead tradition, like the various Scottish brews produced by Heather Ales. Some speciality beers are great and others don't work as well, but all are worth a try.

HEATHER FLOWERS *Heather Ale Fraoch has a sweet, floral, and herbal perfume.*

The most established types are the German smoked beers, and the beers using fruit, especially cherries, like the Brussels Kriek beers. When the malt is smoked over a wood or peat fire, aromas and flavours similar to those found in smoked fish and meats carry through to the finished beer. For fruit beers, which are dry rather than sweet, the technique is to infuse the fruit into an aged lambic beer with plenty of sourness to balance the fruit sweetness. With Heather Ales Fraoch, the method is different and simpler – here heather replaces most of the hops in an otherwise conventional brew.

BARBEQUE BEER *Sausages and barbecued meats bring out the flavours of speciality smoked beers.*

BEER, WINE, OR WHISKY?

Speciality beers include two of the "Holy Grails" in brewing. The first is to link beer with grapes and wine, especially Champagne. Particularly successful are the burgundy-like red ales of Flanders, such as Bourgogne des Flandres. The famous Rodenbach beers use winemaking techniques such as oak ageing to make their beers. The St Lamvinus and Vigneronne beers from the Cantillon brewery in Brussels actually incorporate grapes in the brewing process. The second approach is to treat the malt in order to make a beer which has the character of malt whisky. The best-known brew is Fischer Adelscott from France. However, a new Scottish beer, Innis & Gunn Oak Aged Beer, is making a mark in this area by concentrating instead on whisky-like barrel ageing in American white oak.

BELGIUM

The Belgians are second to none at making speciality beers using fruit, such as cherries and grapes, and some producers even strive to make beers that imitate Champagne. This loose family of styles includes some of the world's finest, and offers incredible variety.

DUCHESSE DE BOURGOGNE

C COLOUR Dark chestnut brown, with a small, short-lived head.

A AROMA Bright red fruits, especially cherry, and quite acidic.

T TASTE Slightly sweet, with red fruits, but also acidic, with a hoppy dry finish.

This excellent beer is made by the Verhaeghe brewery in Flanders. The title Duchesse de Bourgogne is no accident, as the West Flanders red ales have often been compared with wines over the years, and during the last century some of them even adopted the slogan "It's wine"!

This beer is matured in oak casks, rather than the bottle. It is moderately strong at 6.2% ABV, with an overall bittersweet character. It is impossible to avoid comparing it with the classic Rodenbach Grand Cru *(see below)*. I believe the Duchesse can hold its own – you will have to see what you think. This is a great beer for lunchtime drinking, as it is not over-strong, and is wonderful with cold meats, salads, and light food – just like a red burgundy.

DUCHESSE DE BOURGOGNE

BOURGOGNE DES FLANDRES

C COLOUR Dark reddy-brown, with a small head that soon goes lacy.

A AROMA Quite pungent and fruity, with black fruits, spice, and oaky wood.

T TASTE Fairly sour, oaky, and fruity, with cherry and spice.

Timmermans of Itterbeek has been an expert lambic beer brewer since 1888, but it also brews this Flanders red ale. This is a moderately strong ale at 6.5% ABV, and the aromas are typical of the style: quite pungent, with red and black fruits like cherries and plums, spices, and all the signs of time spent in oak barrels. The body of the beer is quite light and very easy to drink, and the stringent fruits and spices give an acidic but refreshing feel. I would go for this one at lunchtime, with a salad or light meal.

VERBODEN VRUCHT

C COLOUR Distinct orange-brown, with a loose, bubbly head.

A AROMA Elegant and delicate; sweet malt, red fruits, spice, wood, and yeast.

T TASTE Bright and fresh, with red fruits and a softer, chocolaty finish.

The name of this fine beer from Hoegaarden means "Forbidden Fruit", and the label is adorned with a slightly risqué picture of Adam and Eve (based on a painting by Rubens) enjoying a glass of beer.

Verboden Vrucht, known as Le Fruit Défendu in France, is an orange-brown beer, with quite pungent aromas that include red fruits and yeast, and some sweetness. The body is moderate, and the overall feel of the taste is fruity and refreshing. This is a very strong beer, at 8.8% ABV, but the alcohol does not dominate. The feeling as you finish a glass of Verboden Vrucht is "Another one, please"!

RODENBACH

C COLOUR Dark orange-red, with a fine, full, creamy head.

A AROMA Pungent fruits, with cherry, grape, herbs, and oaky wood.

T TASTE Quite dry, slightly sour, with red fruits, wood; stringent, fruity finish.

The original owners of this world-famous Belgian brewery came from Germany, and married into a Flemish family. The brewery was established in 1836, in West Flanders, and is very unusual in that it has row after row of upright wooden tuns – a total of 300, some holding more than 50,000 litres. The beer is fermented twice, then stored like wine in the oak barrels, where it sours and develops a complexity from the wood. Hence the epithet for the Rodenbach beers – "the burgundies of Flanders"! In 1998, the business was

RODENBACH

acquired by the Belgian brewer Palm, which withdrew Alexander, a fruity Kriek beer, from production, but retained this beer and the Grand Cru *(see right)*.

Rodenbach, also called Klassic, is a mixture of a vintage brew that has spent at least one year in oak casks, with a young beer matured for just five weeks in metal tanks; 75 per cent of the beer is "young". The resulting beer, at 5% ABV, is moderately strong, but is very dry; so dry that sugar is added to give a bittersweet balance.

This is a red ale and the aromas also have a "red" feel, from the cherry and grape, along with a woody character. The distinctive flavour of this beer is the dry sourness, a bit like balsamic vinegar, which is actually really refreshing. This is balanced with a slight sweetness from the fruit, and at the finish the sourness returns. This beer is unique, and you might want to join its many fans.

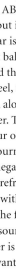

RODENBACH GRAND CRU

C COLOUR Dark, almost opaque chestnut brown, with a good tan head.

A AROMA Very pungent, with red fruits, grape, and red wine.

T TASTE Quite acidic, with sweet cherry balanced by a sharp finish.

Grand Cru is the luxury brand of this famous Belgian brewery, made only from older ales matured in wooden barrels for at least two years. It is dark chestnut brown, and strong at 6.5% ABV. The aromas are pungent and fruity, with a touch of red wine or dry sherry. This beer is an acquired taste. The first mouthfuls are very acidic, but as you get used to it, the quality and the depth of flavour emerge, leaving you with a really refreshing finish.

DEUS BRUT DES FLANDRES

C COLOUR Light gold, with a very foamy head, but thicker than Champagne.

A AROMA Fresh and lively, with malt, citrus, especially grapefruit, and herbs.

T TASTE Quite dry and acidic, with liquorice, mint, and aniseed.

Bosteels in East Flanders is most famous for its red Kwak beer. It has recently introduced this "Champagne" beer, and marketed it in bottles not unlike Dom Perignon. It even boasts the strength of a wine at 11.5% ABV. The manufacturing process is as near to that of Champagne as possible. When you pour this beer, it is visually very similar to Champagne, with a light gold colour and a bubbly head, but the aromas are still quite malty, with citrus notes. The flavours are attractive, with a bright citrus feel, and dry herby notes, especially of liquorice.

RODENBACH GRAND CRU

LIEFMANS GOUDENBAND

C COLOUR Deep red-orange brown, with a slight haze, and a moderate tan head.

A AROMA Complex red fruits, smoke, citrus, cheesy malt, minerals, leather.

T TASTE Medium-bodied, sweet; red fruits and hops; pleasantly sour finish.

It has often been said that Liefmans Goudenband (golden ribbon) is the finest brown ale in the world – and for good reason. This beer has almost infinitely complex aromas and flavours, a near-perfect balance of sweetness and dryness throughout, and the richness and complexity of a vintage wine.

Liefmans Brewery, in Oudenaarde, Belgium, brews its beer for seven days, using a wide range of yeasts and malts. The young beer is stored in the cool cellars of the brewery for several months, usually up to a year, and bottled only when it is perfectly mature. Goudenband can then be laid down for years.

The aromas of Liefmans Goudenband are amazing – ranging from red fruits and citrus, to notes of leather, minerals, smoke, earth, and malt with a kind of cheesy feel to it. I could just smell this beer forever! The flavours are also well balanced, and despite its strength (8% ABV) and complexity, Goudenband is very refreshing. It is neither too full-bodied nor too sweet, and apart from the fine fruit, malt, and hop flavours, you also get a herb-leather-mineral-wood feel. Overall, the fine malt and caramel sweetness of this beer is balanced by a dry finish.

The question is, when do you drink it? Some people like to pair it with light foods, almost treating it like a dry white wine. Others treat it as a party beer, rather like Champagne. I tried it with a chocolate dessert, and it was delicious. Whatever you choose to drink it with, make sure you try it!

LIEFMANS GOUDENBAND

SPECIAL PACKAGE
Liefmans is world famous for its tradition of using corks and wrapping each beer bottle in elegant, decorated paper.

DE DOLLE OERBIER

C **COLOUR** Very dark brown, with a slightly hazy texture.

A **AROMA** Very sweet and fruity, with citrus and smoky notes.

T **TASTE** Quite acidic; red fruits, especially cherries; dry and refreshing finish.

This fine traditional beer is a Scottish-style brown ale, which is strong at 7.5% ABV, and brown with a big, frothy head. Oerbier has a sweet, fruity aroma, with hints of sharper citrus and smoke present in the mix. The flavours have an excellent balance, and although the alcohol is noticeable in a whisky-like feel, it never swamps the flavours. The overall experience is very refreshing, with cherry and apple lighting the way, followed by a smoky malt sweetness and a dry, bitter-chocolate finish.

DE DOLLE OERBIER

HAACHT GILDENBIER

C **COLOUR** Deep chestnut brown, with a full rich head.

A **AROMA** Fresh and bright, with yeast and citrus.

T **TASTE** Quite soft, smooth; sweetish malt and chocolate feel; fruity notes.

If you like brown ale, then you must try this interesting alternative. Gildenbier (guild beer) is a special style of brown ale, traditionally made very sweet and strong, although the modern versions are a little less sweet. It is a dark brown, clear beer, with quite fresh and lively aromas with a hint of citrus sharpness. It is reasonably strong at 6.5% to 7% ABV, but the flavours are well integrated. The sweetness dominates, but the malt is balanced by a woody, tangy, and hoppy dryness.

CANTILLON KRIEK-LAMBIC

C **COLOUR** Deep burgundy red, with a bubbly pink head.

A **AROMA** Very bright and fruity, mainly cherry and almond.

T **TASTE** Light and pleasantly sour; cherry, raspberry; very dry finish.

Kriek is probably the most successful of the lambic beer styles. The dryness and fruitiness of the cherry seem to blend perfectly with the lambic beer base, giving an overall refreshing dryness. Cantillon Kriek-Lambic is one of the driest, if not the driest, in the world. It is dark red, bright, and fruity, with a hint of almond from the cherry stones. The body is light, with the fruit ever-present in an overall dry and refreshing feel. It is a fun beer to drink at any time.

CANTILLON VIGNERONNE

C **COLOUR** Light clear gold, with a short-lived bubbly head.

A **AROMA** Quite vinous and grapy, with a cider-apple and earthy feel.

T **TASTE** Light and dry, with Muscat grapes and notes of wood and nuts.

This beer is blended with white Muscat grapes from Italy. The grapes are added to 18-month-old lambic beer, and the mix is left to mature for six months before it is blended with a younger, year-old beer. It is bottled for release as a Gueuze – a mixture of young and old lambic beers. The result is a lovely golden beer, with the typical lambic aromas of fruit and damp earth. The flavour is dominated by the grapes, but it is also spicy, lemony, and refreshing.

CANTILLON VIGNERONNE

CULTURE AND TRADITION

CHERRY BEERS Fruit beers are very popular in Belgium's cafés, and this style is becoming increasingly popular in many other countries. One of the most popular is Kriekbier (kriek is Flemish for cherry). Unpitted cherries are added to a beer base and allowed to ferment; once the fruit has broken down, the almond flavours of the stone also flavour the beer. The Liefmans brewery, which also makes Goudenband (see opposite), is well known for its Kriek beers, brewed using Danish as well as Belgian cherries. This distinctive beer, which is sold wrapped in light cherry-red paper, has a great balance of fruity aromas, brandy flavours, and a dry finish.

CANTILLON ST LAMVINUS

C **COLOUR** Dark red, with a frothy and bubbly white head.

A **AROMA** Quite yeasty, with dry wine and an earthy feel.

T **TASTE** Light and refreshing, with fruity sweetness and a pleasantly sour finish.

Is it a beer or a wine? The name combines the words lambic, referring to the type of beer, and *vinus*, the Latin for wine.

The Cantillon Brewery is situated in the heart of Brussels, and was established by the van Roy family in 1900. At the heart of Brussels lambic beer brewing, the brewery doubles as a museum.

Lambic beer is a unique style originating in the Senne Valley, not far from Brussels, using a system of spontaneous fermentation from local yeasts, plus the addition of a small amount of wheat.

The young beer is stored in wooden casks for about three years, and the resulting tart, sour, and flat brew is used as the basis of blends with other beers and fruit additives.

St Lamvinus is a two-year-old beer, fermented in oak casks along with red wine grapes – Merlot and Cabernet Franc – from France, and siphoned directly into 750ml Champagne bottles. It is a dark red colour with a bubbly head, which soon vanishes. The aromas are quite fresh and lively, with an earthy, yeasty feel, typical of the style. The flavours are outstanding, a great combination of fresh, red-fruit sweetness and mild bitterness. The grapes are present, and the body is light and refreshing, with a pleasantly sour finish. It is moderately strong, at 6% ABV, and well balanced in every way.

To me this is neither wine nor beer, but a perfect blend of both.

CANTILLON ST LAMVINUS

DREI FONTEINEN KRIEK

C COLOUR Blood-red, with some orange highlights.

A AROMA Cherries dominate, with hints of strawberry and dry nutty notes.

T TASTE Dry and acidic; cherry, plum, herbs; refreshing finish.

Drei Fonteinen is best known for its lambics, and this Kriek is one of the best. It is blood-red, with little or no head, and has a fruity aroma, with cherry set against a dry feel of nuts, earth, vanilla, and wood. The beer is fairly strong at 5% ABV, and the body quite light, but the flavours are massive. Herbs, dry, acidic cherry, plum, and even strawberry really hit you, and the finish is pleasantly sour and refreshing.

BELLE-VUE KRIEK

C COLOUR Medium red, with a creamy-pink head.

A AROMA The cherry dominates, with vinous and almond notes.

T TASTE Dry and creamy; cherry, nuts, and wood; fresh finish.

The Belle-Vue brewery is situated on the outskirts of Brussels, not far from the town of Lambeek, the likely origin of the word lambic, so it is well placed for making excellent Kriek beer. In fact, Belle-Vue is the largest brewer of lambics in Belgium, with 10,000 wooden casks filled with the brew happily bubbling away.

Belle-Vue Kriek is aimed at a wider market than some of the specialist – and expensive – brands, and is therefore a little sweeter than most, and not quite so

BELLE-VUE KRIEK

complex. Although fruit beers look as if they will be sweet, they are basically dry, and some of them are bone dry. To appeal to a broader and younger range of drinkers, the brewers at Belle-Vue have softened this dryness, and as a result these beers are much more popular.

This beer is dark cherry red, with a hint of brown, and a pink, frothy head. The aromas are basically of sweet cherry, with some hints of wine, and almond from the cherry stones. This beer may be a little sweeter than some, but the taste is a lot drier than cherryade! The cherry fruit is dominant, of course, but there is also a woody, almond note to the flavour, which gives you a refreshing finish.

Belle-Vue Kriek is not a super-strong beer, at 5.2% ABV, and the texture is creamy and very drinkable. It makes a lovely drink to sip in the early evening.

KASTEEL BIER BRUIN

C COLOUR Deep ruby- or chocolate-brown, with a small, light-tan head.

A AROMA Sweet malt, rum, raisins, and caramel, with sweet spice.

T TASTE Very rich, fruity, and porty, with lots of caramel, chocolate, and spice.

This would be called "Castle Ale" in English, and in bilingual Belgium it is also known as Bière du Château. The château in question is at Ingelmunster, in West Flanders, and is used to store the beer for up to three months after brewing. This beer is special, and beautifully balanced. It is really strong at 11% ABV, but keeps its aromas and flavours in check, giving a lovely smooth and warming feeling, like a fruit cake mixed with port.

KASTEEL BIER
BRUIN

ST FEUILLIEN CUVÉE DE NOËL

C COLOUR Dark copper; cloudy, with a medium head.

A AROMA Quite sweet and fruity, with notes of herbs.

T TASTE Moderate body, with a malty and fruity sweetness; fresh citrus finish.

This Belgian Christmas ale is brewed by the Friart Brewery, situated in Hainaut, in the west of the country. This old-established brewery brews mainly abbey-style ales, under the St Feuillien brand name. Cuvée de Noël is, of course, its Christmas ale.

You will find this a very strong beer at 9% ABV, easily enough to send you to sleep after your Christmas dinner. This is a warming beer, and the alcohol is not quite overcome by the flavours. It is quite lively, with fruity and herbal aromas, and the flavours are also quite sweet, but with a tangy orange citrus finish. A good, hefty Belgian winter ale, and one to collapse with!

BUSH DE NOËL

C COLOUR Deep orange, with a short-lived frothy head.

A AROMA Sweet malt and caramel, and hints of sweet spice.

T TASTE Smooth, full, lively, and sweet; marzipan and nuts; warming finish.

The strongest beer in Belgium? This beer is made by Dubuisson, which adopted the English brand name Bush in the 1930s to promote an English-style ale. It is marketed in the US as Scaldis to avoid confusion with the giant Anheuser-Busch. Noël is really a Christmas version of Bush's 12% ABV barley wine, and is made to the same powerful strength. This is a well balanced, warming brew, with attractive aromas and lively, spicy, nutty flavours. I love it after dinner on a winter evening.

BUSH DE NOËL

'T SMISJE HONINGBIER

C COLOUR Medium amber, with a thick, white, foamy head.

A AROMA Honey is dominant, along with yeast and sweet caramel.

T TASTE Fairly dry and fruity; smooth body; lively citrus and hop finish.

The De Regenboog (rainbow) micro-brewery near Bruges uses the trademark 't Smisje (the little smith) to show its craft approach to brewing. The brewery specializes in making beers with unusual ingredients; in this case honey, apparently collected from their own hives. The texture of the Honingbier is smooth and attractive, and it is fairly strong at 6% ABV. It is also not too sweet, and the honey blends well with notes of orange at the finish.

ELLEZELLOISE HERCULE

C COLOUR Very dark black, with a thick, creamy head.

A AROMA Dark malty, with black fruits, coffee, and leather.

T TASTE Quite light-bodied, with roasted malt and a sweet feel, but a dry finish.

This Belgian micro-brewery was established in 1993 in the village of Ellezelles, to the west of Brussels. This is its version of an English stout. Hercule is very black, and very strong at 9% ABV. The aromas are also dark, with rich malts, black fruits, and notes of leather and coffee. As you would expect, the roasted malt is also dominant in the flavour, which is mildly sweet, but it has bitter chocolate and a dry, cigar-box finish. The overall feeling is smooth, and the strong alcohol is not quite buried by the flavours. This makes a fine change from the regular English and Irish styles, and it is very welcome.

USA

American breweries love to experiment with new styles, adding new ingredients, developing new processes, or reviving long-lost methods from the distant past. Sometimes they work brilliantly; other times the jury is still out – but they are always worth a try.

ALASKAN SMOKED PORTER

C COLOUR Dark black and opaque, with a rich creamy head.

A AROMA Quite distinctive, with earth and a smoky bacon feel.

T TASTE Full-bodied and oily; sweet malt and bitter hops, all wrapped in smoke.

The Alaskan Brewing Company, in the town of Juneau, is Alaska's oldest brewery; it was only established in 1986, however, by former mining engineer Geoff Larson and his wife Marcy. They have built an impressive reputation with their Amber Ale, an Altbier, which has become a great favourite in the region and won several awards. They also produce a fine Pale Ale and Summer Ale.

This micro-brewery has also branched out into producing Smoked Porter, produced at a moderately strong 6% ABV, but made using the traditional methods of smoked beer. This tradition is usually associated with the German town of Bamberg, in Franconia. The basic principle is that the malt used for making the beer is first smoked over beechwood, which gives the final product a slightly smoky taste.

Alaskan Smoked Porter has been a great success, winning a string of awards. It is smoked over alder rather than beech, and is very dark and brooding, with a small head. The aromas are like smoked meat, with the malt also present. The beer has a very strong burnt wood taste, with bitter chocolate and roasted malt balanced with a very long, dry, hoppy, and smoky finish.

It is fair to say that if you don't like smoked beer or smoked foods, then you probably will not like the Alaskan Smoked Porter. If you do, on the other hand, you will love this beer with food cooked on a barbecue, or any type of smoked food. Why not give this unusual beer a go?

ALASKAN SMOKED PORTER

SENSE OF PLACE *The malt used in Alaskan Smoked Porter is prepared in the same smokery as the local smoked salmon.*

DOGFISH HEAD RAISON D'ÊTRE

C COLOUR Deep mahogany, with highlights of red.

A AROMA Rich, with chocolate, rum, raisins, and sweet malt.

T TASTE Quite sweet, with raisins, molasses, fruit cake, and dark malt.

The Dogfish Head Craft Brewery was established in 1995, initially as a brewpub. They follow the principle of making beers with all kinds of different ingredients, so long as they are natural and "come from the earth and the oven". Organic and natural ingredients include different hops and malts, peat-smoked malt, maple syrup, vanilla, juniper, and brown sugar. Since its establishment, Dogfish Head has made a series of unusual and highly successful beers, beginning with its first hit, Immort Ale, which is brewed with peat-smoked barley, and has vanilla, maple, and much else added.

Raison d'Être is Dogfish Head's version of a Belgian-style old brown ale, made in the manner of Gouden Carolus (*see p466*) and similar rich, sweet beers. Like them, it is very strong, in this case 8% ABV, and has had some success, being voted American beer of the year in January 2000 by Malt Advocate Magazine.

The beer is an impressive mahogany brown, and is slightly cloudy, with rich and complex aromas of sweet malt, molasses, and dark fruit, along with fruit cake. The texture is not too overwhelming, and the strong alcohol is kept under control. The overall feel is like a Madeira wine, with the tell-tale burnt sweetness.

This is the type of beer to sip in a small snifter after dinner, or to drink with quite rich foods, such as game or strong cheese. If you are already a fan of Belgian ales, then Raison d'Être makes a great alternative.

DOGFISH HEAD
RAISON D'ÊTRE

DOGFISH HEAD FESTINA LENTE

C COLOUR Medium apricot, with little or no head.

A AROMA Pungent fruit, with apricot and apple to the fore.

T TASTE Sweet peach at first, with apple and grapes; drier finish.

Dogfish Head produce a range of occasional, special beers in addition to its regular range, including the lambic ale Festina Lente. This beer is produced by both yeast and bacterial fermentation, followed by an ageing process on oak chips and peaches, which gives it a unique, fruity flavour.

The result is a beer with an attractive peach colour and no fizz or head, but with exciting aromas of fruit, nuts, and earth. The initial sweetness of the peaches is overtaken by a much more

FOOD MATCH

BLUE CHEESE Dogfish Head beers are made with the seriousness of wine, and designed to go with food. Raison d'Être and the 90 Minute IPA are both delicious with blue cheeses, such as Stilton or Roquefort.

interesting and citrusy set of flavours, with grapes, apples, and grassy hops. This is quite a strong lambic beer, at 7% ABV, and the body is full and satisfying. You need to take this beer slowly, as it is very full and fruity. If you like lambic beers, then this unusual American version is well worth a try.

DOGFISH HEAD 90 MINUTE IPA

C COLOUR Cloudy orange-brown, with a white head.

A AROMA Hops to the fore, with citrus, yeast, and pine.

T TASTE Smooth and warming, with sweet malt; grapefruit citrus finish.

Dogfish Head brews a range of IPAs including 60 Minute IPA and 90 Minute IPA. The 90 Minute brew has a very attractive aroma, with noticeable pine and citrus, along with grassy hops. It is a very warming beer, and extremely powerful at 9% ABV, but it has just the right amount of bitterness, and is balanced with distinctive flavours of grapefruit, sweet malt, and raisins. I particularly recommend trying 90 Minute IPA with pork chops on a cold winter evening – an excellent beer!

DOGFISH HEAD
90 MINUTE IPA

DOGFISH HEAD WORLDWIDE STOUT

C COLOUR Dark black and deeply opaque, with very little head.

A AROMA Elegant and distinctive, with roasted malts, dark fruits, and port.

T TASTE Extremely rich, with dark roasted malt, rum, and dark fruits.

WorldWide Stout is billed as the world's strongest dark beer, and, at 18% ABV, it might well be. It is best to treat this beer like port, and to drink it in a small snifter, perhaps with a rich dessert. You might expect such a powerful beer to be out of balance, with the alcohol wiping the flavours and the subtlety away. But no, the elegant smoothness, rich fruit, vanilla, and tobacco flavours are all there, and so long as you sip this very slowly, it is a completely satisfying and rich, porty beer.

ROGUE IMPERIAL PALE ALE

C COLOUR Attractive honey brown; fairly cloudy, with a thick foamy head.

A AROMA Floral and very hoppy, with citrus, pine, and resin.

T TASTE Pleasantly bitter, with hops and grapefruit and a lemony finish.

Rogue Ales of Newport, Oregon, is known for its wide range of fine and unusual beers. Imperial Pale Ale (also called I²PA) is billed as "above and beyond an India Pale Ale – not for the faint of heart".

It is a really special and – at 9.2% ABV – really strong beer. It is unfiltered and aged for nine months before it leaves the brewery. This is an outstanding "double" IPA, with a lovely honey-brown colour and

ROGUE IMPERIAL PALE ALE

a full, thick head that stays for quite a while before breaking into lace. As the beer is conditioned in the bottle, it carries sediment, and you should pour it with care if you want a clear beer.

The aromas and the taste are dominated by the hops, and the malt is hardly to be found. Although the beer is strong, the body is medium, and the overall feel is very refreshing. The citrus fruits in the flavours are really stimulating, taking you out on a lemony finish. Watch out for this strong beer – you will want to go back for more than one! Although this is a great beer to drink on its own, I actually prefer to pair it with a fine steak, especially my simple favourite – steak frites – a beer and food combination that, to me, works perfectly.

SAMUEL ADAMS TRIPLE BOCK

C COLOUR Deep opaque brown-black, with no head.

A AROMA Rich malt; Madeira-like, with caramel, molasses, honey, and chocolate.

T TASTE Prunes, raisins, and maple syrup; heavy body; long bittersweet finish.

Brewed with sparkling-wine yeast from California, and aged in American whiskey casks before release, this is a very rich – and very expensive – brew, to be treated essentially as a port or a barley wine. It looks like a deep, dark port, and is very strong – 17.5% ABV! This is a beer you either love or hate. You might try this with a rich dessert, or possibly a very rich paté or terrine.

HEAVYWEIGHT TWO DRUIDS GRUIT ALE

C COLOUR Light translucent orange, with a very small head.

A AROMA Quite pungent and perfumed, with herbal and floral scents.

T TASTE Fairly sweet, with flowers and herbs, licuorice, and a sweet finish.

According to the brewery, one of their colleagues travelled back to meet his ancestors in 15th century Britain and discovered the secrets of medieval brewing! The result is a fairly strong beer that includes herbs such as yarrow, sweet gale, and wild rosemary, along with some spices, based on a medieval formula. This unusual beer is not too dissimilar to cold herbal tea.

HEAVYWEIGHT TWO DRUIDS GRUIT ALE

HAIR OF THE DOG ADAM

C COLOUR Deep brown-black, with dark red highlights.

A AROMA Dark malts and roasted barley, with resin and hops.

T TASTE Dry; hops, smoke, chocolate, coffee, aniseed, and a warm finish.

This "hearty old world ale", as it says on the label, is based on a Dortmund-style German dark beer, itself originally called Adambier. It is bottle-conditioned, and each batch is numbered and aged for two years before it is released. At 10% ABV it is strong, but the alcohol never dominates. This beer is very dark, with a fine, bubbly, long-lasting head, and well-balanced flavours. Too strong to be anything but a sipping beer, this makes a wonderful nightcap, and is one of my favourites.

HAIR OF THE DOG ADAM

MAGIC HAT #9

C COLOUR Attractive, dark orange-gold, with a small head.

A AROMA Dominated by apricot, with a malty sweetness.

T TASTE Light-bodied, with apricot to the fore, some caramel, and a sweet finish.

Magic Hat of Burlington, Vermont, makes some rather unusual but very successful beers, such as Blind Faith IPA. One of the best of its range, #9 is described as "a not-quite pale ale". The "not-quite" is due to the addition of apricots. The aromas and flavours of #9 are dominated by the apricots, with to me not quite enough dryness and citrus balance. The malt and fruit combine well, with some hints of caramel. This is a refreshing alternative summer beer, but is not easy to find outside the region.

CONCORD RAPSCALLION

C COLOUR Deep gold, through to darker orange and dark ruby-red.

A AROMA Rich, spicy malt with orange citrus, pine, and dark fruits.

T TASTE Quite hoppy, with lemon citrus and an attractive bitterness.

Concord Brewers was established in 1993, with a style based on old Belgian ales. All the beers are named Rapscallion. Rapscallion Premier is a golden ale, and the company's flagship brew. It is quite strong at 6.7% ABV, and is fresh, with hops and citrus fruit to the fore. The rich and orange-coloured Blessing is stronger at 8% ABV, and is very hoppy, with aromas of grass and pine, a thick texture, and a dry finish. The third beer, Creation, is darker still, and is ruby red and stronger at 9% ABV. This is similar to a Belgian Rodenbach, with rich chocolate, plum, and sherry aromas, and a rich winey feel to the taste.

JAPAN

The Japanese are experts at adapting and refining products from other cultures, and often improve on the original. Many Japanese specialist beers originated in European styles, but are now made with assurance and skill in Japan.

SAPPORO BLACK BEER

C COLOUR Dark reddy-brown with orange tinges, and a light-tan head.

A AROMA Dark fruit, nuts, and chocolate, with notes of fig.

T TASTE Creamy and full-flavoured, with figs, roasted malt, chocolate, and nuts.

The Sapporo Brewery was founded in 1876, and is the oldest brewery in Japan to have been in continuous operation. Its Black Beer is made from a range of malts, including chocolate malt, and also includes rice. This is an unusual and very full-flavoured beer, and is moderately strong at 5% ABV.

MOKU MOKU SMOKED ALE

C COLOUR Dark reddy-brown, with a fluffy dark-cream head.

A AROMA Rich and peaty, with smoke and wood.

T TASTE Full-bodied, with a slightly oily texture and woody smoke flavours.

Moku Moku is a rural micro-brewery in Nishiyubune, east of Kyoto, and is based around a farming co-operative that concentrates on making country beers. The brewery's unusual name is taken from the Japanese phrase *Moku Moku*, which describes a type of smoke screen used by Ninja warriors.

Moku Moku Smoked Ale looks just like its name – the colour is a smoky, dense, dark brown, and the beer is topped with a fluffy, dark-cream or light-tan head. The aromas display one of the key ingredients in the beer – peated malt from Scotland. When you sip this beer, you get the slight sensation of an Islay whisky, overlain with the stronger, smoky, woody aromas.

The Moku Moku brewery also makes an amber ale and a German-style Weizen, as well as a fine range of food products such as smoked ham and sausage – the perfect accompaniments to the beer! This is a dry, satisfying, and well-balanced beer, and is definitely worth a try if you want something different and unusual.

MOKU MOKU SMOKED ALE

GERMANY

The classic German specialist beer is smoked ale, which originated in the southern part of the country. Other special beers are made using a variety of methods, including freezing – an unusual technique that produces a powerful, syrupy beer known as Eisbock.

SCHLENKERLA RAUCHBIER

C COLOUR Very dark copper, with a foamy, tan head.

A AROMA Very distinctive, dominated by smoke, rather like smoked meat.

T TASTE Quite light-bodied, with smoky meat or fish and dry hop flavours.

The home of smoked beer is Bamberg, in Franconia, the northern region of Bavaria. The tradition was established long ago, when all malt was smoked over wood fires; the most famous producer, now usually called Heller-Trum, was making this style of beer and selling it at the Schlenkerla tavern as early as 1678.

The name of the brewer and the beer often cause confusion. The family who ran the Schlenkerla tavern was called Heller, but for over a century it has been owned and run by the Trum family. So, the brewery is known variously as Heller, Heller-Trum, and Schlenkerla.

Today's smoked beer is made in a modern brewing facility, but its barley malt is still smoked over huge beechwood fires. Schlenkerla Rauchbier is made in a number of variations (including the the strong Urbock), but

generally, Rauchbier is very dark, ranging from copper through to jet black, and the head is usually a tan colour. The aromas are dominated by the smoke, and are suggestive of smoked bacon, or even kippers. The first experience of these aromas may be slightly shocking, but you get used to the bouquet over time!

The flavour of the beer is also very smoky, but the malt and hops come through, bringing some caramel and pleasant woody flavours. The body is fairly light and smooth, and the beer is moderately strong at 4.8% ABV, with stronger versions, such as the Urbock, going up to 6.5% ABV.

To me, Schlenkerla Rauchbier is an excellent drink – though it is an acquired taste, which I am very glad has survived over the centuries. It is a good idea to match it with suitable food, rather than drinking it on its own. It goes very well with mussels, sausages like polony, bockwurst, and bierwurst, or anything from the barbecue.

SCHLENKERLA RAUCHBIER

SMOKE SIGNAL
Rauchbier (smoked beer) is a traditional Franconian style, established long ago, when all malt was smoked over wood fires.

RAUCHENFELSER STEINBIER

C **COLOUR** Deep, attractive orange, with a small, white head that quickly disappears.

A **AROMA** Elegant and balanced, with smoked fish or meat.

T **TASTE** Light-bodied and bright, with wood and a smoky sweetness.

Hot rocks! In the days before copper brewing vessels, rocks were heated and lowered into the wooden brewing vats to start the process, and this "stone beer" revives the technique. The brew caramelizes on the stones, which then influences the flavour, producing an attractive smoky and sweet sensation. The flavour is really subtle and works well with smoked foods, bacon, or the barbecue.

EKU 28

C **COLOUR** Attractive russet orange, with a big bubbly head.

A **AROMA** Very full, with red fruits, grapes, yeast, and cheesy malt.

T **TASTE** Syrupy texture, but fresh and lively with orange and sweet malt.

EKU 28

This powerful Doppelbock, at 11% ABV, is made using a similar method to Eiswein – using freezing to concentrate the strength of the beer – thus the style is termed Eisbock. This beer has a beautiful colour, intense aromas, and a syrupy, concentrated body. The flavours are very firm, with well-balanced sweet malt and citrus. This is a heavy brew, with a very warm finish because of the alcohol – similar to a malt whisky. Treat it like a spirit, but it also goes well with steak, rich paté, and even pickles.

FRANCE

There is a tradition in Alsace of using malt and peat to make a dark beer. The result invites comparison with whisky.

FISCHER ADELSCOTT

C **COLOUR** Bright yellow gold, with a thin small head.

A **AROMA** Lightly peaty, with a toasty malt sweetness, leather, and smoke.

T **TASTE** Medium body and not fizzy; peat, malt, and very little hop bitterness.

Peaty Scottish malt makes this "beer with whisky", according to the hype. The aromas are quite malty and peaty, but the flavour is more a sweet malt with smoky notes rather than the rich depth of a whisky. So to me, this is really a smoked malt beer; it is a fairly good example and is excellent with barbecued meat.

FINLAND

Finland has a long tradition of brewing, going back to the Middle Ages. Unusual ingredients are available in the very cold climate, and where hops are unknown, something else has to be used. People can be very creative when it comes to making beer!

LAMMIN SAHTI

C **COLOUR** Cloudy dark copper red, with little or no head.

A **AROMA** Very yeasty, with vegetables, pine, and juniper.

T **TASTE** Full-bodied and smooth, with juniper, banana, grain, and citrus.

Sahti was the traditional beer of Scandinavia – and particularly Finland – until Carlsberg pioneered lager production in the region in the mid-19th century. Juniper twigs are used in the process, giving a fruity, banana-like flavour. The beer is also typically very full-bodied and strong in alcohol. Lammin is the best-known commercial Sahti producer, although it is really a micro-brewery.

This reddish-brown Sahti is quite strong at 7.5% ABV, and has a very gentle fizz. The juniper is prominent both in the complex aromas and in the flavours, where it is joined by citrus, yeast, and a peppery finish.

Lammin Sahti has been described as "Europe's only primitive beer". Some people might not like it, but give it a try! I can recommend it with hard Finnish rye bread and Dutch Edam or Gouda cheese; even better, with some beetroot.

FINLANDIA SAHTI

C **COLOUR** Cloudy dark orange-amber, with little or no head.

A **AROMA** Yeasty, with pine and juniper to the fore.

T **TASTE** Typical flavours of banana, cloves, and juniper; very full-bodied.

Finlandia Sahti is made mainly from rye, and is produced at Matku. The colour is similar to apple juice and there is hardly any head, just a very delicate natural fizz in the beer. Both the flavour and the body of the beer are very full, with a tangy, sweet, fruity, and caramel feel balanced by herbs, apple, and citrus. The overall experience is bittersweet, and the strong alcohol, at 8% ABV, also gives a warming element to the finish.

FINLANDIA SAHTI

If you are not used to traditional beers of this type, try Finlandia Sahti as an adventure!

UK

In northern regions of the UK, such as Scotland, hops were not always readily available, so local people used other ingredients, including heather and herbs, in their beer. They also drew on their whisky-making traditions to make unusual and sometimes excellent beers.

ANCIENT ALE *Heather Ale Fraoch is based on an ancient Pict recipe that uses heather rather than hops.*

HEATHER ALE FRAOCH

C **COLOUR** Light and bright amber, with a moderate head.

A **AROMA** Very floral scented, with peat and herbs.

T **TASTE** Malty honey sweetness, with spicy herbs and a dry vinous finish.

The ancient people of Scotland – the Picts – used heather to make their beer, a brew known in Gaelic as *fraoch*, pronounced "frook". However, when Scotland became part of the United Kingdom at the beginning of the 18th century, the English parliament passed an act that prevented brewers from using anything other than hops and malt to make beer. The recipe for heather ale became only a verbal tradition passed down through generations.

In 1986, a Gaelic-speaking woman translated the recipe for *leann fraoch* (heather ale) for Bruce Williams, who ran a homebrew shop in Glasgow. In 1993, after several years perfecting the recipe, the beer was launched. Made from heather, malt, sweet gale, ginger root, and some hops, it was a sensation. Because of demand, production was moved to the larger facility of Maclay of Alloa.

Fraoch's aromas are very floral and sweet, reflecting the herbs as much as the heather itself. There is a honey or perfumed sweetness, which some people do not like, somewhat reminiscent of the perfume added to bathroom products. The taste is quite well balanced, as the small amounts of hops and herbs counter the sweetness with a bitterness; the beer is not too cloying and the finish is quite earthy. This is an unusual beer worth looking up.

HEATHER ALE ALBA

C COLOUR Dark orange-amber, with little or no head.

A AROMA Delicate and fruity, with flowers, strawberry, herbs, and pine.

T TASTE Quite sweet malt, with mint, raspberry, flowers – and pine.

Alba – the Gaelic word for Scotland – is one of a series of traditional beers based on ancient Scottish recipes made by Heather Ale Ltd. This company celebrates the Scots' resistance to English attempts to control beer production in Scotland in the 18th century *(see opposite)* by using ingredients other than hops to make their beers.

Heather Ale Alba is an interesting beer brewed from young shoots of Scots pine and spruce. Ale made from these unusual ingredients was first introduced to Scotland by the Vikings, and remained a very popular drink in the Scottish Highlands until as recently as the end of the 19th century. Heather Ale Alba is produced by boiling pine shoots with malted barley; shoots of spruce are added at the last minute for a brief infusion before the mixture is fermented.

This is quite a strong beer at 7.5% ABV. The aromas are scented and fruity, and not too dominated by the pine. The taste is also fruity and fairly refreshing, and has a good balance between sweet malt and pine. I think this is an interesting and very good novelty beer, with a refreshing feel overall.

Other beers in the Heather Ale range include Grozet, which is brewed with Scottish gooseberries; Kelpie, a seaweed ale; the elderberry-infused Ebulum; and of course the famous Fraoch heather ale *(see opposite)*.

HEATHER ALE ALBA

TRAQUAIR JACOBITE

C COLOUR Very dark purple-brown, with a fine foamy head.

A AROMA Rich, with spice, especially coriander, and sweet malt.

T TASTE Light-bodied; full rooty flavours of malt, wood, spice; fruity finish.

This beer is made at the castle of Traquair, in the Scottish Borders. Bonnie Prince Charlie was said to have stayed at the castle during the rebellion of 1745, and the beer was launched in 1995, the 250th anniversary of this event.

Jacobite is a Scottish ale, but spiced with coriander. It has a good balance between the sweet malts, oaky wood, and spice. It is very strong at 8% ABV, and the alcohol comes through at the end for a warming, fruity finish – a little too sweet for some people, but this is one of my favourites for a nightcap.

ST PETER'S KING CNUT

C COLOUR Very dark brown-black, with a dark copper, short-lived head.

A AROMA Quite distinctive, with malt, herbs, and spices, especially juniper.

T TASTE Rich and intense; juniper and orange; caramel and malt sweetness.

Named after the Anglo-Danish King Cnut (or Canute), this herbal ale is based on a recipe from the first millennium AD. and features roast barley, juniper berries, orange and lemon peel, spices, and stinging nettles. No hops are used. St Peter's make the beer once a year and it is usually on sale in June.

Although the beer is only 5% ABV, the flavours are so intense that it can only be sipped, and the citrus, herbs, and spices are all quite powerful. This is an interesting diversion, but I think you would need to be a committed fan to keep drinking this one.

INNIS & GUNN OAK AGED BEER

C COLOUR Attractive light golden amber with orange tinges.

A AROMA Pungent and fruity, with peat, wine, and citrus.

T TASTE Rich orange and vanilla, well-balanced by earthy hops.

Innis & Gunn Oak Aged Beer has created quite a storm. Among other awards, it won the medal as Supreme Champion 2004 in the International Beer Competition. It is the creation of a group of beer enthusiasts in Edinburgh, Scotland, who have great experience in the mainstream brewing industry, but who wanted to make something special. The beer is brewed under contract by the well-reputed Caledonian Brewery, famous for its "shilling" ales – especially

INNIS AND GUNN OAK AGED BEER

Caledonian 80/- and the organic Golden Promise *(see p417)* – and where Dougal Sharp of Innis & Gunn was formerly the head brewer. The beer recipe is, however, Innis & Gunn's alone, and they oversee the brewing process and control the quality.

A "Holy Grail" for some producers is to make the perfect combination of malted beer and malt whisky. The Alsatian beer Fischer Adelscott *(see p481)* claims to have the characters of both but is generally held to have fallen short of the ideal blend. The excitement created by Innis & Gunn Oak Aged Beer is that it is much nearer to a harmonious marriage.

The beer is aged for 30 days in oak barrels and matured for a further 47 days in a "marrying tun" before bottling. This process, totalling 77 days, is well in excess of the brewing industry's norms, but the

PERFECT MARRIAGE The great achievement of Innis & Gunn with their Oak Aged Beer has been to infuse it with some of the genuine characters of malt whisky. They have successfully managed to age Edinburgh ale in American white-oak barrels from Kentucky, home of Bourbon. These are traditionally used in the Scotch whisky industry for aging malts. The beer is stored in a bonded warehouse on Scotland's West Coast while it matures. Once they have been used for the beer, the barrels are sold on to a distillery.

brewers at Innes & Gunn believe this extended period is necessary to create the subtle oak characters and light, natural carbonation.

The colour is a cross between a bitter and a golden ale, with a short-lived head. The aromas are pungent and fruity, with peat and a hint of oaky wine. The beer is lively on the tongue, with a honey sweetness, and very refreshing, with a great, oaky,

malt finish. It is strong at 6.6% ABV, and quite warming.

You could say it is a bit like beer mixed with white wine and whisky, with the best characters of all three to the fore. Look out also for special limited-edition releases, such as the 2004 vintage version, which was bottled at a rather lighter 5.3% ABV. This is really one to watch – and to try without delay!

CIDER

THE GOLDEN APPLE

Cider's reputation is of an old-fashioned drink from rural England or France. However, attitudes are changing. Huge improvements in quality and variety are reviving the fortunes of this great drink.

BLOSSOMING INDUSTRY
The climate and soil of western and southwestern England proved irresistible for the cider apple, and by the 18th century, these areas brimmed with orchards.

The history of cider goes back perhaps as far as ancient Egypt – apple trees are known to have grown along the Nile delta. However, what we know for certain is that the English had a well-established cider culture by the time the Romans arrived in the first century AD. From early Medieval times, the French and English began to plant orchards for the cultivation of cider apples, first in the monasteries and later on private farms. Cider soon became the most popular alcoholic drink in both France and Britain. It was only natural that the English would carry their knowledge of cider-making to the New World, introducing it to America. By the 18th century, cider was well-loved throughout the US, thanks largely to a Massachusetts man known as Johnny Appleseed, who travelled the country planting apple orchards.

However, in the 20th century, cider hit hard times. In both Europe and the US, German brewers began to mass-produce Pilsner lager, and its popularity soon overtook that of cider. Furthermore, the US endured Prohibition – a period between 1920 and 1933 when alcohol consumption was banned throughout the country. Now, though, cider is back – and rightly so. This is a wonderful, refreshing drink that deserves a place behind every good bar.

VARIETY AND STYLE

Cider (known as "hard cider" in the US to distinguish it from apple juice) is not normally made from eating apples, but from dedicated cider varieties, which tend to be too sour to eat. There are four categories of cider apple: sweet, bittersweet, sharp, and bittersharp. Bittersweet apples have low acidity but high tannin; bittersharp are high in both acidity and tannin – and it is these categories that make most cider. The tannins are important because they take the edge off the sweetness and add complexity. The precise character of a cider will depend upon both the varieties of apple in the blend and the production methods. Broadly, however, there are two basic styles of cider: English (including ciders from North America and Australia), and French (including ciders from Spain). Both styles tend to be dry, and English is usually stronger.

SCRUMPY *True scrumpy is traditional, unfiltered English cider, which is flat, rich, and often cloudy. However, some of the commercial brands, such as Scrumpy Jack, are fizzy, light, and fresh – rather more like regular cider.*

" There are few things in life more enjoyable than a cool, crisp glass of cider on a warm afternoon in early summer. "

CHOOSING THE FRUIT *Some ciders are made using up to 20 different varieties of cider apple in the blend. Others use only one, and are often marketed by vintage.*

APPLE HARVEST *Before the age of mechanical harvesting, producers hand-picked the ripe cider apples from the trees. Often a picker would stand below the tree and shake its branches with a long pole (known as a "hooklug") to bring down the apples.*

> " With so many exciting new variations, cider has revived itself as a drink for a new generation. "

CIDER APPLES *There are hundreds of varieties of cider apple – one count gives 365 different varieties in the UK alone. All are known to be high in cancer-fighting antioxidants. Modern cider-making techniques aim to preserve these health benefits in the cider itself.*

English ciders themselves fall into one of two main camps. The traditional English cider is flat and dark and known as "scrumpy". With recent interest in organic beer and other natural products, this type of cider is gaining in popularity, not just in the UK, but all over the world. Most mass-market English cider is highly filtered and carbonated, making it clear and sparkling. This style of cider is light and fresh.

English ciders are often compared to beers, but French cider-makers model their products on sparkling wine, and the results can be extremely complex and well balanced. The best type of French cider is known as cidre bouche, and often comes in Champagne-style bottles, with a cork.

Although they fall into the category of English ciders, those from the US usually tend to be sweeter, and from Canada, less sweet than ciders from the UK. Some of the specialist producers in both these countries make some really excellent dry ciders.

MAKING CIDER

Once the apples are harvested and selected, they are chopped (or "scratted") in a mill and then pressed into a pulp using a cider press. The pulp is mixed with yeast and sugar, and also additional malic acid, a naturally occurring acid in apple juice, which the producer uses to adjust the levels of sweetness and acidity in the pulp. The yeast and sugar set off fermentation, which can take several months. Toward the end of fermentation, the cider is "racked" – it is filtered from one vat into another to leave behind any remaining yeast cells and other unwanted sediment. If the cider is to become fizzy, producers add carbon dioxide into the new vat and this, and the final fermentation of any remaining sugars, creates the bubbles. Most cider is then matured to gain its full flavour and character.

Once the cider has matured, is it blended. French cider-makers, in particular, carefully control the blend of flavours in their product, aiming to get just the right balance of sweetness, bitterness, and acidity in the cider. The results are often quite stunning, with some of the best brands even being comparable to Champagne. After blending, most modern ciders are filtered to make them crystal clear and then pasteurized to stabilize them and preserve their quality for export around the world.

COLOUR, AROMA, AND TASTE

One of the most attractive features of cider is its colour, which is usually light- to medium-gold, often with fine bubbles. However, some styles are darker,

FROM FRUIT TO GLASS *At the Matthew Clark cider mill, Shepton Mallet, Somerset, harvested apples begin their transformation into cider. From here they will enter the "scratter", which chops up the apples ready for pressing.*

MODERN CIDER PRODUCTION *Traditional cider-makers use oak vats for fermenting the apple juice, but most modern producers use gigantic versions made out of stainless steel. In Herefordshire, England, these vats form part of the skyline!*

some lighter. Of course, scrumpy tends to be an amber colour, with little or no fizz at all.

Expect a clean, fruity nose in a good cider. Apples will dominate. Occasionally the apple aromas will be fresh and crisp, but most often ripe, or even baked. Many ciders are also earthy, with a farmyard aroma, and the sweeter versions give aromas of honey and sweet herbs.

The flavours of good cider will find a balance that offers the sweetness of the fruit, but is also refreshingly dry and pleasantly acidic. There should be no burn at the back of your throat.

BUYING CIDER

Most branded cider, such as Strongbow, Woodpecker, and Blackthorn, is widely available on draught and in bottles. But if you are on holiday in a cider-producing region, such as Herefordshire in the UK, Normandy or Brittany in France, or Sonoma (California) in the US, look out for local producers, who often

have really wonderful, high-quality products on offer. Most cider is not meant for ageing, although if sold as a "vintage", it may be suitable for laying down.

SERVING SUGGESTIONS

The differences between English and French ciders are reflected in the way we drink them. In the UK, cider tends to be a pub drink, often used for session drinking, and often with little more than snacks or light meals to accompany it. Serve English cider chilled in a medium-sized beer glass. In France, cider is considered an apéritif, or a serious accompaniment to a meal, especially pancakes. Again, it is served chilled, but this time in a wine or Champagne glass.

For food-matching, a good rule of thumb is anything that works with white wine will work well with cider, especially if the cider is dry. Good examples are cheese, seafood, and most white meats, particularly pork with an apple-and-cider sauce.

POURING AND TASTING *Tilt a clean glass so that it is almost horizontal, but straighten as you pour, and finish with the glass vertical, to bring out any head. The cider should be ice cold and leave a slight bitterness in the finish.*

UK

The UK is the home of commercial cider and is by far the largest producer in the world. Most cider made in this country is for the mass market, but there are also a growing number of specialist producers, making a fabulous range of styles.

WELL-AGED *All Stowford Press ciders are matured in oak vats for six months to ensure that they develop full, fruity characters.*

STOWFORD PRESS

C COLOUR Light gold through to a darker amber for the vintage ciders.

A AROMA Bright and appealing with a good balance of fruit and wood.

T TASTE Well-balanced through the range from dry to sweet.

Stowford Press Cider is one of the flagship brands of Westons, a medium-sized cider producer based in Much Marcle, Herefordshire, in central England. Henry Weston founded the company in 1880, recognizing that his local soil and climate provided the perfect growing conditions for the hard, bitter apples that make such good cider. The company prides itself on its traditional methods – for example, the large apple trees in its orchards do not lend themselves to mechanical harvesting, and so the company still "shakes" the trees to bring down the apples, which are then picked up from the ground and collected by hand.

Stowford Press Cider is light, refreshing, and fruity, with a moderate alcohol content of 4.5% ABV. It is available in dry, medium-dry, and sweet versions. A lighter version (at 3.8% ABV) is medium-sweet.

At 6% ABV, Stowford Press Export Cider is a premium strong cider and is produced using the best cider apples. The drink is matured in old oak vats and then cold filtered, making it crisp, clean, and refreshing. Westons also produces Stowford low-calorie and low-alcohol ciders.

From other parts of the excellent Westons' range, try Henry Weston's Vintage Reserve. At 8.2% ABV this cider is really strong, but it is a wonderful brew made from carefully selected apples and specially blended. The result is smoky and woody with a fine citrus feel. Considering its strength, this cider is dangerously easy to drink!

STOWFORD
PRESS

OLD ROSIE

- **C COLOUR** Cloudy, dark gold to amber, with very little head.
- **A AROMA** Extremely mature apple, with plenty of smoke and oak.
- **T TASTE** Fairly sweet apple at the start, with vanilla and wood; warm, dry finish.

Award-winning Old Rosie is a scrumpy (a natural, flat cider; see p492) with a good reputation. It is produced by Westons, which also make Stowford Press (see opposite). Westons named Old Rosie after the 1920s Aveling Porter steam engine on display at the brewery. Although it is 7.3% ABV, Old Rosie is extremely drinkable, thanks to Westons' commitment to producing well-made cider. It has a distinctive aroma of oxidized apple and a medium palate, which begins with sweetness and ends with smoky wood.

ASPALL

- **C COLOUR** Golden and fizzy, presented in a distinctive green bottle.
- **A AROMA** Obvious apple and yeast, enhanced by high carbonation.
- **T TASTE** Full and quite dry; medium-dry finish with a hint of white wine.

Aspall Suffolk Cyder – spelled with a "y" – is a French-style cider, made in Suffolk, eastern England. The Aspall company was founded in 1728 by Clement Chevallier, originally from Jersey.

The final product is made from a blend of three different base ciders. Each is produced using local apples and fermented using traditional techniques. The range includes Dry, Medium, and Organic. My favourite is the Dry. It is quite strong (6.8% ABV), and has an excellent balance of fruit, spices, yeast, and alcohol.

ASPALL

SHEPPY

- **C COLOUR** Golden and bright, and fizzy for most brands in the range.
- **A AROMA** Fresh apple and yeast, enhanced by carbonation.
- **T TASTE** Bright, well-made; apple, pear; medium-dry finish; hint of white wine.

The Sheppy family has been making cider in Taunton, Devon – in the heartland of English cider-making – since the 1800s. Its range of draught and bottled ciders includes some, such as Kingston Black, Dabinett, and Tremlett's Bitter, that are named after the single variety of apple from which they are made. One of the best is Dabinett, a medium cider, which is quite strong at 7.2% ABV, and is rich, sweet, and full bodied. For something drier and more crisp try the blended Sheppy's Goldfinch.

SHEPPY

KNIGHT'S

- **C COLOUR** Light, bright gold, with very little head.
- **A AROMA** Fresh apple, with hints of vanilla and spice.
- **T TASTE** Full-bodied and medium-dry, with a good balance of apple and spice.

Established in 1973 in Malvern, Worcestershire, award-winning Knight's is a relatively young cider company that prides itself on its use of traditional cider-making methods, as well as the fact that all the cider is produced using apples from its own orchards.

The company's two main products are Malvern Gold, which is full-bodied and quite rich, but without losing its freshness; and the drier and slightly less full-bodied Malvern Oak. Both are traditional still ciders, without any fizz.

THATCHER'S

- **C COLOUR** Dark yellow and quite cloudy, with very little head.
- **A AROMA** Oxidized apple with cinnamon, ginger, and a hint of smoke.
- **T TASTE** Sweetish apple; hints of pear at the start; sweet spice.

Thatcher's Cider Company is based in Somerset, southern England. William Thatcher first started making cider for his farm workers in the early 1900s, and the company continues to produce some cider from his original recipes. The company is proud to base its ciders on only English varieties of apple, selecting the variety specifically for a particular style of cider.

The company's range includes Cox's, which is light, sweet, and juicy; Katy, which is dry and strong; and Premium Press, a cold-filtered, premium cider.

THATCHER'S

SUMMER'S

- **C COLOUR** Fine, dark gold, with a light level of carbonation.
- **A AROMA** Mature apple and a distinct, farmyard earthiness.
- **T TASTE** Medium-dry, with strong tannins and an attractive citrus acidity.

Summer's cider is made in Gloucestershire, southwest England. Founded in 1982, this small producer with a great reputation uses fruit from its own orchards and employs traditional cider-making methods. The results are ciders that offer a fine complexity, with an excellent balance of sweetness and citrus, and a finish rather like a good stilton cheese – earthy and lingering. The company's flagship brand is the award-winning Summer's Medium Cider, which in 2003 won the Campaign for Real Ale's prestigious Gold cider award.

LAND AND PRODUCTION

ENGLISH CIDER THROUGH TIME
Cider-making in England probably began with the Romans, although cider production was not recorded until after the Norman Conquest in 1066. The cool, wet English climate proved perfect for apple orchards, and by the 14th century the English were producing cider in most of the southern half of the country. By the 1700s cider-drinking was a normal part of English life, and even used as a form of payment for farm hands. Now England produces more cider than any other country in the world.

STRONGBOW

C COLOUR Light to golden straw, with only a slight head.

A AROMA Clean and fresh, with a scent of lively apple and yeast.

T TASTE Well-balanced with a medium-dry apple flavour and controlled tannins.

Sold across Europe, the US, Australasia, and the Far East, Strongbow is the flagship brand of Bulmer's, the world's largest cider-maker and part of the drinks group Scottish and Newcastle.

Bulmer's was founded in Hereford, central England, in 1887 by Percy Bulmer, the son of a local clergyman. Percy made the first barrels of his famous cider using apples from the orchard at his father's rectory and an old stone press on the farm next door. Joined in the venture by his brother

STRONGBOW

Fred, Percy eventually built the company's first cider mill just outside Hereford, and in 1911 secured a royal warrant as cider-maker to the British royal family.

Bulmer's ciders – all of which are blended – are now manufactured in a huge, modern facility not far from the original cider mill. The company produces 65 per cent of the 500 million litres (130 million gallons) of cider sold annually in the UK, as well as the lion's share of the country's cider exports. Bulmer's is a big player in the world of cider!

One of Bulmer's most important brands, Strong-bow's name is taken from a nickname for the Norman knight Richard de Clare, later the Earl of Pembroke, who showed great prowess with the longbow. The distinctive "thudding arrow" has been a feature of the brand's television advertising since the 1960s.

MARKET SHARE *Strongbow accounts for more than a quarter of all cider sold in the UK.*

Fresh, lively, and popular, Strongbow has a medium-dry, slightly bitter taste, with a fresh apple and lightly fizzy character. It is moderately strong at 5.3% ABV.

Once it is in the bottle, cider does not continue to mature, so enjoy your bottle of Strongbow as soon as possible. Serve it chilled as a delicious accompaniment to pork, especially some lean chops, and also to spicy, Asian cuisine. Strongbow is also good with general "pub" food, such as a traditional ploughman's lunch with thick cuts of fresh bread, pickle, and a good, strong cheddar cheese – particularly delicious on a hot summer's day.

WOODPECKER

C COLOUR Light golden amber in colour, with a bright, fizzy appearance.

A AROMA Clean and fresh, with distinct apple, yeast, and vanilla aromas.

T TASTE Fairly sweet or medium-sweet apple; a light body.

Woodpecker cider is made by Bulmer's *(see above)* as the sweeter alternative to Strongbow. A medium-sweet style of cider with a low to moderate alcohol content (around 3.5% ABV – although the precise level will vary from country to country), Woodpecker is a traditional cider, which over the years has become one of the mainstays in Bulmer's portfolio. It is widely available in British pubs and stores, and also in stores around the world.

Woodpecker is bright, golden amber in colour with

a frothy head, which soon disappears. Its aromas are fresh and attractive, dominated by apple, but with a slight scent of sweetness and yeast. Its light body makes it infinitely approachable and easy to drink. To me it slightly reminiscent of a semi-sweet white wine, with more fizz – and you can easily drink too much of it! The finish is quite fresh, and slightly drier than the main body of the drink, and there is no heaviness. This is a cider without pretensions – a fun drink to enjoy on sunny afternoons with friends.

Interestingly, Woodpecker is a particular favourite of the Chinese, who generally seem to prefer it to the drier Strongbow. As a result of this popularity, Bulmer's have now established a production plant in China to create a sweet, strong version of Woodpecker called *zhuo-mu-niao* (meaning "pecks-wood-bird"), using Chinese apples.

WOODPECKER

SCRUMPY JACK

C COLOUR Light golden yellow, with no froth or head.

A AROMA Distinctive; sweet and sour apple; cloves and yeast.

T TASTE Medium-dry; fruity apple; fairly full-bodied; dry finish.

Scrumpy is the English word for unfiltered, flat, and cloudy cider, traditionally brewed on a farm – and consumed there. Since the 1980s there has been a surge in interest in "natural" or organic cider, and scrumpy has gained in popularity.

However, Scrumpy Jack is made industrially by Bulmer's *(see above)*, and is widely distributed, so strictly it is not a true scrumpy. It is mildly fizzy, crisp, and fruity, and at 6% ABV, quite strong. Scrumpy Jack is a good, reliable cider; serve it well-chilled with seafood.

SCRUMPY JACK

GAYMER'S

C COLOUR Light yellow-gold, with a hint of green and a small, short-lived head.

A AROMA Apples to the fore, with a little yeast and sulphur.

T TASTE Medium-dry; quite firmly fizzy; dryness lasts through to the finish.

First produced in 1770, Gaymer's is the "traditional" brand produced by Matthew Clark in Bristol, southwest England. Made using only English apples, Gaymer's is soft and light (5.3% ABV), with hints of musty yeast and a touch of sourness in the aroma, and with dry, even tart apples in the flavour. The finish is dry and refreshing.

This is one of my fav-ourite mass-market ciders, and is at its best in the sunshine with a simple potato salad, a plate of cold meats, or any snack.

BLACKTHORN

C COLOUR Attractive gold, with very little head.

A AROMA Sweet; dominated by apple, but also yeast.

T TASTE Medium-dry, with a hint of sweetness, and a tingling finish.

Blackthorn cider is the flagship brand of the Matthew Clark drinks' company. Matthew Clark itself is part of the US Constellation Brands Group, and the second-biggest cider producer in the world. As well as ciders such as Blackthorn, Gaymer's, Diamond White, and K, Matthew Clark owns other well-known drinks brands including Babycham and Stone's Ginger Wine.

Blackthorn is marketed around the world as the main rival to Strongbow (owned by Bulmer's, based in Herefordshire). However,

it is not as dry as its rival, nor quite as full-flavoured – although at between 5.5% and 6% ABV for bottled and canned versions, and 6% ABV on draught, it is no weakling!

This cider is a fine, golden yellow colour, with only a slightly fizzy body and almost no head. It has an array of pleasant aromas, including apple (of course) and a sweet yeastiness, with a hint of alcohol. The flavours are quite well balanced, with the apple giving way to a sweet honey flavour, which itself, after a time, melts into flavours of white wine. Blackthorn has an interesting finish, which has a slight, dry fizziness that leaves you feeling altogether satisfied.

Overall this is a good-value cider, and is easy to find. I think it is best suited for drinking on its own, or with bar snacks, rather than an as a serious accompaniment to food.

BLACKTHORN

K CIDER

C COLOUR Dark gold to light amber with very little head.

A AROMA Fresh and not-so-fresh apple, with some yeast and spirit.

T TASTE Bright, fresh, and somewhere between sweet and dry.

Another cider produced by drinks company Matthew Clark, and aimed at the younger market, K is a strong cider, ranging in strength from 6% to nearly 9% ABV. Most K cider has a dark gold colour and a moderate fizz. There is a good balance of aromas and the flavours are not overly sweet; nor are they too dry, making K easy to drink and rarely disliked. This cider is like a medium-dry white wine, with a little extra caramel and some fizz. Try it in a bar with friends while nibbling a few snacks.

K CIDER

DIAMOND WHITE

C COLOUR Extremely pale yellow (not quite white) with very little head.

A AROMA Oxidized apple, and yeast, with alcohol spirit also present.

T TASTE Quite strong and sharp, with an extremely dry finish.

Diamond White is also produced by Matthew Clark, but it is not quite as sophisticated as other products in the company's range, lying at the budget end of the market.

Diamond White's main feature is its strength (7.5% ABV), and its overall character is fizzy, with a dry taste and finish, and aromas and flavours that are influenced by the alcohol.

This is not a cider with depth and complexity, but if you are looking for something to party with, then it can hit the spot!

FRANCE

France is deservedly famous for its wine, but in Normandy and Brittany, cider is king. The French style of *cidre* is comparable with white wine, and is made with great care, including ageing, vintage registration, and presentation in Champagne-style bottles.

ETIENNE DUPONT

C COLOUR Orangey yellow, presented in a classic Champagne-style bottle.

A AROMA Fresh and fruity, with apple, citrus, earth, and leather.

T TASTE Refreshing and intense apple flavours; long, citrusy finish.

Established in 1837, this is one of the best-known French cider producers, and is still controlled by its founding family. Dupont is based in the Pays d'Auge, in the heart of the Normandy apple region.

The company's core product is Cidre Bouche Brut Etienne Dupont, a dry, aged cider, that at 5.5% ABV is fairly strong. More than one third

of the blend for this cider comes from bitter-sweet and bitter apples, with the remaining part consisting of mostly sweet and some acidic apples. This cider is produced as a vintage, and each vintage will be slightly different, just as with a wine, but generally the result has an excellent balance of sweetness and acidity, especially in the finish. Of course apples dominate the flavour, but there is also a slightly mineral feel to the taste.

Serve this cider chilled as an apéritif, or to accompany poultry, or any dishes with cheese – especially Camembert.

ERIC BORDELET

ERIC BORDELET

C COLOUR Deep gold, rather like apple juice, with a thin, frothy head.

A AROMA Attractive; fresh apple, with earth and herbs.

T TASTE Excellent balance; fruit, pepper, and camomile; perfect, dry finish.

In 1992 Eric Bordelet took over his family's cider-making estate and orchards aiming to raise the profile of cider and make it comparable with fine wine. To achieve this, Bordelet carefully controls the balance of apple varieties (sweet, bitter, and sour) that go into his blends, and uses organic farming and production methods.

The flagship is Sydre Argelette, which is sweet, dry, and herbaceous, with a distinct mineral quality. It retains its wonderful balance and fizziness right through to the finish, and is a must-try!

BELLOT

C COLOUR Rich, attractive gold, with a short-lived, frothy head.

A AROMA Fresh; musty apple with a hint of yeast and baked bread.

T TASTE Gently fizzy; dry and well-balanced; not unlike Champagne.

I think Bellot produces one of the best ciders you could ever taste! Henri Bellot began making cider in the town of Chaorce, northern France, not far from Champagne, in the 1960s. Fresh, fruity, and clean, the traditional cider (Cidre Bouche, which comes in both sweet and dry styles) is made using 30 different varieties of apple and is like a slightly fizzy white wine. It has a lovely, gold colour, and aromas similar to an apple-like Champagne, with just a hint of freshly baked bread. The taste is crisp and refreshingly dry, with a touch of cinnamon at the finish.

I love this cider to accompany roasted duck and turnips, served with a cider sauce – delicious!

CHRISTIAN DROUHIN

C COLOUR Rusty orange through to gold; slightly cloudy.

A AROMA Distinctive, with apple, wood, and hints of minerals and earth.

T TASTE Essentially a dry, apple taste, with hints of smoke and meat; dry finish.

Christian Drouhin began making cider in 1962 and today is one of the best producers of traditionally made French cider in Normandy, northern France. The company uses only top-quality apples, and the ciders are unfiltered and unpasteurized, and moderately strong at 4.5% ABV.

The company's two main products are the dry and elegant Cour de Lion Pays d'Auge and the floral and fruity Bouche Brut de Lauriston. Both of these ciders find the best of the sweet flavours of the apples, and balance them with a dry, fresh taste at the finish.

KERISAC

C COLOUR Light gold, and packaged in a Champagne-style bottle.

A AROMA Extremely attractive; fresh apple, herbs, and earth.

T TASTE Medium-dry and extremely well-balanced with a dry finish.

The Guillet family in Guenrouet, Brittany, northern France, have been making Kerisac according to a traditional family recipe for more than 70 years.

Very popular in France, Kerisac is an award-winning, dry cider, which is only moderately strong at around 4% ABV. Breton ciders tend to be less dry than ciders from Normandy, and so, although dry, this cider is extremely easy to drink. It retains its fizziness throughout, and is an excellent partner for fish, seafood, and white meats.

KERISAC

MANOIR DU PARC

C COLOUR Light, golden yellow; extremely bright and fizzy.

A AROMA Delicate; grapefruit, citrus, and earth.

T TASTE Essentially dry, but well-balanced with an earthy, mineral feel.

Located in St Joseph, Normandy, Manoir du Parc produces bright, golden ciders that are unusual because their aromas and tastes are not openly dominated by apple – they also have a dry, delicate, citrus feel. They come in Champagne-style bottles with wired corks – essential as Manoir du Parc ciders are particularly fizzy!

The excellent Cidre Brut is my favourite. Quite strong for a French cider (5% ABV), it is not very sweet, and both looks and tastes like a dry Champagne. It is great with light meats and fish.

VAL DE RANCE

C COLOUR Very pale gold and only moderately fizzy.

A AROMA Apple, honey, and earth in a swirl of attractive aromas.

T TASTE Less sweet than the aromas suggest, with a medium-dry finish.

Val de Rance ciders are produced in the valley of the Rance River, in northern Brittany, not far from St Malo. These ciders are slightly sweeter than similar ciders from Normandy, which is typical of the Breton style, and they are also reasonably powerful, varying between 5% and 6% ABV.

Overall Val de Rance ciders are extremely well made and are wonderfully approachable and easy to drink. They are not classics, but they represent excellent value for money – sometimes costing half as much as quality brands. If you are not familiar with French-style cider, then these are the ciders to try first.

USA

The term "hard cider" is used by US producers to distinguish the alcoholic beverage from nonalcoholic apple juice. Since the mid-1990s, Americans have begun to appreciate good-quality, imported hard ciders, and now US producers are marketing their own.

HORNSBY'S

C COLOUR Very pale gold through to dark brown, with a frothy head.

A AROMA Quite aromatic; sweetly perfumed apple, and vanilla.

T TASTE Fairly sweet and smooth, with a medium-dry finish.

Winemakers Ernest and Julio Gallo launched Hornsby's hard cider in 1995. There are now a number of ciders in the range, but the best-known is Pubdrafts Draft Cider. This is light gold, and quite sweet (sweeter than most English ciders), but, at 6% ABV, it is fairly strong.

Apples and sugar-candy dominate the aromas and taste of this cider, giving something similar to a semi-sweet white wine.

Amber Hard Cider and Hard Apple Cider are also popular Hornsby's brands, as is the slightly more acidic Dark 'n' Dry, which is dark brown, and has a frothy head.

Although these ciders are more like "fruit beer" when compared with French wine-style ciders, the Hornsby's brands are well made and reliable, and offer a good introduction to mainstream US ciders for those who have not yet tried them.

HORNSBY'S

ACE

C COLOUR Very pale yellow – almost clear – with no head.

A AROMA Dry apple, with just a slight hint of citrus.

T TASTE Very dry and light-bodied, similar to a dry, white wine.

Ace's owner Jeffrey House sees his company at the heart of the "hard cider" revival in the US. Made in north-central California, using apples from Sonoma County (an area of California that is famous for its wine), Ace ciders are light, refreshing, and aimed at a younger market.

The flagship brand is Ace Apple, which is made entirely from local fruit, and is moderately strong at 5% ABV. This cider is bright, fresh, and easy to drink. Ace Apple Honey, fermented from a mixture of apple juice and honey, is sweeter.

ACE

WOODCHUCK

C COLOUR Dark, golden amber; darker than most mainstream brands.

A AROMA Dominant fresh apple, with a hint of sweet spice.

T TASTE Sweeter than ciders from Europe, but smooth and well-balanced.

Made by the Green Mountain Cider Company in Vermont, northeastern US, Woodchuck ciders are among the country's most popular. Green Mountain produces several brands of cider, including Granny Smith and a perry (fermented pear juice).

The flagship cider – and the original Woodchuck cider – is Woodchuck Amber. Made using a blend of apple juices, and fermented using Champagne yeast, this cider is fairly strong (5% ABV), and is lively and fresh, with flavours of sweet apple balanced with white wine and spice.

FARNUM HILL

C COLOUR Clear, light gold, with a frothy, short-lived head.

A AROMA Fresh and floral, with apple and blossom.

T TASTE Fine and fresh, comparable to Champagne, with a dry finish.

Farnum Hill Ciders are produced in New Hampshire, in the eastern US. The Farnum Hill company makes cider according to traditional methods, including using only specially selected cider apples. The company believes that just as winemakers use specific grape varieties cultivated specially for making wine, so cider-makers should use the appropriate varieties of apple for making cider.

The company's range is broad for a small producer. My favourite is the Extra-Dry, which is fresh and citrusy. Other good examples from the range are the well-balanced, crisp, and refreshing Semi-Dry, which has just a slight touch of sweetness at the finish; and Kingston Black – a single-variety cider (from the Kingston Black apple), which displays its vintage on the label and is marketed in numbered bottles. At between 6% and 7.5% ABV, all of the ciders in the Farnum Hill range are strong.

The company claims to make the best ciders in the US, and to me, with products of such high quality and distinctive character, this is no unfounded boast. I would even go so far as to say that these ciders are comparable to the best from France. With such high praise from a Frenchman, Farnum Hill ciders must be worth a try!

VINTAGE APPLES
Farnum Hill makes its ciders using apple varieties originally from the UK, France, and the US, all planted in its own New Hampshire orchards.

SPIRE MOUNTAIN

C COLOUR Light, golden yellow, with little fizz and no head.

A AROMA Fresh apple, with a honey and bubble-gum sweetness.

T TASTE An excellent balance between sweetness and acidity.

Spire Mountain Cider is the US's longest, continuously made and marketed cider brand, and the best-selling craft cider (a locally produced cider) in the Pacific Northwest. The company was established in the 1980s and is now owned by the US's Fish Brewing Company.

There are four styles of Spire Mountain Cider: Hard Apple, Hard Pear, Dark and Dry Apple, and Spiced Apple. The best-selling is Hard Apple – this is well made and well balanced, with a light body and a refreshing feel. Although it is not overly complex, it is a reliable and drinkable regional cider and is well worth a try.

VERMONT

C COLOUR Clear and bright; light straw gold, with a small head.

A AROMA An attractive balance of fresh apple, earth, and spice.

T TASTE Dry and well-balanced, with a fresh, tangy feel and a medium finish.

Vermont Hard Cyders are made by Flag Hill Farm in rural Vermont, in the northeast US. These ciders show how a small, local producer can use traditional cider-making methods and high quality control to create a genuinely great product for a regional market.

The Sparkling Hard Cyder – close to the traditional English style of cider – is lively, fresh, and drinkable, and at 9.5% ABV, extremely strong! The slightly weaker (8.5% ABV) Still Hard Cyder is subtle, complex, and satisfying, with easily distinguishable flavours. These are both excellent ciders from a fine local producer.

AUSTRALIA

Australian cider is in the English, rather than French, style, and production is dominated by the giant beer-maker Carlton United Breweries. It is made in the temperate southeast of the country, which is home to a growing number of small, traditional producers.

BLACK RAT

C COLOUR Medium gold; quite lively and fizzy, presented in modern packaging.

A AROMA Distinctive; tangy and sweet, with spicy apple.

T TASTE Full-bodied, with a good balance between dryness and sweetness.

Established in 1998, the Black Rat Cider Company is based in Eastwood, near Adelaide, South Australia. Aimed at the younger market, Black Rat comes in three flavours – apple, blackcurrant, and lemon. All these versions are fizzy, not too dry or strong, and quite full bodied, with a good balance and a slightly sweet finish.

MERCURY

C COLOUR Dark gold; quite fizzy with a medium head.

A AROMA Apple, honey, and hints of sweet spice.

T TASTE Apple to the fore, with dominant sweetness.

The Mercury Cider company was established more than 100 years ago in Tasmania, Australia, and is now part of Carlton United Breweries, owners of Foster's Lager. The main product is Genuine Draught, produced for the pub market. Medium in strength (5% to 6% ABV), this is a well-made, good-value cider.

GLOSSARY

ABV Alcohol By Volume. The alcoholic strength of a drink measured as a percentage of the whole volume.

ACIDITY The "spine" of a wine; this is essential for the ageing of wine, and for a refreshing flavour.

AGAVE Mexican succulent plant, whose hearts form the basis of tequila and mezcal.

AGEING The process of maturing wine or spirits, usually in wooden containers, especially oak. This develops character and complexity.

ALAMBIC Old term for a pot still, especially as used in making Cognac.

ALCOHOL The by-product of the fermentation of sugars by yeast.

ALTBIER A German beer style with a rich, warm amber colour and a taste of burnt sugar and fruit.

AMERICAN PALE ALE Beer based on the British Pale Ale style but with added hops and alcohol, and a crisper taste.

ANAEROBIC In the absence of oxygen.

AÑEJO Spanish for aged spirit, especially tequila and rum.

ANGELS' SHARE A term used to describe the spirit that evaporates through the wood of barrels containing ageing spirit, especially Cognac.

AOC Appellation d'Origine Contrôlée. The highest classification of French wine, assuring that it has reached a set quality standard *(see also p23)*.

APÉRITIF A drink taken before a meal to stimulate the appetite.

APPELLATION A French geographically designated wine production area; often used more loosely to describe wine from a particular area.

AROMA The perfume or smell of a drink, reflecting its core ingredients. Often used interchangeably with the term bouquet.

AROMATIC A term usually associated with fruity and appealing grape varieties like Riesling, Sauvignon Blanc, and Muscat.

AUSLESE Wine made from grapes left on the vine longer than normal.

AUSTERE Wine in which the fruit is dominated by tannin or acidity. Such wine usually needs time to age and improve.

BALANCE The harmonious relationship between fruit, acidity, tannins, and alcohol, mainly in wine, but important in all drinks.

BAR SPOON Long twist-handled spoon with a flat end; useful for stirring and layering cocktails.

BARLEY WINE A very strong and warming style of beer.

BARRIQUE Small oak cask (France).

BEERENAUSLESE Category of German wine above *Auslese* but below *Trockenbeerenauslese*. The classification is based on the level of residual sugar.

BELGIAN BROWN ALE A very dark, caramelised fruit- and raisin-flavoured style of beer.

BELGIAN STRONG DARK ALE A malty, dark beer, with a smooth, rich texture.

BIÈRE DE GARDE Farmhouse beer of northern France, with fruity malt accents, caramel notes, and spicy hops. Often sold in Champagne-style bottles.

BLANC DE BLANCS A white sparkling wine made entirely from white grapes. Associated with Champagne.

BLANC DE NOIRS A red sparkling wine made entirely from red grapes. Associated with Champagne.

BODEGA Spanish word for cellar or domaine.

BODY The weight of a drink in the mouth, usually related to its fruit and alcohol content.

BOSTON SHAKER Cocktail shaker consisting of a glass and a metal beaker that push together to make a sealed container.

BOTANICALS Herbs, spices, and plants used to flavour spirits, especially gin.

BOTRYTIS CINEREA The fungus that causes the benign disease "noble rot" on grapes. *Botrytis cinerea* is important in the production of sweet wines, such as Sauternes, as it concentrates the sugars in the grapes. Grapes affected by this fungus are referred to as botrytized.

BOUQUET The smell of a wine or other drink, reflecting the ingredients and ageing or maturity.

BOURBON The most important style of American whiskey, made from barley, rye, and corn (maize).

BRANDEWIJN "Burnt wine". Old Dutch name for distilled spirit, and the origin of the word "brandy".

BRANDY A spirit distilled from a base of grape juice; sometimes used more loosely to describe spirits distilled from other fruit bases.

BREATHING Interaction between a drink and the air, leading to the release of aromas.

BRUT French word for "dry", commonly applied to sparkling wines like Champagne.

BUTTERY Pleasant oily, rich, and fat taste usually associated with non-European Chardonnay wines.

CABERNET SAUVIGNON The king of red wine grapes; firm, structured and distinctive. The grape variety of the great Bordeaux, and fine wines from California, Australia and Chile.

CARBONIC MACERATION A technique of fermenting grapes without crushing them, producing deep-coloured and fruity wine; typically used in Beaujolais.

CASK STRENGTH A spirit that has not been diluted from the high alcoholic strength at which it emerges from the maturation process.

CAVA Spanish sparkling wine, made using the same techniques used to produce Champagne (the *méthode traditionnelle*).

CÉPAGE French term, meaning simply "grape variety". As a plural (*cépages*) it refers to the blend of grapes used to produce a particular *cuvée*.

CHANNEL KNIFE Knife designed to easily strip the peel from a lemon, lime, or orange.

CHARDONNAY Grape variety used to make great fruity and off-dry white wines; originally from Burgundy, France, it is now used for wine production in Australia, California, Canada, Chile, New Zealand, and South Africa.

CHARRING Burning the inside of a barrel that is to be used for maturing a spirit; this adds flavour and colour to the spirit, and is particularly used in the production of rum and Bourbon whiskey.

CHÂTEAU Literally French for castle, but used to describe the domaine of origin of some French wines.

CIGAR BOX A descriptive term for the aroma of older wines matured in wood, especially red Bordeaux.

CITRUSY A term to describe the pleasantly acidic and lemony character of a drink.

CLARET English term used to describe red Bordeaux wines. This term is no longer in popular use.

CLOS French term for a small, wall-enclosed vineyard, or a small area within a larger vineyard.

CLOSED Term used to describe the hidden or not-yet-apparent qualities of a wine, which will develop over time.

COFFEY STILL A type of still that allows continuous distillation *(see also pp157–8)*.

COMPLEXITY Term used to describe the many different flavours or aromas found in a high-quality drink. Very desirable.

CORKED WINE Wine that smells mouldy and damp, caused by mould or chemicals in the cork that have tainted the wine.

CÔTE The French term for ridge or slope of one contiguous hillside, the most famous being *Côte d'Or* in Burgundy.

CÔTEAUX French term for non-contiguous slopes and hillsides.

CRIANZA Spanish classification for wine that has spent six months in oak barrels and 18 months in the bottle before release.

CRU French word for "growth", used to define wine quality, as in *grand cru* (the highest) and *premier cru*.

CRU BOURGEOIS A classification that applies only to French wines from the Médoc. It was established in the 1930s to promote the region's lesser-known quality wines, which were not included in the first Bordeaux classification of 1855.

CUVÉE French term, meaning the juice from the wine press. Normally refers to a blend, or special production of a particular wine.

DECANTER Glass container from which drink is served.

DECANTING Separating wine from its natural sediments by pouring into a decanter before serving. Decanting also puts the wine into contact with air, releasing its aromas.

DIGESTIF A drink taken after a meal to settle the stomach and aid digestion.

DISTILLATION Boiling a liquid to produce alcohol vapour, then condensing the liquid alcohol. The basis of spirit and liqueur production.

DO Denominación de Origen. A quality standard for Spanish wine similar to the French classification AOC.

DOC Denominazione di Origine Controllata. With DOCG (Denominazione di Origine Controllata e Garantita), the top classification of Italian wine *(see also p23)*.

DOSAGE The final addition of sugar in the Champagne-making process.

DRAM Originally a Scottish and Irish term for a small glass of spirit, usually whisky.

EAU-DE-VIE "Water of Life". A French term for any spirit distilled from a fruit base.

EISWEIN German term for sweet wine made from grapes harvested when frozen, a process that helps to concentrate the sugars in the grapes. It is called ice wine outside Germany, especially in Canada.

EN PRIMEUR Wine sold by the producer before it has been bottled. Normally the wine is purchased six months after the harvest, for delivery 18 months later.

EURO OR COBBLER SHAKER Metal cocktail shaker consisting of a container and usually a screw cap.

FERMENTATION The process by which sugars are broken down by the action of yeast, forming carbon dioxide and ethyl alcohol.

FINISH The length of time that the flavour of a drink remains on the palate after drinking.

FIRMNESS A measure of the structure and acidity of a drink, as in "firm tannins".

FLOR A scum-like yeast deposit that covers the top of some sherries as they mature, and seals them from the air.

FORTIFICATION Adding spirit, usually brandy, to a wine such as port or sherry, to increase its strength and character.

FRAPPÉ A very cold drink or a liqueur served over crushed ice.

FRIZZANTE Italian expression for a lightly sparkling wine.

FRUIT LAMBIC Belgian beers made by adding fruit during the production process of the beer.

GRAND CRU French term meaning "great growth". This is the top classification of wine quality in Burgundy, but in other regions of France lies just below *premier cru*.

GRASSY A term describing a fresh aroma or flavour; a mixture of new-mown hay, citrus and plants, most often used to describe Sauvignon Blanc wines.

GUEUZE Style of beer originating in Belgium, made by the spontaneous fermentation of wild yeasts. The resulting lambic beer is aged and blended with young beer to produce Gueuze.

HAWTHORN STRAINER Strainer with lugs and a spring around it, enabling it to be attached to the top of a glass. Especially useful in making cocktails.

IPA India Pale Ale. A stronger, hoppier version of Pale Ale; initially a beer designed for export to the British Colonial troops.

JEROBOAM Large bottle size, containing three litres of wine (Bordeaux only), or four of Champagne.

JIGGER Device for measuring the correct amount of a liquid ingredient, especially a cocktail; sometimes designed with a single and double-shot size, like a two-sided eggcup.

KÖLSCH Pale, golden yellow beer from Cologne (Köln); the style is more like an ale than lager, with very complex flavours.

LATE BOTTLED VINTAGE (LBV) Port from a specified vintage that has been matured for between four and six years in wood before bottling.

LEES The remains of grape seeds, yeast, and sediment that settles after the fermentation process of making wine. Also called *lie* in French. In Muscadet, *sur lie* is wine that has deliberately been left in contact with the lees to add character.

LONDON DRY The most important style of gin; clean, fresh, and light.

MACERATION The process of steeping fruits, herbs, and other ingredients in alcohol to extract flavour and colour.

MAGNUM A bottle size containing 1.5 litres of wine.

MALT Grain, usually barley, that has been allowed to germinate; also shorthand for malt whisky.

MASH The mix of raw ingredients used for fermentation.

MERLOT A red grape used to make medium red wines in St-Émilion (France), California, New Zealand, and Australia.

MÉTHODE TRADITIONNELLE Sparkling wines made by the same production process as is used to make Champagne *(see also p129)*.

MEZCAL Spirit made from the agave plant in the Southern Mexican state of Oaxaca. Similar to tequila but smokier and more earthy. Some is made *"con gusano"*– with the worm included in the bottle.

MICROCLIMATE A special and distinct climatic condition within a small area; for example, on a particular part of a hill which faces the sun, or a sheltered spot within a valley.

MOLASSES Substance left behind after the processing of sugar cane. Commonly used as the basis of rum.

MOUTH FEEL Term used to describe the texture of a drink in the mouth.

MUDDLER Cocktail tool rather like a pestle, used for crushing fruit and herbs in the bottom of a glass to release flavour.

MUSCAT Delicate and aromatic white grape variety, the basis of Gewürztraminer in Alsace, Central Europe, and California.

NAVY RUM A dark style of rum originally issued to sailors in the British Royal Navy, where it was traditionally diluted with water to make "grog".

NEBUCHADNEZZAR A bottle size containing 15 litres of wine.

NOBLE ROT A vine disease, caused by the fungus *Botrytis cinerea*, that is important in sweet wine production.

NOSE The aroma of a wine, spirit, or other drink.

OLD ALE Beer that is full of rich malt flavours and usually restrained hop bitterness. Old ales can often be cellared for many years.

OVERPROOF High strength, unaged rum, often white.

OXIDIZED Wine or fruit that has been over-exposed to air.

PALE ALE Often the bottled version of bitter ale, ranging in colour from pale golden yellow to amber, with a good balance between malt and hops.

PEAT Composted and decayed acidic vegetable matter. It is used to fire malt-drying kilns, and imparts a smoky flavour to whisky made from that malt.

PHYLLOXERA A blight that devastated European vineyards in the late 19th century. It is caused by a tiny insect that attacks the vine roots.

PILSNER A classic, bottom-fermented, cold-conditioned lager. It is pale gold in colour, with crisp flowery hop and biscuit flavours. Originally from Pilsen in the Czech Republic, Pilsner is the world's most popular beer style.

PIPE A standard cask measure for port wine (504 litres).

POMACE The remnants of stalks, pips, and crushed berries left after the juice has been pressed from grapes. It is often used to make basic brandies like marc and grappa.

PORTER Traditional London style of dark beer; the predecessor of stout, though not quite so dark or dry.

PREMIER CRU French term meaning "First Growth"; this is the top classification for châteaux or producers in some regions of France; in the Burgundy region, however, it ranks just below *grand cru*.

PROOF American term indicating the alcoholic strength of a spirit; 100-proof is equal to 50% ABV.

QUADRUPEL Rich, warming, and very strong style of Belgian beer.

RANCIO Rich, earthy and highly desirable aroma of dried fruits, chocolate, and spice that appears in very old brandies and some fortified wines, such as Tawny port.

REAMER Device for extracting the juice from citrus fruits by squeezing the flesh inside the fruit.

REHOBOAM A bottle size containing 3.5 litres of wine.

REPOSADO Spanish for "rested". Used to describe a tequila that has been aged for between a few months and one year.

RHUM The name used for AOC rum in the former French islands of Martinique and Guadeloupe. *Rhum agricole* is made from sugar cane, and *rhum industriel* from molasses.

RIESLING Aromatic white grape variety, used to make fruity wines with a mineral character in Germany and central Europe, Alsace in France, and Australia.

SAISON Seasonal ales from Belgium. Usually golden yellow and highly carbonated, with flavours combining fruit and peppery spice; often quite strong.

SALMANAZAR A bottle size containing 9 litres of wine.

SAUVIGNON BLANC White grape used to make intense, complex, and refreshing wines in the Loire in France, New Zealand, Australia, and South Africa.

SCOTCH Whisky made in Scotland; often wrongly used to refer to any whisky.

SEC French wine term meaning dry; *demi-sec* is semi-dry or medium-dry.

SEDIMENT The dead yeast produced during bottle-fermentation of beer or wine; also the tannins and colour pigmentation in very old red wines.

SÉMILLON White grape variety, used to make the sweet wines of Bordeaux, such as Barsac and Sauternes, and also used in aromatic New World wines.

SINGLE MALT Whisky made at a single distillery, and produced only from malted barley, not other grains.

SMOKED BEER A speciality of northern Bavaria based on smoked malts, which give a special smoky flavour.

SOLERA SYSTEM The system used in sherry-making whereby younger wine is gradually blended with older, through a special arrangement of barrels.

SOUR MASH Term used in the manufacture of Bourbon in Kentucky, where soured yeast mash is mixed with other grain, like rye, during fermentation.

STOUT Very dark, heavy and creamy beer; the most famous is the Irish style, epitomized by Guinness, which is very dry.

SYRAH Rich, dark grape variety from the Rhône Valley, making deep, dark, and powerful reds; now important in Australia and California. Also known as Shiraz.

TANNIN A substance contained in the skins of red grapes, which enters the wine during maceration and fermentation, and is a key part of the ageing process. It gives a dry feel in the mouth, rather like green apples.

TERROIR A French word describing the character of any given area in a vineyard, including soil, climate, and aspect. Some include the grower in this evaluation.

TRIPEL Very strong Blonde beers from Belgium, with vibrant fruity flavours, balanced with spicy hops.

TRIPLE SEC Orange-flavoured style of liqueur that is distilled three times during production.

VATTED MALT A malt whisky made from a blend of malts from more than one distillery.

VDQS Vin Délimité de Qualité Supérieure. French wine classification that falls below AOC but above Vin de Pays *(see also p23)*.

VIEUX French term meaning "old", used to describe spirits that have been aged for several years.

VIN DE PAYS French term meaning "country wine"; a classification of French wines that falls between the most basic Vin de Table and the higher quality AOC and VDQS *(see also p96)*.

VIN DE TABLE French term meaning "table wine"; this is the lowest classification of French wine *(see also p96)*.

VINIFICATION The process of turning grape juice into wine.

VINTAGE A wine or spirit from a single year. Also used interchangeably with the word "year" in describing wine.

VS Very Special; the basic grade of Cognac classification.

VSOP Very Special Old Pale. One grade higher than VS in Cognac classification.

WASH Fermented liquid ready for distillation.

WEISSBIER Bavarian speciality beer brewed with at least 50% malted wheat; it is cloudy, because of the yeast and proteins from the wheat, and very refreshing.

WEIZENBOCK / DUNKELWEISSE Darker variations on the Weissbier style. The beers are considerably darker in colour and have added complexity of flavour.

WITBIER Refreshing Belgian beer brewed with around 40% unmalted wheat, and flavoured with coriander and cinnamon.

XO Extra Old; a quality grade applied to aged Cognacs.

YEAST A microscopic fungus, which converts sugar to carbon dioxide and alcohol and is used in the fermentation of wine and beer.

YIELD The total amount of wine produced by a vine or vineyard in a particular vintage.

INDEX

ACKNOWLEDGMENTS

AUTHOR'S ACKNOWLEDGMENTS

Writing this book has been an amazing and rewarding experience, and although all the opinions it contains are my own, I could not have written it without the support of many people, all of whom deserve my sincere thanks and appreciation.

First, of course, thanks to my wonderful and beautiful wife, Amy, for her understanding and to my lovely special children Émilie and George. A very special thank you to Mary and John Fisher, without whose help and support this book would not have been possible. A big merci to my lovely Maman, Brigitte, for all her encouragement through the years and her sacrifices for her sons. A huge thank you to all my Family, in both England and France, especially my brothers Thierry, Fabrice, Laurent, and Ludo, who have been with me all the way.

Also Graeme Souness, the great footballer, manager, wine-lover, and business partner. Thanks Graeme, for your support, faith, and valued friendship over the years. To Robin Hutson, for giving me four great years at the Hotel du Vin; to Nick Jones, Charlie Luxton, and the unit teams at Soho House; to Simon Foderingham at the Oxfords restaurant; to Mike Mason and Andy Gair for the many enjoyable tastings, and to my personal clients and friends, especially Ashley Levett, who have supported me since day one.

To the great team at Cobalt id, especially Marek, Paul, Kati, and Maddy, and to David Lamb, Deirdre Headon, Simon Tuite, and Jo Doran at DK. To my agent, Luigi Bonomi, photographer Ian O'Leary, and the world's greatest beer experts, Michael Jackson and Ian Garrett.

I would also like to thank my teachers, Vincent Courseau and Alain Dussetour; my superb mentors Philippe Bourguignon and Gerard Basset; and Brian Julyan and all my friends and colleagues at the Master Sommeliers' Court.

Thanks to you all. VG.

PUBLISHER'S ACKNOWLEDGMENTS

Cobalt id would like to thank the following for their help with this book: Judy Barratt, Bill Evans, Steve Setford, and Gary Werner for invaluable editorial assistance; Christine Heilman for Americanization; Hilary Bird for indexing; Ane Sesma-Galarraga and Judith Cousins for language services. Our thanks to Ian O'Leary, Laura Forrester, Tim Ridley, and Kerry O'Sullivan at Ian O'Leary Studios; and all at IP Bartenders, Electric House, and Soho House, London, for generous use of their facilities. Our particular gratitude goes to Derek Clark and all the staff at Beers of Europe Ltd, King's Lynn, Norfolk; to Tim Francis and David Attenborough at TheDrinkShop.com Ltd; Magnus Bergquist at drinkalizer.com; and Louise Bull at Berkmann Wine Cellars. Also many thanks to Tim Byne; Stephen Dye and Mike Edwards; Klara and Eric King for technical help; and Sue Metcalfe-Megginson and Richard Dabb at DK.

We gratefully acknowledge the assistance of the following individuals, organizations, and companies, who provided guidance, resources, images, and products without which this book would not have been possible:

THEDRINKSHOP.COM LTD – the UK's foremost online drink store offering a vast choice of wines, beers, spirits and gifts. Visit them at www.thedrinkshop.com

BEERS OF EUROPE – the UK's leading online beer stockist, with more than 1000 different beers from over 50 countries. Visit them at www.beersofeurope.co.uk

42 BELOW vodka & SOUTH gin; Marco Lustenberger at A.Racke GmbH + Co.; Addison Wines; Laura Sperandio at Alivini Company Limited; Allagash Brewing Company; Allez Vins! UK; Allied Domecq Spirits and Wine (UK) Ltd; Allied Domecq Wines, USA; Amathus; Andrew Chapman Fine Wines (www.surf4wines.co.uk); Angostura Ltd; Angove's; Anthony Byrne Fine Wines Ltd; Antigua Distillery Ltd; Araujo Estate Wines; Australian Wineries LLP; Azienda Agricola Fratelli Berlucchi; Bacardi Brown-Forman Brands (BACARDI and the Bat Device are registered trademarks of Bacardi & Company Limited); Bacardi Martini (UK) Ltd; Bardinet Export; Barrels & Bottles; Bass Brewers; Baton Rouge Wines; Louise Bull, Elizabeth Ferguson, and Belinda Stone at Berkmann Wine Cellars Ltd; Berliner Kindl Brauerei; BFG Communications; Bibendum Wine Ltd; Blavod Drinks Ltd; Blue Mountain Winery; María José at Bodegas López de Heredia; Bortársaság; Boutinot Ltd; Boyar International Ltd; Brasserie de Silly; Brauerei Diebels; Brewery Ommegang; Bristol Spirits Limited; Brouwerij 't IJ; Brown Brothers; Buehler Vineyards; C & D Wines Ltd; Cachet Wine; Canadian Iceberg Vodka Corp; Carmel Winery; Cellar Trends Ltd; Chalie, Richards & Co Ltd; Lahcene Boutouba and all at Champagnes & Chateaux Ltd; Charbay Winery & Distillery; Charles Hawkins; Château du Cléray-Sauvion en Eolie; Château du Tariquet; Château La Nerthe; Château Laballe; Château Margaux; Château Moujan; Château Palmer; Jan & Caryl Panman at Château Rives-Blanques; Cisa Asinari dei Marchesi di Grésy; Codorniu UK Ltd; Coe Vintners; College Cellar; Constellation Europe; Coopers Brewery; Coors Brewers; Craft Distillers; Cruzan Ltd; D'Arenberg; Cédric Espitalier Noël at D.A.D. (Didier Absil Développement); Dalmacijav; Decorum Vintners Ltd; Deschutes Brewery; Diageo plc; Distell Group Ltd; Distillerie Stock USA, Ltd; Dogfish Head Brewing; Domaine des Baumard; Domaine Direct; Domaine Laroche; Domaine Zind Humbrecht; DrinkFinder.co.uk (www.drinkfinder.co.uk); Dromana Estate Limited; Durham Brewery; Du Toitskloof Wine Cellar; E. & J. Gallo Winery; Eastwood & Sanders Fine Ales; Teresa at Eaux de Vie Ltd; Eckes & Stock GmbH; Edward Cavendish & Sons Ltd; Emilio Lustau S.A.; Alison Mann at Emma Wellings PR; English Wines Group plc;

Enotria Winecellars Ltd; Eurowines; Farnham Hill Ciders; Finlandia Sahti Ky; Claire Wilson at Fior Brands; Paul Evans at First Drinks Brands Ltd; Folly Wines; Forth Wines Ltd; Fratelli Branca Distillerie SRL; Freixenet (DWS) Ltd; Jill Taylor at Freixenet UK; Fuller, Smith & Turner; G&J Greenall; Marianna Cosmetatos at Gentilini Winery & Vineyards; George Gale and Co.; Georges Barbier; Goedhuis & Co Ltd; Gonzalez Byass UK; Great Western Wine Co Ltd; Gunson Fine Wines Ltd; Hair of the Dog Brewing Company; H & H Bancroft Wines; Hallgarten Wines; Hardy Wine Company; Harrison Vintners; Harviestoun Brewery; Hatch Mansfield Limited; Hayman Barwell Jones Ltd; Heaven Hill Distilleries, Inc.; Howard Ripley Ltd; HwCg Ltd; Innes & Grieve Ltd; Innis & Gunn; Inspirit Brands; Italian Wines Direct Ltd; Jascots Wine Merchants Ltd; Jean-Claude Raspail; Jefferson Hunt Communication Consultants; Jepson Vineyards, Ltd; Jeroboams Group; John E Fells & Sons Ltd; Jose Cuervo International; Julian Baker Fine Wines; Justerini & Brooks Ltd; Kendall-Jackson Vineyard Estates; Keo Ltd; Kiona Vineyards and Winery; KWV International; LacrimaVini; Laird & Company; Lane & Tatham Wine Brokers; Lay & Wheeler Group; Le Bon Vin Ltd; Lea and Sandeman Co. Ltd; Léopold Gourmel; Les Caves de Pyrene; Liberty Wines; Lombard Brands Ltd; Mahrs Bräu; Maison des Futailles; Malcolm Cowen Ltd; Marblehead Brand Development; Marie Brizard & Roger International; Matthew Clark plc; Lindsay Brown and Susy Atkinson at Maxxium UK Ltd; McDowell Valley Vineyards; McWilliam's Wines Pty Ltd; Meantime Brewing Co.; Mentzendorff & Co Ltd; Meridian Wines Ltd; Michael Hall Wines; Milroy's of Soho; Mistral Wines; Moorhouse's Brewery; Morgenrot-Chevaliers PLC; Tom Smith at Morris & Verdin; Myliko Wines; nbpr; Negociants UK Ltd; O W Loeb & Co Ltd; Sarah Winthrop at Oakes Bacot PR; Paragon Vintners Ltd; Perez Barquero, S.A.; Pernod Ricard UK; Peter Lehmann Wines (Europe) Ltd; Pisco Capel; Pol Roger; Porterhouse Brewery; Portsmouth Brewery; Portugalia Wines; Potocki Spirits (Europe) Ltd; Potocki Spirits America; Potocki Wódka; Quinta da Aveleda; Quinta do Portal; Randalls Vautier Ltd; R&R Teamwork; Richards Walford & Co Ltd; Bridget Bottomley at Richmond Towers; Richmond Wine Agencies; Rogue Brewery; Royal Tokaji Wine Co Ltd; Saintsbury; Sazerac Company, Inc.; Scottish & Newcastle; Selected Estates of Europe; Sierra Nevada Brewing Company; Simon Maye & Fils; Simonsig Estates; Smuttynose Brewing Co.; Southcorp Wines Europe Ltd; St George Spirits; St. Peter's Brewery; Stevens Garnier & FSA; Stieglbrauerei zu Salzburg; Karis Hunt at Storm Communications; T & W Wines Ltd; Tanners Wines Ltd; The California Cider Company; The Drambuie Liqueur Co Ltd; The Drinks Group Ltd; The Vintry; Timothy Taylor & Co.; Tortuga Rum Company Ltd; Tsantali Vineyards and Wineries; Umberto Cavicchioli & Figli; United Brands Ltd; V&S Absolut Spirits; Val d'Orbieu Cordier Wines; Victory Brewing Company; Vintage Roots Ltd; Western Wines; William Grant and sons; Wine Importers Edinburgh Limited; Wine Portfolio Group Ltd; Winefare Agencies/A H Rackham Ltd; Wm Cadenhead's; Yapp Brothers Ltd; Zwack Unicum Rt.